The Great Awakening

DOCUMENTS ILLUSTRATING THE CRISIS

AND ITS CONSEQUENCES

THE AMERICAN HERITAGE SERIES

THE

American Heritage

Series

UNDER THE GENERAL EDITORSHIP OF

LEONARD W. LEVY AND ALFRED YOUNG

The Great Awakening

Documents Illustrating the Crisis and Its Consequences

EDITED BY

ALAN HEIMERT

Harvard University

AND

PERRY MILLER

Late Powell M. Cabot Professor of American Literature
Harvard University

THE BOBBS-MERRILL COMPANY, INC.

INDIANAPOLIS AND NEW YORK

FOREWORD

Benjamin Franklin, although not one to be taken in by the antics of a religious pitchman, out of curiosity once attended a sermon by a famous revivalist in favor of a cause which Franklin disapproved. Having resolved in advance to contribute nothing to that cause, when the sermon was over he emptied the gold and silver as well as the coppers from his pockets into the collection plate. The persuasive powers of the preachers of the Great Awakening had to be experienced to be believed. They brought heart as well as head, feeling as well as mind to religion, thereby "awakening" interest in it—and transforming it.

Before the Great Awakening most of the country was religiously parched. Science, reason, and nature—the trinity of the oncoming Enlightenment—with an assist from prosperity and a natural hardening of the religious arteries, had banked the seventeenth century's intense fires of religious emotion, leaving religion with an unsatisfying sobriety, a cold formalism, and a dull, theological pedantry. The time was right, in the 1730's, for a reformation, not in doctrine but in the style of worship. George Whitefield, whom Franklin had heard, Gilbert Tennent, Jonathan Edwards, and a host of others seized and shook their audiences, giving them such an intimate sense of personal sin and an overpowering stimulus to be saved that men and women wept, shrieked, and ecstatically sensed the cleansing experience of conversion. This extraordinary phenomenon of "mass hysteria," this great crescendo of zeal, this revivalistic movement, was the Great Awakening. It convulsed the human spirit and society too, producing paradoxical and lasting results. It split the old churches and provoked religious animosities, yet it also proliferated sects, mainly

Separates, Baptist, and New Side Presbyterian, whose dissenter experiences led them to oppose establishments of religion and advance the cause of religious liberty. It was profoundly anti-intellectual, yet it led to the establishment of four new colleges (Princeton, Dartmouth, Brown, and Rutgers). It was a revolt against religious rationalism, yet it spurred rationalist growth. It accentuated class consciousness, yet it was a popular movement that, as Alan Heimert says, awakened "the spirit of American democracy."

Professor Heimert, initially with the advice and aid of America's foremost intellectual historian—the late Perry Miller, his mentor—has produced a splendid and judiciously balanced collection of primary sources that reveal the religious ideology of the Great Awakening and the opposition to it. Few anthologies are as genuinely deserving of the reviewer's trite encomium, "a highly original contribution to scholarship." Serious students of religious and intellectual history will appreciate the penetrating headnotes and, above all, the invaluable tracts and sermons gathered and scrupulously edited by the most exacting professional standards. Despite its excellences, however, this book, like any on the subject, must, in a certain sense, be deemed a failure: it cannot recapture the performance or the impact of the authors here presented, any more than the sound of a great violinist can be reproduced in type. The voice, the presence, the charisma of the hypnotic orator or histrionic speaker must always elude the historian who can confront only the printed record. But that record, mustered as best it can be, is here for the imaginative to study.

This book is one of a series whose aim is to provide the essential primary sources of the American experience, especially of American thought. The series, when completed, will constitute a documentary library of American history, filling a need long felt among scholars, students, libraries, and general readers for authoritative collections of original materials. Some volumes will illuminate the thought of significant individuals, such as James Madison or Louis Brandeis; some will deal with movements, such as those of the Antifederalists or the Populists; others will be organized around special themes, such as Puritan political thought, or American Catholic thought on social questions. Many volumes will take up the large number of subjects traditionally studied in American history for which, surprisingly, there are no documentary anthologies; others will pioneer in introducing new subjects of increasing importance to scholars and to the contemporary world. The series aspires to maintain the high standards demanded of contemporary editing, providing authentic texts, intelligently and unobtrusively edited. It will also have the distinction of presenting pieces of substantial length that give the full character and flavor of the original. The series will be the most comprehensive and authoritative of its kind.

Leonard W. Levy
Alfred Young

CONTENTS

Part IV · THE AWAKENING: NEW ENGLAND

Part V · THE NEW ORDER: ECCLESIASTICAL

Part VI · THE NEW ORDER: DOCTRINAL

Part VII · LEGACIES

INTRODUCTION

The Great Awakening was the religious revival that swept through the American colonies between 1739 and 1742. A "great and general awakening" was the phrase used at the time by those impressed with the revival's spread from Georgia to New England and, as it seemed, through every element of the populace. As the first in the almost uninterrupted series of revivals America experienced in the following century, the Awakening of the 1740's was the revival by which churchmen and historians measured all others. When in 1800–1801 another great revival, one that touched possibly even more people, occurred, it was called simply—much as the war of 1939–1945 was named—"The Second Great Awakening."

That the first Awakening was somehow "great" has seldom been disputed, not even by those who see in it the sources and archetypes of anti-intellectual fundamentalism: the anxious bench and sawdust trail of later generations. But there is little agreement on just what, if anything, it was an awakening *to*. A "revival" seems almost by definition a return to the past, and a revival of religion, or even of "vital piety," could hardly mark, in the context of the eighteenth century, the dawning of a new future. Accompanied as it was by the resurgence of a"Calvinism"[1] that earlier seemed certain to be swept away by science and reason, the great revival of the

[1] Calvinism is a body of doctrines identified with the reformer, John Calvin (1509–1564), as codified in his *Institutes of the Christian Religion* (1536). The Church of England, as established by Henry VIII, and as it evolved in the later sixteenth century, embodied some of Calvin's ideas, but it was the Puritans who, pressing for further reformation in England, accepted the designation of "Calvinists." Actually, Puritan theology reflected numerous modifications and improvements by Continental and English theologians, but the Puritans, both of Britain and of America, professedly upheld the celebrated "five points" of Calvinism

1740's would appear to be not an awakening at all, but the dying shudder of a Puritanism that refused to see itself as an anachronism.

From another perspective, however, the Awakening clearly began a new era, not merely of American Protestantism, but in the evolution of the American mind. "Historians have variously pointed out that the decade of the Awakening, 1740 to 1750, is a watershed in American development. They have difficulty in putting their fingers on just what precisely the transformation was, since there were no revolutionary changes in political institutions." Churches were divided and reorganized, to be sure, but otherwise "the social scene in 1750 seems fairly much what it was in 1740. And yet you feel, the moment you go to the sources, that after 1750 we are in a 'modern period,' whereas before that, and down to the very outburst, the intellectual world is still medieval, scholastic, static, authoritarian."[2] The Awakening, in brief, marked America's final

---

that were proclaimed when the Synod of Dort repudiated Arminianism. The five "essential" Calvinist doctrines were: 1) unconditional election—God freely chooses those whom he saves and is in no way dependent, nor is his choice conditional, on any human merit or "works"; 2) limited atonement—Christ, by his death, made possible the salvation of some men only, not of all; 3) total depravity—man is, by nature, corrupt, a creature in whom the reigning principle is the sin that was originally Adam's; 4) irresistible grace—man is wholly passive in the work of regeneration, and is powerless to choose, or reject, the grace that is freely given; and 5) the final perseverance of the saints—man, once the subject of grace, will never fall from that state. This last "point," though identified with Calvinism, was probably not so much Calvin's as one inherited by all the Reformers from St. Augustine, who made perseverance the test of whether or not a man had in fact been predestined to sainthood. Calvin's own formulation of the doctrine emphasized predestination (that the choice of the elect was made by God from the beginning of time) in such a way that God was seen to determine, not men's grace merely, but their entire destiny.

[2] Perry Miller, "The Great Awakening from 1740 to 1750," *Encounter* (The Divinity School, Duke University, Durham, N. C., March 1956), p. 5.

break with the Middle Ages and her entry into a new intellectual age in the church and in society. Out of the Awakening came new ideas—the many propositions that "American society, having been shaken by this experience, was henceforth consciously to observe." The Great Awakening thus stands as a major example of that most elusive of phenomena: a turning point, a "crisis," in the history of American civilization.

The tortured process by which this revolution was wrought is itself, apart from its consequences, a fascinating chapter of intellectual history. The half-decade or so of religious exuberance in the 1740's witnessed and exemplified one of the "enduring responses of the American mind to crisis." Before turning either to crisis or to consequences, however: "we are confronted with the problem of whether the Great Awakening is properly to be viewed as a peculiarly American phenomenon at all. It would be possible to write about it—as has been done —as merely one variant of a universal occurrence in Western culture. Between about 1730 and 1760 practically all of Western Europe was swept by some kind of religious emotionalism. It was present in Germany, Holland, Switzerland, and France, and in Catholic circles there was an analogous movement that can be interpreted as an outcropping of the same thing: this the textbooks call 'Quietism.' And most dramatically, it was present in England with the Wesleys, Whitefield, and Methodism.

"Once this international viewpoint is assumed, the American outburst becomes merely one among many—a colonial one at that—and we hesitate to speak about it as a crisis in a history specifically American. What was at work throughout the Western world is fairly obvious: the upper or the educated classes were tired of the religious squabbling of the seventeenth century, and turned to the more pleasing and not at all contentious generalities of eighteenth-century rationalism; the spiritual hungers of the lower classes or of what, for shorthand purposes, we may call 'ordinary' folk were not satisfied by Newtonian demonstrations that design in the universe proved the existence of God. Their aspirations finally found vent in the revivals, and in each country we may date the end of a Calvinist or scholastic, or, in short, a theological era by the appearance of these movements, and therefore mark what is by now called the era of Pietism or Evangelicalism.

"In this frame of reference, the Great Awakening was only incidentally American. It is merely necessary to translate the European language into the local terminology in order to have an adequate account. In this phraseology, the Great Awakening was an uprising of the common people who declared that what Harvard and Yale graduates were teaching was too academic. This sort of rebellion has subsequently proved so continuous that one can hardly speak of it as a crisis. It is rather a chronic state of affairs. And in this view of it, the uprising of 1740 belongs to the international history of the eighteenth century rather than to any account of forces at work only on this continent.

"Told in this way, the story will be perfectly true. Because we talk so much today of the unity of Western European culture, maybe we ought to tell it in those terms, and then stop. But on the other hand there is a curiously double aspect to the business. If we forget about Germany and Holland and even England—if we examine in detail the local history of Virginia, Pennsylvania, and New England—we will find that a coherent narrative can be constructed out of the cultural developments in each particular area. This Awakening can be seen as the culmination of factors long at work in each society, and as constituting, in that sense, a veritable crisis in the indigenous civilization."[3]

---

[3] Perry Miller, "Jonathan Edwards and the Great Awakening," in *America in Crisis,* ed. Daniel Aaron (New York: Alfred A. Knopf, Inc., 1952), pp. 5–7. Copyright 1952 by Alfred A. Knopf, Inc. Excerpts reprinted with permission of the publisher.

THE AMERICAN SETTING OF THE AWAKENING

In examining the American Awakening, a continuing awareness of the international dimensions of the eighteenth-century
revival is helpful. One can thereby resist the temptation to
isolate one or another "cause" of the Great Awakening, which
has on occasion been "explained" in terms of a diphtheria epi-
demic, or the land-bank controversies of the 1730's, or even
of the declining fertility of the unmanured farmlands of the
American backcountry. Each of these phenomena may have
some relevance to the course of the American revival, but none
should be allowed to obscure the fact that eighteenth-century
pietism emerged elsewhere quite apart from any such background. Pietism was a response to the spiritual vacuum left
by the defeat of Puritanism and the disarray of Calvinism.
What concerned American Protestants, a century after the first
planting of Massachusetts Bay, was the sterility—not of colonial soil—but of its spiritual life.

Since the 1660's the ministers of New England had period-
ically arraigned their people for "declension" from the virtues
of their fathers. As embodied in the formula of the "jeremiad,"
New England's lamentation for its departed glory had been
accompanied by increasingly-pointed warnings of calamities
to be visited on a backsliding people by an outraged God. The
earthquake of 1727 seemed such a judgment, and for a moment
the tremors aroused the spiritual concerns of New Englanders.
But the earthquake's effect was not lasting, and in the early
1730's ministers began to call, not for a "reformation" merely,
but a "reviving" of the vital spirit of an earlier New England.

One such spiritual quickening had already been witnessed in
1721, in Windham, Connecticut, and other instances of "re-
markable impressions" had been observed elsewhere in New
England. The most notable were the "harvests" enjoyed in
Northampton, Massachusetts, in the congregation of Solomon
Stoddard, the "pope" of the Connecticut Valley. With Stod-

dard's death in 1729 his grandson, Jonathan Edwards, succeeded to the charge. Five years later Northampton experienced an outpouring of the Spirit more impressive than any before the Great Awakening itself.

The Northampton revival of 1734–1735 was both prelude to the Awakening of 1740 and, in a sense, one of its major causes. Edwards' account of the revival, published in 1736, alerted both Old England and New to the possibility and process of remarkable conversion. The revival also reinforced Edwards' conviction that the working of the Spirit demanded the preaching of "evangelical doctrine." In assessing the Northampton revival Edwards was persuaded that it had been brought about by his decision (one joined in by other ministers) to challenge the "Arminianism"[4] that was corrupting and threatening the inherited religion of New England.

In the seventeenth century, Arminianism had chiefly signified the belief that grace is not irresistible, as John Calvin had declared, but conditional on certain acts of man. By the eighteenth century, however, Arminianism was viewed as a broader challenge, in the name of man's freedom, to the Calvinist idea of the absolute sovereignty of God. It was but one

---

[4] Arminianism is historically, the post-Reformation revolt against extreme Calvinism identified with Jacobus Arminius (or Jakob Harmensen), a Dutch theologian and professor at the University of Leyden. The doctrines of Arminius (1560–1609) challenged all of the five major points of Calvinism and were comprehensively repudiated at the Synod of Dort (1618–1619), which marked the end of the Arminian "Remonstrant" party in the Church of Holland. However, certain of Arminius' views, particularly his objections to Calvinist determinism, came to be espoused by the leaders of the Church of England, which, under the direction of Archbishop Laud (1573–1645), moved away from even the mild Calvinism of its "Thirty-Nine Articles" (1563). When the Puritans attacked the Church of England for adopting "Arminian" theology, they referred specifically to the belief that man is not wholly passive in the process of regeneration but actively chooses ("wills"), or refuses, a proferred salvation.

element in a movement of theological protest expressive of vague, but intense, discomfort with the "harsh" tenets of Calvinism. This new theological mood, which emerged most conspicuously in England, was most appropriately called "rationalism," for each of its forms reflected the scientific and philosophical revolution represented in the thought of Newton and Locke. When Edwards invoked the specter of Arminianism, he was battling the whole of this rationalist impulse, for he saw the doctrine of free will as the central error in a movement that was taking the form of a host of "heresies"— among them "Arianism,"[5] "Pelagianism,"[6] and "Socinianism"[7]—

---

[5] Arianism is a philosophical interpretation of the doctrine of the Trinity, named for a third-century church figure, Arius, who, it is believed, was seeking to make the more mysterious doctrines of Christianity acceptable and comprehensible to the people of pagan cultures. Arius insisted on a complete distinction between the Father and the Son, and on the subordination of the latter. His doctrines were condemned as heresy at the Council of Nicæa (325), which also adopted a creed, embodying the Trinitarian formula of St. Athananius, that remained standard doctrine for more than a millennium. Arian views of the Trinity were revived in late seventeenth-century England, largely in reaction against Puritanism, but these gave way, with the rise of philosophic rationalism, to a more general anti-Trinitarianism, and to the Unitarian view of Christ as a mere man exemplary for his goodness.

[6] Pelagianism is a heresy condemned by the council of Ephesus (431), identified with a British monk, Pelagius, who in Rome and Palestine sought to improve men by affirming that the human will had by nature sufficient power to perform moral duties without relying on supernatural grace. St. Augustine attacked Pelagius as arguing, in his emphases on man's reason and free will, that grace itself could be earned by man's works, or was somehow given by God according to man's meritorious performance of his moral duties.

[7] Socinianism is not a specific heresy, but a mode of theological thinking, anti-Trinitarian in spirit, identified with the sixteenth-century divine, Socinus (Fausto Paolo Sozzini). Socinus emphasized the supremacy of God the Father, and his writings were interpreted as a denial of Christ's divinity. So interpreted, Socinian thought contributed to the rise of Unitarianism in Transylvania, from where it spread to Holland and England. Implicitly, at least, Socinus anticipated the seventeenth-century

that, having arisen in England, now threatened to engulf the colonies.

Many American Calvinists believed that the ultimate tendency of the new theology was outright "Deism."[8] Yet neither this "heresy" nor any of the others that worried Calvinists, had been embraced by more than a handful of Americans before the moment when Edwards mounted his crusade. Indeed, no strictly Arminian doctrine of free will had been overtly or doctrinally propounded in any of New England's Congregational churches. But there, as among the Middle Colony Presbyterians, America's other most numerous Calvinist branch, an Arminian tendency was indeed, as Edwards contended, clearly to be discerned. It appeared in the emphases, and the omissions, in otherwise seemingly orthodox sermons. What actually disturbed Edwards was little more than a logical outgrowth of

---

argument that the atonement was a strategy, not necessary in the very nature of the divine decrees, but chosen by God only for its moral influence on men. This "moral government" theory of the atonement, particularly as developed by Hugo Grotius, pervaded the "rational" theology of the early eighteenth century, as did Socinus' own view of reason as the sole and final arbiter of truth.

[8] Deism is, strictly, a belief in one supreme God, but more specifically, a current of rationalist theological thought that emerged most conspicuously in England in the last years of the seventeenth century. Though Lord Herbert of Cherbury (1583–1648) was the first and most important of the acknowledged English Deists, the figures that loomed largest in the American mind were the later thinkers who, weary of Protestant scholasticism, applied the lessons of Newton and Locke in asserting the sufficiency of natural religion and in denying the unique significance of the supernatural revelation of the Scriptures. Among these Deistic writers were Matthew Tindal (1657–1733), William Wollaston (1659–1724), John Toland (1670–1722), the Third Earl of Shaftesbury (1671–1713), Anthony Collins (1676–1729), and Thomas Chubb (1679–1747). With the possible exception of Benjamin Franklin, the Deists of America reflected, not the influence of these writers, but of later eighteenth-century tendencies (some of them within evangelical religion itself) which, while questioning the divinity of Christ or the inspiration of Scripture, emphasized the ethics of Christianity and the humanitarian teachings of Jesus.

a "rationalist" strain that had been present in Puritanism for more than a century, specifically in the doctrine of "preparation." This doctrine, long central to the self-defined orthodoxy of New England, held that man could not simply await God's pleasure (or, as one of the early Puritans phrased it, hope to go to heaven with his hands by his sides) but must, and could, do something to "prepare" himself as a fit vessel of divine grace. In this respect, the Arminianism that Edwards challenged was no novelty at all, except that, by the second quarter of the eighteenth century, the doctrine of preparation, as it was promulgated from many pulpits, concerned not merely steps to be taken before God would see fit to dispense his grace, but the whole process of salvation. For the old orthodoxy was being reinforced (and having its implications disclosed) by imported notions of "natural religion," and taking the form of a suggestion (not yet a proclaimed doctrine) that men, by use of their rational capacities alone, could come to know God's will, and, knowing, choose to fulfill it, and thus count themselves among the saved.

Such an Arminian rationalism represented a challenging redefinition of the nature of happiness and the manner of its pursuit. The appeal of the new "graceless" dispensation was reflected, not merely in the forms of social behavior that Calvinist ministers bewailed, but in stresses on and within the churches of the colonies. One of the more obvious expressions of the new mood was the defection of New Englanders to the Church of England, which, since the days of Archbishop Laud, had been identified with Arminianism. In the 1720's several Yale tutors and students renounced the faith of their Puritan fathers and took Episcopal orders. Subsequently the appeal of Anglicanism was witnessed less dramatically, but more widely, when, in the 1730's, its attractions were felt in Calvinist churches throughout the colonies. Spokesmen for the "dissenting" churches sought to defend the faith once delivered to the Puritan saints, but many of them were hard pressed to do so, for they themselves were preaching a diluted Calvinism—in the belief that the old formulas were no longer appropriate to the changing circumstances of a growing and more prosperous colonial America. But the 1730's did see efforts to meet the challenge of Anglicanism with the doctrines of a more vital Calvinism. In a long public controversy over the validity of non-Episcopal ordination, the Calvinists, whose spokesman was the New Jersey Presbyterian, Jonathan Dickinson, first manifested the revived intellectual energy that was eventually to be expressed in the Great Awakening.

The Middle Colonies also experienced a revival of religious concern comparable to the one at Northampton. The first occurred among the Dutch Reformed of the Jerseys, under the promptings of Theodorus Frelinghuysen; then in 1735 the Scotch-Irish Presbyterians of New Jersey and Pennsylvania enjoyed a "refreshing." Most Presbyterians had been in the New World less than a generation, but among them no less than in New England there had been much bewailing of a falling off from the ancestral spirit. This was particularly the case with William Tennent and his sons, who rebuked both the rationalism of older Presbyterian ministers and the increasingly secular spirit of the age. By the late 1730's the Tennent party was complaining that too many ministers indulged their favored parishioners in acquisitiveness and displays of conspicuous wealth. Personal ambition, they argued, was inconsistent with a supreme love of God. What men needed, along with an awareness of the Divine sovereignty, was a realization that only in the "excellency of Christ" could the soul be spiritually satisfied.

Both the Tennents and Edwards urged their people to an existential indifference to the things of this world, but they were not in fact otherworldly. Implicit in their mutual assault on rationalism was displeasure with the arrangements of society and a desire for a change in its character. The revivals of

1734–1735, which brought (as Edwards observed) a considerable improvement in the "manners" of the people of Northampton, opened the possibility of a further alteration in man's social condition. Such a promise was the theme of the most significant of pre-Awakening utterances: Edwards' 1739 sermons on the "History of the Work of Redemption." Here Edwards argued that God's great design in history was not the salvation of individuals merely, but the social redemption of mankind.

Edwards also announced in 1739 that the time had nearly come when an outpouring of the Spirit, more extensive than that of 1735, would bring the Kingdom of God to earth. Until this moment, the millenarian speculation of eighteenth-century America had focused on the thought of some catastrophic interruption in the course of history. But Edwards, building on the experience of the earlier arrivals, declared that the millennium would arrive "gradually," by means of the ordinary influences of the Spirit. The "people of God," he added, were capable of "falling in" with the Divine strategy and indeed of "promoting" it. From the delivery of these sermons may be dated the historical optimism that was to be the Awakening's most distinctive legacy. The thought of American Christianity was turning away from past glories and toward the future—and, even more impressively, from the individual to the greater community.

Though the Great Awakening would transform and even destroy the inherited parochial order of colonial America, its drama was played out in a multitude of villages and towns. When the revival erupted in 1740 it was almost everywhere greeted as the harbinger of the millennium, but the fervor of the welcome reflected decades of confusion and discontent within particular communities. Throughout the 1730's the church and religion had been struggling to preserve their social and intellectual primacy. Ministers, their leadership now challenged by editors such as Benjamin Franklin and even by political and economic pamphleteers, were seeking to redefine their status. Congregations were racked by internal dissensions over ministerial qualifications or the requirements of church membership, and communities were aroused by the manner in which the increasing wealth of the colonies was being divided. Whether or not they were directly involved in the pursuit of gain, or caught up on partisan animosity, nearly every American was confronted with a bewildering variety of personal options and ethical choices. Many questions were being asked, but few had been answered satisfactorily, not even in the minds of the clergy. Until, that is, the new light of the Awakening dispelled anxieties by giving a new focus to the thoughts of both ministers and people.

GEORGE WHITEFIELD AND EVANGELICAL PREACHING

The catalyst of the Great Awakening seems to have been the arrival in the colonies, in the autumn of 1739, of the young Episcopal clergyman, George Whitefield. He cannot, however, be called the "cause" of the revival, if only because the American mind was more than prepared for the day of his coming. Even before he arrived Americans were addressing Whitefield in published letters. The theme of all of them was that everyone looked forward to his visit "with much Desire." Whitefield was preceded by his reputation as a stirring pulpit orator, as the main instrument of the English revival, and as a spokesman for "vital religion" against the "decadence" of the Establishment. His discourses, especially the celebrated sermon, "The Nature and Necessity of our New Birth," had already been widely reprinted in the colonies.

Though many American preachers contributed more than

Whitefield to the Awakening, the path of the revival closely followed his tour of the colonies in 1739–1740. Indeed, a realization that a truly "great" awakening was afoot came first to the South, where Whitefield moved after a comparatively brief stay in the Middle Colonies. In Georgia, a center of earlier activity by the Wesleys, Whitefield spoke in early 1740 to ever larger and increasingly enthusiastic crowds. In Charleston, South Carolina, Whitefield first published the revival's distinctive challenges to the standing order. He condemned the "sinful diversions" of the wealthier citizens and he accused the Episcopal clergy of heterodoxy.

In Charleston also Whitefield became the controversial figure he was to remain throughout the course of the Awakening —the symbol, as it were, of the new religious dispensation. "He is the Wonder of the Age," it was noted at the time, "and no one Man more employs the Press, and fills up the Conversation of people, than he does at this Day: None more admir'd and applauded by some, contemn'd and reproach'd by others." The admirers of Whitefield, and those who condemned him, expressed conflicting judgments on the revival of which he was believed the chief instrument. For the Awakening was only briefly, if at all, generally rejoiced in as the long-awaited "pouring out of the grace of God upon the land." Almost immediately it became a subject of debate, and the occasion for a drawing of party lines in every community and within each church. In this respect, the confrontation of Whitefield and Alexander Garden, the leading Anglican minister of the southernmost colonies, was something of a capsule history of the revival's controversies. Garden, who held the Bishop of London's appointment as Commissary, or administrative head of the Episcopal Church in South Carolina, spoke for the Establishment and against the insurgency of Whitefield and the American revival. The exchange of charges between Whitefield and Garden touched on nearly all the issues that were to engage the American religious mind over the next months and years.

First of all, Whitefield spoke as a Calvinist against the Arminianism of the Anglican clergy. The revival in America, unlike that of the Wesleys, built and throve on the preaching of Calvinist doctrine. On May 24, 1740, Whitefield, writing from the colonies, informed John Wesley, who in his sermon on "Free Grace" had recently set English evangelicalism on a non-Calvinist course, that he dreaded the thought of Wesley's coming to America. The "work of God is carried on here," Whitefield wrote, "(and that in a most glorious manner) by doctrines quite opposite to those you hold. . . . There are many worthy experienced ministers, who would oppose your principles to the utmost." In December Whitefield publicly announced his break with Wesley, and thereafter, when questioned by critics of the revival, declared quite accurately that "the constant Tenour of my preaching in *America*, has been *Calvinistical.*" This point bears stressing, not only as an indication of the doctrines of the American revivalists, but as a reminder that none of their sermons were wild, incoherent harangues. The typical sermon of the Great Awakening was a careful disquisition on such points of theology as man's total depravity or the unconditional election of the saints.

However, Whitefield's sermons were by no means traditional Calvinist utterances. Orthodox in their matter, the manner of delivery seemed quite novel, and both admirers and critics noted how Whitefield employed changes in tone and dramatic, though controlled, gestures. From Whitefield's example was derived a radical redefinition of the nature and character of "evangelical preaching." According to critics, such preaching consisted largely in an emphasis on the more "terrifying" of Calvinist doctrines, but the more common complaint was that the revivalists were mere demagogues skilled in arousing the "passions." This issue, first raised by Garden, was central to all the controversies of the Awakening. The position of the revivalists revealed the revolution in logic, as well as rhetoric, that was among the more significant intellectual ramifications of the Awakening.

Before 1740 the efforts of the ministry "could still be described by what Thomas [Aquinas] had defined as the only legitimate function of Sacred Doctrine—that is, to use human reason and the liberal arts 'not, indeed, to prove faith (for hereby the merit of faith would come to an end), but to make clear other things that are set forth in this doctrine.'" With the Awakening, "whole segments of Protestant America have made the fatal break: they have dared to say, or at least to act as though they had said, that the merit of faith is not one whit diminished if a passionate preacher arouses, excites, creates the faith. . . ."[9] Actually, the Awakening began an era in which Calvinism was defended not by the internal logic of its principles nor even in terms of its basis in Scripture, but by the effectiveness of its doctrines in reaching men's "hearts." According to Whitefield's earliest defender, St. Paul himself had "argued the *divinity* of his doctrines from the success and power of them."

Success, in turn, was measured by what Whitefield and his fellow workers termed the "New Birth." Not the Reformation doctrine of justification by faith alone, but the existential fact of the conversion experience, became the "principal hinge" of what Edwards called "the evangelical scheme." To be sure, Calvinists insisted that there was an unerring relationship between doctrine and the revival experience, and that in the phenomena of the Awakening they could be seen "happily combining to illustrate & confirm each other." But the great debate of the Awakening was not, finally, on the question of God's unconditional dispensations of grace, but over the nature and necessity of the experience that the revivalists strove to induce.

---

[9] Miller, "Great Awakening," p. 5.

In the early months of the revival Calvinists defined the New Birth as something that came almost instantaneously and as a "feeling." So often did Whitefield speak of how saving faith was "felt" that his sermons, at least according to his critics, gave rise to a popular notion that grace is a physical presence, as distinctive and as tangible as a bowel ache or a tumor. Some (alluding presumably to the free love charged against revival meetings) observed that "it must be owned that some of the crying or roaring Women among us have brought forth something that may be both seen and felt." Whitefield himself was less than successful in analysing the nature of the conversion experience. "How this glorious Change is wrought in the Soul," he confessed, "cannot easily be explained." The perfecting of a psychological insight appropriate to the emotions of the Awakening was among the many matters left to abler minds than Whitefield's.

Another question raised during Whitefield's invasion of Charleston was that of the opposing claims of ecclesiastical discipline and the liberties of individual ministers and people. Garden attempted to silence Whitefield and to prevent attendance of his sermons, but the itinerant in turn challenged the traditional interpretation of the constitution of the Episcopal Church. A comparable drama was enacted with the various other churches of the colonies, generally, as in Charleston, in a context of fears that the "anarchy" of the revivalists posed a threat to the stability and order, not of the church only, but of all society. Throughout the colonies the name of Oliver Cromwell was echoed in 1740, especially as the number of awakened increased so as to inspire the thought that the millennium was about to dawn, and with it, all earthly authority given over to the saints. Neither this consequence of the "new light" nor any other was viewed in isolation by the critics of the revival, whose stress on "reason and order" in the process of man's salvation was carried over into their responses to other, perhaps more unsettling, aspects of the Awakening. So too with the partisans of the revival, for whom 1740 brought a "new birth," not to individuals merely, but in every area of American thought and life.

DEBATE AND SCHISM IN PRESBYTERIANISM

The issues of the Awakening were essentially the same from colony to colony. But in each of the major centers of revival activity, different questions came to occupy the center of attention and concern, and the pattern in which events unfolded reflected the particular setting. In the Middle Colonies (except in New York) there was no established church, and a history of toleration had produced a greater variety of church groups to be affected by the Awakening. Anglicans in these colonies almost unanimously derided the emotional excesses of the Awakening, as did also the most prominent Philadelphia Friends, who seem to have forgotten (or, guided by their counting-house respectability, wanted to forget) that the seventeenth-century Quakers had themselves been enthusiasts. Some members of Quaker meetings did, to be sure, recognize a parallel between their doctrine of the Inward Light and Whitefield's New Light, and many went, not simply to hear the itinerant's sermons, but to join the churches of other spokesmen of the Awakening. But for the most part the Quakers stood aloof from the revival, perhaps because they were convinced that their "quietism"—with its doctrine of the gradual infusion of the Spirit's illuminating influence—offered a definition of the Christian life superior to that implied by the awakeners' emphasis on abrupt conversion.

Such questions, however, remained for the most part unspoken during the course of the revival in the Middle Colonies, and, like most other doctrinal issues, awaited the waning of the revival to be debated among the various groups touched by the Awakening. Among these were the Baptists, whose growth in New Jersey was enormously stimulated by the revival, and the Moravians, or "Unitas Fratrum," who throughout the Awakening gained new adherents, particularly from the other German-speaking pietistic sects of Pennsylvania. But the highest drama of the Middle Colony Awakening, and nearly all its leading actors, appeared among the Presbyterians. Among them the revival impulse expressed itself largely, though not exclusively, as a force battering at the ecclesiastical structure and, eventually, one that reorganized and liberalized the institutional life of American Presbyterianism. In being so affected by the revival, the Presbyterians were by no means unique, nor were ecclesiastical issues the only ones they debated during the Awakening. But the intellectual history of Presbyterianism in the first years of the 1740's is most striking as an especially vivid illustration of how the Great Awakening "Americanized" the constitution of a colonial church.

Even before the Awakening the Middle Colony Presbyterians were involved in a struggle over the definition of their church structure and the powers of its governing body, the Synod of Philadelphia. Distinct parties emerged during the 1730's, each of them espousing a differing interpretation of the Synod's authority and jurisdiction. One party, centered in the Delaware Valley and composed primarily of ministers born and trained in Scotland, spoke for what they considered a traditional Presbyterianism, tightly and centrally controlled. In the late 1720's this group proposed that all candidates for the ministry be required to "subscribe" to the Westminster Confession—the articles of faith and practice drawn up by the Presbyterians during the Puritan Revolution. Their chief opponents in the "subscription controversy" were the Presbyterian ministers of northern New Jersey and Long Island, organized as the Presbytery of New Brunswick, who served a people mostly transplanted from New England. This group, most of them New England born, and nearly all of them edu-

cated at Yale, was led by Jonathan Dickinson, the most powerful mind in his generation of American divines. The position
they took in the "subscription controversy" bespoke the power
of their distinctive heritage—a Presbyterianism that had its
roots not in Scotland but in the "semi-Presbyterianizing" of
New England Congregationalism over the course of the seventeenth century.

From the very beginning the "New England Way" of
church government had been "impure" by the standards of
the English Congregationalists, or "Independents." In the
Cambridge Platform of 1648, the individual churches of Massachusetts and Connecticut were defined as not wholly independent, but subject, in many respects, to the authority of
"synods" and, on many matters, to "associations" of neighboring churches. Around the turn of the century, the churches of
western Massachusetts were further "Presbyterianized" by
Solomon Stoddard, many of whose ideas were, in the Saybrook
Platform of 1708, enacted into law in the colony of Connecticut. The fifteen "Articles for the Administration of Church
Discipline" adopted by the Connecticut ministers, and approved by the legislature, allowed the laity of each church
somewhat more power than Stoddard thought advisable, but
the Platform did follow Stoddard's lead in calling for "consociations" in each county to oversee and control the major decisions of individual churches. These consociations, that were
to serve such functions as examining candidates for the ministry and hearing appeals from the decisions in matters of discipline of particular churches were not, however, uniformly
welcomed, or given the same sweeping powers throughout
Connecticut. Moreover, the Saybrook Platform followed, in its
articles of faith, the more "Congregational" formula of the
Savoy Declaration (1658), which accepted the Westminister
Confession as only "in substance," and not in every particular,
a valid and standard statement of doctrine.

Thus it was hardly surprising that the Middle Colony Presbyterians of New England descent resisted, as they did in the 1730's, the proposal that all prospective ministers "subscribe" to strict articles of faith, and be judged, ultimately, by the Synod of Philadelphia. Another element in their decision may well have been the intellectual inspiration of Stoddard, who, despite his authoritarian inclinations, had ever been contemptuous of ministers who sought to fix Christian thought in terms of some uniform inherited creed. However, the Dickinson group seems also to have feared that the advocates of subscription intended to place American Presbyterianism under the ultimate control of either the Synod of Ireland or the General Assembly of Scotland. To the degree that such an issue lurked beneath the subscription controversy, the division within Presbyterianism paralleled the concurrent struggle within the Dutch Reformed Church, the government of which by the Classis of Amsterdam was beginning to chafe such New Jersey spokesmen of Dutch Calvinism as Frelinghuysen. Indeed, the issue of trans-Atlantic control, as it was raised in the Presbyterian debates, took precisely the form that focused the question of "Americanism" for the Dutch Reformed—that of where candidates for the ministry were to be educated. For as the controversy within Presbyterianism broadened, it appeared that the Scotch ministers were reluctant to consider anyone qualified as a minister unless he had been certified by a university of Scotland.

The issue of ministerial qualifications, and the hardening lines in the Synod, reflected the emergence within American Presbyterianism of a third element, that of the more recent Scotch-Irish immigration. Migrants from Ulster had begun to arrive in increasing numbers with the second decade of the century and had settled for the most part in the rural areas south and east of Philadelphia. It was to provide for the spiritual needs of these people that William Tennent, himself an emigrant from northern Ireland, began, in the early 1730's, to train young men for the ministry. The Synod of Philadelphia licensed Tennent's first four students, among whom was his son, Gilbert Tennent. But after 1735, when William Tennent established his Log College at Neshaminy, Pennsylvania, a majority in the Synod began to temporize, and, finally, refused to ordain his graduates. The new policy was a symptom of the older Presbyterians' displeasure with the revival of 1734–1735, and with the kind of "evangelical" preaching with which the Tennent party had promoted it.

The controversy within Presbyterianism entered on a new stage when, in the last years of the decade, the Tennent party began to license ministers (among them the fiery young evangelist, Samuel Finley) without the approval of the Synod and to send them into "vacant" parishes. An attempt was made to have the members of the Log College faction submit to ecclesiastical censure and discipline, but the latter replied by challenging the ministerial credentials of their tormentors. A formal education, they declared, was a less valuable qualification than that which was essential to a true minister—a warm faith and a virtuous life. Expanding on the terms of the "subscription controversy," the Tennent group argued that faith did not consist in assent to propositions, but in the experience of grace—a quality, they more than hinted, that was notably lacking in their "dead" opponents. Finally, the Log College men began to charge, not in Synod merely but in public, that certain ministers were not only personally guilty of scandalous vice but were, as preachers, so tolerant of the "sinfulness" of the age that their "easy" doctrine revealed them to be no Calvinists at all, and as such, a clear danger to the souls of their people.

Thus, the materials for an explosion within Presbyterianism had been gathering for more than a decade when, in 1740, the arrival of Whitefield in the Middle Colonies served as an igniting spark. The first hints of an Awakening presented the Log College men with an opportunity to arouse the laity against the "Pharisee-Teachers." The manifesto of the revival party, the most influential sermon of the Awakening and perhaps of the century, was Gilbert Tennent's *The Danger of an Unconverted Ministry.* Here Tennent outlined the various intellectual issues that divided Presbyterianism, and within that context justified the practice that was deemed the head and front of the revivalists' offense against ecclesiastical order: "itinerancy." In arguing that it was proper for a minister to enter a parish other than his own without approval, and that people might properly leave their own ministers in pursuit of the "greater good," Tennent directly challenged the traditional parochial basis of church and society. From the resulting controversy, which can be traced through a series of synodical debates, there emerged opposing conceptions of the church. The antirevival party saw the church as a structured hierarchy, the power and weight of which was felt eventually in a particular community. The prorevivalists, who defined the church as a means of spreading the gospel, emphasized the unalienable rights of the laity. They also envisioned the true Church as transcending denominational, as well as local allegiances, and sought, during the Awakening, to create what the itinerant Samuel Finley called a "party of Christ," in which were united the gracious of whatever persuasion.

In the Awakening, the New England element was drawn to the side of the Log College party, and not merely out of repugnance for the ecclesiastical authoritarianism of the ministers opposed to the revival. Jonathan Dickinson rejoiced in the Awakening itself, and defended its emotions against the scorn of "rational" Presbyterians. Indeed, both prorevival groups offered arguments on behalf of "affecting preaching" and the centrality of the "heart" in religious experience. But they did not in fact produce many significant assessments of the new religious phenomena, perhaps because the opponents of the revival insisted on making the problem of ecclesiastical "anarchy" the central issue of the Presbyterian debate. Moreover, any doctrinal debate was effectively foreclosed as early as 1741, when the Tennent party was ejected from the Synod of Philadelphia. Later they joined the Presbytery of New Brunswick to form the Synod of New York, and the pro- and anti-revival parties thereafter went quite separate ways.

The Old Side Presbyterians, as the opponents of the revival came to be known, and the Tennent-Dickinson New Side carried on no continuing dialogue whatever over the issues raised by the revival experience. When the latter did begin to develop and perfect its thinking about the emotional religion of the Awakening, it was less in response to rationalist objections than in an effort to bring the raging enthusiasm of the later revival years under control. And this intellectual feat the New Side performed, not independently, but with the aid of the wisdom and insight provided them by the Calvinists of New England—to which region was left most of the responsibility of defining the place of the emotions in man's psychic economy, and, with it, the honor of making the most significant of the Awakening's contributions to the evolution of the American mind.

NEW ENGLAND'S TWO ARMIES: REASON AND THE AFFECTIONS

In turning to New England's special role in the Awakening, it should be reemphasized that neither the revival nor the thinking it evoked developed independently in any part of America. Whitefield's self-advertisements made the progress of the revival in each area common knowledge everywhere, and his very person gave those who heard him a sense of participation in an intercolonial experience. Moreover, awareness of the breadth of the Awakening stimulated an interest in what was thought and said elsewhere that caused the revival dialogue to span, almost from the first, nearly the whole of British America. Garden's strictures against Whitefield were quickly answered in Boston, and by mid-1741 the prorevivalists of all the colonies felt themselves united in sympathy with the Awakening and in common cause against its opponents. The Dickinson group, by virtue of its unique position, provided a point of immediate contact between the New England revivalists and the Presbyterians. An actual working alliance of these two prorevival groups was proposed during Whitefield's first visit to New England, and it was in effect sealed during Gilbert Tennent's preaching tour of the northern provinces. The antirevivalists, though less disposed to explicit union, likewise shared in an interdependent intellectual life. The major utterances of the Old Side Presbyterians were common knowledge in Massachusetts well before any local opponent of the Awakening published his own thoughts. In fact, what was said and thought to the southward, both for and against the revival, became part of New England's intellectual life well before the Protestants of the other colonies began to look to the land of the Puritans for definition and resolution of the major issues of the Awakening.

As the revival progressed, however, the eyes of Protestant America were increasingly turned to the north. New England had long been recognized as America's foremost "plantation of religion," and its colleges, whatever their state in 1740, had been the New World's most notable "nurseries of piety." And New England had witnessed the revival of 1734–1735, the publicizing of which had persuaded the pious everywhere that Northampton was somehow the spiritual center of Christendom. When Edwards, in *Some Thoughts Concerning the Present Revival of Religion in New England,* appointed himself the spokesman of the prorevival party in America, no one saw reason to challenge his presumption. Thus during the Awakening, and especially as Edwards' light came to eclipse even that of Dickinson, New England was restored to its traditional role as the colonies' acknowledged source of intellectual inspiration. (Obviously, the very fact of the religious revival effectively challenged Philadelphia's claim to primacy, as staked by Benjamin Franklin in the name of a new secular era.) The shift was in large part a tribute to Edwards' discerning, and portraying in his *Thoughts on the Revival,* what he called the "two armies, separated, and drawn up in battle array." For as Edwards described the contending forces in New England, the fate, not of all American religion, but of Christendom generally, might seem to depend on their fortunes.

Edwards did not see New England's two armies as embattled over ecclesiastical issues, nor was New England in fact ever so clearly divided in this respect as the Presbyterians. This is not to say that the New England revival did not pose, nor was seen to pose, a challenge to church order and government. On the contrary, almost from the outset of the revival New Englanders touched by the Spirit began to leave their "unconverted ministers," and, soon, to organize "Separate" congregations totally independent of the "standing order" of Connecticut and Massachusetts. The Separates, one of the few truly new sects to be spawned by the Awakening in America, came in time to serve as the materials of a revitalized and theologically reoriented New England Baptist Church. Itinerancy was also an issue in New England, where the question was raised, whether or not to admit Whitefield, and a host of other wandering spirits, into particular pulpits. Still, the churches of New England, never so closely organized as those of Presbyterianism, were far from uniform in their practices; the role of "associations" and "consociations," and of the clergy in particular churches, differed widely from area to area. Thus the impact of the revival on church policy was so various as to make difficult at first the drawing of any clear inferences as to the ecclesiastical significance of the Awakening.

In New England, enthusiasm, which seemed to build there

to an unmatched crescendo, was seen as the most distinctive, and controversial, of the revival's phenomena. Whitefield, Tennent, James Davenport, and the other itinerant exhorters who took "*so great* a Hand in the *religious Stir*" were viewed, by critics and defenders alike, not so much as challenging church order as in terms of the emotional experiences of their auditors. This focus was reflected in the names assumed by the parties that emerged in Connecticut—"New Lights" and "Old Lights"—where the issue was from the outset whether the emotional illumination of the revival experience was a witness of the Holy Spirit, or a flagrant departure from God's declared order of operation in his work of conversion. These party names did not come to prevail universally in Massachusetts, in part because Edwards considered such "epithets" unavailing, in larger part because both he and his chief antagonist, Charles Chauncy of Boston, carried the debate over enthusiasm well beyond the terms employed in the early months of the Awakening. Indeed, *the* question in New England became that of the precise nature of "saving knowledge" and the manner in which it is acquired. On such a question the mind of New England was perhaps disposed to fix, for throughout its century of history it had been always more oriented toward epistemological, even psychological, concerns, than most other Calvinists. Whatever the explanation, the "great debate" in New England centered on the human personality, and out of this debate came the reorientations in religious thought that clearly mark the Great Awakening as the "birth-pangs" of a new epoch in the history of American Protestantism.

"The Great Awakening of 1740 was at first hailed by its partisans, we have seen, as a supernatural work. Hence much of the effort in the first delirious months went into formulating the signs or symptoms of authentic conversion, this being still conceived as a seizure from above. The sermon that Edwards delivered on September 10, 1741, at New Haven, entitled *The Distinguishing Marks of a Work of God,* is the best memorial of this early conception, though similar essays were produced by the Tennents. But even in this year, opponents of the Awakening were starting their attack, and everywhere their main charge became that, far from being a supernatural work, the outburst was criminally excited by artificial stimulations. Charles Chauncy's *Seasonable Thoughts on the State of Religion,* published in 1743, is the principal indictment, but the 'Old Lights' and 'Old Side' repeated it again and again. They accused the revivalists of abusing human nature under a pretense that God himself was working the harm. Consequently the revivalists, led by Edwards, were obliged to answer that their techniques did not do violence to the human constitution, either physically or psychologically. Though to the bitter end they contended that the Awakening was a pure act of God, they had progressively so to expound it that in effect they represented Almighty God as accommodating His procedures to the faculties and potentialities of His creature. From the time of Calvin, the focus of Calvinist and of most Protestant thinking had been the will of God; the great divide that we call the Awakening forced both American parties, whether proponents or opponents, to shift the focus of analysis to the nature of man."[10]

The central conflict of the Awakening was thus not theological but one of opposing theories of the human psychology. Edwards' contribution came by way of his reformulation of the propositions of John Locke's *Essay on Human Understanding.* According to Edwards the human personality is an organic unity; its "faculties" are not separate, nor the process of cognition discontinuous. Rather the "understanding" perceives only as the whole being is "affected," and all knowledge—the most important, of course, being "spiritual knowledge"—de-

---

[10] Miller, "Great Awakening," p. 9.

rives from and ultimately depends on a "sense of the heart."
What Edwards accomplished, as he progressively revealed his
insights over the course of the revival debate, was to give
philosophic substance both to Whitefield's fustian about the
"feelings" and to the observable facts of the Awakening. His
"ultimate philosophy of the revival," *A Treatise Concerning
Religious Affections*, was not published until 1746, but well
before then other revivalists (including some, such as Jonathan
Dickinson, who had been independently working toward a
new psychology) incorporated Edwards' insights into their
own thought and sermons.

The Religious Affections has been judged "the most profound exploration of the religious psychology in all American
literature." The same can not be said of any of the "rationalist"
contributions to the discussion, not even those of Edwards'
ablest antagonist, Charles Chauncy. "Chauncy persisted in
arguing the whole case on the grounds of the scholastic psychology." Though he quoted Locke's *Understanding* in the first
of his attacks on enthusiasm, Chauncy wrote throughout the
1740's "as though everybody in Christendom assumed that reason, imagination, and will were distinct 'faculties' and the affections a separate and autonomous power. He used perception
as meaning only to see, and sense was only the register of the
phantasms. Thus he conceived the psychological problem as it
had been conceived since the Middle Ages, that of controlling
the imagination and the will by reason, and of subduing the
emotions to the will; hence all intelligible address must be
directed to the reason, through which decisions are always
given to the will. Any appeal directly to the passions, which
attempts to bypass speculation, was demonstrably immoral.
Whether this affectation was ignorance or a debater's trick, I
cannot say, but it put Edwards under an immense handicap: in
order to make himself understood he had first to expound a
radical and foreign psychology, which few in New England

were prepared to grasp. The irony is that the theological liberal, who in every trait stands for the rational Enlightenment, spoke in the language of outmoded science, and the defender of Calvinism put his case upon a modern, dynamic, analytical psychology in which the human organism was viewed, not as a system of gears, but as a living unit."[11]

It may nonetheless be said that Chauncy, no less than Edwards, announced a new era of religious thought. He laboriously heaped up both Scriptural and Puritan comments on the perversity of the "passions," but his point, finally, was that man is, or must be, an essentially rational creature. "The plain Truth," Chauncy concluded from his reflections on New England's religious disorders, "is, an enlightened Mind, not raised Affections, ought always to be the Guide of those who call themselves Men." Thus out of reaction to revival enthusiasm had emerged a religious persuasion distinguished not so much by an overt avowal of the freedom of the human will as by an insistence on the primacy of the "understanding" among the human faculties. Such a rationalism, soon to be developed in the classrooms of Harvard and Yale as a general philosophy, was the distinguishing mark of the "Liberal religion" of eighteenth-century America. Over the next decades Liberals refined their scheme of salvation, in which "time, exercise, observation, instruction," and the improvement of one's "capacities," were the means of grace—and the only way, as well, for man to pursue his worldly happiness.

Opposed to this philosophy was that inspired by the "joy" of the Awakening and given meaning by Edwards. The experience of conversion, as defined by Edwards, was a delight attendant on the whole being's undifferentiated perception, or "apprehension," as Edwards would have it, of the "excellence of divine things." Man's happiness and his holiness were not

---

[11] Perry Miller, *Jonathan Edwards* (New York: William Sloane Associates, 1949), pp. 177–178.

achieved through study or by way of a mechanically progressive growth in wisdom, but from a heartfelt "consent" to the "divinity of divinity," an order of being that was, by virtue of its beauty, also essentially good. What this involved is really part of another story—that of Edwards' reconstruction of Calvinist philosophy in the majestic dissertations of the 1750's. There he divested Calvinism of the language and conceptual apparatus of the "covenant theology" and portrayed man's salvation (and the redemption of mankind) as part of the divinely-ordered sequence and "attractions" of the universe. His inspiration was of course the physics of Isaac Newton, from which Edwards derived an interpretation of the "law of nature" quite at odds with the more "mechanical philosophy" of Liberal religion.

Among the opponents of the revival, too, there was a casting off from the safe mooring of Puritan theology. In their case the leap was toward the familiar axioms of the Age of Reason. In the 1750's "the religion of nature" emerged as "the instrument of a group, or of an interest," opposed to the doctrines of Calvinism. Their arguments rested "upon the massive authority of Newton," but specifically they were "directed against domestic opponents"—"against revivalists and enthusiasts, against New Light theologians, against those who still insisted upon a strict construction of the doctrines of total depravity and inherent corruption."[12] Among the consequences of this rationalist assault (which was by no means limited to spokesmen of the Church of England) was a reconsideration of the doctrines of the atonement and of the Trinity. In terms of dogma, the spokesmen of rational religion soon began to flirt with what the defenders of Calvinism called Arian or Socinian heresies.

---

[12] Perry Miller, "The Insecurity of Nature. Being the Dudleian Lecture for the Academic Year 1952-1953 . . . ," *Harvard Divinity School Bulletin. Annual Lectures and Book Reviews* (Official Register of Harvard University, Vol. LI, No. 13, Cambridge, Mass. [1954]), pp. 30–31.

But it was not so much a doctrinal revolution that the Awakening introduced as a profound shift in the very character, the perspective and focus, of religious thought and discourse. In the years after the revival, the rationalists began to insist that the Bible must be interpreted "reasonably," divested as it were of all its poetry and mystery. The spokesmen of evangelical religion, on the other hand, stressed the "beauty" of the gospel that was revealed to the gracious eye and mind as the inner meaning of the Testaments. But for both parties, Scripture— once for Protestants the ultimate revelation of the Divine Will —was no longer the final source or test of truth. Almost without fully realizing what they were doing, Calvinists and Liberals alike were converting the Bible into a storehouse of rhetorical devices by which to make truths discovered elsewhere compelling. That Scripture was for Calvinists a vast stock of metaphors, and for Liberals, a body of precedents, was less significant than that both had come out of the Awakening to argue, ultimately, from Nature—the nature of the universe, of man, and of society.

LEGACIES OF THE GREAT AWAKENING

Of course the theological ramifications of the Awakening were immense, and the evolution of American thought in the years after the revival could be traced, as often has been done, in terms of the traditional rubrics of systematic theology. But these consequences of the revival will not be treated here, if only because they were fully disclosed over nearly a full century. One can only hope that the documents of this history will also one day receive the reprinting they merit—and not those only which illustrate the evolution of rational religion from the Liberalism of Charles Chauncy to the Unitarianism of William Ellery Channing. The subsequent development of evangelical religion is equally fascinating, perhaps more so,

since the revitalized Calvinism of the Awakening was transformed, in the remarkable theological renaissance of the late
1750's and the 1760's, into a variety of "Calvinisms," each of
them destined to influence the intellectual life of America, and
also into other faiths, the continuities of which from the religion of the Awakening is not so readily apparent.

By confining himself entirely to dogmatics the historian can
trace Edwards' legacy into what came to be known as the
"New England theology," though it is no easy matter to determine which of the many varieties of the New Divinity most
faithfully preserved Edwards' insights. It has been suggested,
for instance, that Samuel Hopkins, by obscuring the "new
light" of the Awakening, succeeded in perverting Edwards'
lively faith into a sterile creed. In this regard, as in others, it
may be that Edwards' grandson, Timothy Dwight, and Jonathan Edwards, Jr., were not justified in claiming the mantle of
Edwards as their inheritance. Perhaps Edwards' truer heir, at
the close of the eighteenth century, was no such orthodox (and
Federalist) divine but the Baptist evangelist (and Jeffersonian
itinerant) John Leland.

Nor should the heritage of the Awakening itself be hastily
identified with only the frontier revivals of the nineteenth century. The ecstatic outbursts at Cane Ridge and in the Burned-
Over District differed, both in inspiration and in character,
from the outpourings of the 1740's. Indeed, the New York
revivalist Charles Grandison Finney and the Methodist circuit-
rider Peter Cartwright seem quite a different breed from even
Whitefield and Tennent, who, though "far from being clois-
tered and neurotic scholars,"[13] were nonetheless figures of
considerable intellectual dignity and discipline. And there
remains, of course, the commanding figure of Edwards, in
whose thinking if anywhere must be sought whatever "mean-

---

[13] Miller, "Great Awakening," p. 10.

ing" of the Awakening was transmitted through succeeding generations. If Edwards be considered in his role of philosopher merely, divorced from historical relationship to the Great Awakening, the line of spiritual descent can be traced, as has been eloquently done, to the thought of Emerson and the Transcendentalists.[14] But it must not be forgotten that all of Edwards' thinking embodied both the lessons and the aspirations of the Awakening, and that it focused, finally, on the possibility of bringing the Kingdom of God to America. In one sense, it is more than possible that the profoundest insight into the nature of the Awakening impulse was vouchsafed to the historian George Bancroft, who saw the essential spirit of Edwards revived and embodied in the Jacksonian democracy of his day.

To the question of where Edwards' evangelical legacy did ultimately repose, there is obviously no single satisfactory answer. But no worthwhile answer of any sort can be found by pursuing only a single strand of post-Awakening history; all must be viewed together. In the selections that follow, the immediate ecclesiastical and doctrinal consequences of the Awakening are presented separately, for in each realm there was a distinctive progression, and controversies significant in themselves. But such a distinction, however initially useful, proves inappropriate if too long persisted in, and, eventually, misleading—more so even than looking at the course of the Awakening itself purely in terms of self-contained geographical units. For neither the institutional changes wrought by the Awakening nor the intellectual ones emerged separately—either in fact or in the minds of the participants. Thus no post-Awakening issue, nor any single utterance, can be fully comprehended without having in mind the composite pattern of radical

[14] Perry Miller, "From Edwards to Emerson," *Errand into the Wilderness*, p. 184.

change in the religious life of the colonies—a revolution which, it must also be always remembered, arose in, and left its mark on, the whole of American society and culture.

Still, the seamless robe of history must be somewhere touched, and perhaps the best place is at the point where the contemporary evidence indicates whither the revival impulse, as broadly conceived as possible in the early 1740's, was tending. In his *Thoughts on the Revival*, Edwards described the Awakening as an expression of social discontent, and he gave voice to the social aspirations—even goals—of those whom he called "the people of God." Nor was Edwards' *Thoughts on the Revival* simply a defense of "affectionate" religion, for in it he translated the prophetic hopes of the awakened into a program for the redemption of American society. Apart from any assessment of the appropriateness or effectiveness of any of his particular programs (in none of which, Edwards complained, would the "great men" and the "rich men" of colonial society join), it is clear what was implied, in the context of mid-eighteenth-century America, by his prediction that the millennium would "begin in America." The critics of the revival, who from the first moment of the Awakening feared the social implications of the new enthusiasm, were certain that Edwards had issued a call to revolution.

The opponents of the Awakening quickly and consciously strove to strengthen the institutional mechanisms of the colonies and make them over into antipopulist bulwarks against the seemingly seditious energies released in the revival. The most obvious of the pressures being resisted, as also one of the clearest consequences of the revival, was the challenge of the awakened to religious establishments. Everywhere the Awakening issued in a proliferation of religious groups, and a lively competition among them. But in the South the evangelical impulse was resisted by the Episcopal establishment, and so too in New England, where laws were passed, and ministerial resolutions published, denying full freedom to the revival churches. In New England, the separating spirit of the revival gave rise, in most of the larger communities, to two or more competing churches. In many areas critics of the revival formed a new Anglican church; they could not be harassed by colonies which, under royal charter, were obliged to tolerate the Church of England. The weight of the New England establishments fell on the Separates, whose conventicles were formed of those zealously affected by the New Light. The strictly congregational Separates, like the Baptists who succeeded them in New England, were vocal crusaders for religious freedom. But other partisans of evangelical religion, though they hotly debated with these new sectarians, were likewise champions of religious liberty. For out of the Awakening, and consistent with the revival impulse, emerged the notion of "voluntarism," the assumption that church affiliation was not an obligation to be forced on men but a privilege that must be freely exercised.

The evangelical impulse also worked changes in the definition and constitution of the church. The Awakening brought a resurrection of the seventeenth-century Puritan ideal of church membership limited to the "regenerate." In the immediate post-Awakening years the notion of a "pure" or gathered church was most warmly espoused by the New England Separates and the Baptists of the Middle Colonies, both of which defined the church as a communion of those only who had experienced the converting grace of the Spirit. New Side Presbyterians and the Calvinist leaders of New England Congregationalism loudly disputed with these advocates of such a "pure" church. But the argument, it eventually became clear, was not in fact over the question of whether "saints" alone should be admitted to the privileges of church membership. The inner logic of evangelical religion demanded, as Tennent acknowledged, some distinction between the "precious" and the "vile," and even some sort of separation, for, as Tennent also asked during the Awakening, could the children of light be expected to break bread with the children of darkness?

The same question was also asked by Jonathan Edwards when he came, in the course of the Awakening, to reconsider and at last to publicly repudiate the ecclesiastical theories and practices of his grandfather, Solomon Stoddard. "Stoddardeanism" represented the culmination of the process by which, over the seventeenth century, the gate into the New England church had steadily been made less strait. In the first years of settlement only those were admitted as "saints," and allowed to participate in the sacraments, who satisfied the church with a public "profession of saving faith." Subsequently the examination of "professors" was made less rigorous, and under the provisions of the "Half-Way Covenant," adopted by the Synod of 1662, a descendant of any "saint," though he himself could offer no evidence whatever of regeneration, was allowed to present his children for baptism. Such Half-Way members were in theory barred from the other sacrament, the Lord's Supper, but in the late years of the century this barrier too was removed in many churches. Solomon Stoddard decided to admit all citizens of Northampton, the openly scandalous alone excepted, to the Lord's Supper. This practice, along with Stoddard's definition of "visible sainthood" in terms of an evidently sincere assent to the "truth" of the Christian religion, was embraced elsewhere in New England.

All this was challenged by Jonathan Edwards, who decided that both Stoddardeanism and the Half-Way Covenant were inconsistent with the truths and the experience of the revival, which marked some members of every congregation as distinctly "saints." For repudiating Stoddard, Edwards was ejected from Northampton, but his conception of limited church membership was successfully applied in other congregations by his Calvinist colleagues. In time Edwards' system came to be espoused even by many Presbyterians, who thereby broke with that church's tradition of nonexclusion. But such a break had been made at least in part even before the Awakening, when the Tennents had insisted on a much more rigorous examination of applicants for the Lord's Supper. Edwards' polity, however, took the further step of giving to the "saints," and to them alone, not sacramental privileges merely, but the power of governing the church. This power, as Edwards defined it, included disciplining the unregenerate members of the congregation, and distributing, out of a "joint stock" collected from the more prosperous citizens, "charity" to the less fortunate members of society. In sum, Edwards hoped to use the church as an instrument of his (or God's) larger strategy for controlling and redeeming the human community.

Thus Edwards' differences with the Separates were just as significant, and probably more so, than the ideals they held in common. What Edwards shared with the sectarian advocates of a "pure church" was a conviction that the affinities among the elect were much stronger bonds than any of the covenanted relationships into which a man happened to be born. Among the Separates and Baptists this sense of saintly union was expressed in the gathering of "pure" and "independent" churches by way of secession from "corrupt" congregations. Edwards, however, held a vision of the universal Church that transcended local communities and made the godly, wherever they lived or in whatever denomination enrolled, members of a larger Christian commonwealth. Of this greater union the sacrament, defined by Edwards as a "communion" in which was manifested the love of the true saints for each other, was a symbolic reminder—and even a means of making it a reality in human affairs. For "pious union" was, to Edwards, both a taste of millennial felicity and a means of committing the saints to endeavors on behalf of the earthly Kingdom of God. In this respect the Separates were, from Edwards' viewpoint, profoundly irresponsible, for in their communions was expressed, and encouraged, no more than one's sense of difference from (and superiority to) the "impure" neighbors from whom he had withdrawn. Such separated "saints" self-complacently neglected the larger community, except in bewailing its sins and in waiting for God to punish the wicked by intervening in history with the terrors of the Last Judgment. Such an historical pessimism contrasted sharply with Edwards' declaration that "fire from heaven" was not to be looked for, because God intended his kingdom to come into being solely through "natural" causes—by means, that is, of a gradual and progressive improvement in human affairs. To Edwards, the worst of Separate "heresies" was their failure to "fall in" with God's plan (and Edwards') for the redemption of society.

In the Awakening, Edwards believed, God had not simply promised that the millennium would begin in America, but that God had called on his American people to will a reorganized society into being. For Edwards, the ultimate test of sainthood was whether a man was so acting as to "promote" God's historical program. And here precisely was the essential issue as between Edwards and the Separates, which was not ecclesiastical, but doctrinal, and centered on their differing definitions of holiness. Much the same situation prevailed in the Middle Colonies, where the Moravians and the Baptists were persuaded that Gilbert Tennent and Samuel Finley were simply resentful of the competition—and probably envious of the degree to which their more emotional faiths preserved the true spirit of the Awakening, against which, it was charged, the New Side had now turned. The Separates, likewise, thought Edwards had betrayed the warm faith of the revival, and could not understand why he, who had defended "emotional" religion against Charles Chauncy, now referred to the most zealous of the awakened as a "wild, enthusiastical sort of people." The problem was that these sectarians did not understand what Edwards—and the New Side preachers too—had known from the beginning of the Awakening: that true sainthood consisted in much more than unbridled and insubstantial enthusiasm.

Because the Moravians and Baptists seemed to suggest that the regenerate man was released from the obligations of the moral law, Tennent and Edwards identified these enthusiasts as "Antinomians."[15] But such Antinomianism was not to be found, in the post-Awakening years, only among the sectarians. It was a challenge faced in every congregation, including Tennent's and Edwards' own, where there were men and women who had been touched by the Spirit. For everywhere in America there were many who, having "felt" the experience of grace, thereafter simply rejoiced in their good estate and asked no further evidence that they were saved. They believed that their holiness had been assured, and their Christian pilgrimage ended, by the single soul-ravishing experience of the Awakening. It was against such a notion of sainthood—and such an interpretation of the meaning of the Awakening—that Edwards and Tennent and their colleagues were arguing when they rebuked the enthusiasm of the Moravians, Baptists, and

---

[15] Antinomianism is not a specific heresy, but a term generally (and almost always loosely) used to characterize the notions of religious "fanatics" who deny the need for subjection to any law, specifically the moral law of the Old Testament. In America, the term is particularly identified with the party that formed around Anne Hutchinson in the New England "Antinomian Crisis" of 1636–1638. Mistress Hutchinson complained that most of the New England ministers preached that fulfillment of the law was a necessary condition of grace. She insisted that grace was not conditional, and in her defeat, the doctrine of "preparation," with which she was contending, became the official orthodoxy of New England. Her critics accused the Antinomians, however, of arguing that the saint was released from any and all "legal" obligations, and it is in this sense, signifying opposition to all laws whatever, that Antinomianism is often employed—as a sort of metaphysical synonym for anarchism.

Separates. In so arguing against Antinomianism the Calvinists of the colonies evolved a "true religion" which, both in substance and in manner of operation, was one of the most significant of the Awakening's intellectual legacies.

The reconstructed Calvinism of post-Awakening America took for granted the centrality and the necessity of "religious affections," but it condemned as narrow and inadequate any creed that identified holiness with nothing but a momentary emotional experience. The true saint, Tennent insisted, was not so easily comforted; much more was required before he might deem his calling and election sure. In what that "more" consisted was most clearly set forth in the 1740's in Edwards' *Treatise Concerning the Religious Affections,* which provided the Calvinists of all America with the postulates of their more substantial faith. In *The Religious Affections,* Edwards, after defending "affectionate" religion against the barbs of Chauncy, relentlessly exposed as self-deceptive many of the simpler "joys" which the subjects of the Awakening were accepting as proof that they had been saved. Such delight was not, Edwards insisted, the whole of sainthood and was, in fact, if unaccompanied by other affections, presumptive evidence that a man had not been saved at all. Justified happiness, he explained, was attended by a change in man's entire personality (the center of which Edwards called the "heart") and was expressed in the holiest of religious affections, "love." And such holiness of heart must and would manifest itself in a holy "will," as a benevolence, not of thought merely, but of deed.

Having established his principles of psychology, Edwards turned to the question of how a man might know whether he had been so regenerated. In explaining that this could come only by way of "experiment" or "trial," Edwards announced those principles of "experimental religion" which were thereafter to distinguish the evangelical religion of colonial America. To try one's spirit was not to engage in introspective self-examination, but to test the heart by the only appropriate evidence, one's manner of behaving. It was "not in contemplation, but in action," that one must prove, to himself or to others, the legitimacy of his claim to sainthood. "The main and most proper proof of a man's having a heart to do anything, is his doing of it." This was "experimental religion," in which not a single experience, but man's entire subsequent life, provided the evidence he was saved. Herein consisted not merely Edwards' difference with the Separates of the 1740's but that which largely distinguished the evangelical impulse in America from the pietism of eighteenth-century England and Europe. For "experimental religion," as defined by Edwards and embraced by other American Calvinists, was not designed to allow men existential solace in the midst of a troubled world, but demanded of them strenuous exertions bent on setting the world aright. The whole of what "experimental religion" required of the saint was not explicitly revealed by Edwards until his posthumously-published *Dissertation on True Virtue,* wherein he identified true sainthood with total commitment, in heart and in will, to making the social arrangements of mankind as "excellent," or "beautiful," as God intended them to be. But in *The Religious Affections* he made it abundantly clear that the test of sainthood involved endeavors to redeem society and even that the true saint would and could not rest until the Kingdom of God were established on earth.

Edwards' definition of sainthood was embraced by many New Side Presbyterians and, soon after his death, by the Baptists who, under the leadership of the awakened and self-taught preacher Isaac Backus, drew most of the New England Separates back into the evangelical fold. In so regathering, the partisans of "experimental religion" largely fulfilled one of the best-remembered and most frequently-recalled promises of the Great Awakening—that of a "more perfect union" of God's people in America. Such a prospect was revealed early in the revival—in interdenominational communion services and the exchange of pulpits, even between preachers of different colonies, among those who favored the "Work of God." The vision was further illuminated by Edwards' many efforts to realize the prophecy of the millennium, among them the device of concurrent prayer, whereby all the "people of God," of whatever denomination or province, might manifest their unity. Although Edwards' vision extended to all Christendom, it focused most sharply on the possibility of a union of all the pious "in *America*," extending from New England to Georgia. His critics ridiculed Edwards' proposal, for the opponents of the revival were, by contrast, rigidly sectarian and parochial, both in thought and in policy. They sought, for example, to frighten the populace away from Whitefield with the warning that he was an Episcopal "priest," and to keep evangelical ambassadors from other colonies out of their local areas. It was two decades after the Awakening before the spokesmen of rationalism began to evolve their own conception of "union," and when they did, their ideas and program still betrayed the fears aroused by Edwards' suggestion that "God's people" join hands in order to gain "the capacity to act with united strength."

In the second half of the eighteenth century the evangelical aspiration for unity struggled to find formal expression. The impulse was asserted, however, against the strong pull of tradition—a disposition among the spokesmen of the revival to compose differences with those who had opposed them in 1740–1742, and to reunify the old churches divided or strained by the Awakening. Pressure toward pacification was generated in response to real or imagined common external threats—by, at one moment, suspicion of the new sects, at another by fears of a growing Church of England. In the Revolutionary period nearly all the American churches, evangelical or no, made common cause against the "plot" to install an Anglican Bishop in the colonies. But the polarization of American Christianity by the Awakening could not be overcome, and the appeal of a purely evangelical unity, in which communion was limited to men of like mind and affections, proved the stronger and the more enduring.

The shifting alignments of post-Awakening Protestantism were reflected in the histories of the various seminaries of learning that are among the better known legacies of the eighteenth-century revival. The College of New Jersey, which opened in 1747, was the common project of New Side Presbyterians and the prorevivalists of New England. Settled eventually at Princeton, this institution succeeded the Log College as a place for the training of ministers. It was conceived also as an antidote to what seemed the "heresies" of Harvard and Yale, and for a generation its faculty and students were drawn from evangelical New England, as well as from the Middle Colonies and the South. In fact, Princeton was the focus of the intellectual life of Calvinist America generally; in the 1760's Isaac Backus encouraged promising young Baptists to enroll there. Meanwhile, Old Side Presbyterians had cooperated with Anglicans in establishing and running the College of Philadelphia. But after the reunion of Old Side and New Side Presbyterians in 1758, there began a slow process of change at Princeton that resulted, by the early 1770's, in the ejection of the New England element from the intellectual life of Presbyterianism. For a brief period evangelical interest centered on Yale, but the administration of that institution, like the New Light party that rose to dominance in the government of Connecticut, represented a compromising alliance with orthodoxy. Thus in the 1770's two colleges, more distinctively evangelical in inspiration and character, were established: the College of Rhode Island (later Brown), founded by New England Baptists, and Dartmouth, the first president of which was Eleazar Wheelock, one of the surviving itinerants of the Awakening.

The college at Hanover, New Hampshire, was an outgrowth of the school Wheelock had begun in 1743 to educate awakened Indians and to train missionaries for work among that people. Such institutions and enterprises were not, however, the only fruits of the revival spirit, nor the most enduringly significant. What was wrought by the Awakening was a profound alteration in ideas and aspirations, of which any one activity was merely a particular expression. Something of the fulness of that intellectual revolution was captured in the *Diary* of David Brainerd, which Jonathan Edwards presented to the reading public in 1749. Together with Edwards' interpretive memoir of this missionary among the Indians, Brainerd's *Diary* comprises one of the major documents of the Awakening heritage, for it served many generations of evangelical Americans as a standard of faith and practice. Its message was, however, encapsulated in a few sentences of Edwards' concluding observations on Brainerd's "powerful exercise" of true religion:

> How greatly Mr. Brainerd's religion differed from that of some pretenders to the experience of a clear work of conversion wrought on their hearts; who, depending and living on that, settle in a cold, careless and carnal frame of mind. . . . On the contrary, that work on his heart . . . was with him evidently but the beginning of his work, his first entering on the great business of religion and the service of God, his first setting out in his race. His work was not finished, nor his race ended, until life was ended. . . . He continued pressing forward in a constant manner, forgetting the things that were behind, and reaching forth towards the things that were before.

If any one sentence discloses the intellectual significance of the Awakening, it is this last, for the "business of religion," as conceived by post-Awakening Calvinists, was not limited to such traditional endeavors as spreading the Gospel. And as the evangelical impulse pressed forward, many new opportunities, unanticipated even by Edwards, arose (or were created by

Calvinists) for Americans to fulfill the demands of experimental religion by performing the will of God.

In the Awakening, the followers of Edwards believed, God had not simply promised that the millennium would begin in America; he had called on his American people to exert their wills in order to bring that good society into being. Brainerd's endeavors were only one way of "promoting" God's historical design; other men were also required to aid the cause by expressing, at every opportunity, "a great and universal benevolence." Such a definition of true virtue, as embodied in, among other Calvinist writings, Joseph Bellamy's *True Religion Delineated* (which this student of Edwards published in 1750 with the *imprimatur* of the master), was what actually distinguished evangelical religion from the rationalism that arose in post-Awakening America. For the ultimate issue, as between those most conspicuous and persisting streams of American Protestantism, was not the place of emotion in the conversion experience, but the nature and the goals of man's moral endeavor.

At the time of the Awakening, Arminian morality assumed a static, even structured, social order, in which each man's "duties" were defined according to his place and station in society. Eventually rational religion opened the possibility of individual advancement, but it continued to argue that man's happiness and holiness derived solely from a reasonable assessment of, and conformity to, the dictates of his environment. Thus rationalism's two objections to Calvinism were not truly distinct. Critics of Calvinism complained that allowing emotion into man's life put him "out of the Power of distinguishing what is right from what is wrong. For this cannot be done but by man's Reasoning and Perceptive Power, by which he compares things to form his Judgment." The critics also argued (with increasing vehemence in the late 1740's) that Calvinism, by its denigration of "works," encouraged an all-licensed immorality. Both charges assumed that morality was the result of reason and calculation, and, for that matter, strongly implied that worldly prosperity was at least as valuable an end toward which to work as salvation. Evangelical religion, on the other hand, considered true virtue possible only after justification, and virtuous acts as flowing spontaneously (as Edwards conceived the personality) outward from the fountain that was the "vital indwelling principle" of grace. A regenerate heart made it possible for man to choose the good, and to pursue it, "without being at the trouble of a train of reasoning." In this contrast of premises and perspectives was contained no less than opposing judgments of the worth of the existing social order. For Calvinism released men from the vise of traditional obligations and relationships, but not into self-indulgence. It was the duty of the Calvinist "saint" to fulfill "the royal law of love"—to serve, that is, not himself but his fellow men and even, if necessary, to join with him in common endeavors to change society.

At the heart of the evangelical ethic was the hope of human betterment, the vision of a great community in which men, instinctively as it were, would seek the general welfare. Where evangelical virtue might lead America was disclosed in the sermons of the 1740's and 1750's denouncing the acquisitive ethic of Arminian rationalism. But Calvinism was not merely negative in its social attitudes, and much of the drama of the decade after the Awakening consisted in the effort of the Calvinist mind to find new and positive means of applying its definition of true virtue in American society—in the life of the body politic as well as in that of individuals. Rapidly and radically Calvinism's vision of the social good flowed into political protest, into challenges to the "rulers" of colonial society, and, eventually, into the discussion and the activity that preceded and accompanied the American Revolution. But this is another tale, the merest prologue to which (and of that, only glimpses) is offered in the last section of the documents, which includes a few of the more significant utterances of the second decade after the revival.

In turning to that literature, or to the documents of the Awakening years themselves, the reader must bear in mind that the printed page contains the thought and expression of the Awakening, but not its "meaning." Seldom is the fulness of the evangelical revolution made explicit, and then never in any single document. Indeed, several of the documents, taken together, might seem to suggest that there was no definably "evangelical" impulse, that the spirited post-Awakening debates, among the various beneficiaries of the revival, testified to nothing so much as the utter fragmentation of American Calvinism. And it is true that the ecumenical spirit of evangelicalism was sorely tested as the representatives of the older churches argued with those of the new sects. But these evangelicals argued not so much with each other as for the attention of the American mind and, in so doing, actually attested to the death of the old notion of religious uniformity, and the birth of a new ideal of unity. In all their disputes, "the conception of religious liberty was so taken for granted that it had hardly ever to be stated. Therefore, in this open field, the very competition among the denominations . . . becomes, to the analytical eye, not so much a manifestation of individuality, one might say an almost unconscious, method of maintaining some perverse form of solidarity. Rivalry among the churches, even while appearing as contention, proclaimed that they were all members of one single society, that they were not disparate atoms but all conjoined in emulation."[16]

In this new solidarity the advocates of reasonable religion did not participate, at least not in the eighteenth century. For the spokesmen of rationalism neither embraced the ideal of

---

[16] Miller, "Great Awakening," p. 11.

"voluntarism" nor appreciated the kind of unity that evangelical religion affirmed or the goals it pursued. The spokesmen of rationalism defended their own "right of private judgment," not merely against Calvinist critics, but from the demands of an outraged multitude. They viewed themselves as an embattled minority, for Calvinism was, for at least a generation after the Awakening, by far the most popular of the faiths available to Americans. Not surprisingly, the "respectable" citizens of the colonies affiliated themselves with the churches of reasonable religion, but the "lower sort," who, it was generally acknowledged, filled evangelical communions, were by far the more numerous. Among them were many awakened in the 1740's, but others were attracted to evangelical preachers because they, and they alone, continued to sound the jubilee trumpet of the revival. And if the divine light of the Awakening flickered for some of the pious, or even died, by no means all foreswore the Calvinist faith or embraced the "modish divinity" of Arminian "self-sufficiency." On the contrary, many tended, particularly where the policy of rationalists was to deny religious liberty to evangelicals, preachers or people, to lash out against, not rationalist ministers merely, but their smug and prosperous parishioners, and, in so doing, persuade themselves that they were performing the revealed will of God.

Why and how the evangelical multitude did so is not revealed in the documents of the Awakening and its immediate aftermath. But the texts do inform us that in the reconstitution of the churches after the revival, the laity of the evangelical churches were accorded greater power, both in the choice of ministers and in assessing the moral character of their fellow citizens. What such evidence cannot communicate, however, is what this meant in the evolution of the American mind, or to the subsequent history of America—that in the Great Awakening the "will of the people" began its steady march to eventual supremacy. In this case and in many others, it is "entirely a matter of divining nuances." The Awakening liberated Gilbert

Tennent's "Common People" from more than the contumely of their self-appointed betters. In the revival was also removed a more enfeebling intellectual burden, for in the new light of the Awakening was glimpsed the possibility of a people's acting to make their united will prevail as the guarantor of the common good.

"From one point of view, then, this was what actually was at work inside the hysterical agonies of the Great Awakening. This is one thing they meant: the end of the reign over the New England and American mind of a European and scholastical conception of an authority put over men because men were incapable of recognizing their own welfare. This insight may assist us somewhat in comprehending why the pundits of Boston and Cambridge, all of whom were rational and tolerant and decent, shuddered with a horror that was deeper than mere dislike of the antics of the yokels. To some extent, they sensed that the religious screaming had implications in the realm of society, and those implications they—being businessmen and speculators, as were the plutocracy of Northampton—did not like.

". . . In this episode, the Americans were indeed participating in an international movement; even so, they came—or Edwards brought them—to sharper formulations of American experience. What the Awakening really meant for Americans was not that they too were behaving like Dutchmen or Germans or Lancashire workmen, but in the ecstasy of the revival they were discovering, especially on the frontier, where life was the toughest, that they rejected imported European philosophies of society. They were now of themselves prepared to contend that the guiding rule of this society will be its welfare. . . ."[17]

What was awakened in 1740 was the spirit of American democracy.

---

[17] Miller, "Edwards and the Great Awakening," pp. 18–19.

SELECTED BIBLIOGRAPHY

The Bibliography, which is offered by way of suggestions for further reading, does not include articles cited in the Introduction or volumes from which the texts of documents have been extracted.

ORIGINAL SOURCES

EDWARDS, JONATHAN. *Religious Affections*. Edited by JOHN E. SMITH. New Haven: Yale University Press, 1959.

FAUST, CLARENCE H., and JOHNSON, THOMAS H., eds. *Jonathan Edwards: Representative Selections*. New York: American Book Company, 1935. Reprinted as Hill and Wang paperback, 1962.

HOFSTADTER, RICHARD, and SMITH, WILSON, eds. *American Higher Education: A Documentary History*. 2 vols. Chicago: The University of Chicago Press, 1961. Parts I–II.

MILLER, PERRY, ed. "Jonathan Edwards' Sociology of the Great Awakening," *New England Quarterly*, XXI (March 1948), 50–77.

SMITH, H. SHELTON, *et al.*, eds. *American Christianity: An Historical Interpretation with Representative Documents. 1607–1820*. Vol. I. New York: Charles Scribner's Sons, 1960. Chapters 6–7.

COLLATERAL READING

BRIDENBAUGH, CARL. *Mitre and Sceptre: Transatlantic Faiths, Ideas, Personalities, and Politics, 1689–1775*. New York: Oxford University Press, 1962.

GAUSTAD, EDWIN SCOTT. *The Great Awakening in New England*. New York: Harper and Bros., 1957.

GEWEHR, WESLEY M. *The Great Awakening in Virginia, 1740–1790*. Durham, N.C.: Duke University Press, 1930.

GOEN, C. C. *Revivalism and Separatism in New England, 1740–1800*. New Haven: Yale University Press, 1962.

HAROUTUNIAN, JOSEPH. *Piety versus Moralism: the Passing of the New England Theology*. New York: Henry Holt & Co., 1932.

HEIMERT, ALAN. *Religion and the American Mind: from the Great Awakening to the Revolution*. Cambridge, Mass.: Harvard University Press, 1966.

HENRY, STUART C. *George Whitefield: Wayfaring Witness*. New York: Abingdon Press, 1957.

HOFSTADTER, RICHARD. *Anti-Intellectualism in American Life*. New York: Alfred A. Knopf, 1963.

LABAREE, LEONARD W. *Conservatism in Early American History*. New York: New York University Press, 1963. Reprinted as Cornell paperback, 1959.

MAXSON, C. H. *The Great Awakening in the Middle Colonies*. Chicago: The University of Chicago Press, 1920.

MEAD, SIDNEY E. "Denominationalism: the Shape of Protestantism in America," *Church History*, XXIII (December 1954), 291–320.

———. "The Rise of the Evangelical Conception of the Ministry in America (1607–1850)," in H. Richard Niebuhr and Daniel D. Williams, eds., *The Ministry in Historical Perspective*. New York: Harper & Bros., 1956. Pages 207–249.

MILLER, JOHN C. "Religion, Finance and Democracy in Massachusetts," *New England Quarterly*, VI (March 1933), 29–58.

MILLER, PERRY. *Errand into the Wilderness*. Cambridge, Mass.: Harvard University Press, 1956. Reprinted as Harper Torchbook, 1963.

———. "From the Covenant to the Revival," in James Ward Smith and A. Leland Jamison, eds., *Religion in American Life*. Vol. I, *The Shaping of American Religion*. Princeton, N.J.: Princeton University Press, 1961. Pages 322–368.

———. *Jonathan Edwards*. New York: William Sloane Associates, 1949. Reprinted as Meridian paperback, 1958.

MORGAN, EDMUND S. "The American Revolution Considered as an Intellectual Movement," in Arthur M. Schlesinger, Jr. and Morton White, eds., *Paths of American Thought*. Boston: Houghton Mifflin, 1963. Pages 11–13.

NIEBUHR, H. RICHARD. *The Kingdom of God in America*. New York: Harper and Bros., 1937. Reprinted as Harper Torchbook, 1959.

SKLAR, ROBERT. "The Great Awakening and Colonial Politics: Connecticut's Revolution in the Minds of Men," *The Connecticut Historical Society Bulletin*, Vol. 28, No. 3 (July 1963), 81–95.

TRACY, JOSEPH. *The Great Awakening. A History of the Revival of Religion in the Time of Edwards and Whitefield*. Boston, 1841.

TRINTERUD, LEONARD J. *The Forming of an American Tradition. A Re-examination of Colonial Presbyterianism*. Philadelphia: The Westminster Press, 1949.

WRIGHT, CONRAD. *The Beginnings of Unitarianism in America*. Boston: Beacon Press, 1955.

EDITOR'S NOTE

At the time of his death Perry Miller was working on a lecture (to have been delivered at Johns Hopkins University) on the revival impulse of the eighteenth century. He planned to bring his reinterpretation of the Great Awakening to bear on what had been conceived as a joint Introduction to the present volume. Our discussions had not proceeded, however, beyond the most exploratory of stages, and though a few ideas were developed over dinner or on the sidewalks of Cambridge, no decision had been made on the division of tasks. For many reasons it seemed quite appropriate to present this anthology as a collaboration; Perry Miller makes his direct contributions through quotations from his earlier published commentaries on the Awakening. May these excerpts, some of them quite lengthy, serve to lead the reader to the works from which they are taken!

With the exception of the quotations, responsibility for the ideas presented in the Introduction is of course wholly mine. The same is true of the selection of documents. At one point I drew up a possible Table of Contents and submitted it to Perry Miller for approval, but it was never considered anything but tentative. In the course of years several of the items on the original list disappeared, and others were added. In choosing the documents I have been guided by my understanding of the Awakening as both a significant progression of events and as a crisis in the history of the American mind. My goal was a series of texts that would tell the tale of the revival and, at the same time, accurately represent the configuration, and confrontation, of ideas in the Awakening and the years of controversy that followed.

The headnotes to the documents unfold the history of the Awakening in each of the major areas of revival activity and outline the specific issues that inspired publication in the aftermath of the revival. They provide the information necessary to an understanding of the particular setting and context of each utterance, but they do not explore the broader issues implicit in any statement. For this, as for the broader pattern of ideas connecting particular controversies, the reader must turn (preferably before consulting the documents) to the Introduction. This is in the nature of a general essay, dealing with the larger contours of American intellectual life in the era of the Awakening.

Many of the more important utterances of the period are so lengthy that a full reproduction of any would have filled nearly this entire volume. One entitled *A Short Reply to Mr. Whitefield's Letter* ran to nearly one hundred pages, and Tennent, Dickinson, Thomson, Chauncy, and Edwards often took four times that much space to develop their arguments. That such was the case was a tribute to the eighteenth-century mind, which even in sermons only occasionally expressed itself in a form that permits full reproduction in a collection of representative documents. Most of the selections in this volume consist, however, of sections that in the longer originals stood somewhat independently. A few briefer texts, among them instances of lay expression (broadsides or magazine articles), are reproduced in their entirety, as are three longer documents—Gilbert Tennent's Nottingham Sermon, Charles Chauncy's caveat against enthusiasm, and the Harvard faculty's rebuke of Whitefield—central to any understanding of the Awakening. Another, Joseph Bellamy's sermon on the millennium, is possibly *the* essential text for any appreciation of the ramifications of the revival in the mind of later eighteenth-century America. Of these, only two, it might be noted, have previously been made available to the twentieth-century reader, and then in something less than a full text. Most of the documents mark the first time these utterances have come before the public since the era of the Awakening.

I have also tried to present the thought of the Awakening through as many voices as possible. Despite the inclusion of more than one statement by several contributors to the thought of the Awakening, the selections probably do not adequately suggest the special role of certain figures. This is especially the case with Jonathan Edwards, but I comfort myself with the thought that his writings are the most familiar, and available, of all the participants in the revival. With one exception, that of the fairly well-known *Religious Affections,* my selections from Edwards represent a conscious effort to present writings of Edwards that are generally ignored and aspects of his thought that have been too long neglected.

Except in the one instance where a manuscript source has been previously transcribed, and in those cases where the source is a collected edition, the exact original eighteenth-century text is followed. No change has been made in spelling, capitalization, or punctuation, but the modern "s" has been substituted and obvious typographical errors silently corrected. I have also occasionally removed, without notice to the reader, numbers at the heads of paragraphs or what struck me as a superfluity of Scriptural citation. Otherwise excisions have been indicated in the usual manner; but where a selection opens or closes with a complete paragraph, no elision has been marked. Only those references and allusions in the text that are necessary to a proper understanding of the context are identified or explained. Unless otherwise indicated, all footnotes are those of the original authors.

For making the original texts available for study and reproduction I would like to thank the Houghton Library of Harvard University, the Andover-Harvard Library, the Boston Athenaeum, the Boston Public Library, and the libraries of the

Congregational Historical Society, the Massachusetts Historical Society, and the Historical Society of Pennsylvania. I am grateful to Barry O'Connell for his assistance in preparing the texts for publication.

Eliot House   *Alan Heimert*
Cambridge, Massachusetts
December 1965

The Great Awakening

DOCUMENTS ILLUSTRATING THE CRISIS

AND ITS CONSEQUENCES

PART ONE

TOWARD THE AWAKENING

1 · Samuel Wigglesworth

(1688–1768)

AN ESSAY FOR REVIVING

RELIGION

———————

Almost from the time of the settlement of the New England colonies it had been customary for a representative of the clergy to deliver an annual "election sermon." The occasion provided an opportunity to expound political theory, to assess social conditions, and even to propose policies to the legislature. For nearly three-quarters of a century such sermons had followed the formula of the "jeremiad"—the people of Massachusetts (or Connecticut) were warned of the judgments God held in store for his backsliding people. The jeremiad form had first been set in Michael Wig-

———————

Samuel Wigglesworth, *An Essay for Reviving Religion. A Sermon Delivered . . . May 30th. MDCCXXXIII. Being the Anniversary for the Election . . .* (Boston, 1733), pp. 22–26, 30–31.

3

glesworth's long poem of 1662, "God's Controversy with New England." His son, Samuel, was one of the first election preachers to view New England's problems from a different perspective. Unlike his more famous brother, Edward, Harvard's first Hollis Professor of Divinity, Samuel Wigglesworth was subsequently an ardent celebrant of the Great Awakening.

It is a Truth, that we have a *goodly exterior Form of Religion;* Our *Doctrine, Worship* and *Sacraments* are *Orthodox, Scriptural* and *Divine.* There is an external Honour paid to the *Sabbath;* and a professed Veneration for Christ's *Ambassadors* for the sake of their Lord. We set up and maintain the *Publick Worship* of God, and the Voice of the Multitude saying, *Let us go into the House of the Lord,* is yet heard in our Land.

Moreover *Practical Religion* is not quite extirpated among us, and there are, it is to be hoped, a considerable number of serious and vigorous Christians in our Churches, whose *Piety* is acknowledged and respected by their Neighbours, whilst Living; and their *Memories* preserved for it when deceased. Whilst on the other hand, the *prophane and wicked Person* is generally abhor'd; and the more deformed Vices seek the retreats of Darkness to hide their detestable heads.

And yet with what sorrow must we speak, that these things are but the *Remains* of what we *Once* might show; the shadow of past and vanish'd Glory! . . .

If the *Fear of the Lord* be to *Hate Evil,* as *Prov.* 8. 13. Then it is to be feared that our *Religion runs low,* and but little of this Fear is in us: Inasmuch as we find our selves stained with so many most odious Vices, especially *Uncleanness, Drunkenness, Theft, Covetousness, Violence, Malice, Strife,* and others: Which tho', as 'twas said before, they be look'd upon with dishonour, yet multitudes are found who are not ashamed to commit them; and where such *Iniquities abound,* may we not infer that *the Love of many waxeth cold?*

Again, How *Weak is the Testimony that is born by our Good Men against those Transgressions!* Ought not holy Ones when they *Behold the Transgressor, to be grieved!* Will they not hate the things which God hates, and express a suitable indignation at the presumption of the Wicked, and the affronts which they put upon the Majesty of Heaven? *Reproving,* and bringing them to *Punishment?* If therefore our *Professors of Religion* think *Open Prophaneness* unworthy of their Wrath: If our *Ministers of Religion* are sparing to bear their publick Testimony against it; and when also the *Ministers of Justice* are too Complaisant to the Sons of Wickedness, to Execute the wholesome Laws of the Province upon them; unto how low an ebb is our Goodness come! . . .

Nor is it less evident that many of us who have given our *Consent to Religion;* are for *Curtailing* and *Abridging* it as much as we can: contenting ourselves with the *lowest degrees* of it, and carefully avoiding all it's most *Arduous, Mortifying Duties,* such as *Mortification* of our *Beloved Lusts, Self-Denial, Weaning ourselves from the World, Bestowing our Riches on Works of Piety,* and *Overcoming Evil with Good:* As if we were resolved not to *Wrestle with Flesh and Blood,* and to make *Christ's Yoke lighter* than Himself hath done? Many Men are upon Enquiry, *What strict Duty requires of them,* How often they must *Pray,* How often going to *Meeting* will serve the turn; and if they can satisfy their *Conscience,* they care not how seldom: How far *Christian Liberty* may be *extended,* and whither they may not take this or that *Gratification consistently with Religion?* How *sunk* and *debas'd a Temper* is this! And yet 'tis too evidently our own to be deny'd.

And what are we to think of that *Goodness* which is like a *Morning Cloud?* The shocking degree of Apostacy, which is so visible in many of our highest pretenders to Holiness; who having been wrought upon by the *Terrors* of their *Consciences,* and the *Amazing Dispensations of Providence* to *Put away the evil of their Doings;* but have since *turned back,* some to *Open & Scandalous Sins,* and a far greater number to a *Loose unguarded* way of Living, and a *Lifeless Temper;* creates distressing Apprehensions in all them that are sincerely desirous *God's Kingdom* may be advanced in our Land. . . .

I shall only now add, That the *Powerful Love of the World, and Exorbitant Reach after Riches,* which is become the reigning Temper in Persons of all Ranks in our Land, is alone enough to awaken our concerns for abandon'd, slighted and forgotten Religion. 'Tis this that takes up our Time, seizes our Affections, and governs our Views: Straitens our Hands: respecting Works of Charity, and pusheth us into the most wicked Schemes and Methods. This *Worldly Spirit* has in a great measure thrust out Religion, and given it a *Wound* which will prove *Deadly* unless infinite Mercy prevent. . . .

We bless God that we see our Land from time to time cleansed from *Innocent Blood* by the Blood of the Murderer, & other abominable Wickednesses receiving their due Recompence: But it would compleat our Joy if many other Crimes which we think also deserving to be *punish'd by the Judges* were more severely animadverted upon; That so *All Iniquity may stop its mouth.* And would our *Courts of Judicature* please to frown upon those *Litigious* Persons, who make uneasy Work for them, and disturb the repose of their Neighbours; they would do a Work acceptable to God & Man; and Religion would escape the wounds which it daily receives from strife & envy.

. . . It is to be hoped that things have not yet run to so low an ebb with us, but that a good number, if not the greater part of our *Priests* are seen *Cloathed with Righteousness;* That the good and amiable things which they press upon their

Hearers are in some good measure to be found in their own *Personal Characters.* If this be one of the Good things which remain, Let us (my Fathers & Brethren in the Ministry) strengthen it by a more universal Care to live our own Sermons: That we may *Adorn the Doctrine of God our Saviour,* by a *Conversation,* which may convince the World that we believe what we preach, & relish the Duties which we˙ perswade others to embrace. Incredible will be the Influence of such an *Harmony* between our *Doctrine and Life* in setting a new face upon Religion. In such a case, we might reasonably hope, that we should not *Labour in vain nor spend our strength for nought.*

And then as to our *Preaching,* Let us not labour to build up a *Shell,* to form a meer *Carcase of Godliness,* by furnishing our Auditors with *Moral Virtues,* only, void of *Internal Vital Principles;* but *Travail in Birth* with them until *Christ be formed in them,* and they are become holy in Heart, as well as blameless of Life. I know not how we can begin with our Flocks better, than the *Great Prophet & Teacher* did with *Nicodemus, Except a Man be born again, he cannot see the Kingdom of God.*

Our Reasoning with them must tend to perswade them to be *Real and Altogether,* not *Almost Christians,* and therefore we must not heal their wounded Consciences slightly; but wisely suffer *Convictions* to ripen into true *Conversion:* That they may pass from *Death* to *Life* in good Earnest, and not deceive themselves with vain Hopes, and impose upon the World with their *Name* that they *Live.* To prevent which also the Duty of Self-Examination, ought to be frequently urg'd upon them, that they may judge of their state, and rectify what is amiss.

2 · *Jonathan Edwards*

(*1 7 0 3 – 1 7 5 8*)

"JUSTIFICATION BY FAITH

ALONE"

In 1736, the year after the Northampton revival, Edwards'
Faithful Narrative of Surprising Conversions was published in London. Two years later an American edition
appeared, with a preface containing five "Discourses on
Various Important Subjects" delivered by Edwards at the
time of the revival. The most important, to Edwards'
mind, was that on the "great Reformation doctrine" of
justification by faith. It was by recalling his people to this
"principal hinge" of Protestantism, Edwards contended,
that the spread of Arminianism was resisted. More importantly, the outpouring of the Spirit was ample evidence
of "God's approbation" of the "evangelical scheme."

I know there are many that make as though this controversy was of no great importance; that it is chiefly a matter of

Jonathan Edwards, *The Works of President Edwards* . . . (4 vols.; New
York, 1844), IV, 128–131.

nice speculation, depending on certain subtle distinctions, which many that make use of them do not understand themselves; and that the difference is not of such consequence as to be worth the being zealous about; and that more hurt is done by raising disputes about it than good.

Indeed I am far from thinking that it is of absolute necessity that persons should understand, and be agreed upon, all the distinctions needful particularly to explain and defend this doctrine against all cavils and objections (though all Christians should strive after an increase of knowledge, and none should content themselves without some clear and distinct understanding in this point): but that we should believe in the general, according to the clear and abundant revelations of God's word, that it is none of our own excellency, virtue, or righteousness, that is the ground of our being received from a state of condemnation into a state of acceptance in God's sight, but only Jesus Christ, and his righteousness, and worthiness, received by faith. This I think to be of great importance, at least in application to ourselves; and that for the following reasons.

The Scripture treats of this doctrine, as a doctrine of very great importance. That there is a certain doctrine of justification by faith, in opposition to justification by the works of the law, that the Apostle Paul insists upon as of the greatest importance, none will deny; because there is nothing in the Bible more apparent. The apostle, under the infallible conduct of the Spirit of God, thought it worth his most strenuous and zealous disputing about and defending. He speaks of the contrary doctrine as fatal and ruinous to the souls of men, in the latter end of the ninth chapter of Romans, and beginning of the tenth. He speaks of it as subversive of the gospel of Christ, and calls it another gospel, and says concerning it, if any one, "though an angel from heaven, preach it, let him be accursed. . . ."

The adverse scheme lays another foundation of man's salvation than God hath laid. I do not now speak of that ineffectual redemption that they suppose to be universal, and what all mankind are equally the subjects of; but I say, it lays entirely another foundation of man's actual, discriminating salvation, or that salvation, wherein true Christians differ from wicked men. We suppose the foundation of this to be Christ's worthiness and righteousness: on the contrary, that scheme supposes it to be men's own virtue; even so, that this is the ground of a saving interest in Christ itself. It takes away Christ out of the place of the bottom stone, and puts in men's own virtue in the room of him: so that Christ himself in the affair of distinguishing, actual salvation, is laid upon this foundation. And the foundation being so different, I leave it to every one to judge whether the difference between the two schemes consists only in punctilios of small consequence. The foundations being contrary, makes the whole scheme exceeding diverse and opposite: the one is a gospel scheme, the other a legal one.

It is in this doctrine that the most essential difference lies between the covenant of grace and the first covenant. The adverse scheme of justification supposes that we are justified by our works, in the very same sense wherein man was to have been justified by his works under the first covenant. By that covenant our first parents were not to have had eternal life given them for any proper merit in their obedience; because their perfect obedience was a debt that they owed God: nor was it to be bestowed for any proportion between the dignity of their obedience, and the value of the reward; but only it was to be bestowed from a regard to a moral fitness in the virtue of their obedience to the reward of God's favor; and a title to eternal life was to be given them, as a testimony of God's pleasedness with their works, or his regard to the inherent beauty of their virtue. And so it is the very same way that those in the adverse scheme suppose that we are received into God's special favor now, and to those saving benefits that are the testimonies of it. I am sensible the divines of that side entirely disclaim the Popish doctrine of merit; and are free to speak of our utter unworthiness, and the great imperfection of all our services: but after all, it is our virtue, imperfect as it is, that recommends men to God, by which good men come to have a saving interest in Christ, and God's favor, rather than others; and these things are bestowed in testimony of God's respect to their goodness. So that whether they will allow the term *merit* or no, yet they hold, that we are accepted by our own merit, in the same sense though not in the same degree as under the first covenant.

. . . It is no gospel at all; it is law: it is no covenant of grace, but of works: it is not an evangelical, but a legal doctrine. Certainly that doctrine wherein consists the greatest and most essential difference between the covenant of grace and the first covenant, must be a doctrine of great importance. That doctrine of the gospel by which above all others it is worthy of the name gospel, is doubtless a very important doctrine of the gospel.

This is the main thing that fallen men stood in need of divine revelation for, to teach us how we that have sinned may come to be again accepted of God; or, which is the same thing, how the sinner may be justified. Something beyond the light of nature is necessary to salvation chiefly on this account. Mere natural reason afforded no means by which we could come to the knowledge of this, it depending on the sovereign pleasure of the Being that we had offended by sin. This seems to be the great drift of that revelation that God has given, and of all those mysteries it reveals, all those great doctrines that are peculiarly doctrines of revelation, and above the light of nature. . . .

The contrary scheme of justification derogates much from

the honor of God and the Mediator. I have already shown how it diminishes the glory of the Mediator, in ascribing that to man's virtue and goodness, which belongs alone to his worthiness and righteousness.

By the apostle's sense of the matter it renders Christ needless: Gal. v. 4, "Christ is become of no effect to you, whosoever of you are justified by the law." If that scheme of justification be followed in its consequences, it utterly overthrows the glory of all the great things that have been contrived, and done, and suffered in the work of redemption. Gal. ii. 21, "If righteousness come by the law, Christ is dead in vain." It has also been already shown how it diminishes the glory of divine grace (which is the attribute God hath especially set himself to glorify in the work of redemption); and so that it greatly diminishes the obligation to gratitude in the sinner that is saved: yea, that in the sense of the apostle, it makes void the distinguishing grace of the gospel. Gal. v. 4, "Whosoever of you are justified by the law, ye are fallen from grace." It diminishes the glory of the grace of God and the Redeemer, and proportionably magnifies man: it makes him something before God, when indeed he is nothing: it makes the goodness and excellency of fallen man to be something, which I have shown are nothing. I have also already shown, that it is contrary to the truth of God in the threatening of his holy law, to justify the sinner for his virtue. And whether it were contrary to God's truth or no, it is a scheme of things very unworthy of God, that supposes that God, when about to lift up a poor, forlorn malefactor, condemned to eternal misery for sinning against his Majesty, out of his misery, and to make him unspeakably and eternally happy, by bestowing his Son and himself upon him, as it were, sets all this to sale, for the price of his virtue and excellency. I know that those we oppose do acknowledge, that the price is very disproportionate to the benefit bestowed; and say, that God's grace is wonderfully manifested in accepting so little virtue, and bestowing so glorious a reward for such imperfect righteousness. But seeing we are such infinitely sinful and abominable creatures in God's sight, and by our infinite guilt have brought ourselves into such wretched and deplorable circumstances, and all our right-eousnesses are nothing, and ten thousand times worse than nothing (if God looks upon them as they be in themselves), is it not immensely more worthy of the infinite majesty and glory of God, to deliver and make happy such poor, filthy worms, such wretched vagabonds and captives, without any money or price of theirs, or any manner of expectation of any excellency or virtue in them, in any wise to recommend them? Will it not betray a foolish, exalting opinion of ourselves, and a mean one of God, to have a thought of offering any thing of ours, to recommend us to the favor of being brought from wallowing, like filthy swine, in the mire of our sins, and from the enmity and misery of devils in the lowest hell, to the state of God's dear children, in the everlasting arms of his love, in heavenly glory; or to imagine that that is the constitution of God, that we should bring our filthy rags, and offer them to him as the price of this?

The opposite scheme does most directly tend to lead men to trust in their own righteousness for justification, which is a thing fatal to the soul. This is what men are of themselves exceedingly prone to do (and that though they are never so much taught the contrary), through the exceeding partial and high thoughts they have of themselves, and their exceeding dulness of apprehending any such mystery as our being accepted for the righteousness of another. But this scheme does directly teach men to trust in their own righteousness for justification; in that it teaches them that this is indeed what they must be justified by, being the way of justification that God himself has appointed. So that if a man had naturally no disposition to trust in his own righteousness, yet if he embraced this scheme, and acted consistent with it, it would lead him to it.

3 · *Gilbert Tennent*

(*1 7 0 3 – 1 7 6 4*)

THE UNSEARCHABLE RICHES

OF CHRIST

———————

Gilbert Tennent came to America in 1718 with his father, William Tennent, an Episcopal deacon who took Presbyterian orders immediately on his arrival in the colonies. Gilbert and his brothers were educated at the Log College, and in 1726 Gilbert Tennent was installed as minister at New Brunswick, New Jersey. It was in this area that Theodorus Frelinghuysen had had considerable success in promoting a revival in the Dutch Reformed Church by enforcing strict requirements for admission to the Lord's Supper. During and after their brief revival of 1735 the young Presbyterians of New Jersey employed a similar strategy. In a volume of "sacramental" sermons they explained their theory and practice. Gilbert Tennent's preface, dated August 30, 1737, setting forth the

———————

Gilbert Tennent, "Preface," *The Unsearchable Riches of Christ. Considered in Two Sermons on Ephes. iii. 8. Preach'd at New-Brunswick . . . in August, 1737,* in *Sermons on Sacramental Occasions by Divers Ministers* (Boston, 1739), pp. i–v.

larger significance of the remembrance of Christ, anticipated his position in the controversy, formally inaugurated
in 1738, on the nature of happiness and virtue.

Christian Friends and dear Brethren,

The Desire of Happiness is co-natural to the human Soul,
and yet remains with it, notwithstanding the Ruins of its
Apostacy from the blessed God.

But alass, such brutal Blindness infatuates the Understandings, and such sensual Pravity byasses the Wills of the most;
that they pursue wrong Measures to attain the Happiness they
desire.

Some of a lofty Genius, with unwearied Assiduity, labour
to secure Honours, thinking therein to obtain Happiness; and
to that End they climb the aspiring Top of *Parnassus,* emaciate
their Bodies, and waste their animal Spirits in long and deep
Studies, thinking by their labour'd and learn'd Lucubrations,
to spread and eternize their Fame. Others for the same Purpose, boldly tread the Crimson Fields of War, fearlessly open
their senseless Bosoms to all the numerous Engines and sudden
Avenues of pregnant Dangers, and of cruel Deaths, thinking
themselves great Gainers, if through the Loss of their Lives,
they can secure martial Honours and perpetuate Renown for
their heroick Bravery, in the Records of Fame. But alass! how
much is the unhappy Simplicity of those gallant Souls to be
pity'd! for what Good can martial Glory do to the dead?

Others by deeper but securer Policies, & more ungenerous
Methods, seek to mount the Wings of Honour, and reach the
highest Pinacle of Fame, by labouring to enhance great Places
in the Church and State, through the softest Flatteries and
most subtil Stratagems; Methods to be abhorr'd by every hon-

est and ingenious Mind. But when Men have obtain'd Honour, what is it? It is neither a substantial, nor a durable Good; it cannot make us good or happy; it may indeed *corrupt* us, by elating our Pride; but it can never *content* us: We may as easily grasp an Arm full of our own Shadow, as content our Minds with Fame; and as it is a meer empty Bubble in its Nature, and often corrupting in its Effects; so it is various and vanishing in its Continuance, as fickle as the Wind.

Some on the contrary of a baser Temper, and meaner Mould, being void of every Thing sublime or noble, dreaming that Happiness is to be had in terrene Pleasures, plunge themselves in a Pool of lawless Sensuality; so that in order to be happy, they make themselves Beasts, nay worse than they; living in Defiance to all the Dictates of Reason, and of GOD; purchasing at the Price of their eternal Salvation, these poor Pleasures, which being of a gross Nature, limited Degree, and contracted Duration, debase the Dignity of the Soul, and defile its Honours; but can neither suit its noble Nature, and perpetual Existence, nor satisfy its sublime and intense Desires.

But there is yet another Generation, of as mean and sordid Wretches, in whose grovling Bosoms, beats nothing that is great or generous; who imagine Happiness is to be had in temporal Wealth and Riches. *This,* these *Moles* are in the continual and eager Chase of; to *this Mark* all the Lines of their busy Thoughts, anxious Cares, subtle Projects, humerous Speeches, strong Desires, and unwearied Labours bend and terminate. But poor Creatures, if ye did obtain that Measure of Riches ye seek after, do ye think it would better your State, bound your Wishes, or secure your Happiness? No! no! don't ye see the contrary with your Eyes, that the most grow in Wickedness, in Proportion to the Increase of their Wealth, and that instead of satiating, it does but whet their Appetite for more; and ye should remember that the *Redemption of the Soul is precious, and that it ceaseth for ever.* As to these

Things, a high Mountain afar off seems to touch the Clouds, but when we come near, the Distance seems as great as before. Not to add, that temporal Enjoyments are of very uncertain Continuance, *Why then do ye spend your Money for that which is not Bread, and your Labours for that which satisfies not?*

But the noble Subject of the following Discourses, opens a Treasury of inexhaustible Riches, which do indeed better the State, satisfy the Desires, and save the Soul. This is a *Theme* that deserves our most solemn Meditations, a *Mark* worthy of our most sincere and vigorous Pursuits!

O! that I could persuade you, dears Sirs, to seek with restless and persevering Importunity, an Interest in those unsearchable Riches; without them ye cannot be rich, in any valuable Respect, and with them ye cannot be poor. I wou'd direct my Exhortation to graceless Persons, in various Conditions of Life. Are ye poor in Temporals, and do ye find but little Rest and Comfort in this World? Oh! then will ye be persuaded to accept of the most durable and noble *Riches*, *Riches* most dearly purchased, by no less a Price than the Blood of GOD; *Riches* most freely, frequently, and condescendingly offered, by the Love of GOD in the Ministry of his Servants, upon the most easy and most honourable Terms, that the Majesty and Purity of the divine Nature, and the Dignity and Felicity of the human Nature could admit. Poor Sinners, you are under peculiar Obligations to seek for and accept of the Riches of Grace and Glory, least ye be miserable in both Worlds. It is a most dreadful and shocking Consideration, to think that ye should make a hard Shift, to rub through the many Difficulties, Labours, and Sorrows of this present World, to enter into ten thousand Times worse in the next. Where there will be no *Hope*, no *Ease*, no *Interruption*, no *End*. Alas, my Brethren! It had been better for you ye had never been born, than that this should be your *dismal, dismal* Lot. Others have some sorry sensual Comfort in this Life, but ye have none, or next to none. Oh! it is most terrible to think, to be without Comfort and Quiet in both Worlds! Dear Sirs! If ye had but the Riches of a Saviour's Love, it wou'd sweeten your present Difficulties, conform you to the suffering Redeemer, support your sorrowful Souls, with the certain Prospect of perfect Felicity, and distinguished Glory, in the next State. For as the Apostle observes, with a noble Emphasis, 2 Cor. iv. 17. *Our light Affliction, which is but for a Moment, worketh for us a far more exceeding, and eternal Weight of Glory.*

O unhappy Sinners! It would not be hard to persuade you, I suppose, to accept of worldly Riches, and why then will ye not be induc'd to accept of Riches worth Millions of Worlds? Sirs, here, in the blessed Gospel, is the glorious *Pearl* of Price, the inestimable *Jewels* of the Covenant, try'd *Gold*, more pure and noble than that of *Ophir, Peru,* and *Mexico;* and white *Raiment*, to enrich and adorn you; and will ye not accept them, on the reasonable Terms they are offered? O cruel Murder! O vile Ingratitude! O detestable Madness! Be astonished and horribly afraid ye Heavens and Earth at this! Ah ye blessed Angels; ye cannot but wonder to see this terrible Tragedy acted! O ye Saints of God! look how the adorable dying Saviour, and the rich Purchase of his Blood, is slighted, by indigent, ungrateful, and degenerous Rebels! *Matth.* xxv. 4, 5. Oh! Can ye keep your Hearts from Mourning on this Account? See what huge Numbers of Mankind are lying in their Blood and Gore, and yet wont accept of Help and Healing, when it is freely offered. If ye can keep your Hearts from Bleeding upon this Occasion, they are very hard indeed! Ah! It pierces my very Soul, to see my Lord and the Riches of his bleeding Love, treated with such Indifference; while on the contrary, Things of an infinitely meaner Nature, and shorter Duration, are courted and labour'd for with the greatest Vehemence. Truly, Brethren, I know not how to express my Sorrows on this Account; if I could bewail it in Tears of Blood, I would.

Are ye in Bondage and Servitude? here is a spiritual, noble, and everlasting Liberty offered to you, in the Riches of CHRIST! Oh! if the Son of the Father's Love do but make you free, ye will be free indeed.

Are ye rich in worldly Goods? then I beseech you seriously and speedily to consider, that awful Parable of *Dives* and *Lazarus*, and especially the 23, 24, and 25 Verses of it. *And in Hell he lift up his Eyes being in Torments, and seeth* Abraham *afar off, and* Lazarus *in his Bosom. And he cryed, and said, Father* Abraham, *have Mercy on me, and send* Lazarus *that he may dip the Tip of his Finger in Water, and cool my Tongue; for I am tormented in this Flame. But* Abraham *said, Son, remember that thou in thy Life-time receivedst thy good Things, and likewise* Lazarus *evil Things: But now he is comforted, and thou art tormented.* O poor unhappy Sinners! see what a dreadful Change there will be in your Condition in a little Time. Remember ye that now wallow in generous Wines, ye will quickly (except ye repent) want Water to cool your flaming Tongues, but shall not obtain a single Drop; ye will be obliged to make your humble Court to these pious Poor, you now contemn as the Dirt under your Feet.

4 · *Jonathan Edwards*

A HISTORY OF THE WORK

OF REDEMPTION

The sermons on the *Work of Redemption,* first published in 1777, were taken to be Edwards' "uncompleted summa." Shortly before his death Edwards informed the trustees of the College of New Jersey (now Princeton University) that he had on his "mind and heart, (which I long ago began, not with any view to publication,) a great work, which I call a *History of the Work of Redemption,* a body of divinity in an entirely new method, being thrown into the form of a history. . . ." But the text is only that of the thirty-nine sermons Edwards delivered to his Northampton congregation in 1739. They embody, however, the essence of Edwards' radical view of history from the pre-Christian era onward. Where Edwards departed from the standard doctrine of early eighteenth-century New England was in his treatment of the "third stage" of the Work of Redemption: the period of Christ's Kingdom on Earth. Edwards placed the millennium prior to the Final Judg-

Jonathan Edwards, *A History of the Work of Redemption, Works,* I, 470–472, 480–481, 492–493, 510–513.

ment and, most significantly, announced that the spiritual progress of mankind was achievable through human instrumentalities. The impact on his people was such that his doctrines soon were matters of common fame throughout New England.

I proceed now to the last thing that was proposed to be considered, relating to the success of Christ's redemption during this space, viz., what the state of things is now in the world with regard to the church of Christ, and the success of Christ's purchase. And this I would do, by showing how things are now, compared with the first times of the Reformation. And, 1, I would show wherein the state of things is altered for the worse; and, 2, How it is altered for the better.

(1.) I would show wherein the state of things is altered from what it was in the beginning of the Reformation, for the worse; and it is so especially in these three respects.

[1.] The Reformed church is much diminished. The Reformation, in the former times of it, as was observed before, was supposed to take place through one half of Christendom, excepting the Greek church, or that there were as many Protestants as Papists. But now it is not so; the Protestant church is much diminished. . . .

[2.] Another thing wherein the state of things is altered for the worse from what was in the former times of the Reformation, is the prevailing of licentiousness in principles and opinions. There is not now that spirit of orthodoxy which there was then; there is very little appearance of zeal for the mysterious and spiritual doctrines of Christianity; and they never were so ridiculed, and had in contempt, as they are in the present age; and especially in England, the principal kingdom of the Reformation. In this kingdom, those principles, on which the power of godliness depends, are in a great measure exploded; and Arianism, and Socinianism, and Arminianism, and Deism, are the things which prevail, and carry almost all before them. And particularly history gives no account of any age wherein there was so great an apostasy of those who had been brought up under the light of the gospel, to infidelity; never was there such a casting off of the Christian, and all revealed religion; never any age wherein was so much scoffing at, and ridiculing the gospel of Christ, by those who have been brought up under gospel light, nor any thing like it, as there is at this day.

[3.] Another thing wherein things are altered for the worse, is, that there is much less of the prevalency of the power of godliness, than there was at the beginning of the Reformation. There was a glorious outpouring of the Spirit of God that accompanied the first Reformation, not only to convert multitudes in so short a time from Popery to the true religion, but to turn many to God and true godliness. Religion gloriously flourished in one country and another, as most remarkably appeared in those times of terrible persecution, which have already been spoken of. But now there is an exceeding great decay of vital piety; yea, it seems to be despised, called *enthusiasm, whimsy,* and *fanaticism*. Those who are truly religious, are commonly looked upon to be crack-brained, and beside their right mind; and vice and profaneness dreadfully prevail, like a flood which threatens to bear down all before it. But I proceed now to show,

(2.) In what respect things are altered for the better from what they were in the first Reformation.

[1.] The power and influence of the Pope is much diminished. Although, since the former times of the Reformation, he has gained ground in extent of dominion; yet he has lost in degree of influence. . . .

[2.] There is far less persecution now than there was in the first times of the Reformation. You have heard already how dreadfully persecution raged in the former times of the Reformation; and there is something of it still. Some parts of the Protestant church are at this day under persecution, and so probably will be till the day of the church's suffering and travail is at an end, which will not be till the fall of Antichrist. But it is now in no measure as it was heretofore. There does not seem to be the same spirit of persecution prevailing; it is become more out of fashion even among the Popish princes. The wickedness of the enemies of Christ, and the opposition against his cause, seem to run in another channel. The humor now is, to despise and laugh at all religion; and there seems to be a spirit of indifferency about it. However, so far the state of things is better than it has been, that there is so much less of persecution.

[3.] There is a great increase of learning. In the dark times of Popery before the Reformation, learning was so far decayed, that the world seemed to be overrun with barbarous ignorance. Their very priests were many of them grossly ignorant. Learning began to revive with the Reformation, which was owing very much to the art of printing, which was invented a little before the Reformation; and since that, learning has increased more and more, and at this day is undoubtedly raised to vastly a greater height than ever it was before: and though no good use is made of it by the greater part of learned men, yet the increase of learning in itself is a thing to be rejoiced in, because it is a good, and, if duly applied, an excellent handmaid to divinity, and is a talent which, if God gives men a heart, affords them a great advantage to do great things for the advancement of the kingdom of Christ, and the good of the souls of men. . . .

God in his providence now seems to be acting over again the same part which he did a little time before Christ came. The age wherein Christ came into the world, was an age wherein learning greatly prevailed, and was at a greater height

than ever it had been before; and yet wickedness never prevailed more than then. God was pleased to suffer human learning to come to such a height before he sent forth the gospel
into the world, that the world might see the insufficiency of all
their own wisdom for the obtaining of the knowledge of God.
. . . So now learning is at a great height at this day in the
world, far beyond what it was in the age when Christ appeared; and now the world, by their learning and wisdom, do
not know God; and they seem to wander in darkness, are mis-
erably deluded, stumble and fall in matters of religion, as in
midnight darkness. . . .

But yet, when God has sufficiently shown men the insufficiency of human wisdom and learning for the purposes of
religion, and when the appointed time comes for that glorious
outpouring of the Spirit of God, when he will himself by his
own immediate influence enlighten men's minds; then may we
hope that God will make use of the great increase of learning
as a handmaid to religion, as a means of the glorious advancement of the kingdom of his Son. . . . And there is no doubt to
be made of it, that God in his providence has of late given the
world the art of printing, and such a great increase of learning,
to prepare for what he designs to accomplish for his church
in the approaching days of its prosperity. And thus the wealth
of the wicked is laid up for the just, agreeable to Prov. xiii.
22. . . .

We know not what particular events are to come to pass
before that glorious work of God's Spirit begins, by which
Satan's kingdom is to be overthrown. By the consent of most
divines, there are but few things, if any at all, that are foretold
to be accomplished before the beginning of that glorious work
of God. Some think the slaying of the witnesses, Rev. xi. 7, 8,
is not yet accomplished. So divines differ with respect to the
pouring out of the seven vials, of which we have an account,
Rev. xvi, how many are already poured out, or how many
remain to be poured out. . . .

But whatever this be, it does not appear that it is any thing which shall be accomplished before that work of God's Spirit is begun, by which, as it goes on, Satan's visible kingdom on earth shall be utterly overthrown. And therefore I would proceed directly to consider what the Scripture reveals concerning the work of God itself, by which he will bring about this great event, as being the next thing which is to be accomplished that we are certain of from the prophecies of Scripture.

And, first, I would observe two things in general concerning it.

1. We have all reason to conclude from the Scriptures, that just before this work of God begins, it will be a very dark time with respect to the interests of religion in the world. It has been so before those glorious revivals of religion that have been hitherto. It was so when Christ came; it was an exceeding degenerate time among the Jews: and so it was a very dark time before the Reformation. And not only so, but it seems to be foretold in Scripture, that it shall be a time of but little religion, when Christ shall come to set up his kingdom in the world. Thus when Christ spake of his coming, to encourage his elect, who cry to him day and night, in Luke xviii. 8, he adds this, "Nevertheless when the Son of man cometh, shall he find faith on the earth?" Which seems to denote a great prevalency of infidelity just before Christ's coming to avenge his suffering church. Though Christ's coming at the last judgment is not here to be excluded, yet there seems to be a special respect to his coming to deliver his church from their long-continued suffering, persecuted state, which is accomplished only at his coming at the destruction of Antichrist. That time that the elect cry to God, as in Rev. vi. 10, "How long, O Lord, holy and true, dost thou not judge and avenge our blood on them that dwell on the earth?" And the time spoken of in Rev. xviii. 20, "Rejoice over her, thou heaven, and ye holy apostles, and prophets, for God hath avenged you on her," will then be accomplished.

It is now a very dark time with respect to the interests of religion, and such a time as this prophesied of in this place; wherein there is but a little faith, and a great prevailing of infidelity on the earth. There is now a remarkable fulfilment of that in 2 Pet. iii. 3: "Knowing this, that there shall come in the last days scoffers, walking in their own lusts." And so Jude 17, 18, "But, beloved, remember ye the words which were spoken before of the apostles of our Lord Jesus Christ; how that they told you there should be mockers in the last time, who should walk after their own ungodly lusts." Whether the times shall be any darker still, or how much darker, before the beginning of this glorious work of God, we cannot tell.

2. There is no reason from the word of God to think any other, than that this great work of God will be wrought, though very swiftly, yet gradually. As the children of Israel were gradually brought out of the Babylonish captivity, first one company, and then another, and gradually rebuilt their city and temple; and as the Heathen Roman empire was destroyed by a gradual, though a very swift prevalency of the gospel; so, though there are many things which seem to hold forth as though the work of God would be exceeding swift, and many great and wonderful events should very suddenly be brought to pass, and some great parts of Satan's visible kingdom should have a very sudden fall, yet all will not be accomplished at once, as by some great miracle, as the resurrection of the dead at the end of the world will be all at once; but this is a work which will be accomplished by means, by the preaching of the gospel, and the use of the ordinary means of grace, and so shall be gradually brought to pass. Some shall be converted, and be the means of others' conversion. God's Spirit shall be poured out first to raise up instruments, and then those instruments shall be used and succeeded. And doubtless one nation shall be enlightened and converted after another, one false religion and false way of worship exploded after another. . . .

. . . I come now, SECONDLY, To show how the success of redemption will be carried on through that space wherein the Christian church shall for the most part be in a state of peace and prosperity. . . .

And, in the general, I would observe two things.

1. That this is most properly the time of the kingdom of heaven upon earth. Though the kingdom of heaven was in a degree set up soon after Christ's resurrection, and in a further degree in the time of Constantine; and though the Christian church in all ages of it is called *the kingdom of heaven;* yet this time that we are upon, is the principal time of the kingdom of heaven upon earth, the time principally intended by the prophecies of Daniel, which speak of the kingdom of heaven, whence the Jews took the name of *the kingdom of heaven.*

2. Now is the principal fulfilment of all the prophecies of the Old Testament which speak of the glorious times of the gospel which shall be in the latter days. . . . Other times are only forerunners and preparatories to this: other times were the seed-time, but this is the harvest. But more particularly,

(1) It will be a time of great light and knowledge. The present days are days of darkness, in comparison of those days. . . .

There is a kind of vail now cast over the greater part of the world, which keeps them in darkness: but then this vail shall be destroyed: Isa. xxv. 7, "And he will destroy in this mountain the face of the covering cast over all people, and the vail that is spread over all nations." And then shall all countries and nations, even those which are now most ignorant, shall be full of light and knowledge. Great knowledge shall prevail everywhere. It may be hoped, that then many of the Negroes and Indians will be divines, and that excellent books will be published in Africa, in Ethiopia, in Tartary, and other now the most barbarous countries; and not only learned men, but others of more ordinary education, shall then be very knowing in religion: Isa. xxxii. 3, 4, "The eyes of them that see, shall not be dim; and the ears of them that hear, shall hearken. The heart also of the rash shall understand knowledge." Knowledge then shall be very universal among all sorts of persons; agreeable to Jer. xxxi. 34, "And they shall teach no more every man his neighbor, and every man his brother, saying, Know the Lord: for they shall all know me, from the least of them unto the greatest of them. . . ."

(2.) It shall be a time of great holiness. Now vital religion shall everywhere prevail and reign. Religion shall not be an empty profession, as it now mostly is, but holiness of heart and life shall abundantly prevail. Those times shall be an exception from what Christ says of the ordinary state of the church, viz., that there shall be but few saved; for now holiness shall become general: Isa. lx. 21, "Thy people also shall be all righteous." Not that there will be none remaining in a Christless condition; but that visible wickedness shall be suppressed everywhere, and true holiness shall become general, though not universal. . . . And holiness shall then be as it were inscribed on every thing, on all men's common business and employments, and the common utensils of life: all shall be as it were dedicated to God, and applied to holy purposes: every thing shall then be done to the glory of God: Isa. xxiii. 18, "And her merchandise and her hire shall be holiness to the Lord." And so Zech. xiv. 20, 21.—And as God's people then shall be eminent in holiness of heart, so they shall be also in holiness of life and practice.

(3.) It shall be a time wherein religion shall in every respect be uppermost in the world. It shall be had in great esteem and honor. The saints have hitherto for the most part been kept under, and wicked men have governed. But now they will be uppermost. "The kingdoms shall be given into the hands of the saints of the Most High God," Dan. vii. 27. "And they shall reign on earth," Rev. v. 10. "They shall live and reign with

Christ a thousand years," Rev. xx. 4. In that day, such persons as are eminent for true piety and religion, shall be chiefly promoted to places of trust and authority. Vital religion shall then take possession of kings' palaces and thrones; and those who are in highest advancement shall be holy men: . . .

(4.) Those will be times of great peace and love. There shall then be universal peace and a good understanding among the nations of the world, instead of such confusion, wars and bloodshed, as have hitherto been from one age to another: Isa. ii. 4, "And he shall judge among the nations, and shall rebuke many people: and they shall beat their swords into plough-shares, and their spears into pruning-hooks: nation shall not lift up sword against nation, neither shall they learn war any more. . . ."

And then shall malice, and envy, and wrath, and revenge, be suppressed everywhere, and peace and love shall prevail between one man and another; which is most elegantly set forth in Isa. xi. 6–10. Then shall there be peace and love between rulers and ruled. Rulers shall love their people, and with all their might seek their best good; and the people shall love their rulers, and shall joyfully submit to them, and give them that honor which is their due. And so shall there be a happy love between ministers and their people: Mal. iv. 6, "And he shall turn the heart of the fathers to the children, and the heart of the children to their fathers." Then shall flourish in an eminent manner those Christian virtues of meekness, forgiveness, long-suffering, gentleness, goodness, brotherly-kindness, those excellent fruits of the Spirit. Men, in their temper and disposition, shall then be like the Lamb of God, the lovely Jesus. The body shall be conformed to the head.

Then shall all the world be united in one amiable society. All nations, in all parts of the world, on every side of the globe, shall then be knit together in sweet harmony. All parts of God's church shall assist and promote the spiritual good of one another. A communication shall then be upheld between all parts of the world to that end; and the art of navigation, which is now applied so much to favor men's covetousness and pride, and is used so much by wicked debauched men, shall then be consecrated to God, and applied to holy uses, as we read in Isa. lx. 5–9. And it will then be a time wherein men will be abundant in expressing their love one to another, not only in words, but in deeds of charity, as we learn, Isa. xxxii. 5: "The vile person shall be no more called liberal, nor the churl said to be bountiful;" and verse 8, "But the liberal deviseth liberal things, and by liberal things shall he stand."

(5.) It will be a time of excellent order in the church of Christ. The true government and discipline of the church will then be settled and put into practice. All the world shall then be as one church, one orderly, regular, beautiful society. And as the body shall be one, so the members shall be in beautiful proportion to each other. Then shall that be verified in Psal. cxxii. 3, "Jerusalem is builded as a city that is compact together."

(6.) The church of God shall then be beautiful and glorious on these accounts; yea, it will appear in perfection of beauty: Isa. lx. 1, "Arise, shine, for thy light is come, and the glory of the Lord is risen upon thee."

. . . The consideration of what has been said, may greatly serve to show us the consistency, order, and beauty, of God's works of providence. If we behold the events of Providence in any other view than that in which it has been set before us, it will all look like confusion, like a number of jumbled events coming to pass without any order or method, like the tossings of the waves of the sea; things will look as though one confused revolution came to pass after another, merely by blind chance, without any regular or certain end.

But if we consider the events of providence in the light in which they have been set before us under this doctrine, in which the Scriptures set them before us, they appear far from being jumbled and confused, an orderly series of events, all wisely ordered and directed in excellent harmony and consistence, tending all to one end. The wheels of providence are not turned round by blind chance, but they are full of eyes round about, as Ezekiel represents, and they are guided by the Spirit of God: where the Spirit goes, they go: and all God's works of providence, through all ages, meet in one at last, as so many lines meeting in one centre.

It is with God's work of providence, as it is with his work of creation; it is but one work. The events of providence are not so many distinct, independent works of providence, but they are rather so many different parts of one work of providence: it is all one work, one regular scheme. God's works of providence are not disunited and jumbled, without connection or dependence, but are all united, just as the several parts of one building: there are many stones, many pieces of timber, but all are so joined, and fitly framed together, that they make but one building: they have all but one foundation, and are united at last in one top-stone.

God's providence may not unfitly be compared to a large and long river, having innumerable branches, beginning in different regions, and at a great distance one from another, and all conspiring to one common issue. After their very diverse and contrary courses, which they held for a while, yet they all gather more and more together, the nearer they come to their common end, and all at length discharge themselves at one mouth into the same ocean. The different streams of this river are apt to appear like mere jumble and confusion to us, because of the limitedness of our sight, whereby we cannot see from one branch to another, and cannot see the whole at once, so as to see how all are united in one. A man who sees but one or two streams at a time, cannot tell what their course tends to. Their course seems very crooked, and different streams seem to run for a while different and contrary ways: and if we view things at a distance, there seem to be innumerable obstacles and impediments in the way to hinder their ever uniting and coming to the ocean, as rocks, and mountains, and the like; but yet if we trace them, they all unite at last, and all come to the same issue, disgorging themselves in one into the same great ocean. Not one of all the streams fail of coming hither at last. . . .

God doubtless is pursuing some design, and carrying on some scheme, in the various changes and revolutions which from age to age come to pass in the world. It is most reasonable to suppose, that there is some certain great design to which Providence subordinates all the great successive changes in the affairs of the world which God has made. It is reasonable to suppose that all revolutions, from the beginning of the world to the end of it, are but the various parts of the same scheme, all conspiring to bring to pass that great event which the great Creator and Governor of the world has ultimately in view; and that the scheme will not be finished, nor the design fully accomplished, and the great and ultimate event fully brought to pass till the end of the world, and the last revolution is brought about.

Now there is nothing else that informs us what this scheme and design of God in his works is, but only the Holy Scriptures. Nothing else pretends to set in view the whole series of God's works of providence from beginning to end, and to inform us how all things were from God at first, and for what end they are, and how they were ordered from the beginning, and how they will proceed to the end of the world, and what they will come to at last, and how then all things shall be to God. Nothing else but the Scriptures has any pretence for showing any manner of regular scheme or drift in those revolutions which

God orders from age to age. Nothing else pretends to show what God would effect by the things which he has done, and is doing, and will do; what he seeks and intends by them. . . .

Reason shows that it is fit and requisite, that the intelligent and rational beings of the world should know something of God's scheme and design in his works; for they doubtless are the beings that are principally concerned. The thing that is God's great design in his works, is doubtless something concerning his reasonable creatures, rather than brute beasts and lifeless things. The revolutions by which God's great design is brought to pass, are doubtless revolutions chiefly among them, and which concern their state, and not the state of things without life or reason. And therefore surely it is requisite that they should know something of it; especially seeing that reason teaches that God has given his rational creatures reason and a capacity of seeing God in his works; for this end, that they may see God's glory in them, and give him the glory of them. But how can they see God's glory in his works, if they do not know what God's design in them is, and what he aims at by what he is doing in the world?

And further, it is fit that mankind should be informed something of God's design in the government of the world, because they are made capable of actively falling in with that design, and promoting of it, and acting herein as his friends and subjects; it is therefore reasonable to suppose, that God has given mankind some revelation to inform them of this: but there is nothing else that does it but the Bible. . . .

Here we are shown the connection of the various parts of the work of providence, and how all harmonizes, and is connected together in a regular, beautiful, and glorious frame. . . .

How rational, worthy, and excellent a revelation is this! And how excellent a book is the Bible, which contains so much beyond all other books in the world! And what characters are here of its being indeed a divine book! A book that the great

Jehovah has given to mankind for their instruction, without which we should be left in miserable darkness and confusion.

From what has been said, we may see the glorious majesty and power of God in this affair of redemption: especially is God glorious in his power. His glorious power appears in upholding his church for so long a time, and carrying on this work; upholding it oftentimes when it was but as a little spark of fire, or as smoking flax, in which the fire was almost gone out, and the powers of earth and hell were combined to destroy it. Yet God has never suffered them to quench it, and finally will bring forth judgment unto victory. God glorifies his strength in his church's weakness; in causing his people, who are like a number of little infants, finally to triumph over all earth and hell; so that they shall tread on the lion and adder; the young lion and dragon shall they trample under foot. . . .

Let who will prevail now, let the enemies of the church exalt themselves as much as they will, these are the people that shall finally prevail. The last kingdom shall finally be theirs; the kingdom shall finally be given into their hands, and shall not be left to other people. . . .

5 · *Jonathan Parsons*

(1 7 0 5 – 1 7 7 6)

"ACCOUNT OF THE REVIVAL

AT LYME" (1)

Trained in his youth as a mechanic, Parsons entered Yale at the age of twenty. There he decided on a career in the ministry, and later he completed his studies under Jonathan Edwards. Like Edwards, Parsons was sensitive to the winds of change—ecclesiastical and doctrinal—that blew through New England in the late 1720's and early 1730's. Some of this torment was recalled by Parsons in the account he published in the *Christian History* for 1744. Most of the entries in this compilation of revival histories were written with an eye toward proving the "genuineness" of the Awakening. Parsons' contribution, based on a detailed journal of occurrences in his parish, was among the few that attempted to recapture the precise quality of the intellectual life of pre-Awakening America.

Jonathan Parsons, "Account of the Revival of Religion at Lyme West Parish . . . ," in Thomas Prince, Jr. (ed.), *The Christian History, containing Accounts of the Revival and Propagation of Religion in Great-Britain, America, &c. For the Year 1744* (Boston, 1745), pp. 120–125.

I came hither *Febr.* 29th 1729, 30, and had a Call from the People the *May* following to settle in the Work of the Ministry among them: Which Call was again renewed the *latter End* of the *Summer.*

But for some Scruples then upon my Mind about the Validity of our Ordinations, together with the Right of the *civil* Magistrate to impose Forms of Worship, I refus'd to take the Oversight of the Church, until the 17th of the following *March,* tho' I was urged to it. In the mean Time I was endeavouring to find out the Truth respecting these Things; and as one Mean of Light, I made a Visit to the Rev. Dean *Berkley,* since Bishop of *Cloin* in *Ireland,* who was then at *New-Port* on *Rhode-Island.* He treated me with great Humanity, and endeavour'd to convince me that it was my Duty to go over into the Interest of the Church of *England.* And as I had freely told him my Difficulties when I came to take my Leave of him, he made me a Present of Mr. *Richard Hooker's Ecclesiastical Polity.* I took further Pains, by reading, conversing and otherways, to get Satisfaction about my Duty; and by that Time the Day appointed for Ordination came, my Scruples were so far remov'd, that I tho't I might safely receive Ordination from the Ministers chosen, and met together. *Immediately* before I took the Oversight of the Flock, I did, before the *Council* and the *Brethren* of the Church, *expresly* renounce the Articles for Church Discipline drawn up at *Say-Brook,* and took the general *Platform* of the *Gospel* for my Rule; upon which the Church *unanimously* voted me to be their *Pastor,* and the *Council* concur'd, and proceeded to Ordination. I am since that, (tho' for a Time I had rising Doubts) well satisfied that the *Scriptures* make no Difference between *Bishop* and *Presbyter;* that Christ alone is *King* of his Church, and has given *Laws* to it, and Authority to execute them; and that no Man has a Right, by *Fines* or *civil Force,* to bind any Man to Worship God in *this* or *that* particular Form. . . .

The *Summer following* my Ordination there was a great *Effusion* of the HOLY SPIRIT upon the People. There appear'd to be an uncommon Attention to the Preaching of the Word, and a disposition to hearken to Advice; and a remarkable Concern about Salvation. 'Twas a *general Inquiry* among the Middle aged and Youth, *What must I do to be saved?* Great Numbers came to my Study, some almost every Day for several Months together, under manifest Concern about their Souls. I seldom went into a House among my Neighbours, but they had some free Discourse about Religion, or were searching after the Meaning of some Texts of Scripture. I urg'd them very much to *Works,* and gave it as my Opinion (perhaps too hastily) that such awakened Souls ought to attend upon the *Lord's Supper:* and in less than *ten* Months *fifty-two* Persons were added to the Church. There were *several whole Families baptiz'd.* Many of the *young* People were greatly reformed: they turned their Meetings for vain Mirth into Meetings for Prayer, Conference and reading Books of Piety. There was a Number of them kept a religious Society about *two Years;* and they not only behav'd soberly, but took Pains to diswade others from Levity and frothy Conversation. But, altho' there was such a fair Prospect of a considerable Harvest of Souls, I have no *special* Reasons to make me think that many were savingly converted to GOD in that Season of Concern. Many indeed, made an open Profession of Religion, but there were very few did it under a Notion that *saving Grace* is necessary in order to a *lawful Attendance* upon the *Lord's Supper.* Nor have we, in our Admissions to Communion, ever acted upon that Principle, but the contrary. Hence it came to pass that we found no Use for *Relations,* as they are called, but laid them by from the Beginning of my Ministry, tho' they had been of constant Use in my Predecessors Day. And truly I'm of Opinion that the *venerable* Mr. *Noyes* acted right upon his Principle of admitting none but what were, in a Judgment of Charity, *converted* Persons. For tho' we can't attain such positive Marks of Grace as to form an *infallible Judgment* concerning the spiritual State of others, yet such Marks may be had from an Account of their Experiences added to their Life, as are suffi-cient to found a *positive Judgment of Charity* with Respect to their spiritual State. And it looks highly reasonable to me, that the *Community* should be allowed to judge of their *Expe-riences* as well as of their *moral Conduct.* Why any Minister shou'd assume the Prerogative to himself any more than all other Power, without the concurring Judgment of the Church, is what I do not well understand: Nor do I see how a Church, acting upon such a Principle, can give up their Right, or yet give their Vote to admit Persons under a Notion of their being *converted,* without hearing their *Experiences.* I must confess, to me, it looks like *judging a Matter before* they have *heard it.* But then, I think we acted equally right, upon the Supposition that Persons may lawfully come to the Lord's-Table knowing themselves unconverted, or having no good Grounds to hope that they are in a State of Grace: for they being admitted upon such a Principle, have no *Christian Experience* to relate.

But to return from this Digression: In that Day I was greatly in Love with *Arminian* Principles, and especially I abhor'd the Doctrine of God's Absolute Sovereignty; and that might be one Reason why awaken'd Souls fell short of a saving Change, and settled down upon the Righteousness of the Law. The Doctrines that are natural for a Man of such Principles to preach, you know, are calculated to gratify the Pride of Men, to give them exalted Thoughts of their own Duties. I was exceedingly pleased with Dr. *Tillotson's*[1] Notions about the *Power of Man* to perform the Conditions of the Gospel; or to do that to which God has join'd the Promise of special Grace; and some other Sermons of his that seem to be calculated to

---

[1] John Tillotson (1630–1694), Archbishop of Canterbury. [Ed.]

uphold such an Opinion. Dr. *Clark*[2] also, and others of the like
Stamp, that have calculated a Scheme of Religion suited to
the corrupt Views of an haughty Heart, were my beloved
Authors. I had a *Zeal of God*, but *not a laudable* one, because
it was *not according to Knowledge. Being ignorant of* GOD's
Righteousness, I endeavour'd to get others to *establish their
own Righteousness*, and to keep them *from submitting unto
the Righteousness of GOD*.

'Tis now more than *ten Years* since I have seen Cause to
renounce *Arminian* Principles, and turn quite about in some
of the most important Doctrines of the *Christian* Religion: and
consequently, you may well think, *Sir*, that there was as great
an Alteration in my Preaching: for I have all along preach'd,
(as I suppose other Ministers do) agreeable to my own Sentiments. But GOD knows with how little Success I insisted upon
the Things which I had learned and been assured of. Nothing
seem'd to make any deep and lasting Impressions for good
upon the Minds of People in general: it look'd to me, they
liv'd easy without CHRIST, and without GOD in the World. Our
young People took unwarrantable Liberties; *Night-walking*,
Frolicking, and *leud* Practices, some grew bold in, and encourag'd and corrupted others thereby: Others fell into Party-
Quarrels, and grew uneasy with the Plainness of the Preaching,
and were pleas'd sometimes, to call it Censoriousness; especially if I told them, "that I could not, upon our Practice,
reckon Conversions by the Number of those that had joined
to the Church; or that I feared very few had been converted
since my Ministry among them; and when I insisted upon it
that an *external* Profession of the true Religion, join'd with a
good Degree of *doctrinal* Knowledge, *external* Devotion, *nega-*

---

[2] Samuel Clarke (1675–1729), Anglican divine and philosopher, whose
*Remarks upon a Book Entitled A Philosophical Enquiry concerning Hu-
man Liberty* (1717) was one of the earliest, and most influential, of eighteenth-century arguments against the passivity of the human will. [Ed.]

tive Blamelesness, and the like, were not good Evidences that a Person was a *real* Christian; but insisted upon it that all were *spiritually* dead by Nature, must have a Principle of *spiritual* Life implanted, must be converted to GOD, have sensible Communion with CHRIST, and live a Life of Faith, as they would entertain well grounded Hopes of Heaven." These were hard Sayings, and many wou'd not receive them. Thus it was with us for *several Years,* until I was *awfully* deserted of GOD, and got into a very *dull, legal* Frame my self, and then some were better pleas'd.

'Tis now almost *four Years* since it pleased GOD to strengthen and enlarge my Desires after the Increase of CHRIST's Kingdom, and to stir me up to more ardent Endeavours after the *eternal* Welfare of *immortal* Souls. Christ and his Cause grew *exceeding* precious; and one Soul *appear'd* of more Worth than a *Thousand* Worlds; the Souls that were committed to my Charge lay with vast Weight and Tenderness upon my Mind. The State of Religion look'd dismal: But few Instances of Persons that I cou'd meet with among them, that seem'd to be suitably affected with the Miseries of a perishing World, and the decaying State of Religion. The News of Mr. *Whitefield's* rising up with great Zeal for Holiness and Souls, had great Influence upon my Mind: GOD made Use of frequent Accounts about him to awaken my Attention, to humble me for past Deadness, and rouse me up to see my own Standing, and sound an Alarm in some poor Sort, to a drowsy, careless People.

PART TWO

WHITEFIELD IN THE SOUTH

6 · George Whitefield

(1 7 1 4 – 1 7 7 0)

JOURNAL

———————

As a student at Oxford Whitefield was caught up in what came to be known as the "Wesleyan" (and later "Methodist") movement. He was ordained at the age of twenty-two, and a year later, in 1737, he made the first of his several journeys to America. On his return to England Whitefield's preaching met opposition from the Anglican hierarchy, and he soon began to preach "in the fields." In 1739 he sailed again for the colonies, where both his difficulties with the Church of England and his sermons had been well publicized. Whitefield took to publishing a "journal" of his experiences, and by this kind of self-advertising he established a reputation that preceded him on his extensive colonial tour in 1739–1740. One episode that immediately captured the imagination of evangelical

George Whitefield's Journals . . . (London: Banner of Truth Trust, 1960), pp. 400–403.

America was his first confrontation with Alexander Garden, the Bishop of London's Commissary in Charleston, South Carolina.

Friday, March 14 [1740]. Arrived last night at Charleston, being called there to see my brother, who lately came from England, and had brought me a packet of letters from my dear friends. Blessed be God, His work goes on amongst them! Waited on the Commissary, with my brother and other companions; but met with a cool reception. After I had been there a little while, I told him I was informed he had some questions to propose to me, and that I had now come to give him all the satisfaction I could in answering them. Upon this, I immediately perceived passion to arise in his heart. "Yes, Sir," he said, "I have several questions to put to you. But," he added, "you have got above us," or something to that effect. Then he charged me with enthusiasm and pride, for speaking against the generality of the clergy, and desired I would make my charge good. I told him, I thought I had already; though as yet I had scarce begun with them. He then asked me wherein the clergy were so much to blame? I answered, they did not preach justification by faith alone; and upon talking with the Commissary, I found he was as ignorant as the rest. He then sneered me with telling me of my modesty, expressed in my letter to the Bishop of Gloucester; charged me with breaking the Canons and Ordination vow; and notwithstanding I informed him I was ordained by Letters Dismissory from the Bishop of London, in a great rage, he told me, if I preached in any public church in that province, he would suspend me. I replied, I should regard that as much as I would a Pope's bull. "But, Sir," I said, "why should you be offended at my speaking against the generality of the clergy; for I always spoke well of you?" "I might as well be offended," added my brother, "at you saying, 'the generality of people were notorious sinners,' and come and accuse you of speaking evil of me, because I was one of the people." I further added, "You did not behave thus, when I was with you last." "No," he said, "but you did not speak against the clergy then." I then said to him, "If you will make an application to yourself, be pleased to let me ask you one question, 'Have you delivered your soul by exclaiming against the assemblies and balls here?' " "What," said he, "must you come to catechise me? No, I have not exclaimed against them; I think there is no harm in them." "Then," I replied, "I shall think it my duty to exclaim against you." "Then, Sir," he said in a very great rage, "Get you out of my house." I and my friends then took our leave, pitying the Commissary, who I really thought was more noble than to give such treatment. After this, we went to public prayers, dined at a friend's house, drank tea with the Independent minister, and preached at four in the afternoon, to a large auditory in his meeting-house.

Saturday, March 15. Breakfasted, sang a hymn, and had some religious conversation on board my brother's ship. Preached in the Baptist meeting-house; and was much pleased, when I heard afterwards, that from the same pulpit, a person not long ago had preached, who denied the doctrine of original sin, the Divinity and Righteousness of our Lord, and the operation of God's Blessed Spirit upon the soul. I was led to shew the utter inability of man to save himself, and absolute necessity of his dependence on the rich mercies and free grace of God in Christ Jesus for his restoration. Some, I observed, were put under concern; and most seemed willing to know whether those things were so. In the evening, I preached again in the Independent meeting-house to a more attentive auditory than ever; and had the pleasure, afterwards, of finding that a gentle-woman, whose whole family had been carried away for some time with Deistical principles, began now to be unhinged, and to see that there was no rest in such a scheme for a fallen creature to rely on. Lord Jesus, for Thy mercies' sake, reveal Thyself in her heart, and make her willing to know the faith as it is in Thee. Amen.

Sunday, March 16. Preached at eight in the morning, in the Scots' meeting-house, to a large congregation. Visited a sick person. Went to church and heard the Commissary represent me under the character of the Pharisee, who came to the Temple, saying, "God, I thank Thee that I am not as other men are"; but whether I do what I do, out of a principle of pride, or duty, the Searchers of hearts shall discover ere long, before men and angels. I was very sick and weak at dinner. Went to church again in the afternoon; and, about five, preached in the Independent meeting-house yard, the house not being capacious enough to hold the auditory.

> With restless and ungoverned rage,
> Why do the clergy storm?
> Why in such rash attempts engage,
> As they can ne'er perform?
>
> The great in counsel and in might,
> Their various forces bring;
> Against the Lord they all unite,
> And His anointed King.
>
> Must we submit to their commands,
> Presumptuously they say?
> No, let us break their slavish bands,
> And cast their chains away.
>
> But God, Who sits enthroned on high,
> And sees how they combine,
> Does their conspiring strength defy,
> And mocks their vain design.

Felt much freedom after sermon, in talking to a large company at a merchant's house. Supped with another friend, expounded part of a chapter, prayed, and went to our lodgings with my dear companions, praising and blessing God. Hasten that time, O Lord, when we shall join the Heavenly Choir that is now about Thy throne.

Monday, March 17. Preached, in the morning, in the Independent meeting-house, and was more explicit than ever in exclaiming against balls and assemblies. Preached again in the evening, and being excited thereto by some of the inhabitants, I spoke on behalf of my poor orphans, and collected upwards of £70 sterling, the largest collection I ever yet made on that occasion: a further earnest to me, that we shall yet see greater things in America, and that God will carry on and finish the work, begun in His Name at Georgia.

Tuesday, March 18. Preached twice again this day, and took an affectionate leave of my hearers, thanking them for their great liberality. Many wept, and my own heart yearned much towards them; for I believe a good work is begun in many. Generally, every day several came to me, telling me how God had been pleased to convince them by the Word preached, and how desirous they were of laying hold on and having an interest in the complete and everlasting righteousness of the Lord Jesus Christ. Numbers desired privately to converse with me. Many sent me little presents, as tokens of their love, and earnestly entreated that I would come amongst them again. Invitations were given me from some of the adjacent villages; and people daily came to town more and more from their plantations to hear the Word. The congregations grew larger on week days, and many things concurred to induce us to think that God intended to visit some in Charleston with His salvation.

7 · *Alexander Garden*

(*1 6 8 5 – 1 7 5 6*)

TWO SERMONS ON REGENERATION

Whitefield's various impertinences so outraged Commissary Garden that he eventually summoned the young preacher before an ecclesiastical court. Whitefield denied the court's jurisdiction, and the issue of Garden's authority was never actually resolved. On matters of doctrine, however, the lines were clearly drawn, particularly after Whitefield published *A Letter . . . wherein he Vindicates his Asserting that Archbishop Tillotson knew no more of Christianity than Mahomet.* In this tract Whitefield charged nearly the whole of the Church of England with failure to adhere to the Calvinist doctrines on which, according to him, Anglicanism had been founded. Garden replied to this pamphlet, and to Whitefield's southern sermons, with his interpretation of the doctrine of regeneration. Here he contrasted the "reasonable" doctrines of the Church of England with the riotous emotionalism of Whitefield and his followers, and, in a prefatory letter,

---

Alexander Garden, *Regeneration, and the Testimony of the Spirit. Being the Substance of Two Sermons . . . Occasioned by some erroneous Notions of certain Men who call themselves Methodists* (Charleston, S.C., 1740; reprinted Boston, 1741), pp. i–ii, 1–15, 20–25.

indicated that the fundamental issue was Whitefield's manner of preaching. He failed to chasten Whitefield, much less to silence him; the young exhorter's response was a sermon based on II Tim. 4:14: "Alexander, the coppersmith, did me much evil: the Lord reward him according to his works."

To the Inhabitants of the Parish of St.
Philip, Charles-Town.

My dear Brethren,

The following Pages contain the whole Substance of two Short Discourses you lately heard from the Pulpit, and which I now put into your Hands from the Press, to guard you against the Puzzle and Perplexity of some crude Enthusiastick *Notions, which so much prevailed about the* same Period *of the last* Century, *and are now revived and propagated by* Mr. Whitefield *and his Brethren* Methodists. *They were* preached *midst the* Sound *of that* Gentleman's Voice *in your* Ears;*—that* enchanting *Sound! The* natural *and* alone *Cause, which produced all the* Passion *and* Prejudice, *that prevailed 'mong some (the weaker some indeed) of you, in his Favour, against them and every thing else that opposed him; and which would equally have produced the same Effects, whether he had* acted *his Part in the* Pulpit *or on the* Stage. No Proposition in *Euclid more demonstrable to me, than that, not the* Matter *but the* Manner, *not the* Doctrines *he delivered, but the* Agreeableness *of the Delivery, had all the Effect upon you, and as* naturally *as any other Effects in Nature are produced by their proper Causes. Take away this Cause, no more* Multitude *after the* Preacher! *His Discourses will then appear what they really are, viz. a* Medley *of* Truth *and* Falshood, Sense *and* Nonsense, *served up*

*with Pride and Virulence, and other like sawcy Ingredients.
Thus, I say, you heard the Contents of the following Pages
from the Pulpit, 'midst that* inchanting *Sound in your Ears, exciting your Passions, and foreclosing your Understandings
against them.* They *opposed, and breathed only Persecution
and Slaughter against that* Angel! *That* Seraphim! *The* wondrous WHITEFIELD!—*And therefore away with them; they
must be* unregenerate Words, *not fit for regenerate Ears or
Understandings. But Patience, my Brethren;*—a little While,
*and your Passions subsiding, they may find Access to your
Understandings, and by God's Blessing, answer the End for
which they were, and now are designed.*

If I have acted a mistaken Part in opposing Mr. Whitefield,
*as I trust and am daily more and more confirmed I am not; yet
sure I am, that I have acted an honest and faithful one, to the
best of my Capacity and Knowledge;* not as pleasing Men, but
God who trieth our Hearts. *Had I* consulted with Flesh and
Blood;—*consulted my own Ease, and how to avoid that* Storm
of Wrath, Obloquy, *and* Reproach *I sustained from the* zealot
*Party amongst you; I needed only to have acquiesced in the
wild Scene without Opposition, and suffered the Delusion to
have taken such Course and Event as might happen. But how
then could I answer either to God, my lawful Superiours in
his Church, or to my own Conscience?*

No, my Brethren, you are the Flock *lawfully committed to
my Charge, of* whom the Holy Ghost has made me Overseer;
and therefore am I jealous over you with a Godly Jealousie. *I
saw the* Wolf a coming;—*a vain, visionary Creature! Who
would fill your Heads with* Visions *and new* Revelations,—
with speculative perplexing Notions *of Justification,* irresistable
Grace, effectual *Calling, Perseverance, Assurance, Predestination, or,* absolute, eternal *Decrees of* Election *and* Reprobation;
and therefore saw I it my Duty, not to flee, *but to rise up in
your Behalf, for your safety and Defence.*

My Hearts Desire, and Prayer to God for you is, that you may be saved. *This is my Heart's Desire, this my earnest Prayer, this the End of all my Care and Labours among you, who am*   Your most affectionate and
  Charlestown,   humble Servant in Christ,
Nov. 24, 1740.   *ALEX. GARDEN.*

Rom. VIII. 16.

The Spirit itself [Gr. the same Spirit] *beareth Witness with our Spirit, that we are the Children of GOD.*

Forsaking the *ordinary* Ways and Means of attaining the Knowledge of our Religious Duty, *viz.* Natural *Reason* and the *written* Word of God; and substituting in their Place our own *Conceits* of *immediate* Revelations, by certain *Impulses, Motions,* or *Impressions* of the *Holy Spirit* on our Minds, without any rational objective Evidence, or clear and sufficient Proof; —this is proper and direct *Enthusiasm,* in the bad Sense of the Word to which it is now commonly restricted. And of all *Religious* Maladies, this is the most desperate and hardest to be subdued. If the Case be *Atheism, Paganism,* or *Deism,* it is still within the Reach of all the Arguments and Conclusions of natural *Reason,* and which have been often, in such Case, practised with Success; or if the Case be *Judaism, Mahometism* or *Popery,* it is within the Reach of all the Arguments and Conclusions of *Reason* and *Revelation* also;—but if it be *ENTHUSIASM,* it is out of the Reach of *all these,* the alone Means in human Power, wherewith to attempt a *Remedy.* For if once Men be *settled* in this Way; when once they come to place *strong Conceit* or *Imagination* in the Chair of *Reason,* and to subject the *standing* Oracles of God, to the fancied *immediate* Revelations of his *Holy Spirit* to them; they streight assume the Airs of *Infallibility* upon you. If you'll hearken to *their*

Dictates, it is well; but if not, what have *they* to do with your *carnal* Reasonings, or Senses of Scripture? For they have God himself *speaking* inwardly to their Souls; *immediately* teaching, and *infallibly* leading them into all Truth;—and this they are as sure of, as of *seeing* the Light, or *feeling* the Heat of the *Sun,* at Noon-day.

How high soever their *Claims* or Pretences may rise in Process of Time (as often they do, to *Prophecy* and *Working of Miracles*) yet commonly they begin at *Regeneration* or *the New-Birth,* and *the Testimony of the Spirit with* their *Spirit, that they are the Children of God;* that is, *regenerate* or *born again.*—But are not these right and justifiable Claims? Are not *Regeneration,* and this *Testimony of the Spirit,* Scripture Doctrines? Out of all Dispute they are: But then not in the *same* Sense or Meaning, as *they* conceive and insist upon them.

They conceive and insist upon *Regeneration,* to be an immediate, *instantaneous* Work of the *Holy Spirit,* wrought inwardly on the Hearts or Souls of Men, *critically* at some *certain* Time, in some *certain* Place, and on some *certain Occasion;* and by which the whole Interiour is at once, in a Moment, illuminated and reformed; the Understanding open'd, the Will over-ruled, and all the Inclinations, Appetites and Passions, quite alter'd and turn'd from Evil to Good, from being corrupt and vicious, to being pure, virtuous and holy.

Moreover they farther insist, that *before* we *feel* this great Work wrought within us, our *Faith* and *good Works* shall avail us nothing. We may ever so firmly *believe* the Gospel, and *practise* all the Religious and Moral Duties it enjoins;—we may carefully attend the *outward Ordinances,* of *publick* Worship, Preaching, and Sacraments, nor ever neglect our *Closet* and *Family* Devotions;—we may fast, and pray, and give Alms, both in publick and private; and touching the *moral* Duties of Justice and Honesty, Temperance and Chastity, or any other, behave ourselves blameless; and yet alas all to no Purpose!

Except we *feel* this *specifick* Work of Grace wrought in us, we are still in the very Gall of Bitterness and Bond of Iniquity.

Finally they teach and insist, that in this *Act* or Work of *Regeneration,* we are *wholly* and *absolutely passive,* as a Clock or Watch is under the Hands of the Artificer.

This is their Doctrine of *Regeneration.*—And as to *the Testimony of the Spirit,* always accompanying this great Work, they affirm it to be, by certain *Motions, Impulses* or *Impressions,* inwardly on our *Hearts* or Minds, as plainly and distinctly *felt* and known, as those of the *Wind,* or other material Thing, outwardly on our *Bodies* are.

And now, if to *these Doctrines* you demur and object, that you do not apprehend them sufficiently grounded in the Holy *Scriptures,* or ever taught by the *Catholick* Church of Christ in any Age:—The Reason is, they'll answer you, because you are an *unregenerate* Person;—you have not *the Spirit of* God *dwelling in you,* by which alone the Things of *the Spirit* can be discerned; but you see and judge of *spiritual* Things, only by the Eyes of your *carnal* and corrupt Reason.—That this must be your Case, they'll insist is plain; for that, as by the *Indwelling of the Spirit* in themselves, they know and *feel* the Truth of *these Doctrines;* so if you enjoyed the same Benefit with them, and which is the *common Privilege* of all true or regenerate Christians, then and in such Case, you would needs *see* as *they see, feel* as *they feel,* and *act* as *they do.*—Sure a compendious Method to stop every Mouth; shut out all the Powers of Argument and Reason; and so build up *Popery* or *Mahometism,* or *any other* Delusion or Imposture you please!

And thus having briefly stated the Doctrines of *Regeneration,* and the *Testimony of the Spirit,* according to the *Enthusiastick* Turn or System;—we proceed (according to our Measure) to state these Doctrines, as contained in the *Holy Scriptures,* and agreeably taught by the *catholick* Church of Christ in all Ages, and particularly by the Church of

England at this Day. And this, by explaining the Words now before us, under these two distinct Inquiries.

I. What is meant by this Phrase,——*the Children of God.*

II. What is meant, by *the Spirit bearing Witness with our Spirit.*

I. What is meant by *the Children of God.*

Nothing can be more plain or obvious throughout the *Inspired* Writings, than that the Things of God are therein taught by way of *Analogy,* or Allusion taken from natural Things common and known amongst Men.——Thus respecting the *Point* in Hand; (1) As among Men, we are in the most appropriate Sense, *the Children* of those, from whom we immediately derive our Being by *natural* Generation; so *the whole Family in Heaven and Earth* deriving their Being from God by *Creation,* he is thence stiled their *Father,* and they his *Sons* or *Children.* (2) As among Men, Parents *naturally* take Care of, and provide for the Support, Safety, and Happiness of their *Children;* so the Support, Preservation, and Happiness of *all Things* depending on the good Providence of God, he is thence also stiled the *Father of all,* but more *appropriately* of his *intelligent* Creatures. (3) As among Men, *Children* generally partake of the *natural* Temper and Disposition of their Parents, and as brought up under their Authority, Example, and Tuition, do generally obey, imitate, and copy after them, in their *moral* Conduct; so, in Allusion to this, they who *partake* of the *Divine Nature,* in the Frame, Temper, and Disposition of their Minds, and agreeably obey God, and always act and behave with strict Conformity to his Example and sacred Laws, are called *his Sons,* or *Children.*

Now in all these Respects were our first Parents *the Children of God,* in their State of Innocence. They were *his Children* by Creation, the immediate Workmanship of his Hands; he *formed the Man of the Dust of the Ground, and breathed into his Nostrils,* &c. and the *Woman* he immediately *formed out of the Man.* They were *his Children* also, with respect to his provident *Care* for their Support and Happiness. He placed them in the Garden of *Eden;*—he gave them all the Fruits of the Garden for their Food or Sustenance, except of *one Tree* in the Midst of it;—he personally conversed with them, ordered and directed them, and constantly communicated *Lights* and *Graces* sufficient for them. Finally, they were the *Children of God,* as *Partakers of his Divine Nature;—after his Image in Righteousness and true Holiness;* loving him, and him alone, with most intense, pure, and ardent Love, and agreeably obeying his Voice, following his Example, and in all Things conforming to his Will, and *moral* Attributes.

Thus, I say, in all *these* Respects, were our *first* Parents the *Children of God,* in their State of Innocence; but, alas, how *tragically* was the Case altered by their *Apostacy!* For no sooner were they seduced to *disobey* the Voice of God, and transgress his positive Law, by eating the forbidden Fruit, but a certain *Degeneracy* overspread their *whole* Being, their Bodies and their Minds. By the very Act of *Disobedience,* they *ceased* being the *Children of God,* ceased his *moral* Image and Resemblance, and became the *Children* of their *Seducer;* whose Voice they obeyed, whose Example they followed, and whose Works they chose to do. By *judicial* Sentence they are doomed to Labour, and Sorrow, Pains, Diseases and Death. . . .

Thus are our *first Parents t*o be considered, as fallen into the *same* State with the *Apostate Angels;* and in which they must have remained *for ever,* had not the *infinite* Wisdom and Goodness of God interposed, and provided for their *Recovery.*

Now of these *two* Things must their *Recovery* plainly consist, *viz. Pardon* and *Regeneration.* For, as they were thus *fallen* from being the *Children of God,* to be *Children of Satan;* from their *Original* State of Perfection and Innocence, into a State of Sin and Degeneracy; the Case is plain, their Sin must be *pardoned*, and they must be *regenerate* or *new-born*, so as to recover their first State, and become the *Children of God* again.——And lo, the glorious *Provision* of infinite and eternal Wisdom, Love, and Goodness, for both these! The glorious *Provision*, both for the *Pardon* and *Regeneration* of the *Apostate first Parents* of Men; *viz.* the *Second Man, Christ, the Lord from Heaven!* Christ *the Lord their Righteousness!—made unto* them *Wisdom, and Justification, and Sanctification, and Redemption! Christ*, an *immediate* Attonement for their Sin; *Slain from the Foundation of the World;* and an *immediate* Principle of *Regeneration* or new Life in them, by the Influence of his *holy Spirit!* An *immediate* Attonement for their Sin (their Apostacy or *original* Sin) by which it was pardoned, so as not to be imputed to Death eternal;—An *immediate* Principle of *Regeneration*, by which all the evil Effects or Consequences of it, the Degeneracy and Corruption of their Nature it had occasioned, might be gradually done away: And thus an *immediate* and ample *Provision*, by which they are actually *restored* to such a State of Pardon and Reconciliation, as *Life and Death* are once more *set before them*, once more put in their Choice and Power;—*Life* or Salvation again secured them on the easy Terms of Faith, Repentance, and renewed Obedience; and *no* Death or Condemnation to be inflicted, but on their *actual* refusing these Terms, their future *actual* Sins or Transgressions only! . . .

But however our *first* Parents were *thus* restored to a State of *Pardon* and *Salvation;* yet not *so*, but their Sin was still imputed to *many* great and sore Evils; or rather many natural evil Effects still remained, which the provided Remedy was only *gradually* to reach, and *conditionally* to subdue; *viz. Bodies* naked; that is, subjected to many Miseries, Toils, Labours, Pains, Diseases and Death;—*Minds* depraved, weak, ignorant, and incumbered with all the Lusts and Appetites of frail and *mortal Bodies;* exciting the Passions, overbearing the Judg-

ment, and swaying the Will and Affections in their Favour.—
And in this State or Condition, they *begat Sons and Daughters
after their own Image;* that is, of the *same* Frame, State and
Condition with themselves, and to whom they derived all these
temporal Evils, as Conditions of their Nature.

And this miserable Legacy entailed, their *Sons and Daughters,* alas! were not careful to diminish, but greatly enlarged.
They *found out many Inventions,* and daily *corrupted themselves* more and more, by their *actual* Transgressions. . . .

And this being the real State or Condition of the human
World, when *Christ the Redeemer* personally appear'd in it, to
take away the Sins of it, and *bring it out of* that *Darkness into
his marvellous Light; from* that *Power of Satan unto God;* here
opens a more full and clear Idea of *Regeneration,* or what is
meant by *born again;*——*born of God;*——*Sons or Children of
God;—the new Man;*——*the new Creature,* and such like
figurative analogical Terms, used both by *himself* and his
Apostles. . . .

Now of all this the *Pagan,* natural, or carnal Mind can conceive no immediate or direct Idea; because a Thing of which it
has no Experience; because,

Chiefly a Work, not of its *natural,* but, of *Almighty* Power.
I say *chiefly.* Not the *absolute, sole,* or *instantaneous,* but the
gradual co-operative Work of God's *Holy Spirit, for* Mankind,
in them, and *with* them as *moral Agents.* And this Work, in the
ordinary and established Method, consists of these two
Branches.

1. His standing Revelation of the *Law* and the *Gospel* pro-
mulged to the Human World, and written for their Admonition; *to open their Eyes, and bring them out of Darkness into
that marvellous Light;*—for *Faith cometh by Hearing, and
Hearing by the Word of God.*

2. His blessed *Aids* and *Influences* (in fuller Measure conferred now under the *Gospel* Dispensation, in the *Divine* Ordi-

nance of *Baptism*) *indwelling* or abiding in them;——*first*, Breathing, as 'twere, on their corrupt, stony, *dead* Hearts, a Breath of *new* Life, preparing them to receive *the good Seed of the Word;—then,* watering *the good Seed sown,* that it may *take Root downward, and bear Fruit upward,* may *spring* and gradually *grow up, first the Blade, then the Ear, then the full Corn in the Ear;—*in a Word, gently *Co-operating,* assisting, striving together with them, throughout the whole Course of their Lives, that they may *grow in Grace;* advance from *Strength to Strength,* from lower to higher Degrees of Knowledge, of Faith, of Renovation of their Minds, of Virtue, of Righteousness and true Holiness towards that Perfection which is attainable in this present State, of becoming *the Children of God,* by Adoption, *regenerate* or *new born.*

Thus, my Brethren, the Work of *Regeneration* is not the Work of a *Moment,* a sudden *instantaneous* Work, like the *miraculous* Conversion of St. *Paul,* or the *Thief* on the Cross; but a *gradual* and *co-operative* Work of the *Holy Spirit,* joining in with our *Understandings,* and leading us on by *Reason* and *Persuasion,* from one Degree to another, of Faith, good Dispositions, Acts, and Habits of Piety. . . .

To the Law then (my Brethren) *and to the Testimony;—search the Scriptures,* and the agreeable *Interpretations* of the *Catholick* Church in all Ages; if they speak not after this Manner;—if they speak not according to this Doctrine we have now taught, then reject it, as only the private Opinion of a weak and fallible Man: But if they do thus accordingly speak, why then will you be amused with *dark* and *vain Words?* Why will you be carried away with so strange a *Wind of Doctrine,* as persuades to the Belief and Expectation of a certain happy *Moment,* when, by the *sole* and *specifick* Work of the *Holy Spirit,* you shall at once (as 'twere by *Magic* Charm) be *matamorphosed,* stript of your *old* Nature and cloathed with a *new?* Why carried away, I say, with so strange a *Wind of Doctrine* as this, which can blow only from *enthusiastick* Heads, and can serve only to scare and hurry you into *frantick* and *convulsive* Fits of *Religion,* which must terminate either in *Bedlam,* or *Deism,* or *Popery,* or at least in such a Manner as to prove hurtful to true Religion, its real Interest and Concerns?

Thus having endeavour'd to satisfy our first Enquiry, we proceed to

II. The *second,* viz. What is meant by *the Spirit bearing Witness with our Spirit.*

Few Words are used in Holy Scripture in so many various Acceptations as the Word *Spirit;* but besides the first and principal one, denoting the *third* Person of the ever blessed *Trinity,* 'tis used more especially in these three. 1st, To signify the Nature, Genius or Disposition of Persons or Things. 2d, The Gospel in general, as containing the standing Dictates, Doctrines, or Directions of *the Spirit.* 3d, It is put for the Fruits or Effects of it. . . .

Now, if *these Fruits* and *Effects* be the alone certain *ordinary* Testimony *of the Spirit;*—and our *Feelings* or Consciousness of these (*viz.* the good *Dispositions* of our *Hearts,* and agreeable Conduct of our Lives, together with the *Joy, Peace* and *Satisfaction* of Mind, thence naturally arising) be the only true *Feelings* of his *ordinary* Influences or Operations;——if these Things be so, as according to the Scriptures, they manifestly are; then what can our *modern Teachers* mean, when they talk of *Impulses, Motions* and *Impressions,* liken'd to *Pulsations of an Artery,* to *hot Water,* or the *Motions of a Foetus in the Womb?* If they mean the *same* as we have now taught, then why will they talk in another, or rather in an *unknown Tongue?* This can but puzzle and amuse, and therefore can be of no good Design. If their Meaning be *different,* it can be known, I dare say, only by themselves; nor otherwise by themselves (as they offer no sort of rational Proof or Evidence) than as Men know the Meaning of their own Fancies, or the Reveries of a disordered Imagination. Would they be content quietly to enjoy their own *Feelings*, no one would disturb them in the Enjoyment;——but if they will be *running* about the World with their *Feelings*, and telling us, that, tho' they cannot explain or make us conceive *them*, we must yet have the *same* Feelings in *ourselves*, or we *cannot be saved;*——and if to Objections made to this, or any other *their* Doctrines, they will only reply, that their *Motto* is, *Answer him not a Word;*—— this I conceive to be not only *amusing* but *Insulting* of Mankind, instead of *Teaching* them.

What *Opinions* soever Men may have to offer, which they conceive of *Importance* in Matters of *Religion;* if they will offer them with *common* Modesty, (not to say *Christian* Humility) submit them to a fair *Trial* or *Examination,*——and according to the *Apostle's* Rule, *be ready always to render the Reasons* of them *with Meekness and Fear;* they not only ought, but will always be heard and considered by all sober and serious *Christians.* But if instead of this, they will be throwing out their *Opinions* with *Sybilline* Rage and Fury,——*running a Muck* (if I may so speak) on Mankind with them, and cramming them down their Throats with *Anathema's, Hell* and *Damnation* at the End of them, on all that will not *implicitely* receive them; in this Case, I say, be we sure, that such are either Men of *enthusiastick*-Heads or *Emissaries* of Rome. This were easy to demonstrate, but I chuse to detain you no longer, than to expostulate a few Things concerning your tumultuous Assemblies, Preacher and Doctrines.

What went you out, my Brethren, *to see,* or rather *to hear?* Any *new* Gospel, or Message from Heaven? Why, no? but the *old* one explained and taught in a *new* and *better* Manner. But what are the Doctrines you have heard thus taught and explained? Why, the Doctrines of *Regeneration?*——of the *Gift of the Holy Ghost,* or the *Spirit within?*——and of *Justification by Faith only.*

As to the Doctrine of *Regeneration* you have now heard it, as contained in the *Scriptures,* in the various Phrases, *born anew;* ——*born of God;*——*Sons* or Children *of God;*——*the new Man;*——*a new Creature,* &c. and taught by the *Christian* Church in all Ages; *viz.* that 'tis a Work of the *Holy Spirit,* commencing more especially in our Baptism, or entring into the Gospel Covenant, (by which *Infants* are regenerate and fitted for the Kingdom of Heaven) and thence *co-operating* with us, 'till we arrive at *the Measure of the Stature of the Fulness of Christ.*——Thus, I say, you have heard *this* Doctrine now taught and explained; but in another or different, tho' *not new* Manner, you have heard it from your famous *Preacher.* In another and different Manner I say, tho' *not new,* but the *same* with *other* modern *Enthusiasts,* you have heard it taught by him, *viz.* not as a Work of the *Holy Spirit,* regenerating *Infants* in their Baptism, nor as *co-operating,* aiding, or assisting only in the future Course of our *Christian* Warfare:—But as an *absolute, immediate, instantaneous* Work,—darted in upon us like a Flash of Lightning, as upon St. *Paul;* enlightening the *Understanding,* influencing the *Will,* the *Affections* and *Incli-nations,* and in a Word, changing the *whole* Man into a *new Creature,* in the twinkling of an Eye, or a *Moment* of Time.— You have heard this *Doctrine* vehemently asserted; but how have you heard it *proved* or maintained? You have been amused with the *miraculous* Conversions of St. *Paul, Zaccheus,* the *Jailor,* and the *Penitent Thief;* but what are they to the Purpose? Can any good Inference be drawn from those *miraculous Cases,* to what must be the *ordinary* and common Case of all *Christians?* No, my Brethren, such Inference would be idle and absurd: Nor may *Christians* now-a-days conclude, that because St. *Paul* or any others, were converted in a *miraculous* or extraordinary Manner, that therefore that of their own Conversion also must be the same; no more than *ordinary* Ministers of the Church may conclude, that because the *Apostles* were endued with the *Gift of Tongues,* they must therefore be endued with the same also.—But what farther Proofs or Arguments were offered by your *Preacher,* in support of this Doctrine? Why, Proofs and Arguments are all *carnal* Things:—He is *sure* the Doctrine is true, he *knows it,* he *feels it,* and they are all *damned* who will not *believe it;* and if these will not do, you may go look for *Proofs* and *Arguments* where you can find them;—He is a *special* Messenger *sent forth* from God, and therefore not bound to give Proofs or Reasons of his Message.

Moreover you have farther heard, that in this Work of *Regeneration* we are *intirely passive,* as meer *Machines* under the Hand of the Maker: Can do nothing in it or towards it, more or less, of any Sort or Degree whatsoever.——Now in this Case, suppose one of you go to this *Gentleman,* and ask him; "Sir, *What must I do to be saved?* I find myself an *unregenerate Person;*—without *Regeneration* I cannot be saved; what then in such Case must I do to be saved?" Must he not answer, "That the Question was impertinent, for that he had already taught you, that you *can do nothing* at all;—nothing that can avail towards the Work of your *Regeneration,* without which you cannot be saved?" Should he bid you, "fast and pray, or read the Scriptures, or frequent the Ordinances of God, or give Alms, *&c.*" all these *are Works;* and therefore bidding you *do* these as of any Avail, would be an express *Contradiction* to his Doctrine.

Beware, my Brethren, this is an arrant *Jumble* of Contradiction and Confusion, either calculated by a *Romish* EMISSARY, to distract and confound weak Minds; or the Produce of a warm, frantick, *Enthusiastick* Brain.

We know *Rome* has her *Seed* and *Harvest* Missionaries. Her *Seedsmen* sow INFIDELITY and ENTHUSIASM, to distress and unsettle weak Minds, often to *Distraction;* and then appear the *Harvest Men;* to *heal* their Wounds, and *gather* them home into the *Bosom* of their *Mother,* from whom they had gone astray.——But to judge most favourably in the present Case, and that the *Preacher* is honest and in earnest, he's certainly got into the Wilds of *Enthusiasm.* Will he *defend* his Doctrines? No.—Will he *reason* with you, or rationally *answer* your Objections? *No.* How then? Why, *he has the Spirit,* and that must *answer* all Objections.—If a Man comes to me and tells me, "That he is come from God to assure me, that *next Friday* I shall appear at the Bar of Christ;"—if he will raise any one from the Dead, or give Sight to one that was born blind, I will believe him: But if on my demanding the *Credentials* of his Mission, he should only tell me of certain *inward Motions, Impulses,* or *Feelings* he had of the *Spirit,* I shou'd *neglect* the Message, and *pity* the Man. Alas!—My Brethren, we have had enough of such *Pretenders* and *Pretensions* to the *Spirit!*—Look back to the *Oliverian* Days,—what Ruin and Desolation *such Pretenders* brought upon the Kingdom! How did they swarm throughout the Nation! A *Parliament;*—even an *Army* all Saints, Preachers, spiritual and regenerate Men! And yet alas, how were they *divided* and *subdivided* by the *Spirit* into a 1000 Sects, Sorts and Divisions, 'till nothing but *Confusion* as a Cloud covered the whole Face of the Land.

Beware therefore, my Brethren, of such Pretensions;—of the old Story over again! How *intoxicating,* how *fascinating* Things are an agreeable *Voice* and *Manner* of speaking? The only Excellencies of this *Preacher.* Take these away;—put his Discourses into the Mouth of an *ordinary* Speaker, I dare say, no one would step out of his Way to hear them.

In this Particular therefore, my Brethren, be on your Guard. Suffer not your *Passions to be moved,* but as your *Minds are instructed;* And run not away with the *agreeable Voice* of the *Preacher* in your Ears, for the *Soundness of his Doctrine* in your Understandings.

8 · *Josiah Smith*

(*1704–1781*)

WHITEFIELD'S CHARACTER

AND PREACHING

_____

Until 1740 Whitefield had flirted with the possibility that grace was not unconditional, but when John Wesley openly espoused such an Arminianism Whitefield publicly repudiated him. From this point on Whitefield identified himself more with colonial dissent than with his English Methodist friends. Critics of the revival, however, continued to point to his early sermons as evidence of Whitefield's inconsistency, even heterodoxy, and it was necessary for defenders of the Awakening to certify Whitefield's Calvinism while, at the same time, turning back the equally common charge that he preached "Antinomian license." Among the earliest of Whitefield's advocates was Josiah Smith, the first native of South Carolina to be educated at Harvard. As pastor of Charleston's Independent Congregational Church, Smith gained some

_____

Josiah Smith, *A Sermon, on the Character, Preaching, &c. of the Rev. Mr. Whitefield* (1740), in George Whitefield, *Fifteen Sermons Preached on Various Important Subjects* (New York, 1794), pp. 16–21, 26–27.

fame in the 1730's as a proponent of the right of private judgment. His credentials were thus such that his "Character of Whitefield," frequently reprinted in the North, forestalled criticism of Whitefield and even served to stimulate a desire there to hear this "prince of pulpit orators."

. . . I. I shall give you my opinions of the doctrines he insisted upon among us.

To speak more generally, They were doctrines, I am of opinion agreeable to the dictates of reason; evidently founded upon scripture; exactly correspondent with the articles of the establishment; of great use and necessity in forming the Christian life. . . .

To be of more particular;

One of the doctrines, which he has hardly passed over in silence in any single discourse, is that of original sin. A truth so manifest in scripture, that I am almost of opinion, it is impossible any sincere, diligent and unprejudiced inquirer should miss it: for it is written in sun-beams that a man may run and read.

. . . A truth, we feel in every power of our soul! what we read upon our own hearts; and is indeed stamped upon universal nature, within our horizon; and which the more righteous any man is, the more he feels and groans under.——We need not wonder then, our late incomparable preacher should insist upon original sin, when we consider, not only in what an incontestible manner he proved it, but of what vast importance it must be. For to give my opinion freely; I cannot think, I can see, how the Christian scheme can be consistent with itself, or supported with honour, without this basis. I look upon it, not merely as a doctrine of the scriptures, the great fountain of truth, but a very fundamental one; from which, I hope, God will suffer none of you to be enticed, by any sophistry of the subtle disputers of this world, or charms of language.

But to proceed.——

Another doctrine we have lately had in the warmest language impressed upon us, is that Pauline one of justification by faith alone. And here you will remember, how the preacher vindicated himself from all suspicions of Antinomian error, and opening a door to licentious manners: for while on the one hand, he earnestly contended for our justification as the free gift of God, by faith alone, in the blood of Christ, an article of faith delivered to the saints of old; so on the other hand, he took special care to guard against the licentious abuse of it, and would not make void the law, when he asserted that good works were the necessary fruits and evidences of true faith. . . .

Regeneration was another great doctrine, which the excellent man much insisted upon; hardly a single sermon, but he mentioned it, sometimes more than twice; and one, and perhaps the best of his discourses, was *ex professo* upon this subject. Nor can any man be surprised, that a minister of the New Testament should so heartily espouse a principle, which our Lord himself began to speak, and asserted as a fundamental point of Christianity, indispensibly requisite to eternal life; and this with so much vehemency, and earnest repetition. *Verily, verily, I say unto thee, except a man be born again (from above) he cannot see the kingdom of God.* He assures us, *We must be born of water and of the Spirit.* Our regeneration results in its necessity, from original sin. They that are *shapen in iniquity, and conceived in sin,* must be washed and cleansed.—By which is not meant the mere forms and rites of baptism; not the washing away the filth of the flesh, as the corrupt Pharisees might wash their hands, and the outside of the cup; but the answer of a good conscience towards God, purged by the blood of Christ. For we can only be *saved by the washing of regeneration, and renewing of the Holy Ghost:*

the infusion of a new life, a divine, heavenly and prolific principle. As we are by nature dead in trespasses and sins, God must quicken us by his Spirit, and through that we must *mortify the deeds of the body, and crucify the flesh with its lusts and affections.* For until we know (until we feel the exceeding greatness of) the power of Christ's resurrection, we have no part in him: we cannot enter into heaven; or if we should, our first petition would be, to be discharged as soon as possible. Pleasure is the result of harmony; the nature must agree with the object: there must be a great change upon the nature, to make us susceptive of the pleasures of God's presence.——

Cavillers and scoffers, I know, there are enough, in these last days against this doctrine. Some master of Israel may ask, *How can these things be? Can a man when he is old enter a second time into his mother's womb, and be born?*——Who ever said he could? Or what would it avail, if he should? But I hope, there may be such a thing as a spiritual birth, subsequent to the natural.—May we not be again begotten to a lively hope? May not God of his own will do it by his word and Spirit? And may we not then become as *little children* and *new born babes*—— Born not of blood nor of the will of man, nor of the will of the flesh, but of God? Are we not told, in the most express language,—*that which is born of the flesh, is flesh, and that which is born of the Spirit, is spirit?* Are not here two births, one natural, the other spiritual?—I am really astonished, any man should read his Bible and his own heart, and be a stranger to this doctrine of the new-birth; without which all our boasted morality, and ethical virtues, however splendid and rhetoricated upon, can never adorn us in the sight of God, nor qualify us for his redeeming love.

True religion is an inward thing, a thing of the heart; it chiefly resides there, and consists in a right disposition and sanctified temper of the will and affections; and as we have been lately told, *in righteousness, peace, and joy in the Holy Ghost.* Which naturally introduces another doctrine, nearly allied to this, and which was very strongly insisted on, *viz.*

The impressions or (which was the preacher's own phrase) inward feelings of the Spirit. And here you remember how he guarded against the invidious censure, of assuming the character of an apostle.

He renounced all pretentions to the extraordinary powers and signs of apostleship, gifts of healing, speaking with tongues, the faith of miracles; things peculiar to the age of inspiration, and extinct with them. He also allowed these feelings of the Spirit were not in every person, or at all times, in the same degree; and that though a full assurance were attainable, and what every one should labour to obtain, yet not of absolute necessity to the being of a Christian.—Only he asserted that we might feel the Spirit of God, in his sanctifying and saving impressions, and witnessing with our own spirits. And what is there in all this repugnant to reason! What is there in it, but what is perfectly agreeable to scripture! How can we be led by the Spirit, or have joy in the Holy Ghost, without some sensible perceptions of it?—Can I at any time feel my soul in sacred raptures, burning with the love of God, and of Christ, and all my best passions alive? . . . Can I have all these things in me, and do I feel them upon my soul, and yet this doctrine of feeling the Spirit be burlesqued and ridiculed, in an age of infidelity, and of men who love to speak evil of the things which they *know not?* Indeed a sinful and adulterous generation may seek after a sign. But what sign can we give them of things that must be known by being felt? Or what ideas can I convey of light to the blind, and of harmony to the deaf?—Let God touch their hearts as he has done ours, and they shall feel what we feel; and what I would not but feel, for millions of worlds. But till then it is impossible in nature to represent it, in a full adequate light to them; and they may as well ask for mathematical demonstrations in a point of pure morality. This is a doctrine, I have been acquainted with these many years; it is not new or surprising to me; you have heard me preach it scores of times, though perhaps, clothed in other expressions, [as] the influences of the Spirit, the impressions of grace. And however derided by some, who set up and caress a system of rational religion, I hope to have always enthusiasm enough to maintain that the Spirit of God may be felt.—To conclude this head, all the doctrines now mentioned, are primitive, protestant, puritanic ones; which our good fathers, conformists and dissenters, have filled their writings with. . . .

II. I shall next give you my opinion of the manner of his preaching.

And here I need not say, nor can my pen describe his action and gesture, in all their strength and decencies. He is certainly a finished preacher, and a great master of pulpit oratory and elocution, while a noble negligence ran thro' his style. Yet his discourses were very extraordinary when we consider how little they were premeditated, and how many of them he gave us, the little time he was with us.—Many, I trust, have felt, and will long feel the impressions of his zeal and fire, the passion and flame of his expressions. . . .

He appeared to me, in all his discourses, very deeply affected and impressed in his own heart. How did that burn and boil within him, when he spake of the things he had made, touching the King? How was his tongue like the pen of a ready writer? touching as with a coal from the altar! With what a flow of words, what a ready profusion of language, did he speak to us upon the great concern of our souls? . . . The awe, the silence, the attention, which sat upon the face of so great an audience, was an argument, how he could reign over all their powers. Many thought, *He spoke as never man spoke,* before him. So charmed were people with his manner of address, that they shut up their shops, forgot their secular business, and laid aside their schemes for the world; and the oftener he preached, the keener edge he seemed to put upon their desires of hearing him again! How awfully, with what thunder and sound did he discharge the artillery of Heaven upon us? And yet, how could he soften and melt even a soldier of Ulysses, with the love and mercy of God! . . . So methinks (if you will forgive the figure) saint Paul would look and speak in a pulpit, and in some such manner, I have been tempted to conceive of a seraph, were he sent down to preach among us, and to tell us what things he had seen and heard above! . . .

I now proceed, under the last head, to give my opinion, what views providence may have in raising up men of this stamp, now among us.

And this I desire to do with all humility and modesty.

I pretend to no spirit of prophecy, and can only conjecture, and offer the result of observation, reason, and the usual tendencies of things, corroborated by the great promises scattered up and down in our Bibles, wherein *glorious things are spoken of thee, thou city of our God!* The prophesies are usually too dark and mystic to be fully understood: the seals of that book are seldom broken, until the several periods of accomplishment, which makes time the best and surest expositor. But certainly, if we can discern the face of the sky in the morning, we might make some humble and faint conjectures at the times, and seasons, which the Father keeps in his own power. Now we are none of us ignorant, how far the primitive spirit of Christianity has sunk into a mere form of godliness. Irreligion has been rushing in, even upon the Protestant world like a flood: the dearest and most obvious doctrines of the Bible have fallen into low contempt: the principles and systems of our good and pious fathers have been more and more exploded. And now, behold! God seems to have revived the ancient spirit and doctrines. He is raising up our young men, with zeal and courage to stem the torrent. They have been in *labour more abundant;* they have preached with such fire, assiduity, and success; such a solemn awe have they struck upon their hearers; so unaccountably have they conquered the prejudices of many persons; such deep convictions have their sermons produced; so much have they roused and kindled the zeal of ministers and people; so intrepidly do they push through all opposition, that my soul overflows with joy, and my heart is too full to express my hopes. It looks as if some happy period were opening, to bless the world with another reformation. Some great things seem to be upon the anvil, some big prophecy at the birth: God give it strength to bring forth!

PART THREE

THE GREAT AWAKENING:

PRESBYTERIANISM

9 · *Gilbert Tennent*

THE DANGER OF AN

UNCONVERTED MINISTRY

Though Whitefield, on his visit to Philadelphia in the autumn of 1739, preached to as many as six thousand auditors at a time, the revival in the Middle Colonies was less his personal achievement than that of Gilbert Tennent and his fellow graduates of the Log College. In his *Journal* Whitefield saluted the Tennents as "the burning and shining lights of this part of America," and they in turn profited from his example. Before his visit the young Presbyterians were dispatching evangelists only to the

---

Gilbert Tennent, *The Danger of an Unconverted Ministry, Considered in a Sermon on Mark VI. 34* (2nd ed., Philadelphia, 1741; reprinted Boston, 1742), entire.

"vacant" parishes of New Jersey and Pennsylvania. In the last weeks of 1739 they began to enter areas already served by other Presbyterians, often without invitation. The practice was defended and encouraged by Gilbert Tennent in his celebrated Nottingham Sermon of March 8, 1740. This was, in the words of a nineteenth-century Presbyterian historian, "one of the most severely abusive sermons that was ever penned," and Tennent afterward recanted some of his harsher sentiments and language. But this manifesto of the revival party, in its original form, enjoyed continuing publication and popularity throughout the century.

MARK VI. 34.

And Jesus, when he came out, saw much People and was moved with Compassion towards them, because they were as Sheep not having a Shepherd.

As a faithful Ministry is a great Ornament, Blessing and Comfort, to the Church of GOD; even the Feet of such Messengers are beautiful: So on the contrary, an ungodly Ministry is a great Curse and Judgment: These Caterpillars labour to devour every green Thing.

There is nothing that may more justly call forth our saddest Sorrows, and make all our Powers and Passions mourn, in the most doleful Accents, the most incessant, insatiable, and deploring Agonies; than the melancholly Case of such, who have no faithful Ministry! This Truth is set before our Minds in a strong Light, in the Words that I have chosen now to insist upon! in which we have an Account of our LORD's Grief with the Causes of it.

We are informed, That our dear Redeemer was moved with

Compassion towards them. The Original Word signifies the strongest and most vehement Pity, issuing from the innermost Bowels.

But what was the Cause of this great and compassionate Commotion in the Heart of Christ? It was because he saw much People as Sheep, having no Shepherd. Why, had the People then no Teachers? O yes! they had Heaps of Pharisee-Teachers, that came out, no doubt after they had been at the Feet of *Gamaliel* the usual Time, and according to the Acts, Cannons, and Traditions of the Jewish Church. But notwithstanding of the great Crowds of these Orthodox, Letter-learned and regular Pharisees, our Lord laments the unhappy Case of that great Number of People, who, in the Days of his Flesh, had no better Guides: Because that those were as good as none (in many Respects) in our Saviour's Judgment. For all them, the People were as Sheep without a Shepherd.

From the Words of our Text, the following Proposition offers itself to our Consideration, *viz.*

That the Case of such is much to be pitied, who have no other but Pharisee-Shepherds, or unconverted Teachers.

In discoursing upon this Subject, I would

I. *Enquire into the Characters of the Old Pharisee-Teachers.*

II. *Shew, why the Case of such People, who have no better, should be pitied.   And*

III. *Shew, how Pity should be expressed upon this mournful Occasion!*

        And

First I am to enquire into the *Characters of the Old Pharisee-Teachers.* Now, I think the most notorious Branches of their Character, were these, viz. *Pride, Policy, Malice, Ignorance, Covetousness,* and *Bigotry to human Inventions in religious Matters.*

The old Pharisees were very proud and conceity; they loved the uppermost Seats in the Synagogues, and to be called Rabbi,

Rabbi; they were masterly and positive in their Assertions, as if forsooth Knowledge must die with them; they look'd upon others that differed from them, and the common People with an Air of Disdain; and especially any who had a Respect for JESUS and his Doctrine, and dislik'd them; they judged such accursed.

The old Pharisee-Shepherds were as crafty as Foxes; they tried by all Means to ensnare our Lord by their captious Questions, and to expose him to the Displeasure of the State; while in the mean Time, by sly and sneaking Methods, they tried to secure for themselves the Favour of the Grandees, and the People's Applause; and this they obtained to their Satisfaction. *John* 7. 48.

But while they exerted the Craft of Foxes, they did not forget to breathe forth the Cruelty of Wolves, in a malicious Aspersing the Person of Christ, and in a violent Opposing of the Truths, People and Power of his Religion. Yea, the most stern and strict of them were the Ring-leaders of the Party: Witness *Saul's* Journey to *Damascus,* with Letters from the Chief-Priest, to bring bound to *Jerusalem* all that he could find of that Way. It's true the Pharisees did not proceed to violent Measures with our Saviour and his Disciples just at first; but that was not owing to their good Nature, but their Policy; for they feared the People. They must keep the People in their Interests: Ay, that was the main Chance, the Compass that directed all their Proceedings; and therefore such sly cautious Methods must be pursued as might consist herewith. They wanted to root vital Religion out of the World; but they found it beyond their Thumb.

Although some of the old Pharisee-Shepherds had a very fair and strict Out-side; yet were they ignorant of the New-Birth: Witness Rabbi *Nicodemus,* who talk'd like a Fool about it. Hear how our LORD cursed those plaister'd Hypocrites, Mat. 23. 27, 28. *Wo unto you, Scribes and Pharisees, Hypo-*

crites; for ye are like whited Sepulchres, which indeed appear beautiful outward, but are within full of dead Bones, and of all Uncleanness. Even so ye also appear righteous unto Men, but within ye are full of Hypocrisy and Iniquity. Ay, if they had but a little of the Learning then in Fashion, and a fair Outside, they were presently put into the Priest's Office, though they had no Experience of the New-Birth. O Sad!

The old Pharisees, for all their long Prayers and other pious Pretences, had their Eyes, with *Judas,* fixed upon the Bag. Why, they came into the Priest's Office for a Piece of Bread; they took it up as a Trade, and therefore endeavoured to make the best Market of it they could. O Shame!

It may be further observed, That the Pharisee-Teachers in Christ's Time, were great Bigots to small Matters in Religion. Mat. 23. 23. *Wo unto you, Scribes and Pharisees, Hypocrites; for ye pay Tythe of Mint, and Anise, and Cummin, and have omitted the weightier Matters of the Law, Judgment, Mercy, and Faith.* The Pharisees were fired with a Party-Zeal; they compassed Sea and Land to make a Proselyte; and yet when he was made, they made him twofold more the Child of Hell than themselves. They were also bigotted to human Inventions in religious Matters: *Paul* himself, while he was a natural Man, was wonderful zealous for the Traditions of the Fathers: Ay, those poor blind Guides, as our LORD testifies, strained at a Gnat, and swallowed a Camel.

And what a mighty Respect had they for the Sabbath-Day forsooth! insomuch that Christ and his Disciples must be charged with the Breach thereof, for doing Works of Mercy and Necessity. Ah the Rottenness of these Hypocrites! It was not so much Respect to the Sabbath, as Malice against Christ, that was the Occasion of the Charge: they wanted some plausible Pretence to offer against him in order to blacken his Character.

And what a great Love had they in Pretence to those pious

Prophets, who were dead before they were born? while in the mean Time they were persecuting the Prince of Prophets! Hear how the King of the Church speaks to them, upon this Head: Matth. 23. 29—33. *Wo unto you Scribes and Pharisees, Hypocrites; because ye build the Tombs of the Prophets, and garnish the Sepulchres of the Righteous; and say, If we had been in the Days of our Fathers, we would not have been Partakers with them in the Blood of the Prophets. Ye Serpents, ye Generation of Vipers, How can ye escape the Damnation of Hell?*

Second General Head of Discourse, is to shew, *Why such People, who have no better than the Old Pharisee-Teachers, are to be pitied?*   And

1. Natural Men have no Call of GOD to the Ministerial Work under the Gospel-Dispensation.

Isn't it a principal Part of the ordinary Call of GOD to the Ministerial Work, to aim at the Glory of GOD, and in Subordination thereto, the Good of Souls, as their chief Marks in their Undertaking that Work? And can any natural Man on Earth do this? No! no! Every Skin of them has an evil Eye; for no Cause can produce Effects above its own Power. Are not wicked Men forbid to meddle in Things sacred? Ps. 50. 16. *But unto the Wicked, GOD saith, What hast thou to do to declare my Statutes, or that thou shouldst take my Covenant in thy Mouth?* Now, are not all unconverted Men wicked Men? Does not the Lord Jesus inform us, *John* 10. 1. That *he who entreth not by the Door into the Sheep-fold, but climbeth up some other Way, the same is a Thief and a Robber?* In the 9*th* V. Christ tells us, That *He is the Door;* and that *if any Man enter in by him, he shall be saved, by him,* i. e. By Faith in him, (says *Henry.*)[1] Hence we read of a *Door of Faith,* being opened to the Gen-

---

[1] Matthew Henry (1662–1714). His multivolume "Exposition of the Old and New Testament" was a standard Dissenter commentary on Scripture. [Ed.]

tiles. *Acts* 14. 22. It confirms this Gloss, that Salvation is annexed to the Entrance before-mentioned. Remarkable is that Saying of our Saviour, *Matth.* 4. 19. *Follow me, and I will make you Fishers of Men.* See, our LORD will not make Men Ministers, 'till they follow him. Men that do not follow Christ, may fish faithfully for a good name, and for worldly Pelf; but not for the Conversion of Sinners to God. Is it reasonable to suppose, that they will be earnestly concerned for others Salvation, when they slight their own? Our LORD reproved *Nicodemus* for taking upon him the Office of instructing others, while he himself was a Stranger to the New Birth, *John* 3. 10. *Art thou a Master of Israel, and knowest not these Things?* The Apostle *Paul* (in 1 *Tim.* 1. 12.) thanks GOD for counting him faithful, and putting him into the Ministry; which plainly supposes, That GOD Almighty does not send Pharisees and natural Men into the Ministry: For how can those Men be faithful, that have no Faith? It's true Men may put them into the Ministry, thro' Unfaithfulness, or Mistake; or Credit and Money may draw them, and the Devil may drive them into it, knowing by long Experience, of what special Service they may be to his Kingdom in that Office: But GOD sends not such hypocritical Varlets. Hence *Timothy* was directed by the Apostle *Paul,* to commit the ministerial Work to faithful Men. 2 *Tim.* 2. 2. And do not those Qualifications, necessary for Church-Officers, specified 1 *Tim.* 3. 7, 3, 9, 11. and *Tit.* 1. 7, 8. plainly suppose converting Grace? How else can they avoid being greedy of filthy Lucre? How else can they hold the Mystery of Faith in a pure Conscience, and be faithful in all Things? How else can they be Lovers of Good, sober, just, holy, temperate?

2. The Ministry of natural Men is uncomfortable to gracious Souls.

The Enmity that is put between the Seed of the Woman & the Seed of the Serpent, will now and then be creating Jarrs:

And no wonder; for as it was of old, so it is now, *He that was born after the Flesh, persecuted him that was born after the Spirit.* This Enmity is not one Grain less, in unconverted Ministers, than in others; tho' possibly it may be better polished with Wit and Rhetorick, and gilded with the specious Names of Zeal, Fidelity, Peace, good Order, and Unity.

Natural Men, not having true Love to Christ and the Souls of their Fellow-Creatures, hence their Discourses are cold and sapless, and as it were freeze between their Lips. And not being sent of GOD, they want that divine Authority, with which the faithful Ambassadors of CHRIST are clothed, who herein resemble their blessed Master, of whom it is said, That *He taught as one having Authority, and not as the Scribes.* Matth. 7. 29.

And Pharisee-Teachers, having no Experience of a special Work of the Holy Ghost, upon their own Souls, are therefore neither inclined to, nor fitted for, Discoursing, frequently, clearly, and pathetically, upon such important Subjects. The Application of their Discourses, is either short, or indistinct and general. They difference not the Precious from the Vile, and divide not to every Man his Portion, according to the Apostolical Direction to *Timothy*. No! they carelessly offer a common Mess to their People, and leave it to them, to divide it among themselves, as they see fit. This is indeed their general Practice, which is bad enough: But sometimes they do worse, by misapplying the Word, through Ignorance, or Anger. They often strengthen the Hands of the Wicked, by promising him Life. They comfort People, before they convince them; sow before they plow; and are busy in raising a Fabrick, before they lay a Foundation. These fooling Builders do but strengthen Men's carnal Security, by their soft, selfish, cowardly Discourses. They have not the Courage, or Honesty, to thrust the Nail of Terror into sleeping Souls; nay, sometimes they strive with all their Might, to fasten Terror into the Hearts of the Righteous, and so to make those sad, whom GOD would not have made sad! And this happens, when pious People begin to suspect their Hypocrisy, for which they have good Reason. I may add, That inasmuch as Pharisee-Teachers seek after Righteousness as it were by the Works of the Law themselves, they therefore do not distinguish, as they ought, between *Law* and *Gospel* in their Discourses to others. They keep Driving, Driving, to Duty, Duty, under this Notion, That it will recommend natural Men to the Favour of GOD, or entitle them to the Promises of Grace and Salvation: And thus those blind Guides fix a deluded World upon the false Foundation of their own Righteousness; and so exclude them from the dear Redeemer. All the Doings of unconverted Men, not proceeding from the Principles of Faith, Love, and a new Nature, nor being directed to the divine Glory as their highest End, but flowing from, and tending to Self, as their Principle and End; are doubtless damnably Wicked in their Manner of Performance, and do deserve the Wrath and Curse of a Sin-avenging GOD; neither can any other Encouragement be justly given them, but this, That in the Way of Duty, there is a Peradventure or Probability of obtaining Mercy.

And natural Men, wanting the Experience of those spiritual Difficulties, which pious Souls are exposed to, in this Vale of Tears; they know not how to speak a Word to the Weary in Season. Their Prayers are also cold; little child-like Love to God or Pity to poor perishing Souls, runs thro' their Veins. Their Conversation hath nothing of the Savour of Christ, neither is it perfum'd with the Spices of Heaven. They seem to make as little Distinction in their Practice as Preaching. They love those Unbelievers that are kind to them, better than many Christians, and chuse them for Companions; contrary to *Ps.* 15. 4. *Ps.* 119. 115. & *Gal.* 6. 10. Poor Christians are stunted and starv'd, who are put to feed on such bare Pastures, and such dry Nurses; as the Rev. Mr. *Hildersham*[2] justly calls them. It's only when the wise Virgins sleep, that they can bear with those dead Dogs, that can't bark; but when the LORD revives his People, they can't but abhor them. O! it is ready to break their very Hearts with Grief, to see how lukewarm those Pharisee-Teachers are in their publick Discourses, while Sinners are sinking into Damnation, in Multitudes!　　But

3. The Ministry of natural Men, is for the most part unprofitable; which is confirmed by a three-fold Evidence, *viz.* of Scripture, Reason, and Experience. Such as the Lord sends not, he himself assures us, shall not profit the People at all. *Jer.* 23. 32. Mr. *Pool*[3] justly glosseth upon this Passage of Sacred Scripture, thus, viz. *'That none can expect GOD's Blessing upon their Ministry, that are not called and sent of GOD into the Ministry.'* And right Reason will inform us, how unfit Instruments they are to negotiate that Work they pretend to. Is a blind Man fit to be a Guide in a very dangerous Way? Is a dead Man fit to bring others to Life? a mad Man fit to give Counsel in a Matter of Life and Death? Is a possessed Man fit to cast out Devils? a Rebel, an Enemy to GOD, fit to be sent on an Embassy of Peace, to bring Rebels into a State of Friendship with GOD? a Captive bound in the Massy Chains of Darkness and Guilt, a proper Person to set others at Liberty? a Leper, or one that has Plague-sores upon him, fit to be a good Physician? Is an ignorant Rustick, that has never been at Sea in

---

[2] Arthur Hildersham (1563–1632), Puritan author of *A Treatise on the Church of England . . . whether it is to be separated from or joined unto* (1595). [Ed.]

[3] Matthew Poole (1624–1679), English Nonconformist theologian, author of the five-volume *Synopsis criticorum biblicorum* (1669–1676), a summary of the views of 150 commentators on Scripture. His English language *Annotations on the Holy Bible* (2 vols., 1683–1685), which was completed by Poole's friends, was more familiar to American ministers. [Ed.]

his Life, fit to be a Pilot, to keep Vessels from being dashed to Pieces upon Rocks and Sand-banks. *'Isn't an unconverted Minister like a Man who would learn others to swim, before he has learn'd it himself, and so is drowned in the Act, and dies like a Fool?'*

I may add, That sad Experience verifies what has been now observed, concerning the Unprofitableness of the Ministry of unconverted Men. Look into the Congregations of unconverted Ministers, and see what a sad Security reigns there; not a Soul convinced that can be heard of, for many Years together; and yet the Ministers are easy; for they say they do their Duty! Ay, a small Matter will satisfy us in the Want of that, which we have no great Desire after. But when Persons have their Eyes opened, and their Hearts set upon the Work of God; they are not so soon satisfied with their Doings, and with Want of Success for a Time. O! they mourn with *Micah*, that they are as those that gather the Summer-Fruits, as the Grape-gleaning of the Vintage.—Mr. *Baxter*[4] justly observes, *'That those who speak about their Doings in the aforesaid Manner, are like to do little Good to the Church of God.' 'But many Ministers (as Mr.* Bracel[5] *observes) thinks the Gospel flourishes among them when the People are in Peace, and many come to hear the Word, and to the Sacrament.'* If with the other they get the Salaries well paid; O then it is fine Times indeed! in their Opinion. O sad! And they are full of Hopes, that they do

[4] Richard Baxter (1615–1691), a late Puritan divine. His *The Saint's Everlasting Rest* (1650) and *Autobiography* (in the abridgement of Edmund Calamy, 1702) were standard reading in pious households. [Ed.]

[5] I have been unable to identify this as the name of any author, and suspect it is a misprint, probably for "Flavel," although the word "Bracel" (which appeared in the first edition of the sermon) remained unchanged through all but one of the successive reprintings. The exception was the German-language translation, where the name is given as "Barckel." This suggests another, but remoter possibility, that Tennent was taken to be referring to the Quaker apologist, Robert Barclay. [Ed.]

good, tho they know nothing about it. But what Comfort can a consciencious Man, who travails in Birth, that Christ may be form'd in his Hearers Hearts, take from what he knows not? Will a hungry Stomach be satisfied with Dreams about Meat? I believe not; tho' I confess a full one may.

What if some Instances could be shewn, of unconverted Ministers being Instrumental, in convincing Persons of their lost State? The Thing is very rare, and extraordinary. And for what I know, as many Instances may be given, of Satan's convincing Persons by his Temptations. Indeed its a kind of Chance-medly, both in Respect of the Father, and his Children; when any such Event happens. And isn't this the Reason, why a Work of Conviction and Conversion has been so rarely heard of, for a long Time, in the Churches, till of late, *viz.* That the Bulk of her spiritual Guides, were stone-blind, and stone-dead?

4. The Ministry of natural Men is dangerous, both in respect of the Doctrines, and Practice of Piety. The Doctrines of *Original Sin, Justification by Faith alone,* and the other Points of *Calvinism,* are very cross to the Grain of unrenew'd Nature. And tho' Men, by the Influence of a good Education, and Hopes of Preferment, may have the Edge of their natural *Enmity* against them blunted; yet it's far from being broken or removed: It's only the saving Grace of GOD, that can give us a true Relish for those Nature-humbling Doctrines; and so effectually secure us from being infected by the contrary. Is not the *Carnality* of the *Ministry,* one great Cause of the general Spread of *Arminianism, Socinianism, Arianism,* and *Deism,* at this Day through the World?

And alas! what poor Guides are natural Ministers to those, who are under spiritual Trouble? they either slight such Distress altogether, and call it *Melancholy,* or *Madness,* or dawb those that are under it, with untemper'd Mortar. Our LORD assures us, That the Salt which hath lost its Savour, is good for nothing; some say, *"It genders Worms and Vermine."* Now, what Savour have Pharisee-Ministers? In Truth, a very stinking One, both in the Nostrils of God and good Men. *"Be these Moral Negroes never so white in the Mouth, (as One expresseth it) yet will they hinder, instead of helping others in at the strait Gate."* Hence is that Threatning of our LORD against them. Mat. 23. 13. *Wo unto you, Scribes and Pharisees, Hypocrites; for ye shut up the Kingdom of Heaven against Men; for ye neither go in yourselves, nor suffer those that are entering to go in.* Pharisee Teachers will with the utmost Hate oppose the very Work of GOD's Spirit, upon the Souls of Men; and labour by all Means to blacken it, as well as the Instruments, which the ALMIGHTY improves to promote the same; if it comes near their Borders, and interferes with their Credit or Interest. Thus did the Pharisees deal with our Saviour.

If it be objected against what has been offered, under this General Head of Discourse, That *Judas* was sent by Christ; I answer, (1) *That* Judas's *Ministry was partly Legal,* inasmuch as during that Period, the Disciples were subject to Jewish Observances, and sent *only* to the House of *Israel,* Matt. 10. 5, 6. And in that they waited after Christ's Resurrection, for another Mission, *Acts* 1. 4. which we find they obtained, and that different from the former, *Matt.* 28. 19. (2) Judas's *Ministry was extraordinary necessary,* in order to fulfil some ancient Prophesies concerning him. *Acts* 1. 16, 17, 18, 20. *John* 13. 18. I fear that the Abuse of this Instance, has bro't many *Judases* into the *Ministry,* whose chief Desire, like their great Grandfather, is to finger the Pence, and carry the Bag. But let such hireling murderous Hypocrites take Care, that they don't feel the Force of a Halter in this World, and an aggravated Damnation in the next.

Again, If it be objected, That *Paul* rejoiced, that the Gospel was preached, tho' of Contention, and not *sincerely;* I answer,

The Expression signifies the Apostle's great Self-Denial! Some laboured to eclipse his Fame and Character, by contentious Preaching, thinking thereby to afflict him; but they were mistaken; as to that, he was easy: For he had long before learned, to die to his own Reputation. The Apostle's Rejoicing was comparative only: He would rather that CHRIST should be preached out of *Envy,* than not at all. Especially considering the gross Ignorance of the Doctrinal Knowledge of the Gospel, which prevailed almost *universally* in that Age of the World. Besides the Apostle knew that that Trial should be sanctified to him, to promote his spiritual Progress in Goodness, and perhaps prove a Mean of procuring his temporal Freedom; and therefore he would rejoice. It is certain, we may both rejoice and mourn, in relation to the same Thing, upon different Accounts, without any Contradiction.   But the

Third general Head was to shew, *How Pity should be expressed upon this mournful Occasion?*

My Brethren, We should mourn over those, that are destitute of faithful Ministers, and sympathize with them. Our Bowels should be moved with the most compassionate Tenderness, over those dear fainting Souls, that are *as Sheep having no Shepherd;* and that after the Example of our blessed LORD.

Dear Sirs! we should also most *earnestly pray* for them, that the compassionate Saviour may preserve them, by his *mighty* Power, thro' Faith unto Salvation; support their sinking Spirits, under the *melancholy Uneasinesses of a dead Ministry;* sanctify and sweeten to them the *dry* Morsels they get under such blind Men, when they have none better to repair to.

And more especially, *my Brethren,* we should pray to the LORD of the Harvest, to send forth faithful Labourers into his Harvest; seeing that the Harvest truly is plenteous, but the Labourers are few. And O Sirs! how humble, believing, and importunate should we be in this Petition! O! let us follow the LORD, Day and Night, with Cries, Tears, Pleadings and

Groanings upon this Account! For GOD knows there is great *Necessity* of it. *O! thou Fountain of Mercy, and Father of Pity, pour forth upon thy poor Children a Spirit of Prayer, for the Obtaining this important Mercy! Help, help, O Eternal GOD and Father, for Christ's sake!*

And indeed, *my Brethren*, we should join our Endeavours to our *Prayers*. The most likely Method to stock the Church with a faithful *Ministry*, in the present Situation of Things, the publick Academies being so much corrupted and abused generally, is, To encourage private Schools, or Seminaries of Learning, which are under the Care of skilful and experienced Christians; in which those only should be admitted, who upon strict Examination, have in the Judgment of a reasonable *Charity*, the plain Evidences of experimental Religion. Pious and experienced Youths, who have a good natural Capacity, and great Desires after the Ministerial Work, from good Motives, might be sought for, and found up and down in the *Country*, and put to Private Schools of the Prophets; especially in such Places, where the Publick ones are not. This Method, in my Opinion, has a *noble Tendency*, to build up the Church of God. And those who have any Love to Christ, or Desire after the Coming of his Kingdom, should be *ready*, according to their Ability, to give somewhat, from time to time, for the Support of such poor Youths, who have nothing of their own. And truly, Brethren, this *Charity* to the Souls of Men, is the most noble kind of *Charity*–O! if the Love of God be in you, it will constrain you to do something, to promote so noble and necessary a Work. It looks Hypocrite-like to go no further, when other Things are required, than *cheap Prayer*. Don't think it much, if the Pharisees should be offended at such a Proposal; these subtle selfish Hypocrites are wont to be scar'd about their Credit, and their Kingdom; and truly they are both little worth, for all the Bustle they make about them. If they could help it, they wo'dn't let one faithful Man come into the Ministry; and therefore their Opposition is an encouraging Sign. Let all the Followers of the Lamb stand up and act for GOD against all Opposers: Who is upon GOD's Side? who?

THE IMPROVEMENT of this Subject remains.   And

1. If it be so, That the Case of those, who have no other, or no better than Pharisee-Teachers, is to be pitied: Then what a Scrole & Scene of Mourning, and Lamentation, and Wo, is opened! because of the Swarms of Locusts, the Crowds of Pharisees, that have as *covetously* as *cruelly*, crept into the Ministry, in this adulterous Generation! who as nearly resemble the Character given of the old Pharisees, in the Doctrinal Part of this Discourse, as one Crow's Egg does another. It is true some of the modern Pharisees have learned to prate a little more *orthodoxly* about the New Birth, than their Predecessor *Nicodemus,* who are, in the mean Time, as great Strangers to the feeling Experience of it, as he. They are blind who see not this to be the Case of the Body of the Clergy, of this Genera- tion. And O! that our Heads were Waters, and our Eyes a Fountain of Tears, that we could *Day* and *Night* lament, with the utmost Bitterness, the doleful Case of the poor Church of God, upon this account.

2. From what has been said, we may learn, That such who are contented under a *dead Ministry,* have not in them the Temper of that Saviour they profess. It's an awful Sign, that they are as blind as Moles, and as dead as Stones, without any spiritual Taste and Relish. And alas! isn't this the Case of Mul- titudes? If they can get one, that has the Name of a Minister, with a Band, and a black Coat or Gown to carry on a *Sabbath- days* among them, although never so coldly, and *insuccess- fully;* if he is free from gross Crimes in Practice, and takes good Care to keep at a due Distance from their Consciences, and is never troubled about his Insuccessfulness; O! think the poor Fools, that is a fine Man indeed; our Minister is a prudent charitable Man, he is not always harping upon Terror, and

sounding Damnation in our Ears, like some rash-headed Preachers, who by their uncharitable Methods, are ready to put poor People out of their Wits, or to run them into Despair; O! how terrible a Thing is that Dispair! Ay, our Minister, honest Man, gives us good Caution against it. Poor silly Souls consider *seriously* these Passages, of the Prophet, *Jeremiah* 5. 30, 31.

3. We may learn, the Mercy and Duty of those that enjoy a *faithful Ministry*. Let such *glorify* GOD, for so distinguishing a Privilege, and labour to walk worthy of it, to all Well-pleasing; left for their Abuse thereof, they be exposed to a greater Damnation.

4. If the Ministry of natural Men be as it has been represented; Then it is both lawful and expedient to go from them to hear Godly Persons; yea, it's so far from being sinful to do this, that one who lives under a pious Minister of lesser Gifts, after having honestly endeavour'd to get Benefit by his Ministry, and yet gets little or none, but doth find real Benefit and more Benefit elsewhere; I say, he may *lawfully* go, and that *frequently*, where he gets most Good to his precious Soul, after regular Application to the Pastor where he lives, for his Consent, and proposing the Reasons thereof; when this is done in the Spirit of Love and Meekness, without Contempt of any, as also without rash *Anger* or vain *Curiosity*.

Natural Reason will inform us, that Good is desireable for its own sake. Now, as Dr. *Voetius*[6] observes, Good added to Good, makes it a greater Good, and so more desireable; and therefore Evil as Evil, or a lesser Good, which is comparatively Evil, cannot be the Object of Desire.

There is a natural Instinct put even into the irrational Creature, by the Author of their Being, to seek after the greater

---

[6] Gysbertus Voet (1588–1676), a Dutch theologian. As professor and pastor, and in the Synod of Dort, he advocated the strictest Calvinism against the early Arminians. [Ed.]

natural Good, as far as they know it. Hence the Birds of the Air fly to the warmer Climates, in order to shun the Winter-Cold, and also doubtless to get better Food; *For where the Carcass is, there will the Eagles be gathered together.* The Beasts of the Field seek the best Pastures, and the Fishes of the Ocean seek after the Food they like best.

But the written Word of God confirms the aforesaid Proposition, while God by it enjoins us, *to covet earnestly the best Gifts;* as also *to prove all Things, and hold fast that which is good.* 1 Cor. 12. 31. 1 Thess. 5. 2. And is it not the Command of God, that we should *grow in Grace?* 2 Pet. 3. 18. and 1 Pet. 2. 2. Now, does not every positive Command enjoin the Use of such Means, as have the directest Tendency to answer the End designed? namely, *The Duty commanded.* If there be a Variety of Means, is not the best to be chosen? else how can the Choice be called rational, and becoming an intelligent Creature? To chuse otherwise *knowingly,* is it not contrary to common Sense, as well as Religion, and daily confuted by the common Practice of all the rational Creation, about Things of far less Moment and Consequence?

That there is a Difference and Variety in Preachers Gifts and Graces, is *undeniably* evident, from the united Testimony of Scripture and Reason.

And that there is a great Difference in the Degrees of Hearers Edification, under the Hearing of these different Gifts, is as evident to the Feeling of experienced Christians, as any Thing can be to Sight.

It is also an unquestionable Truth, that *ordinarily* GOD blesses most the best Gifts, for the Hearers Edification, as by the best Food he gives the best Nourishment. Otherwise the best Gifts would not be desireable, and GOD *Almighty* in the ordinary Course of his Providence, by not acting according to the Nature of Things, would be carrying on a Series of unnecessary Miracles; which to suppose, is unreasonable. The following Places of holy Scripture, confirm what hath been last observed. 1 *Cor.* 14. 12. 1 *Tim.* 4. 14, 15, 16. 2 *Tim.* 1. 6. *& Acts* 11. 24.

If God's People have a Right to the Gifts of all God's Ministers, *pray, why mayn't they use them, as they have Opportunity?* And if they should go a few Miles farther than ordinary, to enjoy those, which they profit most by; who do they wrong? Now, our LORD does inform his People, 1 *Cor.* 3. 22. That *whether Paul, or Apollos, or Cephas; all was theirs.*

But the Example of our Dear Redeemer, will give farther Light in this Argument. Tho' many of the Hearers, not only of the Pharisees, but of *John the Baptist,* came to hear our Saviour, and that not only upon Week-days, but upon Sabbath-days, and that in great Numbers, and from very distant Places; yet he reproved them not: And did not our Lord love the Apostle *John* more than the rest, and took him with him, before others, with *Peter* and *James,* to Mount *Tabor,* and *Gethsemany?* Matt. 17. and Chap. 26.

To bind Men to a particular Minister, against their Judgment and Inclinations, when they are more edified elsewhere, is carnal with a Witness; a cruel Oppression of tender Consciences, a compelling of Men to Sin: For he that doubts, is damn'd if he eat; and whatsoever is not of Faith, is Sin.

Besides it is an unscriptural Infringment on Christian Liberty; 1 *Cor.* 3. 22. It's a Yoke worse than that of *Rome* itself. Dr. *Voetius* asserts, *"That even among the* Papists, *as to hearing of Sermons, the People are not depriv'd of the Liberty of Choice."* It's a Yoke like that of *Egypt,* which cruel *Pharaoh* formed for the Necks of the oppressed *Israelites,* when he obliged them to make up their stated Task of Brick, but allowed them no Straw. So we must grow in Grace and Knowledge; but in the mean Time, according to the Notion of some, we are confined from using the likeliest Means, to attain that End.

If the great Ends of Hearing may be attained as well, and better, by Hearing of another Minister than our own; then I see not, why we should be under a fatal Necessity of hearing him, I mean our Parish-Minister, perpetually, or generally. Now, what are, or ought to be, the Ends of Hearing, but the Getting of Grace, and Growing in it? *Rom.* 10. 14. 1 *Pet.* 2. 2. *As Babes desire the sincere Milk of the Word, that ye may grow thereby.* (Poor Babes like not dry Breasts, and living Men like not dead Pools.) Well then, and may not these Ends be obtained out of our Parish-line? *Faith* is said to come by *Hearing,* Rom. 10. But the Apostle doesn't add, *Your Parish-Minister.* Isn't the same Word preach'd out of our Parish? and is there any Restriction in the Promises of blessing the Word to those only, who keep within their Parish-line ordinarily? If there be, I have not yet met with it; yea, I can affirm, that so far as Knowledge can be had in such Cases, I have known Persons to get saving Good to their Souls, by Hearing over their Parish-line; and this makes me earnest in Defence of it.

That which ought to be the main Motive of Hearing any, *viz.* our Souls Good, or greater Good, will excite us, if we regard our own eternal Interest, to hear there, where we attain it; and he that hears with less Views, acts like a Fool, and a Hypocrite.

Now, if it be lawful to withdraw from the Ministry of a pious Man in the Case aforesaid; how much more, from the Ministry of a natural Man? Surely, it is both lawful and expedient, for the Reason offered in the Doctrinal Part of this Discourse: To which let me add a few Words more.

To trust the Care of our Souls to those who have little or no Care for their own, to those who are both unskilful and unfaithful, is contrary to the common Practice of considerate Mankind, relating to the Affairs of their Bodies and Estates; and would signify, that we set light by our Souls, and did not care what became of them. For if the Blind lead the Blind, will they not both fall into the Ditch?

Is it a strange Thing to think, that GOD does not ordinarily use the Ministry of his Enemies, to turn others to be his Friends, seeing he works by suitable Means?

I cannot think, that GOD has given any Promise, that he will be with, and bless the Labours of natural Ministers: For if he had, he would be surely as good as his Word. But I can neither see, nor hear of any Blessing upon these Men's Labours; unless it be a rare wonderful Instance of Chancemedly! whereas the Ministry of faithful Men blossoms and bears Fruit, as the Rod of *Aaron. Jer.* 23. 22. *But if they had stood in my Counsel, and had caused my People to hear my Words, then they should have turned them from their evil Way, and from the Evil of their Doings.*

From such as have a Form of Godliness, and deny the Power thereof, we are injoined to turn away, 2 *Tim.* 3. 5. And are there not many such?

Our LORD advised his Disciples, to beware of the Leaven of the Pharisees, *Mat.* 16. 6. by which he shews that he meant their Doctrine and Hypocrisie. *Mark* 8. 15. *Luke.* 12. 1. which were both sour enough.

Memorable is the Answer of our LORD to his Disciples, *Mat.* 15. 12, 13, 14. *Then came his Disciples and said unto him, Knowest thou, that the Pharisees were offended?—And he answered and said, Every Plant which my Heavenly Father hath not planted, shall be rooted up. Let them alone; they be blind Leaders of the Blind: And if the Blind lead the Blind, both shall fall into the Ditch.*

If it is objected, That we are bid to go to hear those, that sit in *Moses'* Chair, *Mat.* 23. 2, 3. I would answer this, in the Words of a Body of dissenting Ministers, viz. *"That sitting in* Moses' *Chair, signifies a Succeeding of* Moses *in the ordinary*

Part of his Office and Authority; so did Joshua, *and the* 70 *Elders,* Exod. 18. 21—26. *Now,* Moses *was no Priest (say they) tho' of* Levi's *Tribe, but King in* Jeshurun, *a civil Ruler and Judge, chosen by God.* Exod. 18. 13." Therefore no more is meant by the Scripture in the Objection, but that it is the Duty of People to hear and obey the lawful Commands of the Civil Magistrate, according to *Rom.* 13. 5.

If it be opposed to the preceeding Reasonings, That such an Opinion and Practice would be apt to cause Heats and Contentions among People;

I answer, That the aforesaid Practice, accompanied with Love, Meekness, and Humility, is not the proper *Cause* of those Divisions, but the *Occasion* only, or the Cause by Accident, and not by itself. If a Person exercising Modesty and Love in his Carriage to his Minister and Neighbours, thro' Uprightness of Heart, designing nothing but his own greater Good, repairs there frequently where he attains it; is this any reasonable Cause of Anger? will any be offended with him because he loves his Soul, and seeks the greater Good thereof, and is not like a senseless Stone, without Choice, Sense, and Taste? Pray must we leave off every Duty, that is the Occasion of Contention or Division? Then we must quit powerful Religion altogether. For *he that will live godly in Christ Jesus, shall suffer Persecution.* And particularly we must carefully avoid faithful Preaching: For that is won't to occasion Disturbances and Divisions, especially when accompanied with divine Power. 1 Thess. 1. 5, 6. *Our Gospel came not unto you in Word only, but in Power*: And then it is added, That they *received the Word in much Affliction.* And the Apostle *Paul* informs us, 1 Cor. 16. 9. That a great Door and effectual was open'd unto him, and that their were many Adversaries. Blessed *Paul* was accounted a common Disturber of the Peace, as well as *Elijah* long before him: And yet he left not off Preaching for all that. Yea, our blessed LORD informs us, That he came not to send

Peace on Earth, but rather a Sword, Variance, Fire, and Division, and that even among Relations. *Mat.* 10. 34, 35, 36. *Luke* 12. 49, 51, 52, 53. As also, That while the strong Men armed keeps the House, all the Goods are in Peace. It is true the Power of the Gospel is not the proper Cause of those Divisions, but the innocent Occasion only: No; the proper Cause of sinful Divisions, is that Enmity against God, and Holiness, which is in the Hearts of natural Men, of every Order; being stirred up by the Devil, and their own proud and selfish Lusts. And very often natural Men, who are the proper Causes of the Divisions aforesaid, are won't to deal with God's Servants as *Potiphar's* Wife did by *Joseph*; they lay all the Blame of their own Wickedness at their Doors, and make a loud Cry!

Such as confine Opposition and Division, as following upon living Godliness and successful Preaching, to the first Ages of Christianity; it is much to be fear'd neither know themselves, nor the Gospel of Christ. For surely the nature of true Religion, as well as of Men and Devils, is the same in every Age.

Is not the visible Church composed of Persons of the most contrary Characters? While some are sincere Servants of God, are not many Servants of Satan, under a religious Mask? and have not these a fixed Enmity against the other? How is it then possible, that a Harmony should subsist between such, till their Nature be changed? Can Light dwell with Darkness?

Undoubtedly it is a great Duty, to avoid giving just Cause of Offence to any; and it is also highly necessary, that pious Souls should maintain Union and Harmony among themselves; notwithstanding of their different Opinions in lesser Things. And no doubt this is the Drift of the many Exhortations which we have to Peace and Unity in Scripture.

Surely, it cannot be reasonably suppos'd, that we are exhorted, to a Unity in any Thing that is wicked, or inconsistent with the Good, or greater Good of our poor Souls: For that would be like the Unity of the Devils, a Legion of which dwelt peaceably in one Man: Or like the Unity of *Ahab*'s false Prophets; all these four Hundred Daubers were very peaceable and much united, and all harped on the pleasing String: Ay, they were moderate Men, and had the Majority on their Side.

But possibly some may again object against Persons going to hear others, besides their own Ministers; the Scripture about *Paul* and *Apollos,* 1 Cor. 1. 12. and say, that it is carnal. Dr. *Voetius* answers the aforesaid Objection, as follows: 'The Apostle reproves (*says he*) such as made Sects, saying, *I am of Paul, and I of Apollos*—and we with him reprove them. But this is far from being against the Choice, which one hath of Sermons and Preachers; seeing at one time we cannot hear all, neither doth the Explication and Application of all, equally suit such a Person, in such a Time, or Condition, or equally quicken, and subserve the Encrease of Knowledge.' Thus far he.

Because that the Apostle, in the aforesaid Place, reproves an excessive Love to, or Admiration of particular Ministers, accompanied with a sinful Contention, Slighting and Disdaining of others, who are truly godly, and with Sect-making: To say that from hence it necessarily follows, That we must make no Difference in our Choice, or in the Degrees of our Esteem of different Ministers, according to their Different Gifts and Graces; is an Argument of as great Force, as to say, Because Gluttony & Drunkenness are forbidden, therefore we must neither eat nor drink, or make any Choice in Drinks or Victuals, let our Constitution be what it will.

Surely the very Nature of Christian Love inclines those that are possessed of it, to love others chiefly for their Goodness, and therefore in Proportion thereto. Now, seeing the Inference in the Objection is secretly built upon this Supposition, That we should love all good Men alike; it strikes at the Foundation of that Love to the Brethren, which is laid down in Scripture, as a Mark of true Christianity, 1 *Joh.* 5. and so is carnal, with a Witness.

Again it may be objected, That the aforesaid Practice tends to grieve our Parish-Minister, and to break Congregations in Pieces.

I answer, If our Parish-Minister be grieved at our greater Good, or prefers his Credit before it; then he has good Cause to grieve over his own Rottenness, and Hypocrisie. And as for Breaking of Congregations to Pieces, upon the Account of People's Going from Place to Place, to hear the Word, with a View to get greater Good; that spiritual Blindness and Death, that so generally prevails, will put this out of Danger. It is but a very few, that have got any spiritual Relish; the most will venture their Souls with any Formalist, and be well satisfied with the sapless Discourses of such dead Drones.

Well, does'nt the Apostle assert, That *Paul and Apollos are nothing?* Yes, it is true, they & all others are nothing as Efficient Causes; they could not change Men's Hearts. But were they nothing as Instruments? The Objection insinuates one of these two Things, either that there is no Difference in Means, as to their Suitableness; or that there is no Reason to expect a greater Blessing upon the most suitable Means: Both which are equally absurd, and before confuted.

But it may be further objected, with great Appearance of Zeal, That what has been said about People's Getting of Good, or greater Good, over their Parish-line, is a meer Fiction; for they are out of God's Way.

I answer, That there are Three monstrous Ingredients in the Objection, namely, A Begging of the Question in Debate, rash Judging, and Limiting of God.

It is a mean Thing in Reasoning, to beg or suppose that, which should be prov'd and then to reason from it. Let it be prov'd, that they are out of God's Way; and then I will freely yield; But till this be done, bold Saysoes will not have much

Weight with any but Dupes or Dunces. And for such who cry out against others for Uncharitableness, to be guilty of it themselves in the mean time in a very great Degree, is very inconsistent. Isn't it rash to judge of Things they have never heard? But those that have received Benefit, and are sensible of their own Uprightness, they will think it is a light Thing, to be judged of Man's Judgment. Let *Tertullus* ascend the Theatre, and gild the Objection with the most mellifluous Ciceronean Eloquence; it will no more perswade them, that what they have felt is but a Fancy (unless they be under strong Temptations of Satan, or scared out of their Wits by frightful Expressions) than to tell a Man, in proper Language, that sees, That it is but a Notion, he does not see: Or to tell a Man that feels Pleasure or Pain, That it's but a deluded Fancy; they are quite mistaken.

Besides there is a Limiting the Holy One of Israel, in the aforesaid Objection; which sinful Sin the *Hebrews* were reproved for. It is a Piece of daring Presumption, to pretend by our finite Line, to fathom the infinite Depths that are in the Being and Works of God. The Query of *Zophar* is just and reasonable, *Job* 11. 7, 8. *Canst thou by Searching find out GOD?*—The humble Apostle with Astonishment acknowledged that the Ways of GOD were past finding out. *Rom.* 11. 33. Surely the Wind blows where it listeth, and we cannot tell whence it cometh, nor whither it goeth. Doesn't JEHOVAH ride upon a gloomy Cloud? and make Darkness his Pavilion? and isn't his Path in the great Waters? *Ps.* 18. *Ps.* 77. 19.

I would conclude my present Meditations upon this Subject, by Exhorting

All those who enjoy a faithful Ministry, to a speedy and sincere Improvement of so rare and valuable a Privilege; lest by, their foolish Ingratitude the Righteous GOD be provok'd, to remove the Means they enjoy, or his Blessing from them, and so at last to expose them in another State to Enduring and greater Miseries. For surely, these Sins which are committed against greater Light and Mercy, are more presumptuous, ungrateful, and inexcusable; there is in them a greater Contempt of GOD's Authority, and Slight of his Mercy; those Evils do awfully violate the Conscience, and declare a Love to Sin as Sin; such Transgressors do rush upon the Bosses of GOD's Buckler, they court Destruction without a Covering, and embrace their own Ruin with open Arms. And therefore according to the Nature of Justice, which proportions Sinners Pains, according to the Number and Heinousness of their Crimes, and the Declaration of Divine Truth, you must expect an enflamed Damnation: Surely, it shall be more tolerable for *Sodom* and *Gomorrah,* in the Day of the LORD, than for you, except ye repent.

And let gracious Souls be exhorted, to express the most tender Pity over such as have none but Pharisee-Teachers; and that in the Manner before described: To which let the Example of our LORD in the Text before us, be an inducing and effectual Incitement; as well as the gracious and immense Rewards, which follow upon so generous and noble a Charity, in this and the next State.

And let those who live under the Ministry of dead Men, whether they have got the Form of Religion or not, repair to the Living, where they may be edified. Let who will, oppose it. What famous Mr. *Fenner*[7] observes upon this Head, is most just, '*That if there be any godly Soul, or any that desires the Salvation of his Soul, and lives under a blind Guide, he cannot go out (of his Parish) without giving very great Offence; it will be tho't a Giddiness, and a Slighting of his own Minister at home.—When People came out of every Parish roundabout, to* John, *no Question but this bred Heart burning against* John,

---

[7] Dudley Fenner (*ca.* 1558–1587), one of the Puritan divines suspended in 1584 for refusing to acknowledge the Queen's supremacy and the authority of the Prayer Book. [Ed.]

*ay, and Ill-will against those People, that would not be satis-
fied with that Teaching they had in their own Synagogues.'*
Thus far he. But tho' your Neighbours growl against you, and
reproach you for doing your Duty, in seeking your Souls Good;
bear their unjust Censures with Christian Meekness, and persevere; as knowing that Suffering is the Lot of Christ's Followers and that spiritual Benefits do infinitely overbalance all
temporal difficulties.

And O! that vacant Congregations would take due care in
the Choice of their Ministers! Here indeed they should hasten
slowly. The Church of *Ephesus* is commended, for Trying
them which said they were Apostles, and were not; and for
finding them Liars. Hypocrites are against all Knowing of
others, and Judging, in order to hide their own Filthiness; like
Thieves they flee a Search, because of the stolen Goods. But
the more they endeavour to hide, the more they expose their
Shame. Does not the spiritual Man judge all Things? Tho' he
cannot know the States of subtil Hypocrites infallibly; yet
may he not give a near Guess, who are the Sons of *Sceva,* by
their Manner of Praying, Preaching, and Living? Many Pharisee-Teachers have got a long fine String of Prayer by Heart,
so that they are never at a Loss about it; their Prayers and
Preachings are generally of a Length, and both as dead as a
Stone, and without all Savour. I beseech you, my dear Brethren, to consider, That there is no Probability of your getting
Good, by the Ministry of Pharisees. For they are no Shepherds
(no faithful ones) in Christ's Account. They are as good as
none, nay, worse than none, upon some Accounts. For take
them first and last, and they generally do more Hurt than
Good. They strive to keep better out of the Places where they
live; nay, when the Life of Piety comes near their Quarters,
they rise up in Arms against it, consult, contrive and combine
in their Conclaves against it, as a common Enemy, that discovers and condemns their Craft and Hypocrisie. And with

what Art, Rhetorick, and Appearances of Piety, will they varnish their Opposition of Christ's Kingdom? As the Magicians imitated the Works of *Moses*, so do false Apostles, and deceitful Workers, the Apostles of Christ.

I shall conclude this Discourse with the Words of the Apostle *Paul*, 2 *Cor.* 11. 14. 15.

And no Marvel; for Satan himself is transformed into an Angel of Light: Therefore it is no great Thing if his Ministers also be transformed as the Ministers of Righteousness; whose End shall be according to their Works.

10 · Jonathan Dickinson

(1688–1747)

THE WITNESS OF THE SPIRIT

When Whitefield returned to Philadelphia in May 1740, he discovered a "general awakening" in progress and the young Presbyterians under attack both for their "intrusions" and for the displays of emotion attendant on their "soul-searching" and "pathetic" preaching. In these circumstances Jonathan Dickinson stepped forward to assess the nature and significance of the revival experiences. The acknowledged intellectual leader of American Presbyterianism, Dickinson was a generation older than the Log College graduates, and his background was quite different. Born in Solomon Stoddard's Massachusetts domain and educated at Yale, Dickinson spoke to and for the New Englanders who since the seventeenth century had been transplanting themselves to Long Island and into the Jerseys. In the disputes of the late 1730's Dickinson had opposed "subscription" but had otherwise managed to avoid identification either with the Tennent party or

Jonathan Dickinson, *The Witness of the Spirit. A Sermon Preached at Newark in New-Jersey, May 7th. 1740. . . . On Occasion of the wonderful Progress of Converting Grace in these Parts* (Boston, 1740), pp. 6–15, 20–21.

their opponents. Thus this sermon celebrating the out-pouring of the Spirit was significant, not only as the Awakening's first sustained analysis of the psychology of conversion, but also because Dickinson gave the revival-ists, already criticized as "anti-intellectual," both public sympathy and his immense prestige.

. . . While Sinners are in an Estate of carnal Security, they will not *know* and consider *the Things of their Peace,* they will not endeavour to *flee from the Wrath to come,* nor to *lay hold on the Hope set before them.* No Means will prevail with them, no Arguments will persuade them to *come to Christ, that they might have Life.* This is a sad Truth, open to our continual Observation & Experience. We see a poor secure World going on boldly in the Paths of Destruction and Death, notwithstand-ing all the Terrors of the Law of God, notwithstanding all the faithful Warnings of the Ministers of Christ, and all the shock-ing Dispensations of Providence. What an astonishing Thought is this! Can rational Creatures cast themselves down the dread-ful Precipice with their Eyes open! Can they run upon the flaming Sword, when it's brandished before their Breasts! Can they venture upon Hell & eternal Damnation, without Care or Fear! When seriously consider'd, it seems impossible: and yet it's obvious to every Observer, that this is the Conduct of the far greatest Part of the World of Mankind; and it will con-tinue to be the Conduct of every unconverted Sinner, until the Spirit of God opens their Eyes, sets their Danger in View, and awakens them out of this stupid and dead State. It is accordingly the first Operation of the blessed Spirit in order to a Sinner's Sanctification, to *convince him of Sin.* This he sometimes does more *suddenly;* and by a more *forceable Im-pression,* filling the Soul with the greatest Agony & Distress, from the most lively Views of his aggravated Sins, and of the amazing Wrath of God. This alarms all the Powers and Passions of the Soul, *pricks* the poor Sinner *to the Heart,* with St. Peter's Hearers causeth him to tremble with the *Jailor* to *tremble and be astonished* with *Saul* at his Conversion.—But in others these Convictions are more *gradually* brought on; and with *lower Degrees* of Terror and Amazement. These have such a Sense of their Sin and Danger, as makes them in earnest inquire *what they shall do to be saved,* tho' they do not approach so near to Desperation, from the astonishing Prospect of their dreadful Deserts. Some Sinners agonize *long* under these *Distresses,* before they can find Rest in Christ. Others are *sooner* brought to act Faith in him; and to the comfortable Evidences of it. But all must hereby be brought to such a discovery of their Guilt & Misery, that they can no longer rest in their present Condition; nor be easy without an Interest in Christ and the Favour of God.

And now my Brethren! It's your Business to consider, whether you have had this *witness of the Spirit with your Spirit,* or not. If you have been thus awaken'd out of your carnal Security, you have the Testimony of *the Spirit himself,* that he has begun a good Work in you. It is true, that this is no certain Evidence of a sanctifying Change. Many have been brought thus far, that have worn off these Impressions; and return'd to Folly, like *a Dog to his Vomit, and like the Sow that was washed to her wallowing in the Mire.* . . . But as for such of you that have had no Experience of these awak'ning Influences of the blessed Spirit, the Case is at once determined against you. There needs no other Evidence, that you are yet in your Sins, and under a dreadful Sentence of Death and Condemnation.

Another Method of the Spirit is by his *humbling* and *Soulabasing* Influences.—A Sinner must be bro't out of himself, or he will never fly to Christ for Refuge, and receive him upon his own Terms. Convictions will awaken him to a solemn Concern about his State; will drive him to Duty, and produce a Reformation of his external Behaviour. But it's too common that these Attainments quiet the Conscience, and procure Peace to the Soul, short of an Interest in Christ, and a real sanctifying Change of Heart & Life. But if the Spirit of God carry on his Work to purpose, he will bring the convinced Sinner to see the infinite Defect of all his Performances and of all his Attainments, of all his Duties, Reformations, Promises, religious Frames, and moral Carriages, and of all he does or can do, to render him acceptable to God. He will bring him to see, that he is undone, and cannot help himself; and that he is utterly unworthy that God should help him. He will bring him to see, that it is a wonder of God's Patience that he is out of Hell; and that it will be a Wonder indeed of sovereign free Grace, if such a polluted guilty Rebel finally escapes eternal Ruin. He will bring him to lie at God's Footstool, as a guilty condemned Malefactor with the Halter about his Neck, having nothing to plead in his own Favour, nothing to depend upon, but abused and forfeited Grace and Mercy.— Convinced Sinners commonly struggle a great while to get out of their Distresses, by some *self-righteous Attempt* or other. One while they'l make *Promises,* and take up Resolutions to watch their Hearts, and to reform their Lives: but alas! they find their Hearts are an inexhaustible Fountain of Corruption, which they cannot cleanse; Their Lusts get the Victory over all their good Designs and strongest Resolutions. Then they'l be ready to fly to *Duty;* and perhaps add new Duties to their old Courses; and hope by these to recommend themselves to God. But here also their Confidence withers away; they find so much deadness and dulness, so many sinful Thoughts and straying Affections in their best Performances, that they cannot hope for Safety from this Refuge. In this Distress, they'l perhaps be ready to flatter themselves with Safety from their

Convictions, from a Sense of their Vileness and Misery. They vainly hope that such Distress for their Sins, such Sorrow and Mourning, such earnest Desires of deliverance from their guilty perishing State, will move God to pity and relieve 'em. But alas! this Bed also will be found too short to stretch themselves upon. The blessed Spirit will still make them sensible that their Convictions, legal Terrors, and Sense of their own vileness and sinfulness, will no more serve to justify them in the Sight of God, than their Resolutions, their Reformations, or their Duties. And what shall they do in this Case? They now see that there is *no Refuge* but CHRIST only; and to Him they would therefore repair, were it not for the same *self-righteous* Principles still obtaining in them. They would commit their Souls to Christ for Salvation; but they can't think he will receive such poor guilty sinful Creatures as they are: They have hard Hearts, and corrupt Affections: They have not been sufficiently convinced of their Sins, or not sufficiently humbled: They have not the necessary Qualifications for coming to Christ and believing in him; and are therefore yet striving in their own Strength to obtain some Preparations, some Fitness of Soul for coming to Christ. But the Spirit of God won't leave those he designs for Mercy, in these unhappy Toils. He'll shew 'em, that they are not to hope, that the Case will ever be better, by any Thing they do or can do; that they neither have, nor ever will have any *Qualifications* at all to *recommend* them to Christ; that it's in vain to strive with their own Hearts, in vain to work in their own Strength, or with a dependance on Creature-Helps. . . .

I proceed to shew you in the next Place, that the *Spirit of God* does in an especial manner *bear Witness* to our Adoption, by working in us *a lively Faith in the Lord Jesus Christ.* We read in *Gal.* iii. 26, that *we are all the Children of God by Faith in Jesus Christ.* If therefore the Sense of our indigent helpless and hopeless Estate in our selves, which I have described, brings us to look to the Fulness and Sufficiency that there is in *Christ,* to receive him upon his own Terms, as revealed in the Gospel, and to depend upon him only as the *Author of our eternal Salvation;* we have therein good Evidence of a glorious Change wrought in us by the Spirit of God, and that *we are the Children of God;* for we are such *by Faith in Jesus Christ.*

This, my Brethren, is the great Concern, this the grand Point that we should be especially careful to clear up to ourselves. If this Foundation be well laid, we are happy for ever: But a Mistake here is the eternal Loss of our immortal Souls. Have we been bro't to yield our unfeigned Assent to Gospel-Truths, and our unfeigned Consent to Gospel-Terms, and to *live by the Faith of the Son of God?* Have we been brought to *rejoyce in Christ Jesus, and to have no Confidence in the Flesh?* Have we *esteem'd all Things as Loss and Dung, in Comparison of Christ, that we may be found in him, not having our own Righteousness which is of the Law, but that which is through the Faith of Christ, the Righteousness which is of God by Faith?* Have we valued an Interest in Christ above all the World; and chosen Him for the Portion of our Souls? Have we received the Lord Jesus Christ in all his Offices, and for all his Benefits? Have we depended only upon the Influences of his blessed Spirit, to renew, sanctify and quicken us; and upon his Righteousness alone, to justify us in the Sight of God? Have we submitted to him as our Lord, as well as our Saviour? Is his Throne set up in our Hearts; and do all the Powers of our Souls bow down to him? . . . Happy beyond Comparison is that Person, who upon an impartial Trial can find these Operations of a saving Faith in his Soul. It is the *Spirit himself,* that has *according to his abundant Mercy, begotten him again to a lively Hope;* and he has a Witness from Heaven to his Adoption & Justification; a Witness that cannot possibly deceive him. He may depend upon it, that *He which hath begun this good Work in him, will perform it unto the Day of Jesus Christ.* The Match is concluded between Christ and his Soul. He may look upon this precious Saviour as his own for ever.

I must yet further go on to shew you, that *the Spirit witnesseth with our Spirits, that we are the Children of God,* by working in us a true sincere *Love to God.* Alas, *Our carnal Minds are Enmity against God;* and this Enmity will remain and reign in the Heart of every Unbeliever, until the Spirit of God by his powerful Influences, renews the Sinner's Nature, sanctifies the Affections, and enables the Soul to live in the Love of God. And whenever this Change is wrought in us, we have thereby *the Witness of the Spirit himself,* to the Safety and Goodness of our State and Hope. Let us make sure of this; and the Case is plain. All Darkness and Doubts will vanish before the clear shining of this Evidence.—If upon a strict Inquisition into our own Hearts we can find, that we sincerely admire and adore the glorious Perfections of God's excellent Nature; and uprightly endeavour universal Conformity to his imitable Properties; and in particular, that we endeavour to be *holy, as our Father which in Heaven is holy:* If we esteem *God's Favour as Life,* and *his Loving-Kindness as better than Life:* If we love what God loveth, and hate what he hateth: If we love his Ordinances, and delight in drawing near to him: If we delight in Communion with God, and cannot content ourselves with an empty Ordinance, without God's special Presence with us therein: If we are greatly uneasy, when he hides his Face from us; and the *Light of his Countenance* is the greatest Joy, Satisfaction, and Comfort of our Souls: If our Imperfections and Sins are our Burthen, peculiarly because dishonourable to God, because against such Love and Compassion as he has manifested to us, and because of the base Ingratitude we are therein chargeable with: If we have much at Heart the Flourishing and Prosperity of his Kingdom and Interest in the World, and exert ourselves with Diligence in our respective Stations to promote it: . . . Then we may conclude we have the *Witness in ourselves,* that we are the Children of God,—Can these Things be the Productions of Nature? Are these the Fruits of that Fountain of Enmity to God, which we have formerly experienced in our own Hearts? No, It cannot be! *The Spirit himself* has wrought these gracious Affections and Dispositions in our Souls. And he thereby gives an incontestable Evidence of our renewed Natures. If *we love him, it is because he has first loved us,* 1 Joh. iv. 19—O that all my Hearers could upon good Grounds take the Comfort of what has been said! But alas! there is just Cause to fear, that the greatest Part of them are *Lovers of themselves,* and not of God; Lovers of their Lusts and sinful Pleasures, Lovers of the World, Neglecters of Godliness; or at the best but formal Protestors: and therefore whatever their Hopes and Expectations are, they can have *no Part or Lot in this Matter.* These do not *love the Lord Jesus Christ;* and therefore must be *Anathema Maranatha,* accursed when the Lord comes, 1 *Cor.* xvi. 22—Oh how different are these two Sorts of Persons; and how very different ought their Views and Expectations to be!

I must furthermore proceed to shew you, that the *Spirit of God beareth Witness with our Spirit,* to our Adoption, and to our Interest in the Favour of God, by giving us *a Love to his Children.* We read 1 Joh. iii. 14. *We know that we are passed from Death to Life, because we love the Brethren.* This cannot imply, that a natural Affection to the Children of God, because of any Relation to 'em, or any personal Friendship, or because of their Kindness to us, their good Neighbourhood, or the like, is an Evidence of our Sanctification. Nor on the other Hand, does it imply, that as an Evidence of our Adoption, we must love or approve the Faults and Mistakes, the Errors and Imperfections of those whom we esteem the Children of God.

But it implies, that if we love the Persons, and especially the gracious Qualifications of those whom we have Reason to conclude the Children of God, for his Sake: if we love the Image of Christ wherever we see it, or wherever we think we see it (for there can be no infallible certainty in this Case) if we love the Brethren as Brethren, love their Company, love Communion and Fellowship with them in religious Exercises; and love an Imitation of them, labour after a Conformity to them in their Graces, their Piety, and vertuous Demeanour; it is a Witness for us, that we are born of God. *The Spirit himself* has wrought these gracious Affections in us. We were naturally in love with Sinners; and how comes it to pass, that their sinful Practices & their sinful Company and Fellowship become so grievous & burdensome to us? On the other Hand, we are naturally full of Enmity to the gracious Attainments, spiritual Dispositions, and religious Lives of the Saints; and how come they to be so delightful to us now? How come they to be our only chosen Companions? How come they to appear to us the only excellent ones of the Earth?

. . . And here I must confess, I am at once nonplus'd, in any Attempt to describe the unspeakable Light and Joy, that flows from this wonderful *Love of God shed abroad in the Heart* of a Believer, *by the Holy Ghost*. This is a *new Name written, which no Man knoweth, saving he that receiveth it.* (Rev. ii. 17.) As no Idea of sensible Objects can possibly be communicated to those that have not the proper Senses to perceive them; so neither can any just Conceptions of this *Fellowship of the Spirit*, this *Joy of the Holy Ghost*, be communicated to any but to those that have had the happy Experience of it in themselves. Thence it is, that some Persons from enthusiastick Heats, from working up their animal Affections and Passions, or else from diabolical Delusions, have pretended to these immediate Influences of the Spirit of God, where the

Consequence has evidently shewn, they have been *Strangers, that have never intermedled with these* Divine *Joys.* This *Witness of the Spirit* is nevertheless distinguishable from any Counterfeits, or false Pretences whatsoever, not only by *its own Light,* which dispels all Doubts and Darkness of the Soul, and gives it an Earnest and Foretaste of its future Blessedness: But it may be also distinguish'd by the *concomitant Graces* of the Holy Spirit. If the Person thus signally favoured of God, has *before* experienced the ordinary Influences of the Grace of God, *renewing* his Nature, *enlightning* his Mind, and *sanctifying* his Heart; if this blessed Experience *humbles* the Soul at God's Foot, in an abasing Sense of his own Vileness and Unworthiness, and in an adoring View of God's distinguishing Mercy and Love to such a base and worthless Worm; if this *purifies the Heart,* and *purges the Conscience from dead Works to serve the living God;* if this mortifies remaining Lusts, makes the Affections more spiritual and heavenly, excites more ardent breathings after the eternal Inheritance; and inkindles a greater Zeal for the Glory of God, as the highest End; and if this be attained in a *Way of Duty;* and makes all the *Ordinances* of God more pleasant to the Soul; if it increases Devotion to God, and Benignity to Men: I say, if the Case be thus with any, he hath doubtless *the Witness of the Spirit himself,* and may well rejoyce *with Joy unspeakable and full of Glory.* —But all Pretences to this extraordinary *Witness of the Spirit,* which are *not* accompanied with these gracious Dispositions of Mind, are false and counterfeit, and are like to end in a dreadful Disappointment.

11 · *John Thomson*

(−*1753*)

THE GOVERNMENT OF THE

CHURCH OF CHRIST

As the Awakening spread through a large area of the Middle Colonies in the spring of 1740, a party in opposition began to form. Its members, among the Presbyterian clergy, were generally men who had long battled the Tennents on other issues. But when the Synod of Philadelphia met in late May, the antirevival party were united in resentment of itinerancy and "censoriousness" and in suspicion of the seemingly unbridled emotionalism of the revival. At the Synod an attempt was made to discipline, even crush, the revivalists by forbidding ministers to enter another parish without synodical permission. Dickinson tried to moderate the controversy by proposing outside arbitration, but Tennent and his adherents proclaimed their presbyteries, in effect, independent units of

---

John Thomson, *The Government of the Church of Christ, and the Authority of the Church Judicatories established on a Scripture Foundation: And the Spirit of rash judging arraigned and condemned* . . . (Philadelphia, 1741), pp. 1–23, 26–27, 30–33, 35, 38, 42, 44–45, 48–49.

the church. Their critics' position hardened into the strictest defense of ministerial prerogative and ecclesiastical forms. The leader of and spokesman for the anti-revival party was John Thomson, who in 1729 had been the most earnest advocate of "subscription." In the years since his ordination at Lewes, Delaware in 1717, Thomson had often moved from church to church—because, as he complained, his parishioners invariably refused to pay him an adequate salary. In 1744 he once again resigned his pulpit, this time to drift into comparative obscurity in Virginia. But in the early months of the revival his eminence was unquestioned, and his extended commentary on the synodical confrontation of May 1740 stands as the major monument of Old Side principles and thought. It is perhaps the most coherent statement to be published by a Middle Colony opponent of the Awakening—and it is surely the least scurrilous.

The divisions and Misunderstandings which have of late all of a sudden arisen to such a Height in this little infant Church, cannot but be Matter of very serious and sorrowful Consideration to every unbyassed Christian, who hath the Peace and Prosperity of Zion in his Heart. Its doleful to think, and Consider, how by these Divisions, so many, and in some Places the greater Part of Congregations are so fill'd with Prejudices against their own Pastors, that altho' they can charge them with nothing exceeding human Frailty, and the sinful Infirmities that in some Measure cleave to the best of Christians; yet they openly, by Speech and Behaviour, declare their utter Disesteem and Contempt of them as if they were the Worst and Vilest of Men, magnifying their failing, misrepresenting their justifyable Conduct, and raising and spreading false and lying Reports, upon them.

Now altho' there are few or none, far or near, but have heard enough, & more than is true, in Relation to these Divisions, yet there hath not, that I know of, been any thing published to the World, setting this Matter in a clear Light. I have thought therefore that it may be to some good Purpose to make an attempt of this Kind, to let the World see the true State of the Case. . . .

So far then as I can see into this Matter, the great Difference between the protesting Brethren and the Synod consists in these two particulars: First these Brethren have conceived so exceeding low and bad Opinion of the generality of their Brethren, judging them to be quite void of Grace yea and Worse, even designed Enemies to the Life of Religion: and accordingly they esteem it a Work of the Highest, and most exalted Charity to resque the Multitudes of perishing Souls, that are under their Care, from the Jaws of everlasting Destruction, by perswading them to believe that these Ministers are as bad as they represent them to be. Any who reads Mr. *Gilbert Tennent*'s Sermon concerning unconverted Ministers, may clearly see this to be the Case, particularly in P. 17. where, after he hath called the Ministers against whom he is declaiming by such Names as these, viz. *Swarms of Locusts, crouds of Pharisees, &c.* He clearly Explains himself and Shews whom he intends while he says, they are blind who see not this to be the Case of the Body of the Clergy of this Generation; which is yet farther evident by comparing this with the introduction to a Discourse which he read in Publick, before the Synod last *May.* . . .

And that Mr. *Tennent* is not alone in thus judging his Brethren does also appear from a Paper much of the same Stamp, which Mr. *Blair*, also read before the Synod, which contains these Words. *But indeed how can such (viz. Min-*

isters) *perform this Duty to any good Purpose, who are Strangers to any such Experience themselves:* Add to this that our Protesting Brethren have been very industrious to entertain their Auditories with Declamations against these *Pharisee* Teachers, in their Itenerations or Travellings amongst us; and all their Admirers and Followers to plainly enough declare that they understand them to intend the Ministers who differ from them: besides that Mr. *Gilbert Tennent* and some others of his Party have been so particular as to Mention the Names of some of their Brethren whom they thus condemn as carnal and unconverted.

A Second particular wherein the Difference between these Brethren and the Synod doth consist is, the vastly different and opposite Judgment and Sentiments of the one and the other, particularly in Relation to Church Government. . . .

. . . [It] is plain and evident that Presbteries and Synods, when regularly constituted, have no Authority at all, in our Brethrens Judgement, either over their Members or People; for first they say that their Determinations are not to be binding upon dissenting Members, which is to sap and overthrow the very Fundamental Laws of all Societies in the World: For how is it possible that any Society can stick together unless either all be Subject to the Authority of one, or the Minisority be concluded and determined by the Majority? Unless we should suppose, what's not to be expected in this imperfect State, that all will still be unanimous in their Votes. Was it ever yet heard of, that any Society was either incorporated, or did incorporate themselves under any Form of Government, but that every one who would enjoy the Benefits and Privileges of such an Incorporation, or social Union, should submit to the Rules and Orders of it, whether they approved of these Rules or not? . . .

It is said also that Presbyteries must not incroach upon the Peoples just Priviledges or Liberties, which doth imply that the

People who are ruled, notwithstanding that they have devolved all their Right in Authority and Government, upon their Representatives, are still the Judges of their own Liberties, even after they have entrusted these Liberties in the Hands of their Representatives, which also overthrows all Authority and Government; for Church Judicatories being a Representatives of the whole collective Body which they represent, must of Course be the only proper Judges of the Just Liberties of the whole Body, and of every particular Member thereof as such, and while he continues a Member. And to be sure no Church Judicatory will ever incroach upon what they judge to be the just Liberties of the Church or Body Collective which they represent.

That these Brethren differ from the Synod in Principles or Order and Government, doth also appear from the Conclusion of Mr. *Gilbert Tennent's* Paper of May last, containing his Reasons for suspecting his Brethren to be unconverted, his Words are these. "Besides the remarkable Success that God has given of late to Mr. *Whitefield's* travelling Labours, and others in this Country, makes me abhor the slavish Schemes of Bigots, as to confinement in preaching the Gospel of CHRIST." which plainly shows with what disdain he beholds and looks down upon that Order which not only Presbyterians, but also all other Churches have, carefully observed; viz. that every Pastor should stick by his own Flock; unless when sent on the Churches Errand elsewhere: And particular Care has been taken to prevent one Ministers preaching in anothers Bounds to the Disturbance of the Peace of the Church; but I will not now further insist upon this, but return and inquire into, and examine the first Ground of Difference between the Synod and the protesting Brethren; viz. the extremely bad Opinion which these Brethren have conceived of the other Members. . . .

I now proceed to examine the Sufficiency of Mr. *Tennent's* Reasons for suspecting his Brethren as unconverted, And his First Reasons is in his own Words as follows.

"First their Unsoundness in some principal Doctrines of Christianity that relate to Experience and Practice, as particularly in the following Points.

"1st. That there is no Distinction between the Glory of God and our Happiness, that self Love is the Foundation of all Obedience. These Doctrines do in my Opinion intirely overset (if true) all supernatural Religion, render Regeneration a vain and needless Thing, involve a crimson Blasphemy against the Blessed God, by putting our selves upon a level with him.

"Secondly, that there is a certainty of Salvation annexed to the Labours of Natural Men. This Doctrine in my Opinion supposes the greatest Falshood, viz. that there is a Free-Will in Man naturally to acceptable Good, and is attended with the most dangerous Consequences, viz. fixing Men upon their own Righteousness, and utterly overthrowing the Covenant of Grace: For if there be a certainty annexed to the Endeavours of Natural Men, it must be by Promise; but a Promise is a Debt. As these Opinions are contrary to the express Testimony of Holy Scriptures, our Confession of Faith, and Christian Experience; they give me Reason to suspect at least that these who hold them are rotten hearted Hypocrites, utter Strangers to the saving Knowledge of God and their own Hearts."

. . . Altho' I will not take upon me to justify these Expressions as sound in their most obvious Meaning, yet I think its a very strange Stretch of censoriousness and rash judging, to conclude the Person unconverted who useth them. Our Happiness and the Glory of God i.e. his manifestative Glory, or declarative Glory, which results from thence are so inseparable, and so near of kin, that to condemn all as unconverted who think they cannot distinguish them, is I think, an uncommon Stretch of rash judging. Our Assemblys Catechisms join the Glory of God and Man's Salvation together, as the Chief i.e. compleat adequate ultimate End of Man. . . .

Again as to the other Expression that Self-Love is the Foun-

dation of all Obedience. Altho' we should grant that it is unguarded and perhaps unsound; yet who, in the World, before
Mr. *Tennent,* ever dreamed, that its of such a Nature as to
prove the User of it intirely unsound in Fundamentals? What
altho' this Expression doth by Consequence, overthrow the
Necessity of Regeneration, and infer Blasphemy against God?
as Mr. *Tennent* alledges, yet perhaps he who useth the Expression doth neither see nor own the Consequence. Yea further
Self-Love is so incorporated with our rational Constitution,
that its simply impossible for us to renounce it, it is supposed
in all the Promises and Threatnings of the Word, of both Law
and Gospel, it is supposed in our Happiness which is joined together with the Glory of God, as Mans chief End, in our
Catechism; and therefore it must be acknowledged to be, tho'
not the Sole and Adequate, yet the partial and inadequate
Foundation, *i.e.* Motive of our Obedience. . . . I think I may
refer it to Mr. *Tennent*'s own Conscience, whether a respect to
the Recompence of Reward hath not Influence upon him, as it
had upon *Moses,* to invigorate and incourage him to his Work
and Duty. . . .

A 2d False Doctrine which Mr. *Tennent* alledges as a Mark
of unconverted Ministers, is that there is a certainty of Salvation annexed to the Labours of natural Men, which Doctrine
he by some Arguments confutes. If there be any of the Members of our Synod of this Judgment, it is more than I know, and
I'm perswaded there are very few, for my own Part I know
not one whom I so much as suspect in this Particular.

Its true, we all may and ought to preach and tell natural
Men, that if they will repent & believe the Gospel they shall be
Saved. But this neither says nor Infers that they can do this,
without the Assistance of divine, renewing, regenerating
Grace: but by complying with the divine Call, i.e. by repent-
ing, and believing, the Person that was natural before, shall
certainly have an Evidence in himself, if he can but see it, that

he is assisted by supernatural Grace, to do what he could not do by any natural abilities which he had before. I really Question whether there be a Member in the whole Synod who maintains the foresaid Doctrine in Terms: altho' it's possible that some unguarded Expressions might inadvertently drop from some, which might be interpreted to that purpose. . . .

It's worthy noticing here, that these Instances of unsound Doctrine which Mr. *Tennent* brings as Marks of an unconverted State, as I think they are far from proving his Point, so I'm perswaded that there are not past two or three if so many that he can so much as alledge to have uttered them, and yet he brings them in as a general ground of Suspicion equally applicable by Hearers to every Member of the Synod; but that eminent Servant of Christ the Rev. Mr. *Whitefield* may print what in all probability is false in Fact, as well as false Doctrine, and yet never be thought the worse of, for his so doing.

2dly, Mr. Tennent takes Notice of some Faults in preaching, which he reckons as so many Marks or Signs of an unconverted State.

. . . I have really better thoughts of the generality of my Brethren that tho' they be not all *Boanergeses,* yet they strive faithfully to warn the wicked, as well as incourage the Godly; nor do they insist so upon external Duties, as to neglect vital Religion and the necessity of Regeneration; and I'm firmly perswaded that many of these, whom he presumptuously condemns, at last will be honour'd with well done good and faithful Servants. Mr. *Tennent,* by saying that Christs Sheep hear his Voice, and living Men have Sence and Savour, would seem to prove that gracious converted Hearers can distinguish between Converted and Unconverted Ministers, by hearing them Preach, which is such a Ridiculous falshood that it deserves not a rational Confutation. . . .

What he says concerning the Unsuccessfulness of Ministers as a Mark of their unconverted State, would with equal Force of Reason condemn some of the most eminent Prophets of old, as Elijah, Jeremiah, &c. and as to the Brethrens Contentedness under this Circumstance, is more than he can know: And besides, how can he know how successful or unsuccessful his Brethren are in their Work? If Conviction of Sin, Reformation from it, and fleeing to Christ for Mercy, may be accounted Success, I hope there is something of that follows upon our Ministry; If Instruction, Edification, and Confirmation in the Ways of Faith and Holiness, be reckoned Success, I hope there is something of this also; altho' we have all Reason to lament that there is so little: But if crying out in our public Assemblies, to the Disturbance of the Worship of God, and if falling down and working like Persons in Convulsions, I say, if those Things only be reckoned Signs of Success, I must own I do not understand it. I think converting Grace works rather on the Soul and rational Parts and Powers than on the Body. And tho' I think it a very desirable Thing to see the inward Concern of the Heart venting itself by Tears and apparent Concern in the Countenance; yet, that public outcrying in a Congregation, to the Disturbing thereof, and the Work of God, I mean the Hearing of the Word, is a sure Mark of the Spirit and Power of God, I am yet to learn. Yea, some of our Protesting Brethren begin now to speak against it, and declare that t's none of God's Work. . . .

Thirdly, Mr. *Tennent* also takes Notice of some Things in a Practice of his Brethren as Symptoms of an unconverted Estate: his Words are these:

". . . *First*, Great Stiffness in Opinion, generally in smaller Matters where good Men may differ, continual Perkness and Confidence, as if they were infallible; which shews, that the Pride of their Understanding was never broken, and that they feel not the Need of Christ as a Prophet. *2ly*. Opposing of God's Servants and Work, insisting much upon the real or supposed Imprudences of God's Servants, but passing over in Silence their valuable Qualities and worthy Actions; this looks *Pharisee-* and Devil-like, notwithstanding all the Colourings of crafty Men. 3*ly,* A Notion that Men may live godly in Christ, and not suffer Persecution. Some among us seem grossly ignorant of this Gospel Doctrine, they think that the Power of Religion may be ordinarily carried on amongst a professing people without Opposition or Division, whereas our Lord informs us that he came to send Fire on Earth, and Division; they seem to imagine that there is a great Difference between the old *Pharisees* and the dry Formalists of this Generation, whereas in Substantials they are the very same, they are both of the same Father, of the same Nature, and under the same Government. 4*ly,* That there is no knowing of People's States; tho' there is no infallible Knowledge of the Estates of some attainable, yet there is a satisfactory Knowledge to be attained; Ministers crying out against this, is an Evidence of their Unfaithfulness in neglecting to use the properest Means to convince Sinners of their damnable State, it also shews their Ignorance of divine Things, or manifests their Consciousness of their own Hypocrisy, and Fear of Discovery. 5*ly,* Letting out Men to the Ministry without so much as examining them about their Christian Experiences, notwithstanding of a late Canon of this Synod, enjoining of the same; how contrary is this Practice to the Scriptures, and to our Directory, and of how dangerous Tendency to the Church of God? Is it probable that truly gracious Persons would thus slight the precious Souls of Men? 6*ly,* More Zeal for outward Order than for the main Points of practical Religion; witness the Committees slighting and shufling the late Debate about the Glory of God, and their present Contention about the Committee Act: This is too much like the Zeal of the old *Pharisees,* in tithing Mint, Annis, and Cummin, while they neglected the weightier Matters of the Law. These Things, my Brethren, I mention in the Fear and Love of God, without personal Prejudice against any; that God who knows my Heart, is Witness that I heartily desire the Conviction of those Ministers whom I suspect, and that they may be as burning and shining Lights in the Church of God: But I am obliged in Faithfulness to God and the Souls of Men, to make mention of these Things, which are distressing to my Heart, as some of the Reasons why I protest against all Restraints in preaching the everlasting Gospel in this degenerate State of the Church. Rules that are serviceable in ordinary Cases, when the Church is stocked with a faithful Ministry, are notoriously prejudicial when the Church is oppressed with a carnal Ministry. Besides, the remarkable Success that God has given of late to Mr. *Whitefield's* travelling Labours, and several others in this Country, makes me abhor the slavish Schemes of Bigots as to Confinement in preaching the blessed Gospel of Christ. I am, Reverend Gentlemen, your Well-wisher and humble Servant,

Philadelphia, May 29, 1740   G.T."

. . . [Here] is nothing but a mere Hotchpotch of incoherent and impertinent Stuff, such as I must confess I have never met with in all my little Reading, since I was capable to take a Book in my Hand. Among all the six Articles which he advances against his Brethren's Practice, there is not one Particular that's commonly ranked among the Vices or Immoralities of wicked Men: Yea, none of the first four, except the second, can, in any Propriety of Speech, come under the Notion of Practice at all. . . .

First thing we are charged with, is our Stiffness in Opinion in smaller Matters. . . . I challenge Mr. *Tennent* and all his Party to give one Instance of any Person or Member in the Synod, yea, I may say in the Province, who either exceeds or is near an Equality to Mr. *Tennent* in this very Particular of Stiffness in Opinion, . . . one Instance of the least Yieldingness of Temper in any one Particular where he hath differed from his Brethren, small or great? . . .

The second Article of Accusation is our opposing of God's Work and Servants: It's true Mr. *Tennent* hath been opposed and contradicted, as to some false Doctrines which he preached, alleging that every true Convert is as sensible of his own good Estate as he would be of a Wound or a Stab, or the blowing of the Wind; if this be the Opposition he complains of, let it be so. I think false Doctrine is none of God's Work; it's like these false Doctrines, together with the Dialect of black-guard Ruffians brought into the Pulpit, such as *old gray-headed stinking Devil, Lamps of Hell, incarnate Devils, your damn'd Duties, you'd go to Hell with your Prayers,* with many other such Expressions, are among the real or supposed Imprudences, which Mr. *Tennent* is offended that there should be taken any Notice of, and alledgeth that it's *Pharisee-* and Devil-like to mention them.

. . . Mr. *Tennent* says that they (*viz.* the unconverted Ministers) seem to imagine that there is a great Difference between the old *Pharisees* and the dry Formalists of this Generation; and I say that Mr. *Tennent* seems to me to imagine that every Imagination of his crazy Brain heated and excited by uncharitable Prejudice against his Brethren, altho' never so groundless, is infallibly true. . . .

In the Conclusion of this Performance Mr. *Tennent* in solemn manner invokes the Heart-searching God to be Witness to the Sincerity of his Affections to his suspected Brethren; as to this I leave him to the God to whom he appeals, both as his Witness and Judge: I shall also leave it to God and the World to judge, whether his monstrous, rash and uncharitable Judgment against his Brethren, being built upon such weak and inconclusive Reasons, be a sufficient Reason for him to cast off all Subjection to the Rules of a Presbyterian Church, whereof he professeth himself to be a Member; as if Irregularity, Anarchy and Confusion were the Properest Means to restore the decayed Life of Religion. . . .

I will now proceed to take a view of what Mr. Blair hath [said] is another Paper of Complaints against his Brethren, wherein, tho' in a much more soft and moderate Stile, yet he is, in my Opinion, guilty of the same rash judging and condemning his Brethren. . . .

The first Part of Mr. Blair's Complaint is against his Brethren's Conduct in their private Conversation; his Words are as follows:

"As to the first Head of Grievances, we cannot but complain of the Unprofitableness of the general Conversation of too many amongst us, whereas they ought to be improving all Opportunities for promoting the great Ends of their high Calling, as Men who are intent upon doing Good to the Souls of Men; upon the contrary, they spend the Time of their occasional Conversation with People generally in discoursing about secular trivial Affairs, with an Air of Pleasure and Satisfaction therein, and Unconcernedness about their great Business, which is too plain an Evidence that that is the Element which is most agreeable to them to live in. . . .

"Another Thing which is worse and of a more pernicous Tendency, is their endeavouring to prejudice People against the Work of God's Power and Grace in the Conviction and Conversion of Sinners, where-ever there are any hopeful Appearances of it amongst us, calling it Enthusiasm and mere working of the Passions, the groundless Fears and irrational Phantasms of ignorant People, entirely owing to their Weakness. . . ."

. . . It's true there are some Things in our Brethren's Conduct which we cannot but condemn, and have condemned and spoken against both in private and public; and some Things also which are the frequent Effects of their Preaching on many of their Hearers, which we cannot esteem so highly of, as both they and their Admirers do.

First, In their Conduct their bold and uncharitable rash judging of their Brethren, and others, as graceless, upon insufficient Grounds. 2ly, Their unwearied Industry to possess our

People with Prejudices against us, and to persuade them to think as meanly of us as they themselves do, by calling us carnal, unconverted, Enemies to the Life of Religion, with an hundred more hard and reproachful Names; see Mr. *Tennent's Sermon concerning unconverted Ministers.* 3ly, Their irregular intruding upon other Men's Charges in a disorderly Way, contrary to all Presbyterian Rules, yea, all Order and Government, which require that every Officer should have and stick by his own Post and Charge, and not intermeddle with anothers, without Order or Consent. Besides, several Things are advanced in Doctrine which we judge erroneous: As, That every true Christian is sure of his own Conversion; Every adult Person when he is converted must be able to tell the Time, Place, and Manner of his Conversion, or else be condemned as a carnal unconverted Person. . . .

Again, There are some Effects which their Preaching have on many of their Hearers, which are cried up as the mighty Power of God going along with these Ministers Labours: *viz.* many Persons crying out aloud in the midst of the Congregations in Time of public Worship, and others falling down half dead, or working like Persons in Convulsion-Fits; which, tho' I will not here take upon me to account for, yet I am sure they are neither the Work of the Spirit of God, *i.e.*, his gracious saving Work, nor yet sure Evidences of it in the Persons who have them. . . .

Again, another Effect is that the Hearers are often seized with such dreadful Fears and despairing Terrors, as can proceed from nothing else but Unbelief, and the Suggestions of the Devil; and others are made to believe strange Delusions, such as that they must die such a Night; that the Day of Judgment is come; that they see Christ, and familiarly converse with him; some see or think they see shining Lights about them when at Devotion; others are seized with strong Fears of seeing or meeting with the Devil; some think they actually see him: Now surely none of these Things can be truly called the Work of God's Spirit or Power of his Grace. . . .

Another Complaint which Mr. *Blair* makes against his Brethren, respects their Manner of Preaching; his Words upon this Head are as follows:

> "In the next place, as to the Strain and Way of Preaching not uncommon among us, it is not adapted, as it ought to be, to the obtaining the great End of preaching, *viz.* the Conversion of Sinners to God, and the carrying on of the Work of Sanctification in his own People: Do not many corrupt the Gospel of the pure Grace of God with legal Mixtures, and so . . . deal with the Word as Hucksters too often do with their Liquors? . . ."

I confess I am at a loss to know what Mr. *Blair* means by this Accusation: Is it not a Minister's Duty and Work to press these Things upon unconverted Hearers? And have we not Commission from God to tell them that if they be sincere and conscientious in them, they shall obtain Pardon and Acceptance through Christ? . . .

What Mr. *Blair* observes concerning the dull and lifeless manner of delivering of Sermons, has, I think, but little in it. The natural Tempers and Gifts of Men are known to be so vastly different, that the truly Zealous may seem to be less lively than many Formalists and Hypocrites, in their Delivery, besides the different Frames that Persons may be in at different Times.

Mr. *Blair* renews his Complaint against us for Undistinctness in Preaching, *viz.* that we make too general Application, not distinguishing between the Precious and the Vile; as if we applied the Promises and Threatnings promiscuously to the Godly and Graceless. . . . Would Mr. *Blair* have us to make a personal Distinction among our Hearers? . . .

. . . There is a Manner of Diction or Phraseology become exceeding common and Much in Vogue, which is a downright Disgrace to the sacred Function of the Ministry of the Gospel, such as . . . asserting that *to judge well of a Person's State by his good Behaviour, is a barbarous bloody murthering Charity;* . . . speaking to Christ is such Words as these, *I summon thee, Lord Jesus, to come down, come down,* you promised me last Night to come down among us this Day, come down, come down, . . . It would be endless to mention the many wicked profane Reveries which are borrowed from *Bilinsgate* rather than from the Holy Scriptures, which are obtruded upon poor abused, amused, ignorant People as Dictates of the Holy Ghost, whereby many weak Minds are terrified out of their Wits and Sense, made to cry out and fall down as Persons dead or in Convulsions; and this is cried up as the mighty Power of God, putting forth itself in the Conversion of Sinners: This Manner of Preaching is not noticed by either Mr. *Tennent* or Mr. *Blair,* which they not being ignorant of, but in part using it, it seems that they look upon it as justifiable. . . .

In [his] last Paragraph Mr. *Blair* goes on to declare his own and others Purpose and Resolution, without Regard to Order or pastoral Relation between Ministers and People, to preach the Gospel where ever they are invited, in Compliance, as he supposes, to the Call of divine Providence, for the Relief of poor starving and perishing Souls under the Care of us grace-less and unfaithful Ministers. He also complains of a violent and extensive Opposition that hath been made unto the Work of God in his and his Brethren's Hands. . . .

As to the violent Opposition which hath been made unto the Work of God in their Hands, I shall not now enlarge, having already observed in what respect any of us have opposed them; leaving the World to judge, whether, what we have opposed or spoken against, be the Work of God, or rather something else, which deserves not so glorious a Title. However, we re-joice that the great God, who over rules all Events for his own

Glory and the Good of his Church, doth make the Truths of the Gospel preached by these Brethren, effectual in many, to stir them up to a more serious Consideration of their Soul's Concerns, than ever before. . . . And I think we had much Need of the Guidance of his Holy Spirit in both Ministers and People, to teach us to distinguish between the Chaff and the Wheat, between what is agreeable to the Will and Word of God and what is not, in our Endeavours after a Reformation, or reviving of true Godliness, which he stand so much in need of; lest we lose our Charity, while we are seeking for Piety; lest, while we look for true Conversion, we be deceived with Delusion; and lest, while we affect a free and unrestrained Preaching of the Gospel, we bring on Anarchy and Confusion, and Overthrow of all Order and Government; and at last be driven off the very Foundation of Gospel-Doctrine contained in the Scriptures, and most excellently summed up in our Confession and Catechisms. . . .

12 · Samuel Blair

(1712–1751)

A PARTICULAR CONSIDERATION

OF "THE QUERISTS"

The counterattack on the revival did not subside with the Synod's failure to discipline the itinerants. In September 1740 some members of New Castle Presbytery (undoubtedly prompted by their ministers) published a pamphlet entitled *The Querists,* in which Whitefield's *Journal,* sermons, and conduct were raked for evidence of inconsistency and error. Whitefield replied with a brief point-by-point defense of his writings and career. A more eloquent answer, however, and one which better revealed the intellectual divisions within Presbyterianism, was that published by Samuel Blair in March 1741. Like Gilbert Tennent, Blair had been born in Ireland and educated at the Log College. In 1739 he was installed as minister at Fagg's Manor, Pennsylvania, where, in late 1740, one of the most remarkable of the Middle Colony revivals occurred. At Fagg's Manor Blair established his own school

Samuel Blair, *A Particular consideration of a Piece, Entitled, The Querists* . . . (Philadelphia, 1741), pp. 3–9.

for the education of ministers. In time Blair's school over-shadowed even William Tennent's institution. Blair was probably the most gifted intellectual among the Presbyterian partisans of the revival. An able theologian, his sermons and tracts were distinguished by their careful logic and methodical argument. But in 1741 Blair was above all the embattled controversialist, one who was persuaded that Whitefield's critics were not defending the faith but pharisaically trying to halt the triumphant progress of the Awakening.

Forasmuch as the Piece before me appears directly calculated to the Prejudice of the Rev. Mr. *Whitefield's* Usefulness in the World, whom I cannot but look upon to be an able and faithful Minister of the New Testament, and One whom the LORD is pleased to make much Use of for Good to perishing Souls; and since there are some bold Strokes in it against the Work of GOD's Power and Grace which he is pleased to carry on in this Land by his and some others Means; (indeed the Whole Seems manifestly designed to bring both it and them under Disgrace, to prejudice the World against both) I therefore, think myself called in Duty, for the Honour and Interest of Religion, and as a Debt to the Publick, a little to consider the Performance.

I would be far from faulting any hearty Lovers of Truth, for writing privately to Mr. *Whitefield* for their Satisfaction about any such Passages of his Writings, as might seem to them either unsound, or dangerous by an unguarded way of expressing Things; and, if in this way they would desire him to revise and correct his Writings, provided it were done with a sincere Mind, with a candid, unprejudiced, and Gospel-Spirit: But as our *Querists* seem not to have been possessed of this Temper, when they composed or adopted the Queries, so neither did they chuse this private Method for their Satisfaction, tho' they pretend that was all they wanted: No; for tho' this would have sufficiently answer'd the pretended End, yet it could never have answer'd the plain real Design at all: This way for obtaining Satisfaction about their Scruples, and a Resolution of their Doubts, would not have painted Mr. *Whitefield* in black and horrid Colours to the World: This would not have made the important Discovery to their Protestant Neighbours, of his being a designing Imposter in League with the *Pope:* They would have entirely lost a good Blow at the Work of GOD in the Country, which must by no means be suffer'd to go on, if it can possibly be stop'd.

The proper Way of Application for a Resolution of their Doubts and Scruples (had that been the Case, and the Thing aimed at, as pretended) was so obvious, and lay so upon the Surface, that they could not but see it; and therefore, they give a Sham of a Reason why they did not make use of it, *viz.* That "Tho' Mr. *Whitefield* himself, by some Part of his Writings, would seem to be a Man of another Spirit and Sentiments from some of his warm inconsiderate Adherents, as appears by many Expressions, &c. But (say they, for so the Connexion runs) when we consider the Treatment a Neighbouring Minister had from Mr. *Whitefield's* warm Adherents, and their Cries still against him, for desiring a Conference with Mr. *Whitefield,* about some Points in his Sermon, which said Minister was in Doubts about; we do despair of Access to him." This, I think, is a pretty remarkable Reason: There is no such Thing, it seems, as Access to Mr. *Whitefield* privately, in the Case; they do *despair* of it: Why? What's the Matter? Is Mr. *Whitefield* such an inaccessible Man? Yes; when they consider the Treatment a Neighbouring Minister had from Mr. *Whitefield's* warm Adherents, and the warm Adherents Cries still against him, for desiring a Conference with him, about some Points in his

Sermon, which said Minister was in Doubts about, they do *despair of Access to him.* But is there no Difference, I beseech you, between sending a discreet Letter privately to Mr. *Whitefield*, and said Minister's furiously pressing thro' a vast crowded Multitude to debate with him before so many Thousands, by that Time he was well got down off the Stage, about something he had said, or rather, which he charged him with having said in his Sermon? Was there such Danger of the warm Adherents Cries in the one Case as the other? Yet after all, tho' they would make the World believe that the Neighbouring Minister received very sad and dismal Treatment upon that Occasion from the warm Adherents, I can't see Ground for it, saving that one Person spoke two or three Words unadvisedly. Indeed there was a very great Tumult and Confusion, People pressing exceedingly upon one another to see and hear, so that some weak Persons had like to have been crushed down: This put the whole Assembly into Confusion and Amazement; some crying, What's the Matter? others answering; and others in a sad Fright lest Mr. *Whitefield* was about to be pull'd in Pieces; as I found, after I had, with much Difficulty, got to the Outside of the Heap (finding a Way thro' under the Stage) in Relief of a Person like to faint with the Press and be trodden down: And was it any Wonder that such a wild Disorder should ensue upon such a Piece of Management? I believe indeed many looked upon this Neighbouring Minister's Conduct as very bad, and a great Evidence of a Spirit of Bitterness against the faithful servants of GOD and the Power of the Gospel, and no doubt would express their Judgment of it to one another accordingly. But then, I think, He that doesn't like the bad Treatment of being called a Thief, shouldn't steal; for if he does, I don't see but he must e'en put up with the Treatment. Let the *Querists* varnish over their Neighbour's Conduct with as smooth-Terms as they please, such as, *Only* DESIRING *a* CONFERENCE *with Mr.* Whitefield, *about some Points in his*

Sermon, which he was in Doubts *about;* yet they will never be able to make the impartial World believe, upon a fair Representation of the Case, that it was any other than a publick warm Opposing of Mr. *Whitefield,* with Hopes, in Confidence of his strong Powers of obtaining a publick Victory and Triumph. And if a Man will run his Head against a Post, who can help it? . . .

But if you would know the Bottom of all; you know that the Work of God, the Power of his Gospel, deep Soul-Exercise about eternal Things, about Soul-Affairs, the most weighty and important of any in the World, is like to make a mighty Inroad upon us: This by all Means must be hindred, if possible from Prevailing; and a Reduction of Things to their former peaceful, quiet and Secure Situation attempted; tho' Thousands should sleep to eternal Destruction. For this Power of Religion is attended with dismal Consequences: Dead secure Formalists, who are entirely destitute of the powerful Operations of the regenerating sanctifying Spirit of God, who can tell nothing of lively Heart-Exercises in Religion, nothing of deep Heart-Distress for Sin and Guilt, of the lively Power and Consolations of Faith in the Redeemer, of sharp Conflicts with Original Corruption, or sweet Communion with God by the Spirit of Adoption; these are like to lose all their former high Reputation for Piety, and find it difficult to keep up their strong groundless Confidences of the Goodness of their Souls State towards GOD, which they can by no means consent to part with. But especially, when People are enlightened and awaken'd by the Word and Spirit of GOD, they can't be satisfied any longer with sapless, careless Ministers; they can get no suitable Nourishment to their hungring Souls from these dry Breasts, and therefore cannot be easy or contented, but must need mourn and grieve under them: And this goes hard with these Pious Ministers. . . . and their warm Adherents. Thus the Success and Power of the Gospel, especially if it be very large and extensive, is, alas, very unwelcome to many of its Professors. Well; you know Mr. *Whitefield* appears much for the Life and Power of Godliness, and earnestly labours to carry on and promote it in the World; he labours to awaken blind and secure Sinners, and bring them off all their false Foundations to a vital Union with Jesus Christ by Faith; and the LORD blesses him with much Success in his Work. This then is one Ground of the Prejudice and Opposition.

Again; there is a certain Club of Preachers among ourselves (for so a Rev. Father was pleased lately to stile them) who are endeavouring to carry on this very unacceptable Work of God with his succeeding Power and Blessing thro' the Land; Mr. *Whitefield* rejoices in these, and has a good Esteem of them, who are esteem'd by many of their professed Brethren no better than a factious and very troublesome CLUB. Alas! what Times are these, when those who are most earnestly labouring and making it their great End to promote the Mediator's Kingdom, and the eternal Interest of immortal Souls, and whose Labours the LORD remarkably owns and blesses to this End, are so opposed and aspersed by Such as profess themselves their Fellow-Labourers in the same high Calling!

Moreover, Mr. *Whitefield* speaks much against unexperienced, blind and unfaithful Ministers, who settle People upon the Lees of their natural and fatal Security by their Ministry, rather than any thing else; and hereupon, as if their own Consciences secretly told them they were the Men, or that their Management was such that they would surely come under the Suspicion, many are exceedingly vexed: They will not have it so much as hinted, if they can help it, that there is the least Danger of any unconverted Person's being in the Ministry amongst us; nay, they would have us believe that it is no great Matter as to their Usefulness in that Station whether they are savingly converted to GOD themselves or not; when Numbers of exercised Souls thro' the Land can witness, that for any faithful Dealing that ever their Ministers used with them, they might have gone on blindfold in a graceless State to eternal Damnation; and not only so, but that their Ministry rather tended to fix them fast in their damnable Presumption and Security.

Now, all these Things concur to raise the swelling Tide of Opposition against Mr. *Whitefield* and his *warm Adherents,* as they are termed. While Mr. *Whitefield* kept within due Limits without disturbing our Borders, and stay'd beyond the Water, he was a brave Man, and doing much Good; but he is not long here among us but he is quite unsufferable. Thus the *Pharisees* in our Saviour's Time, spoke well of the *Prophets that lived in the Days of their Fathers,* at a competent Distance from themselves, while in the mean Time they *persecuted the Prophets of GOD* which they had among them; and so would have done the same to the Prophets which their Fathers persecuted, had they been among them, but whom now they were far enough from, they highly commended: And hereby our LORD convinced them of Hypocrisy.

13 · "The Querists"

A SHORT REPLY TO

MR. WHITEFIELD'S LETTER

Even while Blair was writing, The Querists were draw-ing up a series of "exceptions" to Whitefield's reply to their first critique. The *Second Querists* was more than another brief against Whitefield. Its argument expanded into a criticism of the behavior of the awakened and, finally, into an assault on the revival as an implicitly revo-lutionary movement. As against the cordial union of the pious espoused by the revivalists, The Querists took their stand on behalf of order and subordination in society as well as in the Church.

. . . Is it not Sin and Folly to judge Men's Designs any fur-ther than they appear in their Words or Actions? How then can Men make the vain Notion of a Man's having a good Design, the Ground and Foundation of Judgment concerning their Words or Actions? Is it not as orderly for Men to make use of

A short reply to Mr. Whitefield's letter Which he wrote in answer to the Querists . . . (Philadelphia, 1741), pp. 46–62. A reproduction of the text was provided by courtesy of the Trustees of the Boston Public Library.

their Heads, instead of their Feet to walk upon, as to pretend to make the blind Notion of a Man's having good Designs (which are altogether secret, and because secret, cannot be legal Proofs to us) the Foundation of Judgment concerning his Words? For how doth the Chain of Argument run? But thus first, it is taken for granted, without any Proof, that such a one is a good Man, therefore it is inferred, that he hath good Designs, and from thence 'tis again inferred, that his Words and Actions, tho' inconsistent with the Rule of God's Word, are good and right still; or else, do not Men talk very idly, when they speak of good Designs, to justify plain Errors? And is not such a Way of Arguing, contrary (1) To right Reason? For if we walk by the Rule of right Reason, doth not this teach us to judge secret Things by the Things that are manifest or do appear, and not the contrary? (2) Is it not contrary to plain Scripture-Rule, which teacheth us to know and judge the Tree by its Fruits, and not the Fruits by the Tree, as is done by the aforesaid Way of Arguing? For the wise Man saith, *Even a Child is known by his Doings, whether his Work be pure, and whether it be right.* Prov. 20. 11. How contrary to this is the Practice of judging Men's Works to be pure and right, from the precarious Judgments Men form blindly of their secret State and their Pretensions to good Designs, we leave others to judge at their Leisure. Is it not therefore very evident to all unprejudiced Persons, who have not imbibed Enthusiastick Notions, That the Chain of Argument in such Cases, should run thus: If such a Man's Words and Actions are good and regular, are not we bound by that Charity that hopeth all Things, and thinketh no Evil, not to suspect any Man's State or Designs as evil? For is it not evident that Designs as Designs (no more than the secret State of one's Soul) come not within our Reach to form a positive Judgment of them? Men may have a good Design in a bad Action, and a bad Design in an Action that is seemingly or in Appearance as to the Matter of it, good; and so must pass with Men for a good Action. The Action only we are to judge, and leave the Design to God; without judging any further about it, than it appears in the Action. The Regularity or Irregularity of a Word or Action, is what we are called to judge. If these be good, it is down-right malicious to impeach a Man for having a bad Design therein, unless it some-how appears. On the other-Hand, when Men's Words or Actions are bad, is it not down-right Deceit and Palliation to insinuate Men's good Designs to justify the Matter, unless such a Design can be some-how made to appear? Doth not Scripture as well as Experience tell us, That great Boastings of good Designs, when used to colour and varnish Errors, have a native Tendency to fix and not to remove Suspicions of Men and their Designs, if we consider Matters right? For, who gloried more of their inward Goodness and Designs in all Ages, than bad and designing Men? Is it not easy to shew, that Men's walking by the aforesaid false Rule, was one great Reason of Men's tame Submission to the Antichristian Yoke, and their Wondering after the Beast? What was the Reason of it? Why, surely this was one main Reason, Men believed without any Proof, that the Church of *Rome* was the only true Mother-Church; and from thence it was inferred, That her Missionaries were true Ministers, and from thence that they were good Men, and therefore had good Designs in all they taught and did; and therefore, tho' their Doctrines were never so erroneous, and their Lives never so scandalous, the supposed Conceit of a good Design made Men swallow down one Error after another, till at last they arrived at the great Apostacy or Abomination of the Earth. But what was the Artifice by which Men were induced to believe such Doctrines, as were so vain, fabulous, and wicked, as well as to persevere in such superstitious and idolatrous Practices as were taught them by the *Romish* Clergy? It were too tedious to enter into a Detail of all the Artifices used by them; but probably it may be of some Use, to give Hints of some of the main of them.

(1) They first taught, that the Scripture had a two-fold Sense, *viz.* A *literal* and a *mystical* Sense; and that it belonged to the *Pope* and his Priests or spiritual Men, to give them the true *mystical* Sense; by which Men were induced to believe all their lying and false Glosses, under the Name of the *Mystical Sense* of Scripture.

(2) When they wanted to frame a new Article of Faith, to institute a new Ordinance or Custom, or religious Ceremony, or to appoint the Adoration of some Idol or Saint, or to appoint a new Holy-Day, &c. It was pretended that some one or other had an immediate Revelation or Vision, about the Matter; and then the Populace were ready to fall on their Knees.

(3) To confirm these Things better, they had their Signs or lying Wonders, foretold in Scripture, partly by cunning Craft, and partly by Conjuration; For credible Histories give us an Account of Forty *Popes,* that successively filled the Chair, for the Space of Two Hundred Years and upwards, who were known to be Magicians.

(4) They had their Lying Legends, which were large Volumes of glorious false Accounts of their feigned Saints and Idols, and their lying Miracles.

(5) If any made any Discovery of their false Forgeries and Deceit, he was immediately condemned for an Heretick, and branded with the black Character of being an Impostor or Blasphemer, and dealt with accordingly.

(6) If any appeared stiff, he was presently terrified with the *Pope's* Bulls, Excommunications, Purgatory, and Penance, and the Noise of Fire and Faggot; counting that melting the Heart by discouraging, dispiriting and disheartening Men, was true Conversion.

(7) Besides, Auricular Confession was none of the meanest of their Arts to keep the People in Awe and Terror to offend the Clergy, for fear of their discovering their secret Villanies and hidden Vices confessed to them.

Now, when it is evident and undeniable, that Mr. *Whitefield* symbolizeth with the *Papists,* in using the same or the like Artifices, to establish his Scheme; as *Papists* did to establish theirs; how can Men on good Grounds judge him to be a reforming Protestant? For, is it not evident,

(1) That he expressly asserts, that the Scriptures have a twofold Sense, *viz.* a *literal,* and a *hidden* Sense or Meaning, which he also calls a *spiritual* Sense; and that none but a spiritual Man can understand the hidden or mystical Sense: . . .

(2) Doth not Mr. *Whitefield* make high Pretensions to immediate Revelation, in his professing to think and act by the immediate Guidance of divine Inspiration . . . And doth not he pretend to an immediate Call to the Ministry? And doth not he seemingly condemn the ordinary Call to the Ministry, as a meer human Call? And would not he insinuate, that if the Bishops ordain any, without first obliging Men to give good Proofs of having a special Call and Mission to the Ministry, they would lay Hands too suddenly on Men. . . . And is not this expressly contrary to the very Words of the XXIII. *Article* of the *Church of England,* which are these, "*And those we ought to judge lawfully called and sent, which be chosen and called to this Work by Men who have publick Authority in the Congregation to call and send Ministers unto the Lord's Vineyard.*" And is it not evident, that the contrary Opinion is subversive of all Order in the Admissions of ordinary Ministers to the Ministry?

(3) Have they their Lying Signs and Wonders; Do not these Strange Fits, Convulsions, involuntary Raptures, horrid Noises, and Visions, that accompany the Ministry of the Propagators of this New Scheme, deserve to be ranked in this Class? Were not these ordinarily judged to be the black Marks of Impostors in all Ages, and not of powerful Preaching? And if

it be found that something uncommon this Way happened to fall out upon the Preaching of sound Doctrine, was it ever by the Orthodox accounted Conversion-Work?

(4) Had they their Lying Legends; Is it not easy to shew, that Mr. *Whitefield's* Journal, and History of his Life, is as vain-glorious and fabulous as their Legends, in many Places of it? Which we oblige ourselves to prove, if it be demanded of us: And will any shew us any solid Use that can be made of the one more than the other? For, is it not evident, that the Use of them, is, to amuse the Reader, and to raise a vain Admiration of the Man, and his Party, without any real Edification?

(5) Did they condemn all their Opposers as Hereticks; Doth not Mr. *Whitefield* and his Adherents as loudly make clamorous Exclamations against all the Opposers of his Scheme, as carnal Men, Pharisees, and Hypocrites? And as if this was too little, doth not he rank all the Protestant Ministers in *England* and *Scotland,* as well as the Ministers of our Synod (excepting a few Partizans) with the Priests of *Baal?* And is it not easy to see, what they must expect to be their Lot, if this Party prevail?

(6) Had they their artificial Ways to cause Terrors, as aforesaid; We appeal to the Hearers of these Men, whether there be not another Kind of artificial Roarings and Thunderings used among us, by horribly Devilizing Men, and raging Railings at them as such; as if they judged, that Meltings of Heart by dispiriting Men, was true Conviction and Conversion: But Meltings by meer Terrors is quite another Thing. . . .

(7) Had they auricular Confession; Doth not Mr. *Whitefield* seem to try to establish this every where, as may be seen in his Letter to the Religious Societies in *England* and *Wales,* where he presses them to confess their Faults and communicate their Experiences; and that without reserve, they should

tell each other what is in their Heart; under the fair Pretence of having their Doubts solved about their Soul's State, by meer human Testimony, thereby putting a Bar and Snare in Men's Way, to prevent them from Waiting in the Use of instituted Means, in order to obtain Assurance in God's Way. Is this bringing poor Souls to Christ, or an Artifice to form a Party of blind Admirers of Men, who are greatly loved and admired because they take artificial Ways to deceive? If Mr. *Whitefield* be a good Man, because he thus symbolizeth with *Papists* in some Things, and symbolizeth with *Enthusiasts* in others, as we have shewed elsewhere; or because he mixes a great deal of *Calvinistical* Doctrine with Scraps of *Antinomianism, Arminianism, Quakerism* and *Popery,* which will plainly appear to his considerate Readers: Or is he a good Man, because, as the Report goes, he does but very seldom, if ever, pray for King GEORGE, our lawful and gracious Sovereign, as we are informed by these that have been his Hearers much oftener than ourselves, that they observed him not to do so? Will his praying for Mr. *G. T.* atone for this Defect or Omission? . . . And what is the Design of the vain-glorious, fabulous and boasting Accounts of his Progress published in his *Journals,* and by his Friends in the *Gazette,* but to alarm and amuse the World, in order to make Parties, Factions and Confusions up and down? And are they good Men that are so industrious in such Doings in our Kingdom and Provinces now in a Time of War with a Foreign Nation? Is not the *Catholicism* sometimes spoken of, meer blind, when it is evident, that these pretended *Catholicks* censure all but their own party-coloured Admirers, as carnal Men? . . .

As to your Desire to avoid Bigotry on the one Hand, and confounding Order and Decency on the other Hand; The Scripture tells, That *all the Ways of Man are clean in his own Eyes, but the Lord weigheth the Spirits.* Prov. 16. 2. It has been the Unhappiness of many a good Man, to live among bad

Neighbours; but yet Well-doing hath been found a better Way for such to establish their Characters, than vain-glorious Boastings of their *fine, fine* Hearts. But will you answer us? Who is a greater Bigot than he that ranks all the Protestant Ministers in *England, Scotland* (letting alone our Synod) with the Priests of *Baal;* except a few disorderly Partizans, who are very busy in driving all Order into a confused Anarchy? Seeing we are talking of Order, we would ask you, How is Order in an ordinary Way reconcileable with the Claim of ordinary Ministers to extraordinary and immediate Call and Mission to the Ministry, and the Pretence of immediate Guidance of divine Inspiration in the Fulfilling of it? How can you reconcile Gospel-Order, with the vain, disorderly and illegal Practice of Men's conducting their Deportment, as Church-Members one to another, according to the blind Guesses Men form of one another's carnal or gracious State, upon the bare verbal Declaration of their Experiences? And seeing every ordinary Minister is called to the Oversight of a particular Flock; where is the Order and Decency of leaving a Man's own Flock, and industriously entering other Men's Labours? When Men strive so hard to dissolve the solemn Tye of the sacred Relation between Ministers and People, under the Notion of Liberty; why may not they plead for the same Liberty in other Relations, if it may be supposed to be for the Benefit of the *Orphan-House* in *Georgia?*

We cannot at all doubt the Sincerity of your Wishes, "That the Presbytery when they advised us to publish our Queries, had also cautioned us against dipping our Pen in Gall": For Charity dwells at Home, whether we are abroad or at Home; and it is very often found, that those that shew the least of it expect most of it: And, no doubt, Errors, when Men are attached to them, are as tender a Point as Truth to the Lovers of it; Witness the Women crying for *Tammuz.* But we had wrote before the Presbytery saw our Scruples, and if there was any

Gall at all in the Ink-Powder, the Presbytery or we thought little of it. . . . If Mr. *Whitefield* can shew, that we have meddled at all with his secret State towards God, we will freely own, that it was what we should not have done; it being our Duty to leave it in the Dark as we found it: And seeing you appeal to our Hearts as to your Doctrine, we cannot give a better Account of it in few Words, than this, That it appeared to be a Sort of Motley Mixture, not Day nor Night; many Points scambled over, but none cleared up to any Purpose; the dark Pushes darkening the little Light, that seemed to be peeping out here and there in it; and, if we mistake not, there seems to be a strange Sort of Blinding instead of Illumination, which seems to accompany it: So that it is well known that many of a sudden fall in with Enthusiastick Notions who were never observed to incline that Way before: And if we declare our Experience, we never have observed in our Day, empty Sounds have made such Havock by eating as Canker, as fast as they now seem to do: And if there be not something Diabolick in some of the Fits that accompany your Scheme, we would be glad, if Men can account for them any other Way, that they would speak out clearly, to remove Mistakes; for we are really of that Opinion. And seeing your Doctrine seems not to come up half Way to that of *Calvinist* Ministers, such as ours generally are, and the Orthodox *Independents;* we would be apt to ask you, Whether or no your carrying about a Rush-Candle among the Dissenters, be worth your Pains, were it not, that we read of a certain Humorist, who took great Care to keep his Candle burning in Day-time, for no other Reason, but that the Sun was subject to Eclipses at Seasons: Now, tho' this does not come up to the Point; for your Candle is subject to many Eclipses also; yet this satisfies us, that others might have such mystical Reasons, that cannot bear the Light, as well as this Man had; and that therefore it is in vain to enquire about them.

And now we appeal to your own Conscience, whether we do not lay ourselves fairly open to Conviction, by speaking to the Points in Debate, particularly and plainly, without Evasion, Disguise, or Palliation; so that if you do not do the same in your next Answer, wherein you are remarkably deficient in this; will it not appear an high Degree of Weakness, either in your Cause, or in yourself, to defend it?

And we appeal to the Consciences of our Readers,

Quer. I. Whether or no it be not evident, that Mr. *Whitefield* by confessing some false Divinity, hath not fairly given up his vain Pretence of his Acting and Thinking by the Immediate Guidance of Divine Inspiration?

Qu. II. And whether he doth not discover a very great Weakness in defending some exceptionable Passages, after an Appearance of Christian Spirit in giving up and correcting others?

Qu. III. Whether, as Things now appear, those are to be accounted most Orthodox and Judicious, who applauded all, or those who condemned some of Mr. *Whitefield's* Writings? How shall they be justly reproached as carnal Men, to whom Mr. *Whitefield* seems to allow a better Character?

Qu. IV. Whether the great Out-cry, that some warm Partizans make of their incomparable Enlightnings, and of the Darkness of their Opponents, doth not appear an empty Noise and vain Boasting? For, is it not evident, that this glorious Constellation is now become a meer blazing Comet, a Rush-Candle, or a meer Jack in the Bush, leaving those that walked in its Light, in the midst of the Bog and Quagmire? . . .

Qu. V. And whether it be not evident now to all unprejudiced Persons, that the Opposing of some Part of Mr. *Whitefield's* Writings, be not evidently the Doing of God's Work, and not Opposing it?

Qu. VI. How poor a Notion have they of God's Work, who count the Opposing and Confuting of gross Errors, Persecution? Are not such as make such Out-cries, meer Patrons of Ignorance and Irreligion in this Point? . . .

May the Lord guide us all, to distinguish between Light and Darkness, Truth and Error, Order and Anarchy, Liberty and Licenciousness, the Power of God and lying Signs and Wonders, and between sound Doctrine and meer Wind and Sound of Doctrine; lest, for want of receiving of, and cleaving to the Truth in the Love of it, we may be given up to a Spirit of Delusion, to believe vain Fables and glaring Lies, which seems to prevail very much of late among us, if we mistake not, which we think we do not: For if it be not so, what mean the tumultuous Commotions, the fiery indiscrete Zeal, the outragious Passions, the loud, lying and malicious Out-cries against, as well as the laborious Misrepresentations of Men and Matters; and the uncommon Spurning of the Professors of Truth, at the plain Preaching of Truth, and the Confutation of gilded Errors; and their joining with the wild Rabble, to reflect upon, oppose, belie, slander, and misrepresent *pious* and *godly* Ministers, and serious Professors, to the great Suppression of Truth, Confounding of Order, Disturbing of Peace, Banishment of Charity, Distracting of Communities, and Raising of Factions; to the Strengthening of the Hands of a few thrasonical, vainglorious *Diotrepheses,* who seem to be so thirsty for the Pre-eminence, that they would be content to drive all to Anarchy and Confusion, under the fair Name of Establishing a Catholicism; which is a Thing, tho' in itself desireable, yet neither desireable nor possible in our present Circumstances; unless first the different Apprehensions and religious Sentiments of conscientious Protestants, be removed by clear Scripture-Light, without encroaching upon, or infringing the sacred Rights of Conscience, to the Overthrow of all serious Piety and Order, which are more valuable than our Lives and Fortunes: Can it be supposed that this Catholicism will be brought about by a mobbish factious Rabble, by clamorous Tumults, Lies, and Exclamations, and anarchical Measures, when a legal Establishment, and Force, and Compulsion, tho' too much tried at Seasons, proved not only ineffectual to establish a Catholicism in our Native Land, but also proved the Occasion of Separation and Discord?

Is it not easy to prove, upon a fair Tryal, that Mr. *Whitefield's* Scheme, or what is in Print already, if it was once imposed, would be a more intolerable Yoke than Conformity to the Constitutions of the establish'd Church? For is not Enthusiasm with which his Writings abound, when added to Conformity, more than Conformity itself, as much as the whole is more than a Part? Yea, is not Enthusiasm itself, which is altogether irreconcilable with Gospel-Order, and the stated Order of all and every Community or Society of Orthodox Christians among us, being as opposite thereto as Anarchy is to Order, a more intolerable Burden than the former? Yea, is it not evident, that the Articles of the *Church of England* are unexceptionable, as to the Doctrinal Points of Faith; and therefore are subscribed to by the Orthodox Dissenters in *England* of divers Denominations; and therefore much more fit for a Bond of Union than Mr. *Whitefield's* Scheme, which hath here and there Scraps of *Popery, Antinomianism, Arminianism* and *Enthusiasm* crammed in among *Calvinistical* Tenets? Yea, is it not evident, that his Doctrine and Conduct is contradictory to the Doctrinal Articles of the established Church, as we have given a few Hints already; and we are ready to give more instances, if we are thereunto called? If therefore Mr. *Whitefield,* and others, have good Designs, it is our hearty Prayer that they may be directed to take God's Way to prosecute them, for God's Glory and Welfare of his Church; and not be so far deserted by God as to be suffered in Doctrine or Practice to wound the Truth, promote Error, disturb Order, raise Factions and Animosities to the great Discomfort of the Lovers of Purity, Order and Peace, and Well-wishers of true Scripture.

Reformation, and of the solid, regular Exercises of Religion, to the Hardening of uncircumcised *Philistines* and Runagadoes from God and Godliness, who seem to creep out of their Holes every where to spit out their corrupt Venom at the true Power of Godliness and the Order of God's House, under the fair Pretence of Declaiming against the Corruption of the Times, when in Reality none more corrupt than themselves, and their Corruption never broke out faster than at present. . . .

14 · *"The Wonderful Wandering Spirit"*

Like *The Querists*, which came before the world anonymously, the most venomous of antirevival utterances,
"The Wandering Spirit," was first assumed to be the work
of clergymen hostile to evangelical religion. But it, too,
was probably written by laymen, assisted or encouraged
perhaps, by certain ministerial "advisors." This effusion,
first published in Philadelphia in Benjamin Franklin's
General Magazine, became, much as did Tennent's Nottingham Sermon, itself a point of issue. Long after the
New Side had begun to attempt to heal the breach in the
Presbyterian Church, *The Wandering Spirit* was cited by
a faithful multitude as evidence of the Old Side's unforgivable enmity to the Work of God.

A true and genuine Account of a wonderful WANDERING
SPIRIT, *raised of late (as is believ'd) by some Religious Con-
jurer; but whether in the Conclave at* Rome, *or where else, is
not so certain.*

This Spirit, we are inform'd, does now haunt *Moravia,* and
many other Places in the *German* Empire; has of late been
very troublesome in *England;* and has been seen, felt and
heard by Thousands in *America.* 'Tis raging and proud; censorious and ill-natur'd; deals much by Feelings and Impulses,

The General Magazine, Vol. I, No. 2 (February, 1741), pp. 120–122.

147

in violent bodily Convulsions; and pretends to uncommon Discernments. When it possesses the Mob, which it delights to torture, they swell and shake like *Virgil's* enthusiastick Sybil, or those possess'd with the Devil in the Gospel. Sometimes, like *Balaam,* they fall into Trances, with their Eyes open; or like the honest Folks in *Scotland,* they get by its Influences such a Second-sight, as they can easily see their Neighbours Hearts and Intentions. Like *Proteus,* it assumes most Shapes, and is never easier discovered than when it is moved by the slightest Provocation to ascend the Tribunal, that is always at its Elbow, from whence it sends all that question its Dictates, or divine Extraction, to take up their Lodging with *Cain* and *Judas,* and other Reprobates. It sets up for a Pagod, or Demi-Pope within us; it never openly claims Infallibility, and always acts as if it had it. Sometimes it walks gravely in a *Quaker* Dress; again it appears more brisk, and borrows the Gown; at different Times, as it suits its Humours, it puts on the *Antinomian,* the *Arminian,* the *Calvinist,* or *Anabaptist;* and sometimes is so complaisant to old Mother *Rome* as to disguise itself like a Fryar or a Monk, or a Lay-Clergy-man; tho' it loves rather to be esteemed among us a gifted Brother, or a Lay-holder-forth; and they that are well-acquainted with the Vestments of both Churches, observe, that its Gown has some Ruffles, and other Things in the Sleeves peculiar to *Rome,* rather than *England.* It acts the Busy-Body, is here and there, and every where, and above all Things, hates Rules and good Order, or Bounds and Limits. It is unwearied in issuing Warrants and Commissions under the broad Seal of an inward Call to all that have Conceit and Self-sufficiency enough to run its Errands. It has something in its Nature very different from some other Wandering Spirits, who have been desirous of enriching their Friends, by discovering Gold or hidden Treasure; but it seems to be one of *Mammon's* Squadron, and gripes Money as readily as the greatest Miser. When it ascends the Judgment-Seat it is very magisterial; and upon the slightest Ground, pronounces all its Admirers the dear Children of GOD; but all that doubt its holy Dictates, are condemn'd for incarnate Devils, or carnal Men. Its Proceedings are entirely Partial, appear in what Shape it will. Say-Soes and Declarations, Wry-Faces and Grimaces, Contorsions of the Body and vocal Energy, Faintings and Cryings, delusive Voices and frantick Visions, pass for undeniable Evidences of Conversion, of coming to JESUS and the Power of God: Nay, if little Children are so happy as to cry out when they see their Mothers fainting under its delusive Impulses, they are forthwith canoniz'd for Saints: But such as it cannot lead captive at pleasure, however holy and pious they are in all appearance, are condemn'd upon Whispers and Surmises, and Hear-says, without Proof produc'd, Tryal held, or Summons to appear. 'Tis *Don Quixot* turn'd Saint-Errant, and like him, can see Wonders by Hear-say. It abhors Reason, and is always for putting out her Eyes; but loves to reign Tyrant over the Passions, which it manages by Sounds and Nonsense. It is so blind itself that it walks by feeling; and yet sets up for an unerring Guide to all others. Old *Infallibility* learnt it the Lesson to wrest the Bibles out of Men's Hands, which it performs effectually, by persuading all its Votaries, that nothing but its Suggestions are GOD's Mind in the Scripture: And that all that will not give away Scripture and Reason tamely, for its inward Feelings and Experiences, are proclaimed carnal Men, who cannot understand, but pervert the sacred Oracles. It deals like the same Holy Father, in Confessions and Excommunications, and carefully excludes all from the Number of the Faithful, who will not tell every impertinent hypocritical Canter he meets, his Sins and Experiences. 'Tis always crying out against Persecution, and is a most furious Persecutor to all that will not bow to its Sway. It cries out desperately against Bigotry, and yet will give no quarter to any that will think for themselves, and refuse a blind Obedience to its peculiar and favourite Opinions. 'Tis remarkable for one Quality, that all that it bewitches generally bid farewell to Reason, and are carried by it to the Land of Clouds and Darkness, under the Pretence of divine Light; nor are they yet known, many of them, to be able to break the Spell, nor get rid of the Charm that blinds their Eyes. If we can guess whence it came, by the Effects it has on its Admirers, it must be akin to the lying Spirit that came among *Ahab*'s Prophets. It always sets up for a Preacher of Christ and his Truths, but frequently forgets its Errand, quotes little Scripture, and preaches itself and its Attainments; and, under this sacred Character, acts like a Quack or Mountebank, always telling what mighty Matters it has done in other Places; that it had no other View in undertaking so much Labour and Fatigue in travelling so far, but their eternal Welfare; that it cou'd carry all to Heaven in its Bosom: And seldom stays longer in one Place than it fools them out of their Cash: It seems to have possessed *Judas*, for it loves to finger the Penny, and carry the Bag. It claims Liberty to question and judge all, and refuses Subjection to every proper Judicature. The Pope makes Saints, but it makes Saints, Devils, and Brutes, as it suits its Humours. It hates *Greek* and *Hebrew*, because Holy Languages, and tells its Admirers, that it can make a sanctified Cobler at once an abler Divine than either *Luther* or *Calvin*. It has often haunted our Borders, disguised like an Angel of Light; but its Evil-Speaking and burning Revenge, its Malice and Cruelty toward all that will not renounce Scripture and Reason, discovers to all, that will not wink hard, that it has a cloven Foot, and is either *Moloch*, or *Apollyon* the Destroyer. It has often been spoken to, but can never be laid; and the Reason that is given is, because there are no Conjurers, that deal with Spirits of its Stamp, but soon turn its Admirers. Some surmise, from the Mobs and Disorders that attend it, that it is *Belial*, taking a Tour in Disguise; others surmise, that it must be the Spirit that inspired the *Bachanals* in Days of Yore, because some of is chief Votaries, while under its Impulses, have wallowed in Lewdness. They that are acquainted with the Affairs of the *East,* alledge that it is the same Spirit that was familiar with *Mahomet;* because it has the same fierce and savage Temper, the same falling Fits, and equally hates Learning, and cries up Ignorance. And such as have read the Records of *Germany* and *England,* aledge that it was the same who guided the incomparable *Jacob Behmen*[1] in writing his religious Jargon and dark Nonsense: That possess'd the Enthusiasts of *Munster:*[2] The Ranters in *America,* &c. But all that read the History of the Roman Pontifs, think that it was ador'd in dark Times by Pope *Gregory* or *Hildebrand,* and some others of these Holy Necromancers; who had more Acquaintance with such Spirits as those than with the Spirit of GOD. The Reader may judge for himself in these Things: But, it's hoped, that all true Protestants, whose Forefathers had Courage enough to depose the Thunders of the Vatican, and Anathemas of the great Pope, who pretended to Infallibility, will not be terrifi'd out of their Faith and Reason, by the Roarings of a fallible Pope, or this Spirit of Delusion; but will hold fast the Form of sound Words, which is able to make Men wise unto Salvation. Which that we may all be enabled to do, is the hearty Prayer, of the Historian,

THEOPHILUS MISODAEMON

P.S. Several Memoirs of the Proceedings of this Spirit have been written by way of Journal, or Things of that Nature, and this is humbly offered by way of Supplement.

---

[1] Jakob Behmen (or Boehme) (1575–1624), a German mystical writer. [Ed.]

[2] A city in Westphalia, which for three years (1532–1535) was controlled by a group of radical Protestants, called Anabaptists by their enemies, who believed in absolute equality and a community of property. [Ed.]

15 · *Samuel Finley*

(1 7 1 5 - 1 7 6 6)

CHRIST TRIUMPHING, AND

SATAN RAGING

The vehemence of the revival's critics was occasionally matched by the defenders of Whitefield and the Awakening. The most aggressive of the prorevivalists was probably Samuel Finley, one of the youngest of the insurgent Presbyterians. Born in Ireland, Finley came to the colonies in 1734; he studied with the Tennents and was licensed to preach in 1740. He immediately became a genuine itinerant, without a parish of his own, who traveled throughout the Middle Colonies and eventually into New England. When in 1743 an attempt was made to install him over a Connecticut congregation, Finley was forcibly expelled from that province by order of the legislature. He ended his days as the respected President of the College of New Jersey, but throughout his career

---

Samuel Finley, *Christ Triumphing, and Satan Raging. A Sermon on Matth. XII. 28. Wherein is Proved, That the Kingdom of God is Come unto Us at This Day. First Preached at Nottingham* . . . (Philadelphia, 1741; reprinted Boston, 1742), pp. 16–24, 26–29.

Finley evinced an affinity for—even a delight in—controversy. In his post-Awakening debates with Moravians
and Baptists, as indeed in his "patriot" sermons of the
Seven Years' War, Finley proved himself possibly even
Gilbert Tennent's superior as a master of invective. His
rhetorical skills and combative disposition were first revealed in a brief tract, eventually republished through
the colonies, defending Whitefield, Tennent, and the
practice of itinerancy. But his masterpiece of the Awakening years was undoubtedly the sermon, delivered in
January 1741, in which Finley proclaimed the belief (soon
to be embraced by many of the New Side) that the genuineness of the revival was proved by the bitter opposition
it aroused. The Kingdom of God would come, Finley
announced, by the Spirit's slaying, not merely the sinful
dispositions of man, but the "enemies" of the Awakening.

. . . [When] he that was formerly a Drunkard, lives a sober
Life: When a vain, light, and wanton Person becomes grave,
and Sedate: When the Blasphemer becomes a Praiser of God.
When Laughter is turn'd into Mourning; and carnal Joy into
Heaviness; and that professedly on account of their Souls
Condition: When the Ignorant are fill'd with Knowledge in
divine Things, & the Tongue that was dumb in the Things of
God, speaks the Language of *Canaan:* When the erroneous are
become Orthodox in fundamental Points: When such as never
minded any Religion, do make Religion their only Business:
When busy *Marthas,* & covetous Worldlings, do neglect their
worldly Concerns to seek after God's Ordinances. Now, these
Things, and such like, are discernable to those who are grace-

less; and according to their own Rules they ought to judge that the Devil is cast out. . . .

Besides, to attend the Ordinances of God, to wait on him at his House of Prayer, instead of a Tavern or Play-House; to frequent Christian Societies; to desire Christian Conversation, instead of Balls, Dances, Frolicks, and Merry-Meetings of Good-Fellows; to study Holiness in Heart and Life; to mourn bitterly for Sin, and hate it; to seek the Favour and Presence of God, and Tokens of his Love; to be restless about the State of their Souls, so as nothing will quiet them but Assurance of Pardon; to love God, and rejoice in Christ Jesus above all Things, & c. Now, I say, to do these Things, are not the Works of One that hath a Devil. And if it were the Work of Man, if he were the *Moral Cause* of Conversion; then, surely, the learned and elaborate Discourses, the moral Reasonings, the harmonious and eloquent Preaching of the Clergy, would have still perswaded Mankind to it in every Age. But on the Contrary, since these Characters, and the Properties before described, are contrary to the Nature and Pursuits of *Satan,* and above the Power of both Men and Devils to effect; and only within the Power of God, agreeable to his Word, his Nature, and Perfections: Then it unavoidably follows, That they are the Work of his Spirit.

All that remains now of the Doctrinal Part, is, . . . To prove, *That the Kingdom of God is come unto us at this Day.*

Oh the joyful Sound! *Unto us,* upon whom the Ends of the World are come! Surely all that hear me will rejoice, if I can make it appear.

That there has been a great religious Commotion in the World in our present Day, is so evident, that it cannot be deny'd: But there has been a Murmuring among the People; some saying, That God is with us of a Truth; that the Day spring from on high has visited us; and the Day-star has risen in many Hearts: Others saying, Nay, it is all Deceit, or Delusion, or the Work of the Devil. But that Christ is come to his Church, will appear, I presume, in the Judgment of any considering Person, If I can make these Things appear.

1. That the Church was in the same Circumstances as when he us'd to visit it.

2. If the Manner of his Coming be in Substance the same.

3. If the Treatment he meets with, be the same.

4. If the Consequences and Effects be the same.

5. If the Attempts and Objections made against him, be the same.   And, in a Word,

If the Devil be cast out by Means of true Gospel-Doctrine.

And 1. As to the Circumstances of the Church; He always came when it needed a Reformation, even in the Judgment of graceless Professors; when Religion dwindled into an empty Form, and Professors had lost the Life and Power of Godliness; in a Word, when there was Midnight-Darkness, and little Faith to be found on the Earth. Thus it was when he came in the Flesh; when he sent St. *Athanasius, Luther* and *Calvin,* and at the Reformation of Scotland. We find the graceless *Jews* prayed for the Day of the Lord, in *Amos* 5. 18. And hence were our Pulpits filled with seemingly devout Prayers for a Revival of Religion, and Confessions of its decayed State. And what had we lately but a dry Formality? Did not all in general seem to be at Ease in *Zion,* and in much Peace about the State of their Souls? How few are asking the Watch-men, *What of the Night?* The Lives of Professors careless, unholy, unguarded; Ordinances attended, Duties performed, Sermons preached, without Life or Power, and as little Success. Was not worldly Discourse our mutual Entertainment at our solemn Asiemblies on Holy-days? Thus in Darkness and Security were we: And *like People, like Priest.*

2. As to the Manner of his Coming; It never was in such a Manner as carnal Persons imagined; but still unexpected and out of the common Way. And this is a necessary Consequent of

the State of the Church: For since he comes in a dark Time, we may easily conclude, that the Manner thereof is unobserv'd at first. He must needs come unawares, when a carnal World have forgotten, and do neglect him; and do not know him, or the powerful Operations of his Spirit untill they feel them. For tho' they may pray for the Day of the Lord; yet they know it not when it comes, and so do not know what they ask. *Amos* 5. 18. Now, by this Means he comes always quite cross to the Inclinations of the Clergy, who are generally sunk in Carnality as well as the People. And as a Consequence of this, the Ministers by whom He works, have always at first been few: And thus the Work appears the more eminently to be his own, the less probable that the Instruments appear. Thus it was when he came in the Flesh, He came indeed out of *Bethlehem.* but in a mean Condition; and afterwords unperceivably changing his Place, was mistaken. When he enter'd on his publick Ministry, it was not according to the Traditions of the Fathers; for we find they were surprized, in *Luke* iv. when he began to expound the Scriptures, being neither a Scribe nor Pharisee. And the People not being used with such close and particular Applications, could not bear his new Methods. Passing by the established, but proud, bigotted, gainsaying Clergy, he chuses Twelve unlearned, unpolished Men, most of them Fishers; and gave them a Commission to preach the Gospel, without consulting the *Sanhedrim* about such *unprecedented* Proceedings. Thus was his coming dark, and cross to them.—Now, in our Days the parallel is plain, for supposing the present Commotion to be the Work of God: Every one knows how cross it is to the Inclinations of the Clergy. Surely, our Opposers will confess, they neither did, nor do expect Religion to be reviv'd in such a Manner; while they are so many Things, in their Opinion, wrong. Surely, it is a dark Day to them, and no Light in it; many of them know not what to make of it, by their own Confession. We all know how few it's Propagators are; and they say, that most of us are unlearned: But do they not, by the by, bewray themselves herein? For if unlearned, they must have the less Rhetorick & Oratory; and consequently the less able to bring such Things to pass. If it were the Work of Man, a superior Power of Man would overthrow it.—In a Word, the parallel holds in every Thing, only our manner of Licensing is not *unprecedented.*

3. The Treatment he met with; as a native Consequence of his coming in so dark and mean a Condition, and cross to the Minds of the Clergy; he was rejected by them, and by many of the Noble and Mighty after the Flesh; who imbitter'd against him as many People as they could influence. And as a Consequence of his being disown'd by these, he was chiefly followed by what we call the *Mob,* the *Rabble,* the *common* and *meaner* Sort. And being disown'd by the self-righteous Moralists, was follow'd by the openly profane, the *Publicans,* and *Harlots;* for he is still set for the *Rise* & *Fall of many in* Israel; and many who tho't themselves *first,* and were esteemed so by others in the Dark, did show themselves to be *last.* Thus it was when he came in the Flesh; rejected by the Clergy so generally, and by the Noble and Wise, that it was said, *Have any of the Rulers or Pharisees believed on him?* No: *But this People who know not the Law, are accursed.*—Just so is he treated by the same Ranks of Persons at this Day. May I not ask, Have any of the Rulers, have any of the Ministers embraced the present Work? Do they not rather prepossess & imbitter the carnal People against it? And many who seemed *first* in Religion, are they not become the very *last,* and the *last, first?* For our Opposers confess of their own Accord, That *it is only the ignorant Rabble that embrace it; many of which never minded any Religion,* & *so do not know the Law.* Sure they who know the Law, might know that it is a good Proof of a Day of God's Power when *the Poor have the Gospel preach'd to them,* and do receive it. Mat. xi. 5. Might they not

know that our Lord used this Argument? And also that *God chuses foolish Things to confound the Wise?* But they must confess, that tho' there be not *many,* yet, Glory to God! there are *some* of the *Wise,* and *Mighty,* and *Noble,* on our Side.

4. The Effects & Consequences of his Coming; as a Consequence of the strong Opposition of the Clergy, & others of their Adherents, against him. Contrary to their own Intention, their Speaking of him was a Means of setting the People on the Search; and Numbers flock'd after him, to hear these new *Doctrines* and *new Methods;* and were then caught in the Gospel-net: *As many as were ordained to eternal Life, believed.* Thus in Joh. vii. 11, & *seq.* the Pharisees speaking against him, put him in the People's Minds, who began to talk of him. His Audiences were often deeply affected; and frequently divided between him and the Clergy: And hence we so often read, that *there was a Division among the People.* He never came to send Peace on the Earth, but a *Sword,* & *Division.* Luke xii. 51—58.—Just so it has been in our Day. Many can say by Experience, that their Attention and Curosity was raised by Means of the Contradictions of their Ministers. And hence we have seen unusual Numbers going to hear the Word like thirsty Flocks: And heard a great Mourning, like the Mourning of *Hadadrimmon* in the Valley of *Megiddon.* Also there has been a Division among the Peoples; some praising God for what their Eyes have seen, & their Ears heard, & their Souls felt; others going away mocking, contradicting, blaspheming.

Another Effect was, the Breaking down of Bigotry; partly as a native consequence of the Attention of all Parties being raised to come and hear; and partly by the Example and Directions of Christ, and his Followers. Thus he freely conversed, eat and drank, with different opposite Parties, *Jews* & *Samaritans, Publicans* and *Pharisees;* and justified his so doing from the Need there was of it, that all might come freely and reap

Benefit. And the Apostle, in *Phil*. iii. 15, 16. advises real Christians who hold the Foundation, to walk together in such Things as they are agreed in; for in Things wherein they are disagreed, they cannot.—And just so our Opposers confess it to be now, while they accuse us for holding Communion with different Societies, and would insinuate, that we do so from some politick Design: Indeed there is this Policy in it, to gain some by any Means, and make a Party for Jesus Christ.

5. The Attempts; as a Consequence of the People's following Christ or his Ambassadors, and disregarding the Clergy, the latter always attempted to overthrow the new Scheme; Were (1) unwearied in forming mischievous Devices against him; would tell the People, they had an Imposture, and were deluded, and deceiv'd; follow'd him for no other End but to find something to cavil at; wrested both his Words and Actions to find Matter of Accusation. (2) They were unsatisfied; for after they had been busy all along, they say, *What do we?* q.d. We have been too slack & cowardly; come, let us bestir ourselves, & not suffer all to be overturn'd; we have prevail'd nothing as yet. (3) Their Attempts were still unsuccessful, and always tended to promote the Cause they were set to baffle: Tho' they are still busy, yet are conscious they prevail nothing. Thus when the Scribes & Pharisees sought Christ at the Feast, *John* vii. 11. they put him in the People's Minds, who straight began to talk of him, some good, some evil: When the Pharisees perceived this, they forbid them to speak of him either good or ill; for so much is imply'd in these Words, *Howbeit no Man spoke openly of him for Fear of the Jews*. They hoped that the Thoughts of Christ would wear out of the People's Minds thro' Time.—Just thus do the Opposers now to a tittle. It can be made appear, how Companies of Ministers & People, have met together in a private Manner, to consult how they might suppress the *new Scheme*, and what they could say against it: And indeed, their Cavils, & the Spirit

with which they are urged, do plainly show, that they rather desire Matter of Accusation, than that they really have it. How do they twist and wrest both the Words and Actions, and magnify the Blemishes, of those who stand up for the Work of God? If they can find an unguarded Expression, they draw what horrid Consequences from it they can, & then affirm that this is the Man's Principles. They want some plausible Pretence to blind the People. And they are yet saying, *What do we?*—And I could show, were it necessary, how every Instance of Opposition against the present Work, have all been turn'd to its Advantage. Oh that they would consider whom they fight against! for God is with us of a Truth. And now some of them beg for Peace, and would have us be silent about these controverted Things, that they may wear out of Mind. Their asking Peace & Quietness has an Aspect pleasing to the Flesh, and looks plausible: But God forbid that we should cease to proclaim his wondrous Deeds, to humour the Enemies of his Work! No; let us tell them abroad more loudly, tho' it gall the Consciences, & torment the Minds of all the Opposers on Earth, *Rev.* xi. 10. Thus far we are on a straight Parallel, by the Confession of our Opposers.

6. The Objections made against him, are the same as usual.

For, (1) The Pharisees objected Disorder to our Lord, & his Apostles. How often are they accused of not walking according to the Traditions of the Elders? And our Opposers say, This cannot be the Work of God, because not according to their Order: But they proved not that God is oblig'd to work by their Rules.

(2) When our Lord & his Apostles pleaded for free Grace, they were called Enemies to *Moses* and the Law; and he was often call'd a Blasphemer. So the present Opposers of God's Work, accuse some of us of speaking against the Law, & call us *Antinomians;* and tug & strive, by wresting both the Words and Intentions of some of our Brethren, to prove them Blasphemy. *He hath spoken Blasphemy, why hear ye him?*

(3) It was objected to our Lord and his Apostles, that they held Communion with Persons of different Societies. Hence they stumbled, because he kept Company with *Publicans,* and *Samaritans,* and *Sinners.* And tho't, had he been so much as a common Prophet, he would have known better what Company to keep; and hence concluded he could not possibly be the Christ.—So our Opposers say, that we bring the Church into Confusion by a mixt Communion of different Perswasions; who yet hold the Foundation. And further they ask, Why these who were of no religious Society, are fond of this *new Scheme? Why eateth your Master with Publicanes and Sinners?* He that pretends to be so good a Man, why does he keep such bad Company? They seem now to think it unjust, that Persons who never did so much in Religion as they should enter into the Kingdom of Heaven before them.

(4) It is objected to us, that this Commotion rends the Church; divides Congregations and Families; sets People at Variance; makes them harsh and censorious. So we hear *Tertullus,* Acts xxiv. 5. accuse *Paul* as a *pestilent Fellow, a Mover of Sedition, a Profaner of the Temple.* The Pharisees, *John* ix. 44. ask in a sour Manner, *Are we blind also?* Dost thou judge us to be blind too so rashly? And *Elijah,* because a Son of Thunder, tho' he was the most peaceable, yet he must needs be call'd a *Troubler of Israel,* in I Kin. xviii. 17. And in a Word, both they and we are Turners of the World upside down, Subverters of Peace and Church-Government, and the like. Luke xii. 51. 57. *Suppose ye, says Christ, that I am come to send Peace on the Earth? I came not to send Peace, but a Sword; to divide a Family against it self.*—Why cannot our present Opposers *discern the Signs of* THESE TIMES?

(5) The present Opposers say, they do not quarrel with these Disorders. So, in *John* x. 33. the *Jews* say, *For a good Work we stone thee not:* No: far be it from us, do not so mistake us, we would be ready to encourage every Thing that has the Appearance of Piety; 'tis not for thy good Works, *but for*

Blasphemy. But his good Works, instead of procuring their Favour, did raise their Envy: yet they could willingly have embrued their Hands in his Blood, for no other Crime but his good Works; because he so far out-shined them. But on account of the People, they must first find some plausible Pretence against him. They took no Notice, or laid no Stress on his Miracles; were never satisfied with all the Evidences he gave them; their common Question was, *What Sign showest thou?* Though they seemed resolved not to be satisfied with any Sign. They still found Exceptions against all his Works; and when they could not deny the Matter of Fact, they ascribe it to the Devil sometimes. How often do they ask the Man born blind, how he received his Sight? and would willingly have deny'd that he was blind: How earnest were they to find some Flaw or other? And when they could find none, they put a religious Face upon their Envy; exhort the Man to give God the Glory, but not to mind Jesus; for they were sure he was a Sinner.—Just so it is now a days to a Tittle. Our Opposers have no End of asking for Evidences; without taking Notice of the Power of God, that has appear'd in the Assemblies, or on the Lives of Men: They still muster up Objections, and harp only on what they call Disorder. They gather a great many of their Exceptions together, and then ask, if these Irregularities be the Work of God. Without observing the deep Concern that Souls seem to be under, they only ask about the *Fits* and *Convulsions* that their Sorrow throw them into; and which they would be ready to allow for, in worldly Respects, as the sudden News of the Death of Friends, or the like. And if some unexceptionable Evidence of the Power of God, be alledged against them; they strive to evade its Force some Way or other, by saying, That possibly God may bring Good out of Evil; but yet do speak against the Whole, as a Devilish Work. They seem glad to get any objection against it; not willing that it should be the Work of God. They fix their

Eyes only on the Failures & Blemishes of those who defend it, and magnify Mole-hills into Mountains: And if they can get nothing that has the Appearance of a Fault, they are industrious to forge, and spread slanderous Reports, and false Insinuations; and seem as fond of them, as if they had got a Victory. In a Word; they appear as if their greatest Desire was, to blind their own Eyes, & stop their own Ears, that hearing they might not understand, and seeing they might not perceive, lest they should be *Converts* too, as they call us by the Way of Ridicule.

Thus the Parallel runs clear and undeniable. The same Attempts and Objections, from the same Ranks of Persons, do prove the same Dispositions to be in graceless Persons, now, as formerly; the same Blindness & Enmity. And why should it be tho't strange that Christ's pretended Ambassadors are his bitterest Enemies, seeing it has been always so? The Lord always reformed his Church contrary to their Desires. There is the same kind of Opposition, & Opposers too, in *Scotland* & *England*, at present as here in *America*. And had I Time, I could show, that all Things in every Period of the Church, answer & agree with this, as Face answers to Face in a Glass. But the Coming of Christ in the Flesh, will be found to be analogous to his Coming at other Times; & the Parellel from that is most level to the Capacity of every one; and trac'd with less Difficulty, & more Certainty by common People: And therefore I have chiefly compared that Period, and our present Day. . . .

And how shall any now account for their Opposition to this Work? I desire to speak to such with Bowels of Love.

My Dear Fellow-Mortals! Let me a while expostulate the Matter with you. Why do you not act agreeable to your own Principles? A dry Formalist, who shows no Relish, nor Power of Godliness, seems to live chaste, honest, and sober; and you charitably judge he does so by the Grace of GOD. Another, who was drunken and unclean, becomes chaste and sober, lively and zealous withal; and you insinuate or say, that it is by the Power of the Devil. Why do you not consist with yourselves? Why do you say the one is of GOD, and the other of the Devil, who is a zealous Pleader for the Work of GOD? Do you not see, that God can condemn you by your own Rules? . . .

Do you not perceive a great Change on some of your Neighbours? Do you not observe some of them to be more devout and serious, more sober and knowing, who used to be quite otherwise? And how do you account for these Things? Why do you not either make the Tree good, and its Fruit good; or else corrupt, and its Fruit corrupt? Either say, that Sobriety and Devotion, Temperance and Chastity, diligent Attendance on God's Ordinances, Christian Conference, Sorrow for Sin, Leaving it off, &c. are good, and proceed from a good Cause; or else, say that they are evil, and proceed from an evil Cause. But if you say they are good; why do you ascribe them to Satan? Can he give what he has not? Either speak Things that are consistent, or else be silent. . . .

Perhaps you will say, That you see no Change, only that People are more censorious and uncharitable, judging their Neighbours to be graceless, and seem harsh and passionate against other Ministers, whom they call carnal; and you ask, Are these the Fruits of the Spirit of God?

In Answer, I would desire yourselves to tell by what Rule you would have them judge an Opposer of God's Work to be gracious, who persists against all Evidences of it? Either he does so ignorantly, or knowingly? If ignorantly, does it not prove that he is spiritually blind, & cannot perceive the Things of God, and so must be *Graceless?* But if he does so spitefully, contrary to the Remonstrances of his Conscience, enlightned by the Spirit of God; it seems to be plainly the unpardonable Sin. And why will you accuse me for judging thus, until you prove what I contend for to be the Work of the Devil? Why do you make that Practice an Argument that it is not the Work of God, since it is not the Work will justify the Practice? If I should judge Opposers of God's Work to be gracious, as well as those who plead for it; then I would, like you, be inconsistent with myself; then I would make it, not the Work of God, but some indifferent Thing, where Men might be good, and hold either Side.—It is no new Thing to hear Zeal for God, and Opposition to the Enemies of his Cause, mistaken for Passion and Rage, by such as never have felt the Love of God in their Hearts. And if some Christians, when provok'd by your blasphemous Railery, do speak passionately with Indignation, I think something of it is very justifiable, when I consider *Paul's* Words to *Elymas, O full of all Subtilty, and all Mischief, thou Child of the Devil, thou Enemy of all Righteousness, wilt thou not cease to pervert the right Ways of the Lord?* But, no Doubt, their Zeal may sometimes be as rash as *Peter's*, when he cut off *Malchus's* Ear: The Lord does not approve of this, neither do we: Young Christians have often too much wild Fire mixt with true Zeal. And if ever your Hearts had been warm with Zeal for God and his Cause, if you had ever had a *First Love;* then you would know it to be as I say; and would be ready to make Allowances, especially in some warm Tempers.—But I suppose you would have them be perfect, all Spirit, and no Flesh. They themselves long to be so. But if they were, it would not screen them from your Malice, more than our Lord from the Pharisees. *Malchus* had as good an Argument as you, to prove that *Peter* had no Grace; that Christ and all his Followers were quarrelsome and seditious: And it is probable he did improve it to the same End as you do other Things; asking, if that was any Fruit of the Spirit to cut off his Ear? No Doubt he might say, "If that be Conversion may God keep me from it; these that pretend most of all to it, are the most bitter and outragious; one of the Gang cut off my Ear, from a religious Pretence; there's none of them better; they are all embarqued in the same ship, and have the same sour and harsh Turn of Mind." Just thus you blind yourselves by poring only on the black Spots of God's People, and strive to make them more so: Where then is your boasted Charity? Do you not see that all your Cavils and Objections prove you to be ignorant of the Things of God, and Enemies to his Work? Do you not see that your very Objections prove it to be his Work, and always will? For thus has God always overshot the Devil in his own Bow. Perhaps some of you will say, We are not against it. But don't you show, that you are not for it? Are you not more cordial with its Enemies, than its Friends? Are you not still making Exceptions against it? I look upon all Neutres, as Enemies, in Affairs of Religion. Away with your carnal Prudence! And either follow *God* or *Baal. He that is not* actually *with us, is against us; and he that gathereth not with us, scattereth abroad.* . . .

I tell you further, That *the Sin against the Holy Ghost shall never be forgiven.* And I verily fear, that many, both Ministers and People, in this Generation, will be guilty of it: For God generally leaves a Testimony in the Consciences of his bitterest Enemies; and when they persist against these Convictions, and the clearest Evidences of Matters of Fact, spitefully to reproach the Work of his Spirit; I have small Hopes that they shall ever be renewed to Repentance. For, was it not in these very Circumstances the *Pharisees* were, when our Lord charges them with this unpardonable Sin? *Mat.* xii. 31. Indeed I am afraid, lest I hear, to my Sorrows, that some of you die in a *fearful Looking for of Wrath and fiery Indignation.* But whoever of you do these Things ignorantly, as *Paul,* who verily thought he should do many Things against *Jesus of Nazareth,* there is yet Hope concerning you. I beseech you then, fear and tremble to proceed further: Pray to God, if, perhaps, the Thoughts of your Hearts, and Words of your Mouths, may be forgiven you. And do not resist these Evidences that are as clear as you are capable of, until God give you to know the Things of his Spirit. If you will resist, I tell you in the Fear of God, it will be more tolerable for *Sodom* and *Gomorrah*, for *Tyre* and *Sidon*, in the Day of Judgment, than for you: *Nineveh* together with them, shall rise up in Judgment against you, and shall condemn you; because you have Opportunity of greater Light than they. And tho' you be exalted nearer Heaven, yet wo to you, for with a more dreadful Vengeance will you be plung'd deeper into Hell.

16 · Gilbert Tennent

REMARKS UPON A PROTESTATION

The bitterness of early 1741 bore fruit in the rupture of the Presbyterian Church at the meeting of the Synod in May. The opponents of the revival presented a *Protestation* in which a catalogue of charges was joined with the demand that the revivalists submit to discipline and acknowledge the error of their ways. When the revivalists refused, their critics declared themselves to be the Synod and "ejected" Tennent and his allies. Subsequently Tennent published his account of the entire episode, one which concluded with a ringing defense of his party's conduct and of the principles with which New Side Presbyterianism was thereafter to be identified.

. . . We own that rash Judging is a Sin against God; but we know of nothing in our Principles that leads to it. We are far from such Narrowness and Bigotry as to imagine that all God's Ministers and People are coop'd up within the Verge of any one particular Denomination; or that they are all of our Sentiments, and willing to comply with our Measures in lesser Things.

Gilbert Tennent, *Remarks upon a Protestation Presented to the Synod of Philadelphia, June 1, 1741* . . . (Philadelphia, 1741), pp. 22–31.

Our Brethren alledge, "that rash Judging has been our constant Practice for above Twelve-Months past, as well as of (as they call them) our disorderly Probationers." This Charge, our Opponents, we think, will not be able to prove. Indeed, we have been very jealous about our protesting Brethren's States towards God, because of their inconsistent Conduct in respect of the Work of God, sometimes Approving and sometimes Disapproving of it; and representing of it in a gloomy Dress, because of some uncommon Incidents and Circumstances, which might admit of a favourable Interpretation. Has not Mr. *John Thompson* "term'd the late Revival of God's Work a new-fangled Stir about Religion; as also a spiritual Frenzy?" And have not the Authors of the Pamphlet, entituled, *The Wandering Spirit*, expressed great Bitterness against it? We have Reason to suspect some of our protesting Brethren to be guilty of Forming that malignant Satyr. . . .

We are sorry that our protesting Brethren have, by their Speeches and Conduct, given us such Reason to believe them to be Opposers of God's Work.

As to what is said in the Conclusion of the present Argument, *namely*, that "we (as they say) industriously persuade People to believe, that the Call of God, whereby he calls Men to the Ministry does not consist in their being regularly ordained, *&c*. but in some invisible Motions and Workings of the Spirit: And that the Gospel preached in Truth by unconverted Ministers, can be of no saving Benefit to Souls." In answer to the aforesaid Charge, we declare our Opinions as follows, *namely*, we believe that there is a Necessity of previous Tryals and Ordination in order to the Ministry; and that such who are regularly set apart, being sound in Doctrine, and blameless in Life, however their inward State may be, are true Ministers in the Sight of the Church, and that their Ministrations are valid. But in the mean time, we think that none should undertake the ministerial Work but those that are truly gracious; those that intend therein the Glory of God and Good of Mankind; those that are inclined of God thereto: For we know not how a graceless Man can be faithful in the Ministry. Now, whether those inward, pious Dispositions aforesaid be termed the inward Call of God to the Gospel-Ministry, or only Qualifications necessary or pre-requisitive in the Persons whom God calls, it seems to be the same in Substance. A Debate about Words we judge needless.

As to what is farther alledged in this Paragraph, *namely*, "that the Gospel preached by unconverted Ministers in Truth can be of no saving Benefit to Souls," according to our Opinion. This charge we deny as slanderous. God, as an absolute Sovereign, may use what Means he pleased to accomplish his Work by. We only assert this, that Success by unconverted Ministers Preaching is very improbable, and very seldom happens, so far as we can gather. Alas, for them poor Souls! partly thro' Ignorance of the Nature of vital Religion, and partly thro' a native Enmity against it, and partly thro' Fear of losing their Credit, &c. by its Spread near their Borders; they are under great Temptations (instead of Befriending it) to rise up against it, and try to pull it down by all their Art and Eloquence.

The *Sixth* Reason of the Protest, is, "our Preaching (as they say) the Terrors of the Law in such a Manner and Dialect as hath no Precedent in the Word of God, but rather appears to be borrow'd from a worse Dialect; and seditiously Working on the Passions of weak Minds as to cause them to cry out in a dismal Manner, and fall down in Convulsion like Fits, to the Marring of the Profiting both of themselves and others, who are so taken up in Hearing and Seeing their odd Symptoms, that they cannot attend to, or hear what the Preacher says; after all Boasting of these Things as the Work of God; which we are persuaded do proceed from an inferior or worse Cause."

A. This Reason, when applied to all whom they reject, as

it doubtless is by our Opponents, which their indefinite Manner of Expression signifies, is groundless and slanderous. We challenge our Opponents to prove their invidious Charge against the greater Part of those whom they have rejected: If any one of our Number has been guilty of Indiscretion at any time in his Manner of Address to the People, we will not pretend to justify it; but to charge the Whole with this Fault, is unjust.

We know not that we use any Dialect in inculcating the Terrors of the Law, but what accords with Scripture and Reason; or that we endeavour to excite the lower Passions, but after the Information of the Understanding, and that by scriptural Incentives: Which is so far from being seditious, that it is the Duty of every Gospel Minister. We are bid to cry aloud and not to spare, to shew to *Judah* her Transgressions, and to the House of *Jacob* her Sins. . . . If we speak smooth Things, or please Men, we are not the Ministers of Jesus Christ. . . .

I know of none among the rejected Brethren who look upon the aforesaid Convulsion-like-Fits to be a sufficient Evidence of the Work of God.

We only judge such Appearances to be probable Indications of Concern of Mind, which when it issues in a Closure with Christ by Faith, a Communion with him by Love, and Conformity to him in humble Holiness; we believe it to be a special Work of God's Grace: But even before it has those Effects, while Sinners are only bewailing Sin, chiefly thro' Fear of divine Wrath, we think we have Reason to hope that it is a common Work of the Holy Spirit. . . .

In the mean time it may be observed, that there are but a few that are overcome as aforesaid, in Comparison of the Multitudes that are convinced.

It may be prov'd, by many Witnesses, that several Times when the Truths of God have been preach'd in the wildest Gospel-Strains, that many Persons have been overcome with Love, Joy or Sorrow.

What worse Representation of the Work of God, now Spreading in the World, could be expected from a professed Enemy of all Religion, than we have from our Brethren? Is it not doleful to see Religion thus wounded in the House of its professed Friends?

Do they not manifestly make use of an uncommon Circumstance to blacken the whole Work? . . .

Must they not be stone-blind that do not see, that there be all the Evidences of a Work of GOD now among us, that can reasonably be desired? Are not the Ignorant enlightned, the Secure made solicitous about their Salvation, the Profane reformed, many Formalists shaken off their false Foundations, and brought to experimental Christianity? Have we not all needful Evidence from their Speech and Practice, that the prevailing Temper of many Men's Minds is turn'd into a holy, humble and heavenly Channel?

Divers Opposers of God's Work in several Places of this Land, have been lately struck to the Heart, and made to acknowledge their Wickedness in the most publick Manner. . . .

. . . Several Places in this Continent, are at this Time joining Hand in Hand, in seeking of the LORD; they are setting their Faces Zion-ward, and weeping as they go.

And have not Persons of almost all Denominations been wrought upon by the Word as aforesaid? Do they not unite to give Testimony to God's Work, and celebrate his Praise? Herein *Judah* and *Ephraim* have harmonized. What can be desired more to prove it to be the Work of the Eternal GOD?

If it be objected, that many of those who are said to be under good Impressions, are guilty of rash Judging. A. I can't think it rash Judging to believe those to be graceless, who, in the midst of Means of Conviction, do habitually oppose the Work of God, under the Covert of some supposed or real Indiscretions.

A *seventh* Reason of the Protest is "our preaching and maintaining (as they say) that all true Converts are as certain of their gracious State, as a Person is of what he knows by his outward Senses; and are able to give a Narrative of the Time and Manner of their Conversion, or else we conclude them to be in a graceless State; and that a gracious Person can judge of others gracious State otherwise than by his Profession and Life,—that People are under no sacred Type to Pastors, &c."

A. Our Judgment as to the aforesaid Particulars, is this, *namely*, That gracious Persons may attain a full Assurance of their good State, and some of them do attain it; but we do not believe that all arrive thereto in this Life; and those that do, may, no doubt, lose it again, and get under Clouds and Darkness.

But in the mean time we think, that all who are converted, ordinarily have a lesser or greater Degree of comfortable Perswasion of their gracious State, either immediately upon their Closure with Christ, or some Time afterwards, when Faith is in Exercise, either for a shorter or longer Duration. Surely, those that are rightly humbled by the Spirit of God, will not be satisfied 'til they obtain this.

And altho' those that are converted in adult Age, can generally remember the Time and Means of their Conviction, and give a satisfactory Account of their Experiences to those who are proper Judges of such Things; yet the Case, we supposed, is somewhat different with those who are converted in Infancy and Childhood; yet it must be confessed, that even some Children pass under considerable Convictions. I know of none of our rejected Brethren, that do or ever did believe it to be just or proper, to judge any to be in a natural or graceless State, meerly because they could not tell the Time of their Conversion; if they have Evidences of the Thing, it is enough.

We know of no Way of Judging respecting the gracious State of others, but by their Doctrines, Experiences, and Practice.

No doubt there is a Relation between a Pastor and his People; but the Design of this being to promote their Good, we think it is unreasonable that it should subsist to the Prejudice of that, which it's designed to procure. However, in ordinary Cases, we think it to be the People's Duty, to make regular Application to their Pastors, for Liberty to go where they get the greatest Benefit.

But when Ministers conspire to oppose the Work and faithful Servants of God, in the most open and flagrant Manner, we see no Harm in this Case, in using an extraordinary Method. . . .

We are sorry that our protesting Brethren have given us Reason to suspect them, of being guilty of verging towards the Doctrine of implicit Faith and blind Obedience; this appears from their finding Fault with us (in their Protest) for not obeying the Rules, in the making of which we are in the Negative.

Here we must beg to be excused from Concurring in Sentiment with our Brethren: We are resolved, by the Grace of God, that no gingle or cant of Order and Government shall gull us out of our Reason and Conscience, or rob us of our Priviledges, as Men, as Christians, as Protestants, and as Presbyterians: We declare our utter Abhorrence of all such Pretence to Power in Churches, as is built upon the Ruins of human Nature. . . .

Particular Rules of Churches, are only so far to be valued and obeyed, as they serve to answer their supposed Design, *namely,* the Edification of the Body of Christ. To say that we should regard and obey them when the Case is otherwise, is to say, that we ought to esteem and promote the Injury of Christ's Kingdom; which is absurd.

Our protesting Brethren say, that they doubt not but that when God sees us humbled for our Sins, he will return again in Mercy. No doubt we have at all Times Reason to humble ourselves before God: But if they be not blinded with Prejudice, or otherwise, they may see Reason now to rejoice, that God has returned to his Church in Mercy.

Once more: Our protesting Brethren think that their Protest, which they call their Testimony, may be of use to their Children yet unborn. It may so, for what we know, in shewing them their Fathers Opposition to the Work of God, and schismatical Separation from their Brethren. . . .

17 · Jonathan Dickinson

A DISPLAY OF GOD'S

SPECIAL GRACE

In the late months of 1741 members of the Tennent party (now organized as the Presbytery of New Brunswick) began to grow disturbed by what they thought were noticeable "excesses" in the revival. Concerned by the enthusiasm of the Moravians and Baptists, and preparing to defend Calvinism against the inroads of the sectarian spirit, Tennent wrote Jonathan Dickinson a letter in which he confessed and lamented his own "excessive heat of temper" in the past. Tennent also hinted at his hopes for reunion among Presbyterians, and in May 1742 the New York Presbytery, led by Dickinson, met with the Synod of Philadelphia and attempted to arrange some accommodation. But the Old Side refused to withdraw from their judgment of the previous year. The New York Presbytery thereupon formally protested the manner in which the prorevival ministers had been "illegally" ejected from the Synod.

Jonathan Dickinson, A *Display of God's Special Grace. In a Familiar Dialogue between a Minister & a Gentleman of his Congregation . . .* (Boston, 1742), pp. 28–33.

Further evidence of Dickinson's sympathy was the publication in the summer of 1742 of Dickinson's *A Display of God's Special Grace*. The tract, cast in the form of a dialogue between "Epinetus" and "Theophilus," proved to be Dickinson's most popular work and it was often reprinted in the course of the succeeding century's revivals. It first appeared anonymously, but early in 1743 Dickinson allowed Gilbert Tennent to reissue the volume with the author's name made public. Concurrently Tennent's Presbytery met with the New England group, and the process began whereby, in 1745, the Synod of New York was formed. Out of this formal union of the two dynamic elements of Presbyterianism was to come a distinctly American church, shaped by the experience of the Awakening. But the revival itself can be said to have closed with the publication of Dickinson's *Display*, for in his concluding pages Dickinson turned to argue against the Antinomianism that seemed to be gaining favor among the Awakened. Thereafter the energies of evangelical Presbyterians were to be engaged less in promoting the revival than in preventing the impulse from being dissipated into meaningless emotion, and toward giving institutional embodiment to the spiritual revolution through which they had passed. In his affirmation that the revival had been indeed a "Work of God" Dickinson testified in many ways to the dawning of that new era. Not the least of his contributions was his awareness that the Presbyterianism of the Middle Colonies, however divided within itself, was no longer independent, spiritually or intellectually, of the larger progress of American religion.

EPINET. "How comes it to pass, that we hear so much of these Things of *late,* which former Times and Ages knew so little about?"

THEOPH. This Question makes Way for two further Evidences, that the Spirit of God is the glorious Author of this Work. *First,* I must inform you, that the Fact is quite contrary to your Supposal.—Read all the most famous Authors upon practical Godliness, from the Beginning of the Reformation; and you'l find that they teach the same Doctrines which I have now insisted on.—Read the Narratives of particular Conversions, not only in the Scriptures; but in all the preceeding Ages of the Church, and in all the most distant Countreys and Nations; and you'll find that the Work has always been carried on in Men's Hearts, in a Method substantially the same with what I have described, by the same Progress of Convictions and Humiliations.—And how could this possibly be, unless it proceeded from the same blessed Author? For there could be no Conspiracy, Collusion, or Endeavours of Imitation, in Persons so far removed from, and so unacquainted with one another.—And *Secondly,* whence is it that we hear of so much of these Things now, but from the more plentiful Effusion of the blessed Spirit?—Whence is it that this blessed Work has spread so extensively, far and near, among young and old; and there are so many crying out under the Burden of their Sins; and so earnestly enquiring after the Way of Salvation?— Is not human Nature the same now that it used to be?— Whence is it that the Ordinances, that were before but as a dead Letter, do now make such a lively Impression? Certainly *this is the Lord's Doing; and it is marvellous in our Eyes.*

EPINET. "How do we know that these Convictions are any Thing more, than the natural Effects of those pungent and terrifying *Addresses,* from some warm and zealous Ministers, which we lately hear of?"

THEOPH. I readily allow, that a short temporary Surprize may be this Way excited; but then this Effect could last no longer than the Cause operates. This only could never produce a real effectual lasting Change.—I also allow, that God deals with Mankind as with reasonable Creatures: and when he designs this Change in the Hearts of any, he will provide and bless some suitable Means to effect it. If he save us, it will be in the Way of his own appointing.—But can you yourself imagine, that the most pungent Address of any Teacher under Heaven, can in a natural Way produce those Effects that are frequently seen among us?—Consider I beseech you, the natural State of carnal Men. They *are dead in Trespasses and Sins.* And can a plain Discourse of the most zealous Preacher, how pungent soever, awaken these dead Men to such a lively lasting Concern about their Souls, that they can rest no more until they find Rest in Christ?—They are blind and ignorant, they have no just Apprehensions of their own deplorable Condition; of the Way of Salvation provided for 'em; or of the glorious Excellency of an offer'd Saviour. And will this enlighten their Minds, to a lively View of, and Acquaintance with the Things of their everlasting Peace?—They are proud and self-righteous. And will this lay 'em in the Dust, and bring them to renounce all their own Attainments, Duties, false Hopes, and Refuges?—They have a natural Enmity and Opposition to this Change. And will this so suddenly conquer their Aversation to a Life of Godliness, their Love to their Lusts, Ease and Security, their natural rooted Inclinations to sensual Pursuits; and their habitual Custom in Sin?—Will this cause 'em to lay aside all their Prejudices, beloved Lusts, fleshly Interests and Endearments?—They have strong and mighty Opposition to conquer. And will this overcome all the Craft and Power of Satan? Will it constrain them to forsake all their Pleasures, worldly Pursuits, merry Company, and alluring Expectations; for their present melancholy, fearful, pensive Life? Will it fortify them against all the Persuasions of their carnal Acquaintance, against the Banter and Reproach of their old Companions; and against the Doubts and Misgivings of their own unbelieving Hearts? Could any of the Orators of *Greece* or *Rome* produce such Effects as these upon their Hearers?—If this be a natural Effect, what's the Reason that it was produced no sooner, upon those who have heard so many Scores of Sermons, as pungent and awakening as that which at last prov'd successful? And what is the Reason that it has not a like Effect upon others, naturally as capable of Impression; and as well prepared to receive it, as those who are thus suddenly, thoroughly, and powerfully awaken'd? In a Word, The *Apostle* himself assures us, that *the Excellency of the Power is of God and not of Man;* and that *neither is he that planteth any Thing; nor he that watereth: but God that giveth the Increase.* Let who will oppose the Work, or deny to God the Honour of it, I shall be awfully careful not to ascribe that to poor Worms, which is manifestly (as the *Apostle* speaks) *the Working of God's mighty Power.*

Epinet. "Though I can't reply to the Evidence you have given, that this Work is indeed from the Agency of the Spirit of God: Yet it still remains a great Difficulty in the Way of this, that we hear Nothing of the extraordinary Progress of Convictions, and of what you call Conversions to God, but only under the Ministry of those *warm Preachers,* who directly calculate their Addresses to awaken the Passions of their Hearers; and to put them into Frights and Surprizes."

Theoph. Your Intelligence has been very defective; or else your Prejudice against these Things has call'd off your Attention, from some of the most surprizing Instances of God's Power and Grace, that have been heard of since Apostolick Times.—If you reflect upon the *first Fruits* of this extraordinary and mighty Work of God's special Grace, in the Conversions in *Hampshire* County (*Massachusetts-Bay*) whereof there is so judicious a *Narrative* publish'd to the World, it will be a sufficient Answer to this Objection. Don't you know and don't we all know, that the Ministers there, under whose Instrumentality that Work was carried on, are calm, sedate, and judicious Men, unto whom the greatest Adversaries of this wonderful Work of God could never pretend to impute the least Tincture of *Enthusiasm* or irregular Heat? And if we overlook all the other astonishing Instances of this Nature; and attend to the last refreshing Accounts we have of the like general Progress of converting Grace, at *York, Portsmouth,* and other Places to the Eastward of *Boston*,[1] does it not appear, that no natural Cause has had the least Hand in making a Difference between these Places and others?—The *Ministers* there are some of our grave solid rational Men, and yet the powerful Energy of the Spirit of God, has been as remarkably manisested there as any where else.—Every Objection is therefore now fully silenced; and give me Leave to say, you must be obstinately blind, or acknowledge that *this is the Finger of God*.—O take Heed, when God is in this extraordinary Manner manifesting himself to us, when the Lord Jesus Christ is in these wonderful Works reveal'd from Heaven amongst us, that you ben't found *fighting against God*.—*Beware lest that come upon you, which is spoken of in the Prophets, Behold, ye Despisers! and wonder and perish.* My Friend, Beware lest you *reject the Counsel of God against your self!*

---

[1] *This was wrote before the Work remarkably spread* in many other Towns, *which now might be added.*

PART FOUR

THE AWAKENING:

NEW ENGLAND

18 · *Nathan Cole*

(1 7 1 1 –   )

SPIRITUAL TRAVELS

That Dickinson's *Display* was initially published in Boston, with a preface signed by seven ministers celebrating the "Work of God" in New England, attests that the Awakening did not unfold through each of the colonies in turn. The revival cannot be said to have "spread" from the Middle Colonies into New England, for the descendants of the Puritans seem to have been filled, already in the early months of 1740, with a keen sense of anticipation. Expectation did focus, however, on the available news of Whitefield's triumphs in the other provinces, and ministers wrote letters inviting him to New England.

The William and Mary Quarterly, 3rd Series, vii (1950), pp. 590–591.

When he moved inland from Newport, Rhode Island, in the early autumn of 1740, the populace was quite ready to be awakened. The response to Whitefield's advent was captured in Nathan Cole's account of what happened at Middletown, Connecticut on October 23, 1740. Cole's spiritual autobiography, all but a brief section of which remains to this day in manuscript form, is one of the more remarkable documents of the intellectual life of eighteenth-century America. Its first sentence—"I was born Feb 15th 1711 and born again Octo 1741"—is a tribute to the place of the New Birth in the minds and hearts of the colonial-people.

Now it pleased God to send Mr. Whitefield into this land; and my hearing of his preaching at Philadelphia, like one of the old apostles, and many thousands flocking to hear him preach the Gospel, and great numbers were converted to Christ, I felt the Spirit of God drawing me by conviction; I longed to see and hear him and wished he would come this way. I heard he was come to New York and the Jerseys and great multitudes flocking after him under great concern for their souls which brought on my concern more and more, hoping soon to see him; but next I heard he was at Long Island, then at Boston, and next at Northampton. Then on a sudden, in the morning about 8 or 9 of the clock there came a messenger and said Mr. Whitefield preached at Hartford and Wethersfield yesterday and is to preach at Middletown this morning at ten of the clock. I was in my field at work. I dropped my tool that I had in my hand and ran home to my wife, telling her to make ready quickly to go and hear Mr. Whitefield preach at Middletown, then ran to my pasture for my horse with all my might, fearing that I should be too late. Having my horse, I with my wife soon mounted the horse and went forward as fast as I thought the horse could bear; and when my horse got much out of breath, I would get down and put my wife on the saddle and bid her ride as fast as she could and not stop or slack for me except I bade her, and so I would run until I was much out of breath and then mount my horse again, and so I did several times to favour my horse. We improved every moment to get along as if we were fleeing for our lives, all the while fearing we should be too late to hear the sermon, for we had twelve miles to ride double in little more than an hour and we went round by the upper housen parish. And when we came within about half a mile or a mile of the road that comes down from Hartford, Wethersfield, and Stepney to Middletown, on high land I saw before me a cloud of fog arising. I first thought it came from the great river, but as I came nearer the road I heard a noise of horses' feet coming down the road, and this cloud was a cloud of dust made by the horses' feet. It arose some rods into the air over the tops of hills and trees; and when I came within about 20 rods of the road, I could see men and horses slipping along in the cloud like shadows, and as I drew nearer it seemed like a steady stream of horses and their riders, scarcely a horse more than his length behind another, all of a lather and foam with sweat, their breath rolling out of their nostrils every jump. Every horse seemed to go with all his might to carry his rider to hear news from heaven for the saving of souls. It made me tremble to see the sight, how the world was in a struggle. I found a vacancy between two horses to slip in mine and my wife said "Law, our clothes will be all spoiled, see how they look," for they were so covered with dust that they looked almost all of a colour, coats, hats, shirts, and horse. We went down in the stream but heard no man speak a word all the way for 3 miles but every one pressing forward in great haste;

and when we got to Middletown old meeting house, there was a great multitude, it was said to be 3 or 4,000 of people, assembled together. We dismounted and shook off our dust, and the ministers were then coming to the meeting house. I turned and looked towards the Great River and saw the ferry boats running swift backward and forward bringing over loads of people, and the oars rowed nimble and quick. Everything, men, horses, and boats seemed to be struggling for life. The land and banks over the river looked black with people and horses; all along the 12 miles I saw no man at work in his field, but all seemed to be gone. When I saw Mr. Whitefield come upon the scaffold, he looked almost angelical; a young, slim, slender youth, before some thousands of people with a bold undaunted countenance. And my hearing how God was with him everywhere as he came along, it solemnized my mind and put me into a trembling fear before he began to preach; for he looked as if he was clothed with authority from the Great God, and a sweet solemn solemnity sat upon his brow, and my hearing him preach gave me a heart wound. By God's blessing, my old foundation was broken up, and I saw that my righteousness would not save me.

19 · Jonathan Parsons

"ACCOUNT OF THE REVIVAL

AT LYME" (2)

Possibly because of their intellectual tradition, possibly because they had been forewarned by the turbulence left elsewhere in Whitefield's wake, the Congregational clergy of New England were somewhat more judicious than the Log College men in their welcoming of Whitefield. They gave him every opportunity to speak, and they rejoiced in the fruits of his preaching, but almost from the first moment of the revival the New England ministers took pains to assess the quality of the revival. The result was to give respectability and strength to the revival impulse, especially when a favorable judgment came from ministers whose intellectual standards were unassailable. Parsons' correspondent, Benjamin Colman, had, to be sure, introduced Edwards' narrative of the 1735 revival to the world, but he was also widely known as Boston's most urbane and literary clergyman. When Colman approved both Whitefield's preaching and the effects of it, the Awakening

------

The Christian History for 1744, pp. 125–126, 133.

gained time, as it were, in which to gather momentum, secure from the public abuse of ministers otherwise ill disposed toward emotional religion.

Some time after Mr. *Whitefield* had been thro' this *Colony* (tho' he came not by the Way of *Lyme*) our People were more generally rous'd up to bethink themselves, and converse about Religion. Probably the frequent Accounts of the Success he had in many Places were serviceable among us. But more *especially* my going to hear him at *New-Haven* and some other Places: this gave me a different turn of Tho't about him and his Preaching; and satisfy'd me more fully that there were many Misrepresentations of him and his Views; and, I believe, serv'd as a Means to take off the Prejudices that some among us had conceiv'd against the Effects of his Ministry.

A little after he left *New-England,* I heard of a very great Concern upon the Minds of many People at *Hartford;* especially among the Children and Youth. The various Accounts we had about them stir'd me up to take Pains, that, if it might be, I should understand the true Spring of all their Concern. To this End I frequently conversed with Persons that told me they had seen very surprising Effects of some Cause: they also told me the Effects; and, some of them told me of many Questions they ask'd the Persons under the surprising Operations, and the Answers they gave them; which gave some considerable Hope, that there was a glorious Work of God's Grace among them. But I could not be easy still for want of further Light; and therefore I wrote several Letters to *Gentlemen* in that Town, whom I tho't were *judicious* and *prudent,* desiring particular Accounts of the most extraordinary Facts observable among them: and *one* of them wrote me a prudent and discreet Answer, *relating* to some Matters of Fact, and added, that 'twas his Opinion the Spirit of God was pour'd out among them very gloriously. Yet still, I wanted further Light if it was to be had; and therefore on the 11th of *March* 1740,1. I set out upon a Visit to that Place and People, and to converse with the Ministers there. Mr. *Whitman,* one of the Ministers of that Town gave me a particular & very surprising Account of some Things he had certain Knowledge of; especially of the strong Consolations of some Persons, & the great Distress of others. He *kindly* related some Discourse of a Number once at his own House; and some extraordinary Distresses of many Persons at a religious Meeting: Facts that he knew, and Inquiries that he made to find out the Rise of them: And when I ask'd his Judgment upon the Things he had related, he told, as I remember, that he did not doubt, but the Persons in general, who had been thus affected, were, at that Time, under the Influence of God's Holy Spirit; and that a very gracious Manifestation of Mercy had been made among them.

This Pains I tho't necessary to take, and much more that wou'd be too tedious to relate at present. The Enemy of Souls was very busy, and much Pains were taken to represent the *extraordinary* Things we heard of from Abroad, as the Effect of an *heated* Imagination, or meer *Enthusiasm* and Disorder. 'Twas nois'd about, as if the Country wou'd be undone if such a Spirit shou'd have a general Spread; and Religion wou'd be banish'd from all the Churches. I observ'd that this was the Cry *especially* among those that had been the looser Sort, and seem'd now afraid of any Concern about their *eternal* State; and that gave me some Grounds to think that indeed the Lord was about to do some great Things for the Church which had been so long sunk down into almost meer Formality.

Upon my return Home from *Hartford,* I had further Accounts by Letters from the venerable Dr. *Colman* of the wonderful Progress of the Gospel at *Boston* and the Towns round about, by the Blessing of God upon the fervent Ministry of

Mr. *Tennent,* and their own Pastors. So that by the latter End of *March* I was furnished with a considerable History of the Work from many Places, attested by credible Witnesses; and from what I receiv'd from their Mouths and their Handwriting, I was able to relate certain Matters of Fact, in a Light vastly different from what they had been represented in among us; and to add the Judgment of wise, prudent and judicious Ministers concerning them and the true Spring of them. And therefore on the 29th of that Month I preach'd from *Isai.* 60. 8. from which my *special* Design was to rectify those Mistakes, about the religious Affairs abroad, that had been spread among us; and to give an *History* of *certain Facts,* together with the Opinion of those Ministers and some others, concerning the Rise of those Things, that had been so much the Conversation and Amusement of the People. The History and Application of it in this Sermon, had greater *visible* Effects upon the Auditory, than ever I had seen before in the Course of my Ministry. . . .

Indeed there were no Out-Cries; but a deep and general Concern upon the Minds of the Assembly discovered itself at that Time in plentiful Weeping, Sighs and Sobs. And what appear'd hopeful then, I found, upon conversing with many afterwards, to be true, as far as I could judge. Many told me that they never had such an awaken'd Sense of the Danger of putting off the grand Concern of their Souls to a future Season before, as GOD gave them under that Sermon: They were surprized at their own past Carelesness, and astonished that GOD had born with them so long. Several told me, that tho' they had liv'd *thirty forty* or *fifty Years* under the Preaching of the Gospel, they had never felt the Power of the Word upon their Hearts, so as to be long affected thereby, at any Time as they did then. Before it was the Cry of their Hearts, '*When will the Sermon be over, and the Sabbath be ended*'; but now the Minister always left off too soon, and the Time between Sermons was too long: they long for frequently returning Opportunities to hear. Before, they did not love Soul-searching Discourses, but now never cou'd hear too much of that Nature, together with many other Things of the like Import.

20 · Gilbert Tennent's Powerful

Preaching in Boston

When Whitefield, having addressed more than twenty thousand people on Boston Common, left New England on October 29, 1740, a few newspapers and nearly all the Episcopal clergy expressed relief. But the invasion of New England was not over, for Whitefield had persuaded Tennent to move northward "in order to blow up the divine fire lately kindled there." With Tennent's arrival in Boston in December, the bolder antirevival spirits began to make their voices heard. Tennent himself was abused in print. Still, his success with the multitude was, if anything, even greater than Whitefield's, and he was praised in several clumsily-composed broadsides. One anonymous admirer strove to describe in verse both the matter and the manner of Tennent's preaching.

> We bless the Man sent by the Spirit of Grace
> To turn poor Sinners into Wisdom's Ways;
> To plow the barr'n and break the fallow Ground,
> Dissect the Heart and shew the mortal Wound.

On the Reverend Mr. Gilbert Tennent's Powerful and successful Preaching in Boston . . . (Boston, 1741), entire.

There's few like him that ever we have seen,
Since lovely *Whitefield*—O! how sharp and keen.
He wields GOD's Law—the Holy Spirit's Sword,
And wound the Heart at almost every Word,
A *Boanerges* sometimes he'l appear,
And then a sweet and lovely Comforter.
So skilful Surgeons first rip up the Wound,
Then ply their Medicines 'till the Patient's sound.
The false Professor's by him tri'd and cast,
He shows the Doom they're sure to have at last.
The Formalist he searches to the Root,
And shews they bring forth nought but rotten Fruit.
The Hypocrite he doth anatomize,
Shews they're made up of sordid Falicies.
When he sounds forth the Thunders of the Law,
He strikes the Soul with Trembling and with Awe.
And when the Gospel Charms he doth display,
On Wings of Faith believing Souls away.
They mount, they fly unto the blest Abode
Where JESUS reigns the great incarnate GOD.
While he sets forth the great Redeemer's Charms,
They soar aloft into his blessed Arms.
While for his Master's Son a Spouse he woos,
With pearly Drops his lovely Cheeks bedews.
What mad besotted Disperado can
Take Prejudice against this holy Man?
When all he seeks and with his Soul doth crave,
Is precious and immortal Souls to save.
While scoffing *Ishmaels* rush into the Fire,
I'll fear GOD's Wrath, I'll tremble at his Ire.
While HELL without a Covering they court,
I to the dear Redeemer will resort.
I'll hear the Call the lovely *Tennent* brings,
Because I know it's from the King of Kings.

When *Jonah* unto *Nineveh* was sent,
In Sackcloth clad they generally repent.
The King he leaves his lofty splended Throne,
In Ashes sets before the LORD to mourn.
Shall Gospel Sinners be more vile than they,
In Judgment then will rise old *Nineveh*.
The *Sodomites* and the *Gomorians* too,
Will have a Doom less fearful far than you.
O tell it not in Streets of *Askelon*,
Lest vile *Philistines* vaunt themselves thereon.
Lest Daughters of uncircumcis'd do noies,
And at such Tidings mightily rejoice.
Since GOD has sent his lovely *Whitefield* here,
And blessed *Tennent*, O do not, do not dare,
To slight the Tenders of his wonderous Grace,
Who saves poor Souls in wise and sovereign Ways.
If on a Bed of Languishing you lay,
For some good Surgeon how you'd seek and pray?
You'd spare no Cost so you cou'd but obtain
Ease from Distress and Freedom from your Pain.
How can you then find in your Hearts to slight
Your Souls Physicians—who study Day and Night,
To find a Balsom for your bleeding Soul,
And precious Remedies to make them whole.
The poor, when sick, can scarce a Doctor have
For want of Money which they often crave.
But Soul Remedies are offer'd on free Cost
That you'll not take them, grieves your Teachers most.
Poor wounded Souls, O do not then delay;
To Soul Physicians haste O haste away.
As soon as sick, apply immediately,
Don't perish while you have Relief so nigh.
The Day of Grace may soon a Period have,
And then in vain you'll call, you'll cry and crave,

But all in vain: To Hell to Hell you must
And be for Ever, Ever, Ever curst.
And now he's gone, the heavenly Man is gone,
Bless GOD for faithful Shepherds of our own:
Who loudly call, and fain would Souls allure,
To make their Calling and Election sure.
O prize them, and rejoice in their Sweet Light,
Who're glad to serve your Souls by Day or Night.
They're glad to show the wandering Soul his Way,
From those dark Shades, to an eternal Day.
Follow your Shepherds they'll land you safe ashore,
On Emmanuel's Land, though Men and Devils roar.

21 · *Jonathan Parsons*

"ACCOUNT OF THE REVIVAL

AT LYME" (3)

During his three-month tour of New England Gilbert Tennent passed through many more towns than White-field had reached. At the same time many younger New England ministers began to itinerate, others exchanged pulpits, and the populace itself began to move about in quest of what Tennent had called "the greater good." But the Awakening is not to be measured merely by such mobility. A visit from Tennent, from other itinerants, or from a neighboring minister inspired in a congregation what one minister called "an uncommon Teachableness." Sermons were multiplied, often to four or five a week, and as Jonathan Parsons recalled, the religious life of each community continued to quicken.

On the *Beginning* of the *following Month,* Mr. *Tennent* came thro' this Place, and preached *two Sermons* among us: The first was in the *Evening,* from *Ezek.* 37. 9. But he seem'd to be very dull; and, I tho't, several Times, he wou'd have had

---

The Christian History for 1744, pp. 133–136.

nothing, almost to say. Yet he got thro', and, I believe, he preached the Truth, tho' with no Freedom; nor had the People in general much Sense of what was deliver'd according to the best Observation I cou'd make; yet it was not wholly in vain: one of our Communion was convinc'd of Sin, which after some Days, issu'd, I trust in a saving Conversion to God.—The next Morning he preached again from *Luk.* 13. 24. to a very attentive and deeply affected Auditory. Many that I heard lamenting their own Folly immediately after Sermon, spake as one wou'd expect those to do that had the Arrows of Conviction shot deep into their Hearts. I was not indeed, so sensible of the *extensive* Effects of that Sermon in the Time of it (tho' there was so much visible Concern under it) as afterwards. In a little while a considerable Number came to me and confess'd that they saw themselves undone, that earnestly enquired what they must do to be saved, who dated their first Awakenings from that Sermon.—From us Mr. *Tennent* went over to *Saybrook,* and many of the People of this Place, and the neighbouring Societies went with me to hear him. There he preach'd a rational, searching Sermon, suited to unconverted Sinners and drowsy Saints. I saw but few Instances of Persons much moved by it to Appearance, in Sermon Time; but found some very much enraged with the Preacher afterwards. Some that went from this Town, spent their Time upon the Way home in cavilling, and finding Fault with what had been delivered, and I believe did much Hurt thereby. One especially, who shall be nameless, seem'd exceedingly disaffected, and endeavour'd to disaffect others. But still he could not forget the Sermon, especially that Part of it which was to backward Christians; and tho' he tho't, or endeavour'd to think, that it was a censorious Discourse, yet, as he told me afterwards, it never left him until he was made to see that he was the very Man to whose Case it was suited above any Sermon that ever he had heard.

After this I observed that our Assemblies were greater and more attentive at Times of publick Worship than before. Sabbaths alone wou'd not suffice for hearing Sermons, but greater Numbers still urg'd for frequent Lectures. I was well pleas'd to observe such a flocking to the Windows, and a hearing Ear become general; and therefore I readily consented, upon the Request of the People, to preach as often as I cou'd, besides the stated Exercises of the Sabbath. Once every Week I carried on a publick Lecture, besides several private ones in various Parts of the Parish. And I could not but observe about this Time, that an Evening Lecture I had set up the Winter before in a private House, for the sake of a young Man that was a Cripple, tho' at first exceeding thin (but seven Persons, as I remember, besides the Family) was now greatly increas'd, and in about a Month grew up to several Hundreds, so that I was oblig'd to turn it into a publick Evening Lecture.

Now it pleas'd God to encourage my Heart, give me unusual Freedom, and such a firm State of bodily Health, that I could go thro' three Times the Service I had been able to endure at other Times; so that I was able to study and write three Sermons a Week, and preach several others of my old Notes (for I seldom in all the Time preach'd without Writing.) Sometime in this Month Mr. *Griswold* invited me to preach a Lecture for him, and I consented. While I was preaching from *Psal.* 119. 59, 60. I observ'd many of the Assembly in Tears, and heard many crying out in a very great Bitterness of Soul, as it seem'd then by the Sound of Voices. When Sermon was over I cou'd better take Notice of the Cause; and the Language was to this Purpose, *viz.* Alas! I'm undone; I'm undone! O my Sins! How they prey upon my Vitals! What will become of me? How shall I escape the Damnation of Hell, who have spent away a golden Opportunity under Gospel Light, in Vanity?—And much more of the like Import. . . . As I was satisfied that it was the Truth they had been hearing, so, by their Complaints, it appeared to be the Force of Truth that made them cry out, and threw many of them into Hysterick-Fits: And, if I mistake not, every one that were so violently seiz'd that Night, have since given good Evidence of their Conversion; but that, their Reverend Pastor can give the best Account of.

The visible Success of my Ministry in that and some other Lectures abroad, (tho' I rejoyc'd in the happy Prospect of the Advancement of the Kingdom of our divine Lord) was far from being a Means to damp my Hopes or slacken my Endeavours at Home. My Heart burned with Love to and Pity for the People of my peculiar Charge: I had constant Supplies of Argument flowing into my Mind, and Zeal to urge a speedy Answer.

By the latter End of *April* our young People were generally sick of that vain Mirth, and those foolish Amusements that had been their Delight, and were form'd into several religious Societies for Prayer and reading Books of Piety under my Direction: Many of them were frequently in my Study for Advice; the Bent of their Souls was evidently towards the Things of another World: Whenever they fell into Companies, the great Salvation was the subject of their Conversation. They were so generally displeas'd with themselves for past Carelesness, and spending Time in Revels and Frolicks, that several, at the Desire of others, came to me, and desir'd me to preach them a Lecture upon the 14th of *May* (the Day of our Election in this *Colony*) which they had, for many Years, accustomed themselves to spend in Feasting, Musick, Dancing, Gaming, and the like. I complied with the Request, and preach'd to a great Assembly, from *Mat.* 24. 37, 38, 39. Upon which I observ'd, that *Jesus Christ would certainly come to judge the World;* and that *when he did come, he would find it overwhelm'd in carnal Security;* and from these Considerations I applied my self to those that had been secure and unwatchful, both among Christians and unconverted Sinners, in a Manner, which, I tho't, proper to awaken and convince. Under this Sermon many had their *Countenances changed;* their *thot's* seemed to *trouble* them, *so that the Joynts of* their *Loyns were loosed, and* their *Knees smote one against another.* Great Numbers cried out aloud in the Anguish of their Souls: several stout Men fell as tho' a Cannon had been discharg'd, and a Ball had made its Way thro' their Hearts. Some young Women were thrown into Hysterick Fits. The Sight and Noise of Lamentation, seem'd a little Resemblance of what we may imagine will be when the great Judge pronounces the tremendous Sentence of, *Go ye cursed into everlasting Fire.* There were so many in Distress that I could not get a particular Knowledge of the special Reasons at that Time, only as I heard them crying, *Wo is me! What must I do?* And such sort of short Sentences with bitter Accents.——

22 · *James Davenport*

(1 7 1 0 – 1 7 5 7)

A SONG OF PRAISE

A third invasion of New England, and for the history of the Awakening possibly the most significant, was that by James Davenport in July 1741. He was a great-grandson of the Reverend John Davenport, a founder of New Haven Colony and its first minister. James Davenport received his degree from Yale in 1732 and remained in New Haven for several years pursuing theological studies. In 1738 he received a call from Southold, Long Island, the oldest of the New England-settled towns on the Island. In the early months of the Awakening he and a neighboring minister, Jonathan Barber, commenced holding meetings that lasted as long as twenty-four hours. Davenport also began to pronounce judgment on his parishioners, "almost with the confidence of Omniscience," and to forbid those whom he deemed unconverted to partake of the Lord's Supper. When he crossed the Sound into Connecticut, Davenport was already a controversial figure, his extravagances as worrisome to the prorevivalists as they were offensive to those who were now ready to assail the Awakening. Dav-

---

A Song of Praise for Joy in the Holy Ghost . . . (Boston, 1742), pp. 1–2.

enport's first and possibly most distinctive innovation was his encouragement of singing by the awakened—not only in church but among those who followed him through the streets. His converts did not restrict themselves to the metrical versions of the Psalms that until then had been standard musical fare in the New England churches. He composed "songs" of his own which, though filled with the language of Scripture, represented the revolution in hymnology that was to be among the enduring consequences of the Awakening. One such composition betrayed, however, something of the Antinomian ecstasy which, along with Davenport's other "errors," was eventually to sully the reputation of the revival.

My Soul doth magnify the Lord,
　My Spirit doth rejoice
In God my Saviour, and my God;
　I hear his joyful Voice.
I need not go abroad for Joy,
　Who have a Feast at home;
My Sighs are turned into Songs,
　The Comforter is come.

Down from above the blessed Dove
　Is come into my Breast,
To witness God's eternal Love;
　This is my heavenly Feast.
This makes me *Abba Father* cry,
　With Confidence of Soul;
It makes me cry, My Lord, my God,
　And that without Controul.

There is a Stream which issues forth
From God's eternal Throne,
And from the Lamb a living Stream,
Clear as the Crystal Stone;
The Stream doth water Paradise,
It makes the Angels sing:
One cordial Drop revives my Heart,
Whence all my Joys do spring.

Such Joys as are unspeakable,
And full of Glory too;
Such hidden *Manna,* hidden Pearls,
As Worldlings do not know.
Eye hath not seen, nor Ear hath heard,
From Fancy 'tis conceal'd,
What thou Lord, hast laid up for thine,
And hast to me reveal'd.

I see thy Face, I hear thy Voice,
I taste thy sweetest Love;
My Soul doth leap: But O for Wings,
The Wings of *Noah's* Dove!
Then should I flee far hence away,
Leaving this World of Sin:
Then should my Lord put forth his Hand,
And kindly take me in.

Then should my Soul with Angels feast,
On Joys that always last:
Blest be my God, the God of Joy,
Who gives me here a Taste.

23 · *Jonathan Edwards*

THE DISTINGUISHING MARKS OF

A WORK OF THE SPIRIT

Davenport's tour through Connecticut led many New Englanders to ask whether what was happening was really a "Work of God." Garden's criticism of Whitefield was printed in Boston, and *The Querists* was widely circulated. A few ministers seized on Davenport's extravagance to suggest—although not yet in print—that all the excitement was merely the result of appeals to the passion and even that emotion of the sort now revealed had no place in religion. Then on September 10, 1741, Jonathan Edwards, preaching at New Haven, delivered a ringing defense of the revival. He acknowledged that "imprudencies and errors" had accompanied the Awakening, but he also put such conduct in perspective—one in which this awakening appeared far "purer" than the revival of 1734–1735. In *The Distinguishing Marks* Edwards began the process that was to make, not Divine justification, but human "affections" the principal hinge of the evangelical scheme.

Jonathan Edwards, *The Distinguishing Marks of a Work of the Spirit of God, Works,* I, 548–551, 554–555.

With this sermon, the first extended commentary on the revival to appear in New England, Edwards also began to assume his destined role as spokesman and leader of all the "people of God" in America.

The subjects of these uncommon appearances, have been of two sorts; either those who have been in great distress from an apprehension of their sin and misery; or those who have been overcome with a sweet sense of the greatness, wonderfulness, and excellency of divine things. Of the multitude of those of the former sort, that I have had opportunity to observe, there have been very few, but their distress has arisen apparently from real proper conviction, and being in a degree sensible of that which was the truth. And though I do not suppose, when such things were observed to be common, that persons have laid themselves under those violent restraints to avoid outward manifestations of their distress, that perhaps they otherwise would have done; yet there have been very few in whom there has been any appearance of feigning or affecting such manifestations, and very many for whom it would have been undoubtedly utterly impossible for them to avoid them. Generally, in these agonies they have appeared to be in the perfect exercise of their reason; and those of them who could speak, have been well able to give an account of the circumstances of their mind, and the cause of their distress, at the time, and were able to remember, and give an account of it afterwards. I have known a very few instances of those, who, in their great extremity, have for a short space been deprived, in some measure, of the use of reason; and among the many hundreds, and it may be thousands, that have lately been brought to such agonies, I never yet knew one lastingly deprived of their reason. In some that I have known, melancholy has evidently been mixed; and when it is so, the difference is very apparent;

their distresses are of another kind, and operate quite after another manner, than when their distress is from mere conviction. It is not truth only that distresses them, but many vain shadows and notions that will not give place either to Scripture or reason. Some in their great distress have not been well able to give an account of themselves, or to declare the sense they have of things, or to explain the manner and cause of their trouble to others, that yet I have had no reason to think were not under proper convictions, and in whom there has been manifested a good issue. But this will not be at all wondered at, by those who have had much to do with souls under spiritual difficulties: some things of which they are sensible, are altogether new to them; their ideas and inward sensations are new, and what they therefore know not how to express in words. Some who, on first inquiry, said they knew not what was the matter with them, have on being particularly examined and interrogated, been able to represent their case, though of themselves they could not find expressions and forms of speech to do it.

Some suppose, that terrors producing such effects are only a fright. But certainly there ought to be a distinction made between a very great fear, or extreme distress arising from an apprehension of some dreadful truth—a cause fully proportionable to such an effect—and a needless, causeless fright. The latter is of two kinds; either, first, when persons are terrified with that which is not the truth (of which I have seen very few instances unless in case of melancholy); or, secondly, when they are in a fright from some terrible outward appearance and noise, and a general notion thence arising. These apprehend, that there is something or other terrible, they know not what; without having in their minds any particular truth whatever. Of such a kind of fright I have seen very little appearance, among either old or young.

Those who are in such extremity, commonly express a great

sense of their exceeding wickedness, the multitude and aggra-
vations of their actual sins; their dreadful pollution, enmity,
and perverseness; their obstinacy and hardness of heart; a
sense of their great guilt in the sight of God; and the dreadful-
ness of the punishment due to sin. Very often they have a lively
idea of the horrible pit of eternal misery; and at the same time
it appears to them, that the great God who has them in his
hands, is exceedingly angry, and his wrath appears amazingly
terrible to them. God appears to them so much provoked, and
his great wrath so increased; that they are apprehensive of
great danger, and that he will not bear with them any longer;
but will now forthwith cut them off, and send them down to
the dreadful pit they have in view; at the same time seeing no
refuge. They see more and more of the vanity of every thing
they used to trust to, and with which they flattered themselves,
till they are brought wholly to despair in all, and to see that
they are at the disposal of the mere will of that God who is so
angry with them. Very many, in the midst of their extremity,
have been brought to an extraordinary sense of their fully
deserving that wrath, and the destruction which was then
before their eyes. They feared every moment, that it would be
executed upon them; they have been greatly convinced that
this would be altogether just, and that God is indeed absolutely
sovereign. Very often, some text of Scripture expressing God's
sovereignty, has been set home upon their minds, whereby
they have been calmed. They have been brought, as it were, to
lie at God's feet; and after great agonies, a little before light
has arisen, they have been composed and quiet, in submission
to a just and sovereign God; but their bodily strength much
spent. Sometimes their lives, to appearance, were almost gone;
and then light has appeared, and a glorious Redeemer, with his
wonderful, all-sufficient grace, has been represented to them
often, in some sweet invitation of Scripture. Sometimes the
light comes in suddenly, sometimes more gradually, filling their

souls with love, admiration, joy, and self-abasement; drawing forth their hearts after the excellent lovely Redeemer, and longings to lie in the dust before him; and that others might behold, embrace, and be delivered by him. They had longings to live to his glory; but were sensible that they can do nothing of themselves, appearing vile in their own eyes, and having much jealousy over their own hearts. And all the appearances of a real change of heart have followed; and grace has acted, from time to time, after the same manner that it used to act in those that were converted formerly, with the like difficulties, temptations, buffetings, and comforts; excepting that in many, the light and comfort have been in higher degrees than ordinary. Many very young children have been thus wrought upon. There have been some instances very much like those (Mark i. 26, and chap. ix. 26,) of whom we read, that "when the devil had cried with a loud voice, and rent them sore, he came out of them." And probably those instances were designed for a type of such things as these. Some have several turns of great agonies, before they are delivered; and others have been in such distress, which has passed off, and no deliverance at all has followed.

Some object against it as great confusion, when there is a number together in such circumstances making a noise; and say, God cannot be the author of it; because he is the God of order, not of confusion. But let it be considered, what is the proper notion of confusion, but the breaking that order of things, whereby they are properly disposed, and duly directed to their end, so that the order and due connection of means being broken, they fail of their end. Now the conviction of sinners for their conversion is the obtaining of the end of religious means. Not but that I think the persons thus extraordinarily moved, should endeavour to refrain from such outward manifestations, what they well can, and should refrain to their utmost, at the time of their solemn worship. But if God is pleased to convince the consciences of persons, so that they cannot avoid great outward manifestations, even to interrupting and breaking off those public means they were attending, I do not think this is confusion, or an unhappy interruption, any more than if a company should meet on the field to pray for rain, and should be broken off from their exercise by a plentiful shower. Would to God that all the public assemblies in the land were broken off from their public exercises with such confusion as this the next Sabbath day! We need not be sorry for breaking the order of means, by obtaining the end to which that order is directed. He who is going to fetch a treasure, need not be sorry that he is stopped, by meeting the treasure in the midst of his journey.

Besides those who are overcome with conviction and distress, I have seen many of late, who have had their bodily strength taken away with a sense of the glorious excellency of the Redeemer, and the wonders of his dying love; with a very uncommon sense of their own littleness and exceeding vileness attending it, with all expressions and appearances of the greatest abasement and abhorrence of themselves. Not only new converts, but many who were, as we hope, formerly converted, have had their love and joy attended with a flood of tears, and a great appearance of contrition and humiliation, especially for their having lived no more to God's glory since their conversion. These have had a far greater sight of their vileness, and the evil of their hearts, than ever they had; with an exceeding earnestness of desire to live better for the time to come, but attended with greater self-diffidence than ever; and many have been overcome with pity to the souls of others, and longing for their salvation.—And many other things I might mention, in this extraordinary work, answering to every one of those marks which have been insisted on. So that if the apostle John knew how to give signs of a work of the true Spirit, this is such a work.

Providence has cast my lot in a place where the work of God has *formerly* been carried on. I had the happiness to be settled in that place two years with the venerable Stoddard, and was then acquainted with a number who, during that season, were wrought upon under his ministry. I have been intimately acquainted with the experiences of many others who were wrought upon under his ministry, before that period, in a manner agreeable to the doctrine of all orthodox divines. And of late, a work has been carried on there, with very much of uncommon operations; but it is evidently the same work that was carried on there, in different periods, though attended with some new circumstances. And certainly we must throw by all talk of conversion and Christian experience; and not only so, but we must throw by our Bibles, and give up revealed religion; if this be not in general the work of God. Not that I suppose the degree of the Spirit's influence is to be determined by the degree of effect on men's bodies; or, that those are always the best experiences which have the greatest influence on the body.

And as to the imprudencies, irregularities, and mixture of delusion that has been observed; it is not at all to be wondered at, that a reformation, after a long continued and almost universal deadness, should at first, when the revival is new, be attended with such things. In the first creation God did not make a complete world at once; but there was a great deal of imperfection, darkness, and mixture of chaos and confusion, after God first said, "Let there be light," before the whole stood forth in perfect form. When God at first began his great work for the deliverance of his people, after their long-continued bondage in Egypt, there were false wonders mixed with the true for a while; which hardened the unbelieving Egyptians, and made them to doubt of the divinity of the whole work. . . .

The imprudencies and errors that have attended this work, are the less to be wondered at, if it be considered, that chiefly young persons have been the subjects of it, who have less steadiness and experience, and being in the heat of youth, are much more ready to run to extremes. Satan will keep men secure as long as he can; but when he can do that no longer, he often endeavors to drive them to extremes, and so to dishonor God, and wound religion in that way. And doubtless it has been one occasion of much misconduct, that in many places, people see plainly that their ministers have an ill opinion of the work; and therefore, with just reason, durst not apply themselves to them as their guides in it; and so are without guides.—No wonder then that when a people are as sheep without a shepherd, they wander out of the way. A people in such circumstances, stand in great and continual need of guides, and their guides stand in continual need of much more wisdom than they have of their own. And if a people have ministers that favor the work, and rejoice in it, yet it is not to be expected that either the people or ministers should know so well how to conduct themselves in such an extraordinary state of things—while it is new, and what they never had any experience of before, and time to see their tendency, consequences, and issue. The happy influence of experience is very manifest at this day, in the people among whom God has settled my abode. The work which has been carried on there this year, has been much purer than that which was wrought there six years before: it has seemed to be more purely spiritual; free from natural and corrupt mixtures, and any thing savoring of enthusiastic wildness and extravagance.

. . . Those who are now waiting to see the issue of this work, think they shall be better able to determine by and by; but probably many of them are mistaken. The Jews that saw Christ's miracles, waited to see better evidences of his being the Messiah; they wanted a sign from heaven; but they waited in vain; their stumbling-blocks did not diminish, but increase. They found no end to them, and so were more and more hardened in unbelief. Many have been praying for that glorious reformation spoken of in Scripture, who knew not what they have been praying for (as it was with the Jews when they prayed for the coming of Christ), and who, if it should come, would not acknowledge or receive it.

This pretended prudence, in persons waiting so long before they acknowledged this work, will probably in the end prove the greatest imprudence. Hereby they will fail of any share of so great a blessing, and will miss the most precious opportunity of obtaining divine light, grace, and comfort, heavenly and eternal benefits, that God ever gave in New England. While the glorious fountain is set open in so wonderful a manner, and multitudes flock to it and receive a rich supply for the wants of their souls, they stand at a distance, doubting, wondering, and receiving nothing, and are like to continue thus till the precious season is past.—It is indeed to be wondered at, that those who have doubted of the work, which has been attended with such uncommon external appearances, should be easy in their doubts, without taking thorough pains to inform themselves, by going where such things have been to be seen, narrowly observing and diligently inquiring into them; not contenting themselves with observing two or three instances, nor resting till they were fully informed by their own observation. I do not doubt but that if this course had been taken, it would have convinced all whose minds are not shut up against conviction. How greatly have they erred, who only from the uncertain reproofs of others, have ventured to speak slightly of these things! That caution of an unbelieving Jew might teach them more prudence, Acts v. 38, 39: "Refrain from these men, and let them alone; for if this counsel or this work be of men, it will come to nought; but if it be of God, ye cannot overthrow it; lest haply ye be found to fight against God." Whether what has been said in this discourse be enough to produce conviction, that this is the work of God, or not; yet I hope that for the future, they will at least hearken to the caution of Gamaliel, now mentioned; so as not to oppose it, or say any thing which has even an indirect tendency to bring it into discredit, lest they should be found opposers of the Holy Ghost. There is no kind of sins so hurtful and dangerous to the souls of men, as those committed against the Holy Ghost. We had better speak against God the Father, or the Son, than to speak against the Holy Spirit in his gracious operations on the hearts of men. Nothing will so much tend forever to prevent our having any benefit of his operations on our own souls.

If there be any who still resolutely go on to speak contemptibly of these things, I would beg of them to take heed that they be not guilty of the unpardonable sin. When the Holy Spirit is much poured out, and men's lusts, lukewarmness, and hypocrisy are reproached by its powerful operations, then is the most likely time of any, for this sin to be committed. If the work goes on, it is well if among the many that show an enmity against it, some be not guilty of this sin, if none have been already. Those who maliciously oppose and reproach this work, and call it the work of the devil, want but one thing of the unpardonable sin, and that is, doing it against inward conviction. And though some are so prudent, as not openly to oppose and reproach this work, yet it is to be feared—at this day, when the Lord is going forth so gloriously against his enemies —that many who are silent and inactive, especially ministers, will bring that curse of the angel of the Lord upon themselves, Judg. v. 23: "Curse ye Meroz, said the angel of the Lord, curse ye bitterly the inhabitants thereof: because they came not to the help of the Lord, to the help of the Lord against the mighty."

24 · *David McGregore*

(1710-177?)

THE SPIRITS OF THE PRESENT

DAY TRIED

When an expanded version of *The Distinguishing Marks* was published in Boston in late November 1741, William Cooper supplied a preface in which he stressed the revivalists' consistent invocation of such Calvinist doctrines as original sin and unconditional election. Cooper may have been answering those who, in New England as elsewhere, sought to contain the revival by fostering suspicions of Whitefield's orthodoxy. More likely, however, Cooper was testifying to the conviction—shared by Edwards in his challenge to the opposers of the revival—that behind resistance to the Awakening was a commitment to Arminianism. That such were the battle lines was the message of David McGregore, pastor of a Presbyterian church at Londonderry, New Hampshire, in a sermon delivered in Benjamin Colman's Brattle Street Church on

---

David McGregore, *The Spirits of the Present Day Tried. A Sermon at the Tuesday Evening Lecture in Brattle Street, Boston* . . . (Boston, 1742), pp. 1-3, 11-25.

November 3, 1741. McGregore defined the revival as the fulfillment of genuine and traditional Calvinism and upbraided its "enemies" as traducers of the ancient faith. In a preface to the published version of the sermon several Boston Congregational ministers saluted the Irish-born McGregore as a fellow heir to the faith once delivered to the Puritan saints. Both preface and sermon, however, indicated that the interdenominational "party of the revival," as it was coming to be known, subscribed not to the Westminster Confession, but to the newer and more rousing articles of faith set forth at Nottingham and Northampton.

I. JOHN iv. I.

Beloved, believe not every Spirit, but try the Spirits whether they be of God: because many false Prophets are gone out into the World.

We read *Rev.* 12. 12. That the Devil came down among the Inhabitants of the Earth having great Wrath because he knew his Time was short. When the strong Man armed keepeth his Palace, all his Goods are in Peace: every Thing is then as he would have it to be: his Subjects go sleeping on to Hell, and imagine themselves all the while in the direct Way to Heaven. But on the other Hand, when he perceives that his Policies begin to be detected, the Eyes of his Slaves to be opened to see their Misery and their Need of the Remedy, and that by this Means his Kingdom appears to be going to Wreck; when he sees the Standard of the great Messias erected and the Gathering of the People about it; when sees them flock thereto as a Cloud and as the Doves to their Windows; that Men are daily deserting his Government by Hundreds and Thousands, and going over to Christ the great Deliverer: When (I say) he beholds Things having such an Appearance, he then thinks it is high Time for him to bestir himself, and if possible to support his tottering Empire. To this End he convocates the black Divan, takes Counsel how he may mar God's Work most effectually: and in Pursuance of this Counsel he finds it sometimes necessary to transform himself into an Angel of Light, and to send forth his Ministers; who though inward they are ravening Wolves, yet they come in Sheeps Cloathing: and partly by hellish Lies, partly by aggravating some real Indiscretions, partly by false Parallels, perverting some Texts of Scripture, and misapplying others; they put some of the weaker even of God's own Children to a Stand to that Degree that they know not for some Time what to say: So that they would deceive (were it possible) the very Elect.

Thus it is in this glorious Day of Gospel Grace. As the good Spirit appears to be striving in a remarkable Manner; So Satan and his Instruments, we have Reason to think, are very industrious: Yea so cunningly does this insiduous Adversary manage, that he sometimes gets good Men engaged upon his Side. We have great Reason to fear that it is now a Time in various Places in which there is Ground for the repeating of God's Complaint by his Prophet *Hos.* 4. 6. My People are destroyed for lack of Knowledge; that those who lead them cause them to err: and that by this Means God's Name continually every Day is blasphemed. But blessed be God, that we have our Bibles. So that if it should happen at any Time that those whose Lips ought to preserve Knowledge, should themselves turn aside from the Ways of God either in Doctrine or Morals; that in this Case we are not obliged to follow them implicitly, but that we have a sure Word of Prophesy even the *Law* and Testimony for our Rule, and also the *Promise* that if we ask the Holy Spirit we shall receive him. In sum, we have great Reason to be thankful that our God has given us Liberty and put us in a Capacity of judging for our selves. That I may therefore have an Opportunity of shewing the Necessity and Importance of using this our Christian Liberty aright in trying the Spirits whether they be of God; I have chosen to speak from the above Text as the Ground of the following Discourse: where the Apostle says, *Beloved, believe not every Spirit, but try the Spirits whether they be of God:* &c. . . .

. . . And that I may proceed the more distinctly I shall essay to try (1.) the Spirit of the *Promoters*, (2.) of the *Opposers* of the present Work: and then let every one judge for himself and say, which appears to be most of God. . . .

. . . And in the doing of this I shall essay to try them. (1.) With respect of their *Doctrine*. (2.) With Respect to the *Manner of Life*. (3.) With Respect to their *Labours*. And (4.) With Respect to the *Effects* their Labours have produced.

1. I shall essay to try them with Respect to their *Doctrine*. This is one excellent Mark by which Christians may distinguish between true and false Teachers; and therefore we have it prescribed as a Rule by which we may discern between the Spirit of CHRIST and the Spirit of *Antichrist*, in the Context. Let a Person be never so sober & blameless in his Walk, let him make never so high Pretences to Inspiration or divine Revelation; yet if he bring any Doctrine contrary to Godliness, or which is subversive of the genuine Doctrines of the Gospel, we are not to believe that the Spirit by which he is acted is of God. . . . Now the *Doctrines* which the *Promoters* of this Work teach, are the Doctrines of the *Gospel*, the Doctrines of the *Apostle's Creed*, of the 39 *Articles of the Church of England*, and of the *Westminster Confession of Faith*. To these they often appeal for the Truth of what they preach.—More particularly these Men are careful to teach and inculcate the great Doctrine of *Original Sin*, in Opposition to *Pelagius, Arminius*, and their respective Followers. That this Sin has actually descended from *Adam*, the natural and federal Head, to all his Posterity proceeding from him by ordinary Generation; that

hereby the Understanding is darkened, the Will depraved, and the Affections under the Influence of a wrong Biass, to that Degree that they are utterly indisposed to any Thing that is spiritually good; that Man, as a sad Consequence of the Fall, has lost all Power in Things spiritual. This Doctrine they insist upon, in Order to humble the Pride of Man, to drive him out of himself, and convince him of his own Emptiness?—They teach likewise with due Care the Doctrine of the *Imputation of the Righteousness of the* second *Adam,* viz. JESUS CHRIST, God equal and of the same Substance with the Father, in Order to atone for the Guilt and Cleanse from the Pollution of that Sin descended upon fallen Man from the first *Adam;* that he must be made to Sinners Wisdom, Righteousness, Sanctification, and Redemption; and that he is the Lord our Righteousness, Jer. 23. 6. As also that this Righteousness is apprehended and applied by *Faith* alone, without the Deeds of the Law; that all Works are and consequently all boasting is excluded; that though Works have no Part in our Justification, yet the Faith which justifies the Soul is lively and operative; that which justifies it self in the Sight of the World by Works, which purifies the Soul from the Pollution of Sin, and influences the Person who has it to bring forth the Fruits of new Obedience. They teach likewise that this *Faith is the Gift of God;* that a Man cannot believe by any inherent Power of his own; and that yet notwithstanding Faith being our Act and a commanded Duty, we are to endeavour to believe; and with a due Sense of our own Insufficiency and a humble Dependance upon GOD for Strength, we are to strive to exert the vital Act.—As to *Conversion* or *Regeneration,* they hold this to be absolutely necessary; that the Tree must be made good, before the Fruit be so; that except a Man undergo a supernatural Change by the Operation of the Holy Ghost upon his Soul, or be born of Water and of the Spirit, he cannot enter into the Kingdom of God. And in as much as they find that Man in his

natural State is full of Self-Conceit, that in his own Opinion he
is rich and increased in Goods and stands in need of Nothing,
or as *Job* expresses it, That vain Man would be wise, though he
be born like the wild Asses Colt; they therefore in their Preaching make use of the *Terrors of the Law:* they use the Law, as
God has appointed it to be used, viz. in a Subserviency to the
Gospel, or as a Schoolmaster to bring Men to Christ, *Gal.* 3. 24.
But to say that the Law is the only Topick on which they
constantly insist, endeavouring to work on the lower Passions,
and to drive Men with slavish Fear like brute Creatures, is
false and slanderous. They preach also the *Consolations of the
Gospel,* the intrinsick Beauty of Holiness, and the Reasonableness of Christ's Service.—As to THE SPIRIT, I never heard that
the most considerable Promoters of this Work pretended to the
extraordinary Gifts thereof that were peculiar to the apostolick
Age. I believe I might venture to challenge their Adversaries
to shew that they pretend to the Spirit in any other Sense, than
in his convincing, enlightning, directing and comforting Influences. And in these Respects the Spirit is the Priviledge of all
true Believers. . . .

I am aware it may be said by some; but why do these Men
insist so much upon *Original Sin,* upon the *New-Birth,* and
Justification by Faith alone? Are there not other Doctrines to
be preached as well as these? and is it not the Business of a
Gospel-Minister to declare the whole Counsel of God? To
which I answer 1. That I deny that they always insist upon
these particular Doctrines. 2. I take these to be some of the
Reasons why they insist so much upon them. (1.) Because
these are great important Doctrines. Justification by Faith (as
Luther has observed) is the Article of a standing or falling
Church. And indeed we cannot deny the Observation to be
just, if we allow what the Apostle says, viz. that *if Righteousness come by the Law,* CHRIST *is dead in vain.* (2.) Because
'tis exceeding difficult to bring vain conceited Man in a firm

and stedfast Belief of them. (3.) Another Reason why they insist so much upon these Doctrines is because others insist so little upon them: Nay, some do openly deny them; deny the Necessity of supernatural Grace, hold the Power of Man's Will in Things spiritual, say that we are justified partly by Faith and partly by Obedience, and that CHRIST's Righteousness was only to make up the Defects of our Righteousness. Is it not high Time for all who are faithful to CHRIST's Cause, to appear for and inculcate these Doctrines, when CHRIST is thus wounded in the House of his professed Friends? When the very Foundations of our Religion are shaken, and the distinguishing Doctrines of Christianity are explain'd away? For this I may venture to say; that *Arminianism* tends to *Deism,* and *Deism* superceeds the Christian Scheme: no need of CHRIST to do that which we are supposed to have Power to do our selves; *If Righteousness come by the Law, then* CHRIST *is dead in vain.*

2. Let us try them with Respect to their *Manner of Life.* And can it be denied that this has been very exemplary and heavenly? I grant indeed, that this of it self is no Proof of their being sent of God, if their *Doctrines* were false. The Character of *Socinus* was wise, grave, religious, &c. But when Purity of *Doctrine* & *Life* go together; both united make a very strong Evidence. Now the most famous and successful of them do evidently appear to have much of their Conversation in Heaven, to have got a great Degree of Knowledge of their own Hearts. What a sweet forgiving Spirit do they shew to their most virulent and bitter Enemies? What *Lambs* are they in their own Cause, and yet what *Lions* in CHRIST's? We see an Example of this with Respect to Mr. *Wesley* and Mr. *Whitefield:* The latter of these had a most endeared Affection for the former; and yet, he, viz. *Wesley,* had no sooner stricken at the great Doctrines of Election and the Saints final Perseverance, but the *other* appears openly against him: Thereby shewing

that the Cause of CHRIST was dearer to him than any Friend he had upon Earth, and that he knew no Man after the Flesh, 2 *Cor.* 5. 16.

3. Let us try them with Respect to their *abundant Labours.* And have not several of them been eminent Followers of CHRIST? In this Particular how zealous are they about their Master's Business? How are these Angels or Messengers of God caused to fly swiftly in publishing the everlasting Gospel to them that dwell upon the Earth? What prodigious Fatigue of Body and Mind do they expose themselves to, out of a tender Love to Souls? And how wonderfully are they supported in all their Toil? . . .

4. Let us next try them with Respect to the *Effects* that *their Labours* have produced, and can any have the Front to deny that these have been good? Have not covetous Worldings in a great Measure had their Affections weaned from the Things of the Earth, and set upon those Things that are above: Are there not innumerable Instances of Swearers, Drunkards, unclean Persons, Tattlers, Liars, Sabbath-breakers, &c. who have left off their favourite Vices; have cut off the right Hand, and plucked out the right Eye? Have not several pharisaical self justifying Persons, who thought themselves in a very good State before, had their sandy Foundations discovered; so that they have been made to alter their Tone, and instead of saying *God I thank thee that I am not as other Men are,* they have been made to cry, *Lord be merciful to us Sinners?* Have not many had their secret Sins so particularly touched by the penetrating Sword of God's Spirit, that they have been made to cry out with the Woman of *Samaria, Come see a Man that told me all that ever I did?* Have not many seen both the Heinousness of Sin, and the Desirableness of CHRIST, with other Eyes than ever they did before? Have found a Sweetness in the Bible, a Delight in secret Prayer, and Christian Conference, and Meditation, that before they were Strangers to? Has not Bigotry

been very much subdued? And many of late have so learned CHRIST, as to esteem one another as Christians, and not to place the Kingdom of Heaven in Meats and Drinks? Yea, has not God in his just Sovereignty been revealing the Mysteries of his Kingdom to Babes, while he has hid them from the wise and prudent? Have not little Children been heard singing *Hosanna* to the SON of *David?* God thus perfecting Praises from the Mouth of Babes and Sucklings, and to the stilling of the Enemy and the Avenger.—O my Brethren, are any of you under the malignant Influence of such a woful Prejudice, as to imagine that *these* and many other such desirable *Effects* are the Works of the Devil? It is my Hope and shall be my Prayer that God will remove your Prejudices. . . .

1. Let us try them with Respect to their *Doctrine.* And it will be found upon Examination that some of the most violent Opposers are Men of *Arminian, Pelagian,* and *Deistical* Principles. This is too evident to be denied: Several of them being such as scoff at the Imputation of Original Sin, who deny the Doctrine of Justification by Faith alone, as likewise the high Doctrine of Predestination: And who do strongly assert Man's natural Powers in Things spiritual. I foresee indeed that it may be said that all who oppose the present Work are not Men of such Principles, granting some be. I answer, I charitably hope they are not: But I should rejoice that they would give less Reason, to suspect them of verging that Way.—Is it not a Truth too plain to be denied, that there has been of late a great Growth of the subtile Error of *Arminius* in the protestant World? And I wish I could say that our Side of the *Atlantick* were free of it. Why then are they not more careful to preach against it, to tell their People of the Danger of it, to shew them that it is destructive to true Christianity.—In a Word, when they appear as zealous against it, and make as loud a Cry concerning the Danger of it, as they do against the *New Schemers*

as they affect to term them: We shall then have more Room for Charity towards them in this Regard.

After all, I do charitably believe that there are some weaker Brethren, both of Ministers and People, who are led in to oppose this Work, and yet are no Arminians; but are sound in the Doctrines of Predestination, supernatural Grace, and Justification by Faith alone: But in the mean Time, I believe that the *principal* and *most inveterate Opposers* are Men of *Arminian* and *Pelagian* Principles, and that these others are only Deputy or second Hand Opposers. They are like the two Hundred Men who went up with *Absalom* from *Jerusalem* at the Time of Rebellion: But were not made privy to the Plot? 'Tis said of them that they went in their *Simplicity* and knew not any Thing.— As these are honest in the main; there is the better Ground to hope that God in his own good Time will undeceive them, and let them see their Error. And thus far with Respect to their *Doctrine.*

I come next to try them with Respect to the *Spirit or Temper* with which they oppose the present Work. I shall shew a few of the *Properties of this Spirit,* which in an obvious Manner do discover themselves in the Opposers.   As

1. *Many of them* seem to be acted by a *lying Spirit.* That same Father of Lies, who was a lying Spirit in the Mouth of *Ahab*'s Prophets, is still in Being: And indeed if ever Hell seem'd to be broken loose in horrid Lies and Calumny, now appears to be the Time. I would not say that all who oppose the present Work are wilful Liars because I would be as charitable as possible: but this seems to be the Case; viz. some hatch the Lies, and others labouring under the malignant Influence of a prejudiced Mind do too easily believe them and report them for Truths. How else I pray comes it to pass that so many horrid Lies are forged?—Has not Mr. *Whitefield* been represented as a base, mercenary, covetous Man, one who goes about gathering Money to make an Estate for himself?—Have

not both he and Messieurs the *Erskine's*[1] in *Scotland* been represented as Persons in Confederacy with the Pope, as employ'd by the Man of Sin to bring over People to the cursed Errors of the Church of *Rome?* Have not several of their Doctrines been grosly misrepresented, as any Person may see who will read with Candour what they have written in their own Defence? Have not their unguarded Expressions been laid hold of, yea Words put upon the Rack to extort Meanings from them which it is plain the Authors never intended?—Are there not some who are exceeding industrious in endeavouring to make People believe, that these Men hold it as a Principle, that a few Tears and some Convulsion-like Fits are of themselves sufficient Evidences of a Work of God?—That they pretend to the Gifts of discerning Spirits to such a Degree as to know whether a Person be converted or not by looking in his Face, or by a few Words Discourse with him?—That all converted Persons behoove to be able to give Account of their Conversion with Respect to its Time, Manner, and other Circumstances?—But it would swell to a Volumn to repeat one half of the Slander that is cast upon them. The same Game is play'd against them, which was by the Church of *Rome* against our *Reformers* from Popery, and by the *Scribes* and *Pharisees* against our blessed LORD and his *Apostles.*—Now my Brethren, Say I beseech you what Spirit these Lies do proceed from: Whither it is most probable that they come from the God of Truth or the Father of Lies. One would think a good Cause did not need such Props as these to support it.

2. As it is a lying so it is a most *uncharitable Spirit.* The Opposers of the present Work do blame the Promoters of the same for want of Charity; because these preach (as they say) too much Terror, and make the Gate of Heaven too strait: But

---

[1] Ebenezer Erskine (1680–1754) and his brother, Ralph (1685–1752), were leaders of the revival in Scotland and of the Presbyterian Secession. [Ed.]

what I pray can be more uncharitable than to represent this whole Work in a general undistinguished Manner as the Work of the Devil? To say it is nothing but Phanaticism and Enthusiasm? That it is like a Bubble upon the Water which will quickly be gone? That the Men who promote it are wandering Stars, or blazing Comets, or like raging Waves of the Sea foaming out their own Shame? Are these the Gentlemen of such extensive Charity! Is this the Wisdom that cometh from above; which is pure, peaceable, gentle, easy to be entreated? This that Charity described by the Apostle, I *Cor.* 13? Which vaunteth not it self, doth not behave it self unseemly, which thinketh no Evil? If this be Charity, may God deliver me from the Effects of it! O my Soul come not thou into their Secret, into their Assembly mine Honour be not thou united. *Gen.* 49. 6.

3. As it is an uncharitable so it is an *envious Spirit.*—Envy is a most diabolical Passion: This is thought to be one of the prime Causes of the Devil's first Rebellion against his Creator: And it were to be wished that there was not one Fibre of this cursed Root in Ministers, alas, does not the Conduct of some of them give too much Ground to suspect that they envy the Success of the Lord's Work in the Hands of their Brethren:— That which ought to be Matter of Joy to them, seems to irritate their Spleen, and to fill them with a peevish Discontent. O that such Ministers had more of the Spirit of *Moses;* who when he was told that *Eldad* and *Medad* prophesied in the Camp and desired to forbid them, says to the Messenger, *Enviest thou for my Sake? would to God that all the Lord's People were Prophets* &c.—Or that of *John Baptist;* who rejoiced at the growing Fame of Jesus, saying, HE *must encrease, but I must decrease.*—Or that of *Paul;* who rejoiced that Christ was preached though by some out of Envy and Strife.—O that Ministers instead of weakening, would endeavour to strengthen each others Hands; that they would rejoice in each others Use-

fulness. Is not the Harvest plenty? Are not the Labourers few? Is there not Work enough for all in the spacious Vineyard of Christ? Why need they then stand quarreling with one another; when there is so much planting, watering, pruning and cultivating to be done?

4. As it is an envious so it is a *partial Spirit*. The Apostle *James* gives it as one of the Properties of the *Wisdom that cometh from above,* that it is *without Partiality.*—There is no Perfection in this corrupt sinful State. Many Blemishes are to be seen in the Life of the most eminent Saint; which are the inevitable Consequents of human Frailty and Remains of a Body of Sin and Death. So that if all the Defects of any Author, all the Blemishes of any Person, all the Imprudencies in the Management of any Cause be industriously gathered together and magnified, and in the mean Time no Mention made of that which is commendable in them; it will make the best Person or Cause in the World look with a dark and gloomy Aspect. As for Instance look into the Life of *David* the Man after God's own Heart: Gather all the Blemishes thereof together, his Lying, his vain Glory, his Cruelty, his Murder, his Adultery; and in the mean Time, suffer Partiality to draw a Vail over the bright Part of his Character, which shall conceal whatsoever was excellent in him: And this Picture of him so drawn, shall be so far from amiable, that it will look monstrous and deformed.

Now I appeal to Facts, whither this be not the practice of many of the Opposers of the present Work? They constantly pore upon the dark Side of it: whatever they can hear of that, they imagine will cast a Slur upon it; they greedily lay hold of, and magnify with all their Art and Eloquence. If a Friend of the Work be imprudent, or unguarded in any Part of his Conduct; this shall be industriously improv'd, but not a Word said of what is commendable in him. If he drop an Expression that is somewhat ambiguous, they will be sure to interpret it in the worst Sense: Nor do they stop here, but give out that this is the Opinion of the whole Party.—I appeal to the unprejudiced, whither this be candid, impartial treatment?

5. Lastly, As it is a partial so it is a *profane mocking Spirit.*— I am grieved at Heart that I have Occasion to mention this: But let any Man peruse the Writings of Commissary *Garden* in *Carolina,* and compare these with some ludicrous sarcastical Language that is vented in other Places, both from Press and Pulpit, and then say whether this be a false Charge.—*Felix* trembled when *Paul* reasoned of Righteousness, of Temperance and Judgment to come.—Soul Concern had the same Effect upon the *Jailor.* . . . But now in our Days when God's Word and Spirit produce the same Effects with those mentioned in the above quoted Texts; these Things are all vilified, and undervalued. Men are made to believe that there is no need of Tears and deep Sorrow for Sin; the Work of Conversion may be done in a more smooth, rational and easy Way; that these are no probable Symptoms of a Work of God; they may be all accounted for from physical and mecanical Principles;—Persons must not entertain religious Conversation, use mutual Freedom in talking over their Experiences and communing about the State of their Souls; this favours too much of hypocritical Ostentation, and is inconsistent with Decency and Politeness,—By this Means, alas, alas, the bruised Reed is broken and the smoking Flax quenched; Men are rocked asleep in the Cradle of carnal Security; and instead of being put upon Soul Enquiry, they are made to believe that they are well enough already: So that they go smoothly down the Stream to Hell, singing *Agag's Requiem* to themselves, that *surely the Bitterness of Death is already past.*—O that God would give such Ministers to see what they are doing; whose Interest they are serving, while they are filling the Minds of poor People with groundless Prejudices against the Work of God.

25 · *Charles Chauncy*

(1705-1787)

ENTHUSIASM DESCRIBED AND

CAUTION'D AGAINST

McGregore's sermon, designed as it was to provoke in the laity an animosity toward the ministers who did not support the revival, was the goad that drove the critics of the Awakening into print at last. Whatever the reasons for this delay, it is a fact that the first use of heavy intellectual artillery against enthusiasm by a Congregational minister was Charles Chauncy's sermon of the Sunday following the Harvard Commencement of 1742. Up to this moment Chauncy, the grandson of a Harvard president, had not openly committed his full prestige to the battle. He had written a pamphlet (published anonymously in London) describing the early months of the revival in language that led Whitefield to take it as a personal attack. In several sermons, moreover, Chauncy had warned against the "fashionable" practice of flocking to hear only those min-

------

Charles Chauncy, *Enthusiasm described and caution'd against. A Sermon Preach'd . . . the Lord's Day after the Commencement . . .* (Boston, 1742), pp. 1-27.

isters whose "gifts" were for warm and zealous preaching. He had not, however, clearly condemned the revival, though his very silences, especially as contrasted to the expressed admiration of his colleague, Thomas Foxcroft, for "evangelic preaching," were eloquent. With his sermon on enthusiasm, however, delivered as it was on an occasion that drew many of the Massachusetts clergy into the metropolis, Chauncy was immediately acknowledged to be the leader of all New Englanders who resented or feared the emotions of the revival.

I COR. XIV. xxxvii.
If any Man among you think himself to be a PROPHET, *or* SPIRITUAL, *let him acknowledge that the Things that I write unto you are the Commandments of the* LORD.

MANY Things were amiss in the *Church* of *Corinth,* when *Paul* wrote this Epistle to them. There were envyings, strife and divisions among them, on account of their ministers. Some cried up one, others another: one said, I am of PAUL, another I am of APPOLLOS. They had form'd themselves into parties, and each party so admired the teacher they followed, as to reflect unjust contempt on the other.

Nor was this their only fault. A spirit of pride prevailed exceedingly among them. They were conceited of their gifts, and too generally dispos'd to make an ostentatious shew of them. From this vain glorious temper proceeded the forwardness of those that had the *gift* of *tongues,* to speak in languages which others did not understand, to the disturbance, rather than edification of the church: And from the same principle it arose, that they spake not by turns, but several at once, in the same place of worship, to the introducing such confusion, that they were in danger of being tho't mad.

Nor were they without some pretence to justify these disorders. Their great plea was, that in these things they were guided by the Spirit, acted under his immediate influence and direction. This seems plainly insinuated in the words I have read to you. *If any man think himself to be a prophet, or spiritual, let him acknowledge that the things that I write unto you are the commandments of the Lord.* As if the apostle had said, you may imagine your selves to be *spiritual* men, to be under a divine afflatus in what you do; but 'tis all imagination, meer pretence, unless you pay a due regard to the *commandments* I have here *wrote to you;* receiving them not as the *word of man, but of* GOD. Make trial of your spiritual pretences by this rule: If you can submit to it, and will order your conduct by it, well; otherwise you only cheat yourselves, while you think yourselves to be *spiritual* men, or *prophets:* You are nothing better than Enthusiasts; your being acted by SPIRIT, immediately guided and influenced by him, is meer pretence; you have no good reason to believe any such thing.

From the words thus explained, I shall take occasion to discourse to you upon the following Particulars.

I. I shall give you some account of *Enthusiasm,* in its *nature* and *influence.*

II. Point you to a rule by which you may judge of persons, whether they are under the influence of *Enthusiasm.*

III. Say what may be proper to guard you against this unhappy turn of mind.

The whole will then be follow'd with some suitable Application

I. I am in the first place, to give you some account of *Enthusiasm.* And as this a thing much talk'd of at present, more perhaps than at any other time that has pass'd over us, it will not be tho't unseasonable, if I take some pains to let you into a true understanding of it.

The word, from it's Etymology, carries in it a good meaning, as signifying *inspiration from* God: in which sense, the prophets under the old testament, and the apostles under the new, might properly be called *Enthusiasts.* For they were under a divine influence, spake as moved by the HOLY GHOST, and did such things as can be accounted for in no way, but by recurring to an immediate extraordinary power, present with them.

But the word is more commonly used in a bad sense, as intending an *imaginary,* not a *real* inspiration: according to which sense, the *Enthusiast* is one, who has a conceit of himself as a person favoured with the extraordinary presence of the *Deity.* He mistakes the workings of his own passions for divine communications, and fancies himself immediately inspired by the SPIRIT of God, when all the while, he is under no other influence than that of an over-heated imagination.

The cause of this *enthusiasm* is a bad temperament of the blood and spirits; 'tis properly a disease, a sort of madness: And there are few; perhaps none at all, but are subject to it, tho' none are so much in danger of it as those, in whom *melancholy* is the prevailing ingredient in their constitution. In these it often reigns; and sometimes to so great a degree, that they are really beside themselves, acting as truly by the blind impetus of a wild fancy, as tho' they had neither reason nor understanding.

And various are the ways in which their *enthusiasm* discovers itself.

Sometimes, it may be seen in their countenance. A certain wildness is discernable in their general look and air; especially when their imaginations are mov'd and fired.

Sometimes, it strangely loosens their tongues, and gives them such an energy, as well as fluency and volubility in speaking, as they themselves, by their utmost efforts, can't so much as imitate, when they are not under the enthusiastick influence.

Sometimes, it affects their bodies, throws them into convulsions and distortions, into quakings and tremblings. This was formerly common among the people called *Quakers*. I was myself, when a Lad, an eye witness to such violent agitations and foamings, in a boisterous female speaker, as I could not behold but with surprize and wonder.

Sometimes, it will unaccountably mix itself with their conduct, and give it such a tincture of that which is freakish or furious, as none can have an idea of, but those who have seen the behaviour of a person in a phrenzy.

Sometimes, it appears in their imaginary peculiar intimacy with heaven. They are, in their own opinion, the special favourites of GOD, have more familiar converse with him than other good men, and receive immediate, extraordinary communications from him. The tho'ts, which suddenly rise up in their minds, they take for suggestions of the SPIRIT; their very fancies are divine illuminations; nor are they strongly inclin'd to any thing, but 'tis an impulse from GOD, a plain revelation of his will.

And what extravagances, in this temper of mind, are they not capable of, and under the specious pretext too of paying obedience to the authority of GOD? Many have fancied themselves acting by immediate warrant from heaven, while they have been committing the most undoubted wickedness. There is indeed scarce any thing so wild, either in *speculation* or *practice,* but they have given into it: They have, in many instances, been blasphemers of GOD, and open disturbers of the peace of the world.

But in nothing does the *enthusiasm* of these persons discover it self more, than in the disregard they express to the Dictates of *reason.* They are above the force of argument, beyond conviction from a calm and sober address to their understandings. As for them, they are distinguish'd persons; GOD himself speaks inwardly and immediately to their souls. "They see the light infused into their understandings, and cannot be mistaken; 'tis clear and visible there, like the light of bright sunshine; shews it self and needs no other proof but its own evidence. They feel the hand of GOD moving them within, and the impulses of his SPIRIT; and cannot be mistaken in what they feel. Thus they support themselves, and are sure reason hath nothing to do with what they see and feel. What they have a sensible experience of, admits no doubt, needs no probation".[1] And in vain will you endeavour to convince such persons of any mistakes they are fallen into. They are certainly in the right, and know themselves to be so. They have the SPIRIT opening their understandings and revealing the truth to them. They believe only as he has taught them: and to suspect they are in the wrong is to do dishonour to the SPIRIT; 'tis to oppose his dictates, to set up their own wisdom in opposition to his, and shut their eyes against that light with which he has shined into their souls. They are not therefore capable of being argued with; you had as good reason with the wind.

And as the natural consequence of their being thus sure of every thing, they are not only infinitely stiff and tenacious, but impatient of contradiction, censorious and uncharitable: they encourage a good opinion of none but such as are in their way of thinking and speaking. Those, to be sure, who venture to debate with them about their errors and mistakes, their weaknesses and indiscretions, run the hazard of being stigmatiz'd by them as poor unconverted wretches, without the SPIRIT, under the government of carnal reason, enemies to GOD and religion, and in the broad way to hell.

They are likewise positive and dogmatical, vainly fond of their own imaginations, and invincibly set upon propagating them: And in the doing of this, their Powers being awakened, and put as it were, upon the stretch, from the strong impressions they are under, that they are authorized by the immedi-

---

[1] John Locke, *An Essay Concerning Human Understanding*, Book IV, Ch. 19. [Ed.]

ate command of GOD himself, they sometimes exert themselves with a sort of *extatic* violence: And 'tis this that gives them the advantage, among the less knowing and judicious, of those who are modest, suspicious of themselves, and not too assuming in matters of conscience and salvation. The extraordinary fervour of their minds, accompanied with uncommon bodily motions, and an excessive confidence and assurance gains them great reputation among the populace; who speak of them as *men of GOD* in distinction from all others, and too commonly hearken to, and revere their dictates, as tho' they really were, as they pretend, immediately communicated to them from the DIVINE SPIRIT.

This is the nature of *Enthusiasm,* and this its operation, in a less or greater degree, in all who are under the influence of it. 'Tis a kind of religious Phrenzy, and evidently discovers it self to be so, whenever it rises to any great height.

And much to be pitied are the persons who are seized with it. Our compassion commonly works towards those, who, while under distraction, fondly imagine themselves to be Kings and Emperors: And the like pity is really due to those, who, under the power of *enthusiasm,* fancy themselves to be *prophets; inspired of God,* and *immediately called and commissioned by him to deliver his messages to the world:* And tho' they should run into disorders, and act in a manner that cannot but be condemned, they should notwithstanding be treated with tenderness and lenity; and the rather, because they don't commonly act so much under the influence of a *bad mind,* as a *deluded imagination.* And who more worthy of christian pity than those, who, under the notion of serving GOD and the interest of religion, are filled with zeal, and exert themselves to the utmost, while all the time they are hurting and wounding the very cause they take so much pains to advance. 'Tis really a pitiable case: And tho' the honesty of their intentions won't legitimate their bad actions, yet it very much alleviates their guilt: We should think as favourably of them as may be, and be dispos'd to judge with mercy, as we would hope to obtain mercy.

But I come

II. In the second place, to point you to a *rule* by which you may judge of persons, whether they are *enthusiasts,* meer pretenders to the immediate guidance and influence of the SPIRIT. And this is, in general, *a regard to the bible, an acknowledgment that the things therein contained are the commandments of GOD.* This is the rule in the text. And 'tis an infallible rule of tryal in this matter: We need not fear judging amiss, while we keep closely to it.

'Tis true, it wont certainly follow, that a man, pretending to be a *prophet,* or *spiritual,* really is so, if he owns the *bible,* and receives the truths therein revealed as the mind of GOD: But the conclusion, on the other hand, is clear and certain; if he pretends to be conducted by the SPIRIT, and disregards the scripture, pays no due reverence to *the things there delivered as the commandments of GOD,* he is a meer pretender, be his pretences ever so bold and confident, or made with ever so much seeming seriousness, gravity, or solemnity.

And the reason of this is obvious; viz. that the things contained in the scripture were wrote by holy men as they were moved by the HOLY GHOST: they were received from GOD, and committed to writing under his immediate, extraordinary influence and guidance. And the divine, ever-blessed SPIRIT is consistent with himself. He cannot be suppos'd to be the author of any *private* revelations that are contradictory to the *public standing* ones, which he has preserved in the world to this day. This would be to set the SPIRIT of truth at variance with himself; than which a greater reproach can't be cast upon him. 'Tis therefore as true, that those are *enthusiastical,* who pretend to the SPIRIT, and at the same time express a disregard to the scripture, as that the SPIRIT is the great revealer of the things therein declared to us. And we may depend upon the certainty of this conclusion. We have warrant to do so from the *inspired Paul;* and we have the more reason to rely upon the rule he has given us, as he has made it evident to the world, that he was a *prophet,* and *spiritual,* by signs and wonders which he did before the people, by the power of the SPIRIT of GOD.

But the *rule* in the text is yet more particular. It refers especially to *the things wrote by the apostle* PAUL, and which he wrote to the *church of Corinth,* to rectify the *disorders* that had crept in among them. And whoever the person be, that pretends to be *spiritual,* to be under the extraordinary guidance of the SPIRIT, and yet acts in contradiction to what the apostle has here wrote, he vainly imagines himself to be under the special guidance of the SPIRIT; he is a downright *enthusiast.*

And here suffer me to make particular mention of some of the things, the apostle has wrote in *this Epistle,* which, whoever will not acknowledge, in *deed* as well as *word,* to be the *commandments of GOD,* they are not guided by the SPIRIT, but vainly pretend to be so.

The first thing, in this kind, I would mention, is that which relates to *Ministers;* condemning an undue preference of one to another, the holding one in such admiration as to reflect disgrace on another. This was one of the disorders the Apostle takes notice of, as prevailing in the *church* of *Corinth;* and he is particular in his care to give check to this unchristian spirit, which had crumbled them into parties, and introduced among them faction and contention.

Now, whoever, under the pretence of being guided by the spirit, set up one minister in opposition to another, glory in this minister to the throwing undue contempt on that, thereby obstructing his usefulness, and making way for strife and divisions, they are not really acted by the SPIRIT, whatever they may pretend. For they evidently contradict what the apostle has wrote upon this very head: And if *he* was inspired, the spirit *they* are influenced by, cannot be the SPIRIT of GOD.

Not that one minister may not be preferr'd to another; this is reasonable: But no minister ought to be regarded, as tho' he was the author of our faith; nor, let his gifts and graces be what they will, is he to be so esteemed, as that others must be neglected, or treated in an unbecoming manner. But I shall not enlarge here, having spoken fully to this point, in a Sermon you may, some of you, have in your hands.

Another thing the apostle is particular in writing upon, is the *commandment* of *charity*. And this he declares to be a matter of such essential importance in true christianity, that if a man is really destitute of it, he is nothing, in the sight of GOD: Nay, tho' his pretences, his attainments, his gifts, be ever so extraordinary or miraculous; still, if he is without charity he will certainly be rejected of GOD and the LORD JESUS CHRIST. This is beautifully represented in the three first verses of the 13th chapter of this Epistle, in some of the boldest figures. "Tho' I speak, says the apostle, with the tongues of men and of angels, and have not charity, I am become as sounding brass, or a tinkling cymbal. And tho' I have the gift of prophecy, and understand all mysteries and all knowledge; and tho' I have all faith, so that I could remove mountains, and have not charity, I am nothing. And tho' I bestow all my goods to feed the poor, and tho' I give my body to be burned, and have not charity, it profiteth me nothing." As if the apostle had said, tho' a man had the languages of all nations, and could speak with the eloquence of angels; tho', like an inspired prophet, he had understanding in the deep counsels of GOD, and knew even all things sacred and divine; tho' he had the faith of miracles, and could do impossibilities; tho' he had the zeal of a martyr, and should give his body to be burned; tho' he had a disposition to almsgiving, and should bestow upon the poor his whole substance; still, if he was without charity, "that charity which suffereth long, and is kind; that charity which envyeth not, vaunteth not it self, is not puffed up; that charity which behaveth not it self unseemly, seeketh not her own, is not easily provoked, thinketh no evil, rejoiceth not in iniquity, but rejoiceth in the truth; that charity, in fine, which beareth all things, believeth all things, hopeth all things, endureth all things": I say, if he was without this charity, this love of his neighbour, these things would be all nothing; he would notwithstanding be out of favour with God, without any interest in Christ, and in such circumstances, as that unless there was a change in them, he would certainly perish.

This, in sum, is what the apostle has, in a distinct and peremptory manner, delivered concerning charity.

And in vain may any pretend to be under the extraordinary guidance of the Spirit, while in their practice they trample upon this law of christian love. Men may talk of their *impulses* and *impressions,* conceive of them as the call of God, and go about, as moved by them, from place to place, imagining they are sent of God, and immediately commissioned by him: But if they are censorious and uncharitable; if they harbour in their minds evil surmisings of their brethren; if they slander and reproach them; if they claim a right to look into their hearts, make it their business to judge of their state, and proclaim them hypocrites, carnal unregenerate sinners, when at the same time they are visibly of a good conversation in Christ; I say, when this is the practice of any, they do not acknowledge what the inspired Paul has here *wrote as the commandment of GOD:* They are not therefore acted by the same Spirit with which he spake; but are evidently under a spirit of delusion: And this is so obviously the case, that there is no reasonable room to doubt upon the matter.

Charity, my brethren, is the commandment of the gospel by way of eminence. 'Tis the grand mark by which christians are to distinguish themselves from all others. *By this,* says our

Saviour,[2] *shall all men know that ye are my disciples, if ye have love to one another:* Yea, this is the grand criterion by which we are to judge, whither God *dwelleth in us by his* SPIRIT. *If we love one another, GOD dwelleth in us.*[3] And in the following Verse, *Hereby,* i.e. by our loving one another, *we know that we dwell in him, and he in us, because he hath given us of his* SPIRIT. To pretend therefore that we are led by the SPIRIT, and are under his extraordinary influence, when, in contradiction to the plain laws of Jesus Christ, revealed by the SPIRIT, we *judge our brother,* and *set at naught our brother,* and plead a right to do so, and are in a disposition TO THANK GOD, THAT WE ARE ENABLED TO DO SO; there is not a more sure mark, in all the revelations of God, of a BAD HEART, or a DISTEMPERED MIND. If any thing will evidence a man to be a *prophet* and *spiritual,* only in his own conceit, this must do it: And if this is not allow'd to be sufficient proof, there is no knowing, when a man is under the influence of *enthusiastick* heat and zeal.

Another thing the apostle bespeaks this church upon, is that *self-conceit* which appear'd among them in the exercise of *spiritual gifts:* And 'tis more than probable, there were those among them, who being vainly puffed up in their minds, behaved as tho' they were *apostles,* or *prophets,* or *teachers;* leaving their own station, and doing the work that was proper to others. It was to rectify such disorders, that the apostle, in the 12th chapter, addresses to them in that language, v. 29. *Are all apostles? Are all prophets? Are all teachers?* The question carries with it it's own answer, and means the same thing, as when he affirms in the foregoing verse *God hath set some in the church, first apostles, secondarily prophets, thirdly teachers,* and so on. 'Tis evident from what the apostle here

---

[2] John 13. 35.

[3] I John 4. 12.

writes, and indeed from the current strain of this whole chapter, that there is in the body of CHRIST, the Church, a distinction of members; some intended for one use, others for another; and that it would bring confusion into the *body mystical*, for one member to be employed in that service which is adapted to another, and is its proper business.

'Tis not therefore the pretence of being moved by the SPIRIT, that will justify *private christians* in quitting their own proper station, to act in that which belongs to another. Such a practice as this naturally tends to destroy that order, GOD has constituted in the church; and may be followed with mischiefs greater than we may be aware of.

'Tis indeed a powerful argument with many, in favour of these persons, their pretending to *impulses*, and a call from GOD; together with their insatiable thirst to do good to souls. And 'tis owing to such pretences as these, that encouragement has been given to the rise of such numbers of *lay-exhorters and teachers*, in one place and another, all over the land. But if 'tis one of the things wrote by the apostle as the *commandment of* GOD, that there should be *officers* in the church, an *order of men* to whom it should belong, as their *proper, stated work*, to exhort and teach, this cannot be the business of others: And if any who think themselves to be *spiritual*, are under *impressions* to take upon them *this ministry*, they may have reason to suspect, whether their *impulses* are any other than the workings of their own imaginations: And instead of being under any divine extraordinary influence, there are just grounds of fear, whether they are not acted from the vanity of their minds: Especially, if they are but beginners in religion; men of weak minds, babes in understanding: as is most commonly the case. The apostle speaks of *novices*, as in danger of being *lifted up with pride, and falling into the contamination of the devil:* And it is a seasonable caution to this kind of person. They should study themselves more, and they will see less reason to think their disposition to exhort and teach to be from the SPIRIT OF GOD. And indeed, if the SPIRIT has bid men to *abide in their own callings,* 'tis not conceivable he should influence them to *leave their callings:* And if he has set a mark of disgrace upon *busy-bodies in other men's matters,* 'tis impossible he should put men upon *wandring about from house to house, speaking the things they ought not.*

And it deserves particular consideration, whether the suffering, much more the encouraging WOMEN, yea, GIRLS to speak in the assemblies for religious worship, is not a plain breach of that *commandment of the* LORD,[4] wherein it is said, *Let your* WOMEN *keep silence in the churches; for it is not permitted to them to speak—It is a shame: for* WOMEN *to speak in the church.* After such an express constitution, designedly made to restrain WOMEN from speaking in the church, with what face can such a practice be pleaded for? They may pretend, they are moved by the SPIRIT, and such a tho't of themselves may be encouraged by others; but if the apostle *spake by the* SPIRIT, when he delivered *this commandment,* they can't *act by the* SPIRIT, when they break it. 'Tis a plain case, these FEMALE EXHORTERS are condemned by the apostle; and if 'tis the *commandment of the* LORD, that they should not speak, they are *spiritual* only in their own tho'ts, while they attempt to do so.

The last thing I shall mention as written by the apostle, is that which obliges to a *just decorum in speaking* in the *house of GOD.* It was an extravagance these *Corinthians* had fallen into, their speaking many of them together, and upon different things, while in the same place of worship. *How is it, brethren,* says the apostle? *When ye come together, every one hath a psalm; hath a doctrine; hath a tongue; hath a revelation; hath an interpretation.* It was this that introduced the con-

---

[4] Context, v. 35, 26.

fusion and noise, upon which the apostle declares, if an unbeliever should come in among them, he would take them to be
mad.[5] And the *commandment* he gives them to put a stop to
this disorder, is, that they should *speak in course, one by one,*
and so as that *things might be done to edifying.*[6]

And whoever the persons are, who will not acknowledge
what the apostle has here said is the *commandment of* GOD,
and act accordingly, are influenced by another spirit than that
which moved in him, be their impressions or pretences what
they will. The disorder of EXHORTING, and PRAYING, and SING-
ING, and LAUGHING, *in the same house of worship, at one and
the same time,* is as great as was that, the apostle blames in
the *church of Corinth:* And whatever the persons, guilty of
such gross irregularity may imagine, and however they may
plead their being under the influence of the SPIRIT, and mov'd
by him, 'tis evidently a breach upon common order and decency; yea, a direct violation of the *commandment of* GOD,
written on purpose to prevent such disorders: And to pretend
the direction of the SPIRIT in such a flagrant instance of extravagant conduct, is to reproach the blessed SPIRIT, who is not,
as the apostle's phrase is, *the author of confusion, but of peace,
as in all the churches of the saints.*

In these, and all other instances, let us compare men's pretences to the SPIRIT by the SCRIPTURE: And if their conduct is
such as can't be reconcil'd with an *acknowledgment of the
things therein revealed, as the commandments of* GOD, their
pretences are vain, they are *prophets* and *spiritual,* only in
their own proud imaginations. I proceed now to

III. The third thing, which is to caution you against giving
way to *enthusiastic impressions.* And here much might be said,

I might warn you from the *dishonour* it reflects upon the

---

[5] v. 23.

[6] 26, 27.

SPIRIT of GOD. And perhaps none have more reproach'd the blessed SPIRIT, than men pretending to be under his extraordinary guidance and direction. The veryest fancies, the vainest imaginations, the strongest delusions, they have father'd on him. There is scarce any absurdity in *principle,* or irregularity in *practice,* but he has been made the patron of it.—And what a stone of stumbling has the wildness of *Enthusiasm* been to multitudes in the world? What prejudices have been hereby excited in their minds against the very being of the SPIRIT? What temptations have been thrown in their way to dispute his OFFICE as the SANCTIFIER and COMFORTER of GOD's people? And how have they been over-come to disown HIS WORK, when it has been really wro't in the hearts of men?

I might also warn you from the damage it has done in the world. No greater mischiefs have arisen from any quarter. It is indeed the genuine source of infinite evil. POPERY it self han't been the mother of more and greater blasphemies and abominations. It has made strong attempts to destroy all property, to make all things common, *wives* as well as *goods.*—It has promoted faction and contention; filled the church oftentimes with confusion, and the state sometimes with general disorder.—It has, by its pretended spiritual interpretations, made void the most undoubted laws of GOD. It has laid aside the *gospel sacraments* as weak and carnal things; yea, this *superior light within* has, in the opinion of thousands, render'd the *bible* a *useless dead letter.*—It has made men fancy themselves to be *prophets* and *apostles;* yea, some have taken themselves to be CHRIST JESUS; yea, the blessed GOD himself. It has, in one word, been a pest to the church in all ages, as great an enemy to real and solid religion, as perhaps the grossest *infidelity.*[7]

---

[7] Undoubted instances of these, and many other things of a like nature, are well known to such as are, in any measure, acquainted with the *history* of the *church.*

I might go on and warn you from the danger of it to your-selves. If you should once come under the influence of it, none can tell whither it would carry you. There is nothing so wild and frantick but you may be reconcil'd to it. And if this shou'd be your case, your recovery to a right mind would be one of the most difficult things in nature. There is no coming at a thorow-pac'd *enthusiast.* He is proof against every method of dealing with him. Would you apply to him from reason? That he esteems a carnal thing, and flees from it as from the most dangerous temptation. Would you rise higher, and speak to him from *Scripture?* It will be to as little purpose. For if he pays any regard to it, 'tis only as it falls in with his own pre-conceiv'd notions. He interprets the scripture by *impulses* and *impressions,* and sees no meaning in it, only as he explains it from his own fancy.—'Tis infinitely difficult [to] convince a man grown giddy and conceited under the false notion, that the good Spirit teaches him every thing. His apprehended inspiration sets him above all means of conviction. He rather despises than hearkens to the most reasonable advices that can be given him.

But as the most suitable guard against the first tendencies towards *enthusiasm,* let me recommend to you the following words of counsel.

1. Get a true understanding of the *proper work of the* Spirit; and don't place it in those things wherein the gospel does not make it to consist. The work of the Spirit is different now from what it was in the first days of christianity. Men were then favored with the extraordinary presence of the Spirit. He came upon them in miraculous gifts and powers; as a spirit of prophecy, of knowledge, of revelation, of tongues, of miracles: But the Spirit is not now to be expected in these ways. His grand business lies in preparing men's minds for the grace of God, by true *humiliation,* from an apprehension of sin, and the necessity of a *Saviour;* then in working in them

faith and *repentance,* and such a *change* as shall *turn them from the power of sin and satan unto* God; and in fine, by carrying on the good work he has begun in them; assisting them in duty, strengthening them against temptation, and in a word, preserving them blameless thro' faith unto salvation: And all this he does by the *word* and *prayer,* as the great means in the accomplishment of these purposes of mercy.

Herein, in general, consists the work of the Spirit. It does not lie in giving men *private revelations,* but in opening their minds to understand the *publick ones* contained in the scripture. It does not lie in *sudden impulses* and *impressions,* in *immediate calls* and *extraordinary missions.* Men mistake the business of the Spirit, if they understand by it such things as these. And 'tis, probably, from such unhappy mistakes, that they are at first betrayed into *enthusiasm.* Having a wrong notion of the *work of* the Spirit, 'tis no wonder if they take the uncommon sallies of their own minds for his influences.

You cannot, my brethren, be too well acquainted with what the *bible* makes the *work* of the Holy Ghost, in the affair of salvation: And if you have upon your minds a clear and distinct understanding of this, it will be a powerful guard to you against all *enthusiastical impressions.*

2. Keep close to the *Scripture,* and admit of nothing for an impression of the Spirit, but what agrees with that unerring rule. Fix it in your minds as a truth you will invariably abide by, that the *bible* is the grand test, by which every thing in religion is to be tried; and that you can, at no time, nor in any instance, be under the guidance of the Spirit of God, much less his *extraordinary* guidance, if what you are led to, is inconsistent with the things there revealed, either in point of *faith* or *practice.* And let it be your care to compare the motions of your minds, and the workings of your imaginations and passions, with the *rule* of God's *word.* And see to it, that you be impartial in this matter: Don't make the rule bend to your

pre-conceiv'd notions and inclinations; but repair to the *bible*, with a mind dispos'd, as much as may be, to know the truth as it lies nakedly and plainly in the *scripture* it self. And whatever you are moved to, reject the motion, esteem it as nothing more than a vain fancy, if it puts you upon any method of *thinking*, or *acting*, that can't be evidently reconcil'd with the *revelations* of GOD in *his word*.

This adherence to the bible, my brethren is one of the best preservatives against *enthusiasm*. If you will but express a due reverence to this *book* of GOD, making it the great rule of judgment, even in respect of the SPIRIT's *influences* and *operations*, you will not be in much danger of being led into delusion. Let that be your inquiry under all suppos'd *impulses* from the SPIRIT, *What saith the scripture? To the law, and to the testimony:* If your impressions, and imagined spiritual motions agree not therewith, 'tis because there is no hand of the SPIRIT of GOD in them: They are only the workings of your own imaginations, or something worse; and must at once, without any more ado, be rejected as such.

3. Make use of the *Reason* and *Understanding* GOD has given you. This may be tho't an ill-advis'd direction, but 'tis as necessary as either of the former. Next to the *Scripture*, there is no greater enemy to *enthusiasm*, than *reason*. 'Tis indeed impossible a man shou'd be an *enthusiast*, who is in the just exercise of his understanding; and 'tis because men don't pay a due regard to the sober dictates of a well inform'd mind, that they are led aside by the delusions of a vain imagination. Be advised then to shew yourselves men, to make use of your reasonable powers; and not act as the *horse* or *mule*, as tho' you had no understanding.

'Tis true, you must not go about to set up your own *reason* in *opposition* to *revelation:* Nor may you entertain a tho't of making *reason* your *rule* instead of *scripture*. The bible, as I said before, is the *great rule* of religion, the grand test in mat-

ters of salvation: But then you must use your reason in order
to understand the *bible:* Nor is there any other possible way,
in which, as a reasonable creature, you shou'd come to an
understanding of it.

You are, it must be acknowledged, in a corrupt state. The fall
has introduc'd great weakness into your reasonable nature.
You can't be too sensible of this; nor of the danger you are in
of making a wrong judgment, thro' prejudice, carelessness,
and the undue influence of sin and lust. And to prevent this,
you can't be too solicitous to get your *nature sanctified:* Nor
can you depend too strongly upon the divine grace to assist
you in your search after truth: And 'tis in the way of due
dependance on GOD, and the influences of his SPIRIT, that I
advise you to the use of your reason: And in this way, you
must make use of it. How else will you know what is a revelation from GOD? What shou'd hinder your entertaining the
same tho't of a *pretended* revelation, as of a *real* one, but your
reason discovering the falshood of the one, and the truth of
the other? And when in the enjoyment of an undoubted revelation from GOD, as in the case of the *scripture,* How will you
understand its meaning, if you throw by your reason? How
will you determine, that this, and not that, is its true sense, in
this and the other place? Nay, if no reasoning is to be made
use of, are not all the senses that can be put on scripture
equally proper? Yea, may not the most contrary senses be
receiv'd at the same time, since reason only can point out the
inconsistency between them? And what will be sufficient to
guard you against the most monstrous extravagancies, in *principle* as well as *practice,* if you give up your understandings?
What have you left, in this case, to be a check to the wanton-
ess of your imaginations? What shou'd hinder your following
every idle fancy, 'till you have lost yourselves in the wilds of
falshood and inconsistency?

You may, it is true, misuse your reason: And this is a consideration that shou'd put you upon a due care, that you may use it well; but no argument why you shou'd not use it at all: And indeed, if you shou'd throw by your reason as a useless thing, you would at once put your selves in the way of all manner of delusion.

But, it may be, you will say, you have committed yourselves to the guidance of the SPIRIT; which is the best preservative. Herein you have done well; nothing can be objected against this method of conduct: Only take heed of mistakes, touching the SPIRIT's *guidance*. Let me enquire of you, how is it the SPIRIT preserves from delusion? Is it not by opening the understanding, and enabling the man, in the due use of his reason, to perceive the truth of the things of GOD and religion? Most certainly: And, if you think of being led by the SPIRIT without understanding, or in opposition to it, you deceive yourselves. The SPIRIT of GOD deals with men as *reasonable* creatures: And they ought to deal with themselves in like manner. And while they do thus, making a wise and good use of the understanding, GOD has given them, they will take a proper means to prevent their falling into delusions; nor will there be much danger of their being led aside by *enthusiastic* heat and imagination.

4. You must not lay too great stress upon the *workings* of your *passions* and *affections*. These will be excited, in a less or greater degree, in the business of religion: And 'tis proper they shou'd. The passions, when suitably mov'd, tend mightily to awaken the *reasonable powers,* and put them upon a lively and vigorous exercise. And this is their proper use: And when address'd to, and excited to this purpose, they may be of good service: whereas we shall mistake the right use of the passions, if we place our religion *only* or *chiefly,* in the heat and fervour of them. The *soul* is the *man:* And unless the *reasonable nature* is suitably wro't upon, the *understanding* enlightned, the *judg-ment* convinc'd, the *will* perswaded, and the *mind* intirely

chang'd, it will avail but to little purpose; tho' the passions shou'd be set all in a blaze. This therefore you shou'd be most concern'd about. And if while you are sollicitous that you may be in transports of affection, you neglect your more noble part, your reason and judgment, you will be in great danger of being carried away by your imaginations. This indeed leads directly to *Enthusiasm:* And you will in vain, endeavour to preserve yourselves from the influence of it, if you a'nt duly careful to keep your passions in their proper place, under the government of a well inform'd understanding. While the passions are uppermost, and bear the chief sway over a man, he is in an unsafe state: None knows what he may be bro't to. You can't therefore be too careful to keep your passions under the regimen of a *sober judgment.* 'Tis indeed a matter of necessity, as you would not be led aside by delusion and fancy.

5. In the last place here, you must not forget to go to GOD by *prayer.* This is a duty in all cases, but in none more than the present. If left to yourselves, your own wisdom and strength, you will be insufficient for your own security; perpetually in danger from your *imaginations,* as well as the other enemies of your *souls.* You can't be too sensible of this; nor can you, from a sense of it, apply with too much importunity to the FATHER *of mercies,* to take pity upon you, and send you such a supply of grace as is needful for you. You must not indeed think, that your duty lies in the business of prayer, and nothing else. You must use your own endeavours, neglect nothing that may prove a guard to you: But together with the use of other means, you must make known your request to GOD by prayer and supplication. You must daily commit the keeping of your soul to him; and this you must particularly be careful to do in times of more special hazard; humbly hoping in GOD to be your help: And if he shall please to undertake for you, no delusion shall ever have power over you, to seduce you; but, possessing a sound mind, you shall go on in

the uniform, steady service of your maker and generation, till of the mercy of God, thro' the merits of the Redeemer, you are crowned with eternal life.

But I shall now draw towards a close, by making some suitable *application* of what has been said,   And,

1. Let us beware of charging GOD *foolishly*, from what we have heard of the *nature*, and *influence* of *enthusiasm*. This may appear a dark article in God's government of the world; but it stands upon the same foot with his permission of other evils, whether *natural* or *moral*. And, if we shou'd not be able to see perfectly into the reason of this dispensation, we shou'd rather attribute it to our own ignorance, than reply against God. We may assure ourselves, a wise, and good, and holy God, would not have suffered it thus to be, if there were not some great and valuable ends to be hereby answered.

Greater advantages may, in the end, accrue to true religion, by the sufferance of an *enthusiastic* spirit, and the prevalence of it, at certain times, than we may be capable of discerning at present.

It may furnish both opportunity and occasion for the trial of those, who call themselves christians; whether they have just notions of religion, and courage and faithfulness to stand up for *real* truths, against meer *imaginary* ones.—It may serve as a foil to set off the beauty and glory of true, genuine christianity.—It may tend to the encouragement of reasonable and solid religion; and, in the run of things, recommend it, in the most effectual manner, to men's choice and practice.—In a word, It may put men upon a more thorough examination into the grounds of the christian religion, and be the means of their being, more generally, established in its truth, upon the best and most reasonable evidence.

These are some of the ends capable of being answered by the permission of a *spirit of enthusiasm*, and the prevalence of it, for a while. And as to the persons themselves led aside by it, it is, in the same way to be reconcil'd with the general goodness of GOD towards men, as in the case of *distraction,* and the evil effects consequent thereupon. The persons, heated with *enthusiastic* imaginations are either, in a faulty sense, accessary to this unhappy turn of mind, or they are not: If the *latter,* they may depend upon the pity and mercy of GOD, notwithstanding the extravagancies they may run into; yea, if they are good men, as is, doubtless, sometimes the case, it may be hoped, that this evil which has happened to them, will, after the manner of other sufferings, work together for good to them: But if thro' the pride of their hearts, a vain-glorious temper, accompanied with rashness and arrogance, or the like, they are really accessary to their own delusion, and mad conduct following therefrom, let them not think to cast the blame on GOD: They do but reap the fruit of what they themselves have sown. And if they shou'd be totally delivered up, as has sometimes been the case, to the devices of their own hearts, and the *lying inspirations* of *wicked spirits,* they can fault no body but themselves. GOD is just while he makes them an example for the warning of others, lest they also be given up to believe lies. And he is *good* as well as just; good to others, in putting them hereby upon their guard, tho' he is severe towards *them.*

2. Let none, from what has been offered, entertain prejudices in their minds against the *operations* of the SPIRIT. There is such a thing as his influence upon the hearts of men. No consistent sense can be put upon a great part of the *bible,* unless this be acknowledged for a truth: Nor is it any objection against its being so, that there has been a great deal of *enthusiasm* in the world, many who have mistaken the motions of their own passions for divine operations. This, it must be acknowledged, shou'd make us cautious; putting us upon a careful examination of whatever offers itself, as a communication from the SPIRIT, that we deceive not ourselves: But its no

argument, why we shou'd conceive a flighty tho't, either of the SPIRIT, or his influences, really made upon the minds of men. Much less is it a just ground of exception against the SPIRIT's *operations*, that they may be counterfeited; that men may make an appearance, as if they were acted by the SPIRIT, when, all the while, they have no other view in their pretences, but to serve themselves. This has often been the case; and points it out as a matter of necessity, that we take heed to ourselves, if we would not be impos'd upon by a *fair shew*, and *good words*: But at the same time, 'tis no reason why we shou'd think the worse of the blessed SPIRIT, or of those influences that are really *his*.

Let us be upon our guard as to this matter. Many, from what they have seen or heard of the strange conduct of men, pretending to be under *divine impressions*, have had their minds insensibly leaven'd with prejudices against the things of the SPIRIT. O let it be our care, that we be not thus wro't upon! And the rather, least it shou'd prove the ruin of our souls. This, perhaps, we may not be afraid of: But the danger is great, if we take up wrong notions of the SPIRIT, or encourage an unbecomming tho't of his influences in the business of salvation, least we shou'd grieve the *good* SPIRIT, and he shou'd leave us to perish in a state of alianation from GOD, and true holiness.

'Tis worthy our particular remark, it is by the powerful operation of the holy SPIRIT on the hearts of men, that they are chang'd from the love and practice of sin, to the love and practice of holiness; and have those tempers form'd in them, whereby they are made meet for the glory to be hereafter revealed: Nor can this be done, in any way, without the *special influence* of the blessed SPIRIT.

And is it likely, *He* shou'd be present with men to such gracious purposes, if they suffer their minds to be impressed with contemptuous tho'ts of him? If they begin to call in question his *office,* as the *great dispenser of divine grace,* or look upon his operations as all delusion and imagination.

We must have upon our minds a just tho't of the good SPIRIT, and of his *influences.* This is a matter of necessity. O let us encourage a steady faith in him, as that glorious person, by whom, and by whom alone, we can be prepared in this world, for happiness in the world that is come. And let nothing, no wildness of enthusiasm, ever be able to tempt us to call this in question. And let us so believe in the HOLY GHOST, as to put ourselves under his guidance; and let our dependance be on him for grace to help us in every time of need.

Only let us look to it, that we take no *impressions* for his but such as really are so: And let us not be satisfied, 'till we experience within ourselves the *real effects* of the SPIRIT's operations; such as are common to all that are in CHRIST JESUS; and always have been, and always will be, accompanied with a *holy frame of soul,* and a *conversation becoming the Gospel.*

3. Let not any think *ill* of religion, because of the *ill* representation that is made of it by *enthusiasts.* There may be danger of this; especially, in regard of those who have not upon their minds a serious sense of GOD and the things of another world. They may be ready to judge of religion from the *copy* given them of it, by those who are too much led by their fancies; and to condemn it, in the gross, as a wild, imaginary, inconsistent thing. But this is to judge too hastily and rashly. Religion ought not to suffer in the opinion of any, because of the imprudencies or extravagancies of those, who call themselves the friends of it. Any thing may be abused: Nor is there any thing, but has actually been abused. And why shou'd any think the worse of religion, because some who make more than ordinary pretences to it, set it forth in an ugly light by their conduct relative to it?

There is such a thing as real religion, let the conduct of men be what it will; and 'tis, in it's nature, a sober, calm, reasonable thing: Nor is it an objection of any weight against the sobriety or reasonableness of it, that there have been *enthusiasts,* who have acted as tho' it was a wild, imaginary business. We should not make our estimate of religion as exhibited in the behaviour of men of a *fanciful* mind; to be sure, we should not take up an ill opinion of it, because in the example they give of it, it don't appear so amiable as we might expect. This is unfair. We shou'd rather judge of it from the conduct of men of a *sound judgment;* whose lives have been such a uniform, beautiful transcript of that which is just and good, that we can't but think well of religion, as display'd in their example.

But however religion may appear as viewed in the lives, even of the best men, 'tis a lovely thing, as required by GOD, and pourtrayed in the bible. We shou'd take our sentiments of it from this *book of* GOD; and this, in the calm and sober exercise of our understandings: And if we view it, as 'tis here delineated, we can't but approve of it, the *doctrines* it teaches, and the *duties* it requires, whether they relate to GOD, our selves, or our neighbour; they are all so reasonable in themselves, and worthy of the GOD, the stamp of whose authority they bear.

Let us fetch our notions of religion from the scripture; And if men, in their practice, set it in a disadvantageous light, let us be upon our guard, that we don't take up prejudices against it. This will blind our eyes, and may, by degrees, prepare the way to our throwing off all concern about religion; yea, we may be bro't to treat it even with contempt; than which, nothing can be more dangerous, or put our salvation to a greater risque.

4. Let us esteem those as *friends* to religion, and not *enemies,* who warn us of the danger of *enthusiasm,* and wou'd put us upon our guard, that we be not led aside by it. As the times are, they run the hazard of being call'd *enemies* to the

holy SPIRIT, and may expect to be ill-spoken of by many, and loaded with names of reproach: But they are notwithstanding the best friends to religion; and it may be, it will more and more appear, that they have all along been so. They have been stigmatised as OPPOSERS of the WORK OF GOD; but 'tis a great mercy of GOD, there have been such OPPOSERS: This land had, in all probability, been over-run with confusion and distraction, if they had acted under the influence of the same *heat* and *zeal,* which some others have been famous for.

'Tis really best, people shou'd know there is such a thing as *enthusiasm,* and that it has been, in all ages, one of the most dangerous enemies to the church of GOD, and has done a world of mischief: And 'tis a kindness to them to be warn'd against it, and directed to the proper methods to be preserved from it. 'Tis indeed, one of the best ways of doing service to *real* religion, to distinguish it from that which is *imaginary:* Nor shou'd ministers be discouraged from endeavouring this, tho' they shou'd be ill-tho't, or evil-spoken of. They shou'd beware of being too much under the influence of that *fear of man, which bringeth a snare;* which is evidently the case, where they are either silent, or dare not speak out faithfully and plainly, lest they shou'd be called PHARISEES or HYPOCRITES, and charged with LEADING SOULS TO THE DEVIL. 'Tis a *small matter* to be thus *judged* and *reviled;* and we shou'd be above being affrighted from duty by this, which is nothing more than the *breath* of poor, ignorant, frail man.

There is, I doubt not, a great deal of *real, substantial* religion in the land. The SPIRIT of GOD has wro't effectually on the hearts of many, from one time to another: And I make no question he has done so of late, in more numerous instances, it may be, than usual. But this, notwithstanding, there is, without dispute, a *spirit of enthusiasm,* appearing in one place and another. There are those, who make great pretences to the SPIRIT, who are carried away with their imaginations: And some, it may be, take themselves to be *immediately and wonderfully conducted by him;* while they are led only by their own fancies.

Thus it has been in other parts of the world. *Enthusiasm,* in all the *wildness,* and *fury,* and *extravagance* of it, has been among them, and sometimes had a most dreadfully extensive spread. *Ten thousand* wild *enthusiasts* have appear'd in arms, at the same time; and this too, in defence of *gross opinions,* as well as *enormous actions.* The first discovery therefore of such a spirit, unless due care is taken to give check to its growth and progress, is much to be feared; for there is no knowing, how high it may rise, nor what it may end in.—

The good LORD give us all wisdom; and courage, and conduct, in such a Day as this! And may both *ministers* and *people* behave after such a manner, as that religion may not suffer; but in the end, gain advantage, and be still more universally established.

And, may that grace of GOD, which has appeared to all men, bringing salvation, teach us effectually, to deny ungodliness and worldly lusts, and to live soberly, and righteously, and godlily in the world: so may we look with comfort for the appearing of our SAVIOUR JESUS CHRIST: And when he shall appear in the glory of his FATHER, and with his holy angels, we also shall appear with him, and go away into everlasting life: Which GOD, of his infinite mercy grant may be the portion of us all; for the sake of CHRIST JESUS.

Amen.

CONFESSION AND RETRACTATIONS

Chauncy prefaced the published version of his caveat against enthusiasm with an open letter to James Davenport, reminding him of what their Puritan ancestors had said of the "passions." Davenport was a convenient target, and his antics provided a justification for demanding the revival impulse now be stilled. Actually, New England's Great Awakening was all but over by the early months of 1742. To partisans of the revival it seemed that Davenport was somehow personally responsible for the ebbing of the Spirit, and, though most continued to insist that he was "truly pious," the evangelical leaders increasingly rebuked Davenport for his "errors." Both parties, in short, saw Davenport as something of a symbolic figure, in whom was embodied the meaning of the Awakening. Yet New England seemed reluctant to confront that meaning directly. In June 1742 the General Assembly of Connecticut brought Davenport to trial and declared him a danger to the "peace and order" of the province. He could have been imprisoned, but instead he was sent back to Long Island, the Assembly having decided that Davenport was "under

The Reverend Mr. James Davenport's Confession & Retractations (Boston, 1744), entire.

the influence of enthusiastical impressions and impulses, and thereby disturbed in the rational faculties of his mind, and therefore to be pitied and compassionated, and not to be treated as otherwise he might be." Similarly, when Davenport came to Boston, he was arrested, tried, and declared *non compos mentis.*

It is difficult to determine the precise nature of Davenport's offenses, in part because reports of his career differ according to each commentator's view of the Awakening generally. Probably the most cogent catalogue of his misconduct is provided by his own *Confession.* It was composed at the urging of some Connecticut ministers who thought Davenport, by his behavior, had made it possible for the whole of the revival to be dismissed as an insane aberration. First published in the *Boston Gazette,* July 18, 1744, the *Confession* is useful both as a summary of Davenport's career as an itinerant and as a reminder that his attitudes and activities were never considered a proper expression of evangelical principles. When, for instance, Davenport, at New London, burned his ministerial vestments and a number of "heretical" books, Gilbert Tennent immediately censured the act as both "horrid" and "ridiculous." Davenport, who soon after writing his confession became again a respected pillar of the Presbyterian Church, likewise understood that his worst mistake was not his encouragement of unbridled emotionalism, nor his censoriousness, nor even his provoking of hasty separations. He had forgotten the central evangelical truth that reformation and progress were matters of "internals."

Altho' I don't question at all, but there is great Reason to bless God for a *glorious and wonderful Work of his Power and Grace* in the *Edification* of his Children, and the *Conviction* and *Conversion* of Numbers in *New-England,* in the *neighbouring Governments & several other Parts,* within a few Years past; and believe that the Lord hath favoured me, tho' most unworthy, with several others of his Servants, in granting special Assistance and Success; the Glory of all which be given to JEHOVAH, to whom alone it belongs:

Yet after frequent Meditation and Desires that I might be enabled to apprehend Things justly, and, I hope I may say, mature Consideration; I am now fully convinced and perswaded that *several Appendages* to *this glorious Work* are no essential Parts thereof, but of a *different* and *contrary* Nature and Tendency; *which Appendages* I have been in the Time of the Work very industrious in and instrumental of promoting, by a misguided Zeal: being further much influenced in the Affair by the *false Spirit;* which, unobserved by me, did (as I have been brought to see since) prompt me to *unjust Apprehensions* and *Misconduct* in *several Articles;* which have been great Blemishes to the Work of God, very grievous to some of God's Children, no less in sharing and corrupting to others of them, a sad Means of many Persons questioning the Work of God, concluding and appearing against it, and of the hardening of Multitudes in their Sins, and an awful Occasion of the Enemies blaspheming the right Ways of the Lord; and withal very offensive to that God, before whom I would lie in the Dust, prostrate in deep Humility and Repentance on this Account, imploring Pardon for the Mediator's Sake, and thankfully accepting the Tokens thereof.

The *Articles,* which I especially refer to, and would in the most public Manner *retract,* and *warn others against,* are these which follow, *viz.*

I. The Method I us'd for a considerable Time, with Respect

to some, yea many *Ministers* in several Parts, in openly *exposing such as I fear'd or thought unconverted, in publick Prayer or otherwise:* herein making my private Judgment, (in which also I much suspect I was mistaken in several Instances, and I believe also that my Judgment concerning several, was formed rashly and upon very slender Grounds.) I say, making my private Judgment, the Ground of publick Actions or Conduct; offending, as I apprehend (altho' in the Time of it ignorantly) against the *ninth Commandment,* and such other Passages of Scripture, as are similar; yea, I may say, offending against the Laws both of Justice and Charity: Which Laws were further broken

II. By my *advising and urging to such Separations* from *those Ministers,* whom I treated as above, as I believe may be justly called rash, unwarrantable, and of sad and awful Tendency and Consequence. And here I would ask the Forgiveness of those Ministers, whom I have injured in both these Articles.

III. I confess I have been much led astray by *following Impulses* or Impressions as a Rule of Conduct, whether they came with or without a Text of Scripture; and my neglecting also duly to observe the Analogy of Scripture: I am perswaded this was a great Means of corrupting my Experiences and carrying me off from the Word of God, and a great Handle, which the *false Spirit* has made use of with Respect to a Number, and me especially.

IV. I believe further that I have done much Hurt to Religion by *encouraging private Persons to a ministerial and authoritative Kind or Method of exhorting;* which is particularly observable in many such being much puft up and *falling into the Snare of the Devil,* whilst many others are thus directly prejudic'd against the Work.

V. I have Reason to be deeply humbled that I have not been duly careful to endeavour to remove or prevent Prejudice, (where I now believe I might then have done it consist-

ently with Duty) which appear'd remarkable in the Method
I practis'd, of *singing with others in the Streets* in Societies
frequently.

I would also penitently confess and bewail my *great Stiffness* in retaining these *aforesaid Errors* a great while, and unwillingness to examine into them with any Jealousy of their
being Errors, notwithstanding the friendly Counsels and Cau-
tions of real Friends, especially in the Ministry.

Here may properly be added a Paragraph or two, taken out
of a *Letter from me* to Mr. *Barber* at *Georgia;* a *true Copy* of
which I gave Consent should be publish'd lately at *Philadelphia: "*—I would add to what Brother *T——* hath written on
the awful Affair of Books and Cloaths at *New-London,* which
affords Grounds of deep and lasting Humiliation; I was to my
Shame be it spoken, the Ringleader in *that horrid Action;* I
was, my dear Brother, under the powerful Influence of the
false Spirit almost one whole Day together, and Part of several
Days. The Lord shewed me afterwards that the Spirit I was
then acted by was in it's Operations void of true inward Peace,
laying the greatest Stress on Externals, neglecting the Heart,
full of Impatience, Pride and Arrogance; altho' I thought in
the Time of it, that 'twas the Spirit of God in an high Degree;
awful indeed! my Body especially my Leg much disorder'd at
the same Time,[1] which Satan and my evil Heart might make
some Handle of.—"

And now may the holy wise and good God, be pleas'd to
guard and secure me against *such Errors* for the future, and
stop the Progress of those, whether Ministers or People, who
have been corrupted by my Words or Example in any of the
above-mention'd Particulars; and if it be his holy Will, bless
this publick Recantation to this Purpose. And Oh! may he
grant withal, that such as by Reason of the aforesaid *Errors*

---

[1] I had the *long Fever* on me and the cankry Humour raging at once.

and Misconduct have entertained unhappy Prejudices against Christianity in general, or the late glorious Work of God in particular, may by this Account learn to distinguish the *Appendage* from the *Substance* or *Essence,* that which is *vile* and *odious* from that which is *precious, glorious* and *divine,* and thus be intirely and happily freed from all those Prejudices refer'd to, and this in infinite Mercy through Jesus Christ: and to these Requests may all God's Children, whether Ministers or others say, *Amen.*

July 28. 1744.

James Davenport.

P. S. In as much as a Number, who have fallen in with and promoted the *aforesaid Errors* and *Misconduct,* and are not alter'd in their Minds, may be prejudic'd against this *Recantation,* by a Supposition or Belief, that I came into it by Reason of Desertion or Dulness and Deadness in Religion: It seems needful therefore to signify, what I hope I may say without boasting, and what I am able thro' pure rich Grace to speak with Truth and Freedom; that for *some Months* in the Time of my coming to the *above said Conclusions* and *Retractations,* and since I have come through Grace to them; I have been favoured a great Part of the Time, with a sweet *Calm and Serenity of Soul and Rest in God,* and sometimes with special and remarkable Refreshments of Soul, and these more free from corrupt Mixtures than formerly: *Glory to God alone.*

27 · Jonathan Edwards

THOUGHTS ON THE REVIVAL

OF RELIGION

By focusing so intently on James Davenport, the revivalists of New England themselves confessed bewilderment at the course taken by the Awakening. The original partisans of the revival, here as in the Middle Colonies, were appalled as the energies released by the Awakening flowed into the unexpected, and twisted, channels of Antinomianism and Separatism. The spokesmen of evangelical religion began to dispute among themselves. Some argued that the revival, were it to continue, could do with a little more of Davenport's spirit, and others began to call for an end even to the battle against Arminianism. In these circumstances Jonathan Edwards undertook the seemingly impossible task of isolating the "essence" of the revival and of seeing all the phenomena of the Awakening in a single historical perspective. By doing so, he quietly explained in the preface to his *Thoughts on the Revival,* he

Jonathan Edwards, *Some Thoughts concerning the Present Revival of Religion in New England, Works,* III, 279–282, 313–316, 333–336, 382–383, 390–395.

could prevent the "people of God" from working at cross-purposes, thereby restoring the momentum of the revival and assuring the fulfillment of its hopes. By virtue of its panoramic sweep alone, Edwards' *Thoughts* is the major document of the Awakening. It is also one of Edwards' most significant utterances, for here he drew together for the first time in a single treatise evangelical doctrine, psychological insight, and historical vision. At the center of all was Edwards' dramatic and unforgettable prophecy of the New World's spiritual destiny.

1. Some make philosophy, instead of the Holy Scriptures, their rule of judging of this work; particularly the philosophical notions they entertain of the nature of the soul, its faculties and affections. Some are ready to say, "There is but little sober, solid religion in this work: it is little else but flash and noise. Religion now-a-days all runs out into transports and high flights of the passions and affections." In their philosophy, the affections of the soul are something diverse from the will, and not appertaining to the noblest part of the soul, but the meanest principles that it has, that belong to man, as partaking of animal nature, and what he has in common with the brute creation, rather than any thing whereby he is conformed to angels and pure spirits. And though they acknowledge that a good use may be made of the affections in religion, yet they suppose that the substantial part of religion does not consist in them, but that they are rather to be looked upon as something adventitious and accidental in Christianity.

But I cannot but think that these gentleman labor under great mistakes, both in their philosophy and divinity. It is true, distinction must be made in affections or passions. There is a great deal of difference in high and raised affections, which must be distinguished by the skill of the observer. Some are much more solid than others. There are many exercises of the affections that are very flashy, and little to be depended on; and oftentimes there is a great deal that appertains to them, or rather that is the effect of them, that has its seat in animal nature, and is very much owning to the constitution and frame of the body; and that which sometimes more especially obtains the name of passion, is nothing solid or substantial. But it is false philosophy to suppose this to be the case with all exercises of affection in the soul, or with all great and high affections; and false divinity to suppose that religious affections do not appertain to the substance and essence of Christianity: on the contrary, it seems to me that the very life and soul of all true religion consists in them.

I humbly conceive that the affections of the soul are not properly distinguished from the will, as though they were two faculties in the soul. All acts of the affections of the soul are in some sense acts of the will, and all acts of the will are acts of the affections. All exercises of the will are in some degree or other, exercises of the soul's appetition or aversion; or which is the same thing, of its love or hatred. The soul wills one thing rather than another, or chooses one thing rather than another, no otherwise than as it loves one thing more than another; but love and hatred are affections of the soul: and therefore all acts of the will are truly acts of the affections; though the exercises of the will do not obtain the name of passions, unless the will, either in its aversion or opposition, be exercised in a high degree, or in a vigorous and lively manner.

All will allow that true virtue or holiness has its seat chiefly in the heart, rather than in the head: it therefore follows, from what has been said already, that it consists chiefly in holy affections. The things of religion take place in men's hearts, no further than they are *affected* with them. The informing of the understanding is all vain, any farther than it *affects* the heart; or which is the same thing, has influence on the *affections*.

Those gentlemen that make light of these raised affections in religion, will doubtless allow that true religion and holiness, as it has its seat in the heart, is capable of very high degrees, and high exercises in the soul. As for instance; they will doubtless allow that the holiness of the heart or will, is capable of being raised to a hundred times as great a degree of strength as it is in the most eminent saint on earth, or to be exerted in a hundred times so strong and vigorous exercises of the heart; and yet be true religion or holiness still, but only in a high degree. Now therefore I would ask them, by what name they will call these high and vigorous exercises of the will or heart? Are they not high affections? What can they consist in, but in high acts of love; strong and vigorous exercises of benevolence and complacence; high, exalting and admiring thoughts of God and his perfections; strong desires after God? &c. And now what are we come to but high and raised affections? Yea, those very same high and raised affections that before they objected against, or made light of, as worthy of little regard?

I suppose furthermore that all will allow that there is nothing but solid religion in heaven: but that there, religion and holiness of heart is raised to an exceeding great height, to strong, high, exalted exercises of heart. Now, what other kinds of such exceeding strong and high exercises of the heart, or of holiness, as it has its seat in their hearts, can we devise for them, but only holy affections, high degrees of actings of love to God, rejoicing in God, admiring of God? &c. Therefore these things in the saints and angels in heaven, are not to be despised and cashiered by the name of great heats and transports of the passions.

And it will doubtless be yet further allowed, that the more eminent the saints are on earth, and the stronger their grace is, and the higher its exercises are, the more they are like the saints in heaven; i. e., (by what has been just now observed) the more they have of high or raised affections in religion.

Though there are false affections in religion, and affections that in some respects are raised high, that are flashy, yet undoubtedly there are also true, holy and solid affections; and the higher these are raised, the better: and if they are raised to an exceeding great height, they are not to be thought meanly of or suspected, merely because of their great degree, but, on the contrary, to be esteemed and rejoiced in. Charity or divine love, is in Scripture represented as the sum of all the religion of the heart; but this is nothing but a holy *affection:* and therefore in proportion as this is firmly fixed in the soul, and raised to a great height, the more eminent a person is in holiness. Divine love or charity is represented as the sum of all the religion of heaven, and that wherein mainly the religion of the church in its more perfect state on earth shall consist, when knowledge and tongues, and phrophesyings shall cease; and therefore the higher this holy affection is raised in the church of God, or in a gracious soul, the more excellent and perfect is the state of the church, or a particular soul.

If we take the Scriptures for our rule then, the greater and higher are the exercises of love to God, delight and complacence in God, desires and longings after God, delight in the children of God, love to mankind, brokenness of heart, abhorrence of sin, and self-abhorrence for sin; and the peace of God, which passeth all understanding, and joy in the Holy Ghost, joy unspeakable and full of glory; admiring thoughts of God, exulting and glorifying in God; so much the higher is Christ's religion, or that virtue which he and his apostles taught, raised in the soul.

It is a stumbling to some that religious affections should seem to be so powerful, or that they should be so violent (as they express it) in some persons: they are therefore ready to doubt whether it can be the Spirit of God, or whether this vehemence be not rather a sign of the operation of an evil spirit. But why should such a doubt arise from no other ground than this? What is represented in Scripture, as more powerful in its effects, than the Spirit of God? . . . The Spirit of God is called the spirit of power, and love, and of a sound mind. So the Spirit is represented by a mighty wind, and by fire, things most powerful in their operation.

2. Many are guilty of not taking the holy Scriptures as a sufficient and whole rule, whereby to judge of this work, whether it be the work of God, in that they judge by those things which the Scripture does not give as any signs or marks whereby to judge one way or the other, and therefore do in no wise belong to the Scripture rule of judging, viz., the effects that religious exercises and affections of mind have upon the body. Scripture rules respect the state of the mind, and persons' moral conduct, and voluntary behavior, and not the physical state of the body. The design of the Scripture is to teach us divinity, and not physic and anatomy. Ministers are made the watchmen of men's souls, and not of their bodies; and therefore the great rule which God has committed into their hands, is to make them divines, and not physicians. Christ knew what instructions and rules his church would stand in need of better than we do; and if he had seen it needful in order to the church's safety, he doubtless would have given ministers rules to judge of bodily effects, and would have told them how the pulse should beat under such and such religious exercises of mind; when men should look pale, and when they should shed tears; when they should tremble, and whether or no they should ever be faint or cry out; or whether the body should ever be put into convulsions: he probably would have put some book into their hands, that should have tended to make them excellent anatomists and physicians: but he has not done it, because he did not see it to be needful. He judged, that if ministers thoroughly did their duty as watchmen and overseers

of the state and frame of men's souls, and of their voluntary conduct, according to the rules he had given, his church would be well provided for, as to its safety in these matters. And therefore those ministers of Christ and overseers of souls, that busy themselves, and are full of concern about the involuntary motions of the fluids and solids of men's bodies, and from thence full of doubts and suspicions of the cause, when nothing appears but that the state and frame of their minds, and their voluntary behavior is good, and agreeable to God's word; I say, such ministers go out of the place that Christ has set them in, and leave their proper business. . . .

3. Another thing that some make their rule to judge of this work by, instead of the Holy Scriptures, is history, or former observation. Herein they err two ways: *First,* if there be any thing new and extraordinary in the circumstances of this work, that was not observed in former times, that is a rule with them to reject this work as not the work of God. Herein they make that their rule, that God has not given them for their rule; and limit God, where he has not limited himself. And this is especially unreasonable in this case: for whosoever has well weighed the wonderful and mysterious methods of divine wisdom, in carrying on the work of the new creation, or in the progress of the work of redemption, from the first promise of the seed of the woman to this time, may easily observe that it has all along been God's manner to open new scenes, and to bring forth to view things new and wonderful, such as eye had not seen, nor ear heard, nor entered into the heart of man or angels, to the astonishment of heaven and earth, not only in the revelations he makes of his mind and will, but also in the works of his hands. . . .

And besides, those things in this work that have been chiefly complained of as new, are not so new as has been generally imagined: though they have been much more frequent lately, in proportion to the uncommon degree, extent and swiftness, and other extraordinary circumstances of the work, yet they are not new in their kind; but are things of the same nature as have been found and well approved of in the church of God before, from time to time. . . .

It is not unlikely that this work of God's spirit, that is so extraordinary and wonderful, is the dawning, or at least, a prelude of that glorious work of God, so often foretold in Scripture, which in the progress and issue of it shall renew the world of mankind. If we consider how long since, the things foretold, as what should precede this great event have been accomplished; and how long this event has been expected by the church of God, and thought to be nigh by the most eminent men of God in the church; and withal consider what the state of things now is, and has for a considerable time been, in the church of God, and world of mankind, we cannot reasonably think otherwise, than that the beginning of this great work of God must be near. And there are many things that make it probable that this work will begin in America. It is signified that it shall begin in some very remote part of the world, that the rest of the world will have no communication with but by navigation, in Isa. lx. 9: "Surely the Isles will wait for me, and the ships of Tarshish first, to bring my sons from afar." It is exceeding manifest that this chapter is a prophecy of the prosperity of the church, in its most glorious state on earth, in the latter days; and I cannot think that any thing else can here be intended but America, by the isles that are afar off, from whence the first born sons of that glorious day shall be brought. . . . And what is chiefly intended is not the British Isles, nor any Isles near the other continent; for they are spoken of as at a great distance from that part of the world where the church had till then been. This prophecy therefore seems plainly to point out America, as the first fruits of that glorious day.

God has made as it were two worlds here below, the old

and the new (according to the names they are now called by),
two great habitable continents, far separated one from the
other; the latter is but newly discovered, it was formerly
wholly unknown, from age to age, and is as it were now but
newly created: it has been, until of late, wholly the possession
of Satan, the church of God having never been in it, as it has
been in the other continent, from the beginning of the world.
This new world is probably now discovered, that the new and
most glorious state of God's church on earth might commence
there; that God might in it begin a new world in a spiritual
respect, when he creates the *new heavens* and *new earth.*

God has already put that honor upon the other continent,
that Christ was born there literally, and there made the *purchase of redemption:* so, as Providence observes a kind of equal
distribution of things, it is not unlikely that the great spiritual
birth of Christ, and the most glorious *application of redemption*
is to begin in this. . . .

The other continent hath slain Christ, and has from age to
age shed the blood of the saints and martyrs of Jesus, and has
often been as it were deluged with the church's blood: God
has therefore probably reserved the honor of building the
glorious temple to the daughter, that has not shed so much
blood, when those times of the peace, and prosperity, and glory
of the church shall commence, that were typified by the
reign of Solomon.

The old continent has been the source and original of mankind, in several respects. The first parents of mankind dwelt
there; and there dwelt Noah and his sons; and there the second
Adam was born, and was crucified and rose again: and it is
probable that, in some measure to balance these things, the
most glorious renovation of the world shall originate from the
new continent, and the church of God in that respect be from
hence. And so it is probable that that will come to pass in
spirituals, that has in temporals, with respect to America; that

whereas till of late, the world was supplied with its silver and gold and earthly treasures from the old continent, now it is supplied chiefly from the new, so the course of things in spiritual respects will be in like manner turned.

And it is worthy to be noted that America was discovered about the time of the reformation, or but little before: which reformation was the first thing that God did towards the glorious renovation of the world, after it had sunk into the depths of darkness and ruin, under the great antichristian apostasy. So that as soon as this new world is (as it were) created, and stands forth in view, God presently goes about doing some great thing to make way for the introduction of the church's latter day glory, that is to have its first seat in, and is to take its rise from that new world.

It is agreeable to God's manner of working, when he accomplishes any glorious work in the world, to introduce a new and more excellent state of his church, to begin his work where his church had not been till then, and where was no foundation already laid, that the power of God might be the more conspicuous; that the work might appear to be entirely God's, and be more manifestly a creation out of nothing; agreeably to Hos. i. 10: "And it shall come to pass that in the place where it was said unto them, ye are not my people, there it shall be said unto them, ye are the sons of the living God." When God is about to turn the earth into a Paradise, he does not begin his work where there is some good growth already, but in a wilderness, where nothing grows, and nothing is to be seen but dry sand and barren rocks; that the light may shine out of darkness, and the world be replenished from emptiness, and the earth watered by springs from a droughty desert; agreeably to many prophecies of Scripture. . . .

I observed before, that when God is about to do some great work for his church, his manner is to begin at the lower end;

so when he is about to renew the whole habitable earth, it is probable that he will begin in this utmost, meanest, youngest and weakest part of it, where the church of God has been planted last of all; and so the first shall be last, and the last first; and that will be fulfilled in an eminent manner in Isa. xxiv. 16, "From the uttermost part of the earth have we heard songs, even glory to the righteous."

And if we may suppose that this glorious work of God shall begin in any part of America, I think if we consider the circumstances of the settlement of New England, it must needs appear the most likely of all American colonies, to be the place whence this work shall principally take its rise.

And if these things are so, it gives more abundant reason to hope that what is now seen in America, and especially in New England, may prove the dawn of that glorious day: and the very uncommon and wonderful circumstances and events of this work, seem to me strongly to argue that God intends it as the beginning or forerunner of something vastly great.

I have thus long insisted on this point, because if these things are so, it greatly manifests how much it behooves us to encourage and promote this work, and how dangerous it will be to forbear so to do. . . .

This work, that has lately been carried on in the land, is the work of God, and not the work of man. Its beginning has not been of man's power or device, and its being carried on, depends not on our strength or wisdom; but yet God expects of all, that they should use their utmost endeavors to promote it, and that the hearts of all should be greatly engaged in this affair, and that we should improve our utmost strength in it, however vain human strength is without the power of God; and so he no less requires that we should improve our utmost care, wisdom and prudence, though human wisdom of itself be as vain as human strength. . . . A great affair should be managed with great prudence: this is the most important affair that ever New England was called to be concerned in. When a people are engaged in war with a powerful and crafty nation, it concerns them to manage an affair of such consequence with the utmost discretion. Of what vast importance then must it be, that we should be vigilant and prudent, in the management of this great war that New England now has, with so great a host of such subtle and cruel enemies, wherein we must either conquer or be conquered, and the consequence of the victory, on one side, will be our eternal destruction, in both soul and body in hell, and on the other side, our obtaining the kingdom of heaven, and reigning in it in eternal glory? We had need always to stand on our watch, and to be well versed in the art of war, and not to be ignorant of the devices of our enemies, and to take heed lest by any means we be beguiled through their subtilty.

Though the devil be strong, yet in such a war as this, he depends more on his craft than his strength: and the course he has chiefly taken, from time to time, to clog, hinder and overthrow revivals of religion in the church of God, has been by his subtle, deceitful management, to beguile and mislead those that have been engaged therein; and in such a course God has been pleased, in his holy and sovereign providence, to suffer him to succeed, oftentimes, in a great measure to overthrow that, which in its beginning appeared most hopeful and glorious. The work that is now begun in New England, is, as I have shown, eminently glorious, and if it should go on and prevail, would make New England a kind of heaven upon earth: is it not therefore a thousand pities, that it should be overthrown, through wrong and improper management, that we are led into by our subtle adversary in our endeavors to promote it? . . .

I would take notice of some things, at which offence has been taken without, or beyond just cause.

One thing that has been complained of, is ministers addressing themselves, rather to the affections of their hearers, than to their understandings, and striving to raise their passions to the utmost height, rather by a very affectionate manner of speaking, and a great appearance of earnestness, in voice and gesture, than by clear reasoning and informing their judgment: by which means it is objected, that the affections are moved, without a proportionable enlightening of the understanding.

To which I would say, I am far from thinking that it is not very profitable, for ministers in their preaching, to endeavor clearly and distinctly to explain the doctrines of religion, and unravel the difficulties that attend them, and to confirm them with strength of reason and argumentation, and also to observe some easy and clear method and order, in their discourses, for the help of the understanding and memory; and it is very probable that these things have been of late, too much neglected, by many ministers; yet, I believe that the objection that is made, of affections raised without enlightening the understanding, is in a great measure built on a mistake, and confused notions that some have about the nature and cause of the affections, and the manner in which they depend on the understanding. All affections are raised either by light in the *understanding,* or by some error and delusion *in the understanding;* for all affections do certainly arise from some apprehension in the understanding; and that apprehension must either be agreeable to truth, or else be some mistake or delusion; if it be an apprehension or notion that is agreeable to truth, then it is *light in the understanding.* Therefore the thing to be inquired into is, whether the apprehensions or notions of divine and eternal things, that are raised in people's minds, by these affectionate preachers, whence their affections are excited, be apprehensions that are agreeable to truth, or whether they are mistakes. If the former, then the affections are raised the way they should be, viz., by informing the mind, or conveying light to the understanding. They go away with a wrong notion, that think that those preachers cannot affect their hearers, by enlightening their understandings, that do not do it by such a distinct, and learned handling of the doctrinal points of religion, as depends on human discipline, or the strength of natural reason, and tends to enlarge their hearers' learning, and speculative knowledge in divinity. The manner of preaching without this, may be such as shall tend very much to set divine and eternal things in a right view, and to give the hearers such ideas and apprehensions of them as are agreeable to truth, and such impressions on their hearts, as are answerable to the real nature of things: and not only the words that are spoken, but the manner of speaking, is one thing that has a great tendency to this. I think an exceeding affectionate way of preaching about the great things of religion, has in itself no tendency to beget false apprehensions of them; but on the contrary a much greater tendency to beget true apprehensions of them, than a moderate, dull, indifferent way of speaking of them. An appearance of affection and earnestness, in the manner of delivery, if it be very great indeed, yet if it be agreeable to the nature of the subject, and be not beyond a proportion to its importance, and worthiness of affection, and there be no appearance of its being feigned or forced, has so much the greater tendency to beget true ideas or apprehensions in the minds of the hearers, of the subject spoken of, and so to enlighten the understanding; and that for this reason, that such a way or manner of speaking of these things, does in fact, more truly represent them, than a more cold and indifferent way of speaking of them. If the subject be in its own nature, worthy of very great affection, then a speaking of it with very great affection, is most agreeable to the nature of that subject, or is the truest representation of it, and therefore has most of a tendency to beget true ideas of it, in the minds of those, to whom the representation is made. And I do not think ministers are to be blamed, for raising the affections of their hearers too high, if that which they are affected with, be only that which is worthy of affection, and their affections are not raised beyond a proportion to their importance, or worthiness of affection. I should think myself in the way of my duty, to raise the affections of my hearers as high as I possibly can, provided that they are affected with nothing but truth, and with affections that are not disagreeable to the nature of what they are affected with. I know it has long been fashionable to despise a very earnest and pathetical way of preaching: and they, and they only have been valued as preachers, that have shown the greatest extent of learning, and strength of reason, and correctness of method and language: but I humbly conceive it has been for want of understanding, or duly considering human nature, that such preaching has been thought to have the greatest tendency to answer the ends of preaching: and the experience of the present and past ages abundantly confirms the same. Though, as I said before, clearness of distinction and illustration, and strength of reason, and a good method, in the doctrinal handling of the truths of religion, is many ways needful and profitable, and not to be neglected, yet an increase in speculative knowledge in divinity, is not what is so much needed by our people, as something else. Men may abound in this sort of light and have no heat. How much has there been of this sort of knowledge in the Christian world, in this age! Was there ever an age wherein strength and penetration of reason, extent of learning, exactness of distinction, correctness of style, and clearness of expression, did so abound! And yet was there ever an age, wherein there has been so little sense of the evil of sin, so little love to God, heavenly mindedness, and holiness of life, among the professors of the true religion? Our people do not so much need to have their heads stored, as to have their hearts touched. . . .

. . . In what true Christians feel of affections towards God, all is not always purely holy and divine; every thing that is felt in the affections does not arise from spiritual principles, but common and natural principles have a very great hand; an improper self-love may have a great share in the effect: God is not loved for his own sake, or for the excellency and beauty of his own perfections, as he ought to be; nor have these things in any wise that proportion in the effect that they ought to have. So in that love that true Christians have one to another, very often there is a great mixture of what arises from common and natural principles, with grace; and self-love has a great hand: the children of God are not loved purely for Christ's sake, but there may be a great mixture of that natural love that many sects of heretics have boasted of, who have been greatly united one to another, because they were of their company, on their side, against the rest of the world; yea, there may be a mixture of natural love to the opposite sex, with Christian and divine love. So there may be a great mixture in that sorrow for sin that the godly have; and also in their joys; natural principles may greatly contribute to what is felt, a great many ways, as might easily be shown, would it not make my discourse too lengthy. There is nothing that belongs to Christian experience that is more liable to a corrupt mixture than zeal; though it be an excellent virtue, a heavenly flame, when it is pure: but as it is exercised in those who are so little sanctified, and so little humbled, as we are in the present state, it is very apt to be mixed with human passion, yea, with corrupt hateful affections, pride and uncharitable bitterness, and other things that are not from heaven but from hell.

Another thing that is often mixed with what is spiritual in the experiences of Christians, is, impressions on the imagination; whereby godly persons, together with a spiritual understanding of divine things, and conviction of their reality and certainty, and a strong and deep sense of their excellency or great importance upon their hearts, have strongly impressed on their minds external ideas or images of things. A degree of imagination in such a case, as I have observed elsewhere, is unavoidable, and necessarily arises from human nature, as constituted in the present state; and a degree of imagination is really useful, and often is of great benefit; but when it is in too great a degree, it becomes an impure mixture that is prejudicial. This mixture very often arises from the constitution of the body. It commonly greatly contributes to the other kind of mixture mentioned before, viz, of natural affections and passions; it helps to raise them to a great height.

Another thing that is often mixed with the experiences of true Christians, which is the worst mixture of all, is a degree of self-righteousness or spiritual pride. This is often mixed with the joys of Christians; the joy that they have is not purely the joy of faith, or a rejoicing in Christ Jesus, but is partly a rejoicing in themselves; there is oftentimes in their elevations a looking upon themselves, and a viewing their own high attainments; they rejoice partly because they are taken with their own experiences and great discoveries, which makes them in their own apprehensions so to excel; and this heightens all their passions, and especially those effects that are more external.

There is a much greater mixture of these things in the experiences of some Christians than others; in some the mixture is so great, as very much to obscure and hide the beauty of grace in them, like a thick smoke that hinders all the shining of the fire.

These things we ought to be well aware of, that we may not

take all for gold that glistens, and that we may know what to countenance and encourage, and what to discourage; otherwise Satan will have a vast advantage against us, for he works in the corrupt mixture. Sometimes for want of persons distinguishing the ore from the pure metal, those experiences are most admired by the persons themselves that are the subjects of them, and by others that are not the most excellent. The great external effects, and vehemence of the passions, and violent agitations of the animal spirits, is sometimes much owing to the corrupt mixture (as is very apparent in some instances); though it be not always so. . . .

Thus I have, as I proposed, taken notice of some things with regard to the inward experiences of Christians, by which Satan has an advantage.

I now proceed in the

2d Place, to take notice of something with regard to the external effects of experiences, which also gives Satan an advantage. What I have respect to, is the secret and unaccountable influence that custom has upon persons, with respect to the external effects and manifestations of the inward affections of the mind. By custom I mean both a person's being accustomed to a thing in himself, in his own common, allowed, and indulged practice, and also the countenance and approbation of others amongst whom he dwells, by their general voice and practice. It is well known, and appears sufficiently by what I have said already in this treatise and elsewhere, that I am far from ascribing all the late uncommon effects and outward manifestations of inward experiences to custom and fashion, as some do; I know it to be otherwise, if it be possible for me to know any thing of this nature by the most critical observation, under all manner of opportunities of observing. But yet this also is exceeding evident by experience, that custom has a strange influence in these things: I know it by the different manners and degrees of external effects and manifestations of great affections and high discoveries, in different towns, according to what persons are gradually led into, and insensibly habituated to, by example and custom; and also in the same place, at different times, according to the conduct that they have: if some person is among them to conduct them, that much countenances and encourages such kind of outward manifestations of great affections, they naturally and insensibly prevail, and grow by degrees unavoidable; but when afterwards they come under another kind of conduct, the manner of external appearances will strangely alter: and yet it seems to be without any proper design or contrivance of those in whom there is this alteration; it is not properly affected by them, but the influence of example and custom is secret and insensible to the persons themselves. These things have a vast influence in the manner of persons manifesting their joys, whether with smiles or an air of lightness, or whether with more solemnity and reverence; and so they have a great influence as to the disposition persons have, under high affections, to abound in talk; and also as to the manner of their speaking, the loudness and vehemence of their speech; (though it would be exceeding unjust, and against all the evidence of fact and experience, and the reason of things, to lay all dispositions persons have to be much in speaking to others, and to speak in a very earnest manner, to custom.) It is manifest that example and custom have some way or other, a secret and unsearchable influence on those actions that are involuntary, by the difference that there is in different places, and in the same places at different times, according to the diverse examples and conduct that they have.

Therefore, though it would be very unreasonable, and prejudicial to the interest of religion, to frown upon all these extraordinary external effects and manifestations of great religious affections (for a measure of them is natural, necessary, and beautiful, and the effect in no wise disproportioned to the spiritual cause, and is of great benefit to promote religion), yet I think they greatly err who think that these things should be wholly unlimited, and that all should be encouraged in going in these things to the utmost length that they feel themselves inclined to: the consequence of this will be very bad: there ought to be a gentle restraint held upon these things, and there should be a prudent care taken of persons in such extraordinary circumstances, and they should be moderately advised, at proper seasons, not to make more ado than there is need of, but rather to hold a restraint upon their inclinations; otherwise extraordinary outward effects will grow upon them, they will be more and more natural and unavoidable, and the extraordinary outward show will increase, without any increase of the internal cause; persons will find themselves under a kind of necessity of making a great ado, with less and less affection of soul, until at length almost any slight emotion will set them going, and they will be more and more violent and boisterous, and will grow louder and louder, until their actions and behavior become indeed very absurd. These things experience proves.

Thus I have taken notice of the more general causes whence the errors that have attended this great revival of religion have risen, and under each head have observed some particular errors that have flowed from these fountains. I now proceed as I proposed in the

Second place, to take notice of some particular errors that have risen from several of these causes; in some perhaps they have been chiefly owing to one, and in others to another, and in others to the influence of several, or all conjunctly. And here the

1*st* Thing I would take notice of, is, censuring others that are professing Christians, in good standing in the visible church, as unconverted. I need not repeat what I have elsewhere said to show this to be against the plain, and frequent, and strict prohibitions of the word of God: it is the worst disease that has attended this work, most contrary to the spirit and rules of Christianity, and of worse consequences. There is a most unhappy tincture that the minds of many, both ministers and people, have received that way. The manner of many has been, when they first enter into conversation with any person, that seems to have any shew or make any pretences to religion, to discern him, or to fix a judgment of him, from his manner of talking of things of religion, whether he be converted, or experimentally acquainted with vital piety or not, and then to treat him accordingly, and freely to express their thoughts of him to others, especially those that they have a good opinion of as true Christians, and accepted as brethren and companions in Christ; or if they do not declare their minds expressly, yet by their manner of speaking of them, at least to their friends, they will show plainly what their thoughts are. So when they have heard any minister pray or preach, their first work has been to observe him on a design of discerning him, whether he be a converted man or no; whether he prays like one that feels the saving power of God's Spirit in his heart, and whether he preaches like one that knows what he says. It has been so much the way in some places, that many new converts do not know but it is their duty to do so, they know no other way. And when once persons yield to such a notion, and give in to such a humor, they will quickly grow very discerning in their own apprehension, they think they can easily tell a hypocrite: and when once they have passed their censure every thing seems to confirm it, they see more and more in the person that they have censured, that seems to them to shew plainly that he is an unconverted man. And then, if the person censured be a minister, every thing in his public performances seems dead and sapless, and to do them no good at all, but on the contrary to be of deadening influence, and poisonous to the soul; yea, it seems worse and worse to them, his preaching grows more and more intolerable: which is owing to a secret, strong prejudice, that steals in more and more upon the mind, as experience plainly and certainly shows. When the Spirit of God was wonderfully poured out in this place, more than seven years ago, and near thirty souls in a week, take one with another, for five or six weeks together, were to appearance brought home to Christ, and all the town seemed to be alive and full of God, there was no such notion or humor prevailing here; when ministers preached here, as very many did at that time, young and old, our people did not go about to discern whether they were men of experience or not; they did not know that they must: Mr. Stoddard never brought them up in that way; it did not seem natural to them to go about any thing of that nature, nor did any such thing enter in their hearts; but when any minister preached, the business of every one was to listen and attend to what he said, and apply it to his own heart, and make the utmost improvement of it. And it is remarkable, that never did there appear such a disposition in the people, to relish, approve of, and admire ministers' preaching as at that time: such expressions as these were frequent in the mouths of one and another, on occasion of the preaching of strangers here, viz., *That they rejoiced that there were so many such eminent ministers in the country; and they wondered they had never heard the fame of them before: they were thankful that other towns had so good means;* and the like.—And scarcely ever did any minister preach here, but his preaching did some remarkable service; as I had good opportunity to know, because, at that time, I had particular acquaintance with most of the persons in the town, in their soul concerns. That it has been so much otherwise of late in many places in the land, is another instance of the secret and powerful influence of custom and example.

There has been an unhappy disposition in some ministers toward their brethren in the ministry in this respect, which has encouraged and greatly promoted such a spirit among some

of their people. A wrong improvement has been made of
Christ's scourging the buyers and sellers out of the temple; it
has been expected by some, that Christ was now about thus
to purge his house of unconverted ministers, and this has
made it more natural to them to think that they should do
Christ service, and act as co-workers with him, to put to their
hand, and endeavor by all means to cashier those ministers
that they thought to be unconverted. Indeed, it appears to
me probable that the time is coming, when awful judgments
will be executed on unfaithful ministers, and that no sort of
men in the world will be so much exposed to divine judgments;
but then we should leave that work to Christ, who is the
searcher of hearts, and to whom vengeance belongs; and not
without warrant, take the scourge out of his hand into our
own. There has been too much of a disposition in some, as it
were to give ministers over as reprobates, that have been
looked upon as wolves in sheep's clothing; which has tended
to promote and encourage a spirit of bitterness towards them,
and to make it natural to treat them too much as if they knew
God hated them. If God's children knew that others were
reprobates, it would not be required of them to love them; we
may hate those that we know God hates; as it is lawful to
hate the devil, and as the saints at the day of judgment will
hate the wicked. Some have been too apt to look for fire from
heaven upon particular ministers; and this has naturally excited that disposition to call for it, that Christ rebuked in his
disciples at Samaria. For my part, though I believe no sort of
men on earth are so exposed to spiritual judgments as wicked
ministers, yet I feel no disposition to treat any minister as if
I supposed that he was finally rejected of God; for I cannot but
hope that there is coming a day of such great grace, a time so
appointed for the magnifying the riches and sovereignty of
divine mercy, beyond what ever was, that a great number of
unconverted ministers will obtain mercy. . . .

Nothing has been gained by this practice. The end that

some have aimed at in it has not been obtained, nor is ever like to be. Possibly some have openly censured ministers, and encouraged their people's uneasiness under them, in hopes that it would soon come to that, that the uneasiness would be so general, and so great, that unconverted ministers in general would be cast off, and that then things would go on happily: but there is no likelihood of it. The devil indeed has obtained his end; this practice has bred a great deal of unhappiness among ministers and people, has spoiled Christians' enjoyment of sabbaths, and made them their most uneasy, uncomfortable and unprofitable days, and has stirred up great contention, and set all in a flame; and in one place and another where there was a glorious work of God's Spirit begun, it has in a great measure knocked all in the head, and their ministers hold their places. Some have aimed at a better end in censuring ministers; they have supposed it to be a likely means to awaken them: whereas indeed, there is no one thing has had so great a tendency to prevent the awakening of disaffected ministers in general: and no one thing has actually had such influence to lock up the minds of ministers against any good effect of this great work of God in the land upon their minds in this respect: I have known instances of some that seemed to be much moved by the first appearance of this work, but since have seemed to be greatly deadened by what has appeared of this nature. And if there be one or two instances of ministers that have been awakened by it, there are ten to one on whom it has had a contrary influence. The worst enemies of this work have been inwardly eased by this practice; they have made a shield of it to defend their consciences, and have been glad that it has been carried to so great a length; at the same time that they have looked upon it, and improved it, as a door opened for them to be more bold in opposing the work in general.

There is no such dreadful danger of natural men's being un-done by our forbearing thus to censure them, and carrying it towards them as visible Christians; it will be no bloody, hell-peopling charity, as some seem to suppose, when it is known that we do not treat them as Christians, because we have taken it upon us to pass a judgment on their state, on any trial, or exercise of our skill in examining and discerning them, but only as allowing them to be worthy of a public charity, on their profession and good external behavior; any more than Judas was in danger of being deceived, by Christ's treating him a long time as a disciple, and sending him forth as an apostle, (because he did not then take it upon him to act as the Judge and Searcher of hearts, but only as the Head of the visible church). Indeed, such a charity as this may be abused by some, as every thing is, and will be, that is in its own nature proper, and of never so good tendency. I say nothing against dealing thoroughly with conscience, by the most convincing and searching dispensation of the word of God: I do not desire that that sword should be sheathed, or gently handled by ministers; but let it be used as a two edged sword, to pierce, even to the dividing asunder soul and spirit, joints and marrow; let conscience be dealt with, without any compliments; let ministers handle it in flaming fire, without having any more mercy on it, than the furnace has on those metals that are tried in it. But let us let men's persons alone: let the word of God judge them, but do not let us take it upon us until we have warrant for it.

Some have been ready to censure ministers because they seem, in comparison of some other ministers, to be very cold and lifeless in their ministerial performances. But then it should be considered that for aught we know, God may hereafter raise up ministers of so much more excellent and heavenly qualifications, and so much more spiritual and divine in their performances, that there may appear as great a difference between them, and those that now seem the most lively, as there is now between them, and others that are called dead and sapless; and those that are now called lively ministers may appear to their hearers, when they compare them with others that shall excel them, as wretchedly mean, and their performances poor, dead, dry things; and many may be ready to be prejudiced against them, as accounting them good for nothing, and it may be calling them soul murderers. What a poor figure may we suppose, the most lively of us, and those that are most admired by the people, do make in the eyes of one of the saints of heaven, any otherwise than as their deadness, deformity, and rottenness is hid by the vail of Christ's righteousness?

Another thing that has been supposed to be sufficient warrant for openly censuring ministers as unconverted, is their opposing this work of God, that has lately been carried on in the land. And there can be no doubt with me but that opposition against this work may be such, as to render either ministers or people truly scandalous, and to expose them to public ecclesiastical censure; and that ministers hereby may utterly defeat the design of the ministry, as I observed before; and so give their people just cause of uneasiness; I should not think that any person had power to oblige me constantly to attend the ministry of one, who did from time to time, plainly pray and preach against this work, or speak reproachfully of it frequently in his public performances, after all Christian methods had been used for a remedy, and to no purpose.

But as to determining how far opposing this work is consistent with a state of grace, or how far, and for how long time, some persons of good experience in their own souls, through prejudices they have received from the errors that have been mixed with this work, or through some peculiar disadvantages they are under to behold things in a right view of them, by reason of the persons they converse with, or their own cold and dead frames, is, as experience shows, a very difficult thing; I have seen that which abundantly convinces me that the business is too high for me; I am glad that God has not committed such a difficult affair to me; I can joyfully leave it wholly in his hands who is infinitely fit for it, without meddling

at all with it myself. We may represent it as exceeding dangerous to oppose this work, for this we have good warrant in the
word of God; but I know of not necessity we are under to
determine whether it be possible for those that are guilty of it
to be in a state of grace or no.

God seems so strictly to have forbidden this practice, of our
judging our brethren in the visible church, not only because
he knew that we were too much of babes, infinitely too weak,
fallible, and blind, to be well capacitated for it, but also because he knew that it was not a work suited to our proud
hearts; that it would be setting us vastly too high, and making
us too much lords over our fellow creatures. Judging our
brethren and passing a condemnatory sentence upon them,
seems to carry in it an act of authority, especially in so great
a case, to sentence them with respect to that state of their
hearts, on which depends their liableness to eternal damnation; as is evident by such interrogations as these (to hear
which from God's mouth, is enough to make us shrink into
nothing with shame and confusion, and a sense of our own
blindness and worthlessness), Rom. xiv. 4, "Who art thou that
judgest another man's servant? To his own master he standeth
or falleth." And Jam. iv. 12, "There is one lawgiver that is able
to save and to destroy; who art thou that judgest another?"
Our wise and merciful Shepherd has graciously taken care
not to lay in our way such a temptation to pride; he has cut
up all such poison out of our pasture; and therefore we should
not desire to have it restored. Blessed be his name, that he has
not laid such a temptation in the way of my pride! I know that
in order to be fit for this business I must not only be vastly
more knowing, but more humble than I am.

Though I believe some of God's own children have of late
been very guilty in this matter, yet by what is said of it in the
Scripture, it appears to me very likely, that before these things
which God has lately begun, have an end, God will awfully
rebuke that practice; may it in sovereign and infinite mercy

be prevented, by the deep and open humiliation of those that have openly practised it.

As this practice ought to be avoided, so should all such open, visible, marks of distinction and separation that imply it; as particularly, distinguishing such as we have judged to be in a converted state with the compellations of *brother* or *sister;* any further than there is a visible ecclesiastical distinction. In those places where it is the manner to receive such, and such only to the communion of the visible church, as recommend themselves by giving a satisfying account of their inward experiences, there Christians may openly distinguish such persons, in their speech and ordinary behavior, with a visible separation, without being inconsistent with themselves: and I do not now pretend to meddle with that controversy, whether such an account of experience be requisite to church fellowship: but certainly, to admit persons to communion with us as brethren in the visible church, and then visibly to reject them, and to make an open distinction between them and others, by different names or appellations, is to be inconsistent with ourselves; it is to make a visible church within a visible church, and visibly to divide between sheep and goats, setting one on the right hand, and the other on the left.

This bitter root of censoriousness must be totally rooted out, as we would prepare the way of the Lord. It has nourished and upheld many other things contrary to the humility, meekness, and love of the gospel. The minds of many have received an unhappy turn, in some respects, with their religion: there is a certain point or sharpness, a disposition to a kind of warmth, that does not savor of that meek, lamblike, sweet disposition that becomes Christians: many have now been so long habituated to it, that they do not know how to get out of it; but we must get out of it; the point and sharpness must be blunted, and we must learn another way of manifesting our zeal for God.

28 · *Charles Chauncy*

SEASONABLE THOUGHTS ON

THE STATE OF RELIGION

In his *Thoughts on the Revival* Edwards moved from an assessment of the experience through which New England had passed to a consideration of the shape of things to come. Charles Chauncy almost accepted the challenge— at least to the extent of making his *Seasonable Thoughts on the State of Religion in New-England* something more than what it had evidently been conceived as: a compendium of horror stories about the worst emotional extravagances of the Awakening. Chauncy solicited such material from correspondents throughout New England and even toured the provinces personally to collect eye-witness accounts. Together these accounts and letters would provide irrefutable evidence that what had taken place was not a "Work of God." But when Chauncy was confronted with Edwards' manifesto and the necessity of answering it, his commentary on the revival expanded into

Charles Chauncy, *Seasonable Thoughts on the State of Religion in New-England* . . . (Boston, 1743), pp. 319–325, 366–375.

a sustained argument against, not enthusiasm merely, but all the major points in the "program" of his mighty opposite. His *Seasonable Thoughts,* its list of subscribers comprising New England's "social register" of the day, was unquestionably the official utterance of the antirevivalists. Chauncy codified the many criticisms of the revival, to all of which he had special access by virtue of his role as chieftain of the opposition. "I wrote and printed in that day more than two volumes in octavo," Chauncy later recalled. "A vast number of pieces were published also as written by others; but there was scarce a piece against the times but was sent to me, and I had labour sometimes of preparing it for the press, and always of correcting the press. I had also hundreds of letters to write, in answer to letters received from all parts of the country." But the *Seasonable Thoughts* is more than the capstone of Chauncy's indefatigable labors against the Awakening. In it Chauncy established the rubrics under which enthusiasm would be assailed for several generations. Indeed, his *Seasonable Thoughts* was the first comprehensive statement of the new American rationalism. Yet Chauncy's volume never enjoyed the popularity of the work it was designed to refute. Eleazar Wheelock, an itinerant of the 1740's who was later to be Dartmouth's first president, believed that Chauncy's volume was "never vendible," except among a handful of Connecticut Arminians. Even those religious leaders who later honored Chauncy for his efforts to prevent the creation of an American bishop seemed to prefer that his strictures against the Awakening be forgotten. Most evangelical spokesmen, of course, considered them unforgivable, and one suspects that enlightened Americans found Chauncy's *Seasonable Thoughts* disturbing. For here Chauncy revealed how darkly pessimistic a vision of the American future could be seen through the newly-opening eye of reason.

. . . The true Account to be given of the *many* and *great* Mistakes of the present Day, about the SPIRIT's Influence, is not the *Newness* of the Thing, the not having *felt it before;* but a *notorious* Error generally prevailing, as to the *Way* and *Manner* of judging in this Matter. People, in order to know, whether the Influences they are under, are from the SPIRIT, don't carefully examine them by the *Word of GOD*, and view the *Change* they produce in the *moral State* of their *Minds* and of their *Lives*, but hastily conclude such and such *internal Motions* to be *divine Impressions*, meerly from the *Perception* they have of them. They are ready, at once, if this is *unusual*, or *strong*, to take it for some Influence from above, to speak of it as such, and to act accordingly. This is the Error of the present Day; and 'tis indeed the *proton Pseudos*, the first and grand Delusion: And where this prevails, we need not be at a loss to know the *true Spring* of other Errors.—As to the *Multitudes* who are bro't into such *new*, and (to them) *unheard of Circumstances*, 'tis true, they are *illiterate*, and *young* People; but this notwithstanding, if the *Newness* of their Circumstances is such as is proper to *new Creatures*, they will, in their *general Behaviour*, discover the *true Spirit* and *Genius* of this Sort of Persons. 'Tis a great Mistake to think, that the *new Nature*, or those *Influences* that produce it, however extraordinary, are apt to put Men upon making *wrong* and *strange* Judgments, either of *Persons* or *Things:*

They have a contrary Tendency: and 'tis a Reproach to them both, to suppose otherwise. A *meer passionate* Religion, 'tis true, has always led to this, and always will; but not that, which enlightens the Understanding, renews the Will, and makes the Heart good and honest.—How far 'tis a Truth, that *this People* have *scarce* heard of such a Thing as the *Outpouring* of the SPIRIT of GOD, or had *no Notion* of it, may admit of Dispute; but that the *Outpouring* of the SPIRIT should introduce *such a State of Things,* as that those *upon whom* he has been *poured out,* should *not know how to behave,* will, I think, admit of no good Plea in its Defence. 'Tis a plain Case, one of the *main Ends* of the *Out-pouring* of the SPIRIT, is to dispose and enable People to behave as *Christians,* in their various *Stations, Relations* and *Conditions* of Life; and if instead of this, they are thrown into such a *strange State,* as that they can't behave as they ought to do, not in here and there a perplext Case, but in some of the most *obvious* and *essential* Points of Practice; let who will call this an *Out-pouring* of the SPIRIT, 'tis not such an one as the *Bible* knows any Thing of. And 'tis nothing short of a gross Reflection on the *blessed SPIRIT,* to speak of *him* as *wonderfully* poured out upon a People, and, at the same Time, to suppose such a State of Things arising therefrom, as that People may run into *very ill Conduct,* and it not be thought *strange,* if they do so.— What is observ'd of People's *Readings* to hearken to those, who have been the *Instruments* of bringing them into their present Circumstances, I own, is no other than might be expected: Nor have I any Doubt, upon my Mind, whether the *Disorders,* so *general* in this Land, had their *Rise* from these Persons. But *Schism,* and *Confusion,* and other *evil Works,* won't change their Nature, be their *Origin* in *People* themselves, or their *Leaders.*

It is still urged, "That when Persons are *extraordinarily* affected with a recent Discovery of the Greatness and Excellency of the divine Being, the Certainty and infinite Importance of eternal Things, the Preciousness of Souls, and the dreadful Danger and Madness of Mankind, together with a great Sense of GOD's distinguishing Kindness and Love to them; no Wonder that now they think they must exert themselves, and do something extraordinary, for the Honour of God, and the Good of Souls, and know not how to forbear speaking and acting with uncommon Earnestness and Vigour. And in these circumstances, if they ben't Persons of uncommon Steadiness and Discretion, or han't some Persons of Wisdom to direct them, 'tis a Wonder, if they don't proceed without due Caution, and do Things that are irregular, and will, in the Issue, do more Hurt than Good." 'Tis readily granted, Persons under a just and strong Sense of divine Things, will exert themselves with an awaken'd Activity in the Business of Religion. 'Twould be no Wonder, if those who had *extraordinary* Discoveries of GOD, were, to an *extraordinary* Degree, filled with Lowliness and Humility, and such an Awe and Reverence of the divine Majesty, as would make them *eminently* circumspect in their whole Deportment towards him; if from the *uncommon* View they had of his Perfections, they were, in an *uncommon* Manner, transformed into his Likeness, appearing in the World *lively Images* of that Goodness, Righteousness, Faithfulness, Kindness, Mercy, Patience and Long-suffering, which are the *moral Glory* of the infinitely perfect Being. 'Twould be no Wonder, if those, who had upon their Minds an *extraordinary* Sense of the *Preciousness of Souls*, discovered extraordinary Care and Pains in working out the Salvation of their *own Souls*; if they were observably *diligent* in *adding to their Faith, Vertue; to Vertue, Knowledge; to Knowledge, Temperance; to Temperance, Patience; to Patience, Godliness; to Godliness, Brotherly-Kindness; and to Brotherly-Kindness, Charity: For they that lack these Things are blind* to the Worth of their *own Souls*; whereas, they *that do them* make it evident that they regard their Souls: *For so an Entrance shall be ministred to them abundantly, into the everlasting Kingdom of our* LORD *and* SAVIOUR JESUS CHRIST. In like Manner, 'twould be no Wonder, if those who had an *extraordinary* View of the *Danger* and *Madness* of those who neglect their Souls, were *proportionably* active, within their *proper Sphere,* in Endeavours to do them all the Service they could; if they were ready with their Advice, their Counsel, their Prayers, their Intreaties, to beget in them a just Concern about Salvation: Nor would they be "worthy of *Indignation,* and be beyond *Compassion*," if, through an *indiscreet Zeal* they should, now and then, be betray'd into Weaknesses and Excesses. These are Things, not to be wondered at; they are no other than might reasonably be expected. But the Wonder is, how an *extraordinary* Discovery of the Greatness and Excellency of GOD, the Importance of eternal Things, and the Preciousness of Souls, and the Danger of their perishing, should make Men vain and conceited, full of themselves, and apt to throw Contempt on others; how it should loosen Men's Tongues to utter such Language as would not be seemly, even in those who profess no Sense of GOD, or divine Things; how it should lead them into wrong Sentiments in Religion, blind their Eyes as to some of the most plain Points of Doctrine; and in a Word, dispose them to such Things as are called in Scripture, the *Works of the Flesh.*

These don't look like the Fruit of *extraordinary* Discoveries of GOD; but they are the very Things which may be expected, where Men's *Passions* are rais'd to an *extraordinary* Height, without a proportionable Degree of Light in their Understandings.

Such *high Affections,* I know, are freely spoken of as owing to the Influence of the SPIRIT of GOD; and this, when there is not given "*Strength* of *Understanding* in *Proportion;* and by Means hereof, the *Subjects* of these Affections may be driven, through Error, into an *irregular* and *sinful Conduct.*" But it may justly be question'd, whether *extraordinary Warmth* in the *Passions,* when there is not *answerable Light* in the *Mind,* is so much owing to the SPIRIT of GOD, as some may be ready to imagine. For is it reasonable to think, that the *Divine SPIRIT,* in dealing with Men in a Way of Grace, and in Order to make them good Christians, would give their *Passions* the *chief* Sway over them? Would not this be to invert their Frame? To place the Dominion in those Powers, which were made to be kept in Subjection? And would the alwise GOD introduce such a State of Things in the human Mind? Can this be the Effect of the *Out-pouring* of his SPIRIT? It ought not to be supposed. One of the most *essential* Things necessary in the *new-forming* Men, is the Reduction of their *Passions* to a proper Regimen, i. e. The Government of a *sanctified Understanding:* And 'till this is effected, they may be called *New-Creatures,* but they are far from deserving this Character. *Reasonable* Beings are not to be guided by *Passion* or *Affection,* though the Object of it should be GOD, and the Things of another World: They need, even in this Case, to be under the Government of a *well instructed Judgment:* Nay, when Men's *Passions* are raised to an *extraordinary* Height, if they have not, at the same Time, a due Ballance of *Light* and *Knowledge* in their Minds, they are so far from being in a more desirable State on this Account, that they are in Circumstances of extreme Hazard. There is no Wildness, but they are liable to be hurried into it; there is no Temptation, but they are expos'd to be drawn aside by it: Nor has the Devil ever greater Advantage against them, to make a Prey of them, and lead them captive at his Will. And this has often been verified by sad Experience. Who can boast of greater Transports of Affection, than the wildest Enthusiasts? Who have had their Passions excited to a higher Pitch, than those of the ROMISH Communion? Who have been more artful in their

Addresses to the *Passions,* than *Popish Priests?* And who more successful, by *heating* the *Affections* of People, to establish Error and Delusion? Nay, what Engine has the *Devil* himself ever made Use of, to more fatal Purposes, in all Ages, than the *Passions* of the *Vulgar* heightened to such a Degree, as to put them upon acting without Thought and Understanding? The plain Truth is, an *enlightened Mind,* and not *raised Affections,* ought always to be the Guide of those who call themselves Men; and this, in the Affairs of Religion, as well as other Things: And it will be so, where GOD really works on their Hearts, by his SPIRIT. 'Tis true, "the End of the Influence of the SPIRIT of GOD is not to increase Men's natural Capacities:" But 'tis to fit their Powers for religious Exercise, and preserve them in a State of due Subordination. 'Tis as much intended to *open the Understanding,* as to *warm the Affections;* and not only so, but to keep the *Passions* within their proper Bounds, restraining them from usurping Dominion over the *reasonable* Nature. 'Tis true likewise, "GOD has not oblig'd himself immediately to increase *civil Prudence,* in Proportion to the Degrees of *spiritual Light.*" But if it shall please GOD to visit Men with the Influences of his SPIRIT, it may justly be expected, that he should increase their *moral* or *religious* Prudence; that, if he should give them *spiritual Light,* it should be for their Instruction in the Knowledge of what is *Sin,* and what is *Duty.* . . .

I have hitherto considered *Ministers* as the Persons, more especially obliged to discountenance the bad Things, prevailing in the Land; and now go on to observe.

That this is the Duty of *all in general.* Not that I would put any upon acting out of their *proper Sphere.* This would tend rather to Confusion than Reformation.—Good Order is the Strength and Beauty of the World.—The Prosperity both of *Church* and *State* depends very much upon it. And can there be Order, where Men transgress the Limits of their Station, and intermeddle in the Business of others? So far from it, that the only effectual Method, under GOD, for the Redress of *general Evils,* is, for *every one* to be faithful, in doing what is *proper* for him in his *own Place:* And even *all* may *properly* bear a Part, in *rectifying the Disorders* of this Kind, at this Day.

Civil Rulers may do a great deal, not only by their *good Example,* but a wise Use of their *Authority,* in their various Places, for the Suppression of every Thing hurtful to Society, and the Encouragement of whatever has a Tendency to make Men happy in the Enjoyment of their Rights, whether *natural* or *Christian.* And herein chiefly lies, (as I humbly conceive) the Duty of Rulers, at this Day. 'Tis true, as *private Men,* they are under the same Obligations with others, to make their Acknowledgments to CHRIST; and doubtless, if HE was *visibly* and *externally* (according to the Custom among *Kings* and *Governors*) to make his solemn Entry into the Land, as their SAVIOUR and LORD, "it would be expected they should, as *public Officers,* make their Appearance, and attend him as their *Sovereign* with sutable Congratulations, and Manifestations of Respect and Loyalty; and if they should stand at a Distance, it would be much more taken Notice of, and awaken his Displeasure much more, than such a Behaviour in the common People."[1] But the Case is widely different, where his supposed Entry is in a *spiritual Sense only, and after such a Manner* even in this Sense, as that there is a *great Variety of Sentiments* about it, among the *best Sort* of Men, of all Ranks and Conditions: Nor does it appear to me, when the Case is thus circumstanc'd, that it is either the *Duty* of *Rulers,* or would be Wisdom in them, by any *authoritative Acts* to determine, whose Sentiments were the most agreable to Truth. And as to their Appointment of Days of *Thanksgiving,* or *fasting,* on this

---

[1] Vid. Mr. EDWARDS's Book of the *late Revival of Religion.*

Account, there must be an Impropriety in it, so long as that Complaint of GOD against the *Jews* is to be seen in the *Bible, Behold ye fast for Strife and Debate!* Their *Duty* rather lies in keeping Peace between those, who unhappily differ in their Thoughts about the State of our religious Affairs: And their Care in this Matter ought to be *impartial*. Each Party, without Favour or Affection, should be equally restrain'd from Out-rage and Insult. Those, who may think themselves Friends to a *Work of GOD*, should be protected in the Exercise of all their *just Rights*, whether as *Men*, or *Christians:* So on the other Hand, those who may be Enemies to *Error* and *Confusion*, have the same Claim to be protected.

And if, on either Side, they invade the Rights of others, or throw out Slander, at Random, to the Hurt of their Neighbour's Reputation and Usefulness, and the bringing forward a State of Tumult and Disorder; I see not but the *civil Arm* may justly be stretched forth for the Chastisement of such Persons; and this, though their Abuses should be offered in the Name of the LORD, or under the Pretext of the most flaming Zeal for the REDEEMER's *Honour*, and serving the Interest of *his Kingdom:* For it ought always to be accounted an Aggravation of the Sin of *Slander*, rather than an Excuse for it, its being committed under the *Cloak of Religion*, and Pretence for the *Glory of GOD;* as it will, under these Circumstances, be of more pernicious Tendency. I am far from thinking, that any Man ought to suffer, either for his *religious Principles*, or *Conduct* arising from them, while he is no Disturber of the *civil Peace;* but when Men, under the Notion of appearing zealous for GOD and *his Truths*, insult their Betters, vilify their Neighbours, and spirit People to Strife and Faction, I know of no Persons more sutable to be taken in Hand by *Authority:* And if they suffer 'tis for their own Follies; nor can they reasonably blame any Body but themselves: Nor am I asham'd, or afraid, to profess it as my Opinion, that it would probably have been

of good Service, if those, in these Times, who have been publickly and out-ragiously reviled, had, by their Complaints, put
it properly in the *Magistrates* Power, to restrain some Men's
Tongues with *Bit* and *Bridle*.

Private Christians also, of all Ranks and Conditions, may do
something towards the Suppression of these *Errors*, by mourning before the LORD the Dishonour which has hereby been
reflected on the Name of CHRIST, and Injury done to Souls; by
being much in Prayer to GOD for the Out-pouring of his
SPIRIT, in all desirable Influences of Light, and Love, and
Peace; by taking good Heed that they ben't themselves drawn
aside, avoiding to this End, the Company and familiar Converse of those, who, by *good Words* and *fair Speeches,* might
be apt to deceive their Hearts, but especially an Attendance
on religious Exercises, where the *Churches* and *Ministry* are
freely declaimed against by those who have gone out from
them, under the vain Pretence of being more holy than they;
and in fine, by a faithful Performance of those Duties, which
arise from the various Relations they sustain towards each
other: As thus, if they are *Children,* by hearkening to the
Advice of their *Parents,* and obeying and honouring them in
the LORD; and if they are *Parents,* by counseling, reproving,
warning, restraining, and commanding their *Children,* as there
may be Occasion: If they are *Servants,* by pleasing their *Masters* well in all Things, not defrauding them of their Time or
Labour, but accounting them worthy of all Honour, that the
Name of GOD be not blasphemed; and, if they are *Masters,*
not only by providing for their *Servants* Things honest and
good, but by keeping them within the Rules of Order and
Decorum, not suffering them to neglect the Religion of the
Family at home, under Pretence of carrying it on elsewhere;
especially, when they continue abroad 'till late in the Night,
and so as to unfit themselves for the Services of the following
Day.

In these, and such like Ways, *all* may exert themselves in making a Stand against the Progress of Error: And *all* are oblig'd to do so; and for this Reason, among others I han't Room to mention, because the *last Days* are particularly mark'd out in the *Prophecies* of *Scripture*, as the Times wherein may be expected, the Rise of SEDUCERS. . . .

'Tis true, we read of the coming on of a *glorious State* of Things in the LAST DAYS: Nor will the *Vision fail.*—We may rely upon it, the Prophesies, foretelling the Glory of the REDEEMER's *Kingdom*, will have their Accomplishment to the making this Earth of *Paradise*, in Compare with what it now is. But for the *particular Time* when this will be, it *is not for us to know it, the Father having put it in his own Power:* And whoever pretend to such Knowledge, they are wise above what is written; and tho' they may think they know much, they really know nothing as to this Matter.

It may be suggested,[2] that "the *Work of* GOD's SPIRIT that is so extraordinary and wonderful, is the *dawning*, or at lest, a *Prelude* of that *glorious Work of GOD*, so often foretold in Scripture, which, in the Progress and Issue of it, shall renew the whole World." But what are such Suggestions, but the Fruit of Imagination? Or at best, uncertain Conjecture? And can any good End be answered in endeavouring, upon Evidence absolutely precarious, to instill into the Minds of People a Notion of the *millenium* State, as what is NOW going to be introduced; yea, and of AMERICA,[3] as that Part of the World,

---

[2] Mr. Edwards late book.

[3] While I was writing this Page, I received a Letter from a worthy Gentleman, in which, speaking of Mr. EDWARDS's late *Book*, he has these Words, "I am surpriz'd at his long Labour to prove the *Millennium* shall begin in AMERICA.—He has been so modest as to conceal the Reason of this; but it may easily be gathered from what he has *often said to private Persons*, viz. that he doubted not, the *Millennium* began when there was such an Awakening at NORTH-HAMPTON 8 Years past."—So that Salva-

which is pointed out in the *Revelations* of GOD for the Place, where this glorious Scene of Things, "will, probably, first begin?" How often, at other Times, and in other Places, has the Conceit been propagated among People, as if the Prophecies touching the Kingdom of CHRIST, in the *latter Days,* were NOW to receive their Accomplishment? And what has been the Effect, but their running wild? So it was in GERMANY, in the Beginning of the Reformation. The *extraordinary* and *wonderful* Things in that Day, were look'd upon by the Men then thought to be most under the *SPIRIT's immediate* Direction, as "the Dawning of that glorious Work of GOD, which should renew the whole World;" and the Imagination of the Multitude being fired with this Notion, they were soon perswaded, that the Saints were now to reign on Earth, and the Dominion to be given into their Hands: And it was under the Influence of this vain Conceit, (in which they were strengthened by *Visions, Raptures* and *Revelations*) that they took up *Arms* against the lawful *Authority,* and were destroy'd, at one Time and another, to the Number of an HUNDRED THOUSAND. . . .

And 'tis well known, that this same Pretence of the near Approach of the MILLENIUM, the *promised Kingdom of the* MESSIAH, was the *Foundation-Error of* the *French Prophets,* and those in their Way, no longer ago than the Beginning of this Century: And so infatuated were they at last, as to publish it to the World, that the glorious Times they spake of, *would*

---

tion is gone forth from NORTH-HAMPTON, and NORTH-HAMPTON must have the Praise of being first brought into it.

To which let me add a few Words, from the late venerable Dr. INCREASE MATHER, which will shew, how widely good Men may differ from one another, in Matters of *meer Conjecture.* They are these, "I know there is a blessed Day to the visible Church not far off: But it is the Judgment of very learned Men, that, in the glorious Times promised to the Church on Earth, AMERICA will be HELL. And, although there is a Number of the Elect of GOD to be born here, I am verily afraid, that, in Process of Time, NEW-ENGLAND will be the wofullest Place in all AMERICA."

be manifest over the whole Earth, within the Term of THREE
YEARS. And what Set of Men have ever yet appear'd in the
Christian World, whose Imaginations have been thorowly
warmed, but they have, at length, wrought themselves up to
a *full Assurance,* that NOW was the Time for the Accomplishment of the Scriptures, and the Creation of the *new Heavens,*
and the *new Earth?* No one Thing have they more unitedly
concurred in, to their own shameful Disappointment, and the
doing unspeakable Damage to the Interest of Religion.—A
sufficient Warning, one would think, to keep Men modest; and
restrain them from Endeavours to lead People into a Belief
of that, of which they have no sufficient *Evidence;* and in
which, they may be deceived by their *vain Imaginations,* as
Hundreds and Thousands have been before them.

There are unquestionably many Prophecies concerning
CHRIST, and the *Glory of his Kingdom,* still to be fulfilled; and
it may be of good Service to labour to beget in People a Faith
in these Things; or, if they have Faith, to quicken and strength-
en it: But it can answer no good End to lead People into the
Belief of any *particular* Time, as the Time *appointed* of GOD
for the Accomplishment of these Purposes of his Mercy; because this is one of those Matters, his Wisdom has thought fit
to keep conceal'd from the Knowledge of Man. Our own Faith
therefore upon this Head can be founded only on *Conjecture;*
and as 'tis only the like *blind Faith* we can convey to others,
we should be cautious, lest their Conduct should be agreeable
to their Faith. When they have imbib'd from us the Thought,
as if the *glorious Things,* spoken of in Scripture, were to come
forward in their Day, they will be apt (as has often been the
Case) to be impatient, and from their *Officiousness* in tendring
their Help where it is not needed, to disserve the Interest of
the Redeemer.

29 · *Isaac Stiles*

(*1 6 9 7 – 1 7 6 0*)

A LOOKING-GLASS FOR

CHANGELINGS

———

The able logic of Chauncy's treatise was by no means the only weapon wielded by the opponents of the revival. They also exercised what the New England Baptist leader Isaac Backus called "a more powerful way of reasoning," such as the Connecticut laws, passed in May 1742, forbidding, and providing punishments for, deviations from the established ecclesiastical constitution. It was under the provisions of these laws that Davenport and Finley were removed from Connecticut. The laws, an extension of Connecticut's Saybrook Platform, were designed to prevent itinerancy, separations, and the removal of ministers by congregations who preferred warmer preaching or greater zeal for the revival. The laws may have succeeded in stemming the progress of the Awakening, but they also converted the revival spirit of that province into a political

———

Isaac Stiles, *A Looking-glass for Chang[e]lings. A Seasonable Caveat against Meddling with them that are given to Change* . . . (New London, 1743), pp. 11–32, 34–37.

movement. A New Light party emerged, determined to remove the legislators—"great men and rich men," the itinerant Benjamin Pomeroy called them—who had acted to thwart the "Work of God." The defenders of the restraining laws, many of them ministers, were likewise drawn into political activity, and their party came to be known as the "Old Lights." The most articulate Old Light spokesman was Isaac Stiles, who throughout the Awakening had been harassed by a vocal and enthusiastic minority in his congregation. In 1742 Stiles declared, in his Election Sermon, that the inherited ecclesiastical and political system of New England, and not the millenarian visions of the revivalists, constituted the true New Jerusalem. When the laws of May 1742 (for which Stiles' Election Sermon was the intellectual justification) aroused partisan opposition, Stiles was the first to realize that the safety of the standing order required direct appeals to the electorate. *A Looking-Glass for Changelings,* delivered before the assembled "freemen" of New Haven, was a hortatory utterance, in which Stiles, the Old Lights' most accomplished orator, used every rhetorical device available to an advocate of reason and order.

The Enacting human Laws & civil Statutes for the Punishment of evil doers and the Encouragement of them that do well; the maintaining and promoting Peace and good Order, the protection of the Church and furthering of the Commonweal, the suppressing all Disorders, frowning away Seducers, and preventing the prevailing and spreading of dangerous

Errors, &c. is one (and none of the least) of those ways wherein they that are invested with Legislative Power and Authority are the Ministers of God unto their People for good: And it is a despising the Divine goodness herein; a contemning and dishonouring our Political Fathers, and a shameful violation of the fifth Commandment for any to disregard, go abrest to or counter-act such Laws.

Further, We are bound in all proper ways and methods, to express our gratitude and thankfulness not only to God, but likewise to these wise and good Patriots; these Patrons of our Civil and Religious Enjoyments, Liberties, Rights and Privileges; for all the Quietness we injoy by their Providence,—To testify our Fidelity to them; to stand by 'em, to stand up for them and endeavour to Encourage their Hearts and strengthen their Hands; and not imagine Mischief against them, nor consult to cast them down from their Excellency. See Ezra, 10. 4. *Arise, for this matter belongeth unto thee: we also will be with thee. . . .*

. . . III. We come now to consider the last and Cautionary Branch or part of the Text,—*And meddle not with them that are given to Change.*

And here I shall endeavour to shew,

1. *Who or what manner of Persons these are.*

And

2. *That these are not to be meddl'd with.*

To begin with the first.

1. I am to draw the ugly, mishapen and forlorn Picture of them that are given to Change.

And this must be done in *Miniature:* For it would be endless to trace them in their almost infinite mutations, mazes, meanders, intricate turnings & windings, in all their Excentrick, Progressive and Retrograde, Apogee and Perigee motions.

But to come to the Point and to the Case in hand.

They that are given to Change, are men that (being under

the direction, influence & government of no fix'd steady Principles) are frequently altering their Mind, shifting and changing their Opinion, and in consequence hereof their Practice and Conduct, not for the better but for the worse.

There is a good as well as a bad Change: A Change which all of us are, or must be the Subjects of as ever we hope to be happy, *viz.* That which St. Paul speaks of; 2 Cor. 3. 18. *We all with open face beholding as in a glass the glory of the Lord, are chang'd into the same Image from glory to glory, even as by the Spirit of the Lord.* There is such a thing as a man's changing from bad to good, and from good to better, which cannot be condemned. If men have imbib'd unsound Principles, embrac'd Errors and espous'd false Maxims and acted upon them; 'tis fit they should change their Sentiments and alter their Course of acting.—'Tis strictly Just, 'tis Honorary to our Profession as Christians, and our Glory as Men to Embrace Truth when ever it offers it self to our Choice: 'Tis highly commendable for any when they find themselves in an Error, whether in Opinion or Practice, speedily to renounce, relinquish and abandon the same: To exchange falshood for truth, darkness for light, and bitter things for sweet. 'Tis praiseworthy to do all we can to rectify our Mistakes and false Judgments of things, and to turn from crooked and perverse Ways into such as are right and strait, and the paths of Peace.

But this (I conceive) is not the Change here intended. No, but a changing from good to bad, or from better to worse; a changing true Maxims and Opinions for false ones: turning away from the truth and turning unto fables, and turning from the right ways of the Lord to commit works with the workers of Iniquity.

Changlings there are of this sort too too many. There are, who love and use Changes, and are so addicted hereunto, that they are here said *to be given to Change;* even as one that inordinately loves and follows strong Drink is said to be given to it, I *Tim.* 3. 8.

Some there are who are Unstable in all their ways, in their Obedience to God, and to the King, and are prone to Rebellion against both. They change their mind & manners almost as often as the *Camaleon* is said to change his Colour: Are as changeable as the Weather & variable as the Wind: Meer Weather-Cocks—Constant in nothing, save only in Inconstancy.

(1) *They are given to change in matters of Religion.* They seem always as tho' they had their Religion to chuse, in regard they are never fix'd in any thing; but are for ever wavering like a wave of the Sea, driven to and fro and carried about with diverse & strange Doctrines. One while these are allow'd to be sound Doctrines; anon, these are condemn'd and discharged. One while these are good Preachers, orthodox and sound in the Faith; presently, these are deferred and stigmatiz'd by them as *Hereticks, Legalists, Letter-learned Pharisees, Soul-daubers, &c.* And others set up Caress'd and Canoniz'd, even such as come from the Ends of the Earth, and for ought they Know may be *Missionaries from the Pontificate of Rome. (For these that have turned the World upside down, are come hither also,* whom some have receiv'd—). . .

One while these are some of the best of Books; after a while these are rejected, are nigh unto Cursing and their End is to be *Burned.* Nor can the departed Spirits of their Authors be found (by the Extensive Charity of these right Catholick men) any where but in the devouring Flames of Hell: and because (as they think) the Smoke of their Torment will ascend up for ever and ever, they can sing Hallelujahs on this Joyful Occasion: *So Pityful, Tender-hearted and full of Compassion are these dear Children and distinguish'd Saints.*——

One while this the best and the only true Form of Worship & Church-Discipline; the only likely Method to promote Religion, to further Awakenings, &c. By & by this Scheme is dislik'd, cry'd down, laid aside and superseded by another that is bran-new. Thus moveable are their ways that you cannot know them. Perhaps a Hare does not oftener alter her course, interchange ground, turn short about, wind & twist, than some of these change their Faith and Practice. They are like Children tossed to & fro and carried about with every wind of Doctrine, and led aside by the cunning Craftiness of them that lie in wait to deceive. Like a silly Dove wandring from Mountain to Valley, seeking rest but finding none to their unsettled & wavering Minds. Like Ephraim of old *feeding on the wind, and following after the East wind.* Their goodness is as a morning Cloud and early Dew, it goeth away, *Hos.* 6. 4.

This is to be *given* to Change.—

So those men that wickedly forsake God & break his Laws, are said to *change their God, Jer.* 2 11 And to change GOD's Judgment & Ordinances Isa. 24 5. *The Earth also is defiled under the inhabitants thereof, because they have transgressed the Laws, changed the Ordinances and broken the everlasting Covenant.* See also *Ezek.* 5 5, 6.—So they did in the Prophet Elijah's day, *The children of Israel* (says he) *have forsaken thy Covenant, thrown down thine Altars and slain thy Prophets with the sword.* So in the time of the Prophet Hosea; *My people* (says he) *ask Counsel at their Stocks, and their Staff declareth unto them; for the Spirit of Whoredom hasth caused them to Err, and they have gone a whoring from under their God. . . .*

. . . And in Ezekiel's time what Abominations were committed, not only by Others, but by some of the Ancients of the house of *Israel* in the dark, in the Chambers of their Imagery: which the Prophet saw in Vision, *Ezek.* 8. 11. And in the time of the last Prophet, how shamefully did they despise and forsake God's Ordinances, prophane his Day, *&c.? The Table of the Lord was polluted by them,—They Vow'd and then Sacrificed unto the Lord a Corrupt thing:— The Table of the Lord is Contemptible.* (This was their Language) They *said, What a weariness is it? And they snuffed at it.* See a black Bill of Indictment summarily drawn up &

exhibited against them by God Himself, Mal. 3. 7 *Even from the days of your Fathers ye are gone away from mine Ordinances, and have not kept them.*

Thus did they gad about to change their way; like a common Prostitute whose Love is never fix'd, but sometimes set on this, sometimes on that Paramour; playing the Harlot with many Lovers. And are there none at the *present Day* who might here behold their Face & proper Features as in a Glass?

(2) *This sort of Men are likewise given to Change with reference to Civil Affairs.* In consequence of this *Vertigo,* or dizziness in the Head, this instability, fickleness & variation in Opinion and Judgment, they are ever & anon for change of Government, and thence are raising a Dust, making a Bustle, and endeavouring to Overset the Government; to turn things *topsy turvy* and bring all into Confusion.——

One while they are for this Model & Form of civil Government, another while for that, & oftner for none at all. Those men they esteem the best Qualified for Rulers (and accordingly will Vote for them) who are most like themselves, viz. *given to Change:* well knowing that such are most likely to abett & encourage, or at least to connive at their Fluctuating & extravagant Principles & Practises. Not the upright & steadfast Oak, but the bending cringing Willow is the Tree which they chuse should Rule over them. Wise men and understanding and known, *i.e.* approv'd among our Tribes, known to be strong Rods and fast Friends to the Government; Men who have for many Years Rul'd us in the Integrity of their Hearts and by the Skilfulness of their Hands, these must by all means be laid aside, turn'd out, and Changlings set up—Thus using their Liberty for a cloak of Maliciousness and not as the Servants of God. . . .

But I must pass on,

2. To shew, *That these men are not to be meddled with.* To make way for which, it may not be amiss if we take some brief

Notice of what is implied in this Caution,—*And meddle not with them that are given to Change.*

According to the Original, it is, *Mix not thy self with them,—* "*i.e.* Either in their Counsels and Practises, or in familiar Conversation." But there is moreover a Miosis in the words, more imply'd & intended than is express'd. 'Tis not enough that we mix not our selves with them in their Counsels and Practises, but we must use all lawful Methods and Endeavours that the Counsel of these *Ahithophels,* these Changlings, may be turned into Foolishness, that their Devices may be disappointed; that they may be taken in their own Craftiness, that their Counsel may be carried headlong, and that their hands may not perform their Enterprise.

When we plainly see them attempting to introduce a Change, whether in Church or State, or both; a Change which is likely to be subversive of and destructive to our most dear and valuable Interests: When we hear them say one to another, *Rase it, rase it, even to the Foundation thereof!* Does it not concern us to Counter-act them, and do what we can to prevent the growing & important Mischief?

When they that are given to Change, are opening a wide and perillous Door for the letting in of *Enthusiastical Impulses, Trances, Visions & Revelations, Antinomian & Familistical Heresy,* and the like; and what loudly threatens a Subversion to all the peaceable Order in a Government, and when the most barefac'd Contempt is cast upon Authority both Civil & Ecclesiastical; in this case Neutrality seems hardly sufficient. Eph. 5. 10. *Have no fellowship with the unfruitful works of Darkness, but rather reprove them.* 'Tis doubtless best that such *Grapes of Sodom & Clusters of Gomorrha* be nipp'd in the Bud, that the *Cockatrice* be crush'd in the Egg. The way to do which (one would think) is not to sit still and do nothing: Prov. 22. 3. *A prudent man foreseeth the Evil and hideth himself; but the simple pass on and are punished.*

Proceed we now to make it out, that men given to Change are not to be meddled with. And this may appear in the light of these following particulars.

1. The meddling with men of this Character is expressly Forbidden by the Holy Ghost in this and implicitly in sundry other Texts of Scripture: Particularly where we are Caution'd not to be *Partakers of other mens Sins; To withdraw from them that walk Disorderly; To mark them that cause Divisions and avoid them.*—

2. Their being oppos'd in the Text to such as Fear GOD and the King, plainly intimates that they are men of no Religion, men void of Piety and Loyalty; and therefore they are not to be meddl'd with.

The mixing our selves with them in common Conversation, but especially in their Counsels, is unprofitable, yea, 'tis hurtful: *For their Heart studieth Destruction and their Lips talk of Mischief,* Prov. 24. 2. Hence Job could say, Chap. 21 16 *The Counsel of the wicked is far from me.* He that walketh with the wise shall be wise; but a companion of fools shall be destroyed. And persons that Fear not GOD neither regard men cloath'd with Authority, must needs be unqualify'd and unfit to sustain any publick Post either in the Church or in the State. *Shall even he that hateth right, govern?* Job 34. 17. So that they are to be let alone and not meddl'd with in this respect. If they that are given to Change are men that fear not GOD nor the King, what profit can we expect to reap from intermeddling or mixing ourselves with them in their Counsels and Practises?

O my Soul, come not thou into their Secret! It was David's honour and happiness that he could Appeal to Almighty GOD and profess, *I am a Companion of all them that fear Thee, and of them that keep thy Precepts.* And again, *I have not sat with Vain Persons, neither will I go in with Dissemblers: I hate the congregation of Evil doers and will not sit with the Wicked.*

So Jeremiah, Chap. 15. 17. *I sat not in the Assembly of the Mockers, nor rejoiced.—Blessed is the man that walketh not in the Counsel of the Ungodly, nor standeth in the way of Sinners, nor sitteth in the seat of the Scornful. The thoughts of the righteous are right: but the counsels of the wicked are deceit,* Prov. 12. 5.

3. If we view them in the light (or rather in that darkness) wherein they have been plac'd in the foregoing Discourse, we shall see sufficient Reason to steer clear of, and have nothing to do with these men,—

'Tis true, these are in their own Opinion, the only Lights of the World, burning and shining Lights: But as the Moon is known to be an Opake Body, void of innate Light, by its frequent Lunations & Changes; so their being given to Change, is Evidential that the Light which is in them is Darkness, yea, 'tis Darkness that may be felt: 1 Joh 2 9 *He that saith he is in the Light and hateth his Brother, is in Darkness even until now. He walketh in Darkness & knoweth not whither he goeth, because Darkness hath blinded his Eyes.* Those that are Unstable as Water don't Excell: No, but render themselves many ways mean & contemptible & very unfit for publick Trust & Improvement. There is no trust to be put in them, there is no depending upon them. Confidence in such men is like *a broken tooth & a foot out of joint,* Pr. 25. 19.

4. The meddling with & preferring such men to places of publick Trust & Improvement, is like to be of very pernicious Consequence, and tends greatly to hurt the Publick. *When the Righteous are in Authority the people rejoice; but when the Wicked beareth Rule the people mourn. As a roaring Lion and a ranging Bear, so is a wicked Ruler over the poor People. They that work Wickedness must not be set up,* Mal. 3. 15. When Vile men are exalted they have it more in their Power to injure the Publick,—And they seldom want a Will.

So what a Tumult and Rout was caus'd in the State by

Absalom (a Seditious Villain) and those that Tagg'd after him? Some of whom had little Wit, and others as little Honesty: For of some 'tis said, *That when called they went in their simplicity and knew not any thing,* i.e. of Absalom's wicked & rebellious design. But this some were well appriz'd of, particularly the Spies or such as rid Post, whom he sent throughout all the Tribes of Israel, saying, *As soon as you hear the sound of the Trumpet, then ye shall say Absalom Reigneth in Hebron.*

Again, What an ill-boding Change was made in the Republick by another ambitious Top and aspiring Coxcomb, together with that disaffected and designing Crew of changlings with whom he conferred, consulted and consorted, and *who following Adonijah helped him?*

I might further Instance in Jeroboam, (one mightily given to Change, especially when 'twould serve his own ambitious and aviritious Ends & Designs) who first made a change in Civil, and then soon introduc'd one in Sacred and Ecclesiastical affairs; whose Name is left on sacred Record with this brand of Infamy fix'd upon it, to his immortal Dishonour,— *Jeroboam the son of Nebat, who made Israel to sin.*

But what shall I more say? For the Time would fail me to speak of the great and manifold Disturbances, Disorders, Convulsions and Confusions both in Church & State, and the infinite Mischiefs which have been fomented and brought forward by men of this make & character; especially when they have been promoted to Honour, had the plaudit of the Populace, and have been hail'd & even hosanna'd by the giddy Multitude of unthinking Mortals.

5. Another Reason wherefore we shou'd not meddle or mix our selves with them that are given to Change, is, because the more such Changlings there are, the *greater* Mischief they are capable of perpetrating & pushing forward. *Vis unita fortior.* 'Tis pity there should be so much as one such belonging

to a Community,–*One Sinner destroys much good,*—But when such are multiplied, under one or more Ringleaders & Arch-changlings (like the Plague of Locusts or Lice brought upon the Egyptians) they carry all before them, darken a Land and make a most fearful Desolation. (Nor is such a Plague when begun & spreading, like to be stay'd, except Phinehas rise up & execute Judgments.) Like the tail of some baleful, baneful red-hot Comet, they scatter and diffuse their malignant Influences far & wide, kindle a destroying Fire and make a rueful Conflagration wherever they come. And were there enough such Phaetons, they would soon set the whole World on Fire in good earnest, not in fiction but in fact.

Very grievous are they when once they get the lead, in so much that were a Land as the garden of Eden before them, behind them it would be a desolate Wilderness, yea and nothing could escape them. . . .

6. If we meddle with them & become partakers of their Sins, we must expect to receive of their Plagues & Punishment. *Tho' hand join in hand, the wicked shall not go unpunished.* The wicked, such are they whose bold transgressions of the Laws of GOD & Man plainly saith, *that there is no fear of God before their eyes.* We are told that a participation or partnership with such in their wickedness, very awfully exposes to divine Vengeance, See *Ps.* 50. 17–

The Day is hastning when Christ the Judge will speak unto them in his Wrath and vex them in his sore Displeasure; will break them with a rod of Iron, and dash them in pieces like a Potters vessel: Will say, Bring hither these mine Enemies, who would not that I should Reign over them and slay them before my face: Bind them in bundles & burn them together. Is not destruction to the wicked, (to all such as fear not the LORD & the King) and a strange punishment to the workers of iniquity? The hypocrite in heart heap up wrath, *Job* 36. 13 The wicked plotteth against the just; the LORD shall laugh at him, for he seeth that his day is coming: Into smoke shall they consume away; the transgressors shall be destroyed together, *Psal.* 37. 12,—

How awful to this purpose are those words of St. *Peter?* 2 Pet. 2. 1, 2, 3. *But there were false Prophets also among the people, even as there shall be false Teachers among you, who privily shall bring in damnable Heresies, and bring upon themselves swift destruction: And Many shall Follow their Pernicious Ways, by reason of whom the way of truth shall be evil spoken of: And through Covetousness shall they with feigned words make merchandise of you; whose Judgment now of a long time lingreth not and their Damnation slumbereth not.* And let it be remembred, that he that receiveth such into his house and biddeth him God speed, is partaker of their evil deeds, *John*'s Epist, 2 ver 10, 11.

But I hasten to make some brief *Improvement.*

I. *It is matter of deep Lamentation that there are so many among us who fear not GOD and the King, but are given to Change.* The bad changes both in Principle & Practise visible in many, and that proximate preparedness hereunto, which appears in more than a few, may well fill every thoughtful Mind with deep Concern, and constrain us to cry out with the weeping Prophet, *O that my head were waters and my eyes a fountain of tears, that I might weep day & night.* Does not this spirit and practise which is so prevalent and rife among us, argue a most lamentable decay (instead of revival) of Religion? And what can be thought of, that is of more hurtful & dangerous Tendency or bodes more ill to the Community? Alas! that there should be such Numbers who have changed their glory for that which doth not profit: Who have left their first-love, left off to be wise & do the godly deed: Whose just character is that, I Thes. 2. 15. *They please not God, and are contrary to all men.* God planted us a noble Vine; how then are we turned into the degenerate plant of a strange

Vine unto him. Be astonished O ye Heavens at this, and O
Earth be horribly afraid and very desolate. For these things I
weep; mine eye, mine eye runneth down with water,—When
I remember I am afraid and trembling taketh hold on my flesh.
Would to God, there were not so many of these gray Hairs
here & there upon us, threatning symptoms of approaching
ruin.

Are not these the Horns that have scatter'd our Judah, the
Eyes that mock their Fathers, the Vipers that eat through
their Mothers bowels? Is not much of the glory departed from
our *Israel?* How is our gold become dim, how is our most fine
gold changed? And is there no cause (in a sense) to renew
that complaint of the *Psalmist?* Ps. 74 –2, 8–*Thine Enemies rore
in the midst of thy Congregations. They brake down the
carved works thereof: They have defiled the dwelling place
of thy Name; they have cast fire into thy Sanctuary.* For in
truth it is come to pass, that instead of a sweet smell there is a
stink, and instead of a girdle there is a rent, and burning instead of beauty, *Isa* 3 24.

I see not but that the Abomination of desolation spoken of
by Daniel (in some degree) is now standing in the holy Place,
even in these *American* goings down of the Sun. Are not the
stones of the Sanctuary (in a sense) poured out in the top of
every Street, and the precious Sons of our Zion, comparable
to fine gold, how are they esteen'd as earthen Pitchers? Our
Nobles are yet of our selves (Blessed be GOD) and our *Governour* of our own chusing; but are not these (as it were)
hang'd up by their hand? and the faces of the Elders are not
honoured. Don't the very Child behave himself proudly
against the Ancient; and the Base against the Honourable?

For my part, I think it's high time to blow the Trumpet in
Zion, to sound an Alarm in God's Holy Mountain, and bear
the most publick Testimony & Remonstrance against that horrid and insufferable Contempt that is cast upon Authority both

Civil and Ecclesiastical, not a little owing to the wild & over officious Zeal of pragmatical restless Spirits, who like Self-conceited & Rebellious Absalom, are ever wishing, *Oh! That I were made Judge in the Land, that every man that hath any Suit or Cause might come unto me and I would do him Justice?* And to a spirit of Choraism, with which too many, are deeply Tinctur'd. These (with but too many others which are the reigning Evils of this *Unhappy Day,* and which are the Fruits of our being *given to Change*) I can't but be of Opinion, have a more gloomy and threatning Aspect upon the Land, than should the punishment of the Sword, Famine or Pestilence be sent among us.

The Kings of the Earth and all the Inhabitants of the World would not have believed that the Adversary & the Enemy should have thus entred into the gates of this *Jerusalem,* and kindled such a Fire, that it's well if it don't devour the Foundation thereof.

Who ever reads the History of the rise & progress of the *Anabaptists* in *Germany* in the *Sixteenth Century,* may have a taste of the bitter & fatal Fruits of being *given to Change,* and see to what a prodigious Bulk & Size *Enthusiasm* & *Fanaticism* may grow.

God forbid that any should imagine that Reformation consists in Changes that tend to the utter Extirpation of Religion & Government; in Principles & Practises which want a new Bible to justify them. . . .

We have great reason to Adore the Unchangeable JEHOVAH, for all the showers of divine Grace and that Righteousness which He has rain'd upon the unworthy People of this Land from time to time: But have cause (I think) to be deeply Humbled for, to Mourn and Lament some of the Changes that have of late been among us, usher'd in by them who professing themselves to be wise (*and are wise above what is written*) have changed the truth of God into a lie; and whrshipped & served the Creature, more than the Creator who is blessed for ever. For GOD is not the Author of Confusion, but of Peace in all the Churches of the Saints. GOD will be sought and served after *the due Order,* I *Chron.* 15. 13.

II. *Our Subject furnishes us with a Rule by which to proceed in the important Affair we are* now *Conven'd upon and to be Active in.* We are here Instructed (in giving in our Suffrage or Votes for men to be intrusted with the weighty Affairs of Government.)

1 Not to meddle with them that are given to Change. Them, that (if ever they were otherwise) appear *now* to be Back-friends to the Government, and its effectual Adversaries. Them, that (if they ever were subject to good & wholsom Laws) are *now* tack't about, and are steering quite another Course; breaking the Laws themselves, and teaching others to do the like. These deserve to be least in the Kingdom of Men, and are by no means to be preferr'd to places of Publick Trust. When a man has got the rounds, Phlebotomy or Bleeding is more proper for him than Promotion. And would we hit such men in the right Vein, in order to work a more thorough Cure, we must let 'em see and feel that we don't look upon such Changlings qualified for publick Improvement. No, should such be set on high, 'twould serve only to make their Heads still more dizzy and put their Brains into a more violent Rotation. It's dangerous venturing the Sword of civil Government in the hand of one that is Delirious or in a Phrensy: And we know there is more than one sort of Phrensy. *The Spiritual man* may be *mad,* See *Hos.* 9. 7.

What a pitiful Stick must he be for a Pillar to support and bear up the Common-wealth, who may be twisted like a meer Wythe, or who is for ever shifting, veering & wheeling about like a Windmill. If he that is at Helm be addle Headed & can't stand Steady, he will make but wild Steerage, especially in a Stormy and Tempestuous Season; when the Winds are Boistrous, the Seas Roar, the Billows run high and Deep calleth unto deep. The steady Trade-wind is an Emblem of one that is fit to Rule over men, and not the blustering & hurtful Whirlwind. Good Rulers are Eyes to the Blind, and Feet to the Lame, *Job* 29 15. But if such as have lost their Way & are themselves got Bewildr'd, were set to Lead and Conduct others, that would soon be fulfill'd, Isa. 9. 16. *The Leaders of this people cause them to Err, and they that are led of them are destroyed.*

We may allow Solomon to be a good Polititian, a wise & experienc'd Statesman. Well, his Sentence, you see, is, *That men of this Character are not to be meddl'd with.*

2. 'Tis imply'd (tho' not express'd) in our Text, that we ought in this case to make Choice of men that are of fix'd & steady Principles and uniform in their Practice: Men that may be confided in and depended upon; Men of a true greatness, stability & constancy of Mind; and such as appear to bear the nearest Resemblance to the Supream Ruler of the Universe, in Wisdom & Knowlege, in Holiness, Justice, Goodness & Truth; with whom there is no Variableness nor shadow of turning. *He is in one mind, and who can turn him: Job* 23. 13.

Civil Rulers should resemble the fix'd Stars, acting and shining in their exalted Spheres; and not be like the inferior Planets, which are given to Change. They should be like a company of Horses in Pharaoh's Chariots, whose necks are cloath'd with Thunder, and who can't be made afraid as a Grashopper.—Men that can't be sway'd or turn'd about by Fear, or Hopes, or Gifts: That won't basely Betray the cause of Truth & Sacrifice the most valuable Interests of their People for fear of being turn'd out of their Posts, or least they should rise no higher: That don't love the Praise of Men more than the Praise of GOD.

Blessed be GOD, such there are who have hitherto been the Chariots of our Israel and the Horsemen thereof; Strong &

very Couragious in Protecting, Maintaining & Promoting our best Interests Civil & Religious; and can say with the renowned David, who Rul'd with GOD and was Faithful with the Saints, *Wherefore should I be afraid in the days of Evil, when the Iniquity of my heels should compass me about?* And I pray GOD blast the Designs and bring to nought the Devices of any that may be attempting to deprive the Publick of so great a Blessing.

30 · *Elisha Williams*

(1 6 9 4 – 1 7 5 5)

THE ESSENTIAL RIGHTS AND

LIBERTIES OF PROTESTANTS

However special the political-ecclesiastical situation in Connecticut, the issues raised there clearly transcended the provincial context. The most extensive critique of the laws of 1742 was published anonymously in Boston; first it was assumed to have been written by a citizen of Massachusetts. The actual author of *The Essential Rights and Liberties* was, however, one of the most prominent citizens of Connecticut. Elisha Williams, a member of New England's leading family of divines, was one of the most widely trained men of his generation. After his graduation from Harvard, Williams practiced law and served as a representative to the Connecticut General Assembly and as clerk of the lower house. Later he became a tutor at Yale and in 1721 was ordained as a minister. In 1721, during the agitation that followed the reversion of two Yale

Elisha Williams, *The essential Rights and Liberties of Protestants. A seasonable Plea for The Liberty of Conscience, and the Right of Private Judgment* (Boston, 1744), pp. 44–53, 60–65.

instructors to Episcopalianism, Williams was appointed rector of the College. Isaac Stiles' son Ezra, later the president of Yale, remembered Williams as "a good classical scholar, well versed in logic, metaphysics and ethics, and in rhetoric and oratory." In 1739 Williams resigned the rectorship and was again chosen to represent Wethersfield in the legislature. He was appointed a judge of the Superior Court just as the Awakening became a matter of public dispute. Williams was charged with using his position, and his political prestige, to support the revival and religious liberty for reasons of personal and partisan ambition. What the *Essential Rights* indicates, however, is that Williams continued to view religion as the most important of human affairs. His argument, though clearly derived from John Locke's thoughts on toleration, is imbued with the warmer faith that fed the emerging American philosophy of voluntary church affiliation. Williams assumed that the policy of a state, and even its social order, must give way if either hinders the fulfillment of a people's religious aspirations.

. . . That being the *End* of civil Government (as we have seen) *viz*, the greater Security of Enjoyment of what belongs to every one, and *this Right of private Judgment*, and *worshipping* God according to their *Consciences*, being the *natural and unalienable Right* of *every Men*, what Men by entering into civil Society neither did, nor could give up into the Hands of the Community; it is but a just Consequence, that they are to be *protected* in the *Enjoyment* of *this Right* as well as any other. A worshipping Assembly of Christians have surely as much Right to be *protected* from Molestation in their Worship, as the Inhabitants of a Town assembled to consult their civil Interests from Disturbance &c. This Right I am speaking of, is the most valuable Right, of which every one ought to be most tender, of universal and equal Concernment to all; and *Security* and *Protection* in the Enjoyment of it the just Expectation of every Individual. And the civil Magistrate in endeavouring and doing this, most truly comes up to the Character of a *nursing Father* to the Church of CHRIST. If this had been *protected* as it ought to have been, what infinite Mischief to the Christian Church had been prevented? From the Want of a due Care of this, the *Clergy* through Pride and Ambition assumed the Power of prescribing to, imposing on and domineering over the Consciences of Men; civil Rulers for their own private Ends helping it forward; which went on 'till it produced the most detestable *Monster* the Earth ever had upon it, the *Pope*, who has deluged the Earth with the Blood of Christians. This being the true Spirit of *Popery*, to impose their Determinations on all within their Power by any Methods which may appear most effectual: and those *civil Magistrates* that suffered and helped that *Beast* to invade this Right, did therein *commit Fornication with her, and give her their Strength and Power;* and so instead of proving *Fathers* to their People, proved the cursed *Butchers* of them. It has been by asserting and using this Right, that any of the *Nations* who *have been drunk with the Wine of her Fornication,* have *come out from her Abominations:* and would the civil Magistrates of those Nations, who at this Day worship the Beast, but protect their Subjects in *this natural Right* of *every one's judging for himself in Matters of Religion,* according to that alone Rule the *Bible;* that settled Darkness of Ignorance, Error & Idolatry, which now involves them, would vanish as the Darkness of the Night does by the rising of the Sun. How unspeakably would the Advantages be, arising from the Protection of this Right, did they reach no further than to the Estates, Bodies, and Lives of Men?

All *Reformations* are built on this single Principle I have been pleading for, from which we should never depart: yet it must be owned and deserves to be lamented, that the Reformed have too much departed from this Principle upon which they at first set up; whence it has come to pass that Reformations in one Place and another have not been more perfect. For the Prince of Darkness has always found Means this Way to make a Stand against the most vigorous Efforts; and if any Advantages have been gained in any Point, to secure a safe Retreat, by infatuating Men with that strange Sort of Pride, whereby they assume to themselves only, but allow to none else, a Power of domineering over the Consciences of others. Religion will certainly lie under Oppression if this unjust Authority be transferred, to *Decrees of Councils, Convocations, Injunctions of civil Magistrates*, or from one Man or any Order of Men to another; as it is if we have any other Rule of Faith and Practice in Religion, besides the *Bible*. It were easy to enlarge on the vast Advantages and Happiness of admitting no other Rule or Guide but the sacred *Scriptures* only: thence would flow the greatest Blessings to Mankind, Peace and Happiness to the World: so that if there be any Rights and Liberties of Men that challenge *Protection* and *Security* therein from the civil Magistrate, it is *this natural Right* of *private Judgment in Matters of Religion*, that the sacred *Scriptures only may become the Rule to all Men in all religious Matters*, as they ought to be. In a Word, this is the surest Way for the Ease and Quiet of Rulers, as well as Peace of the State, the surest Way to engage the Love and Obedience of all the Subjects. And if there be divers religious Sects in the State, and the one attempts to offend the other, and the Magistrate interposes only to keep the Peace; it is but a natural

Consequence to suppose—that in such Case they all finding themselves *equally safe,* and *protected* in their Rights by the civil Power, they will all be equally obedient. It is the Power given to one, to oppress the other, that has occasioned all the Disturbances about Religion. And should the Clergy closely adhere to these Principles, instead of their being reproached for Pride and Ambition, as the Sowers of Strife and Contention and Disturbance of the Peace of the Church of God; they would be honoured for their Work's sake, esteemed for their Character, loved as Blessings to the World, heard with Pleasure, and become successful in their Endeavours to recommend the Knowledge and Practice of Christianity.

It also follows from the preceeding Principles, that *every Christian* has *Right* to *determine* for himself *what Church to join himself to;* and *every Church* has *Right* to *judge* in *what Manner* God is to be *worshipped* by them, and *what Form of Discipline* ought to be observed by them, and the *Right* also of *electing their own Officers.* (For Brevity Sake I put them all together) From this *Right* of *private Judgment* in Matters of *Religion,* sufficiently demonstrated in the foregoing Pages, it follows, that no Christian is obliged to join himself to *this* or *the other Church,* because any Man or Order of Men command him to do so, or because they tell him the Worship and Discipline thereof is most consonant to the sacred Scriptures; For no Man has Right to judge for him, whether the Worship and Discipline of *this* or *the other* Church be most agreeable to the sacred Scriptures; and therefore no other can have Right to determine for him to which he ought to join himself: This Right therefore must lie with every Christian. As this is the Right of each *Individual;* so also of a *Number* of them agreeing in their Sentiments in these Things, to agree to observe the Ordinances of Christ together, for their mutual Edification according to the Rules of the Gospel, which makes a particular Christian Church. And having voluntarily agreed together for such an End, no Man or Order of Men has any Authority to prescribe to them, *the Manner* of their *worshipping* GOD, or enjoining any *Form of Church Discipline* upon them. So a *Number of such Churches* (who are all endowed with Equality of Power) have Right to judge for themselves, whether it be most agreeable to the Mind of CHRIST, to *consociate* together in any *particular Form;* as far Instance, of *Presbyteries,* or *Synods,* or the like. . . . So also from the same Premisses it follows, that every Church or worshipping Assembly has the *Right* of *choosing its own Officers:*—Tho' it may ordinarily be a Point of Prudence for a Church destitute of a Pastor, to consult Pastors of other Churches where they may be supplied with a Person suitable for that Office; yet that no Way supposes, the full *Power of Election* does not lie with the Church. It is for the *better improving* their *Power of Election,* that such a Method is ever to be taken, and not because they have not the Power of Election in themselves. Nor can they be bound to this, if they see good Reason to act otherwise, (as the Case has sometimes hapned and often may.) *Nor can they be at all bound* to *elect* the *Person recommended:* They are to prove him themselves, and be fully satisfied in his Ministerial Gifts and Qualifications, and may herein be controuled by no Power whatever. It is their own good, their everlasting Interest that is concerned, and if they judge his Doctrine not agreeable to the sacred Scriptures, that he is not qualified as he ought to be for a Gospel Minister they have Right to reject him. As they have a Right of judging the Doctrines taught them by the sacred Scriptures, and of rejecting the same if not agreeable thereto, so it necessarily follows they have equal Right to refuse such a one for their Teacher, who does not teach according to the Scriptures.

But if it be demanded how this Power can be exercised, must every Individual be agreed in the Person, or no Election made?

I answer,

1. Such a universal Agreement is not necessary, the Election may be made by a Majority. Experience has shewn where the Candidate has had the Gospel Qualifications for the Office, the Concurrence in the Choice has been universal, at least so general as to bring no Difficulty in the Exercise of this Right. So when there has been any considerable Number who judged they had any weighty Reason against the Election made by a Majority, Experience has also shewn the Majority's denying themselves of that Choice, and trying farther, has issued happily for the whole. In such Cases, 'tis certain, *Wisdom is profitable to direct.* And that Rule of our Saviour's, *Math.* 7. 12. will go a great Way in keeping Churches in the peaceable Exercise of this Right.

2. Where a minor Part cannot in Judgment acquiesce in the Choice made by the major Part of the worshipping Assembly, they have a Right to withdraw and choose a Minister for themselves, or if not able to support one may attend divine Worship in a neighbouring Church, where they find they may do it to greater Edification. They are all equally vested in the same Right, and hold it independent one of another, and each one independent of the whole, or of all the rest. So that the greater Number can have no Right to impose a Minister on the lesser. It is not here as in civil Societies where the Right of each Individual is subjected to the Body, or so transferred to the Society, as that the Act of the Majority is legally to be considered as the Act of the whole, and binding to each Individual. As to what concerns Men's civil Interests, there is nothing in the Nature of Things to hinder or prevent its being lawful or best, so to transfer their Power to the Community. But it is not so in religious Matters, where Conscience and Men's eternal Interests are concerned. If the Power of acting be transferred in this Case, as in that of civil Societies (now mentioned) Thus, if for Instance, the Majority should elect an *Arminian* Teacher, the minor Part must be so concluded by that Choice, as to submit to such a One as their Teacher,

when at the same Time it may be directly against their Consciences to receive such Doctrines or such a Teacher. But since the Rights of Conscience may not be touched, the Right of electing a Teacher is not transfer'd to the Body by the Individuals, as civil Rights may be in civil Societies. That Principle or Supposition, which any Ways infer, an Infringement upon the Rights of Conscience, cannot be true; as that does, which supposes a Majority may impose a Minister on a lesser Part. . . .

By what I have said you will find some other of your Queries answer'd, without my making particular Application, and therefore I leave that for you to do at your own Leisure: And should here finish my Letter, but that you insist on my giving you my Sentiments on a Law made in your Colony *May* 1742, Intitled *An Act for regulating Abuses, and correcting Disorders in Ecclesiastical Affairs:* Which it seems, thro' the fond Opinion some Persons among you had of it, was thrust into one of our publick News Papers, soon after it was passed; under which every wise By-stander, that was a hearty Friend to your civil and religious Interests, was ready to write, *Tell it not in Gath* &c.

I shall not descend into every Particular that might be offered upon it—Some few Remarks may suffice.

I. The Law is founded on this false Principle, *viz.* That the civil Authority hath Power to establish a Form of Church-Government by penal Laws. The Act relates wholly to Matters of an ecclesiastical Nature: and as it supposes, the civil Magistrate has Authority by penal Laws to regulate ecclesiastical Matters, so consequently to establish an ecclesiastical Constitution by penal Laws. It appears from the Preamble to the Act, that the declared Design of it is to keep Persons from deviating from the ecclesiastical Discipline established by Law, in the Year 1708. and that under the Penalties by this Law enacted.—But that they have no such Authority, has been fully demonstrated in the foregoing Pages, which I need not repeat. Whence it must follow, that the Act is fundamentally wrong, being made without any Authority. Be pleas'd to reflect one Minute on this Power challenged by this Law, to correct, and that by penal Laws, such Disorders as are purely of an ecclesiastical Nature, and see the Consequence of it. One Disorder to be corrected is, A Minister's preaching out of his own Parish undesired by the Minister and major Part of the Church where he shall so preach. If the civil Magistrate has this Power the Act supposes, if he judges it to be a Disorder for the Minister to preach in his own Parish on a Week Day, he may then restrain him: or if he thinks it a Disorder that there should be any public Prayers but by a set printed Form, he may then restrain all to such a Form. It is plain, if the civil Magistrate has Authority to correct ecclesiastical Disorders, he has a Right to judge what is a Disorder in the Church, and restrain the same. If he may execute this in one Instance, he may in another: and every Thing is on this Principle liable to be disallowed in the Worship of God, which does not suit with the civil Magistrate's Opinion. Whatever he judges to be a Disorder, is so by this Principle, and may be restrained accordingly. And so farewell all Christian Liberty. . . .

Having made this general Observation, I go on, to consider the first Paragraph, which runs thus—"That if any ordained Minister or other Person licensed as aforesaid to preach, shall enter into any Parish not immediately under his Charge, and shall there preach or exhort the People, he shall be denied and secluded the Benefit of any Law of this Colony made for the Support and Encouragement of the Gospel Ministry; except such ordained Minister or licensed Person shall be expresly invited and desired so to enter into such other Parish, and there to preach and exhort the People, either by the settled Minister, and the majort Part of the Church of said Parish; or in Case there be no settled Minister, then by the Church or Society in said Parish."

The Minister's heretofore supposed Right to have Assistance and Help from his Brethren in the Ministry by preaching, is hereby cut off. None may preach unless the major Part of the Church desire it; tho' the Minister and one Half of the Church and all the rest of the Congregation, which make up much the greater Part of the Number, who have Right to hear the Word preached, are ever so desirous of hearing the Word from another, and apprehensive (as the Case may be) of the great Necessity of it. Before this Law was passed, I should have presumed, there was not one Minister on the Continent, but what thought he had good Right to invite any orthodox Minister to preach in his Pulpit: not only Ministers, but Churches in every Part of the World, have so supposed and practised. But it seems by this Law this Supposition is a Mistake, and the Practice a Disorder in the Church. . . . Such now being the plain Sense of this Paragraph; I say then,—

II. That it is apparently inconsistent with itself, deprives Ministers and particular Christians of their Rights and Liberties, and invests a lordly Power in a small Part of a Parish-Society, *viz.* a major Part or one Half of a Church, over a worshipping Assembly, since they never had nor can have any rightful Power to hinder other Christians in the Parish from hearing such Ministers as they judge may promote their spiritual Good, as by this Law they are enabled to do.

III. It invests an exorbitant Power in Ministers over a Church and Congregation. This may look very strange, especially when you reflect, that by the Preamble to this Law the Ministers are represented as having departed from the established ecclesiastical Discipline, and been guilty of disorderly and irregular Practices; and therefore are such Persons as are not fit to be left to conduct themselves, in their ministerial Office, nor to be governed by their own ecclesiastical Constitution, but must of Necessity be laid under some extraordinary legal Restraints. I say, they are thus plainly represented (whether truly, or not, is not the Question) by the Preamble; yet, notwithstanding all this, they are by this Law vested with an exorbitant Power over the Churches. Christians, it seems, must be strip'd of an invaluable Branch of Liberty Christ has vested them with, & the same must be lodged in that Order of Men, who are represented as unfaithful in the Execution of their Trust. For by this Law every Minister has not only Power given him, to prevent any other Minister's preaching in his Parish, not only if a small Number desire it, but if the whole worshipping Assembly desire it; not only in the Pulpit, but in any private House, which is directly inconsistent with the Rights of Christians: but also in Case a Parish be under a Necessity of settling another Minister thro' the Incumbent's Disability to discharge his Pastoral Office, it is put into his Power to negative any Choice they shall make of a Minister, and so Churches are really stript of their Right of electing their own Ministers. . . .

VII. I come now to the last Paragraph, which runs thus: "That if any *Foreigner* or *Stranger* that is not an Inhabitant within this Colony, including as well such Persons, that have no ecclesiastical Character, or License to preach, as such as have received Ordination or License to preach by any Association or Presbytery, shall presume to preach, teach or publickly to exhort in any Town or Society within this Colony, without the Desire and License of the settled Minister and the major Part of the Church of such Town or Society; or at the Call and Desire of the Church and Inhabitants of such Town or Society, provided that it so happen that there is no settled Minister there; that every such Teacher or Exhorter shall be sent (as a *vagrant* Person) by Warrant from any one Assistant or Justice of the Peace from Constable to Constable, out of the Bounds of this Colony". Since which, you tell me, there has been last *October* an Addition made, *viz.* "That whoso thus offends shall pay the Costs of his Transportation; and if he returns again and offends in such Sort, it is made the Duty of any Assistant or Justice of the Peace that shall be informed thereof, to cause such Person to be apprehended and brought before him, and if found guilty, to give Judgment that such Person shall become bound in the penal Sum of an *hundred Pounds* lawful Money, to his peaceable and good Behaviour until the next County Court, in the County where the Offence shall be committed, and that such Person will not offend again in like Manner; and the County Court may (if they see Cause) further bind &c. during their Pleasure."—Occasioned, as I am informed, by that good Gentleman Mr. *Finley*'s coming at the Direction of a *Presbytery* in the *New-Jersey* Government, who had been applied to for a Minister, and preaching to a Presbyterian Church at *Milford,* who had join'd themselves to that Presbytery, and put themselves under their Care; for which being transported out of the Government, he returned and preached to a congregational Church at *New-Haven,* who had been allowed, as well as the former at *Milford,* to be a Society for the worshipping of God, by the County Court at *New-Haven,* by Virtue of a Law formerly made for the Ease of such as soberly dissent from the Way of Worship and Ministry established by the Laws of *Connecticut;* and for this he was adjudged by the civil Authority to be transported again, which was but in Part effected thro' the Negligence of some Officer; and, I'm told, he returned and preached again.— This his Preaching and Exhorting, it seems, *greatly disquieted and disturbed the People;* as the Preamble to this Act expresses it.—Is it not strange, the preaching of that peaceable and humble Christian (as you confess his Behaviour bespoke him to be while in the Colony) unto a Number of People, who had Right to hear the Gospel preached from him, should *greatly disquiet and disturb* such as had their Choice in hearing others! Or could it *disquiet* and *disturb* any Minds except such as can't bear their Christian Neighbours should enjoy their unalienable Rights!—But to return to the before mentioned last Paragraph, I observe, that *any Stranger, not an Inhabitant in the Colony, who has received Ordination or License to preach from any* Association *or* Presbytery, *that shall presume to preach undesired,* as expressed in the Paragraph, is liable to be treated as a *Vagrant,* unworthy to tread on that Spot of Earth: But if he should happen to be licensed by the Patriarch of *Greece,* a Super-intendant of *Denmark,* or any Bishop, he may escape the Lash of this Law. If the coming in of a Stranger and preaching in such a Manner be such a Breach of the Peace, as is punishable by the State, why should there be such *Partiality?* Why should Dr. *Watt's* preaching in such Manner in *Connecticut* be a greater Crime, because ordained by a *Presbytery,* than any other Stranger's doing so that was licensed by a Patriarch or Bishop, &c.—However, that is much less to be wondered at, than such Treatment as this Law subjects orthodox Ministers to, even the best Ministers of Christ upon Earth, for a mere Non-conformity to a certain Point of Order, that never took Place (I suppose) in any Church upon Earth.

But to be as brief as may be in the Consideration of this Paragraph; Let the Question be, if you please, exactly according to the Words, *viz.* Whether a civil State has rightful Authority to *banish* or thrust out a confessedly *orthodox Minister* of Jesus Christ, tho' a Foreigner or Stranger, for only *preaching the Gospel* to a Number, without the Desire of the Incumbent, and major Part of the Church in the Parish wherein he shall so preach; the said Minister being supposed to have a *Right* to Protection, and a *Right* to remain in that State, until he does something to *forfeit* it?—I have truly stated it, because I have mentioned the very supposed *Crime* for which such Foreigners or Strangers are to be thrust out of the Government; and I must necessarily suppose them *true* or *orthodox* Ministers of Christ, because *this Law* supposes them so, since it speaks of such as are *ordained* or *licensed by any Association or Presbytery* not within that Government; which includes all such as are on this Continent, as well as *Great-Britain* (at least) all of which are esteemed *orthodox.* I put in the last Words, because they really relate to the Subjects of the King of *Great Britain,* from whom the Government holds it *Charter,* and so to any Persons in the Plantations, as well as on the Isle of *Great Britain,* who have a Right therefore to be treated as *Englishmen,* or Fellow-Subjects under King GEORGE, and so may be truly said to have a Right to remain in the Colony, in such a Sense as you will not allow to any belonging to another Kingdom. I don't mention this because I would go into the Consideration of what particular Powers may be in your *Charter,* different from others; tho' I confess, I can't find any Words in your *Charter,* that express or imply a Power to do any Thing that is pretended to be done by this Law, to establish or regulate by Law any Matters of an ecclesiastical Nature, to impose any civil Pains or Penalties in Matters of Conscience, relating to the Worship of God. But neither your Colony, nor any other in the King's Dominions, have any rightful Authority to do as is here supposed, according to the Question, as I have truly stated it. Let me here take a plain Case to illustrate the Point. *Wickliff*[1] arose a Light in *England,* while Popery prevailed: be it supposed, he instructed a few in the Truth, but neither Bishop nor Incumbent of the Parish would give Leave for his preaching. However, he goes on preaching the Gospel, and the People will hear him. In this Case, the King and Parliament had no rightful Authority to banish *Wickliff,* or turn him out from the Island, for his so preaching. . . . It alters not the Nature of

---

[1] John Wycliffe (*ca.* 1320–1384), urged popular reforms in the church and by virtue of his communistic views, is blamed for the Peasants' Revolt in 1381. [Ed.]

civil Government, whether the Magistrate be Protestant or Papist, Christian or Pagan. What of Right appertains to the civil Magistrate by Virtue of his *Office*, must also necessarily belong to him, tho' Popish, or Heathen. The supposal therefore that the civil Magistrate in *England* at that Day had rightful Authority to have sent away *Wickliff*, for preaching the Gospel without Leave of the Clergy, is big with too great an Absurdity, for a consistent Protestant to swallow. Suppose then these *Colonies* to have existed at that Time, or *Great Britain* and these Colonies *Popish* now, as *Great-Britain* was then, and *Wickliff* to come into any of them and preach in some Parish without the Consent of the Incumbent, at the Desire of a Number of People, it is certain, in this Case none of these Colonies could have any rightful Authority to thrust him out of their Borders, or do any Thing like it.—The *same Reasons* must conclude against these Colonies Authority to transport him, for coming and preaching *now* without an Incumbent's Leave at the Desire of a Number, as in the former Case; the same Principles and Reasoning will hold equally true, applied to any such Instance as now before us, any Time since the Reformation from Popery. The civil *Peace* is no Ways broken by this Action of *preaching*, of which we are speaking: But indeed if any should take Occasion from it, to contend and quarrel with their Neighbours, as Papists and Heathens have sometimes done, the Apostle (*James* 4. 1.) has shown us the true Spring thereof, the *Lusts* in Men's Hearts; the Outbreakings of which in *Injuries* to their Neighbours, fall under the civil Magistrate's Cognizance.—And the Rights of *Conscience and private Judgment* in Matters of *Religion* are unalterably the same: And 'tis a Scandal to Christians, to contend and quarrel with their Neighbours for enjoying them, and inexcusable in a Protestant State to make any Infringement upon them. And it was on these very Principles, which I here Advance (and by which this Law must fail) that our first *Reform-*

ers acted, and on which all Reformations must be built. And tho' our Nation in Times past under the Influence of a bigotted Clergy, and arbitrary weak or popish Princes, have made Laws founded on Principles contrary to these I have been pleading for; yet they seem in a great Measure rooted out of the Nation: and these Principles of Truth have taken Root, and been growing ever since the happy *Revolution*, and Act of *Toleration;* and 'tis to be hoped, will prevail & spread more and more, until all spiritual Tyranny, and lording it over the Consciences of Men, be banished out of the World.

But I shall finish with observing, That by Virtue of the *Act of Toleration*, all his Majesty's Subjects are so freed from the Force of all *Coercive Laws* in Matters of *Religion*, relating to Worship and Discipline, that they act their own *private Judgment*, without Restraint:—That *any Number* of Christians, greater or less, hear *any Protestant Minister* they desire, without Controul from the Will of others, or Authority of the civil State:—Since this is the Case, and withal as plain as the Sun in the Meridian, that where such a *Law* as this I have been considering, takes Place, *There* People are abridged of that *Christian Liberty*, which the same Persons would enjoy under the present Constitution, if they were in *England*. And how far therefore it falls short of denying and secluding them from the Benefit of the *Act of Toleration*, I leave you to say, who well know, that it is expressly provided by the Terms of your *Charter*, that *the Laws to be made in Virtue of it, shall not be contrary to the Laws of* England. This Right of private Judgment and Liberty now mentioned, is confessed and secured to you by that Law which was the Glory of the Reign of WILLIAM and MARY; but by your Law now before me, it is denied to you. How you will clear it from a *Contrariety* to the former, I know not. Nor is this about a trivial Matter, or what is dependent upon the Will of your Legislature. The Rights of *Magna Charter* depend not on the Will of the Prince, or the

Will of the Legislature; but they are the inherent natural Rights of *Englishmen:* secured and confirmed they may be by the Legislature, but not derived from nor dependent on their *Will.* And if there be any Rights, any Priviledges, that we may call natural and unalienable, this is one, *viz.* the Right of *private Judgment,* and Liberty of worshipping God according to our Consciences, without controul from human Laws. A Priviledge more valuable than the civil Rights of *Magna Charta.*—This we hold, not from *Man,* but from GOD: which therefore no Man can touch and be innocent. And all the Invaders of it will certainly find, when they shall stand at his Bar, from whom we hold this, *that* CHRIST *will be King in his own Kingdom.*—In the mean Time, it stands Christians in Hand to hold fast this Priviledge, and to be on their Guard against all Attempts made upon it. . . . It has commonly been the Case, that Christian *Liberty,* as well as Civil, has been lost by little and little; and Experience has taught, that it is not easy to recover it, when once lost. So precious a *Jewel* is always to be watched with a careful Eye: for no People are likely to enjoy Liberty long, that are not zealous to preserve it.

31 · *The Testimony of Harvard College*

against George Whitefield

───────────

In Massachusetts the dispute over religious liberty was confined largely to the church. In the spring of 1743 a meeting of ministers resolved that it was right and necessary to forbid itinerant preachers admission to their parishes. A dissident group (the more numerous, as it turned out) repudiated this resolution as unrepresentative of ministerial opinion and as an unwarranted abridgement of Christian liberty. The larger issue, however, was the character of what, by 1743, were known as the "late religious commotions," and the convention's stand was an evident effort to prevent any recurrence of those phenomena. In 1744 George Whitefield announced his intention to visit New England again, and opposing parties braced to resist or to welcome him. The assault on Whitefield opened with a lengthy criticism of his career drawn up by the president and faculty of Harvard College, whom Whitefield had earlier offended with his strictures on New England's institutions of higher learning. "As for the Universities," Whitefield had observed in his published *Journal,* "I believe, it may be said, their Light is become Darkness."

───────────

The Testimony of the President, Professors, Tutors, and Hebrew Instructor of Harvard College, against George Whitefield (Boston, 1744), entire.

340

Though the *Harvard Testimony* touched on nearly every aspect of Whitefield's thought and conduct, its primary significance rests in its statement of the judgment of reasonable men on the "anti-intellectualism" of the revival.

In regard of the Danger which we apprehend the People and Churches of this Land are in, on the Account of the Rev. Mr. *George Whitefield,* we have tho't ourselves oblig'd to bear our Testimony, in this public Manner, against him and his Way of Preaching, as tending very much to the Detriment of Religion, and the entire Destruction of the Order of these Churches of Christ, which our Fathers have taken such Care and Pains to settle, as by the Platform, according to which the Discipline of the Churches of *New England* is regulated: And we do therefore hereby declare, That we look upon his going about, in an Itinerant Way, especially as he hath so much of an enthusiastic Turn, utterly inconsistent with the Peace and Order, if not the very Being of these Churches of Christ.

And now, inasmuch as by a certain Faculty he hath of raising the Passions, he hath been the Means of rousing many from their Stupidity, and setting them on thinking, whereby some may have been made really better, on which Account the People, many of them, are strongly attach'd to him (tho' it is most evident, that he hath not any superior Talent at instructing the Mind, or shewing the Force and Energy of those Arguments for a religious Life, which are directed to in the everlasting Gospel). Therefore, that the People who are thus attach'd to him, may not take up an unreasonable Prejudice against this our Testimony, we think it very proper to give some Reasons for it, which we shall offer, respecting the Man himself, and then his Way and Manner of Preaching.

First, as to the Man himself, whom we look upon as an Enthusiast, a censorious, uncharitable Person, and a Deluder of the People; which Things, if we can make out, all reasonable Men will doubtless excuse us, tho' some such, thro' a fascinating Curiosity, may still continue their Attachment to him.

First then, we charge him, with *Enthusiasm.* Now that we may speak clearly upon this Head, we mean by an *Enthusiast,* one that acts, either according to Dreams, or some sudden Impulses and Impressions upon his Mind, which he fondly imagines to be from the Spirit of God, perswading and inclining him thereby to such and such Actions, tho' he hath no Proof that such Perswasions or Impressions are from the holy Spirit: For the perceiving a strong Impression upon our Minds, or a violent Inclination to do any Action, is a very different Thing from perceiving such Impressions to be from the Spirit of God moving upon the Heart: For our strong Faith and Belief, that such a Motion on the Mind comes from God, can never be any Proof of it; and if such Impulses and Impressions be not agreeable to our Reason, or to the Revelation of the Mind of God to us, in his Word, nothing can be more dangerous than conducting ourselves according to them; for otherwise, if we judge not of them by these Rules, they may as well be the Suggestions of the evil Spirit: And in what Condition must that People be, who stand ready to be led by a Man that conducts himself according to his Dreams, or some ridiculous and unaccountable Impulses and Impressions on his Mind? And that this is Mr. *Whitefield's* Manner, is evident both by his Life, his Journals and his Sermons: In which, the Instances of this dangerous Turn are so many, that we cannot touch on more than a very few of them. From these Pieces then it is very evident, that he us'd to govern himself by his Dreams; one Instance we have of this, is in his Life, pag. 12. *Near this Time I dream'd that I was to see God on M. Sinai.*

This made a great Impression upon me. Another like Instance we have *p.* 39, 40. *I prayed that God wou'd open a Door to visit the Prisoners, quickly after I dream'd that one of the Prisoners came to be instructed by me; the Dream was impress'd much upon my Heart; in the Morning I went to the Door of the Goal.*—Once more, a like Instance we have *pag.* 43. *I dream'd I was talking with the Bishop*——*and that he gave me some Gold, which chinked in my Hands;* and p. 44. The Guineas *Chinking in my Hand, put me in Mind of my Dream.*

Now if we consider these Instances, we must suppose him conducting himself by his Dreams: Nay, the Second looks as if he wou'd have us think, that it was a divine Direction to him, as was that of the divinely inspir'd Apostle, which caus'd him to attempt to preach the Gospel at *Macedonia.* And as plain it is, that he usually governed himself by some sudden Impulses and Impressions on his Mind; and we have one Instance that may satisfy us, that his first setting out upon his Itinerant Business, was from an Enthusiastic Turn. Journal from *London* to *Gibraltar,* p. 3. He says, *He will not mention the Reasons that perswaded him, that it was the divine Will that he should go abroad, because, they might not be deemed good Reasons by another;* but saith, *He was as much bent as ever to go, tho' strongly sollicited to the Contrary, having asked direction from Heaven about it for a Year and an half.* Other Instances there are, wherein he shews it to be his Custom to attribute any common Turn of his Mind to a Motion of the Holy Spirit upon him, without any more Reason than any Man may, any Recollections of his Memory, or sudden Suggestions of his own Understanding. Such an one you have, Journ. from *Gibral.* to *Savan. p.* 6. *I went to Bed with unusual Tho'ts and Convictions, that God wou'd do some great Things at* Gibraltar——: Another, Journ. from *Savann.* to *England,* p. 22. where he Says, That the Lesson before he left *Savannah* being St. *Paul's* Shipwreck; and *that,* before his leaving

Charlestown being the First of *Jonah,* made such a deep Impression upon him, that he wrote to his Friend to acquaint him, he was apprehensive he should have a dangerous Voyage, and it happening to be bad Weather accordingly, he says, *God hath now shewed me, wherefore he gave these previous Notices.* So that every Scripture that came to his View, was receiv'd as the *Bath Kol* of the *Jews,* and he plainly shews himself as much directed by this Way of finding out the Will of God, as he calls it, as the old Heathen were by their *Sortes Homerciæ, Virgilianæ,* &c. And of this we have a very full Instance, same Journ. Pag. 38. where you have a particular Application of the Words which appear'd upon the Doctor's first opening the Book of Common Prayer, *viz. The Lord hath visited and redeemed his People;* upon which he wisely observes, *so it was, for about* 8 *of Clock the Men saw Land.* Sometimes he speaks as if he had Communications directly from the Spirit of God, Journ. from *Gibral.* to *Savann.* p. 5. *God was pleased to shew me, it was not his Will.* Journ. from *Savann.* to *N. E.* p. 31. *The Power of the Lord came upon me:* So also, p. 38. and again, *p.* 68. *The Spirit of the Lord was upon me:* Journ. from *N. E.* to *Falmouth* in *Engl.* pag. 6. *The Lord gave me that Freedom that the Spirit came down upon them as a rushing mighty Wind.* Sometimes, and indeed very frequently, he (in a most enthusiastic Manner) applies, even the historical Parts of Scripture particularly to himself, and his own Affairs; and this Manner he endeavours particularly to vindicate. Serm. of *Searching the Scriptures,* p. 246. of his Sermons. *It is this Application of——the historical Parts of Scripture when we are reading, that must render them profitable to us;* and appeals to the Experiences of the Christian, that if he hath so consulted the Word of God, he has been as plainly directed how to act, as tho' he had consulted the *Urim* and the *Thummim.* For in this plain and full Manner, he says, p. 38. of his Life, *The holy Spirit hath, from Time to Time, let him into the Knowledge of divine Things, and hath directed him in the minutest Circumstances.* And no doubt hence it is that he says, formention'd Serm. p. 247. *That God, at all Times, Circumstances and Places, tho' never so minute, never so particular, will, if we diligently seek the Assistance of his holy Spirit, apply general Things to our Hearts:* Which tho' it may be true in some Measure as to the doctrinal and preceptive Parts of Scripture, yet is it evidently enthusiastical, to say so, as to the historical Parts of it. In this Manner he pretends a Direction from God to go to *England* from *Savannah,* p. 28. of that Journ. The like use we have made of Scripture, p. 36. so p. 42. *That he shou'd be cast upon Karrigholt Island, because he had an Impression upon his Mind, as to what the Apostle tells the Mariners, That they must be cast upon a certain Island.*

But we proceed to mention one Piece of *Enthusiasm* of a very uncommon Turn, which shews to what a great Length this unhappy pernicious Disposition of the Mind may carry a Man. When Pag. 32 of his Life, he personates our blessed Lord himself, when in his Passion, says he, *It was suggested to me, that when Jesus cried out, I thirst, his Sufferings were near at an end; upon this I threw my self upon the Bed, crying out, I thirst, I thirst: Soon after I felt my Load go off——, and knew what it was truly to rejoice in the Lord.* And certainly it is easy enough to conceive, from what Spirit such a *Suggestion* must come. To mention but one Instance more, tho' we are not of such Letter-learned as deny, that there is such an Union of Believers to Christ, whereby *they are one in him, as the Father and he are One,* as the Evangelist speaks, or rather the Spirit of God by him; yet so Letter-learned we are, as to say, that that Passage in Mr. *W—*'s Sermon of the *Indwelling of the Spirit,* p. 311: vol. of Sermons, contains the true Spirit of Enthusiasm, where he says, *to talk of any having the Spirit of God without feeling of it, is really to deny the Thing.* Upon which we say, That the Believer may have a Satisfaction, that he hath the Assistance of the Spirit of God with him, in so continual and regular a Manner, that he may be said to dwell in him, and yet have no feeling of it; for the Metaphor is much too gross to express this (however full) Satisfaction of the Mind, and has led some to take the Expression literally, and hath (we fear) given great Satisfaction to many an Enthusiast among us since the Year 1740, from the swelling of their Breasts and Stomachs in their religious Agitations, which they have tho't to be *feeling the Spirit,* in its Operations on them. But it is no way necessary to instance any further upon this Head; for the aforesaid Compositions are full of these Things.

The whole tends to perswade the World (and it has done so with respect to many) that Mr. W. hath as familiar a Converse and Communion with God as any of the Prophets and Apostles, and such as we all acknowledge to have been under the Inspiration of the Holy Ghost.

In the next Place, we look upon Mr. W. as an uncharitable, censorious and slanderous Man; which indeed is but a natural Consequence of the heat of Enthusiasm, by which he was so evidentally acted; for this Distemper of the Mind always puts a Man into a vain Conceit of his own Worth and Excellency, which all his Pretences to Humility will never hide, as long as he evidently shews, that he would have the World think he hath a greater Familiarity with God than other Men, and more frequent Communications from his Holy Spirit. Hence such a Man naturally assumes an Authority to dictate to others, and a Right to direct their Conduct and Opinions; and hence if any act not according to his Directions, and the Model of Things he had form'd in his own heated Brain, he is presently apt to run into slander, and stigmatize them as *Men of no Religion, unconverted,* and *Opposers of the Spirit of God:* And that such hath been the Behaviour of Mr. W. is also sufficiently evident as was the former Head. Hence were his monstrous Reflections upon the great and good Archbishop TILLOTSON, (as Dr. *Increase Mather* Stiles him) comparing his Sermons to the conjuring Books which the Apostles perswaded the People to destroy.

Hence also is that Reflection made upon Mr. Commissary *Garden,* Journal from *Savana* to *N. E.* p. 22. where he says, *he was oblig'd to tell him he believ'd he was an unconverted Man.* But what oblig'd him to tell all the World of it in his Journal? and why did he believe so? *Because* (he says) *all his Discourses were so inconsistent with and contrary to the Gospel.* But this (considering Mr. *Garden's* Character) must be only according to his peculiar Notions of Inconsistency. If the Commissary were too severe upon Mr. *W.* his Spirit might indeed be naturally irritated thereby; but he shou'd have consider'd, that it is no new Thing, that true Christians shou'd persecute (in some Degree) one another. Again, p. 44. He insinuates in a very unchristian Manner, *That Mr.* H——n *of* Newp—t *had no experimental Knowledge of the N. Birth.*

The next Instance we shall note, is the reproachful Reflections upon the Society which is immediately under our Care. p. 55. Where are observable his Rashness and his Arrogance. His Rashness, in publishing such a disadvantageous Character of *Us, viz.* Because some Body had so inform'd him. Surely he ought, if he had followed our Saviour's Rule, to have had a greater Certainty of the Truth of what he publish'd of us to the whole World. But his Arrogance is more flagrant still, that such a young Man as he should take upon him to tell what Books we shou'd allow our Pupils to read. But then he goes further still, when he says, p. 95. both of *Yale College* as well as ours, *As for the Universities, I believe it may be said, Their Light is now become Darkness, Darkness that may be felt.* What a deplorable State of Immorality and Irreligion has he hereby represented *Us* to be in! And as this is a most wicked and libellous Falshood (at least as to our College) as such we charge it upon him. But why doth he say thus? Why, *because this is complain'd of by the most godly Ministers*. Here we are at a Loss to think whom he means by *the most godly Ministers*. Certainly not the Rev. Gentlemen of the Town of *Boston* (with whom nevertheless he was most acquainted) for they are in the Government of the College, have assisted in making the Laws by which it is govern'd, and constantly visit us by a Committee, and themselves four Times in a Year, and make Examination how the Laws are executed. Besides, we don't know that he hath been pleas'd to allow to any one of them any such religious Character, in any one of his Journals, as should make us think he means them, but rather the reverse. Vid. p. 76 of his Journal from *N. E.*

But we shall finish this Head of his Censoriousness, when we have mentioned his pernicious Reflections upon the Ministers of the Churches in this Land. We say *this Land;* for it is far from a torturing of the Words, to suppose he directly means them, when he says, p. 70. *He is perswaded the generality of Preachers talk of an unknown unfelt Christ;* tho' he hath evasively said (since he came this time) that *he did not restrain the Expression to the Ministers of* N. England, *tho' he did not exclude them.* Admirably satisfactory this Explanation! But he can't come off so easily in the Reflection he makes upon our Ministers, *p.* 95. *Many, nay most perhaps that preach, I fear, do not experimentally know Christ*—Is it possible he should say, this is no Charge upon the Ministers of these Churches? It is true, it is not so in Form; but is it not one of the most uncharitable Things he cou'd have done, to manifest these his Fears to all the World, without Ground? Without Ground, we say; for as to the greatest Part of them by far, their Conversation is as becomes the Gospel, and we may challenge him and all the World to shew the contrary.

And now let the World judge, if we have not the highest Reason to tax Mr. *W.* as an *uncharitable, censorious* and *slanderous* Man; that he has been guilty of gross Breaches of the *Ninth Command* of the moral Law, and an evident disregard to the Laws of Christian Charity, as they are delivered to us in the N. Testament. And now is it possible that we should not look upon him as the blameable Cause of all the Quarrels on the Account of Religion, which the Churches are now engaged in? and this not only on account of his own Behaviour; but also as the coming of those hot Men amongst us afterwards (who, together with the *Exhorters* that accompanied them, cultivated the same uncharitable Disposition in our Churches) was wholly owing to his Influence and Example. So that all the Errors, Confusions and Quarrels that our Churches are now in, are owing to this censorious, most unchristian Carriage and Disposition; and it is, to us, a very marvellous Thing, when such Behaviour as Mr. *W.* &c. have used, is plainly and directly contrary to the moral Law, and all the Rules of Christianity, that the People, in general, should not be able to see it.

Again, We think it highly proper to bear our Testimony against Mr. *W.* as we look upon him a *Deluder of the People.* How he designs to manage in this Affair now, we know not: but we mean, that he hath much deluded them, and therefore suppose we have Reason in this respect to guard against him. And here we mean more especially as to the Collections of Money, which, when here before, by an extraordinary mendicant Faculty, he almost *extorted* from the People. As the Argument he then used was, *the Support and Education of his dear Lambs at the Orphan-House,* who (he told us, he hop'd) might in Time preach the Gospel to us or our Children; so it is not to be doubted, that the People were greatly encouraged to give him largely of their Substance, supposing they were to be under the immediate Tuition and Instruction of himself, as he then made them to believe; and had not this been their Tho't, it is, to us, without all Peradventure, they would never have been perswaded to any considerable Contribution upon that Head; and this, notwithstanding, he hath scarce seen them for these four Years; and besides hath left the Care of them with a Person, whom these Contributors know nothing of, and we ourselves have Reason to believe is little better than a *Quaker;* so that in this Regard we think the People have been greatly deceiv'd.

Furthermore, the Account which Mr. W. hath given the World of his Disbursement of the several Contributions, for the use of his Orphan House (wherein there are several large Articles, and some of about a *Thousand Pounds,* our Currency, charg'd in a very summary Way, *viz.* For sundries, no Mention being made therein what the Sum was expended for, nor to whom it was paid) is by no means satisfactory. And as we have so much Reason to be dissatisfied with the Man, so *we think,*

Secondly, We have as much Reason to dislike and bear Testimony against the *Manner* of his Preaching; and this in Two respects, both as an *Extempore* and as an *Itinerant* Preacher.

And first, as to his *extempore* Manner of preaching; this we think by no means proper, for that it is impossible that any Man should be able to manage any Argument with that Strength, or any Instruction with that Clearness in an *extempore* Manner, as he may with Study and Meditation. Besides, it is observable that your *extempore* Preachers give us almost always the same Things in the applicatory Part of their Sermons, so that it is often very little akin to their Text, which is just open'd in a cursory, and not seldom in a perverted Manner, and then comes the same kind of Harangue which they have often used before, as an *Application;* so that this is a most lazy Manner, and the Preacher offers that which cost him nothing, and is accordingly little Instructive to the Mind, and still less cogent to the reasonable Powers. Now Mr. W. evidently shows, that he would have us believe his Discourses are *extempore,* and indeed from the Rashness of some of his Expressions, as well as from the dangerous Errors vented in them, it is very likely: Hence, no doubt, were the many unguarded Expressions in his Sermons when he was here before; and since he has come again, he hath told us, "That Christ loves unregenerate Sinners with a *Love of Complacency:*" Nay, he hath gone rather further, and said, *"That God loves Sinners as Sinners;"* which, if it be not an unguarded Expression, must be a thousand times worse: For we cannot look upon it as much less than Blasphemy, and shows him to be stronger in the *Antinomian* Scheme than most of the Professors of that *Heresy* themselves; and that this is not unlikely, is to be suspected, because the Expression was repeated, and when he was tax'd with it, by a certain Gentleman, he made no Retractations.

But, *lastly,* We think it our Duty to bear our strongest Testimony against that *Itinerant* Way of preaching which this Gentleman was the first promoter of among us, and still delights to continue in: For if we had nothing against the *Man,* either as an *Enthusiast,* an *uncharitable* or *delusive* Person, yet we apprehend this Itinerant Manner of preaching to be of the worst and most pernicious Tendency.

Now by an *Itinerant* Preacher, we understand One that hath no particular Charge of his own, but goes about from Country to Country, or from Town to Town, in any Country, and stands ready to Preach to any Congregation that shall call him to it; and such an one is Mr. *W.* for it is but trifling for him to say (as we hear he hath) That he requires in order to his preaching any where, that the Minister also should invite him to it; for he knows the Populace have such an Itch after him, that when they generally desire it, the Minister (however diverse from their's, his own Sentiments may be) will always be in the utmost Danger of his People's quarrelling with, if not departing from him, shou'd he not consent to their impetuous

Desires. Now as it is plain, no Man will find much Business as an *Itinerant* Preacher, who hath not something in his Manner, that is (however trifling, yea, and erroneous too, yet) very taking and agreeable to the People; so when this is the Case, as we have lately unhappily seen it, it is then in his Power to raise the People to any Degree of Warmth he pleases, whereby they stand ready to receive almost any Doctrine he is pleased to broach; as hath been the Case as to all the Itinerant Preachers who have followed Mr. *W's.* Example, and thrust themselves into Towns and Parishes, to the Destruction of all Peace and Order, whereby they have to the great impoverishment of the Community, taken the People from their Work and Business, to attend their Lectures and Exhortations, always fraught with Enthusiasm, and other pernicious Errors: But, *which is worse, and it is the natural Effect of these Things,* the People have been thence ready to despise their own Ministers, and their usefulness among them, in too many Places, hath been almost destroy'd.

Indeed, if there were any thing leading to this manner of Management in the Directions and Instructions given, either by our Saviour or his Apostles, we ought to be silent, and so wou'd a Man of any Modesty, if (on the other hand) there be nothing in the N. Testament leading to it. And surely Mr. W. will not have the Face to pretend he acts now as an *Evangelist,* tho' he seems to prepare for it in Journ. from *N. E.* to *Falmouth* in *England,* p. 12. where he says, *God seems to shew me it is my Duty to Evangelize, and not to fix in any particular Place:* For the Duty of that Officer certainly was not to go preaching of his own Head from one Church to another, where Officers were already settled, and the Gospel fully and faithfully preached. And it is without Doubt, that the Mind and Will of Christ, with respect to the Order of his Churches, and the Business of his Ministers in them, is plainly enough to be understood in the N. Testament; and yet Mr. W. has said of late, in one of his Sermons, he thinks that an Itinerant Manner of preaching may be very convenient for the furtherance of the good of the Churches, if it were under a good Regulation. Now we are apt to imagine, if such an Officer wou'd have been useful, Christ himself wou'd have appointed him; and therefore (under Favour) this is to *be wise above what is written,* and supposes either that our Lord did not know, or that he neglected to appoint all such Officers in the Ministry, as wou'd further in the best manner the Truths of the Gospel: And it is from such Wisdom as this, that all the Errors of *Popery* have come into the *Christian Church,* while the Directions of the Word of God were not strictly adhered to, but one tho't this Way or that Ceremony was very convenient and significant, and another another, till they have dress'd up the Church in such a monstrous heap of Appendages, that at this Day it can hardly be discern'd to be a Church of Christ.

And now, upon the whole, having, we think, made it evident to every one that is not prejedic'd on his Side (for such as are so, we have little hope to convince) that Mr. W. is chargeable with that *Enthusiasm, Censoriousness* and *delusive Management* that we have tax'd him with; and since also he seems resolv'd for that Itinerant Way of preaching, which we think so destructive to the Peace of the Churches of Christ; we cannot but bear our faithful Testimony against him, as a Person very unfit to preach about as he has done heretofore, and as he has now begun to do.

And we wou'd earnestly, and with all due respect, recommend it to the Rev. Pastors of these Churches of Christ, to advise with each other in their several Associations, and consider whether it be not high Time to make a stand against the Mischiefs, which we have here suggested as coming upon the Churches.

Harvard College, Dec. 28. 1744.

Edward Holyoke, *President.* .

32 · *William Shurtleff*

(1 6 8 7 – 1 7 4 7)

LETTER TO THOSE WHO REFUSE

TO ADMIT WHITEFIELD

———————

The Yale faculty likewise called on the clergy to take action against Whitefield. The laws of 1742 did not apply
(nor could they have, without endangering the Connecticut charter) to ministers of the Church of England. So in
Connecticut, as in Massachusetts, ministerial associations
met and announced—generally in language quoted or borrowed from the collegiate testimonies—their reasons for
refusing to give Whitefield another hearing. Included
among the signers of such declarations were a few ministers who had warmly received the Awakening and who
were to remain staunch Calvinists. But the greater number, and invariably those who took the lead, were Old
Lights and rationalists. An occasional association proclaimed its members' willingness to admit Whitefield, but
such a decision did not need to be defended. Whitefield's

———————

William Shurtleff, *A Letter to those of his brethren in the Ministry who
refuse to admit the Rev. Mr. Whitefield into their Pulpits* (Boston,
1745), pp. 3–9.

opposers knew they were flouting both the desires of the people and the traditions of Congregationalism. Several ministers and even some representatives of the laity published statements declaring that the decision for or against Whitefield was not for the clergy to make, that such power was given only to the "people." The last position was soon to be recognized as the only one consistent with the spirit and principles of the Awakening, but in the debates of 1745 few New England minds were focused clearly or exclusively on the future. The argument over Whitefield actually represented New England's effort to assess the occurrences of the previous half-decade—in order, possibly, thereby to comprehend the nature of the new dispensation. William Shurtleff's letter to his fellow ministers shows how one of New England's older divines judiciously, but nonetheless warmly, welcomed the beginning of the evangelical era.

Reverend and Beloved,

Having many of you seen fit to publish your Determination of not admitting the Rev. Mr. *Whitefield* into your Pulpits, and more than implicitly censur'd your Brethren who have conducted themselves towards him in a different Manner: It can't be just Matter of Offence, that one of them takes the Liberty of addressing you in this public Way; especially seeing you are some of you grown so shy, and become such Strangers of late, that he is depriv'd of the Opportunity he has sometimes wish'd for of privately conferring with you upon the foregoing Head.

That so many are turn'd aside to *vain Jangling,* I think calls for Lamentation, and if I know my self, I am a hearty Mourner for that Spirit of Discord that is gone forth, and so far prevails among *Ministers* as well as *private Christians.* If what I am now writing should have any Tendency to increase it, and be a Means of further alienating your Affections, I shall be very sorry: Tho' let what will be the Event, it will be some Support to me, that I am acted by right Views. And as I find my self in the Exercise of brotherly Love, I shall endeavour to pre- serve that *Gentleness* and *Meekness* that so peculiarly becomes our high and heavenly Profession.

To come then to the Matter in Hand; in refusing Mr. *White- field* the Liberty of your Pulpits, you go upon *this Supposition,* that he has been already the Instrument of much Mischief to the Churches of CHRIST in this Land, and that there is a Prospect of yet more Mischief, should he be indulg'd the Lib- erty of preaching to the People of your Charge.

I. You suppose, and many of you expresly say, 'That Mr. *Whitefield* by his former preaching among us, has been the Occasion of much Mischief to the Churches of this Land.'

You allow that there is a considerable *Alteration* in the *State of Religion* in these Churches now, from what it was some Years ago, and that Mr. *Whitefield* has been one great Instru- ment of it, and so far we are agreed. But then you affirm, 'That this *Alteration* that there is in the *State of Religion* is for the *worse,* and that he is to be look'd upon as the *blameable Cause* of all the Disorders that have arisen among us.' And herein I am obliged to differ from you.

[1.] I can by no Means allow that the *State of Religion* in the Churches of this Land is really alter'd for the *worse* within these *four* or *five Years* past: and that you and I may form a right Judgment of the Matter, let us view it, as it was before that Time, and as it has been *since.*

1. Let us look a little back, and take a View of the *State of Religion* as it was in these Churches *five Years ago,* and for *some Time before.*

An affecting Spectacle I confess! what no serious Christian could behold in the Time of it, without a heavy Heart, and scarce without a weeping Eye. To see that solid and substantial Piety for which our Ancestors were so justly renowned, having long languish'd under sore Decays, brought so very low, and seemingly just ready to expire and give up the Ghost.

How did not only *Pelagianism,* but *Arianism, Socinianism,* and even *Deism* itself, and what is falsely call'd by the Name of *Free-thinking,* here and there prevail? How much was it grown into Fashion to throw off all Manner of Regard to strict and serious Godliness? How many seem'd asham'd of the Dress? and of those that wore the Garb, and kept up the *Form,* what Numbers were there that were content with this, and had but little else? The *instituted Means of Salvation,* it's evident in many Places, were but lightly esteem'd, and a horrid Contempt was put upon the *Ministry of the Word!* When there was no more than a *Monthly Lecture* even in a large Parish, what a small Handful should we find attending upon it? Indeed upon the *Lord's-Day,* when the Season was inviting, and there was nothing in the Way, there would (it may be) be what some call a handsome Appearance: That is, there would be a Number of Persons of both Sexes, especially in some Congregations, richly and curiously dress'd, and making as fine and glittering a Shew as if this was the Thing they chiefly aim'd at; which, with some might possibly be what they had principally in View. Accordingly how remote were they for the most Part from that Seriousness and Solemnity that became the Place where they were, and the Business they were about? How little did they behave as those that came to converse with an infinitely holy and glorious GOD; and to secure the Salvation of a Soul, which, tho' immortal, and of more Worth than the whole World, was in Danger of being lost for ever? Even whilst the Word of God was dispensed, how many Eyes, if they were not slumbering, would be wandering and gazing? And how little Heed did the Generality give to the Things that they heard? What Numbers were there, who having after a Sort attended on the Sermon, and so perform'd their Task, went away satisfied as if there was nothing further required? How seldom was it that the Word made any abiding Impressions on the Hearers? And sometimes it may be it was but poorly adapted to this Purpose.

We who took upon us to be *Masters of Assemblies,* upon Reflection may find Occasion to charge our selves with being too dull and sluggish, careless and negligent in our public Ministrations. I would not be understood to insinuate that this was universally the Case. There were doubtless Exceptions to the contrary. But what I intend is, that it was too commonly so, or at least that there were too many mournful Instances of it. It's well if we were none of us among those *that corrupt the Word.* But if we were not Teachers of Doctrines that are grosly and notoriously false; are there not *some weighty Points,* such as that of *Original Sin, Regeneration* and *Conversion, Justification by Faith only,* &c. that have not been so fully and throughly handled, so clearly explained, and so strongly pressed as they might, and ought to have been? By which Means too many of our People have had but very confused and indifferent Notions of them; and if they have own'd them as Truths, have not had a just Sense of the *Importance* of them. And tho' we saw but little Fruit of our Labours in those Times I am speaking of, how many Ways did we find to satisfy our selves, and how easy were we in our want of Success? Were we, one and another of us upon this Account, crying out with the Prophet, *Wo is me, for I am as when they have gathered the Summer Fruits,* &c? Did we constantly make it the Matter of our most bitter Lamentation before God, or was it the Subject of our Complaint one to another? No; when we met together, our Conversation too generally turn'd upon Points of a lower Nature. *Religious Conference* was so much laid aside, not only among *private Christians,* but even among

Ministers; that it could not always be easily introduc'd. Our *Association Meetings* had not always that Seriousness in them that might be expected from Persons of our sacred Character: Insomuch that some have since told me, that being occasionally present, it was Matter of Stumbling to them to see us behave as if we had nothing further in View than to smoke and eat together, to tell a pleasant Story, and to talk of the common and ordinary Affairs of Life. To be sure, if our Discourse reach'd to Matters of Religion, it was seldom any further than to Externals and Circumstantials. You and I must own, and GOD grant we may make suitable Reflections upon it, that the greatest and weightiest Matters were too much neglected; that our Time was not so much of it spent as might and ought to have been in concerting Measures how to advance the Kingdom of that dear REDEEMER, to whose special Service we were solemnly devoted; and how to secure the Salvation of the precious Souls we had taken under our Watch and Charge.

These Hints may serve to give us some Representation of the *State of Religion* as it was in the Generality of the Churches in this Part of the Land, and as far as I am able to judge, in most other Parts of it, *some Years ago.* And were those such glorious and happy Days, that you should so earnestly wish, as some of you seem to do, for their Return?

I must confess that they don't appear to me in that Light. But it may be you may be ready to say; 'Tho' Things were bad then, look upon them and see if they are any Thing better; nay, whether all Things being considered, they are not less desirable now?'

Accordingly I come,

2. To take a View of the *State of Religion* in these Churches *since* the Time I was before Speaking of.

The Reports that were brought among us of Mr. *Whitefield* and his Ministry; of the Multitude that attended it, and the Manner in which they were wrought upon by it, had excited a

Thoughtfulness in a great many, even before his Arrival among us: And when he came, you are sensible what Crowds came to hear him, and how generally they were wrought upon by his Preaching. As it made saving Impressions upon some; so where it failed of this, it raised in a great Number a deep and lasting Concern as to their spiritual and eternal Interests. When Mr. *Tennent* came among us, this Concern increased and became more extensive; so it continued after he went from us. As *People* long'd more to *hear;* so *Ministers* lov'd more to *preach* than they had used to do, and usually spoke with greater Power. Some of them that were Strangers to true and vital Piety before, became now acquainted with it; and others that were grown in a great Measure dead and formal, were quicken'd, stir'd up, and had new Life put into them. Some great and *important Doctrines* that before, if not wholly omitted, were but gently touch'd; were now more largely insisted on, more clearly unfolded, and more warmly press'd. *Our Assemblies* were vastly throng'd; and it was rare to see a careless and inattentive Hearer among them all. Their thirsty Souls seem'd greedily to drink down every Word that drop'd from the Preacher's Lips. They heard as for their Lives. And then what a divine Power accompanied the Word from one Time to another? What Numbers are there that have been awaken'd out of their Security in Sin; that have seen the lost and perishing State they were in; that being in the utmost Agony and Anguish of Soul from the Apprehensions of divine Wrath, have made it their anxious Inquiry how, and in what Way to escape; and that have been applying themselves to their Ministers, and others for Direction in this great and weighty Affair? And tho' some soon lost their Convictions, and others that went a great Way, have since apostatiz'd and drawn back; yet upon a strict and fair Inquiry, you will find a great many in one Place and another that are exhibiting all the Evidence that can be expected of an effectual and thorough

Chance; a great many that having been *sometimes Darkness, but being now Light in the Lord, walk as Children of the Light;* and by their good Conversation are bright and shining Ornaments to their Christian Profession.

But now, tho' this be acknowledg'd, and tho' as far as has been said, it be allow'd that a very glorious and delightful *Scene* is open'd to our View; I know you will be ready to object, 'That the Brightness of it is eclipsed and obscured by Reason of the Disorders that have occur'd.' And tho' as I may hereafter have Occasion to observe, it could hardly be expected we should be perfectly free from every Thing of this Kind; yet I heartily mourn that so much of it has arose. *Some Ministers* that were great Friends to the Revival of Religion, thro' an ungovern'd, tho' well meant Zeal, have been carried into unbecoming Extreams; and whilst they have been much admir'd and almost idoliz'd by the People, have been left (and partly it may be for that Reason) to fall into great Indiscretions. And so it has been as to *some others,* and I make no Doubt as to some gracious Persons; they have run into Errors of Judgment, and Errors of Practice. Some have strangely given Way to Spiritual Pride; they have discover'd too much of a censorious Spirit one towards another; have been rash and uncharitable in judging the Ministers of CHRIST, and too ready to separate from them. I have heard of mournful Instances of this Nature in the *Colony* of *Connecticut:* and we have had too many Examples of it in *these Provinces.* Some have separated for no Cause, and others upon too slender Grounds. Tho' as to some that have withdrawn from the Communion to which they have belong'd; I have sometimes thought, that if many of those that make a great Noise about Separations and other Disorders, had been treated just in the same Manner, they would have left their Ministers long ago. For you know this *dividing Spirit* is not confin'd to those that are Friends to what we esteem as a remarkable Work of GOD's

Grace that has been going on among us. No; those that have been disaffected to this Work have, in sundry Instances, withdrawn from their Ministers, for their firm and conscientious Attachment to it; and where they have set up a separate Congregation, if I have been rightly inform'd, have been encourag'd and assisted in it by such as have made the loudest Complaints of the like Disposition in others. Thus I have taken a short View of the *State of Religion* as it was in these Churches *some Years ago,* and as it has been *since.*

And now Brethren, let us weigh Things maturely in our own Minds; and consider whether the *latter State,* tho' attended with some disagreeable Circumstances, be not really, taking all Things together, more desirable than the *former?* How many disorderly Things does the Apostle *Paul* complain of in the Church of *Corinth,* where the Preaching of the Gospel had been accompanied with a remarkable Effusion of the Holy Spirit? He tells them of *Envying, and Strife, and Divisions, that were among them,* which was a Sign of their being too carnal: *One said, I am of* Paul, *another I am of* Apollos. They were too apt to magnify and adore one Minister, and to debase and despise another. But notwithstanding all this, so far is the Apostle from thinking they had better continued in their former State, that he could not forbear admiring and gratefully acknowledging *the Riches of divine Grace* that had been display'd among them. *I thank my God,* says he, *always on your Behalf, for the Grace of God that was given you by Jesus Christ.* In the late Times, amidst all the Disorders that have arose, there has been a deep and serious Concern among great Numbers as to the Salvation of their Souls. Not a few we have good Reason to think have been rescued from the *Powers of Darkness,* and become the Subjects of the Redeemer's Kingdom. Now does not this which has occasion'd so much Joy in Heaven, and diffused such a Pleasure thro' the whole angelic Hosts, call for Rejoicing from us here upon Earth, and demand our chearful Praises to the *GOD of all Grace?* Is not such a State as this preferable to that we were formerly in? when it was a rare Thing for any to be converted from the Error of their Way, and effectually brought home to God; when the Generality of those that were not openly vicious, were sunk into a dead, lifeless and formal State; when they were, the most of them it is to be fear'd, resting in their Attendance upon Ordinances, and in an external Conformity to the divine Will; and it may be too many without a just Sense and Apprehension of there being any Thing more requir'd in order to their Acceptance with GOD.

Now if it be really so, as I conceive it to be, that the Alteration there has been as to the State of Religion in these Churches, all Things being consider'd, be for the better and not for the worse; and if Mr. *Whitefield* has had any Hand in the Change which you seem to acknowledge, and I readily allow; I think he ought to be highly valued and regarded by us; that it becomes us to be very thankful to *him*, but above all to give *Glory* to GOD, that has raised up such an Instrument, and made him the Means of so much Good to us.

PART FIVE

THE NEW ORDER:

ECCLESIASTICAL

33 · Gilbert Tennent

IRENICUM ECCLESIASTICUM

The most obvious of the many ecclesiastical effects of the Awakening was undoubtedly that which first took institutional form—the dramatic and violent schism in Presbyterianism that occurred during the revival itself. After the Tennent party was read out of the Synod of Philadelphia, and united with the Yankee-descended Presbyterian partisans of the Awakening, the New Side and the Old Side operated, not simply as distinct Presbyterian bodies, but as different churches. For a while, the members of the Tennent group continued to protest that they were still "lawful" members of the Philadelphia Synod,

---

Gilbert Tennent, *Irenicum Ecclesiasticum, or a Humble Impartial Essay upon the Peace of Jerusalem* . . . (Philadelphia, 1749), pp. 76, 78–81, 90–91, 120–125.

perhaps because they realized that such a divided Presbyterianism, joined neither constitutionally nor even by a
sense of Christian fellowship, was an anomaly. The division clearly perplexed and troubled Gilbert Tennent, particularly after some of his own converts began to secede
into the more enthusiastic Baptist churches. In 1748 he
broached the possibility of Presbyterian reunion, for
which he argued in his sermon of the following year,
Irenicum Ecclesiasticum. In this sermon Tennent displayed a passion for Christian union that was characteristic, by the end of the revival decade, of many former
partisans of the revival and which, throughout all the
ecclesiastical controversies of the post-Awakening years,
silently controlled and directed all the divisions and alignments of American evangelicals.

At the time, Tennent's overtures for Presbyterian union
were ignored by the Old Side and bitterly assailed by
members of his own party. The New Side laity, it would
seem, were even less willing to forget, and to forgive, than
their clergy, for the argument of Tennent's *Irenicum*
assumes intense and widespread popular displeasure with
his second thoughts about the schism. It may well be that
Tennent unconsciously sought to be rebuked by his followers, as the *Irenicum* clearly disclosed Tennent's own
psychological reaction to the role that history, and popular
acclaim, had almost thrust upon him. In effect, Tennent
refused the crown, and did so because he wanted to make
Christ, and not himself, the center of Christian attention,
and his people members, not of a sect, but of the universal
church. Such a vision of the church eventually served to

bring the New Side into a reunited American Presbyterian church. In 1758, the Synods of New York and Philadelphia were restored to communion, and out of the merger arose a church, dominated by the New Side, that was not simply an organ of discipline but an instrument of evangelism. But Presbyterianism continued to be plagued by the two issues that Tennent, in his irenic rewriting of Awakening history, curiously chose to dismiss: the qualifications of a gospel minister and the propriety of communion with the unregenerate. And in these questions was embodied the most persistent of the revival's challenges to the ideal of Christian union: whether men could be of like mind and judgment when some worshipped a more reasonable God than others.

. . . Now we beseech you Brethren by the Name of our Lord Jesus Christ, that ye all speak the same Things, and that there be no Divisions among you (or Schisms as it is in the Original, Chismata) but that ye be perfectly joined together in the same Mind, and in the same Judgement, (I Cor. i. 10.)

By *Schisms,* the Apostle means new *Factions, Sects* and *Parties* within the *Church,* whereby it is *torn, Ferments* promoted in its *Bowels,* the Affections of the People uncharitably and unreasonably alienated from each other, not upon the Account of Differences in Essentials of *Doctrine, Worship,* or *Discipline,* but *circumstantial Matters;* while some gloried in this, and some in the other *Patron;* some *carnally* crying up *Paul,* and some *Apollos,* and some *Cephus,* to the *Disparagement* of each other, and the *Prejudice* of the Church's *Peace* and *Union;* so *Calvin, Beza, Pareus, Grotius,* and *Symachus.*

The Conduct of the Apostle *Paul* upon this critical Occasion, was truly amiable, and worthy of a Minister of JESUS

CHRIST, he refused their immoderate *Respect,* and spake DI-
MINUTIVELY of HIMSELF, with Design to stop the perilous
CAREER of the *People,* in making new *Parties, Sects,* and *Factions,* and setting *himself* at the *Head* of one of them, he would
by no Means accept of such a false *Honour,* to the Prejudice
of CHRIST's *Kingdom,* No! He abhorr'd it! He would rather be
condemned and despis'd by the *Corinthians,* than condemned
by GOD, and his own *Mind;* for being the Instrument of *uncharitable Schisms* and *Factions!*

He therefore nobly ventures his *Character* in the *Cause* of
GOD, the Cause of the Church's *Peace* and *Union,* and fearlessly exposes himself to all the *Fury* of their *Reflections,* for
his *Fidelity* to his Master: *Reflections* that were as unreasonable as they were well intended.

That blessed Man, endeavoured to stop the violent *Torrent*
of *Faction,* by addressing the *Corinthians* in this humble
Language.

But *is* CHRIST *divided? Was* Paul *crucified for you? Or were
ye baptiz'd in the Name of* Paul? I Cor. i. 13. How came these
Parties? There is but one CHRIST. Did I enlist any that I
baptiz'd, under my own *Banner?* Seeing the *Head* is but *one,*
whay should the *Body* be *divided?*

Now compare the aforesaid Scriptures with what the same
Apostle says *Phil.* iii. 15, 16, and you may easily perceive, that
he urges *Forebearance* in lesser Things, and only proposes
Essentials as Terms of Communion. . . .

Angry *Debates* and *Divisions* about Circumstantial Matters
in Religion, dishonour GOD, render the Church *Contemptible,*
make the several Members of it *terrible* to each other, instead
of being desirable and amiable, *engines* of mutual *Sorrow* and
Mischief, instead of *Comfort* and *Benefit;* and likewise Marr
the publick *Good,* which every generous Mind has a principal
regard to. . . .

Yea my Brethren such *Divisions* and *Contentions,* tend to

and wou'd certainly issue in, did not Almighty Power interpose, the utter Destruction of the visible *Kingdom* of *Christ,* upon the *Earth;* for as he himself who is the Wisdom of the Father, justly and excellently observes; *how can a House that is divided against itself stand.*

But by Peace and Union, on the Terms before observ'd, GOD is *glorify'd,* in our *obedience* to his *Precepts,* and *Conformity* to his *attributes, Religion* is *honoured,* by a real, a visible and amiable *Representation,* of its peaceful, kind and beneficent *Nature.*

The visible Church is *strengthened,* and made awful to its inveterate Enemies, its implacable opposers: Our own *Minds* are *delighted* with the most agreeable prospect and sweet sensations; and others Benefit is thereby promoted, for being at Peace with them they are the more ready to receive our Council and Reproofs!

But shou'd we join with those who we fear are Graceless?

I answer the Terms of Church *fellowship,* that God has fix'd was soundness in the Main *Doctrines* of *Religion,* and a *regular Life. . . .*

The Standard of our *King* and *Master* we must buckle to, and not follow our own fickle and often partial and byass'd *Fancies* and Humours. . . .

The aforesaid Terms that *Christ* has fix'd may be certainly known, and therefore they are *rational.* But some of the novel and superstitious *Terms,* which some good Men have invented, tho' with a pious design, are *irrational,* because they cannot be certainly known, unless it be suppos'd that Churches are infallible in their Determinations; a claim which the *Protestants,* (some Enthusiasts excepted) have not pretended to, at least in Words; but the Bible is a stranger to such Terms of Communion. I know not one Passage in it, that proves converting Grace, or the Churches Judgment of it, to be a Term of Christian *Communion* of divine Appointment. . . .

But must not we adhere to our former Testimony to Conversion?

I *Answer,* Yes, and we do so by declaring our assent to the Holy Scriptures, and by maintaining our excellent *Westminster Confession of Faith* and *Catechisms,* which open the Nature, and assert the Necessity of Conversion agreeable to the sacred Oracles.

And as to our fallible Opinion concerning the late religious Appearances, which is a distinct Thing from the Doctrine of Conversion in general; we may and ought to maintain it. But in a consistency with Peace, Love and Charity.

There is a vast difference between our holding our uncertain *Opinion* concerning the *reality* of this or that Instance of Conversion, and our imposing it upon others as a *Term* of *Communion,* either Ministerial or Christian. Such as are for imposing their private Opinion about Matters of Liberty, which they cannot certainly know, of which Kind particular Instances of a Work of Conversion in any (in our Times) undoubtedly are, as a Term of Church Fellowship, refusing to join with them in Communion, unless they be of their Sentiment; should either produce their Charter from the Holy-Scriptures, for such an extraordinary claim of Power, for such an unprecedented kind of Proceeding, or at least be silent, if they are not free to do what perhaps they urge upon others, viz. to confess their *Error* in *Principle,* and *Indiscretion* in *Practice. . . .*

And seeing in a Case of such uncertainty, as Mens *Judgment* of gracious Experiences of others, good Men are apt to be of contrary Sentiments because of their different Degrees of *Knowledge,* different *Experiences* in some Things, different *Tryals, Byasses,* and natural *Tempers,* it has a direct Tendency to alienate their Affections from each other, and so disturb the Churches *Peace,* weaken her mutual *Love,* and break her social *Union,* and consequently tear the seemless Coat of CHRIST into an infinite Number of *Parts;* Yea and prevent a desirable *re-union,* after unhappy Breaches. . . .

If it be a commanded Duty to pray for the *Peace* of *Jerusalem,* to long for it, to pursue after it, with Vehemence, rejoice in its Approaches, and to bewail its Absence; it must needs be a great Iniquity to fly from it, as if it were a *Buck-bear,* to reject the Offers of it upon reasonable Terms, to be *grieved* for and *frightned* at its approaches, as if it were an Enemy, and pleased with its Distance: This shews a distorted Judgment and distemper'd Heart: This *Religion,* or rather misguided and ill-temper'd *Zeal,* and severe narrowness of Soul, is directly contrary to right Reason and to the Christian Revelation; Contrary to all social Offices, and every valuable Interest of Society. Alas its pitty that any who are sincere in Heart, should have such contracted, gloomy, and irregular Views of Things! May it please the GOD of *Mercy, Love* and *Peace,* to instruct, enlighten and reclaim them, and soften their well meant Rigours, and untamn'd Fierceness into *Gentleness* and *Love! . . .*

If it be said, that there is no necessity of this *Peace* and *Union,* we are well enough as we are.

I answer, that there is always a *Necessity* of *Obedience* to GOD's commanding *Authority. . . .*

But perhaps some may object, to this Purpose, that to join with a Company of dead Men, is the ready way to make us deader than we are.

Answer, It is cruel and censorious Judging, to condemn the States of those we know not; and to condemn positively and openly the spiritual *States* of such as are sound in *fundamental Doctrines,* and *regular in Life.* The Way to obtain quickning Grace, is the Path of *Duty,* and not the sacandalous Practice of that God-provoking and Church-rendring *Iniquity* RASH-JUDGING, this may quicken indeed, but not to any Thing that is good; but to *Back-biting, Slandering, Wrath, Malignity,* and all Manner of Mischief! O! that a gracious GOD would open the Eyes of the Children of Men, to see the inexpressible Baseness and Hoorors of this detestable IMPIETY, that is pregnant with inumerable *Evils!*

Again, if may be objected, that we are enjoined in divers Places of Scripture, to beware of *Wolves* in Sheep's cloathing, of *Dogs,* of *Foxes,* &c.

I answer, these *Places,* and others of like tendency, if they are strictly examined, together with the Context, where they are they will be found to respect in my OPINION, primarily, principally and directly *erroneous* and *heretical Teachers,* such may be known, and such should be with Care avoided; but to *separate* from such as are sound in essential and necessary Articles, of Faith, regular in Life, and edifying in their Ministry, meerly or only because they differ from us in some circumstantial Points which they do not impose, or are judg'd by us to be unregenerate, is uncharitable, unscriptural, and of dangerous Tendency! As this Practice wants a divine *Warrant,* so it puts the Peace and Union of the visible Church of CHRIST, upon a very uncertain and precarious *Bottom,* and opens a *Door* to inumerable mischevious and scandalous *Rents* and *Divisions!* And if it be sinful to make a Breach on such a Foundation, (which has been ever my Opinion, tho' now I confess, thro' GOD's Mercy, I have a more distinct and enlarged View of the Case than formerly,) it must needs be so to keep up the *Breach,* or refuse reasonable *Overtures* of *Peace,* upon such a Foundation.

If it be farther said, that the Church is now in a cold *declining State,* and that when there was more *Liveliness,* and more Good done, no Proposals of *Peace* or *Union* were made, nor was there any Prospect of it.

I answer, the *Church* is now in its ordinary *State,* in which Men being *calm,* can best examine and judge concerning the *Doctrines* of *Religion,* altho' not so many are alarmed out of their *Security,* as some Time since, yet thro' divine *Goodness,* some are awakened and to Appearance *converted;* and the body of CHRIST is edify'd, for which there is great Cause of Thankfulness. . . .

Some Years past, the *Church* in this *American Wilderness,* was in an extraordinary Situation, by Reason of a very uncommon *Effusion* of divine *Influence,* in the *Conviction,* and *Conversion* of *Sinners,* (to all Appearance) in much greater Numbers than what is usual, but the *Ignorance* of Some, and corrupt *Passions* of *others,* mixing therewith, cast a *Cloud* over the blessed *Work* of GOD, and were at least the Occasion of *Offence* and *Stumbling* to some (which if they had more PATIENTLY ENDURED *for a Time,* would probably have *prevented unhappy Consequences,*) These Things together with some difference of *Sentiment* about *lesser Matters* and warm *Disputes pro* and *con* respecting them, raised the *Ferment* so high, that it was to no *Purpose,* to make Proposals of *Peace,* speedily after the *Rupture,* till the *Minds* of the contending *Parties,* became more *calm,* and took more Time to reflect upon, and examine Matters with more Impartiality and Exactness. . . .

Give me leave to consider one *Objection* more, which is this, *viz.* That our Brethren of the present *Synod* of *Philadelphia,* have oppos'd the *whole* of the late *Work of God* in this Land, and ascribed it to the *Devil,* in support of which, these Things following are alledg'd, viz.

A Satyrical *Lampoon,* entitled, *the Wandering Spirit.* But seeing that Piece was Anonymous, (had no Name affix'd to it) and was never own'd by our Brethren, *as a Body,* it cannot, without manifest Injustice, be ascrib'd to them, as such. . . .

Again, the *Querists* are produc'd as another Proof, in Confirmation of the Charge; to which it may be reply'd, That notwithstanding some slighty representations of the late religious Commotions, interspers'd in some Passages of those Writings; yet I know not that they assign any of them, and much less all of them, to the *Devil:* Moreover it should be considered, that these Books were *Anonymous,* and never approv'd by the *Synod* of *Philadelphia,* by any authoritative judicial Act. . . .

In a Word, whatever unadvised Expressions, in private Conversation, might possibly drop from the Lips of some of our *Brethren* in a heat of *Passion,* or *ferment* of *Dispute,* (in disparagement of the Work of GOD) many Years agone, which Methinks it is now high Time to forget, yet upon Enquiry I cannot find any UNITED TESTIMONY of their BODY upon *Record* against the late REVIVAL of RELIGION (truly so called) not one by which they deny the *Reality* of it, and far less ascribe it to the *Devil.* . . .

Pray may not an Acknowledgement be as reasonably desir'd of us, for LICENCING and ORDAINING contrary to the Act of the Synod, as we can desire an Acknowledgement, upon the Account of the PROTEST? But can we make such an Acknowledgement? No! for whither [sic] we did right or wrong in Licencing &c. we did it in the integrity of our Hearts, as believing it to be our Duty; & if we wou'd exercise the same Charity towards our Brethren, as we desire towards ourselves, in this Case, wou'd not we believe that they protested against us with the like Integrity, from an Apprehension "that the *Church* was in no small Danger of expiring out right, and that quickly as to the Form, Order and Constitution of an Organiz'd Church. . . ."

Now in order to avoid uncharitable *Divisions,* and *Tumults;* it is necessary to beware of *Pride.* . . . Pride inclines us to obtrude with Violence our Opinion even in lesser Things upon others, and unjustly deny them the Liberty we desire for ourselves. . . .

Nor is it less necessary, to beware of *narrowness* of *Soul;* which not only the *Warmth* of some Men's *Tempers,* disposes them to, as well as their *conversing* with *such only* who are of their *turn* of *Mind,* and *small Stature* in respect of *Knowledge;* but especially their Unacquaintedness with the *History* of the *Church* of CHRIST in past Ages, as well as with its present

State throughout the World. If religious People did but know the great *Mischief* that Divisions have done in former Times, to the Church of CHRIST, they would not pretend to *reform* her, by that which has almost proved her *Ruin:* Or uncharitably confine the *Church* of CHRIST within the narrow *Compass* of a *Nut-shell,* I mean a few *Societies* of their own superfine *Cast* or *Party;* and so rob the *Redeemer,* of his visible *Kingdom* on Earth almost altogether. . . .

It is also necessary, Sirs, to beware of enslaving ourselves, to any *Party* of Men, by confining all our Respect to them, to the Neglect of others; and making them *Masters* of our *Consciences,* because of their *Piety;* so as to take for granted what they say, by an *implicit Faith,* without examining it; or so as to be slavishly *afraid* to contradict them: No! my Brethren, we must not judge of *Doctrines* by the Persons that hold them. . . .

Nevertheless the *Judgment* of the *aged* and experienced, in whom the fierce *Fires* of *Youth* are abated, (which some call *Zeal,* but falsely) not only by the Influence of *Years,* but by farther Acquaintance with themselves, (in a great *Variety* of *Vicissitudes,* and *tossings* upon this turbulent *Ocean*) as well as with the rest of Mankind, and by more deep and calm *Searches,* into the *Meaning* of the *Scriptures,* and *History* of *past Ages:* I say the *Judgment* of such, is more to be valu'd, and especially in Matters that concern the Peace of the *Church* of GOD, than the indigested *Notions* of *rash-headed,* fiery and unexperienced *Youth:* Yet the Judgment of none should be taken without Tryal, as the great Apostle *Paul* humbly acknowledges concerning himself, that when he was a *Child,* he *spake as a Child;* so had others his *Humility* they would acknowledge the same Thing; . . . when the Apostle grew to the Stature of a *Man,* he was not ashamed to *put away Childish Things;* nor should others, to follow his Example, how much soever they may suffer for it, by such, who would seem to have it understood, that they are infallible, and that Wisdom must die with them.

34 · Samuel Davies

(1723–1751)

THE STATE OF RELIGION

IN VIRGINIA

In the older areas post-Awakening Presbyterianism was occupied largely with the problems of schism and reunion, and, to a degree, of defections to the Baptist church. But in the South, the Presbyterian church was a continuing beneficiary of the revival impulse, especially in Virginia, where the Awakening, late to begin, lasted well through the decade of the 1740's, and even beyond. In Virginia, the evangelical impulse quickly took the form of a struggle for religious freedom—against an overtly Arminian Episcopal Establishment. The leading instrument of the southern revival, and the spokesman for Virginian dissent, was Samuel Davies, the most notable of the American-born generation of Presbyterians. Davies began his studies

---

Samuel Davies, *The State of Religion among the Protestant Dissenters in Virginia; in a Letter to the Rev. Mr. Joseph Bellamy* . . . (Boston, 1751), pp. 4–15, 18–19, 28–29, 38, 41–43.

under Abel Morgan, the guiding intellectual spirit of the Middle Colony Baptists, and finished his education at Samuel Blair's academy. In 1747 Davies was ordained as an evangelist to Virginia, where the valleys were filling up with a large number of Scots-Irish from Pennsylvania. Soon afterward he entered into public debate with the Anglican critics of the revival, and then into the battle to secure Presbyterians their rights under the Act of Toleration. Davies did not achieve the latter goal until after the French and Indian War, in which he and his people did the state no little service. Davies' reputation as a poet, hymn writer, and classical scholar earned him the presidency of the College of New Jersey (Princeton) in 1758 as Edwards' successor. But he was probably best known as a "rousing preacher," not of the evangelical gospel merely, but of patriotic sermons that were admired and imitated by the proponents of the Revolution.

I hope I may observe without the Umbrage of Calumny, what glares with irresistable Evidence on the Eyes of the Serious of all Denominations among us, that Religion has been, and in most Parts of the Colony still is, in a very low State. A surprizing Negligence appears in attending on publick Worship; and an equally surprizing Levity & Unconcernedness in those that attend. Family-Religion is a Rarity, and a solemn Solicitude about eternal Things is still a greater. Vices of various Kinds are triumphant, and even a Form of Godliness is not common. The Clergy universally, as far as my Intelligence extends, have embraced the modish System of *Arminian* Divinity, (tho' I allow my self the Pleasure to hope there are sundry consciencious Persons among them) and the *Calvin-istic,* or rather PAULINE Articles of their own Church are counted horrendous and insufferable.—But I suppose universal Fame has superseded my Information; and therfore I willingly exempt my self from the disagreable Talk. . . .

I have Reason to hope Sir, there are and have been a *few Names* in various Parts of the Colony, who are sincerely seeking the Lord, and groping after Religion, in the Communion of the Church of *England;* which I charitably presume from my finding there were a few of this happy Character in & about *Hanover* before the late Revival of Religion. Such were awakened, as they have told me, either by their own serious Reflections, suggested and enforced by divine Energy; or on reading some Authors of the last Century, particularly Bolton,[1] Baxter, Flavel,[2] Bunyan, &c. Some of them were wont to attend on publick Worship in the established Church without much murmuring at the Entertainments there; tho' they were sensible these were vastly inferior to what past Ages were favoured with, and often wondered if there were such Doctrines taught any where in the World at present, as they found in the Writings of these good Men. Others of them, tho' they had no Objections against the Ceremonies of the Church of *England,* except a few who were shocked at the impracticable Obligations imposed upon the Sponsors in Baptism, were utterly dissatisfied with the usual Doctrines taught from the Pulpit. Tho' these were generally true, and would have been useful, in their Connection with the Scheme of evangelical Doctrines; yet so many necessary Truths were neglected, as

---

[1] Robert Bolton (1572–1631), author of *Some Generall Directions for a comfortable Walking with God* (1625), a Puritan "guide to godliness" that went through five editions in its first three years and became a classic of "practice." [Ed.]

[2] John Flavel (*ca.* 1627–1691), English Presbyterian, whose most famous work, *Husbandry Spiritualized* (1698), was continually in print in America well into the nineteenth century. [Ed.]

rendered those that were inculcated of very little Service. The whole System of what is distinguished by the Name of *experimental Religion,* was past over in Silence. The *Depravity of humane Nature,* the *Necessity of Regeneration, and it's Prerequisites, Nature and Effects, the various Exercises of pious Souls according to their several Cases,* &c. these were omitted; and without these, you know Sir, the finest Declamations on moral Duties or speculative Truths, will be but wretched Entertainment to hungry souls. Such a maim'd System is not the compleat Religion of JESUS, that glories in the amiable *Symmetry,* mutual *Dependency* and *Subserviency* of all its Doctrines, as its peculiar Characteristic. Had the *whole Counsel of God* been declared, had all the Doctrines of the Gospel been solemnly and faithfully preached in the established Church; I am perswaded there would have been but few Dissenters in these Parts of *Virginia;* for, as I observed, their first Objections were not against the peculiar *Rites* & *Ceremonies* of that Church, much less against her excellent *Articles;* but against the general Strain of the *Doctrines* delivered from the Pulpit, in which these Articles were opposed, or (which was the more common Case) *not mentioned at all:* so that at first they were not properly *Dissenters from* the original Constitution of the Church of *England,* but the most strict *Adherents to* it, and only dissented from those that had forsaken it, tho' they still usurped the Denomination. But tho' such Impartiality in preaching the Gospel might have prevented the Advancement of the Interest of the Dissenters *as* a Party, it would have tended to promote the infinitely more valuable Interests of the blessed Redeemer: and had this been the Case, our Zeal and Industry to convert them to *Presbyterianism,* would have been almost superfluous, and quite disproportioned.——And here Sir, it may be proper to observe, That when in this Narrative I speak of the Increase of Dissenters in these Parts with an Air of Satisfaction, I do not boast of them as meer *Captures* from the Church of *England,* but as hopefully sincere *Prose-*

lytes to living Religion, or at least as lying open to Conviction, and in the Way of more profitable Means. I cannot indeed but conscienciously dissent from some of the Peculiarities of that Church; and it tends a little to heighten our Satisfaction, when such as agree with us in *Essentials,* and appear truly pious, do also agree with us in *Circumstantials;* for as Agreement is the Foundation and Measure of social Love, *this* must be co-extended with *that:* Yet as I am fully perswaded *the Kingdom of God is not Meat & Drink, but Righteousness and Peace and Joy in the Holy Ghost;* and that Persons of superior Piety and Judgement have used there Rites and Ceremonies with Approbation; I think the Alteration of Men's Principles and Practice with Respect to these Things *only,* without being born again of God, is a wretched Conversion; and it would inspire me with much greater Joy to see a *pious Church-man,* than a *graceless Presbyterian.* . . . The chief Reason Sir, why I call upon you to congratulate the Increase of the Dissenters here, and rejoyce in it my self, is, because I have Ground to hope that the Number of the Heirs of Heaven is augmented in some *Proportion,* tho' alas! not to an Equality; and to triumph on inferior Accounts, would argue the narrow Genius of a *Bigot.*——But to return.

The Few that profess'd a Dissatisfaction with the general Strain of Preaching in Church, and therefore either absented themselves, or attended with Murmuring and Reluctance, were generally counted whimsical Creatures, and hypocritical Affectors of Singularity: and indeed they could not but own their Sentiments singular; for they knew of none in the present Age of the same Mind with them; and therefore had no Prospect of obtaining a Minister to preach to them those Doctrines they thirsted for. Their Notions, as far as I can learn, were found in the main; tho' intermix'd with some corrupt Notions verging towards *Antinomianism,* the opposite Extreme to that they had left. And tho' this rendered them more

odious to their Adversaries, and furnished them with Occasions more plausibly to expose them; yet, considering their
Circumstances as being destitute of a judicious Minister to
instruct them in the Doctrines of the Gospel, and caution
them against Mistakes; and as labouring under the Prejudices
of Education and transported with the Sallies of their first
Zeal, which is generally imprudent and wild; I am more surprized at their Soundness and Regularity in most Things, than
at their Mistakes and Extravagancies in a few.

In this Case about ten or twelve Persons who are now
Members of my Congregation, had been for some Time before the Revival of Religion which began in the Year 1743.
One Mr. *Samuel Morris* (for I am not ashamed publickly to
mention his Name, notwithstanding the Calumnies flung upon
it by many) a Person of a forward, sociable Spirit, who had
for some Time been extremely anxious about his eternal State,
& unweariedly seeking Relief by all Means within his Reach,
at length obtain'd a Discovery of that glorious Method of
Salvation thro' Jesus Christ, to which Sinners *from all the
Ends of the Earth look, and are saved,* and where they universally agree to fix all their Hopes, notwithstanding the great
Diversity of their Circumstances as to Situation, Education,
outward Instruction, &c. The distinct Relation he has given
me of his Exercises at that Time and since, and the prevailing
Piety of his common Behaviour, leave me no Room to be
anxious about the Sincerity of his Religion; tho', as it is common in such Cases, his former pious Zeal to do Good, with a
few very pardonable Imprudences that attended it, have
fix'd an indelible *Odium* on his Character among many who
opposed the religious Concern he attempted to promote. After
this Discovery of the Gospel, his Soul was anxious for the
Salvation of his Neighbours, and inflamed with Zeal to use
Means to awaken them. This was the Tendency of his Conversation; and he also read to them such Authors as had been

most useful to him, particularly *Luther's Comment upon the Galatians,* which first opened to him the Way of Justification thro' Christ alone, and his *Table-Discourses;* sundry Pieces of honest *Bunyan's* &c. By those Means a few of his Neighbours were made more tho'tful about Religion than usual, and doubtful they had lived 'till then in a careless Ignorance of it; but the Concern was not very extensive.

I have prevailed, Sir, on my good Friend before mentioned, who was the principal private Instrument of promoting the late Work, and therefore well acquainted with it, to write me a Narrative of its Rise & Progress from this Period 'till my Settlement here: and this, together with the Substance of what he and others have told me, I shall present to you without any material Alterations, and personate him, tho' I shall not exactly use his Words.

"The Reverend Mr. *Whitefield* had been in *Virginia,* I think, in the Year 1740, and at the Invitation of the Rev. Mr. *Blair,*[3] our late Commissary, had preached in *Williamsburg,* our Metropolis, about 60 miles from *Hanover.* His Fame was much spread abroad, as a very warm and alarming Preacher; which made such of us in *Hanover* as had been awakened, very eager to see & hear him; but as he left the Colony before we heard of him, we had no Opportunity. But in the Year —43, a young Gentleman arrived from Scotland with a Book of his Sermons preached in *Glasgow,* & taken from his Mouth in short Hand, which with Difficulty I procured. After I had read it with great Liking & Benefit, I invited my Neighbours to come & hear it; and the Plainness, Popularity, & Fervency of the Discourses, being peculiarly fitted to affect our unimproved Minds, and the Lord rendring the Word efficacious, many were convinced of their undone Condition, and constrained to

---

[3] James Blair (1656–1743), probably the only prominent Anglican to welcome Whitefield to the colonies in 1739–1740 and to encourage his preaching. [Ed.]

seek deliverance with the greatest Solicitude. A considerable Number convened every Sabbath to hear these Sermons, instead of going to Church, and frequently on Week Days. The Concern of some was so passionate and violent, that they could not avoid crying out, weeping bitterly, &c. and that when such Indications of religious Concern were so strange and ridiculous, that they could not be occasioned by Example or Sympathy, and the Affectation of them would have been so unprofitable an Instance of Hypocrisy, that none could be tempted to it. My Dwelling-House at length was too small to contain the People; whereupon we determined to build a Meeting-House, meerly for Reading; for we knew of no Minister in the World whom we could get to preach to us according to our Liking; and having never been accustomed to social *extempore* Prayer, none of us durst attempt it in Company. By this single Mean sundry were solemnly awakened, and their Conduct ever since is a living Attestation of the Continuance and happy Issue of their Impressions. When the Report of these Sermons and the Effects occasioned by reading them was spread Abroad, I was invited to several Places to read them, at a considerable Distance; and by this Means the Concern was propagated.

"About this Time, our absenting our selves from Church, contrary, as was alledged, to the Laws of the Land, was taken Notice of; and we were called upon by the Court to assign our Reasons for it, and to declare what Denomination we were of. As we knew but little of any Denomination of Dissenters, except *Quakers,* we were at a Loss what Name to assume. At length recollecting that *Luther* was a noted Reformer, and that his Doctrines were agreable to our Sentiments, and had been of special Service to us, we declared our selves *Lutherans;* and thus we continued till Providence afforded us an unexpected Opportunity of hearing the Rev. Mr. *William Robinson.*" Here Sir, it may be proper for me to lay aside the Person of my Informer for a while, and interrupt the Connection of his Relation, to give you some Account of the Travels & Successes of that zealous, faithful and laborious Minister of Christ, the late Mr. *Robinson,* whose dear Memory will mingle with my softest & most grateful Thot's, as long as I am capable of Reflection. He was in the Ministry about six Years, and never took the Charge of a Congregation 'till a few Months before his happy and triumphant *Exit.* The necessitous Circumstances of many Vacancies, and the Prospect of more extensive Usefulness engaged him to expose his shattered Constitution, to all the Hardships & Fatigues of almost uninterrupted Itinerations; and it has been my Lot to trace his Travels in sundry Parts of *Pennsylvania, Maryland,* and *Virginia;* and I cannot recollect one Place in which he had officiated for any Time, where there were not some illustrious Effects of his Ministry. He had a noble disinterested Ambition *to preach the Gospel, where Christ was not named;* and therefore, by the Permission of the Presbytery, he took a Journey thro' the new Settlements in *Pennsylvania, Virginia,* and *North-Carolina,* in which he continued about two Years, oppress'd with the usual Difficulties a weakly Constitution finds in travelling a Wilderness, and animated only by his glorious Successes. . . .

I shall now re-assume the Person of my Informer and proceed in his Narrative——"On the 6th of July—43, Mr. *Robinson* preached his first Sermon to us from *Luk.* 13.3. and continued with us preaching four Days successively. The Congregation was large the first Day; and as the Report of him spread, it vastly encreas'd on the three ensuing. 'Tis hard for the liveliest Imagination to form an Image of the Condition of the Assembly on these glorious Days of the Son of Man. Such of us as had been hungring for the Word before, were lost in an agreable Confusion of various Passions, surprized, astonished, pleased, enraptured! so that we were hardly capable of Self-Government, and some could not refrain from publickly declaring their Transport: we were overwhelmed with the Tho'ts of the unexpected Goodness of God, in allowing us to hear the Gospel preached in a Manner that surpassed even our former Wishes, and much more our Hopes. Many that came thro' Curiosity were *pricked to the Heart;* and but few in the numerous Assemblies on these four Days appeared unaffected. They returned astonished, alarmed with Apprehensions of their dangerous Condition, convinced of their former entire ignorance of Religion, and anxiously enquiring, what they should do to be saved; and there is Reason to believe there was as much Good done by these four Sermons, as by all the Sermons preached in these Parts before or since.

"Before Mr. *Robinson* left us, he successfully endeavoured to correct some of our *Antinomian* Mistakes, and to bring us to carry on the Worship of God more regularly at our Meetings. He advised us to meet to read good Sermons, and to begin & conclude with Prayer and singing of Psalms, which 'till then we had omitted. When we met next, we complied with his Directions; and when all the rest refused, I read and prayed with Trembling and Diffidence; which Method was observed in sundry Places 'till we were furnished with a Minister. The Blessing of God remarkably attended these more private Means; and it was really astonishing to observe the solemn Impressions begun or continued in many, by hearing good Discourses read. I had repeated invitations to come to many Places round, some of them 30 or 40 Miles distant, to read; with which I generally comply'd. Considerable Numbers were won't to attend, with eager Attention and awful Solemnity; and sundry were, in a Judgment of Charity, Thoro'ly turned to God, and thereupon erected Meeting-Houses, and chose Readers among themselves, by which the Work was more extensively carried on.

"Soon after our Father, Mr. *Robinson,* left us, the Rev. Mr.

John Blair paid us a short visit; and truly he came to us *in the Fulness of the Gospel of Christ.* Former Impressions were ripened, and new formed on many Hearts. One Night in particular a whole House-full of People was quite over-come with the Power of the Word, particularly of one pungent Sentence that dropt from his Lips; and they could hardly sit or stand, or keep their Passions under any proper Restraints, so general was the Concern during his Stay with us; and so ignorant were we of the Danger Persons in such a Case were in of Apostacy, which unhappy Observation has since taught us, that we pleased our selves with the Expectation of the *gathering* of more *People* to the divine *Shiloh* than now seem to have been actually gathered to him; tho' there be still the greatest Reason to hope that sundry bound themselves to the Lord in an everlasting Covenant, never to be forgotten.

"Some Time after this, the Rev. Mr. *John Roan,* was sent by the Presbytery of *New-Castle,* (under whose immediate Care we had voluntarily placed ourselves to supply us.) He continued with us longer than either of the former; and the happy Effects of his Ministrations are still apparent in many Instances. He preached at sundry Places at the earnest Solicitations of the People, which was the happy Occasion of beginning and promoting the religious Concern, where there were little Appearances of it before. This, together with his speaking pretty freely about the Degeneracy of the Clergy in this Colony, gave a general Alarm, and some Measures were concerted to suppress us. To incense the Indignation of the Government the more, a persidious Wretch deposed, he heard Mr. *Roan* use some blasphemous Expressions in his Sermon, and speak in the most shocking & reproachful Manner of the established Church. An Indictment was thereupon drawn up against Mr. *Roan,* (tho' by that Time he had departed the Colony) and some of the People who had invited him to preach at their Houses, were cited to appear before the

General Court, (which in this Government consists of the Governour or Commander in Chief, and His Majesty's Council) and two of them were fined *twenty Shillings* Sterling, besides the Costs, which in one of the Cases would have amounted to near *fifty Pounds,* had the Evidences demanded their Due. While my Cause was upon Trial, I had Reason to rejoyce that the Throne of Grace is accessible in *all Places,* and that helpless Creatures can waft up their Desires *unseen,* to God, in the midst of a Crowd. Six Evidences were cited to prove the Indictment against Mr. Roan; but their Depositions were in his Favour; and as for the Evidence mentioned just now, who accused him of Blasphemy against God and the Church, when he heard of Messirs. *G. Tennent*'s and *S. Finley*'s Arrival he fled, and has not returned since; so that the Indictment was drop'd. I had Reason to fear being banished the Colony, and all Circumstances seem'd to threaten the Extirpation of Religion among the Dissenters in these Parts.

". . . [Our] present Pastor, was sent by the Presbytery to supply us about six Week, in Spring, *Anno* 1747, when our Discouragements from the Government were renewed and multiplied: For on one Sunday the Governour's Proclamation was set up at our Meeting-House, *strictly requiring all Magistrates to suppress & prohibit, as far as they lawfully could, all itinerant Preachers,* &c." which occasion'd us to forbear Reading that Day, 'till we had Time to deliberate and consult what was expedient to do; but how joyfully were we surprized before the next Sabbath, when we unexpectedly heard that Mr. *Davies* was come to preach so long among us; and especially, that he had qualified himself according to Law, and obtained the Licensure of four Meeting-Houses among us, which had never been done before! Thus when our Hopes were expiring, and our Liberties more precarious than ever, we were suddenly advanced to a more secure Situation. *"Man's Extremity is the Lord's Opportunity."* For this seasonable

Instance of the Interprosition of divine Providence, we desire to offer our grateful Praises; and we importune the Friends of *Zion* generously to concur in the delightful Employ."

Thus, Sir, I have given you a brief Account of the Rise and Progress of Religion here 'till my first coming into the Colony; and the Facts themselves I know to be well attested, tho' the Order in which I have related them, is in some Instances preposterous.——I shall now proceed in my Narrative from my own Knowledge, and inform you of the State of Affairs since *April* 1747.

The Dissenters here were under peculiar Disadvantages for want of a settled Minister. By this they were not only deprived of the stated Ministrations of the Gospel, but also exposed to great Difficulties from the Government, which could not be wholly removed while they continued vacant; for it was alledged, (this is no proper Place to enquire with how much Law or Reason) that 'till they were an organized Congregation, and had a Minister qualified, and their Meeting-Houses licens'd, according to Law, they could not claim the Liberties and Immunities of the Act of Toleration. Besides, the Itinerations of my Brethren, tho' occasioned by Necessity, were misconstructed, as turning all Things upside down, as a meer Artifice to wheedle People out of their Money, and as an Evidence there were such prodigious Swarms of us to the Northward, that we were obliged to make Excursions into distant Parts: When indeed the chief Reason was the small Number of our Ministers & Candidates, which was vastly disproportioned to the Vacancies in *Pennsylvania,* and much more to those in *Maryland* and *Virginia,* (not to mention the Discouragements that would be naturally suggested to young Ministers, at the Thoughts of removing to a strange Colony, separated from their Brethren, exposed to peculiar Fatigues, and the Embarrassments of so limitted and precarious a Toleration as they then had Reason to expect.)

On these Accounts the Synod, and particularly the Presbytery of *New-Castle,* were very solicitous to settle a Minister among them as soon as possible. I was therefore sent by said Presbytery into *Hanover* at the Time mentioned above, both to officiate for some Time, and to see if my Way should be cleared to settle there. Upon my Arrival, I petitioned the General Court to grant me a License to officiate in and about *Hanover,* at four Meeting-Houses; which after some Delay, was granted, upon my qualifying according to the Act of Toleration. . . .

I forgot to inform you, Sir, in its proper Place, that the Rev. Mr. *Davenport* was sent by the Synod to *Hanover* last Summer, & continued here about 2 Months. There appeared some Evidences then, and I have discovered more since, that he did not labour in vain. Some were brought under solemn Impressions, which seem to have a happy Issue; and many of the Lord's People were much revived, and can never forget the Instrument of it.

Thus, dear Sir, I have given you a brief Narrative of the Rise and Progress of Religion among us; and I doubt not but you will readily acquiesce in the Conclusion after which sufficient Scrutiny I have drawn, *That this is the Lord's Doing.* I claim no *Infallibility;* but I must not under the modest Pretence of renouncing it, scruple a Matter attested with all possible Evidences, and so rush into *Skepticism.* If I could form no Judgment of so public a Work, I should renounce my Function this Moment; for with what Face can I pretend to promote a divine Work in the Conversion of Men, if I cannot have any satisfying Knowledge of it, when it appears? I act in the Dark, and promote I know not what. Indeed the Evidence of its Divinity here is so irresistible, that it has extorted an Acknowledgement from some, from whom it could hardly be expected. The Rev. Mr. *John Thomson,* who, tho' a Man of Judgment, and, I hope, Piety, unhappily opposed the late

Revival in *Pennsylvania* with the most industrious Zeal, has repeatedly declar'd, "That whatever our Ministers had done elsewhere, they have undoubtedly done MUCH GOOD in *Hanover;* and that he heartily rejoyced in it." Were your Soul, Sir, contracted with the narrow Spirit of a Bigot, you would no doubt indulge an ignoble Joy at the Tho't, that there are now some *Hundreds* of Dissenters in a Place where a few Years ago there were not *ten* that I know of within a hundred Miles;[4] but I assure my self of your Congratulations on a nobler Account, because a considerable Number of perishing Sinners are gained to the blessed Redeemer, with whom, tho' you never see them in these Regions of Mortality, you may spend a blissful Eternity in the divinest Intimacy, and mutually assist each other in ascribing immortal Praises to *the Lamb that was slain, and has redeemed* his People *by his Blood, out of every Kindred, and Tongue, and People, and Nation.*—After all, poor *Virginia* demands your Compassion; for Religion at present is but like the little Cloud which *Elijah's* Servant saw; and sometimes I am afraid of its unseasonable Dissipation. Oh! that it may spread, and cover the Land, and *drop down Fatness upon it!* and may the Lord keep us from *despising the Day of small Things!*

'Tis likely, Sir, you may desire some Account of the State of Religion in other Counties where Dissenters are settled; and therefore, as I have undertaken this History, and as I know not any other Way in which you may receive as full Information, I shall endeavour to gratify you. . . .

There was a great Stir about Religion in a Place called

---

[4] There are and have been in this Colony a great Number of Scotch Merchants, who were educated Presbyterians; but (I speak but what their Conduct more loudly proclaims) they generally upon their Arrival here, prove Scandals to their Religion and Country by their loose Principles and immoral Practices, and either fall into an Indifferency about Religion in general, affect to be polite by turning Deists, or fashionable by conforming to the Church.

Buckingham, on the Sea-shore, about four Years ago, when I was there; but it was not then come to Maturity. It has spread since, and issued in a hopeful Conversion in sundry Instances; and I am informed they are now sufficient to constitute a Congregation, and are waiting for a Minister.

But the most glorious Display of divine Grace in *Maryland* has been in and about *Somerset* County, which lies at some Distance from *Cheasapeak* Bay on the Eastern Shore. It began, I think, in the Year 1745, by the Ministry of Mr. *Robinson;* and was afterwards carried on by sundry Ministers that preach'd transiently there. I was there about two Months, when the Work was at its Height; and I never saw such a deep and spreading Concern among People in my Life as then appeared among them: The Assemblies were numerous, tho' it was in the Extremity of a cold Winter, and unwearied in attending the Word; and frequently there were very few among them that did not give some plain Indications of Distress or Joy. Oh! these were the happiest Days that ever my Eyes saw, or are, as I fear, like to see. Since that, the Harvest seems over there; tho' considerable Gleanings, I hear, are still gathered; and many of the late Converts give the utmost Reason to presume their final Perserverance. . . .

APPENDIX.

I at first intended, Sir, to have said Nothing of a particular Restraint impos'd upon us at present by the civil Government; lest I should seem fond of raising the Cry of *Persecution,* which is very indecent in the Followers of the uncomplaining Lamb of God, especially when there is in Truth so little Occasion for it; or to fling injurious Reflections on His Majesty's Council for this Colony, for whom I have the profoundest Veneration on Account both of their honourable Character and their Accomplishments for it; and under whose indulgent Administration we enjoy so many civil and sacred Liberties.

But as I know not, Sir, but this Narrative may come into the Hands of some who may have some Influence to secure our Priviledges, or procure their Enlargement, Disadvantage to us in *Hanover*, because we might easily apply to the Commander in Chief, or the General Court; and therefore 'tis of small Importance with me how it be determined; tho' it would occasion a considerable Difficulty to those that live 2 or 300 Miles distant from *Williamsburg*.

But the restraining a dissenting Minister to but *one* Meeting-House would be a prodigious Grievance to the People in their present Circumstances.—This, Sir, is not a proper Place to debate the Legality of it, nor does it belong to my Province to determine it; yet I may inoffensively suggest the following Remarks upon it, as Matters of Speculation to the Curious, and of Determination to those in Authority. . . .

The Act of Toleration (which has been received by our Legislature) does not determine the Number of Meeting-Houses, but only gives a general Toleration to legally qualified Ministers to officiate in Places legally licensed: And may it not be reasonably presumed from hence, That the *Number* is left to be determined according to the peculiar Circumstances of particular Congregations?

35 · "The Safety of the Church of England"

In the South the Awakening ended the near-monopoly of the Episcopal Church, but in New England, and to a degree in the areas of Philadelphia and New York, the revival made Anglicanism more appealing by contrast. The revival years were marked by several dramatic secessions (in some instances, of both ministers and people) to the church that seemed a haven of reason and order. The Anglicans of New England were particularly prompt to take advantage of the situation, both by proselytizing and by asking the hierarchy in England for assistance in setting up new churches in the colonies. Their appeals, as well as many tributes from lay groups attracted to Episcopalianism, were addressed to the corresponding secretary of The Society for the Propagation of the Gospel in Foreign Parts. This organization, which had been chartered as an instrument of bringing Christianity to the Indians, had over the years assumed responsibility for the general direction of the Episcopal Church in New England, where Congregationalism was historically and legally the established religion. Even before the Awakening the Society had installed "missionaries" in several New England com-

Francis L. Hawks and William S. Perry (eds.), *Documentary History of the Protestant Episcopal Church . . . Connecticut* (2 vols.; New York, 1863–1864), I, 178–179, 190–191, 210–211.

munities to serve the English population. Such activity intensified during and after the revival, in response to what the reports of New England Episcopal spokesmen called the "anarchy" of the New World. To deal with the threat, as well as to seize the golden opportunity for expansion offered by the revival, Connecticut Anglicans privately suggested that an American bishop be appointed. When subsequently such a proposal was made public, there began the controversy that would eventually help to unite rationalist and evangelical Americans in resistance to British tyranny. The more immediate response, however, was among the Old Lights of Connecticut and the Liberals of Boston, who had their special reasons to resent the fact that the revival had made Episcopalianism the "fashionable" religion of the "respectable" and socially conservative.

N. Groton, March 30th, 1742.

Reverend Sir,

There never was more pressing need of good books among us than in this astonishing season, in which the wildest enthusiasm and superstition prevail; and it is attended with the most bitter fruits of uncharitableness and spiritual pride, an instance or two of which I shall trouble the honourable Society with. Some time since, immediately after I had preached a sermon in Norwich, one of these enthusiasts came to me and demanded my experience; (which is very common;) his request being denied, he pronounced me unconverted, and, not only going myself, but leading all under my charge, down to hell. Soon after, he was attended with a dumb spirit, and uttered nothing for five or six days, except two or three blasphemous expressions, viz., Go tell the brethren I am risen; at another time, Suffer little children to come unto me, &c. There also came another of these exhorters (as they are called here) to my house, attended by many; declared me as upright and as exemplary a person as any he knew in the world, yet he knew I was unconverted, and leading my people down to hell; he affirmed that he was sent with a message from God, and felt the Spirit upon him, &c.; he seemed sincere. Soon after, Mr. Croswell, the dissenting teacher in this parish, with two attendants, came singing to my house, pronounced me unconverted, yet, at the time, declared that he did not know me guilty of any crime. I assured him that, in my opinion, it was a greater crime for him thus to murder my soul, useful-ness and reputation in the world, than for me to attempt his natural life; and that he certainly must be a worse man, thus, in cool blood and under a religious pretence, to pronounce damnation against me, than for a common swearer to say to another "God damn you;" since this he is not so fierce as before.

At the first rise of this enchanting delusion, I was under melancholy apprehensions that the infant Church of England, in this and the adjacent places, would be crushed, those being the centre of the religious delirium; some have gone after it, but more been added, and I am more and more convinced of the promise of our blessed Lord, that the gates of hell shall never prevail, &c. My labours abundantly increase, and I have scarce been at home a week together the past winter; some-times I preach two or three sermons a week, beside constantly on the Lord's-day, and I have good hope that my labour is not in vain.

Your and the honourable Society's
Real friend and servant,
Eben'r Punderson.

Reading, in New-England,
April 20th, 1743.

Reverend Sir,

The enclosed is the state of my parish, which is very little altered in this last half year. My people are not at all shaken, but rather confirmed in their principles by the spirit of enthusiasm that rages among the Independents round about us, and many of the Dissenters, observing how steadfast our people are in their faith and practice, while those of their own denomination are easily carried away with every kind of doctrine, and are now sunk into the utmost confusion and disorder, have conceived a much better opinion of our Church than they formerly had, and a considerable number in this colony have lately conformed, and several Churches are now building where they have no minister. Indeed, there is scarce a town in which there is not a considerable number professing themselves of the Church of England, and very desirous to have it settled among them; but God only knows when and how they can be provided for. Were there in this country but one of the Episcopal order, to whom young men might apply for ordination without the expense and danger of a voyage to England, many of our towns might be supplied which now must remain destitute. To express this opinion to the venerable Society (I am sensible) may be deemed impertinent, but I am moved to it by hearing so frequently numbers of serious people of our Church lamenting their unhappiness, that they can rarely enjoy that worship which they hunger and thirst after, there being so small a number of Clergymen in this country; while Presbyterians, Independents, and all sects are here perfect in their kind. But, although we have not the utmost that we could wish for, yet I bless God for the pious care and charity of the venerable Society, to which it is owing that so many hundreds of souls are provided for in this government; and had it not been for that, we have reason to think there would not have been at this day as much as one congregation in this colony worshipping God according to the Church of England.

I have this day drawn upon the treasurer for my half year's salary.

> I am, Reverend Sir, yours,
> And the venerable Society's
> Obliged and obedient servant,
>
> JOHN BEACH.

Northbury, May 28th, 1744

The representation and humble petition of the members of the Church of England, in Northbury, in the township of Waterbury, in the colony of Connecticut, in New-England, and the members of said Church, dwelling in other places nearby adjoining, humbly sheweth:

We were all educated in this land, under the instruction of Independent teachers, or (as they would be called) Presbyterians; and consequently, we were prejudiced strongly against the Church of England from our cradles, until we had advantage of books from your Reverend missionaries and others, whereby we began to see with our own eyes that things were not as they had been represented to our view; and Mr. Whitfield, passing through this land, condemning all but his adherents, and his followers and imitators, by their insufferable enthusiastick whims and extemporaneous jargon, brought in such a flood of confusion amongst us, that we became sensible of the unscriptural method we had always been accustomed to take in our worship of God, and of the weakness of the pretended constitution of the Churches (so called) in this land; whereupon, we fled to the Church of England for safety, and are daily more and more satisfied we are safe, provided the purity of our hearts and lives be conformable to her excellent doctrine; and that it is the best constituted Church this day in the world.

HENRY COOK, BARNABY FORD, ISAAC CASTEL,
JOHN HOW, THOMAS CLASELEE

Though Jonathan Dickinson, for one, spent his last years fighting the Anglican counterreformation, other Calvinists were disposed, at least through 1750, to concentrate their energies on resisting the sectarian spirit bred by the Awakening. In New England this impulse was embodied in the Separates, who sought to gather, out of the established churches, "pure" communions composed of the converts of the revival. One of the early leaders of the Separates—their "Moses," he was later called—was Elisha Paine (1693–1775). Paine was a lawyer who in 1721 had been touched, along with his brother Solomon, by the brief religious revival in Windham County, Connecticut. With the Awakening of 1740–1741 Paine quit the courts and became an itinerant preacher. At first his relationship with the other ministers of the county was quite cordial. Two of them, Eleazar Wheelock and Benjamin Pomeroy, initially approved Paine's attempt to establish a school for the training of lay exhorters. Later they repudiated Paine, largely because of his extravagant, and to them heretical, theological notions. In 1745 the associated ministers of Windham published a documentary history of Paine's career as an admonition against his ideas and the

A Letter from the Associated Ministers of the County of Windham, To the People in the Several Societies in said County . . . (Boston, 1745), pp. 3–12, 14–15.

sect he led. Their letter, signed by New Lights as well as Old, also contained yet another commentary on the "excesses" of the Awakening. It represented an effort to recapture, by means of common opposition to the Separates, something of the lost unity of Connecticut Congregationalism.

Dear Brethren and Friends,

We are well satisfied there has been of late, in a few Years past, a very great and merciful Revival of Religion in most of the Towns and Societies in this County, as well as in many other Places in this Land; which we desire to acknowledge to the Praise of Divine Grace: So we are fully satisfied there have been many Things which have accompanied this Work, which have really been of a different Kind. When it pleased GOD to send down the HOLY SPIRIT to convince and convert Sinners, and the Prince of Darkness was no longer able to keep them in that fatal Security and Formality in which they had lain, he was then obliged to act a different Part to carry on the Designs of his Kingdom of Darkness, and oppose the Conquests and Triumphs of the Redeemer. And this he has done by imitating, as nearly as he could, the Work of the HOLY GHOST, both by setting on imaginary Frights and Terrors, in some Instances, on Men's Minds, somewhat resembling the Conviction of the Blessed Spirit, and awakenings of Conscience for Sin; and also filling their Minds with Flashes of Joy, and false Comforts, resembling somewhat, in a general Way, the Consolations of the HOLY GHOST. . . . As these Designs of the grand Adversary have opened more, and we have great Reason to fear that many Persons, in several of the Places we have the especial Charge of, have been suffered by GOD's righteous Judgment to be deceived, and have run into such Errors and Miscarriages, as evidently to become the Instruments of Satan to carry on some of these Designs and Occasions of stirring up others to such severe Treatment of them, as hardens them more and more in their Errors, and many are drawn away after them, partly out of pity to them, and by wrong Conclusions, that their Sufferings are an Evidence that they are right, and partly out of Opposition to others whom they think to be carnal and ungodly Men: We have in our respective Places, as GOD has enabled us, endeavoured to convince and recover them, and help them to discern the Snares of the Devil; but since private Endeavours have proved insufficient, we have lately united to give our publick Testimony against some Things, which we dare no longer forbear openly to testify against; and therein told you that we purposed by GOD's help more particularly to do it in a little Time: And the rather, as you well know there are diverse Persons in several of our Societies, who have of late separated themselves from the Congregations to which they did belong, and have vented diverse erroneous and dangerous Principles, calculated to overthrow the Institution of the Gospel Ministry; to render vain the Ordinances of CHRIST's Appointment; to the perverting of the holy Scriptures, and making some of the great and most important Doctrines of the holy Scriptures, appear in a ridiculous Light, and have followed several Persons who have set up for publick Teachers and Exhorters (as far as we can find on the same Principles) and draw away the People after them, to the Neglect and Contempt of the instituted Worship of GOD.

Some of the most considerable of those Errors are these that follow;

1. That it is the Will of GOD to have a pure Church on Earth, in this Sense, that all the Converted should be separated from the Unconverted.

2. That the Saints certainly know one another, and know who are CHRIST's true Ministers, by their own inward Feel-

ings, or a Communion between them in the inward Actings of their own Souls.

3. That no other Call is necessary to a Persons Undertaking to preach the Gospel, but his being a true Christian, and having an inward Motion of the Spirit, or a Perswasion in his own Mind that it is the Will of GOD he should preach and perform ministerial Acts: The Consequence of which is, that there is no standing instituted Ministry in the Christian Church which may be known by the visible Laws of CHRIST's Kingdom.

4. That GOD disowns the Ministry and Churches in this Land, and the Ordinances as administered in them.

5. That at such Meetings of Lay-preaching and Exhorting they have more of the Presence of GOD, than in His Ordinances, and under the Ministration of the present Ministry, and Administration of the Ordinances in these Churches. And hereupon many Persons have chosen to follow after such as have set up themselves to be Preachers, Exhorters and Expounders of the Doctrines of the Scriptures; several of which there have sprung up of late in this County, the most famous of which is Mr. *Elisha Paine,* of whose Mistakes and Errors in these Points, we have had diverse Informations, and some of us have taken Pains to recover him, and others who practice in like manner, though to no purpose: But as the People's Errors and wild Zeal encrease, so the Admiration of these Teachers encreases, so that they are often crying, *Never Man spake like these Men,* at least, crying them up above all their Teachers. Now as to our own Parts, we hope we could be content to have our Names sink and be despised, if CHRIST was but honoured, and the Souls of his People edified; but being sufficiently convinced of the contrary, and that our blessed Saviour, the LORD JESUS, is abused, and his Name reproached under a shew of great Zeal and Love to it, his Laws broken, his Word perverted and his Ordinances despised, under a pretence of advancing his Glory; the People in danger of being led into still more fatal Errors; and yet all to promote their

Salvation: We could not answer it to our divine Lord, nor to your Souls, any longer to forbear giving our most open Testimony against these Things.

Having therefore set down these Errors and corrupt Principles, which some of you have drank in, we shall endeavour, by the Help of God, plainly to show you the Falshood of them, their Danger and evil Tendency, and the Sinfulness of your Practice upon them, and to give a fair Answer to your Reasonings and Objections about them, so far as they are known to us: But since many Informations have been sent us of the Errors, which are taught by the Preachers and Exhorters now mentioned, we look upon ourselves obliged to let you see some of the Testimonies which have been sent to us, concerning the Performances of Mr. *Elisha Paine* (who is by most in this County) known to be of much superiour Abilities to the others: And we must leave you and all Christians to judge, what sort of Teachers you put yourselves under, when you contemn and forsake the Ministry which Christ has set up.

Mr. James Cogswell, *who now preaches in* Canterbury, *Testifieth in the Words following;*

There was a Lecture appointed here sometime ago, with an Expectation that Mr. *Davenport* would preach it, but he fail'd of coming and I preach'd the Lecture. Sometime after the Lecture was over Mr. *Elisha Paine* came to see me, and a considerable number of People were in the Room: He began his Discourse in this Manner, with a grave Countenance, I am come on purpose to discourse with you concerning your Sermon. I replied, Sir, you have Liberty to say any Thing that is reasonable cencerning it. He answer'd immediately, I must needs tell you, I had rather have been burnt at the Stake than to have heard such a Sermon, if I had not a Mind to get better Satisfaction concerning you. I replied, if the Sermon be so dreadful, doubtless you can make some reasonable Objections against it. He answer'd, the whole Discourse was no thing but

Trifling; it was spending Time to prove what both Sides allowed to be true, like a young Attorney at the Bar, trying to prove what is allowed on all hands to be true; which the Judges always condemn as Trifling: But, says he, there were two Points of false Doctrine in it; the first was, that I asserted, "We must have recourse only to the Word of GOD, to prove that CHRIST suffered and died for Sinners;" and said, The direct Tendency of such an Assertion was, to make Men believe there was no Necessity of the Influences of the Spirit of GOD in order to Conversion. The next Sentence which he condemn'd as false was this, that I asserted, "the Reason why the unpardonable Sin cannot be forgiven, is not, because there is not Power and Ability enough in CHRIST to forgive it; but GOD has determined in his Word it shall not be forgiven." I asked him wherein the Falsity of it lay? He said, in the first Place, it was making the Attributes of GOD clash together; and supposing GOD had Power to do what he has told us he cannot do. I told him, that what I meant by Power and Ability in CHRIST, was, that there was enough in the Merits of CHRIST to procure a Pardon for that Sin, as the next Sentence of my Discourse sufficiently manifested: And he said farther, the Reason why I believe there is a Sufficiency in the Blood of CHRIST to procure Pardon for this Sin is, because CHRIST is an infinite Person, and consequently there was an infinite Merit in what he did and suffered. He replied, Sin is an infinite Evil also. I answered, that Sin was in a Sense infinite, yet not absolutely infinite, for that would make every Sin of an equal Magnitude; but that the Value of CHRIST's Death and Sufferings was absolutely infinite, and therefore in its own Nature sufficient to procure a Pardon for all Sin, for the Sins of the World. After some farther Discourse, I asked him, Mr. *Paine*, do you not think there is sufficient Merit in the Blood of CHRIST to procure Pardon for the Sins of the whole World? He answer'd, GOD has made Provision sufficient for the Salvation of them that are saved, and no more; and to suppose otherwise would be to render GOD unjust. Then, said I, you do deny there is a Sufficiency in the Merit of CHRIST to procure Pardon for the Sins of the whole World? He said, No, he did not say so; But, said he, you talk just like the rest of the unconverted World. After some farther Discourse, he said, I will tell you how GOD convinced me of this; In the first Place he convinced me I was a Sinner; then he shewed me there was enough in CHRIST for Sinners; and then he discovered that CHRIST died for me: This, said he, was the general Truth which was discerned; but to know whether this Faith was true or no, we must look to the Fruits produced by it. I asked him, whether he thought that was saving Faith? He answered in the Affirmative. I told him, I thought it was not, and offered an Argument against it: He said my Fathers taught me so, and they could have taught me better Arguments than that. I told him I thought saving Faith was this, when a Soul was convinced of his lost undone Estate and Condition; had a Discovery of the Fulness and Sufficiency of CHRIST, and the Sincerity and Universality of the Call of the Gospel, and that he was invited to come to CHRIST; that saving Faith was a Receiving and Embracing CHRIST in all his Offices, and so resting on him for Salvation. He replied, that I talked like the Papists, or that this was Popish Doctrine; and that this was the very Dispute between the Papists and Protestants; that this Doctrine which he held was the old Puritan Doctrine, and that it was much safer to hold so than that a Person might be Converted, and not know it.

James Cogswell.

We being present at the same Time, according to the best of our Memories, heard the above Discourse for Substance the same as it written.

October 9.   *Jabez Fitch.*
1744   *Lydia Fitch.*

Canterbury, Octo. 7. 1744

These may signify to whom it may concern, That we the Subscribers being in Company with Mr. *Elisha Paine* sometime past, and being upon some Discourse about spiritual Things, heard him declare, That it was made manifest to him, that CHRIST was about to have a pure Church, and that he had not done his Duty in Time past in promoting Separations and Divisions among the People, and that for Time to come he should endeavour to promote and encourage Separations; and that likewise CHRIST's own Ministers would have their Churches rent from them by reason of their not doing their Duty in that Respect, and Mr. *Moseley's* Church in special Manner: And Mr. *Paine* being asked, what their Duty was which they neglected? He replied thus, Because they did not separate those who were Converted from the Unconverted in the Church; and being asked likewise, what he thought of our Saviour's Parable, where it is said to the Servants, *that they should not gather up the Tares from the Wheat, lest they rooted up the Wheat also?* He replied, that the Meaning of that Parable was, that they should not kill those Persons who were unconverted, for, says he, if they are unconverted now, they may be converted, if not themselves, some might spring from them who should be converted. These are, according to the best of our Remembrance, the Words which we heard Mr. *Paine* say.

Elisabeth Darbe.
Jabez Fitch.

What follows is a Letter from Mr. Paine *to Capt.* Fitch, *occasion'd by the Exposition he had given in the foregoing Evidence.*

Capt. FITCH, *Sir,*
I am informed that the Discourse I had with you concerning

the Parable of the Tares, is grievous to you: It is what I have been taught from my Youth, *viz.* That it was the World, and not the Church of Christ, in contradistinction from the World, that is there meant; and that the Servants were Christ's Children that would run into the same Mistake that his Disciples did, when they would have Fire come down from Heaven to destroy, *&c.* had not Christ forbad: Thus Christ himself shews us in the following Texts, *Matth.* 13. 24,—30. and Verses 36,—43. It is clear from Scripture, that Christ never designed to hinder his Church from Discipline, but that all should grow together, and that there should be no Difference between the vile and the pure in his Church in this World; for you see it bear Fruit before the Tares appeared, and Christ tells us in abundance of Texts that the Church must keep herself pure both in the old Testament and new, and hath given her Rules and Authority so to do; a few of which I have here set down, as, *Jer.* 15. 19, 20, 21. *Zech.* 3 7. *Ezek.* 22 26. Chap. 44 5, 6, 7, 8, 9, 23. Now I believe GOD loves his Church as well, and takes as good Care of it in the new as in the old Testament: See *Matth.* 18. 15, 16, 17, 18. *Rev.* 2d & 3d Chapters. Christ shews us also in the 7th Chap. of *Matth,* the Rule to know the Tares: So *Luke* 6. 43. *By their Fruit they are to be known,* and so it was; the Tares appeared when the Fruit appeared: So the Apostle, 1 *Cor.* 5 Chap. shews us a plain Difference between the World and the Church, even such as were apparently of the Church, but not Sound, and so condemned by the Church, Verses 9, 10, 12, 13, 19. *Galat.* 6. 1, 2, 3. *Colos.* 4. 5. 1 *Thes.* 4. 12. 2 *Tim.* 4. 5. Here the Apostle shews that there is to be a Difference in this Life or World, so *Tit.* 1. 9. so Chap. 2. 8. There is a Difference even in *Teachers*[1], *Tit.* 1. 10, 11. *Rom.* 16. 17. 18. *Phil.* 3. 2, 19. *Jude* ver. 3, 4. *Rev.* 2. 2. 1 *Job* 4. 1, 5, 6. 2 *Pet.* 2. 1. *Rom.* 2. 20. *Matt.* 7. 15. We are to *beware of them.*

---

[1] Would to GOD Mr. *Paine* and his Followers understood and believed these Texts.

Having thus shewn you a few of the many Texts that might be shewn, to prove that tho' Christ's Children must live in this World, among worldly Men, yet they are not to join with them in their Ways, &c. Neither is the World to be killed, as the Romish Church doth those that will not adhere to her Ways: Yet you see by the above Texts that the Church is to cast her Tares out when they appear, or the whole Church is Leavened: Now if you can find one Scripture to warrant your Opinion, that it is the Church that is meant in the above Parable, I shall be oblig'd if you will let me know it, for I can find none: So I rest, praying that Your's and every one's Eyes may be opened, that thinks it is the Church there meant, for it opens a Door to pollute the Church.

Elisha Paine.

. . . November 21. 1744.

Israel Everet, jun testifieth, That about the Middle of *October* last, I went to the Prison in *Windham,* to discourse with Mr. *Elisha Paine,* and after some Discourse, a Question was put to Mr. *Paine,* to this Purpose, Whether the Saints, by Virtue of Grace in themselves, know the Certainty of Grace in another? Mr. *Paine* and Mr. *Douglass* answer'd in the Affirmative; Which I denied; for which they charged me with Blasphemy. I told them the most eminent Divines held the contrary, and particularly Mr. *Stoddard:* Mr. *Paine* replied, he cared not for Mr. *Stoddard,* nor nobody else, but would prove it by Scripture, and alledged that 1 Cor. 2. 15 *He that is spiritual judgeth all Things, yet he himself is judged of no Man.* 1 John 3. 14. *We know that we have passed from Death unto Life, because we love the Brethren.* Upon this, some Scripture was brought in Opposition to Mr. *Paine,* viz. *GOD searcheth the Heart, and trieth the Reins;* and that, 1 Sam. 16. 7. *Man looketh on the outward Appearance, but the Lord looketh on the Heart;* and therefore this Work was GOD's Prerogative. Mr. *Paine* replied, We don't judge by Man's Judgment, but by GOD in us. Mr. *Paine* asked me to expound that Scripture, *By this we know that we have passed from Death unto Life, because we love the Brethren.* I answered, that it meant this, That when a Man was conformed to the Image of GOD, he loved GOD, and consequently loved his Image, and that when he had reason to think a Man was converted by external Evidence agreeable to the Word of GOD, and felt his Soul drawn out answerably in Love to that Man, because he was a good Man, he had as good an Evidence that he himself was a Child of GOD, as if he certainly knew it. Mr. *Paine* replied, he did not think the Devil could have wrested that Scripture, as I had done, by Craft; but told me it was in vain to try to teach a Man in a State of Nature any thing about Religion: Whereupon Mr. *Paine* went to Prayer, and blessed GOD for that Priviledge he had given to Saints to know the Certainty of Grace in others; and prayed that the young Man might be enlightened to know the Truth. This I can safely make Oath of.

Witness my Hand,   *Israel Everit,* jun.

We the Subscribers, can testify to the Truth of the above and within-written Evidence.

James Tracy.
Joseph Hutchison.
Nathanael Tracy.

. . . We have published none of these Things with any Design to expose Mr. *Paine* to Reproach, but as we thought it our Duty, we were very desirous to have had Opportunity to converse with him about these Things, and accordingly . . . we wrote to Mr. *Paine,* earnestly desiring him to meet us at *Ash-*

ford on the 9th of *October,* but at that Time Mr. *Paine* was confined in Prison at *Windham.* We wrote to him again, the 13th of *November,* some Account of several Errors we heard he had vented, as before-named and hinted at, and prayed him to meet us at *Mansfield,* this 11th of *December;* and sent the Letter by the Rev. Mr. *Moseley,* desiring him to use his Interest with Mr. *Paine,* to prevail with him, if he could, to come and see us. Mr. *Moseley* informs us, that he sent him the Letter, and did use his utmost Endeavours to perswade him, that the Honour of GOD, and the Interest of Religion, and Cause of Truth call'd him to comply with our Desire; but could not prevail with him. We thought ourselves bound, for the Honour of CHRIST, and the Welfare of Souls, to give you an Account of these Things, that you may see to what Danger Persons are exposed in running after such Teachers, and how false are their Pretences to the special Impulses of the Holy Ghost in calling them to preach, or teaching the Mind of GOD in his Word. And we beseech you to take Notice how GOD has testified against their Practice in his Providence, since you will not hear his Word: Diverse of those who have undertaken this Work having fallen into scandalous Sins and Miscarriages, and others into foul and dreadful Errors, and even Mr. *Paine,* who in other Things is known to be a Man of the most Sense of any in these Parts, who have set themselves above the Word of GOD, who might probably have done much Service for GOD if he had obeyed his Command, 1 Cor. 7. 24. *Brethren, let every Man wherein he is called therein abide with God;* but having undertaken a Business which GOD has not called him to, has been left to great Errors, miserable Weakness, and a strange perverting of the Word of GOD. . . .

37 · Solomon Paine

(–1754)

A SHORT VIEW OF THE
CHURCH OF CHRIST

The Old Lights did not merely argue against the Separates. In many parts of Connecticut, the insurgents were
outlaws and, as Solomon Paine's account of the 1740's
indicates, persecuted in a variety of ways. Paine, like his
brother Elisha, was not trained for the ministry, but he
too revealed, during the Awakening, a gift for preaching.
It was for attending Paine's sermons that John and Ebenezer Cleaveland, both of them subsequently noted and
honored evangelical spokesmen, were expelled from Yale.
Paine himself was tried and jailed for flouting Connecticut
law by accepting the pastorate of the most important
Separate conventicle in the province, that at Canterbury.
While in prison Paine seems to have refined his thesis that
the Connecticut Establishment was the "Anti-Christ,"

Solomon Paine, *A Short View of the Difference between the Church of
Christ, and the established Churches of the Colony of Connecticut . . .
Being discovered by the Word of God . . .* (Newport, R.I., 1752), pp.
3–13.

doomed to destruction by the God of the Separates. "The Author's Apology" which prefaced his *Short View* attests, by its confessional tone and quasi-mystical use of Scripture, the spiritual ardor that made Separatism one of the most dynamic elements of post-Awakening religion.

If you inquire, why I publish this Treatise, and ask, as Eliab did, *With Whom I have left them few Sheep?* &c. 1 *Sam.* 17. 28.

I answer: *What have I now done? Is there not a Cause?* And if your Heart fails, and you say with *Saul, Thou art not able to go against this* Constitution, ver. 32, 33. I Answer: *The Lord that delivered me out of the Paw of the Lion,* I Pet. 5. 8. Prov. 26. 13. *and out of the Paw of the Bear, Prov.* 28. 15. *he will deliver me out of the Hand of this* Constitution, 1 *Sam.* 17. 37.

And the Reason why I do not go armed with Man's Wisdom, and flattering Titles, or railing Accusations upon Men's Persons, is because I have not proved them in the Work of God, lest your Faith should stand in the Wisdom of Men, and not in the Power of God. Neither have I shunned to speak the Truth for Fear.

And if with the uncircumcised *Philistine* you disdain me, because I am a poor little Creature, and come with nothing but a Staff; I Answer: This Constitution *cometh to me with a Sword and with a Spear, and with a Shield, but I come to that in the Name of the Lord of Hosts,* the God of the Churches of Jesus Christ, whom that hath defied, ver. 45.

If you say as the Priest of *Bethel* did to the Prophet *Amos,* that I have conspired against the Governor, *&c. and bid me go Home and eat my Bread and Prophecy, for it is* the Established Religion, *Amos* 7. 10, 11, 12, 13.

I Answer: I was no Prophet, nor Prophet's Son, but I was an Herdman, and a Gatherer of the Fruit of the Field, *and the Lord took me as I followed the Flock; and the Lord said, Go Prophecy,* Ver. 19.

I have not put myself in the Ballance with the Men of the Established Religion; No, they and I too are quite out of the Question, unless the Truth by our Fruit ranks us in one, and shews which of the Constitutions each one is of: But I have put the Truth of God's Word, the Constitution of the Church of Christ under his supream Government, in one Scale of the Ballance of the Sanctuary, and the Ecclesiastical Laws and Constitution of the Established and Tolerated Churches under the Supream Government of the Major Vote of the Inhabitants of the Towns and Societies of the Colony of Connecticut, in the other Scale, and find *Mene Mene Tekel* written upon the latter, all over the Scriptures.

And seeing God's Name dishonoured, and my dear Country ruined, and many following, as the Men did *Absalom, in Simplicity, and know not any Thing,* 2 Sam. 15. 11. And the Lord spoke unto his Watchmen, *When I say unto the Wicked, Thou shall surely die, if thou dost not speak to warn the Wicked from his wicked Way, that wicked Man shall die in his Iniquity; but his Blood will I require at thine Hands. Nevertheless, if thou warn the Wicked,—thou hast delivered thy Soul,* Ezek. 33. 8, 9.

The Word of the Lord was like a Fire shut up in my Bones, and the Cry of the poor Innocents, who are some of them shut up in Prisons, and others with their little Children crying for Milk, and could get none, for the Collector had taken their Cow for the Minister; and the very grey-headed stript of their necessary Household-stuff: And poor weakly Women, their's taken away, even to their Warming-Pan. Men's Oxen taken out of their Teams; Horses stript of their Tackling; All the Meat taken away from some, just at the setting in of Winter, when the poor Men had nothing in the List, but their Head and one Creature: And when they have nothing but a Family of small Children, to prison with the Head of the Family, and all to support the Minister. And seeing the dreadful Hardness of Heart that hath seized the People which do this Violence to their Neighbour's Persons and Estates, selling and buying for a Tenth Part of the Value, added to their former awful Opposition to the Work of the Spirit of God, and stopping Men from preaching the Gospel, and exhorting the People to the Duties of Christianity. And seeing the just Judgment of God falling upon this Land, according to his just Threatnings in his Word, and knowing that this Constitution in the very Nature of it, lays the Subjects of it under a fatal Necessity to bring forth such corrupt Fruit, and bring upon themselves all the Righteous Blood shed upon Earth, and sudden and eternal Destruction, unless they renounce it, and turn to the Lord with all their Hearts.

And seeing the Advantage that Satan by this Oppression, and the Remainder of corrupt Nature in the Saints, to tempt the weak Believers to try to get from under the Rod of the Wicked, by putting forth their Hands to Iniquity, either first in giving what they demand to support that God-provoking Idolatry, for fear they will take more, or cast them into Prison; or second, to dissemble, as *Peter* did, into some other Sect, to escape the Cross, and lead others away with their Dissimulation; or thirdly, secretly to consent to a mobbish Spirit, whereby many are defiled, and fall from their first Love: *And the Time is come, that Judgment must begin at the House of God, and if it first begin at us,* I *Pet.* 4 17, 18, 19. and the Spirit of God withdrawn in a great Measure, as to his convincing and inviting Influences. The Bowels of the Saints who were wont in Times past to sigh bitterly, even to the breaking of their Loins before Sinners, are now almost shut up. This Day is so evil, that the Prudent hold their Peace in a great

Measure, and the Inhabitants of the great City (*which is spiritually called* Sodom *and* Egypt, *where also one Lord was crucified*), rejoice and send Gifts one to another, *Rev.* 11. 7, 8, 9, 10.

While I mused on these Things, and on the Zeal God hath for his own Glory, *which he will not give to another, nor his Praise to Graven Images*, the Fire burned in me, my Sleep departed from me; when I said my Bed should ease me, Behold, I was like one whose Bones are out of Joint, while he is yet alive; when I said that walking alone should divert my Mind, Behold, I heard the same Cries going up and entring into the Ears of the Lord of *Sabaoth*, so that I could no more rest than if I saw an House on Fire; if I said, Christian Conversation should ease my troubled Breast, Behold, I heard the same, so that I was like a Stranger among my Friends while they spake of Religion; if I said I would pray it away, Behold, when I drew near to God, I heard the Cry of Blood! Blood! Blood! louder than Thunder, from *Abel* to this Day, the Streams all pointed by the Word and Providence of God, and the Fruit of this Constitution, right down upon *Connecticut*, 'till my Strength failed me, and I seized with such a constant Pain in my Vitals, that I could scarce speak sometimes with an audable Voice: I tryed to pray and preach that away, as I had done other Ails, by Faith in Christ many Times, but this failed me, for I could scarce see any Thing but like the flying Roll, *Zech.* 5. 8. against this Constitution, and I thought that it was not best to preach that, because it might not edify the Hearers to preach it.

This continued several Weeks, and I freely confess to God and Man, that it was my Ignorance and Pride that held me in this perplexed, tho' blessed be God, not in a despairing Condition; for all this while when I cried, saying, Lord, What wilt thou have me to do? I had a secret Conviction, that it was best to publish by the Press, the Light that God had given me,

to discover the destructive and damning Nature of the Established Constitution of Religion in this Colony; but I shifted it
off in some Measure from Day to Day, by the following
Excuses, 1. That I had held it out in Love to the Inhabitants
of this Society, both in Writing, which they have upon File in
their Clerk's Office, and by Word of Mouth, both publickly,
and in private, intreating them not to usurp over the Church
of Christ, and grieve the Spirit of God away. 2. I had with the
Church, warned the Man the Society were going to settle,
against the Vote of the Church. 3. We all held it out to the
Con-sociation, which came to ordain him. 4. To the Courts
which *Mitimus'* us to Prison for not going to hear their Society's Ministers, and for preaching the Gospel, and exhorting
the People to the Duties of Christianity, as their Law calls it,
without Leave of this Supream Head: And 5. after they had
ordained him against the Vote and solemn Warnings and Intreaties of the Church and Children of God, as abovesaid, and
they began to oppress the Church; and also all the settled
Ministers of the County left the Church, and never have
preach'd one Sermon to them since the Church disobeyed the
Society in their Sovereign Act of settling a Minister. Then I
went to the General Assembly in Behalf of the Church, with a
Petition, shewing them that the Church was usurp'd over, and
oppress'd as abovesaid, and prayed them to interpose, and
forbid the Society, or grant Relief, &c. The Society's Attorney
objected, and said, that it would spoil the Society, for if these
were released, the Charges would be so heavy upon the rest,
that they would forsake the Minister to save their Rates, &c.
and thereupon we got no Temporal Relief; but I got the
Answer of a good Conscience, in bearing a Testimony to the
Rulers against the Evil of Oppression, which is carried on by
the Force of their Laws, to clear my Garments of their Blood,
and that the Justice of God may shine in their aggravated
Damnation, if they will, against all these Intreaties and Warn-

ings, go on in their Sins 'till they are destroyed from the Face of the Earth, as Jeroboam was. 6. After this, when I see the Oppression increase in the Land, in other Towns as well as in this, I went with a Memorial, shewing that Violence is done by them Ecclesiastical Laws, and that they are right against the Law of God and the King, and prayed them to repeal them, but got no Temporal Relief, nor did I desire any by any Sectary Denomination that would release me, and leave one Child of God to suffer by this *Pharoah*; No, I had rather *suffer Affliction with the People of God, &c. Heb.* 11. 24, 25. But I had thro' the Grace of God, cleared my Garments of their Blood once more, but still the Cry of Violence and Spoil increased in the Colony, and dreadful Tokens in the Providence of God, as well as Threatnings in his Word, of a dreadful Storm of Judgment for such Oppression, which was like a Fire shut up in my Bones, until I warned the Saints in the several Towns to meet at a general Meeting at *Windham*, to cry to the Lord for Direction what to do in such a Day as this, and it appeared evident, by the Word of God, and sealed by his Spirit, that God called us to go once more to the Assembly, and tell them to let the People go, &c. Accordingly it fell upon *Matthew Smith* and I to go, and there was a Memorial writ as followeth:

"*To the Honourable General Assembly of His Majesty's Colony of* Connecticut, *in New-England, to be holden at* Hartford *in said Colony, on the second* Tuesday *of May, A.D.* 1748: *The Memorial of* Solomon Pain *of* Canterbury, *in the County of* Windham, *and* Matthew Smith *of* Stonington, *in the County of* New-London, *and Colony aforesaid, and other Inhabitants of said Colony, and most of them Freemen of this Corporation, and all of them loyal Subjects to his Royal Majesty, King* George *the Second, whom God preserve; all whose Names are hereunto subscribed, humbly sheweth:*

"That whereas the living and true God in his Holy Word,

hath commanded all Men to fear God and honour the King, and that their Fear towards God ought to be taught by his unering Word, and not by the Precepts of Men; and hath given to every Man an unalienable Right in Matters of the Worship of God, to judge for himself, as his Conscience receives the Rule from God, who alone hath Right to challenge Sovereignty over, and Propriety in them: And he hath shewed the Zeal he hath for his own Worship, both by Threatnings, and inflicting heavy Judgments upon those who dare to usurp this Authority over the Consciences of others, and teach for Doctrine the Commandments of Men; and also in promising to, and confering great Favours upon those who have appeared uprightly to stand for the Glory of God, in Liberty of Conscience in all Ages, and particularly upon our Fore-Fathers, who left their Native Country for an howling Wilderness, full of savage Men and Beasts, that they might have Liberty of Conscience; and they found the merciful and faithful God was not a Wilderness to them, but drove out the Savages, and planted Churches and Colonies, and he gave them Favour in the Sight of the Kings and Queens, so that their Majesties granted to, and indulged their Subjects of this Colony with a Charter, in which, among other great Favours, this of Liberty is not abridged. And their Majesties King *William* and Queen *Mary,* tolerated Liberty of Conscience to all, without any Allowance to any Company or Body of Dissenters from the Church of *England,* to oblige any of a different Opinion from them, to pay towards the Building of their Meeting Houses, or Maintaining of their Ministers, and forbids or disallows, of any of whatsoever Profession, to impose upon, or to disturb others in their Worship, by Fines, Imprisonments, &c. in Case they give Satisfaction when called thereto, that they do not hold treasonable Meetings by taking the Oaths, &c. as in said Act, which is still upheld by our gracious Sovereign King *George;* so that when his Majesty's

Subjects of this Colony, who were Conscience-bound to worship in the Way called the *Church of England,* and of the *Quakers,* and also the *Anabaptists,* who were obliged by some Laws called Ecclesiastical, of this Colony, to suffer the Loss of Goods or Imprisonment, and they made their Application to the Honourable Assembly, they had the Force of said Ecclesiastical Laws abated, so far as they respected their Profession; yet all this notwithstanding, forasmuch as said Ecclesiastical Laws are still understood, by those who have to execute civil Power, to stand in full Force against all who do not worship with some one of them Churches, or with the major Part of the People in the Society where they live.

"And whereas, your Honours Memorialists, and many more of their Neighbours, who worship with them in the Fear of God, cannot without doing Violence to their own Consciences, profess to be of any of the above said Churches, or of their Way of Worship, and so neglect to worship God according to their own Consciences, as they understand the Word of God by his Holy Spirit. But since the Grace of God hath appeared to them, teaching them to deny all Ungodliness, *&c.* they are determined, by Divine Assistance, to obey God, and worship him in Spirit and in Truth, altho' that Way be called *Independent* or *Separate,* and to honour the King as supream, and Governors as sent by him, in yielding Obedience to them in all civil Matters.

"And yet they are all exposed, either to make Shipwreck of a good Conscience, or to suffer by Fines or Imprisonment, as many of them have already suffered, for preaching the Gospel, and other Acts of Divine Service, in Obedience to the Commands, and by the Power of God's Spirit; and great Quantities of their temporal Goods, with which they should serve God and honour the King, are taken from them to support that Worship which they cannot in Conscience uphold: And they knowing that the doing such Violence, indangers

Souls, and also Common-wealths, and is threatned in the Word of God, with public Calamity, or eternal Punishment, he shall have Judgment without Mercy, that hath shewed no Mercy, and Mercy rejoiceth against Judgment, for they shall be judged by the Law of Liberty. And seeing the Judgments of Almighty God are coming upon this Land, and the abovesaid Imposition and Oppression still carried on: Whereupon your Honours Memorialists pray, That your Honours may be the happy Instruments of unbinding these Burdens, and enact universal Liberty, by repealing all those Ecclesiastical Laws that are or may be executed, to the debaring of any of this Colony of the Liberty granted by God, and tolerated by our King; or forbid the Execution of said Laws: And they, as in Duty bound, shall ever pray." *Subscribers* 330.

This was preferred to the Assembly, but they refused to grant it; but so ignorant was I and foolish, that seeing that all this had been done, went about to excuse myself thus; saying within myself, What doth it avail? it will only inrage them, and make them lay on heavier Burdens upon the poor Saints, thinking we had better go to the King, &c. for they will take no Notice of it. Again, I put it off under the following Excuses: 1. That I had not the Gift that some had, like a great Eagle, &c. to take off the Top of the tall Cedars; but this Excuse was taken off, by a Conviction, that I am a Worm which God hath prepared at the Root of this Gourd, and my Happiness is to serve God, and my Generation, in the Work he calls me to: But (2) I was afraid I should neglect my publick Calling, and lose my spiritual Life in preaching. And this Excuse lay with the greatest Weight by far, and here I thought sometimes, that I should shake the Conviction off as to writing; but as I said before, my Health and Strength, and preaching and Life, and all seemed to be going together, the Cry seemed louder and more intelligible; it seemed when I lay down to sleep (as abovesaid) as real as if I had heard Thousands saying unto me, We are in the Dark about this

Thing, and know not what to do; we are afraid to join with the Established or Tolerated Churches, and if we do not, we see nothing, but that we must have all our Estates taken away, and sold for less than a tenth Part of what they are worth, and then our Bodies cast into Prison forever, unless we will pay to support that Worship, and that we are afraid to do; for we see that those who pay to support it, lose the Life of Religion. And we have heard that you have Light in those Things, so that it is no Trial or Temptation to you to join with them, for fear of Fines, Rates, or Imprisonments, or even Death itself, you knowing that you must deny Christ to join with them; therefore we pray you to set these Things in the Light of the Scriptures before us, peradventure the Lord will bless it to us as well as to you, for all that hath been done yet of that Nature, hath not so particularly described the Foundation of those Churches to us, as that we fully understand them, and yet there is so much currupt Fruit, we are afraid to join with them as aforesaid.

And when I went to put off these Cries, the Lord said unto me, *No Man lighteth a Candle, and putteth it under a Bushel,* Matt. 5. 15. Luke 8. 16. and my Conscience testified unto me, that God had given me that Light by his Word and Spirit; and the Laws of this Constitution, and of the Nature of Idolatry, that I knew as perfectly that this is Idolatry, as I do that *Nebuchadnezzar's* or *Jeroboam's* was, and that it is no more of a Question with me, whether I ought to give what they demand to support it, than it is, whether *Israel* ought to give to support *Jeroboam's* Priests, which he made for his Calves: And I could as freely go into the Fiery Furnace for not supporting it, as I could for not worshipping *Nebuchadnezzar's* Golden Image; neither did I ever lose one Minute's Sleep by all that they have taken from me (but it was the Evil and Destruction abovesaid, and the Cries of the Oppressed, that trouble me) not unto me, but unto God, be the Glory.

And when I thus mused, the Fire burned in my Heart with

Love to the Sovereign Lord Jesus, to whose Blood I was made to flee for Pardon of my Pride and Ignorance, and backwardness to receive his Teachings, which are always contrary to my wicked Self; and in Love and Pity to my dear Country People, I yielded to the Conviction to give them one public Warning more.

And when I began to write, I found my Health of Body return, and instead of losing my Spiritual Life in preaching, I had rather a double Portion. I afresh, fell in Love so with the dear Church of Christ, that had I a Thousand such poor Bodies as this is, I could have been willing to have sacrificed them all, rather than that the Spouse of the blessed Lord Jesus Christ should be defiled with other Lovers, and be dethroned, and *Mammon* set in his Throne. And when I girded myself, and served him, he bid me sit down and eat; and I can truly say, he is an infinite good Master, and I am an unprofitable Servant, for I have done that which was my Duty to do, but he is so good to me, that he hath given me to be willing. If he pleases to take every Drop of my poor Blood to seal these Truths, tho' I should pity the poorest of all the Human Race if he must be so unhappy as to indure Guilt of Conscience one Night for taking of it away.

Now to the King Eternal, Immortal, Invisible, the only wise God, be Glory, Honour, and Majesty, both now and ever. *Amen.*

38 · Jonathan Edwards

QUALIFICATIONS FOR

COMMUNION

In theory the whole prorevival party shared the Separates' belief in religious liberty. Many New Lights also practiced the belief, and Jonathan Edwards, who was outraged by the enthusiasm of the Separates, condemned those who would interfere with sectarian worship by banning ministers. It is "the people's right," Edwards insisted, "to choose the food with which they will be fed." His sympathy with the Separates seemed even more evident when in 1747 Edwards announced to his congregation that he had decided to limit participation in the sacraments to "visible saints." In so doing he repudiated the theories of his grandfather, Solomon Stoddard, who in *An Appeal to the Learned* (1709), had defined the "visible church" (the church, that is, on earth) as consisting, not of the regenerate merely, but

---

Jonathan Edwards, *An Humble Inquiry into the Rules of the Word of God, Concerning the Qualifications Requisite to a Complete Standing and Full Communion in the Visible Christian Church*, Works, I, 119–120, 144–145, 188–191.

of all who would "profess" the truth of the Christian religion. Since Edwards' scheme would have deprived many members of his Northampton congregation of their traditional privileges, a bitter controversy ensued, one which ended with Edwards' removal from his charge by a vote of the congregation and the approval of a ministerial council. In 1749, when the controversy was nearing its climax, Edwards published his *Humble Inquiry*. He hoped thereby to acquaint his critics with the reasoning behind his decision and to answer their complaint that he, in seeking to "purify" the church, had "fallen in" with the Separates.

Edwards reasoned that the "visible church" should be as close an approximation as possible to the "invisible church," that holy company, here and hereafter, of those whom God alone knew for certain he had elected to sainthood. Men could not infallibly determine who on earth were saints, but they must devise some test whereby it might be discovered who were "visibly" such as in all likelihood had a heart conformed to love of God. Both "profession" and "practice" must be judged, he concluded—the former in order to establish that the applicant had enjoyed some religious experience, the other to certify that his experience was not a mere transient flight of enthusiasm. Behind Edwards' ecclesiastical theory lay the central premise of his *Religious Affections*—that a man's actions, not his words, were the surest evidence of his inner dispositions. The same premise informed his objection to the ecclesiastical practice of the Separates, who, in Edwards' day, accepted as "saints" those who loudly and frequently described their experiences of personal communication with God. Such declarations, Edwards argued, were more than likely evidence, not of sainthood, but of spiritual pride, especially if they were not accompanied by a course of conduct that indicated the impression was not merely transient.

Where Edwards also differed from the Separates was in his desire to give both dignity and discipline to the process of examining prospective church members. The Separates, as Edwards saw it, acted as though one saint intuitively knew the inner holiness of another by a "spirit of discerning." Although for Edwards the ultimate test of sainthood was an aesthetic one, he would not allow mere taste or intuition to serve as the sole judge of sainthood. Careful and strict, yet charitable "public" examination was, for Edwards, a means of reminding those who aspired to "sainthood" of their communal obligations, while the Separate system, he believed, produced a mere mutual admiration society, its members rejoicing in their privileges but neglecting their responsibilities. Herein was the explanation of why Edwards, after being ejected from Northampton, spurned the suggestion that he form a separate church composed of those who could fulfill his standards of sainthood. Such a communion, Edwards believed, could accomplish nothing, except to instill in its members an unproductive sense of their own superior virtue.

What the church might accomplish was ever uppermost in Edwards' mind during his arguments over the qualifications for communion. The fatal flaw in Separatism, according to Edwards, was that it failed to see the church as an instrument. They established their "pure" churches by "coming out" from the corruptions of the world, and thereby forswore both responsibility for contending with that corruption and the opportunity to do so. Edwards did not intend, had he succeeded in changing the constitution of the Northampton church, to dismiss the unregenerate from his congregation. Far from it, he wanted to keep them in the society, under the watchful eyes of the "saints"—into whose hands alone the government and discipline of the church would be given. Their "communion" would serve, not only as an expression of the peculiar love saints bore for one another, but to confront the minds of the as-yet-unconverted citizens with an emblem of the pleasures and the privileges—and the power—of the saints. Such a church was one element (but not the only one) in Edwards' program for mobilizing the "people of God" to carry out God's plan for the redemption of society.

. . . The nature of things seems to afford no good reason why the people of Christ should not openly profess a proper respect to him in their hearts, as well as a true notion of him in their heads, or a right opinion of him in their judgments.

I can conceive of nothing reasonably to be supposed the design or end of a public profession of religion, that does not as much require a profession of honor, esteem and friendship of heart towards Christ, as an orthodox opinion about him; or why the former should not be as much expected and required in order to a being admitted into the company of his friends and followers, as the latter. It cannot be because the former is in itself not as important, and as much to be looked at, as the latter; seeing the very essence of religion itself consists in the former, and without it the latter is wholly vain, and makes us never the better; neither happier in ourselves, nor more acceptable to God. . . . When persons only manifest their doctrinal knowledge of things of religion, and express the assent of their judgments, but at the same time make no pretence to any other than a being wholly destitute of all true love to God, and a being under the dominion of enmity against him, their profession is, in some respects, very greatly to God's dishonor; for they leave reason for the public greatly to suspect that they hold the truth in unrighteousness. . . .

Another evidence, that such as are taken into the church, ought to be in the eye of a Christian judgment truly *gracious* or *pious* persons, is this, that the Scripture represents the *visible church* of Christ as a society having its several members united by the bond of *Christian brotherly love.*

Besides that general benevolence or charity which the saints have to mankind, and which they exercise towards both the evil and the good in common, there is a peculiar and very *distinguishing* kind of affection, that every true Christian experiences towards those whom he looks upon as truly gracious persons, whereby the soul, at least at times, is very sensibly and sweetly knit to such persons, and there is an ineffable oneness of heart with them. . . .

Now this intimate affection towards others as *brethren in Christ* and *fellow members* of him, must have some apprehension of the understanding, some judgment of the mind, for its foundation. To say, that we must thus *love* others as visible members of Christ, if any thing *else* be meant, than that we must love them because they are visibly, or *as* they appear to our judgment, real members of Christ, is in effect to say, that we must thus love them without any foundation at all. In order to a real and fervent affection to another, on account of some amiableness of qualification or relation, the mind must first judge there is that amiableness in the object. The affections of the mind are not so at command that we can make them strongly to go forth to an object *as* having such loveliness, when at the same time we do not positively *judge* any such thing concerning them, but only *hope* it may be so, because we see no sufficient reason to determine the contrary. There must be a *positive* dictate of the understanding, and some degree of satisfaction of the judgment, to be a ground of that *oneness of heart and soul* which is agreeable to Scripture representations of φιλαδὲλφια, or *brotherly love*. And a supposition only of that *moral sincerity and virtue,* or *common grace,* which some insist upon, though it may be a sufficient ground of *neighborly* and *civil* affection, cannot be a sufficient ground of this intimate affection to them as *brethren* in the family of a heavenly Father, this fervent love to them *in the bowels of Jesus Christ;* that implying nothing in it inconsistent with being *gospel sinners* and domestic *enemies* in the house of God; which Christians know are the most hateful enemies to Christ, of all the enemies that he has.

It is a thing well agreeing with the wisdom of Christ, and that peculiar favor he has manifested to his saints, and with his dealings with them in many other respects, to suppose, he has made a provision in his institutions, that they might have the comfort of uniting, with such as their hearts are united with in that holy intimate affection which has been spoken of, in special religious exercises and duties of worship, and visible intercourse with their Redeemer, joining with those concerning whom they can have some satisfaction of mind, that they are cordially united with them in adoring and expressing their *love* to their common Lord and Saviour, that they may *with one mind, with one heart, and one soul,* as well as *with one mouth, glorify him;* as in the forementioned Rom. xv. 5, 6, compared with Acts iv. 32. This seems to be what this heavenly affection naturally inclines to. And how eminently fit and proper for this purpose is the sacrament of the *Lord's supper,* the Christian church's great feast of *love;* wherein Christ's people sit together as *brethren* in the family of God, at their Father's table, to feast on the love of their Redeemer, commemorating his sufferings for them, and his dying love to them, and sealing *their* love to him and one another?—It is hardly credible, that Christ has so ordered things as that there are no instituted social acts of worship, wherein *his saints* are to manifest their respect to him, but such as wherein they ordinarily are obliged (*if the rule for admissions be carefully attended*) to join with the society of fellow worshippers, concerning whom they have no reason to think but that the *greater part* of them are *unconverted* (and are more provoking enemies to that Lord they love and adore, than most of the very Heathen), which Mr. Stoddard supposes to be the case with the members of the visible church. . . .

As to the two last arguments in the *Appeal to the Learned,* concerning the subjects of the Christian sacraments, their being members of the *visible* church, and not the *invisible;* the force of those arguments depends entirely on the resolution of that question, Who are *visible saints?* Or what adult persons are regularly admitted to the privileges of members of the *visible church?* Which question has already been largely considered: and, I think, it has been demonstrated that they are those who exhibit a credible profession and visibility of *gospel holiness* or vital piety, and not merely of moral sincerity. So that there is no need of further debating the point in this place.

I might here mention many things not yet taken notice of, which some object as *inconveniences* attending the scheme I have maintained: and if men should set up their own wit and wisdom in opposition to God's revealed will, there is no end of the objections of this kind, which might be raised against any of God's institutions. Some have found great fault even with the *creation* of the world, as being very inconveniently done, and have imagined that they could tell how it might be mended in a great many respects. But however God's altar may appear homely to us, yet if we lift up our tool upon it to mend it, we shall pollute it. Laws and institutions are given for the general good, and not to avoid every particular inconvenience. And however it may so happen, that sometimes inconveniences (real or imaginary) may attend the scheme I have maintained; yet, I think, they are in no measure equal to the manifest conveniences and happy tendencies of it, or to the palpable inconveniences and pernicious consequences of the other. I have already mentioned some things of this aspect, and would here briefly observe some others.

Thus, the way of making such a difference between outward duties of *morality* and *worship*, and those great inward duties of the *love of God* and *acceptance of Christ*, that the former must be *visible*, but that there need to be no *exhibition* nor *pretence* of the latter, in order to persons being admitted into the visible family of God; and that under a notion of the latter being *impossibilities*, but the other being *within men's power*; this, I think, has a direct tendency to confirm in men an *insensibility* of the heinousness of those *heart sins* of unbelief and enmity against God our Saviour, which are the source and sum of all wickedness; and tends to prevent their coming under a humbling *conviction* of the greatness and utter inexcusableness of these sins, which men must be brought to if ever they obtain salvation. Indeed it is a way that not only has this tendency, but has actually and apparently this effect, and that to a great degree.

The effect of this method of proceeding in the churches in New England, which have fallen into it, is actually this. There are some that are received into these churches under the notion of their being in the judgment of rational charity *visible saints* or *professing saints*, who yet at the same time are actually open *professors* of heinous *wickedness;* I mean the wickedness of living in known impenitence and unbelief, the wickedness of living in enmity against God, and in the rejection of Christ under the gospel: or, which is the same thing, they are such as freely and frequently acknowledge, that they do not profess to be as yet *born again*, but look on themselves as really *unconverted*, as having never unfeignedly accepted of Christ; and they do either explicitly or implicitly number themselves among those that *love not the Lord Jesus Christ;* of whom the apostle says, let such be *Anathema, Maranatha!* And accordingly it is known, all over the town where they live, that they make no pretensions to any *sanctifying grace* already obtained; nor of consequence are they commonly looked upon as any other than *unconverted* persons. Now, can this be judged the comely *order* of the gospel? Or shall God be supposed the *author* of such *confusion?*

In this way of church proceeding, God's own children and the true disciples of Christ are obliged to receive those as their *brethren*, admit them to the *communion of saints*, and embrace them in the highest acts of Christian society, even in their great *feast of love*, where they feed together on the body and blood of Christ, whom yet they have no reason to look upon otherwise than as *enemies of the cross of Christ*, and haters of their heavenly Father and dear Redeemer, they making no pretension to any thing at all inconsistent with those characters; yea, in many places, as I said before, freely professing this to be actually the case with them.

Christ often forbids the members of his church *judging one another:* but in this way of ecclesiastical proceeding, it is done continually, and looked upon as no hurt; a great part of those admitted into the church are by others of the same communion judged *unconverted, graceless* persons; and it is impossible to avoid it, while we stretch not beyond the bounds of a *rational* charity.

This method of proceding must inevitably have one of these two consequences: either there must be *no public notice* at all given of it, when so signal a work of grace is wrought, as a sinner's being brought to repent and turn to God, and hopefully becomes the subject of saving conversion; or else this notice must be given in the way of *conversation,* by the *persons themselves,* frequently, freely, and in all companies, declaring their own experiences. But surely, either of these consequences must be very unhappy. The former is so, viz., the forbidding and preventing any *public* notice being given on earth of the *repentance of a sinner,* an event so much to the honor of God, and so much taken notice of in *heaven,* causing *joy in the presence of the angels of God,* and tending so much to the advancement of religion in the world. For it is found by experience, that scarce any one thing has so great an influence to awaken sinners, and engage them to seek salvation, and to quicken and animate saints, as the tidings of a sinner's repentance, or hopeful conversion: God evidently makes use of it as an eminent means of advancing religion in a time of remarkable revival of religion. And to take a course effectually to prevent such an event's being notified on earth, appears to me a counteracting of God, in that which he ever makes use of as a chief means of the propagation of true piety, and which we have reason to think he will make use of as one principal means of the conversion of the world in the glorious latter day. But now as to the *other* way, the way of giving notice to the public of this event, by particular persons *themselves* publishing their own experiences from time to time and from place to place, on all occasions and before all companies, I must confess, this is a practice that appears to me attended with many inconveniences, yea, big with mischiefs. The abundant trial of this method lately made, and the large experience we have had of the evil consequences of it, is enough to put all sober and judicious people forever out of conceit of it. I shall not pretend to enumerate all the mischiefs attending it, which would be very tedious; but shall now only mention two things. One is, the bad effect it has upon the persons themselves that practise it, in the great tendency it has to spiritual *pride;* insensibly begetting and establishing an evil habit of mind in that respect, by the frequent return of the temptation, and this many times when they are not guarded against it, and have no time, by consideration and prayer, to fortify their minds. And then it has a very bad effect on the minds of *others* that hear their communication, and so on the state of religion in general, in this way. It being thus the custom for persons of all sorts, young and old, wise and unwise, superiors and inferiors, freely to tell their own experiences before all companies, it is commonly done very *injudiciously,* often very rashly and foolishly, out of season, and in circumstances tending to defeat any good end. Even sincere Christians too frequently in their conversation insist mainly on those things that are no part of their *true spiritual experience;* such as impressions on their fancy or imagination, suggestions of facts by passages of Scripture, &c.; in which case *children* and weak persons that hear, are apt to form their notions of religion and true piety by such experimental communications, and much more than they do by the most solid and judicious instructions out of the word they hear from the pulpit: which is found to be one of the devices whereby Satan has an inexpressible advantage to ruin the souls of men, and utterly to confound the interest of religion. This matter of making a public profession of godliness or piety of heart, is certainly a very important affair, and ought to be under some *public regulation,* and under the direction of *skilful guides,* and not left to the management of every man, woman, and child, according to their humor or fancy: and when it is done, it should be done with great seriousness, preparation and prayer, as a solemn act of public respect and honor to God, in his house and in the presence of his people. Not that I condemn, but greatly approve of persons speaking sometimes of their religious experiences in private conversation, to proper persons and on proper occasions, with modesty and discretion, when the glory of God and the benefit or just satisfaction of others require it of them.

In a word, the practice of promiscuous admission, or that way of taking all into the church indifferently as *visible saints*, who are not either ignorant or scandalous, and at the same time that custom's taking place of persons' publishing their own *conversion* in common *conversation;* where these two things meet together, they unavoidably make *two* distinct kinds of *visible churches,* or different bodies of professing saints, one within another, openly distinguished one from another, as it were by a visible dividing line. One company consisting of those who are *visibly gracious* Christians, and open professors of godliness; another consisting of those who are *visibly moral* livers, and only profess common virtues, without pretending to any special and spiritual experiences in their hearts, and who therefore are not reputed to be converts. I may appeal to those acquainted with the state of the churches, whether this be not actually the case in some, where this method of proceeding has been long established. But I leave the judicious reader to make his own remarks on this case, and to determine, whether there be a just foundation in Scripture or reason for any such state of things; which to me, I confess, carries the face of glaring absurdity.

39 · *Solomon Williams*

(*1 7 0 0 – 1 7 7 6*)

THE TRUE STATE OF

THE QUESTION

———

Though Edwards was exiled to Stockbridge, his conception of the church was eventually to gain a considerable
measure of triumph within New England Congregationalism and even, surprisingly enough, among New Side Presbyterians. In the 1760's it was everywhere being argued
that admitting the unregenerate to church privileges
confirmed them in their "complacency" and thus disposed
them to Arminianism. Many who considered themselves
strict Calvinists chose, however, to preserve the older
polity. Herein they followed Solomon Williams, Jonathan
Edwards' cousin and his chief antagonist in the controversy over church membership. Williams had been an outspoken supporter of the Awakening, and he had also been
instrumental in persuading Davenport to publish his
Confession. It seems to have been Williams' fear that

Solomon Williams, *The True State of the Question Concerning the Qualifications Necessary to lawful Communion* . . . (Boston, 1751), pp. 140–
143.

435

Edwards' ecclesiastical theory, with its evident denigration of "mere morality," would encourage enthusiasm. Williams was also plagued by Separates in his own community and convinced that the duty of Calvinists, in the context of 1750, was to unite in defense of New England's inherited faith.

But Williams' confutation of Edwards was in effect the charter of a new orthodoxy, for though he claimed to be disturbed as much by a resurgent Arminianism as by Antinomian Separatism, his arguments sacrificed central evangelical principles. Williams defended the Half-Way Covenant with the traditional notion of New England's "special relationship" to God, while the true church of Calvinism, as Edwards reminded his cousin in a subsequent reply, was a much larger Kingdom, composed of saints wherever they happened to have been born. However, the thrust of Williams' orthodoxy appeared in his declaration that it was irrelevant whether "outward Duties of Morality and Worship proceed from some other Causes than the Love of God." He was, in sum, unwilling to accept the most radical and unsettling of the implications of the Awakening—those that fixed in the minds of the godly a sense of their differences from their neighbors who remained enemies to God's Kingdom.

I agree with my dear Brother *Edwards*, that if Men should set their own Wit and Wisdom in Opposition to God's revealed Will, there's no End of Objections which may be raised against any of God's Institutions, and if we lift up our Tool to mend

God's Altar, we shall pollute it.—And I am of Opinion that Inconveniencies both real and imaginary may attend the Scheme which he has undertaken to maintain: And that they are not only equal to the manifest Conveniences and happy Tendencies of it, or to the Inconveniencies and bad Consequences of the other, but vastly greater, and that it is a Scheme contrary to God's Dispensation to his Church in all Ages, and inconsistent with it self.

The outward Duties of Morality and Worship, when to Appearance they are sincerely performed, are by the Church in their publick Judgment to be charitably thought to be the Product of the great inward Duties of the Love of God, and Acceptance of Christ. The latter ought not only to be pretended to, but exhibited by the former; and God never appointed any other Way of their being made visible to the World: And he who is the Searcher of Hearts has only a Right and Ability to determine of them otherwise. But in this State of Things, he neither has given us a Rule, nor will allow us to judge otherwise in order to Persons being taken into his Family, and to the outward Priviledges of his House.—The Notion of Men's being able and fit to determine positively the Condition of other Men, or the certainty of their gracious Estate; has a direct Tendency to decieve the Souls of Men; to harden some in Hypocrisy, and lift up others with Pride and Self-Conceit. The Effect of such a Way and Practise in Admission of Persons into the visible Church seems naturally this, and these Effects speak out themselves: That since the outward Duties of Morality and Worship may proceed from other Causes than the Love of God, and Faith in Christ, therefore some Persons look upon these as not giving any Evidence at all of those Graces: But judge of some Accounts which they hear of Persons relating their Experiences, or some inward Feelings; (which can only be said to evidence their Grace if they be not decieved themselves, nor aim to decieve others) and which without those Duties of Morality and Worship, or separate from them, can't be so good Evidences of Grace as these are without them. And so they determine that if Men live never so strictly conformable to the Laws of the Gospel, and never so diligently seek their own Salvation to outward Appearance, they give no more publick Evidence that they are not Enemies of God, and Haters of Jesus Christ, than the very worst of the Heathen. Nor do they stick any more to speak of them, and act openly towards them in such a Manner; thereby violating in the most open & scandalous Manner the Law of Christ, wherein he solemnly forbids them to judge one another: Which yet they continually do in open Defiance of his Law, the Rules of his visible Kingdom, and his own Example as King of the visible Church. And the greatest Part of those who are in Covenant with God, and to whom Christ has commanded Baptism the Seal of the Covenant to be administered, whom he hath bound by the most solemn Engagements to attend all his Ordinances, and wait at his Foot for all the Blessings of the Covenant of Grace; are forbidden to do it by their Brethren, tho' they own them at the same Time to be in Covenant with God; because they think them not good enough to recieve the Food which Christ has provided for them.

Mr. *Edwards* proposes one of two Evil Consequences inevitably following the Method of Proceeding which he opposes.—"Either there must be no publick Notice given of the Conversion of a Sinner, or else this Notice must be given in a Way of Conversation by the Parties themselves."

And how are these Evils remedied upon his Scheme? Supposing it be necessary that some publick Notice be given of the Conversion of every Person in a Town, what Way can it be done? According to him the best visible Exercise of the Worship of God, and most sincere Practise of moral Virtues to outward Appearance; the greatest visible Appearance of the

Love of God, and Concern to please him that is compatible to the State of an unconverted Man, is not so much as the least Evidence of any Pretence to Godliness.

What other Way is there left but a Declaration of inward Experiences? For as to Persons saying they are converted, this I believe will by few be thought to be so good an Evidence as the former. Now what Way has the Church to judge of these Experiences? Are they to take the Minister's Word for them; and so admit the Person? If this is the Way, it may indeed give him as great Advantage in some Respects as the Romish Priests have, or make him something like *Nebuchadnezzer, Dan.* 5. 19. But it will leave the Church as much in the Dark as they were before; and if they offer unto God Thanksgiving upon his Information, it must surely be done upon an implicit Faith; if the Church are to judge for themselves, there can be no Way but by hearing the Man relate his Experiences. "And this must be done by Persons declaring their Experiences from Time to Time, and Place to Place," or else the Church must all meet together to hear them, and this amounts to the same Thing. So that I can't see how one of these Evil Consequences is avoided by Mr. *Edwards*'s Scheme. "He supposes the Matter ought to be under some Regulation, and the Direction of skilful Guides &c."—Shall these skilful Guides direct every Man, Woman and Child, what Experiences to relate, and what to omit, what are fit to be published, and what not? If so, I believe the Church will soon judge, or if they don't others will, that this is as artificial a Sort of Conversion, as the making a common Draught, and Formula, for the Experiences of all that are to be taken into the Church. Whether this is like to promote the Honour of God, or be a Scandal & Reproach to his Name, seems not very difficult to determine.—One would think the late dreadful Consequences of such Sort of Doings in this Land had been enough to convince every judicious Christian of the Sinfulness of it. Neither upon Mr. *Edwards*'s Scheme can I conceive the making two distinct Kinds of visible Churches, or visible Bodies of professing Saints any more unavoidable than on the other. Indeed the very Doctrine itself makes two such Bodies within one another, and openly distinguish'd one from another. One Company consisting of such as openly declare that they judge themselves gracious Christians: And the other of those whom these own to be in Covenant with God, who have been sealed with the Seal of his Covenant, and Christ has taken into his Family, but only they have no Right to so much as the outward Priviledges of it belonging to the visible Kingdom of Christ, and yet at the same Time visibly and openly belonging to the Kingdom of the Devil; declaring that they desire above all Things in the World to partake and enjoy the Blessings of the Kingdom of Christ, having sworn that they will make it their chief Business to obtain them, and use every Method which Christ has appointed therefor; moral or visibly Religious in their Conversation, and yet treated as open and avowed Enemies of Jesus Christ, and his Kingdom, making no Pretence to Godliness; and this by the declared & publick Judgment of the Church, in the same visible Covenant with them. I appeal also to the common Sense of Mankind, whether this be not the Case where that Method of Proceeding Mr. *Edwards* contends for, is established; and with Mr. *Edwards*, leave it to the judicious Reader to make his own Remarks, whether there be a just Foundation in Scripture or Reason for such a State of Things; and whether this is the comely Order of the Gospel which Christ hath instituted.

40 · Ebenezer Frothingham

(*1719–1798*)

THE ARTICLES OF THE

SEPARATE CHURCHES

Not all criticism of Edwards came from the spokesmen of cautious orthodoxy. The Separates also responded negatively to his inquiry into the qualifications for church members—in part because Edwards had continued to rebuke the Separates' notion of a "pure" church, but largely because it seemed to them that Edwards was stubbornly refusing to accept the logical and radical implications of his premise that communion should be limited to the regenerate. But though the Separates, or at least their successors the Baptists, were eventually to claim Edwards as their own, his differences with them were fundamental. Edwards preserved a vision of the universal Church, while the early Separates tended to view each individual conventicle as distinct and unaffiliated with any other or

---

Ebenezer Frothingham, *The Articles of Faith and Practice, with the Covenant that is confessed by the Separate Churches* . . . (Newport, R.I., 1750), pp. 33–37, 50–51, 100–103, 105–109, 176–177, 256–261, 351–355, 374–377, 386–387, 422–428.

larger communion. It was the profounder "independence"
of Separatism, however, that offended Edwards and set
him apart from his enthusiastic critics—an individualism
that Edwards rebuked in 1749 in his memoir of the young
missionary to the Indians, David Brainerd, as more spiritually selfish than that of reasonable Arminians.

How valid Edwards' criticisms were may be judged from
the first comprehensive statement of Separate principles
to be published, Ebenezer Frothingham's *Articles of Faith
and Practice*. Though Frothingham does not define religion as mere emotions and impressions, and though he
does attend to the saints' moral duties, he focuses, to a
degree that Edwards would not allow, on the individual
saint's sense of personal communion with the Deity. Moreover, Frothingham's separated holy men, however "social"
their worship, have neither "dependence" on one another
nor any program for overcoming the corruptions of the
society from which they have withdrawn. Rather they
merely bewail the sins of the age, taking comfort in the
thought that they, having assuredly tasted the joys of salvation, will one day watch with delight while God inter-
venes in history to rain retribution on the unrighteous.

Frothingham was one of the original Separates of
Wethersfield, Connecticut, where for many years Edwards' father Timothy had been the established minister.
In 1747 Frothingham was installed as pastor of the Separate church of Wethersfield; he was jailed for preaching
without permission. On the basis of such treatment, Frothingham concluded that even the best of New England's

ministers had betrayed the revival. But he could not bring himself to include Jonathan Edwards in this indictment. In the *Articles*, Frothingham's bitter disappointment in the other erstwhile revivalists is matched by a longing to march once more under the banner of Jonathan Edwards. Such a reunification of New England's evangelical party was in fact eventually achieved, though not in Edwards' lifetime nor with Frothingham as a participant. Frothingham did not, as did so many New England Separates, become a Baptist, but those who did came, under the guidance of Isaac Backus, to profess Edwards' definition of true virtue and to follow his vision of the church and its role in history.

A Discourse Treating upon the great Privileges of the Church of Jesus Christ

In prosecuting this Discourse we shall first endeavour to prove the fifteenth Article before recited in this Book, which is, that real Believers, and none but such, are Members of the true Church of Jesus Christ, *&c.*

But we find the Work considerably shortened by one that we trust the Truth will be received more freely from, without Prejudice, viz. Mr. *Edwards,* in his late Book, entituled, 'An Enquiry into the Qualifications for full Communion in the visible Church.' But we would observe to the Reader, that altho' we don't join with Mr. *Edwards* in every particular thing laid down in the Book, yet as to the Substance of the

Arguments and Scriptures brought to prove that none have a Right to the Lord's Supper but real Saints, and that there is no half-way Covenant; we say, as to the Substance of the Arguments and Scriptures brought by the Author to prove these Points, and also the Duty of the Saints visibly covenanting with God and each other, and there frequently renewing the same, we do highly esteem, as being agreable to sound Doctrine, and the eternal Standard of Truth; therefore we would heartily recommend the Book (excepting some Particulars in it) to the serious Perusal of every Person of all Ranks and Denominations, earnestly praying that the all-wise and merciful God would bless it, and make it Instrumental of bringing the Saints in *New-England* into the real order of the Gospel, that so we may be of one Heart, and brought onto one Practice in attending the institutions of the Gospel of Jesus Christ. Here we shall take Occasion to observe some Things from the Caution that the Author gives the World in his Preface to the fore-cited Book, respecting his Opinion of the People called Separates; and we do it the more readily, inasmuch as he himself laid a Foundation for it in the same Preface in his Apology, &c. And here first, since it is not a Transgression to judge a Tree according to the Fruits, or speak of a Person according to the Fruits made visible and manifest in his Performance, therefore we are exceedingly prone to think that the Author was under a prejudiced Frame of Mind when he gave his Caution against the Separates, and spake in his Zeal without knowledge, and made himself guilty of the same Sin that he charges them with, i.e. of censorious judging; for it is more than probable that the Author has never had any Knowledge, either by personal Acquaintance, or true Report of an hundred part of the Separates in this Land, by Reason that there are Thousands of them in this Land, and scarce any of them live near him; and the Author has made no Reserve or Distinction among them, but judg'd them all off at one uncharitable

Declaration, and call'd them ill-minded People, and wild enthusiastical Sort of People, and self-confident, contentious, uncharitable, and such like Expressions he writes. Now although we hold the Author to be founded upon the Rock of Christ, yet it no ways follows that all he builds upon that Foundation is pure Gold. Now we ask whether it would not be censorious, wicked, and unreasonable for one that is a Separate to say that all the standing Churches or People that meet in such Congregations, are a Company or Companies of Drunkards, or wicked scandalous Persons, because there was a few such wicked Persons among them; the Answer must be, Yes. . . .

We now pass on to consider and enquire into the Visibility that the Author holds as the Door of Admission into the Church; and if it should so happen, that we should prove from the Author's writing, the same Visibility as the Door of Admission into the visible Church as we hold, we would hope that he and others may have an Occasion to reflect upon themselves for marking us out by way of Reproach and Contempt, as the only Persons in the Land that pretend to a pure Church, when he and they hold to a visible Evidence of gracious Sincerity, or real Saintship, even of that Sort of Saintship which the Saints in Heaven have. Now this we confess is the Truth in fact; and we know not of one Saint that is in regular Standing in any of the Separate Churches in the Land, that holds to any fuller or further Evidence than this Testimony is: And notwithstanding this clear Truth the Author has laid down, yet by some other Passages, we are prone to think that he don't understand himself, or else contradicts himself; which brings us into a further Enquiry into this Visibility the Author insists upon: . . .

A Church of Christ has no right to take in one Member but upon certain Evidence of visible Fruits of a new-born Principle of Grace in the Soul, or visible Saintship; and for the Proof of this, the Reader may see that the Churches upon sacred Record try'd the Profession, when they had any Fear or Suspicion that the Person professing, had not the Truth of saving Grace in their Hearts. *Rev.* 2 chap. 2 & 9 ver. *Acts* 5 chap. from the 1 to 14 ver. chap. 3. 20, 21 and 37. chap. 9 26, 27, 28 ver. *Gal.* 2 chap. 4, 5, 6, ver. 1 *Cor.* 4 chap. 19, 20 ver. We conclude that every unprejudic'd Person will see that these Passages which we have cited out of the Author, are according to the Visibility that we hold; and if the Author should be tempted to deny what he has writ, or to explain the Substance of it some other Way, because the Separates join with it; yet what he has written according to sound Doctrines, will stand, let the Author turn which Way he will God's Truths don't stand upon Creatures Stability; and although the Author is so careful in his Preface to let the World know that he don't join with the People called Separates, yet notwithstanding, they crave the Liberty, and by God's Grace assisting, determine to join with him, so far as he joins with and publishes the Truths of the living God.

Having thus considered this Visibility which we hold to be the Door into the Church of Jesus Christ, which is a true Convert or Saint of God, made manifest to the Understanding by visible Fruits of saving Grace; publickly requesting to partake of all the Privileges that Jesus Christ hath purchased for, and given to his Church, in her militant State: So joining this with the Substance of what the Author has written, respecting the Qualifications for full Communion in the visible Church, we agree as one. And although the Author has improved his five Talents, yet inasmuch as one Member has no just Right to say unto another, I have no Need of you, and the Feeble are necessary. . . .

But to return I must entreat the Reader always to keep in your Mind the Distinction between a Person's being actuated in and by the Spirit of God, or by Nature, and human Wisdom. The Apostle *Paul* speaks of two Eyes or Principles. *Rom.* 7 chap. 19, 20 ver. *For the Good that I would, I do not; but the Evil which I would not, that I do. Now if I do that I would not, it is no more I that do it, but Sin that dwelleth in me.* Observe, one Eye here spoken of, is the Eye of Grace, of Divine Light shining into the Soul, that sees in Kind as God seeth because it is a Ray of Divine Light from God and yet the Creature is and will eternally remain a Creature, depending upon the Rays of Divine Light from the Creator. We are all called to be holy, as God is holy; and a Believer has the same kind of Holiness and Light as God has; for the Scriptures testify, that in the Light we see Light. A Soul is no further happy than he is holy, and like his Divine Head. The other Eye is spoken of Nature or the Law of Sin, which is Darkness itself Having only this Eye of Nature, a Person cannot know his own Heart, nor see the Fountain of Corruption there: But under the Improvement of the Eye of Divine Light, he sees the Fountain of Corruption in his Heart, and also what Principles of Grace God has implanted there. 1 *John* 4 chap. 13. *Hereby know we that we dwell in him, and he in us, because he hath given us of his Spirit.* chap. 2. 27 ver. *But the Anointing which ye have received of him, abideth in you: And ye need not that any Man teach you; but, as the same Anointing teacheth you of all Things, and is Truth, and is no Lie.* Observe here, we would always be understood, when we write of the Person's knowing as writing of this new Principle, or Eye, that is implanted in the Soul; for Nature and Grace, Darkness and Light (in strictly speaking), never mix together, but are and will be separate forever. It is in the same Faith and Light that we know ourselves to be Saints; that we know the Apostles and holy Men of God upon sacred Record, to be Saints; and by the same Rule, the Saints know each other now. The Knowledge comes by the Spirit of God witnessing to the Spiritual Fruits manifested in the Saint; which Fruits never was, nor never will be found in an Unbeliever, or the most refined Hypocrite under Heaven. It is pure Charity or Love which comes from God, implanted in the Heart of a Saint, that goeth forth to God's Image, or the new born Principle in another; and this Love or Charity cannot be deceived: God never giveth his Spirit to witness to a Falshood or Lie; and tho' a Saint under the Influence of Nature, or the old Eye, may imagine he is the Image of God in this or the other Person, and thinks he has Charity for them; here he may be deceived an Hundred Times, and yet this does not destroy the Certainty of his Knowledge, when under the Divine Influence of that new Eye, or the Spirit of God witnessing to its own Fruits. . . . [The] Saints have the same Spirit of God, to lead, instruct, and give them Knowledge now, as the Apostles and Disciples of old had. God is a Sovereign, as to Dispensing the Measures of his Gifts and Grace. But the same Holy Ghost, is the Gift of God to every Saint, 'till Christ come the second time, in the Glory of his Father, and of the Holy Angels. 15 ver. *Beware of false Prophets which come to you in Sheep's Clothing, but inwardly they are ravening Wolves.* First observe the Caution Christ giveth, and what it implieth, *Beware of false Prophets;* which plainly implieth, that they may be known: For it casts reflections upon a wise God, to suppose he should charge us to beware of false Prophets, and at the same Time we should have no Way to come at the Knowledge of them: But Christ has plainly told us, *That by their Fruits we shall know them;* which Fruits we shall search after. But first observe their Appearance, namely, *which come to you in Sheep's Clothing:* As much as if Christ had said, They will come to you in their external Profession, just like the true Ministers of Christ, assenting to the same Doctrines in general, and externally much alike. . . .

We shall endeavour to write something of the Fruits that these two Trees bear: First, the corrupt Tree, as it represents a false Teacher or Wolf, in order to hide their Fruits; they come in Sheep's Clothing (as has been described), with a Pretence of much Love and Concern for Souls, and perhaps he and a Society agree pretty well, they generally like his Preaching, and all Points are settled but one and that is his Maintainance, Settlement, and Salary; the Society propose a Sum, but it does not suit his Covetousness and Pride, for doubtless he has layed out in his Mind to live in such Grandeur, Plenty, and Honour, therefore he refuses the Offer; and whilst the Society is a Consulting to come up to the Price that will suit him, behold there is a bigger Flock with a larger Fleece presents; and now the Heart or inward Fruits appear by his Practice (when at the same Time outwardly he is very moral, and pleads Duty, to provide well for his Family), for this ravening Wolf will soon strike a Bargain, and the Matter quickly settled; and likely no other Reason can be given for his leaving the first Flock, only because the second offered more Money. Now observe that a little more Money can turn the Concern of this Hireling from one Flock to another as quick as the Prospect of increasing his Goods presents; and many Times some of these false Teachers are so crafty, that they will get their Salary stated upon Silver, at so much per Ounce, so that if Providence send Famine and Scarcity, or our common Currency run never so low they will take Care of one, and the poor intangled Flock may shift as they can: And after they have been some Time settled, they will begin to complain; not of the Security of the Congregation, and his Unfruitfulness in his Labours, and the Want of the Spirit of God to assist him in dispensing the Word; No; But the Times are hard, Money fall very fast. And instead of getting the Church together once for solemn Fasting and Prayer, for the Out-pourings of God's Spirit, that Sinners may be converted, and that the Saints quickened, and built up in the most Holy Faith, they will have the Society together thrice to consult about more Salary. . . .

Now if you follow them further, you will find they visit scarce any but the Rich and Honourable of the Flock; and could you hear their Conversation, you would hear them discourse about the World; or if upon Religion, it would be in generals, and what this and that Author has writ upon this and the other Point, and not one Word about what God has writ by his Holy Spirit upon their Hearts. Now the Poor of the Flock are generally neglected 'till a sick Bed, and then they must be sent for to pray over the Sick, that perhaps is launching forth into a vast and boundless Eternity, and they will parrot over a Prayer in such a cold Manner, as 'tho the Soul was little worth. But let us follow them into their Studies, and there instead of strong Cries by Prayer in Faith to Jesus Christ, that can loose the Seals, and open the Book, and unfold the Misteries of the Gospel to their Understanding, and of searching the Scriptures directly; we say, instead of this (and much more that might be writ), you would find them likely scarce breathe out a cold dead Form, and at the same time perhaps their Mind is upon this and that Author that they Purpose to study and write their Discourse out of, and by their human Wisdom, they put their sermons into a connect Form, to smooth, and in such general Terms, that no Conscience is awakened, or Saints quickened, for God does not own such legal Improvements. And if it is a Custom to have a Lecture once in a Month or two, they will attend it, and that is all. Once more, follow them into the Pulpit, and there you may hear the same Prayer from Sabbath to Sabbath, with scarce any Alteration; a dead lifeless Form (which God's righteous Soul abhoreth): And if you chance to look upon the Minister, you will possibly see his Eyes roving around the Meeting House, if not follow Persons from the Door into their Seats: And when they come to preach, they preach in a legal old Covenant Spirit, which bears the Fruits that we know them by. The Saints of God know it to be a Stranger's Voice, which they will not follow. . . .

Now it has been Manifest to all, that a few Years ago, in the Year 1741–2 or 3, there was two Sorts of Ministers, of the Learned among us; one sort came to us with the Message of the Lord of Hosts, and was as a Flame of Fire; whose Ministry was Instrumental, under God's Blessing, for the awakening, convicting, and converting Sinners: And also of rouzing up the few slumbering Saints that there was in the Land, to trim their Lamps, and be ready for their Lord's coming, *&c.* The other sort was a great Number of Wolves, as we have Reason to fear, that come in Sheep's Cloathing, *Matt.* 7 chap. 15 and as the Scriptures tell us, run, and God has not sent them, and they steal the Word from their Neighbor (or get their Sermons out of other Men's Works,) and say, Thus saith the Lord, and the Lord hath not sent them, and they shall not Profit the People, *Jer.* 23 chap. 30, 31, 32. These two sorts of Ministers was distinguished by one sort being called the *New-Lights*, and the other sort the *Old-Lights.* The first sort was soon shut out of the other's Pulpits and Societies; only as the Grace of God constrained some of them for a short Time, to break over Society Lines; and at this Time, there was manifestly two Companies of them; the Christian Ministers would flock to-gether to their own Company with the Saints, like the Disci-ples of old; and the other sort would gather together in their own Company, to consult how to insnare, and bring back, or stop those Messengers of the Lord of Hosts; and the Lord in his Sovereignty, for wise and holy Ends, has permitted the Thing: And doubtless the first Stroke that was given, was by a Number of *Balaams* that passed for New-Lights or Christians. They had the Spirit for a while, but no Union to Christ by a living Faith; and when their Salaries and Honours was likely to go for the Truth, behold then they cried a Confederacy, with them that God said there should be no Confederacy; and also returned to them to whom God said they should not return. *Isa.* 8 chap. 12. *Say ye not, A Confederacy to All them whom this People shall say, A Confederacy; neither fear ye* *their Fear, nor be afraid. Jer.* 15 chap. 19. *Let them return into thee, but return thee not unto them.* So right against the Word of God, these Ministers joined in with the false Teachers; so that it was properly by the Tail of the Dragon that these Christian Ministers was caught, and cast down, and their Testimony slain. . . .

If that Beast which hath two Horns like a Lamb, and speaks as a Dragon, has no rule in this Land, we enquire then, Whence it is that the Saints of God have been so imprisoned of late Years, who did their fellow Men no wrong, nor was they guilty of the Breach of any moral Precept that is to be punished by Man; but on the contrary, endeavouring in the Fear of God, and Order of the Gospel, to seek and promote the best Peace, Good, and Happiness of their fellow Men? Some have been haled before Rulers, and to Prison, for nothing else but preaching the Gospel of Jesus Christ. The very Face of their Complaints, or Charge laid against them was nothing more criminal than this, that they had preached the Gospel so and so, which was contrary to the Laws of this Colony. And now *O New-England! Connecticut! Connecticut!* for the Lord's Sake, consider what Laws are them that confront an infinite God, and are set in Array against the Lion of the Tribe of *Judah,* out of whose Mouth proceedth a two-edged Sword; for God is jealous for *Zion* with great Jealousy (yea, he is), jealous for her with great Fury. . . .

Again, Where does the Power come from, that has put the Saints of God in Prison, because they have endeavoured to obey God in that great Duty of Exhortation? Heb. 3 chap. 13. 8. chap. 10, 24, 25. *And let us consider one another to provoke unto Love, and to good Works. Not forsaking the Assembling of ourselves together, as the Manner of Some is, but exhorting one another.* And further, What Power is that which hath imprisoned the Saints for not attending and supporting that Worship which they know by God's Word and Spirit, is not according to Divine Appointment, but contrary to the plain Letter of the Word of God? Again, What Power is that which hath once and again turned out and rejected solid, substantial Men (that consult the best good of the Colony), from the General Court, who have been lawfully chosen according to our Charter, when nothing in Equity could be brought against them, only they stood up for and acknowledged the Work of God in the Land (which every Ruler ought to do, and heartily embrace it too), or they were called *New-Lights* or *Separates;* when at the same Time, Mockers and Scoffers at the Work, Ways, and Power of God, have been rather indulged by the same Court? And at such a Practice as this, the true Ministers of Christ have great Reason to cry out and say, *Be astonished, O ye Heavens, at this, and be terribly afraid* (O Connecticut!) *for the Day of thy Visitation cometh. . . .*

Once more, we enquire whether or no that antient Law Book, called the Bible, is not too, too much laid aside and not duly consulted by them that are the Law-makers and by them also that set to judge in the Courts of Common Pleas, as of civil Justice and Equity between Man and Man? And whence is it that there are such Volumes of Men's crafty Wisdom and human Tradition brought into the Courts of civil Justice, that when an honest Man comes to have Justice done him in the Court, that unless he comes in such a critical Shape and Form, marked out by Men's Traditions, the poor Man is non-suited, and his Case drops through, or he that has done his Neighbor wrong, gets his Case, and the Man brought under greater Charge, instead of being righted in his honest Case; and after great Charge, he brings his Action so as it will suit the Scheme, and it enters upon Tryal; and yet it is almost three to one but he loses his Case at last, by Reason of some Craft or another, especially by them Time-Wasters the Lawyers, who many times by their subtilty, make the Case more obscure and dark, by their crafty pleading, than it was before they said a Word;

and so by this Means, with other Things, wrong Judgment may proceed, and the innocent Person further oppressed, and the wicked Oppressors goes free for the Present, 'till an impartial Court of eternal Equity and Righteousness shall set, where a true Witness shall be given, and a righteous Plea made, and perfect decisive Judgment proceed, to set all Things right for one Eternity. Hab. 1 chap. 4. *Therefore the Law is slacked, and Judgment doth never go forth; for the Wicked doth compass about the Righteous, therefore wrong Judgment proceedth.* Gen. 18 chap. 25. *Shall not the Judge of all the Earth do right?* Eccles. 12 chap. 14. *For God shall bring every Work into Judgment, with every secret Thing, whether it be Good or whether it be Evil.* Read *Micah,* 3 chap. & chap. 7, 2, 3, 4.

Again, since the great Sin-hating God has appointed Rulers to be the Ministers of God for Good to them that fear his great Name, and also to be a Terror to them that do Evil. *Rom.* 13 chap. 3, 4. Therefore we enquire further, that we may the better know what we have to mourn for before God, and what we must look for, if speedy Repentance prevent not. First, How comes it to pass, that reveling and banqueting, fiddling and dancing, wicked, prophane, and filthy Conversation is so much connived at, and no more suppressed by the Rulers of this Land? And how have these wicked Practices been indulged by some in publick Office, when at the same Time the Saints of the most high God have been frowned upon by the same Rulers, and punished for nothing else, but because they assembled together to worship the living God? And why is it that so much Pains have been taken in some places, to keep out the everlasting Gospel of Jesus Christ, and prevent the Saints of God meeting together for to worship God, whilst at the same Time very little Pains, if any, in a proper Manner has been taken to prevent that dreadful destructive Practice, both to Body and Soul, viz. of Tavern-hunting, drinking to Excess, and Drunkeness; Town dwellers

sitting whole Evenings tippling at the Tavern, sporting themselves over the everlasting Flames of an eternal Hell, and at
some Times cursing and swearing, taking God's Name in vain,
talking in such awful Language which is enough to make a
Person's Flesh crawl upon his Bones, that has any solid
Thoughts of a future Judgment. . . .

Now how many there are in *New-England,* of Ministers, and
the common Sort of People, whose Conversation and Practice
make manifest, that they are in the same wicked envious Spirit
that *Zedekiah* was in (and cannot bear that the Spirit of God
should leave the great and learned Ministers, and rest upon,
and open the Scriptures to the poor ignorant Laymen, enabling
them to preach the Gospel) we shall leave the Reader to judge
from the Fruits made visible. So also, there are many that have
the same Language as they had in *Jeremiah*'s Time, who are
trying all Ways possible to set up the Priest and the Ruler, the
Great and Learned, even against the Sovereignty of God.
These Persons talk may be read in *Jer.* 18 chap. 18. *Then said
they, Come, and let us devise Devices against* Jeremiah; *for
the Law shall not perish from the Priest, nor Counsel from the
Wise, nor the Word from the Prophet; come and let us smite
him with the Tongue, and let us not give Heed to any of his
Words.* Thus in the same Line, is the Talk of many in this Day,
saying "Come, and let us devise Devices against these crazy,
deluded Separates; come and let us smite them with the
Tongue: Report say they, and we will report it, chap. 20 10
ver. And let us not give Heed to any of their Words; they
think to make us believe that they understand the Scriptures,
and that God is doing a great Work in the Land, and amongst
them, for our good and learned Ministers, that have all their
Days searched the Scriptures, say, It is nothing but Delusions;
and what do you think, that our Ministers do not understand
the Law or Work of God? and do not our wise Men understand Counsel, and knew how to make good and wholesome

Laws, to prevent such Disorders as the Separates make? and is not the Word of God with our great and good Men? Etc." This and the like, is the horrid Talk of ignorant idolatrous Persons; and their false Refuge will quickly fail them. . . .

As to our separating from the Churches. Observe when a single Person is fully satisfied from the Word and Spirit of God, that it is his Duty to leave a Church, by Reason that it is gone off from the Gospel Foundation, and is so corrupt, that Christ's kingly Power and Rule is denyed, then that Person has no Right to wait for others to be brought, to see Eye to Eye with him, in order for him to practice what he sees and believes. True it is, that he ought to use proper Means, agreeable to the Mind of Christ, to shew the Church where they are wrong (if they will allow it) and leave the Event with God; and obey God singly for himself, in practicing according to the Divine Teachings of his Holy Spirit; and not neglect his own Duty, 'till there are a sufficient Number to come out as a Body, and set up a Church in Gospel Order: For one Christian ought not to make another practice a Foundation for himself to practise upon. That Person that meets in any Place whatever, to worship God, because some godly Person meets in the same Place, and so takes that to be right; *mark:* That Person's Foundation of Action, is upon the Sand; and yet are there not Multitudes, whose Consciences tell them, their Foundation is no better? Reader, let thy Conscience speak as in the Sight of an omniscient God. Would you not join to worship God, and attend the Gospel Institutions, with the People of God, who have left the common Churches in the Land, provided some godly Men you esteem, or Christian-learned Minister joined with them, or the Separate Part were the biggest or ruling Part in the Land? If so, depend upon it, that the Foundation of your Practice is false, and will surely fail you.

Observe. That Person that has not his Foundation of Faith and Practice directly and intirely in and from the Word and

Spirit of God, as much as if there was not another human Creature upon Earth, will assuredly suffer Loss sooner or later; for the Day is at hand, that will burn and consume all such Foundations, as Stubble is consumed before devouring Flames, 1 *Cor.* 3. 13. *Every Man's Work shall be made manifest. For the Day shall declare it, because it shall be revealed by Fire; and the Fire shall try every Man's Work, of what sort it is.* Thus if we rightly consider the Nature of Practice in Religion, on Obedience to God, we shall see an absolute Necessity for every Person to act singly, as in the Sight of God only; and this is the Way, under God, to bring the Saints all to worship God sociably, and yet have no Dependance one upon another. . . .

Altho' there be Divisions and Contentions amongst us, which to our Shame we would confess; yet it no ways followeth, that the Work we are engag'd in, is not the Work of God; nor doth it prove, that God's special Presence is with us from time to time. To take the Sins and Infirmities of the Saints for a Rule, to know whether God is amongst them with his gracious Presence, is a very wrong Way of Tryal; and this Objection stands as against the Work of God in all Ages of the Church, as it doth against us in God's present Work. . . . These Scriptures shew, that the most eminent Saints have been divided; and *Paul's* Epistles to the Churches, shew that there were Contentions often amongst them; and yet notwithstanding God did a great Work amongst them in that Day: so also, God is doing a great Work amongst us in this Land, at this Day, and we have great Reason to be humbled before God and Man, that there is such Contention, Sin, and Infirmity amongst us; yet the Discord that is amongst us, is no Proof that God is not carrying on a great Work, any more than *Luther,* and *Calvin's* contending, did prove that God was not carrying on a great Work in their Day.

As to the false Religion and Power that is objected against, we do not know but such as make the Objection, call the real Spirit and Power of God, a false Religion. But that there has been a false Operation and Power amongst us at times, we do readily own. We will endeavour to give some Distinction between the false Operation and the true. Here first; the false Operation or Power, usually puffs the Person up, who is under the Influence of the same; and if he goeth to reprove others, he goeth in an harsh, hard Spirit, which is as cruel as the Grave; and instead of leaving a Conviction in the Person's Conscience, of his Sin, it rather raiseth the like hard Spirit in the Person reproved. But here we must observe, that a Person under the genuine Influence of the Holy Spirit, in Love reproving another, is many times opposed, even when it strikes the Person's Conscience that is reproved. But then he that reproves in Love, usually hath Peace and Sweetness in his Soul; and he that is under the false Religion, has Hardness and Dryness in his Soul. Again. A Person under this false Frame, may have great Power in Exhortation (or whatever Improvement) and speak with great Fluency of Words, and yet it Affects no body in a right Kind. The Hearers that have not been brought to distinguish this false Power from the true Power of God, commonly under such Improvement, set in a Sort of careless Condition, or else they are wondering what the Matter is they cannot feel something of the Power upon their Hearts. Now all that are intangled with such a false Religion will have Fellowship with such as improve in it, and their Souls at the same Time be as dry as a Husk. When any of the Saints which are now in the standing Churches, have been at such a Meeting, they find nothing but an empty Sound, and so are prone to think that the Separates Religion is all like that, and cry out, 'Delusions, a false Religion, Etc.' Now the Person that exhorts or preaches under the influence of this false Religion, is all the Time destitute of any true Brokenness of Heart; and the Reason is, because there is no Charity or true Love ruling in his

Heart; therefore all such Improvements are, as *Paul* expresses it in the 1 *Cor.* 13. 1, 2. This false Religion may be compar'd to the barren Fig Tree which Christ came to, and found nothing on but Leaves. So this Religion makes a flourishing shew of Power and Freedom of Speech, as tho' it did bear Fruit; but upon Search, there is no Figs or true Love to be found, and hungry Souls may starve for all they can get in such Improvements, &c. Observe here; Persons are usually caught in this false Religion, by indulging Pride, when they are under Barrenness, and no Religious Frame, and are a going to improve in Public, the Pride of their Heart is not willing that they should appear just such Creatures as they are, empty, barren, nothing Creatures; therefore the Persons are under a Temptation to act in a Frame and Power which is not of God, &c. The Saints want more Honesty and Uprightness of Heart before God and Man, that when they are called to any Improvement, they may appear just as they be; if they are under Barrenness and Desertion, then honestly to confess it, and not try to work a Frame and Power, which is not in pure Love and Solemnity. Indeed, Divine Light begins to shine so clear in the Understanding of some Saints, that it is very difficult for any Person to cheat them with a Shew of Religion, as if they had the Religion of Christ, when they have it not. . . .

And in our dispensing the Word, the Truths of the Gospel are opened to our Understandings, and fall with Weight upon our Hearts, and is sweeter than the Honey and the Honeycomb; and as we are delivering it out, it goeth from our Hearts, and is carried by God's Spirit to the Hearts of the Hearers; and usually at such a Time, the Saints are corrected, instructed, and blessedly quickened, and the Arrows of Convictions have been fastened on Sinners Hearts, as a Nail in a sure Place, from which they could not get Relief, only by having the Virtues of Christ's Blood savingly applyed to their Souls: And at such Times, the Peace and Love of God has flow'd among the Saints like a living Stream, whereby their Hearts have been knit together in fervent Love or Charity, which covers a Multitude of Sins, 1 *Pet.* 4. 8. Again. At other Times, when we have been called to preach, we have been exceedingly press'd down with Concern for the Cause and Honour of God, and the Good of Souls, and have seen how God's dreadful Name would be dishonour'd and his Cause wounded, if we should run in our own Name; and at such a Time, we have been stript from all human Schemes, and brought to stand as in the Presence of the flaming Eye of God, and all the Powers and Faculties of our Souls have been siez'd with Reverence and awe of God's Greatness. We have had some sight also of the Worth of them Souls with whom we have been about to treat, not knowing but at the next Meeting, we should have, with the whole Assembly be before the great white Throne, with the righteous Judge of Quick and Dead; at which Time there has been a great Tenderness upon our Spirits, lest we or some others should do something which would grieve God's Holy Spirit. We have also a strong Thirst in our Minds, that we might be enabled to deliver the whole Counsels of God, and so quit our Garments of the Blood of them that perish. . . .

But the Work that the same Spirit of God is carrying on among the Separates, is to enlighten their Understanding, and to lead them into a more sound and thorough Understanding of the true Doctrines and Practices of the Gospel, and in leading them to a more clear and right Understanding of the Corruptions and Idols of their Hearts, and in bringing them off from a traditional and formal Worship, teaching them to worship God in Spirit and in Truth. Now we have good Reason to think, that *Mr. Brainerd* was ignorant that the Lord was carrying on such a Work among us, and likely he drank in a Conceit, that there was nothing but a heated Zeal, and false Religion among us, *&c.* Therefore the Reader ought to weigh these Things carefully, in a candid Mind, and not make up a

Judgment, before he knows where God's Spirit is at work, and what the Work is that it is doing. Again. I shall make some Observations from what *Mr. Edwards* has wrote . . . and no doubt his Aim was at the Separates; and when I read it, my very Soul trembled, and was in Pain for poor deluded formal Hypocrites, and the dear Saints of God, that are in woful Captivity, by Men's Inventions, for in that Page, there is no proper Distinction made between Truth and Error; and the natural Tendency of such Writing, to Prejudice the poor ignorant Persons against the Power of God, and all the powerful Appearances of the Goings of our God and King in his Sanctuary, *Psa.* 63. 2. *To see thy Power and thy Glory, so as I have seen thee in the Sanctuary.* And also to seal down poor formal deluded Hypocrites in Hundreds, for Damnation: May God in Mercy prevent it. Again. What is there writ, is exceedingly likely to perplex and intangle the Saints of God, and wound some who may be longing and thirsting to see God's Power and Glory again; and also to harden others who have got a Prejudice against the Power of God, and thereby to keep them still under that cruel Spirit, *&c.* Now had *Mr. Edwards* applyed what he has writ upon the top of the next Page, to himself, and others that oppose the Separates, he would have no doubt have hit the right Nail in the Head (as we used to say). He has writ thus: 'Or 'tis like the Conduct of some unskilful rash Person, who finding himself deceived by some of the Wares he had bought at that Shop, should at once conclude that all he saw there, was of no Value, and pursuant to such a Conclusion, when afterwards he has true Gold and Diamonds offered him, enough to inrich him, and enable him to live like a Prince all his Days, he should throw it all into the Sea, *&c.*' Now if this is not the very Case to a Tittle, of those that oppose the Separates, I think I am greatly mistaken indeed: For observe; because there has sometimes been among the Separates, a false Power and Zeal, Hay, Wood, and Stubble (which

God is in Mercy, a consuming and purging out of our Hearts and Practices); therefore *Mr. Edwards* and others, are rashly refusing the true Gold, or Religion, which is from the Divine Influence of the Spirit of all Grace, which if they would heartily receive, would enable them to live more like the Priests of the most high God (1 *Pet.* 2 chap. 9) and remove away that Barrenness, and hard Temper of Mind, which we abundantly fear they are chiefly under. But not to inlarge: I readily grant, that there is such a Thing as Satan's bringing Scripture to Persons Minds, upon which, they may be transported, and filled with Joy, and they may have sudden Impulses also, and Satan may transform himself into an Angel of Light, and delude Persons; but then I would observe, that the Scripture that Satan brings, does not come with any renewing, instructing, or sanctifying Influence upon the Heart, neither is a Person, by such sudden Impulses upon the Mind, brought to see the Divinity and Connection of the Scriptures: But when the Spirit of God brings or applies Scriptures to a Person, these Things are wrought more or less upon the Heart; so also the Joy that is raised from vain Imaginations, or Sparks of a Person's own kindling, such Joy has no Substance in it, nor does it yield any solid Comfort; and when such Joys go off a Person, there is no more Tenderness nor Watchfulness wrought in the Person's Mind, of sinning against an holy God; which the true Believer has when his Joys go off. Again. The sudden Impulses upon the Mind, that come from a false Spirit, serve to lead a Person away from God, and not to cleave to the Scriptures, but to puff them up with Pride, and lead them out of the Pathway of Duty; but the sudden, immediate Influences of the Spirit of God, always more or less, leads the Heart towards God, and seizes the Mind with Reverence, and the Fear of God, and inclines the Person to search, that he might know the Mind and Will of God in the Path-way of Duty; and there is a tender Care begotten in the Mind, lest he should go contrary to the Will of God: These sudden Influences that are from God's Spirit, never lead a Person contrary to the Scriptures. . . .

But Mr. *Edwards* and others, have mustered up a Number of Errors, and made a Scarecrow of them, by not making proper Distinctions, so that tender Lambs of Christ's Flock are scared from the Gospel Fold, and are almost worried out of all the powerful Influences and Operations of the Spirit of God; and in his Application of these Errors, saith, 'It is the Separates Religion.' So also in his trying to cut off our Religion, he cuts across the Spirit of God in its divine Teaching, and sealing Influences, and, as it were, takes away the Key of Knowledge, and shuts up the Way to Heaven, and will neither enter in himself (for the present) nor suffer them that have a Mind to enter, to go in; and therefore makes sad the Hearts of the Righteous, and strengthens the Hands of the Wicked: And will the Lord in Mercy look upon him, and forgive him this great Sin.

The Reader may remember, if he has read Mr. *Brainerd's* Life, that Mr. *Edwards* improves Mr. *Brainerd's* Experiences and Religion, in order to shew that the Separates Experiences, is Delusions, and their Practice, Erroneous; and he has not writ one Word, as I remember, but what the learned Ministers in the Land, and their Congregations hold with, and experience the same Religion that Mr. *Brainerd* had, and the Separates are the only Persons that are deluded, and out of the Way, in the Land: Therefore this brings me to make a brief Inquiry, who it is that holds to and professes that Religion, and them Influences, or Experiences, and Practice, that Mr. *Brainerd* had from time to time: And here first; Did not Mr. *Brainerd* from time to time, experience and express a great Sense of his own Nothingness, and great Vileness, and his intire Dependance upon God, for Help to assist him in the Discharge of all Duties that lay before him? Now is this the Experiences of the learned Ministers, and their Churches in general in the Land; or is it not rather the daily Experience of the Saints in the Separates?

So I conclude; earnestly praying, that God would give Mr. *Edwards* to see wherein he has opposed and stood against God's Work of late in the Land; and that he might have a Pardon sealed to his Soul, and that God would once more make his Face as Flint and his Brow as Brass, against the Enemies of God and his Church: And that he might be made as a Flame of Fire, in dispensing the everlasting Gospel. Amen.

41 · John Bass

(fl. 1740-1751)

NARRATIVE OF AN

UNHAPPY CONTENTION

———

The impact of the Awakening was most distinctly felt neither in separations nor even in great debates over ecclesiastical principles but in the affairs of every particular church. Each congregation was eventually forced to apply the lessons of the revival in its choice of a minister—or, as at Northampton, in his removal. The decision was seldom made calmly, and almost never without raising questions about the power structure of both church and community. What was the authority of the clergy, of councils and synods, and of the laity, and were the "keys" given to the whole congregation or only to the "saints"? In New England the answers were not revealed for nearly a century, and the result was generally a Unitarian secession. From the beginning the source of contention was the preference, by a majority or minority of a church, for a minister

———

John Bass, *A True Narrative of an Unhappy Contention in The Church of Ashford* [Connecticut] . . . (Boston, 1751), pp. 3–7, 22–27.

of one of the two doctrinal persuasions emerging from the Awakening—or, perhaps more accurately, for a "rational" or an "evangelical" style of preaching. Which was the more popular is suggested by the fact that Edwards was nearly unique as a Calvinist who was dismissed in the period after the Awakening. The more typical case was that of John Bass, whose account of his removal provides a rigid glimpse into both the communal turmoil of these years and "reason's" response to the challenge of an evangelically-disposed majority.

The Controversy which has for some Months subsisted between the aggrieved Brethren of the Church of Christ in *Ashford*, and my self, together with the Dissolution of my pastoral Relation to Them, being noised abroad in the Land, has drawn on Us the Censure of Multitudes, who before this were great Strangers to Us, and many of whom remain so still, I make no doubt, notwithstanding all they have heard. And as Mankind are generally fond of News, and of prying into the State of Others, however willingly ignorant many are of Themselves, by sending abroad the following Lines I may hope to gratify their Curiosity a little, and to prevent their commending or blaming us at Random. I design not to injure or offend any Body; No, the most I have in View, is to tell some of my Fellow-Mortals the true State of the Case; but if after this, when I have wronged no Body, I am maligned and reviled as I have been, I matter it not as to any Hurt such snarling Bigots can do me. I am not fond of making my self known in this manner; but should have been glad to have enjoyed my former Obscurity, could it have been consistent with a good Conscience; but this could not be: I am forced abroad, and made a

gazing Stock to the World, and therefore I think I may claim
the Liberty to tell my own Story, though I do it poorly.

When I was settled in the Ministry at *Ashford*, which was in
the Year 1743, I was, and professed my self to be, of the
Calvinian Class; and as such I remained for several Years; yet
all that Time suspected by some of my very zealous and critical Hearers; and was accordingly harassed by them, charged
with *Arminianism* and what not, accused before Counsels and
pelted with Insults: Yet so long as I remained Orthodox I stood
my Ground, and always came off with Victory. But, alas! alas!
when this failed, though my Adversaries will not say I wanted
any Thing else, I fell.—*Calvinistic* Principles I then found to
be at this Day a Clergy-man's main Defence; the best he can
hit upon to provide him Food and Raiment, and to fix him in
the good Graces of the Populace: Interest set this Way.
Nevertheless so imprudent was I, that to please my Conscience, I must examine anew the Foundation of my Faith, the
Truth of those Principles, I had professed and preached for
Years before. And the Effect of this was, I found my self
obliged to recant some former Sentiments; and, as you will see
by and by, to come into a new and different Scheme, or Set of
Notions[1]—Then I must leave out of my public Performances
those Notions which were peculiar to *Calvinism;* which being
discovered by some of my eagle-eyed People, their Jealousy
revived and grew Stronger than ever; and though for a Time
this was but whispered among them, at length it broke out in a
flaming Contention, which has unhappily issued in such a
Breach, not only betwixt the greater Part of the People and my
self; but also betwixt the People themselves, as 'tis highly
probable will never be healed.

'Twas some Time in *December* last, that I entertained my

---

[1] These I did not in my Sermons publish to my People; because I thought
they could not bear them as yet.

People with a publick Discourse from those Words of St. *Paul*, in 1 Thes. 5. 21. *Prove all Things, hold fast that which is good.* At which Discourse, though I medled with no controversial Point, yet as I advised them to a careful, unprejudiced Enquiry after the Will of GOD as revealed in the BIBLE, and not to content themselves with a Religion at Second-Hand: They were some of them extreamly displeased, supposing (I conclude) such Advice had on favourable Aspect upon their particular Notions.—Now it was, that some were too uneasy to sit still any longer; and as the Administration of the Supper was to be on the next Sabbath, something they thought must be immediately done—They itched, it seemed, to have me in their Clutches; but how to attack me they were at a loss.—I had not, as yet, spoke out my Sentiments upon the controverted Points hereafter mentioned, except to a Friend in the Corner: But as two Brethren of the Church of CHRIST, who were known to be my Friends had, it was resolved to fall upon them in the first Place.—Being strongly importuned by some of the Dissatisfied, I went with them to converse with those two Brethren; and though I did not then, as I remember, declare my own Sentiments upon the Points in Dispute, but, to excite them to mutual Charity and Forbearance, endeavoured to let them see, that much could be said on both Sides: They apparently became more confirmed in their Suspicion of me than before; and to such a surprising Length did some carry their groundless Resentment, that on the next Lord's-Day they withdrew from the Ordinance of the Supper, thereby proclaiming abroad their Discontent; which spread among the People, as they became acquainted with the Grounds of it. There was presently a general Commotion among them; and within a few Days after, a Detachment from the Aggrieved came to my House, and requested a Church-Meeting. My Answer was, That as the People were generally in a Ruffle, 'twas, in my Opinion, best to defer calling them together, till they were cooler and so fitter for Action. This was not at all pleasing to them; and all I could say was to little Effect: For on the 10th Day of *January* 1750,1 I received the following Letter from the Aggrieved.—

Rev'd Sɪʀ,

These are to let you know, that we the Subscribers think you cannot but be sensible, that there is great Uneasiness among us on account of some Principles that you and some others hold, as we think, which appear to us very dangerous: We therefore humbly desire that you would forthwith warn a Church-Meeting to look into the Affair; if not, you will put us under a necessity of taking some other Course.

		Nathanael Eaton
Theophilus Clark	Benjamin Walker	²Zechariah Bicknell
Jonathan Baker	James Bicknell	Jacob Dana
William Chub	William Watkins	Jedediah Dana

In pursuance of which Request, I appointed a Church-Meeting to be on the 23d of the same Month; When the Church met, and several Brethren with my self, made the following Declaration in Writing to the Church,—

We the Subscribers being desirous to maintain Peace and Concord in the Church of Christ, and always ready to con-tribute, according to our Power, towards the Removing of such Difficulties as arise among us,

Do now say,

1. That We do really believe the Scriptures both of the Old and New-Testament to contain the Truth of Gᴏᴅ—And that therein are contained all that Gᴏᴅ requires of Men to believe and do in order to their enjoying his Favour in this World and that to come.

2. As we apprehend our Church-Covenant to be agreable to the Scriptures of Truth, we yet adhere to it, and to every Article of it.

---

² The gentleman with this mark is since dead.

3. We esteem this to be a true Church of CHRIST, purchased by his own Blood, and are really desirous of continuing in the Communion of it.

4. We are sensible there be different Sentiments among us about the Meaning of some Scripture-Passages, and different Sentiments we are apt to think there always will be among Men, while in the present State of Frailty and Imperfection.

5. As we claim the Liberty of judging for our selves in Matters of Religion, so we are ready to grant the same Liberty to every Member in this Church, and to every Man in the World; and while we impose not upon any one, we hope none will be so unchristian-like as to impose upon us.

6. We stand ready to converse freely with this Church and every Member of it, upon any Article of Religion whatsoever; and we hope every one in this Church is open to Conviction, and ready to receive Truth upon real Evidence, as we Trust we are our selves.—

> *Edward Tiffany*   *Thaddeus Watkins*   *John Bass*, Pastor
> *Timothy Eastman*   *John Pitts*
> *Nathaniel Spring*   *John Parry*.

All this was not, as I could find, in the least Satisfactory: 'Twas hissed at—And the following accurate Draught was brought upon the Carpet, and read.

Rev'd Sir,

These are to let you know the Grounds of our Uneasiness. In the first Place, *We think you are gone from what you profest to the Council that ordained you in the Matter of* Original Sin: *You then profest to believe, That it was not only our Infelicity, but our Sin, that we fell in* Adam; *and now you seem to hold only the Depravity and deny the Guilt; it appears so to us by your Preaching, Praying and Conversing;* 1st, *In your Preaching you neglect to preach up the Doctrine of* Original Sin, *and the Necessity of the* New-Birth *as we find recorded in* John 3d, *where are* CHRIST's *own Words; and you seem to lay the chief*

Stress of our Salvation on our moral Obedience (we hold Obedience Necessary, as the Fruit and Effect of Faith; but in the Matter of our Justification to have no Part.) 2dly, You don't preach up the Doctrine of Election, *as it is recorded in* Romans 11. 5, 6. Eph. 1. 3, 4, 5. *and Multitudes of other Texts, too many here to be recited, that plainly point out Personal absolute Eternal Election; also the Doctrine of Particular Redemption, and the Doctrine of Perseverance; which are Doctrines plainly set forth in the Word of God, and necessary to be preached by every Minister of Christ, as fundamental Articles of the Christian* Religion: *In which we say you are very defective. Again, When some signify'd their Uneasiness with one or two of the Brethren for denying the above said Points, you seem to justify them, by preaching from* Acts 5 Ch. 38 & 39 Ver. *Also a further Confirmation of your holding these same Principle is, When you baptize Children you don't so much as mention one Word of the Child's being Guilty of Sin, or of Christ's Blood being applied to the mystical Washing from Sin, or any other Words that represent the Child being guilty of Original Sin. Again we say, that in your Conversation you discover the same Principles while you approve of and plead for Mr.* Taylor's *Book,*[3] *that so plumply denies the Doctrine of Original Sin. Now from all these Things we think neither your Preaching nor your Principles are good*

		James Bicknell
Joseph Snow	Nathaniel Eaton	William Watkins
Samuel Snow	Theophilus Clark	Jacob Dana
Benjamin Snow	James Hall	Jedediah Dana

With the abovesaid Letter, this sifting Question was directed to me by one of those Subscribers; *Sir, Don't you think that a Child brings Sin enough into the World with it to damn it*

[3] John Taylor, *The Scripture-Doctrine of Original Sin Proposed to Free and Candid Examination* (London, 1738). [Ed.]

forever? And being determined to deal fairly, I answered in the Negative.—This Answer, with a little frank Conversation of the like Tenor, gave the Aggrieved as much Advantage against me, as they seemed to wish for; and the main Thing insisted on by them afterwards, was the Calling of a Council to hear and determine these Difficulties. And all I could obtain was to have the Meeting adjourned to the 6th of the next Month; when the Church met, and I attempted to shew from my Sermons, that my Preaching upon sundry Points of Doctrine, (concerning which I was charged with Error and Deficiency) was not contrary to the sacred Scriptures, and consequently no ways dangerous: But some of the Church expressing their Dislike at it, and a strong Desire of having the Matters of their Grievance laid before a Council: The following Questions were put to the Church.

1. Whether the Church would send for a Number of Ministers with Delegates from their respective Churches, to come and give Us Advice under our present Difficulties.

Voted in the Affirmative.

. . . [The] Council (having before tried the Mind of the Church respecting my being dismissed from them, and heard and over-ruled a Plea in Bar made by sundry Brethren of said Church) . . . drew up the following decisive Result. . . .

This Council having been called here by the Moderator of the last Consociation, upon the Advice of the Association, and the Motion and Desire of the aggrieved Brethren of this Church, after humble Supplication to the Father of Lights, for his gracious Guidance and Direction; It was first desired by some Brethren of the Church of *Ashford,* that the Vote of the Church *March* 10th 1746, 7, which was offered to the last Council, in which the Concurrence of Pastor and Church was made necessary towards perfecting any Act, and also their mutual Agreement in calling Councils, &c. might be reconsidered as an Objection against the Consociations setting, &c.

Upon this, it was put to the Church (warned to be present at this Time) whether they desired it to be reconsidered.—It was voted in the Negative. Mr. *Bass* also said, that he did-n't insist upon it himself.—In the next Place, Mr. *Bass* offered a Paper, giving an Account of his Sentiments respecting the Principles objected against him, with the Reasons thereof.—This the aggrieved Brethren submitted to the Judgment of the Council.—Mr. *Bass* having declared to this Council, that if the People in general were not desirous of his Continuance in the Ministry among them, he was willing to leave them, or be dismissed from them, desiring the Mind of the Church might be known.—The following Question was then put to the Church, *viz.* Whether notwithstanding Mr. *Bass's* present Sentiments (about the Points in question) as declared before the Council—the Church are desirous he should be still their Pastor.—Two thirds of the Brethren present were in the Negative.——

It now appearing to this Council that the most of this Church are dissatisfied and aggrieved with the Principles of their Pastor the Rev'd Mr. *John Bass;* and complaining that he has departed from those Principles he professed and declared in the Confession of Faith, which he subscribed when he settled here, and declared to be his leading Principles, which he was resolved by the Grace of CHRIST to maintain and inculcate;—and that most of the Church remain firm in the belief of those Principles: and therefore desire the said Mr. *Bass* may be dismissed and removed from them.

This Council find that the Sentiments and Principles of the Rev. Mr. *Bass* (as himself has expressed and declared them in the said Paper, delivered in to us) are now very different from what they were as contained in the aforesaid Confession of Faith; and we think that this Difference (which we apprehend to be a Departure from the true Doctrine of the Gospel, and also from the Principles to whom the Generality of the Church do adhere,) is sufficient Ground for the Dissolution of the Pastoral Relation of the said Mr. *Bass* to this Church; and do according to the Desire of the Church declare the Pastoral-Relation of Mr. *Bass* to this Church to be dissolved——And that he is dismissed from this Church and People.——

Though the Doctrine of *Original Sin,* and those Points which have gone under the Name of the Quinquarticular Points, have been the Subject of much Controversy in the Christian Church, for which, as well as other Reasons, we think the Brethren of this Church should be careful to treat one another with great Meekness; yet we think it our Duty, for our own Parts, to declare we are clearly perswaded that the *Calvinistical* Sense of those Articles is agreable to the Word of GOD, and have been fairly proved to be Doctrines delivered to the Saints in the holy Scriptures; and the contrary Principles we look upon to be great Mistakes and of dangerous Tendency to the Souls of Men: And think it our Duty to warn and beseech the Brethren to contend meekly and yet earnestly for the Doctrines once delivered to the Saints, and to hold fast the Truth which they have heard and received; that they be not moved from the Doctrines of the Gospel, nor driven to and fro, and tossed with every Wind of Doctrine; but by diligent Study of the holy Scriptures and fervent Prayer to GOD, labour that they may be united and established in the Truths of the Gospel. And as we heartily lament our Brother *Bass's* falling into those Errors and Mistakes, we do sincerely pray GOD may give him Light; and that He would cause this Church and People to understand the Grounds of his Controversy with them, in leaving them to the Difficulties they are fallen into, and humble them therefor; and that He would return to them in Mercy and build them up, and establish and preserve them to his heavenly Kingdom.

Signed by Order of the Consociation,

Jacob Eliot, *Scribe.*

This Result and Judgment of the venerable Consociation was published before a large Assembly; and followed with solemn Prayer to GOD for Success. After which One of the Council in few Words exhorted the poor, bereaved, divided People to exercise mutual Charity, and pursue the Things which make for Peace. And then every one retired to his Quarters; the Council no doubt pleased with the Stand they had made against encroaching Error, and the Relief they had afforded to the dissatisfied Brethren, though they left many thinking Persons at a loss, as to the direct Tendency such Conduct of Councils has to serve the Interest of Truth and Religion: And I can't see how it could be otherwise; for a mere Judgment or Opinion, without any proper Arguments produced in Vindication of it, will be satisfactory to none, in such a Case, but those who are well enough pleased with implicit Faith.—However, I believe the Council thought they had acted right; and I shall not dispute their Integrity. Good Men may be guilty of Mistakes; and I leave it with the unprejudiced to say whether they are not in the following Particulars,—

1. In saying no more in their Result than they do, respecting the Pleas I grounded upon that Vote and Agreement made *March* 10th 1746, 7. They only remark thus, 'Mr. *Bass* said, He did not insist upon it himself.' As though I in Form gave it up as insufficient to Support a Plea in Bar; when the Gentlemen may remember (though it might slip their Minds in the Time of it) That I expressed my self after this Manner, 'I shall not insist any more upon it, or shall not multiply Words upon it,' as I say in the Preamble to the Declaration of my Sentiments, *&c.* then delivered to them.—The Consociation on *March* 12th set this Vote aside; and sundry Gentlemen of the Association, in my Hearing, at their last Meeting declared, before a Number of the Aggrieved, then present, that they looked upon it as nothing: For which Reason it was, I did not

think it worth while to multiply Words about it. Tho' I think still that Vote was good: And it appears to me, that if Consociations have Authority to nullify such Acts, particular Churches have little or no Priviledge allowed them, but to send their Delegates with their Ministers to Councils; and to ask and receive the like Kindness in their Turn.—O precious Priviledge!

2. They say, That I declared to them, That if the People in general were not desirous of my Continuance among them in the Ministry, I was willing to leave them, or be dismissed from them; desiring the Mind of the Church might be known.—The natural Construction of which is, That I expressed a Willingness to be determined in that Affair, by the Vote of the Church only; when at the same Time the Council might have remembred, that I, with sundry others, insisted, That the Congregation should have their Voice in the Affair, as well as the Church.—This was denied Us.—And all the Reason given for it, that I remember, was, that the Congregation were not warned to meet them according to Law; though at the same Time, I informed them, that such a Meeting had been requested of the Select-Men, but refused.—But as I thought it expedient, that the Congregation should have their Voice; I did, (and nothing more could be done) on the Sabbath-Day Evening before, desire the Congregation to meet before the Council, and shew their Mind.—The Congregation came, and were ready to do it.—This was plead,—but it availed nothing.—And was it right for the Council, after this, to predicate their Result, in any Measure upon my declared Willingness to be dismissed, when that was upon a Condition they refused to act up to. Take away this, and they can't say, I declared any Willingness at all to be dismissed; and then surely their Result in this Respect is without Foundation.—But now, As to the Councils refusing to hear the Congregation before they proceeded to my Dismission; How this can be justified, I know not.—The Congregation, 'tis allowed, have as good a Right to

Vote in the Call and Settlement of a Minister, as the Church.—
For 'tis the Congregation, and not the Church, that indent
with him for his Salary, and see it paid: And wherefore then
is it, they shall be denied their Voice in his Dismission. Shall
the Fifth Part of a Society rule in this Matters and involve
them in what Difficulties and put them to what Charges they
please? This in my Opinion is out of all Proportion in the
World.—I know of nothing that can be said, to vindicate the
Council in this Point, except they can prove their Judgment of
my Opinions, to be founded upon Scripture, which (it may
be) they will find hard Work to do.—But then supposing they
are found in the Faith; does this give them a Right to deprive
any Religious Society of their Teacher, without their Consent;
I trow not. Much less when their Orthodoxy is disputed.—The
good Gentlemen no doubt are Orthodox to themselves, and so
are many others that differ from them. And they will not deny,
but that I have on my Side the Question in dispute, Gentlemen
of as bright Characters for Learning, Ingenuity and Virtue, as
they on theirs.—Great Names we see then will not decide the
Controversy, nor perhaps will it ever cease in the Church
militant.—Arguments indeed are the best Weapons that can
be used in the Cause.—And I should have been pleased, to
have heard the Council reasoned a little in Publick, as they
were desired, upon those Points they are so well setled in:
This they refused;—supposing, it seems, their Judgment sufficient to settle the Controversy, and reduce those that were
wandering with me into Errors of dangerous Tendency to
their Souls.—But if we had not Reasoning; we had Wailing:—
The Gentlemen heartily lament my falling into Errors: And
I am obliged to them for their Compassion; yet, should have
been more so, if with their Compassion, they had shewn a
little more Lenity. But it may perhaps be replied, The Distemper is so malignant, that the severer Remedy was not to be
any longer neglected.—Though I as heartily subscribe to every
Passage of sacred Scripture as they do themselves. We inter-

pret them differently, and my Interpretation is in their Judgment big with Errors of dangerous tendency to the Souls of Men: But this I never yet saw proved. And I can't see any Danger in telling People, they are the *Offspring of GOD,* and *made after his Similitude;*—That they are indebted to Him for their Being and all their Natural Capacities, Dispositions, Affections and Passions. In this I see no Danger, no Tendency to swell Men with Pride, and to encourage them in Sin; but on the contrary, a natural Tendency to induce Them to love and serve Him as obedient Children, to render them humble and penitent for their Sins, to excite the most grateful Regards to Him for the Love and Compassion He exhibits to Sinners in the glorious Scheme of our Redemption by JESUS CHRIST; to inspire the best Resolutions, and to influence them to a right Conduct;—whereas the representing our Nature as exceeding Corrupt and Wicked as soon as formed, odious to GOD's Holiness and under his Wrath and Curse; has, so far as I can see a natural Tendency to fill the Mind with the most gloomy Apprehensions of the Author of our Being, to damp our Spirits, to turn away our Hearts from Him; and, in a Word, to the Destruction of all Religion.

Again, Where is the Danger of a Minister's telling his People, He can't find the Doctrine of absolute personal Election to eternal Life any where in the Bible: And at the same Time that the Voice of Scripture is, That Faith and Obedience, in whomsoever it is found, lead to Life eternal; but on the other hand, Unbelief and obstinate Wickedness, to final Ruin.—If such Talk as this has a dangerous Tendency, then so far as I can see, the New-Testament is the most dangerous Book in all the World: For to believe in Christ and keep his Commandments is there made necessary in order to a Man's being his Disciple indeed, and to his enjoying the Blessedness of the future World.

But now, to believe that GOD Almighty from all Eternity has

absolutely elected a certain Number of *Adam's* Race to eternal Life, and sent his Son into the World to redeem them; and that the Residue are non-elect, and denied that *purchased Assistance* without which a Man can never comply with the Terms of Salvation, and so must of necessity, after all his Endeavours to the contrary, be miserable forever:—This, in my Opinion, has a very dangerous Tendency. For, though the *Sublapsarian* Divines say, the Sentence of Reprobation is in Consequence of a Man's Wickedness; yet, as upon their Scheme his Wickedness is inevitable, his Damnation must be so too, notwithstanding all he can do himself, or any other Being has done or will do for him.

After all, I freely own, That the Scheme of Religion I espouse, as Things now go in the Country, has a Tendency to fling all that are known to fall in with it, out of the good Liking of the Generality of People, and to deprive such, if Clergymen, of their Livings: Which, as it is known, is no small Temptation to a temporizing Conduct, to unfairness and down-right Hypocrisy: than which nothing has a more pernicious Tendency to the Souls of Men.—*O Tempora! O Mores!*——

PART SIX

THE NEW ORDER: DOCTRINAL

42 · *Samuel Quincy*
(*fl. 1735–1750*)

REGENERATION

The Puritans' perilous balance of piety and reason had been disturbed long before the Awakening. What the revival accomplished was to make fixed doctrine of what had been tentative notions and to create parties of the affections and of the understanding. The latter party evolved, in response to the revival, a simpler and more authoritative faith and did not attempt, as did the partisans of evangelical religion, to translate the experience of the revival into a subtler reading of the nature and operation of the human mind. Rather they simply proclaimed reason as an absolute good, and emotions as a clear and present danger to be exorcised from the religious life of the colonies.

The belief that "Christianity is a Rational Religion" was first confidently expressed in a series of sermons delivered by Samuel Quincy in Charleston, South Carolina. The Boston-born Quincy served in the 1730's as a missionary of the Society for the Propagation of the Gospel in Georgia. There he attracted the attention of Alexander Garden,

-----

Samuel Quincy, "The Nature and Necessity of Regeneration," in *Twenty Sermons . . . Preach'd in the Parish of St. Philip . . .* (Boston, 1750), pp. 274–281, 284–291.

and was installed early in the 1740's as a "lecturer" at St. Philip's. Several of the sermons Quincy delivered in the years after the Awakening were published in Boston in 1750—with a subscription list representing the Episcopalian elite from Georgia to New Hampshire. His thoughts, however, were not narrowly Anglican, rather they were typical of the doctrines being evolved out of a negative reaction to the revival.

Now some Men in their Notions concerning the new Birth, seem to confound these two Things, very distinct in themselves, *viz.* the ordinary, with the extraordinary and miraculous Gifts of the Holy Spirit. Hence they give strange and unwarrantable Interpretations of this Matter, contrary to Reason, Experience, and express Scripture. Yet supposing themselves to be led by the immediate and infallible Guidance of God's Holy Spirit, they are notwithstanding mighty confident that they only are in the right; because they feel and are certain that they are so. Whereas if we interpret Scripture by Scripture, i. e. the more obscure and difficult Parts, by such as are plain and easie to the Understanding; we shall not fall into any fatal Error, neither with regard to this particular Doctrine of the new Birth, nor any other Matter. The written Word of God is at present our only Rule, and a rational Interpretation of it, the only Secure and warrantable one we ought to fix upon Scripture: For to suppose that the Father of Lights has dictated to his Creatures Absurdities and Contradictions, is to think very unworthily of God, and throw the utmost Indignity on divine Revelation that we can possibly do.

And this alone distinguishes the Enthusiast from the sober, rational Christian. The one renounces his Reason, and believes implicitely without Examination; but the other, having duly weighed and considered Arguments and Proofs, embraces

Religion upon the most firm and solid Grounds; and hence, according to the Advice of St. *Peter,* is always ready to give an Answer to every Man that asketh a Reason of the Hope that is in him.

It is true, there are some Things in Religion far above our Comprehension, which it would therefore be absurd for us to reason upon, and which nevertheless we ought not to reject; but this is not the Case of the Doctrine before us. For our Saviour does not reckon this among those sublime Mysteries of which we can have no adequate Ideas; but plainly distinguishes it from such. *Verily,* says he, *we speak that we do know, and testifie that we have seen, and ye receive not our Witness: If I have told you earthly Things* (i. e. such Things as are palpable to Sense, and obvious to common Observation) *and ye believe not; how shall ye believe if I tell you of heavenly Things?* Of such heavenly Things as it is likewise necessary you should know and believe in order to receive my Doctrine, and acknowledge me for the Son of God, the true Messiah. How that the Son of Man came down from Heaven, and must suffer Death upon the Cross for the Redemption of Mankind, of which the Serpent lifted up by *Moses* in the Wilderness, was an Emblem or Type. These Things being supernatural Discoveries of God's Grace and Goodness to Men, might fill *Nicodemus* with Surprize and Wonder, that God should so graciously condescend to sinful Creatures, and he might with some Colour of Objection have replied; *How can these Things be?* But when our Saviour only told him of that Power and Influence which his Doctrine, accompanied with the Assistances of the divine Spirit, was designed to have over Men, making an intire Change and Renovation in their Hearts and Lives; this he might easily have understood, tho' convey'd under a metaphorical Similitude, but yet strongly expressive of the Thing intended: And no doubt upon Reflection, he soon became sensible of his Mistake.

This Doctrine then of Regeneration, or the new Birth, being

an easy, intelligible, and rational Doctrine; encumber'd with no kind of Difficulty or Obscurity, and suited to every Man's Capacity; I shall in the following Discourse endeavour to treat of it as such. And to this End shew,

I. What is the true Doctrine of the Text; or the proper Meaning of this Phrase, To be born of the Spirit.

II. Take Notice of the different Explications of this Doctrine which some Men have advanced, and thereby occasioned very grievous Mistakes concerning it.

III. Shew the Necessity of being born of the Spirit, according to the plain Sense and Meaning of this Phrase, in order to qualifie us for the Kingdom of Heaven.

I. I am to shew what is the true Doctrine of the Text; or the proper Meaning of this Phrase, To be born of the Spirit.

Now this is a figurative Manner of Expression and means, as I have before observed, that intire Change which is made in the Hearts and Lives of Men, when from a vicious and wicked Life they become sincere and good Christians. This Change our Saviour asserts the absolute Necessity of, and says that without it Men cannot enter into the Kingdom of Heaven. They may become formally and externally Christians by being baptized into his Name; but they cannot be truly and realy so, unless they are also born of the Spirit; renewed by the Influences of that divine Spirit whose Fruits appear in Men by a holy and unblameable Conversation. This our Saviour calls being born again. And that this is the full Sense and Meaning of the Words, will appear by comparing other Places of Scripture where this Matter is spoke of more clearly, under the same Kind of Allegory. St. *Paul* in his Epistle to the *Ephesians,* speaking of those Vices and Corruptions which Christians were obliged by their Profession to forsake, and walk contrary to them, says; *But ye have not so learned Christ; if so be that ye have heard him, and have been taught by him as the Truth is in Jesus.* He probably alludes to the Doctrine of the New-Birth as taught by our Saviour; for he proceeds. *That ye put off concerning the former Conversation, the old Man, which is corrupt according to the deceitful Lusts, and be renewed in the Spirit of your Mind; and that ye put on the new Man, which after God is created in Righteousness and true Holiness.* Being born again; undergoing, as it were, a new Creation, and becoming a new Creature, are the same Figures of Speech, and plainly signifie no more than that great and mighty Change which visibly appears in Men after they become true Converts to Christianity, and take upon them, not only the Profession, but the Life and Behaviour of a Christian. For so the Apostle explains himself in the following Verses, where he shews in what this Change consists, *viz.* In putting away all those vicious Habits and immoral Practices, which are inconsistent with pure Religion; and in being Followers of God as dear Children; walking in Love, as Christ also hath loved us. This is called being born of, or by the Spirit; because all good Motions and Actions proceed from the Suggestions and Assistances of the divine Spirit of God, who is the Author of all that is good in us, whether Principles or Actions. By him God worketh in us both to will and to do of his own good Pleasure. And therefore we ought to ascribe to this divine Spirit of God, as the immediate Cause, all good Desires and Inclinations in us; the Beginning, Progress, and final Perseverance of a religious and godly Life. And altho' the Manner how this divine Spirit operates on the Mind may be mysterious to us; yet the Fruits and Effects of this divine Operation are not so, but very plain and visible to our selves and others, *The Fruits of the Spirit are in all,* without Exception, *Goodness and Righteousness and Truth.* These are the constant and never-failing Effects which the Holy Spirit of God produces in Men, and therefore to these we must attend if we would be assured that this good Work is wrought in us, and we are indeed renew'd in the Spirit of our Minds after the Image of Him that has created us. And these are Fruits that cannot be hid; but are as manifest as their opposites, the Works of the Flesh.

Light and Darkness cannot be more distinct in their own Nature, than are those Fruits which proceed from carnal and corrupt Affections, and those which are the genuine Offspring of the divine Spirit. And therefore when Men forsake all their evil Courses, and embrace true Religion; receive it into their Hearts, and practice it in their Lives; it produces so great a Change in them as every one must be sensible of. Indeed this Change is more or less apparent according to the former Course of Men's Lives. When such who have lived in open and notorious Wickedness, are converted from the Evil of their Ways, and become truly religious and good Men, this Change is very conspicuous, and every one is ready to take Notice of it, and cannot help observing what a mighty Alteration there is in them for the better; so as to say of them that they are in reality *new Men*, quite different Sort of Persons to what they were before. And as to those who have never run into any Excess of Impiety, but have behaved with more Regularity, tho' this Change cannot be so remarkable in them; yet Religion when sincerely embraced, produces the same Effects in all Men. It possesses their Minds with quite different Principles, and puts them upon very contrary Views and Designs to what carnal and vicious Men pursue. . . .

I proceed,

II. To take Notice of the different Explications of this Doctrine, which some Men have advanced, and thereby occasioned very grievous Mistakes concerning it.

It is a very safe Rule in Divinity which ought always to be observed by those who expound Scripture; That Doctrines should not be raised, nor Conclusions drawn from metaphorical Passages beyond what is the first and obvious Meaning of such Metaphors: Because this would lead Men into unavoidable Mistakes, and make Room for abundance of Errors, as it has notoriously done with respect to the Doctrine before us. For some Men who give Way to a warm Imagination, and are not contented with a plain and rational Interpretation of Scripture, extend this Doctrine beyond all reasonable Bounds, and maintain; That because Conversion from a wicked Life is represented by the Metaphor of a new Birth; therefore this second or spiritual Birth, must in some Respect or other, be analogous to whatever can be said of our natural Birth; and from hence they draw many absurd Conclusions, as contrary to Scripture, as they are to Experience and common Sense. For they say it is necessary in this new Birth that every Man, whatever his former Course of Life has been, should feel great Horrors and Agonies of Mind; be fill'd with the most dreadful Apprehensions of God's avenging Wrath, and labour under the utmost Terrors of a guilty Conscience. Thus they represent Persons undergoing, as they call it, the Pangs of the new Birth, in all the frightful Circumstances of Despair, rather than under the gentle Calls of the Spirit of God. And though some Men, who have lived very wickedly, may have been brought to Consideration by some extraordinary, awakening Providence, and so have felt great Terrors of Mind; yet this is not the ordinary Course of God's Dealings with Men; nor, in any Case, the necessary Consequence of his Spirit working in them. On the contrary, these violent Perturbations of Mind always proceed from Men's own natural Fears, and inbred Passions, and on whatever Occasion they have been excited, must subside again before Men can be brought to that calm and sober Reflection which is necessary to real Conversion. So that a greater Injury cannot be done to Religion, than to persuade Men that these violent inward Emotions are necessary to true Conversion. If Men by considering their Ways, become so far sensible of the Guilt and Danger of their sinful Courses, as to forsake them, and turn their Feet to God's Testimonies; this is what is required of them; and tho' they may have been thrown into ever such unatural Frights, and terrifying Apprehensions of their future Damnation, if they continue still in their Wickedness, all this is but mere Delusion. And whatever be the Event (for God can bring Good out of Evil) yet these

Things are bad in themselves, and have no Tendency in them to promote the Work of Conversion. Conversion is described in Scripture by coming to a Man's Self, or returning to his right Mind; and surely it can never be the Way to produce such good Effects as are the Result of Sober Reason and calm Consideration, by raising unnatural Ferments, and filling the Mind with such distracting Fears as put Men beyond the Use of their Reason, and even drive them from their Senses. What Sort of Conversions have been realy effected by these wicked and unwarrantable Means, have been too evident where these Practices have prevailed, and Men have been taught to ascribe to the good Spirit of God, those Excesses of Grief and Joy, of Hope and Fear, as have plainly proceeded from their own disturb'd and over-heated Imaginations. Such Men, as their Passions only have been raised, but their Judgments never informed; so their Religion subsists wholly in the former; and generally too in such kind of evil Affections, as apparently discover to what Spirit they ought properly to be ascribed. For Envying, Revilings, censorious and rash judging of others, and vainboasting of themselves, are not the Works of the Spirit of God, but the contrary. And therefore where Men are notoriously given to these worst of Vices, the Tree is known by its Fruits, and we may certainly conclude, notwithstanding all their solemn Pretences to inward Feelings and Experiences, that they are Strangers to true Conversion, They have neither Part nor Lot in this Matter; for their Hearts are not right with God. They are still in the Gall of Bitterness, and in the Bond of Iniquity.

Again;

Other Misinterpretations of this Doctrine are, that this Work of Conversion or the New Birth, is sudden and instantaneous, and wrought by an irresistable Degree of God's Grace and Power. These Mistakes likewise proceed from too strict an Adherence to the Metaphor, for they say; that as the Work of Creation was wrought in an Instant, and we were at first called out of Nothing into Being by the Almighty *Fiat;* for he only said, *Let it be, and it was so;* So our second Creation, likewise, must be an instantaneous Work, the Effect of almighty, irresistable Power. That Conversion from a wicked Life may not, in some extraordinary Instances, have been very suddenly effected, cannot be doubted; and that without any known Preparatory Work, as some affect to call it; because they will allow that Men may perform preparatory Works, tho' they maintain that they are intirely passive in the Work of Conversion itself: But then that this is the ordinary Method of God's Grace; or that Conversion, in any Instance, is the Effect of irresistable Power, does not at all appear; nay is contrary to the Nature of this great and mighty Change in the Hearts and Lives of Men, which is called Conversion, or the New Birth. For no one is made either very bad, or very good in an instant; Conversion is a progressive Work, and the Principles and Habits of Grace and Goodness, are not infused into us by Miracle, all at once; as the extraordinary Gifts of the Holy Ghost were bestow'd on the first Christians. This some seem to think, who speak of Conversion as an instantaneous Work; but this is not the Case of the ordinary Operations of God's Holy Spirit. He works upon us by way of rational Conviction, and the several Graces of Christianity are acquired by degrees; one Virtue is added to another, and we grow up to the Christian Life by insensible Gradations. And then, if we were wholly passive in the Work of Regeneration; it cou'd by no Means be fitly pressed upon us to convert and turn to God from our evil Ways; All Exhortations and Persuasions of this Nature, as there are many in Scripture, wou'd be a mere Mockery of Mankind, and to no Manner of Purpose, if Men had no Power to do any thing themselves; but depended intirely on irresistable Grace to effect their Conversion. And that God should punish Men notwithstanding for neglecting their Salvation; and not doing what was not in their Power; conveys so unworthy an Idea of God, as we should be far from entertaining.

THE NECESSITY OF HOLDING

FAST THE TRUTH

The Calvinism that emerged from the Awakening was more than a simple counterstatement to the new, and increasingly bolder, Arminian rationalism. Evangelical doctrine evolved also from the struggle to curb the emotional excesses of the revival, to give substance to the New Light without sacrificing its essential spirit. The first post-Awakening doctrinal utterances of the New Side Presbyterians were responses to an Antinomianism that Gilbert Tennent, among others, identified with the "errors" of the Moravians. This church group consisted originally of the German pietists, members of the "Unitas Fratrum," who had come to Pennsylvania shortly before the Awakening. They were members of a sect founded in Bohemia in the middle of the fifteenth century by the more spiritually-minded followers of the reformer Jan Hus. After nearly two centuries of persecution, the Moravians entered on a

Gilbert Tennent, *The Necessity of Holding Fast the Truth. . . with an Appendix, Relating to Errors lately vented by some Moravians* (Boston, 1743), pp. 60–71.

new era of expansion, in which they were devoted to evangelizing and to missionary work. Those who migrated to Pennsylvania settled chiefly at Bethlehem, but the group also established Indian missions in the interior. The acknowledged leader of the eighteenth-century Moravians, Count Zinzendorf (1700–1760) came to America in December 1741, partly in response to reports of the Awakening sent him by his correspondent, George Whitefield. Zinzendorf hoped to unite all the German-speaking Protestants of Pennsylvania, and it is more than likely that his ideal of the unity of all true Christians, founded on a liberty to uphold different "non-essential" doctrines, helped to reinforce the Presbyterian evangelists' vision of a revival "party of Christ" and to encourage Tennent's later ecumenical program.

But by the time that Zinzendorf returned to Europe in early 1743, Gilbert Tennent and Samuel Finley viewed the Moravians as corruptors of the Awakening. Tennent published a critique of Moravian doctrine and practice that set forth Moravian "errors" in such a way that one New England opponent of the revival was able to publish a tract in which, by means of parallel columns, the author of the Nottingham Sermon was made to appear condemned out of his own words. Yet it cannot be assumed that Tennent's thoughts represented simply a conservative reaction to a new insurgency; he saw in Moravian doctrine a heresy just as dangerous as Arminianism. According to Tennent, the Moravians offered an assurance of salvation based on no more than a man's own assured sense of his "good frame," or inner feelings, and by denying the saint's need to perform any "Law-work,"—the duties, that is, of the moral law. Actually Moravian theology had long proclaimed the necessity of good works as evidence of true faith, and Zinzendorf's own German-language sermons, published in the colonies during the Awakening, urged men to mistrust any assurance of faith that had no other basis than feelings and impressions. Still, it is clear that the Moravians did serve, in the Middle Colonies, something of the same function as that of the New England Separates—one of offering an institutional channel for the Antinomian enthusiasm of the revival. Particularly in their proselytizing appeals to Whitefield's converts, the Moravians tended to accept the moment of conversion, and its joy, as nearly the whole of religion. To Tennent this seemed too easy a faith, one indifferent both to God's law and the needs of society—and, most importantly, a form of self-delusion that needed to be chastened among his own followers.

It signifies little, my Brethren, to profess Regard and Love to Holiness, while Truth, precious Truth is slighted. It is a childish Weakness, to call it no worse; it is a beginning at the wrong End of Religion; it is just as if a Man should shew great Regard to the Superstructure of a House, and neglect the Foundation. What signify fair Shews of Love and Holiness, without Truth for their Foundation? They are only Blinds to deceive the Simple, Rattles to please Children.

It is a plain Sign of an *enthusiastical* and deluding Spirit, to slight that precious *System* of Truths, which we have laid before us, in a most plain consistent and excellent Manner, in our *Westminster-Confession* of Faith, and *Catechisms;* among which we see a strong Connection, and charming Harmony; and in which, if we are not blinded with Ignorance or Prejudice, we may perceive a transcendent Beauty, a direct Tendency to exalt all the Honours of the divine Attributes, to humble the Pride of Man, and conform him to the Deity, in universal Goodness and Holiness: There Vice, of every Kind & Form, is justly represented in its own native Dress of Horror and Meanness: There sincere Holiness is fix'd upon it's proper and impregnable Basis; and open'd in it's vast Extent and attractive Magnificence, and encourag'd with all proper pertinent and powerful Incentives: There the Creatures Crown is cast at the dear Redeemer's Feet, and all the Glory of it's Happiness, ascrib'd to the Mediation of our great Immanuel: There are astonishing Beauties of the pure, free, Sovereign, rich, inexhaustible and glorious Grace of God, are unvail'd, in a consistency with the Creatures Duty; so as hereby to establish the Interests of Vertue and Piety, upon the most prevailing and ingenuous Motives! Now I say to slight such a blessed Self-consistent System of Principles, and in the Room thereof, under a Pretence of Holiness in a superior Degree, to introduce a Bundle of inconsistent Jargon, Contradictions, Nonsense, and damnable Errors; Errors that affect the very Foundations of Religion, both in Doctrine and Practice;—is it not vile Enthusiasm, and detestable Delusion?

Certainly the Case of such who have known the Truths of Christ, and turn from them to Vanity, Lies, and Nonsense, is more inexcusable, than of those who have been breed up in Ignorance. O what a foolish Choice do they make, in bartering away the finest Gold for the basest Dross? What unaccountable Ingratitude do such express to the great and good God, for all the religious Privileges & Means of Improvement they have had? They turn their Backs upon the unsullied

Snow, and sacred Sweets of *Lebanon,* and pursue after poisonous Streams and muddy Waters.

To pretend to introduce into *one Communion,* all that have an Appearance of Experience, Affection, and Piety, without searching into their main *Principles,* without a Concurrence in them (as I have Reason to think the *Moravians* do) is to build *Babel* over again, and promote the Confusion of Languages.

It cannot be reasonably expected, that such a confus'd Medley, such a heterogeneous Mixture will stand long, for it has no solid Foundation to stand upon. To pretend to promote Love and Union, by concealing our Principles and lessening our Regard to Truth, is to do Evil that Good may come. Indeed it is the direct Road to Division and Contention; and this the Event proves. To love Persons in a general View as Christians, without due Respect had to their main peculiar *Principles,* is an unreasonable childish Passion, more fit for Children and Simpletons, than for Men of Understanding. For, as *Solomon* observes, *the Simple Man believes every Word,* Prov. 14. 15. A pretended Union without a System of *Principles* acknowledged, is rather a Confederacy, than a Scriptural Union. It is infinitely more candid, to let others freely know our Scheme of Principles, that so they may judge of them; and in Things of smaller Moment, to use Moderation and Forbearance; and to make no more Terms of Communion, than Christ himself has fixed. Any other Union is neither rational, nor desirable, and deserves not the Name of Union.

But the *Moravian* Concealment of their pernicious Principles, seems to be a Fulfilment of St. *Peter's* Prophesy, concerning false Teachers, that they should *privily* (or covertly) *bring in damnable Heresies.* *Plutarch's* Story of a Boy that carried something under his Cloak, may be applied to them. The Boy was asked by a Stranger, What it was he carried so closely under his Cloak? To whom the Boy answered, you may well know, that it is something I don't intend you shall know, by so carrying it. All Religion that is worth a reasonable Man's Choice is gone, when Truth is gone. All that is left is childish Fancy, enthusiastical Folly, and painted Pageantry.

For any Men to pretend to *know* certainly who are *gracious,* as one of the *Moravians* did in my hearing, is to assume an incommunicable Prerogative of God: and to run upon this *false* Plan in Church-Matters, is to turn all into the wildest *Disorder* and *Confusion.*

Methinks the Consideration of the Truths of God, may justly *alarm the Secure* and *Impenitent,* and excite them to fly from Sin to God, and humble themselves before him, and seek his Favour; seeing that all the Threats of God are pointed at them like so many burning Thunderbolts, which the Truth of God will oblige him to discharge at them, except Repentance intercept the falling Blow. All the Examples of the divine Severity against the Impenitent, which are recorded in both the Testaments, are shocking Momentos to a secure World!

But let all *devout Souls,* who have felt the proper Influence of Truth upon their own Hearts and Practices, and still retain a Regard thereto, *Rejoyce.* Go on, my dear Brethren, in the blessed Way of Truth, and ye shall receive a Crown at last! The Consideration of God's blessed Truths may *support* you, in all Manner of Distresses, whither it be by *Persecution* from open or covert *Enemies,* or misguided *Friends.* The God of Truth, whose Cause you plead, will sooner or later comfort your Hearts, and crown you with Protection, and Songs of Deliverance.

It is true, Enthusiasts and Errorists themselves will talk of Persecution; but it is not the Punishment, but the *Cause* that makes a *Martyr.* Those that suffer for Error, suffer for Sin, and not for God. Blessed be Jehovah, that so many in the Land, have a Regard to the dear and precious Truths of Christ! O may God increase their Number, their Zeal, and their Love!

The Consideration of the Truths of Christ, yields sweet

Support under *Temptation, Desertion,* and every other Calamity. God is faithful who has promised to relieve his People, and able also, as well as willing and gracious. He has given many Examples of his Kindness this Way in Times past; yea, he has confirmed the Truth of his Promises, by an Oath, that we might have stronger Consolation. The Truths of God are firmer than the Foundations of Mountains. They are try'd in the Fire seven Times. The Heavens and Earth may and shall pass away, but the Truths of God shall stand stedfast to all Generations. We may lean the Weight of our everlasting Salvation upon the Truth of the least Promise of God. Indeed Brethren, it will never fail us.

He that hath an Ear to hear, let him hear the Command of our Lord, *viz. to beware of false Prophets, who shall come unto you in Sheep's cloathing, but inwardly they are ravening Wolves.* This Scripture (in my Opinion) is justly applicable to the *Moravian* Brethren. They have a Sheep's Coat on, they seem to be mighty mild, harmless and innocent in their Looks, but inwardly they hold dividing dangerous Principles: You may know them by their Fruits, like Wolves they cruelly scatter the poor Sheep of Christ, by their damnable Doctrines. Beware, my dear Brethren, of the Leaven, the false infectious Doctrine of those *Moravians,* who like the Pharisees of old, are proud *Seperatists,* make broad Philacteries, and compass Sea and Land to make Proselytes. Some of which, become seven-fold worse, if possible, than themselves. . . .

I can't but think, and that from some particular Knowledge of the Conduct of some of them, that they fall far short of many other Enthusiasts, in *Candor* and *Honesty.* Watch therefore, my dear Brethren, stand fast in the Faith, quite you like Men, be strong. O be not as Children tossed to and fro with every Wind of Doctrine, by the Craftiness of those who lie in wait to deceive. Away with those *sorry Shews* of Zeal, Piety and Meekness, which have not Truth and Humility for their Foundation. May the God of Truth graciously baffle all the crafty Schemes, and coloured Intrigues, of all schismatical, enthusiastical and deceitful *Babel-builders!* who under the Mask of Humility and Love, declare their Pride and Enmity in *separating* from the Protestant reformed Churches, and in despising and tearing of them in Pieces, as far and as fast as they can. Who that has got the least Spark of Love to the God of Truth, can be altogether tame and silent upon so mournful an Occasion, and patiently suffer the carved Work of the Temple to be pull'd down by proud *Seperatists?* Was not *Meroz* cursed, because he did not *come up to the Help of the Lord against the Mighty?* What, my Brethren, shall we thro' base Indifferency, let those dear and amiable Truths, which have cost our Ancestors Blood, slip away by *Moravian* Hands? God forbid! Let us awake, my Brethren, out of stupid Indolence, and fordid Lukewarmness, and with humble, impregnable Fortitude, contend for the Faith once delivered to the Saints!

But pray, *why* do any esteem this new upstart *Moravian* Sect? Is it,

1. For their Shew of *Meekness* and *Harmlessness?* But may not Persons, under this Guise, have cruel Designs and Dispositions? Don't our Lord tell us, that Wolves shall come in Sheeps Cloathing? And what is this Sheeps Cloathing, but a Covert of Meekness and Harmlessness? But what Evidence have we that the Moravians are really meek, when we see them not exposed to Temptations? They generally shun Debate, which would try their Meekness: but if any of them happen to be try'd a little, they shew their Weakness as much as other People. Besides, it ought to be considered, that there is a threefold Meekness, *viz.* 1. Natural; springing from a natural Temper of a milder Mould. 2. Moral; proceeding principally from selfish Considerations; these two are of little Moment. And 3. There is a sinful Meekness; that is, when Persons are Lukewarm about God's Truths, as the Moravians are. But while the Moravians cover themselves with a Sheep-Skin, like cruel

Wolves they scatter the poor Sheep of Christ. Like Foxes they craftily and sneakingly creep into the Vineyard, and spoil the tender Grapes with their detestable Delusions. How very different are the Fruits of their coming into this Country, from the Reverend Mr. WHITEFIELD's? His plain and pungent Preaching of the Truths of the Reformation, united generally the Hearts of good Men thro' the Land. But the Moravians where-ever they have any Influence, divide the People of God, and set them a jangling.

How very different are these Men from the Spirit of *Luther*, whom they pretend a Respect to. He was so zealous for Truth, that he expressed himself thus, respecting it, *viz.* That Madness was better than Mildness in the Cause of God: Rather, said he, let Heaven and Earth rush together, than one *Crumb* of Truth should perish. *Potius Cælum et Terra ruerent, quam una mica veritatis periret.*   Or,

2. Is it because they *smile* generally, and appear *loving?* But, Brethren, is not this *Judas*-like, to betray us with a Kiss? For while they shew such Love, they draw pious People into Error, and so set them a quarrelling with one another. If this be their Love, may the good Lord deliver us from it! Shall we suffer them to smile us out of our Principles? Then I'm sure we are poorly grounded in them. Away, away with such sordid Complyance!

3. Is it because they profess they are *Catholick*, or against all Sectarianism? This is indeed a most subtle Devise: for while they talk so, they are busily making a new Sect; and those that join with it, how ever ignorant, erroneous, or dark in Experience they be, they are presently esteemed and caressed, while all others who will not join with them, how knowing and experienced soever they be in Christianity, are despised. Besides, as I am informed, they will join with no Church but their own.   Or,

4. Is it because of their Shew of *Humility*, while in the mean Time they *undervalue all but themselves?* Some of the Heads

of that Party, have spoken most reproachfully in *New-Brunswick* of all the Protestant reformed Churches. One of them in my hearing compared them to *Babel.* Is this Humility, to imagine themselves more advanced in Grace, than all the World besides? I'm sure, it's of a different Stamp from that of the Apostle *Paul,* who look'd upon himself to be less than the least of all Saints. And those whom they *proselyte,* in the midst of their ignorant Zeal, betray horrible Arrogance, in proudly disdaining all the Churches of Christ when compared with their Sect.

5. Is it because they have the Appearance of great *Mortification?* I answer, their Mortification is not agreable to the Scriptures; because they are ignorant of a preparatory Work of the Law. If we may believe Count *Zinzendorf,* when they are converted in their Way, they are free from Complaints of Sin and Struggles with it, and so get into a Sleep. What is this but the Fruit of Blindness & Delusion? *To the Law and to the Testimony: if they speak not according thereto, it is because there is no Light in them.*   Or,

6. Is it because they *say* they have *Communion with God,* and in Consequence hereof *Joy and Sweetness? I answer;* When we consider the *Antinomian* Principles they hold, concerning Faith and Justification, as well as the proud Effects of their pretended good Frames, and that under a Mask of Humility; as also their denial of a Law-Work; We have great Reason to suspect their *Communion* to be but a Delusion of the grand Enemy, and their *Joys* to be the Joys of Time-Believers, and Stony-Ground Hearers. See *Heb.* 6. 4. True Communion with God does certainly *humble* the Soul. *Isai.* 6. 4. *Job* 42. 5, 6. It's no new Thing for *Antinomians* and *Enthusiasts* to talk of Joys and Comforts. The old *Antinomians* were won't to commend their Principles to others by this, that they were an experienced Cure to all Soul-Trouble. And it's true enough, they are a Cure, but a false one.

The *Moravians,* with their Brethren the *Antinomians,* and

other Enthusiasts, seem to forget both the Doctrine and Practice of *Repentance.* I don't remember to find any thing of it in the *Count's* Sermons, neither can I perceive any thing of it in their Practice. But why should they *repent,* while they pretend to *Perfection?* No, no; they have got above that in their own Conceit. Now seeing their Comforts don't come after the Exercise of Repentance for Sin, have we not Reason to suspect them?

7. Is it because they *travel* and *take great Pains?* I answer, Did not the *Pharisees* of old *compass Sea and Land,* to make one Proselyte; and when he was made, was he not twofold more a *Child of Hell* than themselves? And do not *Jesuits,* and many other Enthusiasts, travel still? But what Good do the *Moravians* do by their travelling, unless it be good, to *sow Tares,* to corrupt and divide religious People? Or what Good can reasonably be expected from Persons, who reject the *Law* of God, and think it not their Duty to make Application to *unconverted* Persons in a State of Security, either to alarm or direct them. See the *Count's* Sermons, Pages 69, 70.

But they are *deny'd to the World.* Ans. So was *Diogenes* in his Time. So were the *false Teachers* in *Paul's* Time, who try'd to Reproach him. 2 *Cor.* 11. 12. And do not the begging *Friars* among the Papists, as also their *Monks* and *Nuns,* give up all their worldly Goods? *Peter* seems to boast of their *leaving all for Christ,* Mat. 19. 27. But did not *Judas* do this, as well as the rest? Did not *Ananias* and *Saphira* put the chief of their Estate into a common Treasury, for the Maintenance of others? *Acts* 5. And this they did *freely,* for there was no Necessity laid on them to sell their Possession. *Acts* 5. 4. . . .

But methinks, my dear Brethren; the Consideration of that *glorious State,* which the Sons of *Truth* shall be introduced into, after a few Moments expire; should invite them to be earnest in Defence thereof against all Seducers, and patient in enduring their unjust Reproaches. After a few Moments more are elapsed, the Children of *Truth* shall walk with God in

White, in a Robe of Honour, in a State of Blessedness. I say, they shall walk in the Galleries of Paradise, and drink the Streams of Nectar and Ambrosia. There all Sighing and Sorrow will for ever expire; and in Place thereof shall succeed the greatest, sweetest, surest, most satisfactory, and sinless Joys. There Reproach, Error and Contest will be for ever banished; and pure *Truth*, unfading Honour, and uninterrupted Rest, take Place thereof!

The Children of *Truth* (such who have experienced its Energy, and walk'd according to its Direction) shall carry Crowns of Victory upon their Heads, and Palms of Honour in their Hands!

There Impurity and Sin will not be so much as mentioned!

There the *eternal God* will be beheld, in all the dazling Glory of his Attributes, in all the shining Charms of his Word and Works!

There the dear *Redeemer* will be admir'd, and adored, by all the Hosts of Heaven; while they attentively view his mediatorial orient transcendent Excellency!

There the *Understanding* will be pleas'd, with the noblest Entertainments, of the sublimest Knowledge, attain'd with Ease, and to the utmost Perfection!

There the pure Springs of Truth will be fully open'd and run in liquid and incessant Rivulets, thro' all the Paradise of God: The Understanding shall no more be clouded with Ignorance, or tainted with Mistake!

There the *Will* shall be satisfy'd, with enjoying the supream Good!

There the noble Soul of Man in all its Powers, will be freed from its present Clogs and Incumbrances, which obscure its Views, obstruct its Peace, and retard its Motions!

There it will expand all its Wings, and embrace a Good suited to its spiritual Nature, noble Original, vast Desires, and incessant Duration!

There the eternal God will be worshipped in the perfection

of Beauty, without Sin and without Uneasiness: No discording Sound shall ever be heard from the Harps of those heavenly Choristers!

There the inferiour *Passions* of the Soul, shall ever keep their proper Channel, and observe due Degrees of Motion!

There the original Beauty, and ancient Harmony, that adorn'd the Soul, before its fatal Fall from God, shall be restor'd to the highest Perfection; and that which is in Part shall be done away.

There no Fear of any impending Evil or Calamity shall ever perplex, disturb or distress the pious Bosom: No, they shall be fully assur'd of the perpetual Continuance of the divine Favour; a pleasing Calm and undisturbed Serenity, shall still possess the Soul, without Murmur or Uneasiness!

There no *erroneous Sentiments,* no *ungenerous Jealousies,* shall stain the Beauty, interrupt the Pleasure, or mar the Harmony of Society; neither of these shall have any Access to, or Residence in that Seat of Truth and Purity, of Love and Peace!

There *Temptations* shall come to a perpetual End; that envious and malignant Spirit shall no more sully our Innocence, or disturb our Peace, by his Temptations which will then cease for evermore: What amazing Sweetness, must issue from the View of the divine *Attributes?* When the Vail which now intercepts our Sight is removed, and they appear in their native Charms, their open'd Oriency and Lustre! If the smallest Glimpse of one of the divine Perfections, sometimes transports the Soul into Extasy and Ravishment, what will the immediate uninterrupted and united View of them all, effect! O the inexpressible Blessedness of the Glorify'd!

What endearing Sentiments of Soul must inspire the Children of Truth, while they behold the enthroned *Jesus* array'd with the brightest Majesty, and most awful Glory; while they see the Signatures of his dying Love, and recount the Labours of his Life, and Sorrows of his Soul for *them!*

O when they revolve in their Minds the humble and astonishing Stoop of condescending Majesty, in the whole of our Lord's *Humiliation,* with the gracious Design thereof, how deeply will it affect their Hearts, that he who was the Sovereign of the World, should come in the Form of a Servant, that we might be made the Sons of God; that he who was Rich should become Poor, that we thro' his Poverty might be made Rich; that the Chastisement of our Peace was laid upon him, that thro' his Stripes we might be healed!

There the Contrivance of the gracious *Covenant* will be perfectly laid open, wherein the harmonious Display of God's venerable Attributes has appeared to the Astonishment of the angelick Throng, who stoop down to behold the unsearchable Depths of divine Grace in the Redemption of Mankind by the Blood and Obedience of the Lord Jesus Christ! Herein Wisdom devis'd a Way to satisfy divine Justice, and yet save the guilty Criminals from merited Destruction. So that Justice can demand no more, and Mercy is cloathed with a Coat of Arras, vested with stately Charms, and attractive Magnificence.

There the Works of *Nature* and Depths of *Providence* will be fully unfolded, to the equal Astonishment and Delight of all the Inhabitants of Heaven. The secret Springs, the strong Connection, and sweet Relation of Providences, with their Conduciveness to compass one uniform noble Design, namely, the manifestative Glory of God, and in Subordination thereto, the special and enduring Good of his People, will be discovered!

Here sometimes the great God makes Darkness his Pavilion, and hides the Face of his Throne; his Footsteps are in the great Deep, and we cannot sound the Depths of his providential Actings by the Line of our shallow Reason: but the End will crown the Scene, beautify the whole Piece, and magnify the Glory of it's Author.

There will be no Objects of Misery, on Account of Error in Principle, or Impiety in Practice, to invite our sympathetick

Tears and Sorrows; no Allay of Grief or Pain to disturb our incessant Felicity!

There our Father's Face will never be hid from us any more, by a gloomy *Desertion;* but we shall without Interruption and Period, enjoy the bright Meridian of his Love, which is better than Life itself!

There no *Diversity of Sentiment* shall mar the Sweets of social Worship, but unallay'd Harmony and inimitable Beauty, shall ever adorn the Courts above, and bless those calm Regions of Light, of Life, of Day!

But indeed all Words and Images of Thought, even of the boldest and most exalted Kind, faint before the Paradise of God, and cannot convey sufficient Ideas of it.

44 · *Andrew Croswell*

(1 7 0 9 – 1 7 8 5)

WHAT IS CHRIST TO ME,

IF HE IS NOT MINE?

———

In the ecstasies of 1740–1741 many revivalists so fixed on the New Birth as to make inner feeling seem the essence of saving faith, and even its guarantor. Not only the more exuberant itinerants spoke of the "assurance" of faith; Jonathan Dickinson for one deemed such a definition of justification to be something of an immutable Calvinist truth. Yet by the time of Davenport's tour the notion that grace carried its own conviction was counted among the Antinomian "heresies" that needed to be contained. Not surprisingly, one of Davenport's most unyielding partisans, Andrew Croswell, rose in defense of the "good old faith." Croswell's role in the Awakening, and in eighteenth-century American religion generally, was a peculiar one. Always the outspoken controversialist, he was the first New Englander to reply to Garden's criticisms of White-

Andrew Croswell, *What is Christ to me, if he is not mine? Or a season-able Defence of the Old Protestant Doctrine of Justifying Faith* . . . (Boston, 1745), pp. 4–7, 28–31, 44–45.

field. Later he complained that Edwards' *Thoughts on the Revival* was too soft on Arminianism. In 1742 Croswell, then minister to a church in Groton, Connecticut, began to itinerate; he drew large crowds, especially in Charlestown, where he was later installed as pastor. According to his critics, Croswell's sermons were admired chiefly, even exclusively, by "the Rabble." In his attacks on Harvard College and in his egalitarian sentiments Croswell might be taken as a spokesman for what can be called the left wing of the New England revival. Yet he probably represented no one but himself, and much of his thinking is representative only of the intellectual confusion of the postrevival era. He did not condemn separations, but he was at the same time an earnest critic of that movement's Antinomian tendencies. The one constant in Croswell's long career seems to have been his "harping upon" (as he once wrote of St. Paul) the "great joy" of true believers. In his later years he criticized the "New Divinity" as well as Harvard's rationalism for denying men this personal delight. To Croswell faith was always "particular," and the Spirit's work was the redemption of individuals. Where he deviated from the mainstream of evangelical thought was in failing to integrate his social criticisms with the New Light of the revival.

. . . I see plainly that the World hates Christ's Religion *now*, as mortally, as it ever hated *him;* that (as *Luther* saith) " 'tis not the Gospel Men preach, if it is preach'd in Peace; and that whosoever will be a faithful Preacher of the glorious Gospel of

Jesus Christ, *must* (as *he* hath foretold) have the World for an Enemy, and live in the Wars all the Days of his Life."

Indeed, did I call that preaching the Gospel, which commonly passeth for it, viz. Ministers telling poor Sinners they must believe Jesus Christ to *be an all-sufficient Saviour of Sinners in general, but not their Saviour in particular;* I should be of another Sentiment: For the World doth not *hate,* but *love* this Religion; 'tis the Religion of *Nature;* at least *Nature* is not puzzled with it; all the Ministers Hearers have got *something* of it already; or, however it appears an easy Thing to get *dark* Religion at any Time: So that Ministers will be more likely to be *deify'd* than *persecuted* by the World for preached *this* Gospel. . . .

This is the View in which the Thing appears to me: In Proportion therefore, as *Jesus Christ* appears to me to be a *great* Saviour, my *Heart always burns within me,* with Zeal against *that* Religion which makes him a *little* Saviour. Nay, sometimes when I ascribe *Glory to the Lamb* in my Heart, and *lift him up in* my very Soul, it seems that if I had as many Lives as Hairs on my Head, I could willingly and chearfully part with them all, rather than *come into their Secret,* who are for banishing a *particular* Faith out of the World, and thereby *pulling down* the Lord Jesus Christ, and *trampling* him under their Feet.

And, 'tis because *God who is rich in Mercy, for the great Love wherewith he loved me, when I was dead in Trespasses and in Sins,* hath *quickned* me by making me to know that Christ is *mighty to save,* that I have undertaken, and, at Length finished the ensuing Treatise; the great Design of which (*he* knows) is to speak a good Word for the *Lord Jesus Christ,* and to set the Crown upon *his* Head, when so many are going Traiterously to rob him of it, and to place it upon the Head of *Rebellious Man.*

And as I know that *Jealousy* for the Honour of *Zion's King,* hath made me *bold in my God,* to draw my Pen in *his* Cause, and to maintain *his* Right, notwithstanding a great *Host* of *Terrors* that were set *in Array* against me; so I am persuaded, *my God who stood by me, and strengthened me* to go through the Work, will bless it now it is done, to the *praise of the Glory of his Grace:* Nay, I *can't* doubt but it will redound more to his Glory than any Work I have been enabled to do *by* him, and *for* him, ever since I *knew the Grace of God in Truth.*

Here, I expect it will be said by *some,* "For *their* parts, *they* think I have been writing a Book that confutes *no body;* since all the Ministers they can find agree with me, that a *meer General* Faith is good for *nothing,* and that Believers should have a particular Application of the Blood of Christ to their *own* Souls." I answer; Ministers may agree together in saying *all this,* and yet be no nearer together in the Matter of *Justifying* Faith than *East* and *West.*

Accordingly, Dr. *Perkins*[1] observes, that both "*Papists* and *Protestants* agree together in holding that Believers should have a *particular* Application of the Blood of Christ unto their *own* Souls: and yet, (saith he) the Agreement is only *in Words:* For *we* hold a *particular* Application *by Faith; they* only *by Hope* and *Conjecture.*"

Just so it is with many Ministers at this Day: all the Application *they* hold is only *by Hope* and *Conjecture:* they teach that when Men see the Fruits of Faith in themselves, good Frames, and good Duties, *they* should thereby *humbly hope* and *conjecture* they have an Interest in the Blood of Christ; but they will not allow that one who is now an Hell-deserving Sinner, should *directly, immediately, before* he sees any good Thing in himself, believe that the *Blood of Jesus Christ*

---

[1] William Perkins (1558–1602), "that famous minister of Christ in the Universitie of Cambridge," one of Puritanism's foremost intellectuals, whose thought profoundly influenced the mind of seventeenth-century New England. [Ed.]

cleanseth him from all his Sins. In order to satisfy my self, whether these Men really held a *particular Faith,* notwithstanding all their Talk *for a particular Application,* I have often asked them, what was the first Thing a Man believes about Christ, when he believes *to Salvation?* Whether he believes that *he himself hath* (not *may* have *for* accepting, or, *if* he will accept upon Gospel-Terms, as the Phrase is, but actually *hath now*) *Redemption through his Blood,* even *the Forgiveness of Sins, according to the Riches of God's Grace?* And whether he will not have *as much* Assurance of the Forgiveness of *his* Sins, as he hath Faith?[2] And being try'd *this Way,* they are found *wanting,* and can say nothing but *Sibboleth, Sibboleth.*

I freely own I have had great Fears, lest *Antinomians* and *Libertines* who are always too plenty, and who shew themselves after a Day of *great Grace,* should like *vile Spiders* (as Mr. *Erskine* calls them) suck Poison out of the *Flower of the*

---

[2] *It having been reported that Mr.* Whitefield *held a* general *Faith, inasmuch as he had said, in a Sermon, that* Assurance was not of the Essence of saving Faith; *after I had found, that all he meant was, that* Assurance *was not* so necessary, *but that a Man might be a* true Believer, *tho' he should be* now *in* the dark, *or even* die in the dark *about his State: (which Thing I also held) I ask'd him whether a Man hath* not *as* much Assurance *as he hath* Faith: *To which he reply'd, Yes, Yes. I heard him preach* eight *Sermons, and discours'd with him I believe more than* eight *Times upon the Subject; and by all he appear'd to me, to speak out* Shibboleth *without any Hesitation. I could never believe that he denied a* particular *Faith, were it only for* this; *that* he knows *that he is of God; there being an heavenly* necessity *laid upon all such Persons to be Friends to that Faith. Accordingly, it may be observed to the Honour of a* particular *Faith, that of all the Men in the World who are Enemies to it, whether* Protestants, *or* Papists *(for the great* embattell'd *Army who are now against it, is a* confederate *Army made up of* Protestants *and* Papists, *especially the* latter; *the* Pope *himself being* Generalissimo *of the Host) there is not one single Person who knows that* he is of God. *For, whoever knows that he is of God, can know it only by a* particular *Faith: And such an one had rather be burnt to Ashes, than be against* that *Faith by which he knows himself to be of God.*

Gospel, and pervert what I have written to their *own Destruction.* But this I know, the Doctrine I advance is *essentially* different from *their's:* (Tho' *Luther* and *Calvin,* and St. *Paul* were tho't *Antinomians* for holding it: perhaps never any one preached *pure Gospel* without being *honour'd* with the *reproachful* Name of an *Antinomian:*) For *their* Faith is a Man's believing that he *hath been* forgiven, and *was actually* in a *State* of Favour with God, *before* Faith. . . .

Besides, The *Antinomians* don't hold it material, that there should be a Work of *Conviction before,* and a Work of *Sanctification* after Faith; whereas *we* maintain that no Man can *truly* believe *his* Sins are *freely* forgiven, till he sees himself *slain by the Law;* and that whosoever believes that he is *cleansed* in the *Blood of Christ,* will be *constrained* by the *Love of Christ to cleanse himself from all Filthiness of Flesh and Spirit, and to perfect Holiness in the Fear of God:* So that if *our* Faith is guarded (as it *always* should be) with a Work of *Conviction before,* and Work of *Sanctification behind,* *Antinomians* and *Libertines* have nothing to do with it; instead of speaking Comfort to *such,* it condemns them all to the Flames of Hell.

There is also one Thing more, which hath been Matter of much Concern to me, viz. An Apprehension lest those who are *Antiministerial,* and of a *Separating Spirit,* should get any Advantage by my Writings, and strengthen themselves in a *Way that is not good.* . . .

Another Argument against this *general* Faith is, That it is an Enemy, i.e. it makes Men Enemies to that glorious and Soul-ravishing Doctrine of *Assurance,* of which we read *so much* in the Scriptures of Truth.

Time would fail to enumerate all those Passages which either assert, or else plainly suppose, the *Assurance* of Faith to be what Believers *commonly* attain to. Very many to this Purpose may be seen in St. *John's* I. Epistle: Nay, St. *Peter* in his I. Epist. 1. Chap. Ver. 1, 8 takes it for granted, that all the Believers who were scattered throughout *Pontus, Galatia, Cappadocia, Asia* and *Bythinia,* knew something of *Assurance* by their own Experience. For which Reason, I have often thought with my self, what dreadful *Antinomians Peter* and *John,* and other Apostles would be looked upon were they to live at this Day; and how fast most Pulpit-doors in Town and Country would be shut against them! For the Generality of Ministers are so far from being of the same Mind with *them,* that they don't seem to think that scarce one in a thousand ever arrives to *Assurance;* when they speak of it, they *run it down* as a Thing that People are better *without* than with. 'Tis represented by them as a Thing that would make Persons *lazy* and *proud;* Nay, one of Note declared it to be so dangerous a Thing, that he said "an *assured Believer,* would be in great Danger of murdering himself, that he might go to Heaven the sooner."

Now, to what can it be owing that the Apostles and these Ministers agree no better in the Article of *Assurance?* The *Root of Bitterness* is the above-mention'd *dark* and *general* Faith: Take away *that* and the *Contention* ceases: Whereas that being *held fast* there *can* be *no Reconciliation.* Nay, I have sometimes wonder'd how it comes to pass, that the *Men of this Device,* agree with the Apostles as far as they do, in owning Assurance to be so much as a *possible Attainment:* For even *this* is more than their Principle will admit of. Let us make the Trial—Suppose some one hath actually attain'd to *Assurance;* I would ask, How did he come *by it?*

Now, if the Faith by which he was justified, was, as *they* say, only a Belief of *Jesus Christ's* being a sufficient Saviour for Sinners *in general;* every one may see that *this* Faith, though strain'd to the *highest Pitch,* will not *come up* to *Assurance.* For there can be nothing in the *Superlative,* of which there was not *something* in the *Positive.* If therefore there was no *Assurance* in the *positive* Degree, 'tis *impossible* there should be *any* in the *Superlative*. Since therefore the Man's Faith (let him be never so *strong in the Faith*) don't help him *at all* to *Assurance*, it follows that his *Assurance* if he hath *any*, can be only the *Assurance of Works*. Now that there can be no such Thing as the *Assurance of Works*, or *Assurance* rising *only* from the Observation of our good Frames, and good Duties, is evident enough from this single Consideration, viz. That every Believer knows how *unlike* a Child of God he is *sometimes:* And if he asks himself whether he who is *sometimes like* a Child of God, and *oftentimes unlike* one, be really a true Child of God, or else only a reformed Hypocrite; the most he can arrive to *this Way* will be a *Probability* that his State *may* be good. This Thing must needs be so: And if it is so, then it will follow, that though a Man hath never so much of *their* Faith, and withal *abounds* in good Works, he can't hereby come to any *Assurance:* And if Faith and Works together will not bring *Assurance*, I know not what will; all Men must live and die *without* it. The *small* Agreement therefore which there is between these Men and the Apostles, is *too much* for *their* Principles to bear: to be consistent with themselves, they must deny even the *Possibility of Assurance*. The Papists have gone this length: They were *resolved* to follow *their general* Faith as far as it would carry them; and since it led them to contradict the Apostles entirely, and to deny all *genuine Assurance*, they have done it with *great Boldness*. Nor, can I see how *these Calvinists,* (for *Calvinists* they will be called, though against *Calvin* in the main Point of a justifying Faith, as well as in other important Articles, as may be shewn in the Sequel) can *rationally* stop 'till they come to the same Conclusion.

Is not *this* therefore enough to spoil the Credit of a general Faith (if only *this* could be said against it) that it constrains Men by necessary Consequence to deny the Doctrine of Assurance, which the Bible is every where bespangled with? And, is it not clear from hence, that *true* Faith is of a *particular* Nature, whereby every one believes Christ to be *his* Saviour, and hath just so much *Assurance* as he hath Faith?

Nor, doth this Account of justifying Faith at all derogate from the Honour which the Scriptures put upon good Works, in making them *evidential* of a Man's good Estate. Indeed when a poor Sinner believes to Salvation, he looks upon God in Christ to be his Friend (according to his Word) without seeing any good Thing in himself; for before Faith there can be none: But a Man can never determine that he *hath* believ'd, and is *passed from Death to Life,* without seeing the *Fruits* of Faith in himself; because *if any Man is in Christ Jesus, he is a new Creature.* 2 Cor. 5. 17. Observing this Change in our selves, is what the Apostle, in Rom. 8. 16, calls the *Witness* of our *own Spirits;* and our looking upon God in Christ, to be our *Friend,* which we are enabled to by his Spirit, is in the same Verse, called the *Witness* of *his Spirit:* So that in Order to our being *quite sure,* that our *State* is good, there must be *two Witnesses,* and God must be *one* of them. . . .

Thus have we fairly try'd a general Faith at the Bar of Scripture and Reason, having examin'd many Evidences *for* it, and *against* it; and upon the whole, it appears, that it is so far from *justifying,* that 'tis only *Christ-despising, Man-exalting,* and *Soul-condemning* Faith; for which Reason it ought itself to be *condemned,* and *sentenced to die the Death.* And would to God that the *Sentence* might *speedily be executed!* O that Believers would join their Forces together, and *pray it to Death:* May we all with one Heart, and one Soul, besiege the Throne of Grace, and give God *no Rest,* 'till he *destroys* it out of the World, by the *Breath of his Mouth, and the Brightness of his Appearing.*

The CONCLUSION

The Conclusion of the whole Matter, shall be to exhort every one into whose Hands this little Book may come, not to be so cruel to his own Soul, as to venture it any longer upon a *general* Faith; But to see to it, that he hath a *particular* and *assured* Faith, that Christ is *his* Saviour, and that all his Benefits do really belong to *him.*

I know the World hates the Doctrine of *Assurance* (perhaps all the Errors and Imprudences that have been in the Land these few Years past, have not vext the World so much as this one *glorious* Doctrine of *Assurance,* which they have heard so often ringing in their Ears:) Because it *condemns* the World; because this *Light* being held up against their Religion, discovers it to be *Darkness:* And hence it is that *many* who love the *Name* of *Protestant* Ministers, are full as bad as the *Papists* and *Jesuits* themselves, in prejudicing their Hearers against the *full Assurance of Faith.*[3] But let me intreat you, not to *give Heed* to any of their Words; *The Poyson of Asps is under their Lips; Destruction and Misery are in their Ways:* If *they* can be brisk and chearful, though every Time they shut their Eyes to sleep, they do not *know* but that they may awake in Hell; do you have Pity upon your immortal Souls, and give your selves no Rest, 'till you have made *sure* of the *one Thing needful.*

Methinks I hear some poor Souls saying: "If we had a Thousand Worlds, we would part with them all, for this *Assurance* of which you are speaking." I answer; I wish you were willing to have it *for Nothing:* Do but let go your own Righteousness, and I dare pawn my Soul, that you shall have it before I have done speaking with you. *Come now, let us*

---

[3] *The* Jesuits *say, that the Apostles themselves, were not quite sure of their own Salvation; and that Christians now a days, must not think of having* full Assurance; *for this would be to go beyond the Apostles.* All *the* Arminians *preach this Divinity; which is not to be wonder'd at; (for it is easy to make out to the World that every* Arminian *is* more than three Quarters of a Papist:) *But is it not strange that professed* Calvinists *should symbolize with them?* . . .

reason together: What is the Difficulty, what is the *Wall of Partition* that lies in the Way to your having *Assurance?* Is it that you are old Sinners, great Sinners, *Sinners against God exceedingly?* Why, my dear Friends, Sin is *no Impediment* at all; you have no more Reason to doubt of God's good Will towards you, than if you had never sinn'd, you are in as good a Case as if you had never offended him, in Thought, in Word, or in Deed, *having such an High-Priest:* Though your Sins *have abounded,* the Grace of God hath *abounded much more;* though your Sins have reached unto the very Heavens, the Mercy of God in Christ is *above the Heavens.* Indeed, was *Jesus Christ* but a *little Saviour,* there would be good Reason for *great* Sinners to be afraid; nay, I myself should not have one Thought of being saved by him. But he is a *great* Saviour, *able to save unto the uttermost,* I know him to be such a Saviour, and therefore, I, though a *great* Sinner, though the *Chief of Sinners,* am not afraid to venture my Soul upon him: And if I had all your Souls to take Care of, I would *this Moment* venture them all upon *him,* without one Doubt of his being willing to save them.

A TREATISE CONCERNING

RELIGIOUS AFFECTIONS

———

Croswell was directly answered by Solomon Williams, who wrote in the name of New England's inherited faith. But the most telling confutation of Croswell's notion of "particular faith" was the volume in which Edwards most successfully translated traditional doctrine into the axioms and postulates of a new and distinctively American Calvinism. Nowhere in *The Religious Affections* was Croswell (nor, for that matter, any particular "heresy") mentioned by name. The rebuke came by way of Edwards' general reorientation of evangelical thought away from the momentary joys of conversion ("mere flowers") to sanctification and the "fruits" by which it was known. *The Religious Affections* began as a series of sermons delivered in 1742–1743, and it contained a defense of emotional religion and analyses of the varieties of Awakening experiences. But when Edwards came to publish

———

Jonathan Edwards, *A Treatise Concerning Religious Affections, Works,* III, 18–20, 70–76, 112–114, 186–189.

the work in 1746, he was no longer primarily concerned with refuting the rationalist view of the human personality. Only one section of *The Affections,* and that the shortest, was devoted to upholding "the religion of the heart." Edwards' main effort was to show how and why the joys of many who thought themselves converted were not truly "spiritual." His arguments were largely negative, but at every point he relentlessly exposed the prideful selfhood of any feeling or vision short of an apprehension of the "divinity of divinity." Not until the *Dissertation on True Virtue* was Edwards to disclose the whole of his meaning—by identifying the "excellency of excellency" with the sweet beauty of social union. Still, the doctrines of *The Religious Affections* required, and were designed to encourage, heartfelt and active commitment to the ultimate good of mankind. Only by the preaching of such doctrines, Edwards insisted, could the momentum of history be restored, and New England regain "that fair prospect, we had a little while ago, of a kind of paradisaic state."

Upon the whole, I think it clearly and abundantly evident, that true religion lies very much in the affections. Not that I think these arguments prove, that religion in the hearts of the truly godly, is ever in exact proportion to the degree of affection, and present emotion of the mind: for undoubtedly, there is much affection in the true saints which is not spiritual; their religious affections are often mixed; all is not from grace, but much from nature. And though the affections have not their seat in the body; yet the constitution of the body may very much contribute to the present emotion of the mind. And the degree of religion is rather to be judged of by the fixedness and strength of the habit that is exercised in affection, whereby holy affection is habitual, than by the degree of the present exercise; and the strength of that habit is not always in proportion to outward effects and manifestations, or inward effects, in the hurry and vehemence, and sudden changes of the course of the thoughts of the mind. But yet it is evident, that religion consists so much in affection, as that without holy affection there is no true religion; and no light in the understanding is good, which does not produce holy affection in the heart: no habit or principle in the heart is good, which has no such exercise; and no external fruit is good, which does not proceed from such exercises.

Having thus considered the evidence of the proposition laid down, I proceed to some inferences.

1. We may hence learn how great their error is, who are for discarding all religious affections, as having nothing solid or substantial in them.

There seems to be too much of a disposition this way, prevailing in this land at this time. Because many who, in the late extraordinary season, appeared to have great religious affections, did not manifest a right temper of mind, and run into many errors, in the time of their affections, and the heat of their zeal; and because the high affections of many seem to be so soon come to nothing, and some who seemed to be mightily raised and swallowed up with joy and zeal, for a while, seem to have returned like the dog to his vomit; hence religious affections in general are grown out of credit with great numbers, as though true religion did not at all consist in them. Thus we easily and naturally run from one extreme to another. A little while ago we were in the other extreme; there was a prevalent disposition to look upon all high religious affections as eminent exercises of true grace, without much inquiring into the nature and source of those affections, and the manner in which they arose: if persons did but appear to be indeed very much moved and raised, so as to be full of religious talk, and express themselves with great warmth and earnestness, and to be filled, or to be very full, as the phrases were; it was too much the manner, without further examination, to conclude such persons were full of the Spirit of God, and had eminent experience of his gracious influences. This was the extreme which was prevailing three or four years ago. But of late, instead of esteeming and admiring all religious affections without distinction, it is a thing much more prevalent, to reject and discard all without distinction. Herein appears the subtilty of Satan. While he saw that affections were much in vogue, knowing the greater part of the land were not versed in such things, and had not had much experience of great religious affections to enable them to judge well of them, and distinguish between true and false; then he knew he could best play his game, by sowing tares amongst the wheat, and mingling false affections with the works of God's Spirit: he knew this to be a likely way to delude and eternally ruin many souls, and greatly to wound religion in the saints, and entangle them in a dreadful wilderness, and by and by, to bring all religion into disrepute.

But now, when the ill consequences of these false affections appear, and it is become very apparent, that some of those emotions which made a glaring show, and were by many greatly admired, were in reality nothing; the devil sees it to be for his interest to go another way to work, and to endeavor to his utmost to propagate and establish a persuasion, that all affections and sensible emotions of the mind, in things of religion, are nothing at all to be regarded, but are rather to be avoided, and carefully guarded against, as things of a pernicious tendency. This he knows is the way to bring all religion to a mere lifeless formality, and effectually shut out the power of godliness, and every thing which is spiritual, and to have all true Christianity turned out of doors. For although to true religion there must indeed be something else besides affection; yet true religion consists so much in the affections, that there can be no true religion without them. He who has no religious affection, is in a state of spiritual death, and is wholly destitute of the powerful, quickening, saving influences of the Spirit of God upon his heart. As there is no true religion where there is nothing else but affection, so there is no true religion where there is no religious affection. As on the one hand, there must be light in the understanding, as well as an affected fervent heart; where there is heat without light, there can be nothing divine or heavenly in that heart; so on the other hand, where there is a kind of light without heat, a head stored with notions and speculations, with a cold and unaffected heart, there can be nothing divine in that light, that knowledge is no true spiritual knowledge of divine things. If the great things of religion are rightly understood, they will affect the heart. The reason why men are not affected by such infinitely great, important, glorious, and wonderful things, as they often hear and read of, in the word of God, is undoubtedly because they are blind; if they were not so, it would be impossible, and utterly inconsistent with human nature, that their hearts should be otherwise than strongly impressed, and greatly moved by such things. . . .

They who condemn high affections in others, are certainly not likely to have high affections themselves. And let it be considered, that they who have but little religious affection, have certainly but little religion. And they who condemn others for their religious affections, and have none themselves, have no religion.

There are false affections, and there are true. A man's having much affection, does not prove that he has any true religion; but if he has no affection, it proves he has no true religion. The right way, is not to reject all affections, nor to approve all; but to distinguish between affections, approving some, and rejecting others; separating between the wheat and the chaff, the gold and the dross, the precious and the vile. . . .

The true saints only have that which is spiritual; others have nothing which is divine, in the sense that has been spoken of. They not only have not these communications of the Spirit of God in so high a degree as the saints, but have nothing of that nature or kind. For the Apostle James tells us, that natural men have not the Spirit; and Christ teaches the necessity of a new birth, or of being born of the Spirit, from this, that he that is born of the flesh, has only flesh, and no spirit, John iii. 6. . . . And the Scripture speaks of the actual being of a gracious principle in the soul, though in its first beginning, as a seed there planted, as inconsistent with a man's being a sinner, 1 John iii. 9. And natural men are represented in Scripture, as having no spiritual light, no spiritual life, and no spiritual being; and therefore conversion is often compared to opening the eyes of the blind, raising the dead, and a work of creation (wherein creatures are made entirely new), and becoming new-born children.

From these things it is evident, that those gracious influences which the saints are subjects of, and the effects of God's Spirit which they experience, are entirely above nature, altogether of a different kind from any thing that men find within themselves by nature, or only in the exercise of natural principles; and are things which no improvement of those qualifications, or principles that are natural, no advancing or exalting them to higher degrees, and no kind of composition of them, will ever bring men to; because they not only differ from what is natural, and from every thing that natural men experience, in degree and circumstances, but also in kind; and are of a nature vastly more excellent. And this is what I mean, by supernatural, when I say that gracious affections are from those influences that are supernatural.

From hence it follows, that in those gracious exercises and

affections which are wrought in the minds of the saints, through the saving influences of the Spirit of God, there is a new inward perception or sensation of their minds, entirely different in its nature and kind, from any thing that ever their minds were the subjects of before they were sanctified. For doubtless if God by his mighty power produces something that is new, not only in degree and circumstances, but in its whole nature, and that which could be produced by no exalting, varying, or compounding of what was there before, or by adding any thing of the like kind; I say, if God produces something thus new in a mind, that is a perceiving, thinking, conscious thing; then doubtless something entirely new is felt, or perceived, or thought; or, which is the same thing, there is some new sensation or perception of the mind, which is entirely of a new sort, and which could be produced by no exalting, varying, or compounding of that kind of perceptions or sensations which the mind had before; or there is what some metaphysicians call a new simple idea. If grace be, in the sense above described, an entirely new kind of principle, then the exercises of it are also entirely a new kind of exercises. And if there be in the soul a new sort of exercises which it is conscious of, which the soul knew nothing of before, and which no improvement, composition, or management of what it was before conscious or sensible of, could produce, or any thing like it; then it follows that the mind has an entirely new kind of perception or sensation; and here is, as it were, a new spiritual sense that the mind has, or a principle of a new kind of perception or spiritual sensation, which is in its whole nature different from any former kinds of sensation of the mind, as tasting is diverse from any of the other senses; and something is perceived by a true saint, in the exercise of this new sense of mind, in spiritual and divine things, as entirely diverse from any thing that is perceived in them, by natural men, as the sweet taste of honey is diverse from the ideas men have of honey by only looking on it, and feeling of it. So that the spiritual perceptions which a sanctified and spiritual person has, are not only diverse from all that natural men have after the manner that the ideas or perceptions of the same sense may differ one from another, but rather as the ideas and sensations of different senses do differ. Hence the work of the Spirit of God in regeneration is often in Scripture compared to the giving a new sense, giving eyes to see, and ears to hear, unstopping the ears of the deaf, and opening the eyes of them that were born blind, and turning from darkness unto light. And because this spiritual sense is immensely the most noble and excellent, and that without which all other principles of perception, and all our faculties are useless and vain; therefore the giving this new sense, with the blessed fruits and effects of it in the soul, is compared to a raising the dead, and to a new creation.

This new spiritual sense, and the new dispositions that attend it, are no new faculties, but are new principles of nature. I use the word principles for want of a word of a more determinate signification. By a principle of nature in this place, I mean that foundation which is laid in nature, either old or new, for any particular manner or kind of exercise of the faculties of the soul; or a natural habit or foundation for action, giving a personal ability and disposition to exert the faculties in exercises of such a certain kind; so that to exert the faculties in that kind of exercises may be said to be his nature. So this new spiritual sense is not a new faculty of understanding, but it is a new foundation laid in the nature of the soul, for a new kind of exercises of the same faculty of understanding. So that new holy disposition of heart that attends this new sense is not a new faculty of will, but a foundation laid in the nature of the soul, for a new kind of exercises of the same faculty of will. . . .

From what has been said it follows, that all spiritual and

gracious affections are attended with and do arise from some apprehension, idea, or sensation of mind, which is in its whole nature different, yea, exceeding different, from all that is, or can be in the mind of a natural man; and which the natural man discerns nothing of, and has no manner of idea of (agreeable to 1 Cor. ii. 14), and conceives of no more than a man without the sense of tasting can conceive of the sweet taste of honey, or a man without the sense of hearing can conceive of the melody of a tune, or a man born blind can have a notion of the beauty of the rainbow.

But here two things must be observed, in order to the right understanding of this.

1. On the one hand it must be observed, that not every thing which in any respect appertains to spiritual affections, is new and entirely different from what natural men can conceive of, and do experience; some things are common to gracious affections with other affections; many circumstances, appendages and effects are common. Thus a saint's love to God has a great many things appertaining to it, which are common with a man's natural love to a near relation; love to God makes a man have desires of the honor of God, and a desire to please him; so does a natural man's love to his friend make him desire his honor, and desire to please him; love to God causes a man to delight in the thoughts of God, and to delight in the presence of God, and to desire conformity to God, and the enjoyment of God; and so it is with a man's love to his friend; and many other things might be mentioned which are common to both. But yet that idea which the saint has of the loveliness of God, and that sensation, and that kind of delight he has in that view, which is as it were the marrow and quintessence of his love, is peculiar, and entirely diverse from any thing that a natural man has, or can have any notion of. And even in those things that seem to be common, there is something peculiar; both spiritual and natural love cause desires

after the object beloved; but they be not the same sort of desires: there is a sensation of soul in the spiritual desires of one that loves God, which is entirely different from all natural desires: both spiritual love and natural love are attended with delight in the object beloved; but the sensations of delight are not the same, but entirely and exceedingly diverse. Natural men may have conceptions of many things about spiritual affections; but there is something in them which is as it were the nucleus, or kernel of them, that they have no more conception of, than one born blind, has of colors.

It may be clearly illustrated by this: we will suppose two men; one is born without the sense of tasting, the other has it; the latter loves honey, and is greatly delighted in it, because he knows the sweet taste of it; the other loves certain sounds and colors; the love of each has many things that appertain to it, which is common; it causes both to desire and delight in the object beloved, and causes grief when it is absent, &c., but yet that idea or sensation which he who knows the taste of honey has of its excellency and sweetness, that is the foundation of his love, is entirely different from any thing the other has or can have; and that delight which he has in honey is wholly diverse from any thing that the other can conceive of, though they both delight in their beloved objects. So both these persons may in some respects love the same object: the one may love a delicious kind of fruit, which is beautiful to the eye, and of a delicious taste; not only because he has seen its pleasant colors, but knows its sweet taste; the other, perfectly ignorant of this, loves it only for its beautiful colors: there are many things seen, in some respect, to be common to both; both love, both desire, and both delight; but the love and desire, and delight of the one, is altogether diverse from that of the other. The difference between the love of a natural man and a spiritual man is like to this; but only it must be observed, that in one respect it is vastly greater, viz., that the kinds of excellency which are perceived in spiritual objects, by these different kinds of persons, are in themselves vastly more diverse than the different kinds of excellency perceived in delicious fruit, by a tasting and a tasteless man; and in another respect it may not be so great, viz., as the spiritual man may have a spiritual sense or taste, to perceive that divine and most peculiar excellency but in small beginnings, and in a very imperfect degree.

2. On the other hand, it must be observed that a natural man may have those religious apprehensions and affections, which may be in many respects very new and surprising to him, and what before he did not conceive of; and yet what he experiences be nothing like the exercises of a principle of new nature, or the sensations of a new spiritual sense; his affections may be very new, by extraordinarily moving natural principles in a very new degree, and with a great many new circumstances, and a new co-operation of natural affections, and a new composition of ideas; this may be from some extraordinary powerful influence of Satan, and some great delusion; but there is nothing but nature extraordinarily acted. As if a poor man that had always dwelt in a cottage and, had never looked beyond the obscure village where he was born, should in a jest be taken to a magnificent city and prince's court, and there arrayed in princely robes, and set on the throne, with the crown royal on his head, peers and nobles bowing before him, and should be made to believe that he was now a glorious monarch; the ideas he would have, and the affections he would experience, would in many respects be very new, and such as he had no imagination of before; but all this is no more than extraordinarily raising and exciting natural principles, and newly exalting, varying, and compounding such sort of ideas, as he has by nature; here is nothing like giving him a new sense.

Upon the whole, I think it is clearly manifest, that all truly gracious affections do arise from special and peculiar influences of the Spirit, working that sensible effect or sensation in the souls of the saints, which are entirely different from all that is possible a natural man should experience, not only different in degree and circumstances, but different in its whole nature; so that a natural man not only cannot experience that which is individually the same, but cannot experience any thing but what is exceeding diverse, and immensely below it, in its kind; and that which the power of men or devils is not sufficient to produce the like of, or any thing of the same nature.

I have insisted largely on this matter, because it is of great importance and use evidently to discover and demonstrate the delusions of Satan, in many kinds of false religious affections, which multitudes are deluded by, and probably have been in all ages of the Christian church; and to settle and determine many articles of doctrine, concerning the operations of the Spirit of God, and the nature of true grace.

Now, therefore, to apply these things to the purpose of this discourse.

From hence it appears, that impressions which some have made on their imagination, or the imaginary ideas which they have of God or Christ, or heaven, or any thing appertaining to religion, have nothing in them that is spiritual, or of the nature of true grace. Though such things may attend what is spiritual, and be mixed with it, yet in themselves they have nothing that is spiritual, nor are they any part of gracious experience.

Here, for the sake of common people, I will explain what is intended by impressions on the imagination and imaginary ideas. The imagination is that power of the mind whereby it can have a conception, or idea of things of an external or outward nature (that is, of such sort of things as are the objects of the outward senses) when those things are not present, and be not perceived by the senses. It is called imagination from the word *image;* because thereby a person can have an image of some external thing in his mind, when that thing is not present in reality, nor any thing like it. All such things as we perceive by our five external senses, seeing, hearing, smelling, tasting, and feeling, are external things: and when a person has an idea or image of any of these sorts of things in his mind, when they are not there, and when he does not really see, hear, smell, taste, nor feel them; that is to have an imagination of them, and these ideas are imaginary ideas: and when such kinds of ideas are strongly impressed upon the mind, and the image of them in the mind is very lively, almost as if one saw them, or heard them, &c., that is called an impression on the imagination. Thus colors and shapes, and a form of countenance, they are outward things; because they are that sort of things which are the objects of the outward sense of seeing; and therefore when any person has in his mind a lively idea of any shape, or color, or form of countenance; that is to have an imagination of those things. So if he has an idea, of such sort of light or darkness, as he perceives by the sense of seeing; that is to have an idea of outward light, and so is an imagination. So if he has an idea of any marks made on paper, suppose letters and words written in a book; that is to have an external and imaginary idea of such kind of things as we sometimes perceive by our bodily eyes. And when we have the ideas of that kind of things which we perceive by any of the other senses, as of any sounds or voices, or words spoken; this is only to have ideas of outward things, viz., of such kind of things as are perceived by the external sense of hearing, and so that also is imagination: and when these ideas are livelily impressed, almost as if they were really heard with the ears, this is to have an impression on the imagination. And so I might go on, and instance in the ideas of things appertaining to the other three senses of smelling, tasting, and feeling.

Many who have had such things have very ignorantly supposed them to be of the nature of spiritual discoveries. They have had lively ideas of some external shape, and beautiful form of countenance; and this they call spiritually seeing Christ. Some have had impressed upon them ideas of a great outward light; and this they call a spiritual discovery of God's or Christ's glory. Some have had ideas of Christ's hanging on the cross, and his blood running from his wounds; and this they call a spiritual sight of Christ crucified, and the way of salvation by his blood. Some have seen him with his arms open ready to embrace them; and this they call a discovery of the sufficiency of Christ's grace and love. Some have had lively ideas of heaven, and of Christ on his throne there, and shining ranks of saints and angels; and this they call seeing heaven opened to them. Some from time to time have had a lively idea of a person of a beautiful countenance smiling upon them; and this they call a spiritual discovery of the love of Christ to their souls, and tasting the love of Christ. And they look upon it a sufficient evidence that these things are spiritual discoveries, and that they see them spiritually, because they say they do not see these things with their bodily eyes, but in their hearts; for they can see them when their eyes are shut. And in like manner, the imaginations of some have been impressed with ideas of the sense of hearing; they have had ideas of words, as if they were spoken to them, sometimes they are the words of Scripture, and sometimes other words: they have had ideas of Christ's speaking comfortable words to them. These things they have called having the inward call of Christ, hearing the voice of Christ spiritually in their hearts, having the witness of the Spirit, and the inward testimony of the love of Christ, &c.

The common and less considerate and understanding sort of people, are the more easily led into apprehensions that these things are spiritual things, because spiritual things being invisible, and not things that can be pointed forth with the finger, we are forced to use figurative expressions in speaking of them, and to borrow names from external and sensible objects to signify them by. Thus we call a clear apprehension of things spiritual by the name of *light;* and a having such an apprehension of such or such things, by the name of *seeing* such things; and the conviction of the judgment, and the persuasion of the will, by the word of Christ in the gospel, we signify by spiritually hearing the call of Christ: and the Scripture itself abounds with such like figurative expressions. Persons hearing these often used, and having pressed upon them the necessity of having their eyes opened, and having a discovery of spiritual things, and seeing Christ in his glory, and having the inward call, and the like, they ignorantly look and wait for some such external discoveries, and imaginary views as have been spoken of; and when they have them are confident, that now their eyes are opened, now Christ has discovered himself to them, and they are his children; and hence are exceedingly affected and elevated with their deliverance and happiness, and many kinds of affections are at once set in a violent motion in them.

But it is exceedingly apparent that such ideas have nothing in them which is spiritual and divine, in the sense wherein it has been demonstrated that all gracious experiences are spiritual and divine. These external ideas are in no wise of such a sort, that they are entirely, and in their whole nature diverse from all that men have by nature, perfectly different from, and vastly above any sensation which it is possible a man should have by any natural sense or principle, so that in order to have them, a man must have a new spiritual and divine sense given him, in order to have any sensations of that sort: so far from this, that they are ideas of the same sort which we have by the external senses, that are some of the inferior powers of the human nature; they are merely ideas of external objects, or ideas of that nature, of the same outward, sensitive kind; the same sort of sensations of mind (differing not in degree, but only in circumstances) that we have by those natural principles which are common to us with the beasts viz., the five external senses. . . .

From what has been said, therefore, we come necessarily to this conclusion, concerning that wherein spiritual understanding consists, viz., that it consists in "a sense of the heart, of the supreme beauty and sweetness of the holiness or moral perfection of divine things, together with all that discerning and knowledge of things of religion, that depends upon, and flows from such a sense."

Spiritual understanding consists primarily in a sense of heart of that spiritual beauty. I say, a sense of heart; for it is not speculation merely that is concerned in this kind of understanding; nor can there be a clear distinction made between the two faculties of understanding and will, as acting distinctly and separately, in this matter. When the mind is sensible of the sweet beauty and amiableness of a thing, that implies a sensibleness of sweetness and delight in the presence of the idea of it: and this sensibleness of the amiableness or delightfulness of beauty, carries in the very nature of it the sense of the heart; or an effect and impression the soul is the subject of, as a substance possessed of taste, inclination and will.

There is a distinction to be made between a mere notional understanding, wherein the mind only beholds things in the exercise of a speculative faculty; and the sense of the heart, wherein the mind does not only speculate and behold, but relishes and feels. That sort of knowledge, by which a man has a sensible perception of amiableness and loathsomeness, or of sweetness and nauseousness, is not just the same sort of knowledge with that by which he knows what a triangle is, and what a square is. The one is mere speculative knowledge, the other sensible knowledge, in which more than the mere intellect is concerned; the heart is the proper subject of it, or the soul, as a being that not only beholds, but has inclination, and is pleased or displeased. And yet there is the nature of instruction in it; as he that has perceived the sweet taste of honey, knows much more about it, than he who has only looked upon, and felt of it.

The apostle seems to make a distinction between mere speculative knowledge of the things of religion, and spiritual knowledge, in calling that the form of knowledge, and of the truth in the law, Rom. ii. 20, "Which hast the form of knowledge and of the truth in the law." The latter is often represented by relishing, smelling, or tasting: 2 Cor. ii. 14, "Now thanks be to God, which always causeth us to triumph in Christ Jesus, and maketh manifest the savor of his knowledge, in every place." Matt. xvi. 23, "Thou savorest not the things that be of God, but those things that be of men." 1 Pet. ii. 2, 3, "As new born babes, desire the sincere milk of the word, that ye may grow thereby; if so be ye have tasted that the Lord is gracious." Cant. i. 3, "Because of the savor of thy good ointments, thy name is as ointment poured forth, therefore do the virgins love thee;" compared with 1 John ii. 20, "But ye have an unction from the Holy One, and ye know all things."

Spiritual understanding primarily consists in this sense, of taste of the moral beauty of divine things; so that no knowledge can be called spiritual, any further than it arises from this, and has this in it. But secondarily it includes all that discerning and knowledge of things of religion, which depend upon and flow from such a sense.

When the true beauty and amiableness of the holiness or true moral good that is in divine things is discovered to the soul, it as it were opens a new world to its views. This shows the glory of all the perfections of God, and of every thing appertaining to the divine Being. For, as was observed before, the beauty of all arises from God's moral perfection. This

shows the glory of all God's works, both of creation and providence. For it is the special glory of them, that God's holiness,
righteousness, faithfulness, and goodness, are so manifested
in them; and without these moral perfections, there would be
no glory in that power and skill with which they are wrought.
The glorifying of God's moral perfections, is the special end
of all the works of God's hands. By this sense of the moral
beauty of divine things, is understood the sufficiency of Christ
as a mediator; for it is only by the discovery of the beauty
of the moral perfection of Christ, that the believer is let into
the knowledge of the excellency of his person, so as to know
any thing more of it than the devils do; and it is only by the
knowledge of the excellency of Christ's person, that any know
his sufficiency as a mediator; for the latter depends upon, and
arises from the former. It is by seeing the excellency of Christ's
person, that the saints are made sensible of the preciousness
of his blood, and its sufficiency to atone for sin; for therein
consists the preciousness of Christ's blood, that it is the blood
of so excellent and amiable a person. And on this depends
the meritoriousness of his obedience, and sufficiency and prevalence of his intercession. By this sight of the moral beauty of
divine things, is seen the beauty of the way of salvation by
Christ; for that consists in the beauty of the moral perfections
of God, which wonderfully shines forth in every step of this
method of salvation, from beginning to end. By this is seen
the fitness and suitableness of this way: for this wholly consists in its tendency to deliver us from sin and hell, and to
bring us to the happiness which consists in the possession and
enjoyment of moral good, in a way sweetly agreeing with
God's moral perfections. And in the way's being contrived so
as to attain these ends, consists the excellent wisdom of that
way. By this is seen the excellency of the word of God. Take
away all the moral beauty and sweetness in the word, and
the Bible is left wholly a dead letter, a dry, lifeless, tasteless

thing. By this is seen the true foundation of our duty, the worthiness of God to be so esteemed, honored, loved, submitted to, and served, as he requires of us, and the amiableness of the duties themselves that are required of us. And by this is seen the true evil of sin; for he who sees the beauty of holiness, must necessarily see the hatefulness of sin, its contrary. By this men understand the true glory of heaven, which consists in the beauty and happiness that is in holiness. By this is seen the amiableness and happiness of both saints and angels. He that sees the beauty of holiness, or true moral good, sees the greatest and most important thing in the world, which is the fitness of all things, without which all the world is empty, no better than nothing, yea, worse than nothing. Unless this is seen, nothing is seen that is worth the seeing; for there is no other true excellency or beauty. Unless this be understood, nothing is understood that is worthy of the exercise of the noble faculty of understanding. This is the beauty of the Godhead, and the divinity of divinity (if I may so speak), the good of the infinite fountain of good; without which, God himself (if that were possible) would be an infinite evil; without which we ourselves had better never have been; and without which there had better have been no being. He therefore in effect knows nothing, that knows not this. . . .

Things being thus, it plainly appears, that God's implanting that spiritual supernatural sense which has been spoken of, makes a great change in a man. . . .

. . . And thus it is that holy affections have a governing power in the course of a man's life. A statue may look very much like a real man, and a beautiful man; yea, it may have, in its appearance to the eye, the resemblance of a very lively, strong, and active man; but yet an inward principle of life and strength is wanting; and therefore it does nothing, it brings nothing to pass, there is no action or operation to answer the show. False discoveries and affections do not go deep enough to reach and govern the spring of men's actions and practice. The seed in stony ground had not deepness of earth, and the root did not go deep enough to bring forth fruit. But gracious affections go to the very bottom of the heart, and take hold of the very inmost springs of life and activity.

Herein chiefly appears the power of true godliness, viz., in its being effectual in practice. And the efficacy of godliness in this respect, is what the apostle has respect to, when he speaks of the power of godliness, 2 Tim. iii. 5, as is very plain; for he there is particularly declaring, how some professors of religion would notoriously fail in the practice of it, and then in the 5th verse observes, that in being thus of an unholy practice, they deny the power of godliness, though they have the form of it. Indeed the power of godliness is exerted in the first place within the soul, in the sensible, lively exercise of gracious affections there. Yet the principal evidence of this power of godliness, is in those exercises of holy affections that are practical, and in their being practical; in conquering the will, and conquering the lusts and corruptions of men, and carrying men on in the way of holiness, through all temptations, difficulty, and opposition.

Again, the reason why gracious affections have their exercise and effect in Christian practice, appears from this (which has also been before observed), that "the first objective ground of gracious affections, is the transcendently excellent and amiable nature of divine things, as they are in themselves, and not any conceived relation they bear to self, or self-interest." This shows why holy affections will cause men to be holy in their practice universally. What makes men partial in religion is, that they seek themselves, and not God, in their religion; and close with religion, not for its own excellent nature, but only to serve a turn. He that closes with religion only to serve a turn, will close with no more of it than he imagines serves that turn; but he that closes with religion for its own excellent and lovely nature, closes with all that has that nature: he that embraces religion for its own sake, embraces the whole of religion. This also shows why gracious affections will cause men to practise religion perseveringly, and at all times. Religion may alter greatly in process of time, as to its consistence with men's private interest, in many respects; and therefore he that complies with it only for selfish views, is liable, in change of times, to forsake it; but the excellent nature of religion, as it is in itself, is invariable; it is always the same, at all times, and through all changes; it never alters in any respect.

The reason why gracious affections issue in holy practice, also further appears from the kind of excellency of divine things, that it has been observed is the foundation of all holy affections, viz., "their moral excellency, or the beauty of their holiness." No wonder that a love to holiness, for holiness' sake, inclines persons to practise holiness, and to practise every thing that is holy. Seeing holiness is the main thing that excites, draws, and governs all gracious affections, no wonder that all such affections tend to holiness. That which men love, they desire to have and to be united to, and possessed of. That beauty which men delight in, they desire to be adorned with. Those acts which men delight in, they necessarily incline to do.

And what has been observed of that divine teaching and leading of the Spirit of God, which there is in gracious affections, shows the reason of this tendency of such affections to a universally holy practice. For, as has been observed, the Spirit of God in this his divine teaching and leading, gives the soul a natural relish of the sweetness of that which is holy, and of every thing that is holy, so far as it comes in view and excites a disrelish and disgust of every thing that is unholy. . . .

The reason of this practical tendency and issue of gracious affections, further appears from what has been observed of such affections being "attended with a thorough conviction of

the judgment of the reality and certainty of divine things."
No wonder that they who were never thoroughly convinced
that there is any reality in the things of religion, will never be
at the labor and trouble of such an earnest, universal and
persevering practice of religion, through all difficulties, self-
denials, and sufferings in a dependence on that, which they
are not convinced of. But on the other hand, they who are
thoroughly convinced of the certain truth of those things,
must needs be governed by them in their practice; for the
things revealed in the word of God are so great, and so infinitely more important than all other things, that it is inconsistent with the human nature, that a man should fully believe
the truth of them, and not be influenced by them above all
things in his practice.

Again, the reason of this expression and effect of holy
affections in the practice, appears from what has been observed of "a change of nature, accompanying such affections."
Without a change of nature, men's practice will not be thoroughly changed. Until the tree be made good, the fruit will
not be good. Men do not gather grapes of thorns, nor figs of
thistles. The swine may be washed, and appear clean for a
little while, but yet, without a change of nature he will still
wallow in the mire. Nature is a more powerful principle of
action, than any thing that opposes it: though it may be violently restrained for a while, it will finally overcome that
which restrains it: it is like the stream of a river, it may be
stopped a while with a dam, but if nothing be done to dry the
fountain, it will not be stopped always; it will have a course,
either in its old channel, or a new one. Nature is a thing more
constant and permanent, than any of those things that are the
foundation of carnal men's reformation and righteousness.
When a natural man denies his lust, and lives a strict, religious
life, and seems humble, painful, and earnest in religion, it is
not natural; it is all a force against nature; as when a stone is
violently thrown upwards; but that force will be gradually

spent; yet nature will remain it its full strength, and so prevails again, and the stone returns downwards. As long as corrupt nature is not mortified, but the principle left whole in a man, it is a vain thing to expect that it should not govern. But if the old nature be indeed mortified, and a new and heavenly nature infused, then may it well be expected, that men will walk in newness of life, and continue to do so to the end of their days. . . .

The tendency of grace in the heart to holy practice, is very direct, and the connection most natural, close and necessary. True grace is not an unactive thing; there is nothing in heaven or earth of a more active nature; for it is life itself, and the most active kind of life, even spiritual and divine life. It is no barren thing; there is nothing in the universe that in its nature has a greater tendency to fruit. Godliness in the heart has as direct a relation to practice, as a fountain has to a stream, or as the luminous nature of the sun has to beams sent forth, or as life has to breathing, or the beating of the pulse, or any other vital act; or as a habit or principle of action has to action; for it is the very nature and motion of grace, that it is a principle of holy action or practice. Regeneration, which is that work of God in which grace is infused, has a direct relation to practice; for it is the very end of it, with a view to which the whole work is wrought; all is calculated and framed, in this mighty and manifold change wrought in the soul, so as directly to tend to this end.

. . . Christian practice, taken in the sense that has been explained, is the chief of all the evidences of a saving sincerity in religion, to the consciences of the professors of it; much to be preferred to the method of the first convictions, enlightenings, and comforts in conversion, or any immanent discoveries or exercises of grace whatsoever, that begin and end in contemplation.

. . . Reason plainly shows, that those things which put it to the proof what men will actually cleave to and prefer in their practice, when left to follow their own choice and inclinations, are the proper trial what they do really prefer in their hearts. Sincerity in religion, as has been observed already, consists in setting God highest in the heart, in choosing him before other things, in having a heart to sell all for Christ, &c. But a man's actions are the proper trial what a man's heart prefers. As for instance, when it is so that God and other things come to stand in competition, God is as it were set before a man on one hand, and his worldly interest or pleasure on the other (as it often is so in the course of a man's life); his behavior in such case, in actually cleaving to the one and forsaking the other, is the proper trial which he prefers. Sincerity consists in forsaking all for Christ in heart; but to forsake all for Christ in heart, is the very same thing as to have a heart to forsake all for Christ; but certainly the proper trial whether a man has a heart to forsake all for Christ, is his being actually put to it, the having Christ and other things coming in competition, that he must actually or practically cleave to one and forsake the other. To forsake all for Christ in heart, is the same thing as to have a heart to forsake all for Christ when called to it: but the highest proof to ourselves and others, that we have a heart to forsake all for Christ when called to it, is actually doing it when called to it, or so far as called to it. To follow Christ in heart is to have a heart to follow him. To deny ourselves in heart for Christ, is the same thing as to have a heart to deny ourselves for him in fact. The main and most proper proof of a man's having a heart to any thing, concerning which he is at liberty to follow his own inclinations, and either to do or not to do as he pleases, is his doing of it. When a man is at liberty whether to speak or keep silence, the most proper evidence of his having a heart to speak, is his speaking. When a man is at liberty whether to walk or sit still, the proper proof of his having a heart to walk, is his walking. Godliness consists not in a heart to intend to do the will of God, but in a heart to do it.

46 · *Lemuel Briant*

(1 7 2 2 – 1 7 5 4)

THE ABSURDITY OF

DEPRECIATING MORAL VIRTUE

The young Calvinists who followed Edwards' lead in preaching "experimental religion" came under attack, from Separates and even among their own people, as "legalists." But Edwards' thought urged the performance of the "works of the law," not as a means of procuring or earning salvation, but as the only evidence by which men who thought themselves touched by the Spirit might come to know they were in fact saved. Moreover, the "moral law" of post-Awakening Calvinism held quite different ethical imperatives from those contained within the creed of Arminian rationalism. Indeed, most spokesmen of rational religion recognized the radical social implications of "experimental religion," but they attacked Calvinism, not on this score, but as releasing men from all social duties whatever. Unless men thought their works could win them

Lemuel Briant, *The Absurdity and Blasphemy of Depreciating Moral Virtue* . . . (Boston, 1749), pp. 6–11, 22–31.

God's favor, argued the new Arminianism, there could be no compelling motive to moral behavior. Such a critique of Calvinism was made by Lemuel Briant in a sermon first delivered in Scituate and then repeated, on June 18, 1749, from the pulpit of Jonathan Mayhew's West Church in Boston. Briant's sermon was immediately recognized, and answered, as the first charge in a rationalist counterattack on post-Awakening Calvinism. Indeed John Adams, one of Briant's North Braintree parishioners, considered this "jocular and liberal" preacher the founder of New England Unitarianism. But Briant's "Liberalism" was hardly the generous and full-blown faith of William Ellery Channing. His response to criticism of his sermon was to qualify his words in order to defend his official orthodoxy and then, when pressed, to complain that his "liberty" was being infringed by inquisitorial Calvinists. Briant's sermon was not so much a statement of doctrine as an expression of attitudes—those of the lonely few who were fighting the seeming tyranny of the post-Awakening era and its enthusiastic rabble.

Certain it is, that the Word of God (as the best Things are liable to Corruption and the Corruption of the best is the worst) has either thro' the Weakness, Inattention and Ignorance, or more criminal Designs of its Expositors, (by some such I say,) in all Ages of the World been wretchedly abused to serve the Purposes of Error, Superstition and Vice. And perhaps nothing has had a more fatal Tendency to delude the Simple and harden the Profane, than judging of Scripture

Doctrines from particular Scraps of Scripture, and from the bare jingle of Words, without attending to the general Drift and Design of the Author, and the whole Current of Inspiration as to the Point under Examination.

Hence it has come to pass that when Men read of God's choosing whole Nations to certain Priveleges (and those in this Life only) they have rashly concluded that *particular Persons* are *unconditionally* chosen to eternal Life hereafter. —That when they have laid before them the Character of a very loose and abandoned People, who by their *own* long practised Wickedness, have rendered themselves the Children of Wrath, and fitted themselves for Destruction, they are induced to vilify humane Nature itself with the same vicious Character.—That when they hear of our being *saved by Grace,* they conceive of it so as to destroy all moral Agency, and set themselves down with this vain Thought, that nothing on their Part is necessary to Salvation, but if they are designed for it, they shall irresistably be driven into Heaven, whether they will or not.—And if they are not, no Prayers, nor Endeavours will avail.—And finally; when they meditate on the constant unchangeable Affection God bears to *good Men,* they make this groundless Inferrence from his Unchangeableness, that they are unchangeable also.

Thus "stupified and bewildered with Sounds, without attending to the true Sense of Revelation," the pure and perfect Religion of Jesus, (which contains the most refined System of Morality the World was ever blessed with; which every where considers us as moral Agents, and suspends our whole Happiness upon our *personal* good Behaviour, and our patient *Continuance* in the Ways of Well-do-ing) is in many Places turned into an *idle Speculation, a mysterious Faith, a senseless Superstition, and a groundless Recumbency;* and in short, every Thing but what in Fact it is, viz. a Doctrine of Sobriety, Righteousness and Piety.

The like Delusions, and by the same Means have been introduced in judging of our spiritual State.

Some (and those not a few) are full of Hope in God. Because as they imagine he has from all Eternity and that not only without any Reason, but in direct Opposition to the very Nature and essential Constitution of his moral Government, *set his Love upon them*—Others you will find amusing themselves with a vain and groundless (*however no Matter since 'tis a strong*) Perswasion that there is no Need of their being righteous themselves, because they have the perfect Righteousness of Christ imputed unto them: But if they should happen to think any Thing is required of them, they will be sure to fix their Duty in some Thing of very cheap and easy Performance, many Degrees short of actual, and much more universal Goodness.—As in an affected Sorrow and groaning for Sin, especially for the Sins of *others* they never had any Hand in, without any Reformation of themselves. . . .

And (not to forget my Text) no Passage perhaps in the whole Book of GOD has been more shamefully perverted to the propagating of such Libertine Notions than this I have now chosen to discourse upon. The Words, as they are commonly received, are a standing Reflection on all Virtue and good Manners; the most effectual Discouragement that could be given to the Practice of Christian Morality, and consequently one of the most fatal Snares that could be laid for the Souls of Men. The common Notion of them is, that the Prophet is here giving us a just and literal Description of the Righteousness of the best, while he is only confessing and lamenting the aggravated Sins of the worst of Men. From hence, this odious Character has been transferred to the moral Attainments of Men under the Gospel; and the best Righteousness of the most improved Christians hath been generally spoken of, as no better a Qualification (even according to the merciful Tenour of the Gospel, and considered as the Condition of that final Happiness which is in the Hands and at the Disposal of Jesus Christ, who according to the good Pleasure of the Supreme Father of all is constituted the only Mediator between GOD and Man) no better a Qualification, I say, even in this mediatorial and infinitely gracious Scheme, to appear before GOD with Acceptance, than filthy Rags are to dress and adorn the Body for a Visit to the King and Court on Earth.

But the true Sense of the Words (as I trust will appear in the Progress of this Discourse) is not, that their Righteousness would have been as *filthy Rags,* if they had really been a righteous People: (The sacred Writer suggests no such thing,) But his whole Design is to shew that they had no real true Righteousness, being, as to their general Character, of a corrupt Heart and polluted Life, or as 'tis said in the former Part of the Verse, *all of them as an unclean Thing.*

It must therefore, be a Matter of great Importance, a Design richly worth our Undertaking to deliver the Text (which is the Business of the present Discourse) from this false Gloss, this horrid Abuse that has been put upon it: and demonstrate to the contrary, (as may very easily be done) that neither all, nor any part of *our* Righteousness when true and genuine, sincere and universal, can possibly, consistent with Reason, Revelation, or indeed so much as common Sense, deserve this odious Character of *filthy Rags.* . . .

The most rational and divine Scheme of Religion may become despicable in the Eyes of the World, by Misrepresentations. Even *Christianity* itself, tho' capable of a rational Defence, well attested by external Evidence, and when viewed in it's native Purity and Simplicity, void of all corrupt Glosses and human Additions, carrying in it the clearest internal Marks of its divine Original; even this Religion, I say, may be so represented, as to render it ridiculous in the Opinion of sensible thinking Men. For with what Air of Infallibility

soever Men may vent the Fictions of their own weak or disordered Brains for the Doctrines and Precepts of the Gospel;
and tho' the greatest Absurdities, the most palpable Nonsense;
in Times of Ignorance and implicit Faith may be winked at;
tho' the unthinking Multitude may be best pleased with that
they understand least, and be carried away into any Scheme,
that generously allows them the Practice of their Vices, tho'
every Article be a downright Affront to common Sense; yea,
by a few rabble charming Sounds be converted into such
fiery Bigots, as to be ready to die in the Defence of Stupidity
and Nonsense, as well as to kill (and that purely for the
Glory of God) all that are so *heretical* and *graceless* as not
to renounce their Reason in Complaisance to their sovereign
Dictates; notwithstanding all this, I say; There always was
and always will be some in the World (alas that their Number is so few) that have Sense eno' and dare trust their own
Faculties so far, as to *judge in themselves what is right.* That
by no Arts, how sanctimonious soever, can ever be bro't to
believe, (and much less profess when they don't believe)
Things repugnant to the first Principles of Reason. And therefore are naturally led to conclude, That no Scheme can be
right, no Doctrine from God that abates the Motives of Vertue, or discourages the Practice of any one Duty. For the
Existence of God is not more certain than this: That it must
be the grand Design, the ultimate View of God, in all his
Dispensations, to promote the moral Rectitude and Happiness
of his Creatures. And exactly in Proportion to it's Tendency
this Way arises the true intrinsick Value of every Revelation
he gives us. But if this be *Revelation* and *Grace,* to vilify
human Nature, and disparage all our Improvements in those
divine Vertues wherein essentially consists all our Glory and
Felicity; If the Scriptures are used to affront human Reason,
and debauch Men's Manners, and the most glorious Dispensation of the Gospel in particular, instead of teaching us to deny

Ungodliness, and every worldly Lust, and to live soberly righteously, charitably and devoutly in this present World, be conceived of only as a Scheme calculated to allow Men the Practice of their Vices here, with Impunity hereafter; If this be the Liberty and peculiar Privilege of the Saints to be discharged from their Obligations to obey their Master, and they that break his Commandments, stand fairer for his *Grace*, than they, who conscienciously keep them, for fear they should trust to what they do; so far, I say, as any take their Conceptions from such Corruptions of Christianity, they must necessarily be prejudiced against it.—Thunder we ever so loud, without any previous *Lightning*, HE THAT BELIEVETH NOT SHALL BE DAMNED, it will signify nothing, for they will be DAMNED before they will believe. 2*dly*. The loading of moral Vertue with such opprobious Terms, has a natural Tendency to encourage and harden wicked Men in their Vices. What can tend more to dispirit Men's Endeavours after Purity of Heart and Sanctity of Manners, to stop their Mouths from ever putting up one Petition to Heaven for Assistance in carrying on the Work of Righteousness in them, than thus to asperse moral Vertue, as nothing worth in the Sight of God, no more than *filthy Rags!* It is evident to common Sense, that this must lead Men into an utter Contempt of those Things that are of infinite Importance for them to esteem and practice. Surely Men will never take much Pains for that, which will be of no Service to them when they have got it. To speak freely, I confess I never yet saw with what Face a Man can pretend to exhort others to the Practice of Righteousness, who is constantly telling them, perhaps in the same Breath, that *all their Righteousness,* when they have obtained it, will be nothing but *filthy* Rags. . . .

. . . The plain Truth of the Case is this; Either our Righteousness is of some Use and Significancy in the Affair of our Salvation, or it is not. Either it has some Connection with, and actual Influence on our Happiness, or it is of no real Necessity as to us. If the Latter, then there is not one Word to be said in favour of it, but the greatest Advocates for Licentiousness may be the best Friends to Christianity, and the most Vicious the highest in the Grace of God. But if the Former, then 'tis a sure Thing, that in Proportion to it's real Worth, and final Advantage, arises the Folly of those who neglect it, and the Strength of all our Arguments to recommend it to Mankind.

. . . The Consequences of depretiating moral Vertue are very injurious to such as are sincere upright Christians, in robbing of them of that divine Comfort they are the proper Heirs of, and filling their Minds with needless Fears and Scruples about their spiritual State.

The great Rule the Scriptures lay down for Men to go by in passing Judgment on their Spiritual State, is the sincere, upright, steady and universal Practice of Vertue. This they speak of as the only sure Rule, to which all others are reducible, as what we may with Confidence rely on, and ought to adhere to, in Opposition to all other delusive Marks whatever. 1 *John* 3. 7. *Let no Man deceive you: He that doth Righteousness, is righteous.* Ver. 10. *In this the Children of God are manifest, and the Children of the Devil: Whosoever doth not Righteousness, is not of God.*

But now if we are perswaded to think that all our Righteousness, when we are become sincere good Men are nothing but *filthy Rags,* we are naturally led to seek for some other Evidence of our good State, than what results from our Goodness; and it being impossible to find any other to be relied on, for the Scriptures propose none but this, it necessarily follows that we must either be filled with vain Hopes and empty Joys, or else after all our vertuous Attainments we must be subjected to all the Horrors we can suppose the most vicious of Men to be exercised with. We must fear where no Fear is; And in a Word, put the Matter in the most favourable Light, we must walk to Heaven on the confines of Hell, while our Path would be smooth and easy, our Prospect serene and bright, and we should anticipate future Enjoyments in our present Hopes, if we were but allowed to think (and that while all necessary Evidences are in our Favour) that our present Condition is safe.

These, to be brief, are the natural unfailing Consequences of thus depretiating the moral Vertues of good Men.—It ministers to the Growth of Infidelity, and of Vice among professed Christians, and to the great Disquiet of sincere good Christians, who are the proper Heirs of Comfort. And thus I have finished what I at first proposed.

To conclude the whole Matter; I expect by this Time, some are ready to break forth—*Ah! all this directly tends to build People up in their own Righteousness—Not one Word of Christ, nor the least Savour of true gospel soul-saving Preaching in all this Discourse.*

To the first Part of which Charge, I answer—If by it's building People up in their *own* Righteousness, be meant, That it recommends Hypocrisy and counterfeit Vertue; that it places Religion in any external Duties separate from a corresponding good Temper within (all which Sort of Righteousness would indeed, as to our final Acceptance with God, thro' the Mediation of Christ, be no better than *filthy Rags*) or, in short, in any Righteousness of our own contriving and not taught of God; in any Thing but what the Bible, from the Beginning of *Genesis* to the End of *Revelations,* makes the Substance of our present Duty, and the Condition of our future Happiness; If this, I say, be the Force of the present Objection, I have no other Answer to make, but to leave every one to judge for himself, how groundless it is.

But if by it's tending to build People up in their *own* Righteousness be designed, that it is any Ways calculated to encourage *personal* Goodness, and promote the Practice of moral and christian Vertue in the World; the least Tendency it has this Way, I shall heartily rejoice in, and instead of being sollicitous to prove the Objection groundless, my greatest Concern, upon a Review of the preceeding Discourse, is really this, that there is not *more* Ground for it; and that so good a Design is so poorly served.

In the next Place; As to its not being *preaching of Christ;* the Difficulty, perhaps will entirely vanish when we come to adjust our Notions of the Thing. "To PREACH CHRIST (says a late very elegent Writer) is universally acknowledged to be the Duty of every Christian Minister. But what doth it mean? It is not to use his Name as a Charm to work up our Hearers to a warm Pitch of Enthusiasm; without any Foundation of Reason to support it.—'Tis not to encourage undue and presumptuous Reliance on his Merits and Intercession, to the contempt of Virtue and good Works. No: But to represent him as a Lawgiver as well as a Saviour, as *a Preacher of Righteousness,* as one who hath given us a most noble and compleat System of Morality, enforced by the most Substantial and worthy Motives."

. . . Therefore, "to explain and press the eternal Laws of Morality by all the peculiar Motives which the christian Religion suggests, and making all it's Doctrines subservient to Holiness, is beyond Comparison the most *useful* Way of preaching."—To preach up chiefly what Christ himself laid the chiefest Stress upon (and whether this was not *moral Vertue,* let every One judge from his Discourses) must certainly, in the Opinion of all sober Men, be called truly and properly, and in the best Sense, *preaching of Christ.*

After all; tho' this Sort of Preaching is evidently conformable, both to the Design of the Gospel, and the Example of our Saviour, yet I am sensible 'tis not calculated for the general *Taste* of the present Age. *It is not to walk in the*

Way of their Heart, and in the Sight of their Eyes. It may not, at present, be the Way to *popular* Applause, nor to *priestly* Favours. However, if it be the Way of Truth (and I hope this is no certain Evidence that it is not) the Way, I say, of Truth, of Honesty and Integrity, we are sure it is the Way that will endure forever. And while this Assurance is fixed in a Man's Mind, tho' the asserting of it should expose him to Poverty and Contempt, and, in short, all Manner of temporal Inconveniences, a stedfast Faith and inflexible Vertue will readily reply—*None of these Things move me, neither count I my Life dear unto me, if so be I may finish my Course with Joy, and the Ministry which I have received of the Lord, to testify the Gospel of his Grace.* And both these truly great and infinitely important Ends, will infallibly be secured, if we not only in Doctrine, but in Practice, inviolably Adhere to that pertinent Advice of St. *Paul's* to his beloved Son according to the common Faith, *Titus* 3. 8. *This is a faithful Saying, and these Things I will that thou affirm constantly, that they which have believed in God, be careful to maintain good Works.* THESE *Things are* GOOD, *and* PROFITABLE *unto Men.*

47 · *Joseph Bellamy*

(1 7 1 9 – 1 7 9 0)

TRUE RELIGION DELINEATED

The 1750's witnessed regroupings of the forces of rational and evangelical religion and further reconstructions of their thought. Prominent among spokesmen of the new Calvinism was Joseph Bellamy, who had participated in the Awakening as one of the youngest itinerants. At the age of eighteen Bellamy had been installed pastor at Bethlem, Connecticut, where he later conducted the school from which many theologians of the "New Divinity" graduated. His doctrinal treatises were, in their enduring influence, second only to those of his teacher and friend, Jonathan Edwards. Bellamy's *True Religion Delineated*, published in 1750 with a laudatory preface by Edwards, added little of substance to the ideas of *The Religious Affections* (which Bellamy considered "the best book on experimental religion since the days of inspiration"). But Bellamy did make more explicit the humanistic

Joseph Bellamy, *True Religion Delineated; or, Experimental Religion, as Distinguished from Formality on the One Hand, and Enthusiasm on the Other, Set in a Scriptural and Rational Light. . . , The Works of Joseph Bellamy, D.D. . . .* (3 vols.; New York, 1811), I, 49–51, 67–68, 187–196.

tendency of "experimental religion." In his hands Calvinism became more concerned, if not in doctrine then surely in precept, with man's benevolence to his fellow men. Bellamy never betrayed, however, *the* central insight of the Awakening and of Edwards: the supreme worth, in all human experience, of an affecting sense of beauty.

. . . It has doubtless appeared as a thing strange and dark to so many pious persons, and occasioned not a little perplexity of mind, to observe what has come to pass in *New England* since the year 1740.—That there should be so general an outpouring of the spirit—so many hundreds and thousands awakened all over the country, and such an almost universal external reformation, and so many receive the word with joy; and yet, after all, things come to be as they now are: so many fallen away to carnal security, and so many turned enthusiasts and heretics, and the country so generally settled in their prejudices against experimental religion and the doctrines of the gospel, and a flood of *Arminianism* and immorality, ready to deluge the land; but, as strange and dark as it may have seemed, yet doubtless if any of us had lived with the Israelites in the wilderness, or in the first three ages after Christ, or in the time of the reformation from *Popery*, the dispensations of Divine Providence would, upon the whole, have appeared much more mysterious than they do now. And yet those were times when God was doing glorious things for his Church. . . . Thus it has always been.—This is a state of trial, and God has permitted so many sad and awful things to happen in times of reformation, with design to prove the children of men, and know what is in their hearts. . . .

A compassionate sense of the exercises, which godly persons, especially among common people, might be under, in these evil days, while some are fallen away, and others are clapping their hands and rejoicing with all their hearts to see Zion laid waste; while *Arminians* are glossing their scheme, and appealing to reason and common sense, as though their principles were near or quite self-evident to all men of thought and candour; and while *enthusiasts* are going about as men inspired and immediately sent by the Almighty, pretending to extraordinary sanctity, and hold in it that they are so holy in themselves, and so entirely on the Lord's side, that all godly people must, and cannot but see as they do, and fall in with them, unless they are become blind, dead, and carnal; and gotten back into the world; a compassionate sense, I say, of the exercises of mind, which pious persons among common people might have, in such a trying situation of things, was the first motive which excited me to enter upon this work, which I now offer to the public: and to make divine truths plain to such, and to strip error before their eyes, that they might be established, and comforted, and quickened in their way heavenward, was the end I had in view: and, accordingly, I have laboured very much to adapt myself to the lowest capacities, not meaning to write a book for the learned and polite, but for common people, and especially for those who are godly among them.

. . . And I design here to take a general view of all the reasons and motives which ought to influence us to love the Lord our God; all which are implied in those words, *The Lord thy God. Thou shalt love the Lord thy God with all thy heart,* i.e. because he is the Lord and our God.

1. The first and chief motive which is to influence us to love God with all our hearts, is *his infinite dignity and greatness, glory and excellency;* or, in one word, *his infinite amiableness.* We are to love him with all our hearts, because he is the Lord; because he is what he is, and just such a Being as he is. On this account, primarily, and antecedent to all other consid-

erations, he is infinitely amiable; and, therefore, on this account, primarily, and antecedent to all other considerations, ought he to appear infinitely amiable in our eyes. This is the first and chief reason and ground upon which his *law* is founded, I AM THE LORD. (*Exod.* xx. 2. *Lev.* XIX.) This, therefore, ought to be the first and chief motive to influence us to obey. . . . But why need I multiply words? For it seems even self-evident that God's loveliness ought to be the first and chief thing for which we love him.

Now, God is infinitely lovely, because he is what he is; or, in other words, his infinite dignity and greatness, glory and excellency, are the result of his natural and moral perfections. So that it is a clear sight and realizing sense of his natural and moral perfections, as they are revealed in his works and in his word, that make him appear, to a HOLY soul, as a Being of infinite dignity and greatness, glory and excellency. Thus, the Queen of *Sheba*, seeing and conversing with *Solomon*, and viewing his works, under a sense of the large and noble endowments of his mind, was even ravished; and cried out, *The one half was not told me!* And thus the holy and divinely enlightened soul, upon seeing God, reading his word, and meditating on his wonderful works, under a sense of his divine and incomprehensible perfections, is ravished with his infinite dignity, majesty, greatness, glory, and excellency; and love, admires, and adores; and says, *Who is a God like unto thee!*

. . . To love God with all our heart, lays a foundation, and prepares the way for us to love our neighbours as ourselves. It removes and takes away those things which are contrary to this love; such as pride, selfishness, worldliness, a narrow, stingy, envious, revengeful temper. True love to God mortifies and kills these things at the root. And, secondly, True love to God assimilates us to the divine nature, and makes us like God in the temper of our minds.—But God is love: and the more we are like God, the more are our hearts, therefore, framed to love and benevolence. *He that dwelleth in love, dwelleth in God, and God in him.*—Love to God sweetens the soul, and enlarges our hearts to love our fellow-men. And, *thirdly,* The more we love God, the more sacred is his authority with us, and the more glorious, amiable, and animating does his example appear, and the greater sense have we of our obligations to gratitude to him; all which tends jointly to influence us to all love and goodness towards our neighbours. So that, he that knows God, and loves him, will be full of love to mankind; and, therefore, *he that loveth not, knoweth not God.* 1 John iv. 8. On the other hand, where there is no true love to God, there is no true love to mankind; but the heart is under the government of pride, selfishness, and other corruptions, which are contrary to love. So that a genuine love to mankind is peculiar to the godly. 1 *John* iv. 7, 8.

And now, from what has been said, we may evidently see these following sorts of love to our neighbour are, neither of them, the love required, however nearly they may sometimes seem to resemble it.

1. What is commonly called *natural compassion,* is not the love here required; for the most wicked, profane man, may be of a very compassionate temper: so may the proud, the selfish, the envious, the malicious, and spiteful man—as experience plainly shows. And besides, natural compassion does not take its rise from any sense of the rectitude and fitness of things, or any regard to the divine authority, but merely from the animal constitution: and men seem to be properly passive in it. It is much the same thing in the human, as in the brutal nature: It is, therefore, a different thing from the love here required.

2. The same may be said of what is called *good-nature:* It arises merely from animal constitution, and is not the love here required; for such a man is not influenced in his love by the reason and nature of things, or the authority of the great

Governor of the world, or from a consideration of the infinite goodness of the divine nature, any more than the beasts are, who are some of them much better tempered than others: so that this sort of love has nothing of the nature of religion in it. And it is evident that many wicked and ungodly men have much of this natural good temper, who yet have no regard to God or duty: yea, a secret grudge against a neighbour, reigning in the heart, may be, in the *good-natured* man, consistent with his *good-nature*, but it is not consistent with the love here required; and therefore they are evidently *two* things.

3. That love which is commonly called *natural affection,* is not the love here required. It is true, *that* man is worse than the beasts, who is without natural affection, for they evidently are not; but every man is not a saint, because he has natural affection: and it is true we owe a peculiar love, according to God's law, to our relatives; but natural affection is not this love: for there are many ungodly wretches, who care neither for God nor his law, who have as much natural affection as any in the world; yea, it is a common thing for ungodly parents to make very idols of their children; for them, they go, and run, and work, and toil, by night and day, to the utter neglect of God and their own souls: and surely this cannot be the very love which God requires. And besides, as natural affection naturally prompts parents to love their children more than God, and be more concerned for their welfare than for his glory, so it is commonly a bar in the way of their loving others as they ought. They have nothing to give to the poor and needy, to the widow and the fatherless; they must lay up all for their children: yea, many times they rake and scrape, cheat and defraud, and, like mere earth-worms, bury themselves in the world; and all this for the sake of their children. And yet all this love to their children does not prompt them to take care of their souls. They never teach their children

to pray, nor instruct them to seek after God: they love their bodies, but care little for their souls. Their love to the one is beyond all bounds, but, to the other, is little or nothing: it is an irrational fondness, and not the love required. Indeed, if parents loved their children as they ought to do, their love would effectually influence them to take care of their souls, and do all their duty to them—which *natural affection* evidently does not; and therefore it is not that love with which God, in his law, requires parents to love their children: nor, indeed, does there seem to be any more of the nature of true virtue or real religion in the *natural affection* of men, than there is in the natural affection of beasts—both resulting merely from animal nature and a natural self-love, without any regard to the reason and nature of things.

4. Nor is that the love here required, which arises merely from a *party-spirit;* because such a one is of their party, and on their side, and loves those whom they love, and will plead, stand up, and contend for them, and maintain their cause: for such a love is pregnant with hatred and ill-will to every body else; and nothing will humour and gratify it more than to see the opposite party hated, reviled, and blackened: and besides, such a love is nothing but self-love in another shape.— *Ye have heard that it hath been said, Thou shalt love thy neighbour, and hate thine enemy: But I say unto you, love your enemies.* Mat. v. 43, 44.

5. Nor is that the love here required, which arises merely from *others' love to me:* As if a rich man is kind and bountiful to poor people all around him, and appears to love and pity them, they, though almost ever so wicked, will feel a sort of love to him. But if this rich man happens to be a civil magistrate, and is called to sit as a judge in their case, and passes judgment against them for their crimes, now their love dies, and enmity, and hatred, and revenge begin to ferment in their hearts. In this case, it is not the *man* they love, but rather his

kindnesses: and their seeming love is nothing but a certain operation of self-love. And indeed, however full of love persons may seem to be to their neighbours, if all arises *merely from self-love,* or is for *self-ends,* nothing is genuine: and that, whether things worldly, or things religious, occasion their love. A poor man will love and honour those who are rich, if he hopes to get any thing by it. A rich man may be kind to the poor, with an eye to his credit. An awakened sinner will love an awakening preacher, in hopes he shall be converted by his ministry. A minister may seem to show a world of love to the souls of sinners, and all with an eye to applause. Hypocrites will love a godly minister, so long as he thinks well of them, and happens not to detect their hypocrisy in his public preaching. Even the *Galatians* were very full of love to Paul for a while, so long as they thought he loved them, and had been the instrument of their conversion; yet, afterwards, they lost their love, and turned his enemies, for his telling them the truth; while others, who loved him truly for what he was, were more and more knit unto him for those very doctrines for which the *Galatians* hated him. *If ye love them which love you, what reward have ye? Do not the publicans the same?* Mat. v. 46. There is no virtue nor religion in such a kind of love, and it is evidently *not the thing* required by the divine law. And indeed it is a thing as difficult, and as contrary to corrupt nature, for us genuinely to love our neighbours as ourselves, as it is to love God with all our hearts; and there is as little true love between man and man, as there is between men and God. It is for our interest to love God, and it is for our interest to love our neighbours, and therefore men *make as if* they did so, when, really, there is nothing genuine and true. And, at the day of judgment, when a wicked world comes to God's bar, and their past conduct is all brought to light, nothing will be more manifest than that there never was a spark of true love to God or man in their hearts, but that, from first to last, they were actuated and governed either by their animal constitution, or else merely by self-love.

6. I may add, nor is that the love required, when men love others *merely because they are as bad, and so just like themselves.* Nature and self-love will prompt the worst of men to do so. The vain and profligate love such as are as bad as themselves: and, from the same principle, erroneous persons have a peculiar regard for one another. And the enthusiast and blazing hypocrite may, from the same principle, seem to be full of love to their own sort, though full of malice against all others: and they may think that it is *the image of God* which they love in their brethren, when, indeed, it is only *the image of themselves.* Persons of a *bad taste* may greatly delight in those things in others, which are very odious in the sight of God: but surely this cannot be the love required; and yet, by this very thing, many a hypocrite thinks himself a true saint.

Thus we see what it is to love God with all our hearts, and our neighbours as ourselves, and see these two distinguished from their counterfeits. And so we have gone through the two great commands of the law, in a conformity to which the very essence of religion does much consist. . . .

So that now, in a few words, we may here see *wherein true religion does consist,* as it stands distinguished from all the false religion in the world. The godly man, from seeing God to be just such a one as he is, and from a real sense of his infinite glory and amiableness in being such, is thereby influenced to love him supremely, live to him ultimately, and delight in him superlatively: from which inward *frame of heart,* he freely runs the way of God's commands, and is in his element when doing God's will. He eats, he drinks, he works, he prays, and does all things, with a single eye to God, who has placed him in this his world, allotted to him his peculiar station, and pointed out before him all the business of life: always looking to him for all things, and always giving thanks unto his name, for all his unspeakable goodness to a wretch so infinitely unworthy. And, with a spirit of disinterested impartiality, and genuine benevolence, he views his fellow-men; gives them their places; takes his own, and loves them as himself: their welfare is dear to him; he is grieved at their miseries, and rejoices at their mercies, and delights to do all the good he can, to every one, in the place and station which God has set him in. And he finds that this *new* and *divine temper* is inwrought in his *very nature;* so that, instead. of a forced religion, or a religion merely by fits, his *very heart* is habitually bent and inclined to such views and apprehensions; to such an inward temper, and to such an outward conduct.

This, this is the religion of the Bible; the religion which the law and the prophets, and which Christ and his apostles too, all join to teach; the religion which Christ came into the world to recover men unto, and to which the spirit of God does actually recover every believer, in a greater or lesser degree. Thus those *who are dead in sin, are quickened;* Eph. ii. 1. *Have the law written in their hearts.* Heb. viii. 10. *Are made new creatures,* all *old things being done away, and all things become new;* 2 Cor. v. 17. And are effectually *taught to deny all ungodliness and worldly lusts, and to live soberly, righteously, and godly in this present world.* Tit. ii 12. *And so serve God without fear, in holiness and righteousness, all the days of their lives;* Luke i. 74, 75.

And *this* is specifically different from every sort of false religion in the world: for all kinds of false religion, however different in other things, yet all agree in this, to result merely from a principle of self-love, whereby fallen men, being ignorant of God, are inclined to love themselves supremely, and do all things for themselves ultimately. All the idolatrous religion of the heathen world, in which some took much pains, had its rise from this principle. They had some notion of a future state; of a heaven and a hell, as well as of temporal rewards and punishments, and so were moved by hope and fear, from a principle of self-love, to do something to pacify the anger of the gods, and recommend themselves to the favour of their deities: and all the superstitions of the seemingly devout papist; his *pater-nosters,* his *ave-marias,* his *penances,* and *pilgrimages,* and endless toils, still arise from the same principle: so does all the religion of formalists, and legal hypocrites, in the reformed nations. It is a slavish fear of hell, and mercenary hope of heaven, which, from a principle of self-love, sets all a going; yea, the evangelical hypocrite, who mightily talks of supernatural, divine light; of the spirit's operations; of conversion, and a new nature, still, after all, has no higher principle in him than self-love. His conscience has been greatly enlightened, and his heart terrified, and his corruptions stunned: and he has, by the delusions of Satan, obtained a strong confidence of the love of God, and pardon of his sins; so that, instead of being influenced chiefly by the fear of hell, as the legal hypocrite is, he is ravished with heaven; but still, all is from self-love, and for self-ends: and, properly and scripturally speaking, he neither knows God, nor cares at all for him. And this is the very case with every *graceless* man living, of *whatever denomination;* whether a Heathen, or Jew, or Christian; whether Papist, or Protestant; whether Church-man, Presbyterian, Congregationalist, or Separatist; whether a Pelagian, Arminian, Calvinist, Antinomian, Baptist, or Quaker. And this is the case with every *graceless* man living, *whatever his attainments may otherwise be;* though he hath all knowledge to understand all mysteries, and can speak with the tongues of men and angels, and has faith to remove mountains, and zeal enough to give all his goods to feed the poor, and his body to be burned; yet he has no *charity;* he is perfectly destitute of this genuine love to God and his neighbour, and has no higher principle in his heart, from which all his religion proceeds, but a supreme love to himself. For, ever since our first parents aspired to be as gods, it has been the *nature* of all mankind to love themselves supremely, and to be blind to the infinite beauty of the divine nature; and it remains so to be with all, until renewed by divine grace: so that self-love is the highest principle from which unregenerate men do ever act, or can act.

Here, therefore, we have true religion; a religion specifically different from all other sorts of religion in the world, standing in a clear view: yea, and we may be absolutely certain that this is the very thing which has been described: for this conformity to be the moral law is, throughout all the Bible, by Moses and the prophets, by Christ and his apostles, represented to the very thing in which the essence of religion originally consists. "Blessed be the name of the Lord for ever, who has given us so clear a revelation of his will, and so sure and certain a guide as his word." Come here, all you poor, exercised, broken-hearted saints, that live in this dark benighted world, where many run to and fro, and where there are a thousand different opinions, and every one confident that he is right; come here to the law and to the testimony; come here to Christ himself, and learn what the truth is, and be settled; be confirmed, and be established for ever; and remember, and practise upon those words of Jesus Christ, in John vii. 17. *If any man will do his will, he shall know of the doctrine, whether it be of God....*

PART SEVEN

LEGACIES

48 · *Jonathan Edwards*

THE VISIBLE UNION OF
GOD'S PEOPLE

That the Great Awakening shattered the parochial order of early eighteenth-century America was everywhere almost immediately understood. More dimly seen at the time was how, out of the revival, was also being born that spirit which was to become American nationalism. Edwards briefly tapped this undercurrent of the Awakening when he proposed, in his *Thoughts on the Revival,* that "all God's people in America" join in a common day of prayer. Two years later a number of Scottish divines called for such a "Concert of Prayer" among all who, on both sides of the Atlantic, hoped for an expanding and continu-

---

Jonathan Edwards, *An Humble Attempt to Promote Explicit Agreement and Visible Union of God's People in Extraordinary Prayer, for the Revival of Religion and the Advancement of Christ's Kingdom on Earth...,* Works, III, 461–463, 467–469, 471–474.

ing revival. Edwards agreed to introduce the proposal to America, and he chose this opportunity to expound the metaphysics of his vision of the progressive unfolding of the Work of Redemption. The crucial sections of Edwards' tract were those in which he argued the impossibility of a reversal in the direction of history and delineated "The Beauty and Good Tendency of Union." Over the next century the "Concert of Prayer" became something of an established ritual in the American churches, and it proved to be an instrument of interdenominational cooperation. But the fuller import of Edwards' hope of the great community emerged, subtly perhaps and elusively, in America's continuing effort to comprehend a destiny that could not be contained in ecclesiastical forms. In the 1790's, for instance, a minister who publicized Edwards' thoughts grew convinced at last that only through the election of Thomas Jefferson as president could God's American people achieve the more perfect union promised by Edwards. The "republican millennium," as it was styled in 1801, seemed to many citizens the partial fulfillment, at least, of Edwards' social and historical vision.

As the present state of things may well excite earnest desires after the promised general revival and advancement of true religion, and serve to show our dependence on God for it, so there are many things in Providence, of late, that tend to encourage us in prayer for such a mercy. That infidelity, heresy, and vice do so prevail, and that corruption and wickedness are risen to such an extreme height, is that which is exceeding deplorable; but yet, I think, considering God's promises to his church, and the ordinary method of his dispensations, hope may justly be gathered from it, that the present state of things will not last long, but that a happy change is nigh. We know that God never will desert the cause of truth and holiness, nor suffer the gates of hell to prevail against his church; and that it has usually been so from the beginning of the world, that the state of the church has appeared most dark, but before some remarkable deliverance and advancement. . . .

The late remarkable religious awakenings, that have been in many parts of the Christian world, are another thing that may justly encourage us in prayer for the promised glorious and universal outpouring of the Spirit of God. . . .

. . . In the years 1734 and 1735, there appeared a very great and general awakening, in the county of Hampshire, in the province of the Massachusetts Bay in New England, and also in many parts of Connecticut. Since this there has been a far more extensive awakening of many thousands in England, Wales and Scotland, and almost all the British provinces in North America. There has also been something remarkable of the same kind, in some places in the United Netherlands: and about two years ago, a very great awakening and reformation of many of the Indians, in the Jerseys, and Pennsylvania, even among such as never embraced Christianity before: and within these two years, a great awakening in Virginia and Maryland. Notwithstanding the great diversity of opinions about the issue of some of these awakenings, yet I know of none that have denied that there have been great awakenings of late, in these times and places, and that multitudes have been brought to more than common concern for their salvation, and for a time were made more than ordinarily afraid of sin, and brought to reform their former vicious courses, and take much pains for their salvation. If I should be of the opinion of those that think these awakenings and strivings of God's

Spirit have been generally not well improved, and so, as to most, have not issued well, but have ended in enthusiasm and delusion, yet, that the Spirit of God has been of late so wonderfully awakening and striving with such multitudes, in so many different parts of the world, and even to this day, in one place or other, continues to awaken men, is what I should take great encouragement from, that God was about to do something more glorious, and would, before he finishes, bring things to a greater ripeness, and not finally suffer this work of his to be frustrated and rendered abortive by Satan's crafty management; and that these unusual commotions are the forerunners of something exceeding glorious approaching. . . .

How condecent, how beautiful, and of good tendency would it be, for multitudes of Christians, in various parts of the world, by explicit agreement, to unite in such prayer as is proposed to us.

Union is one of the most amiable things, that pertains to human society; yea, it is one of the most beautiful and happy things on earth, which indeed makes earth most like heaven. God has made of one blood all nations of men, to dwell on all the face of the earth; hereby teaching us this moral lesson, that it becomes mankind all to be united as one family. And this is agreeable to the nature that God has given men, disposing them to society; and the circumstances God has placed them in, so many ways obliging and necessitating them to it. A civil union, or a harmonious agreement among men in the management of their secular concerns, is amiable; but much more a pious union and sweet agreement in the great business for which man was created, and had powers given him beyond the brutes; even the business of religion; the life and soul of which is love. Union is spoken of in Scripture as the peculiar beauty of the church of Christ, Cant. vi. 9: "My dove, my undefiled is but one, she is the only one of her mother, she is the choice one of her that bare her; the daughters saw her and blessed her, yea, the queens and the concubines, and they praised her." Psal. cxxii. 3, "Jerusalem is builded as a city that is compact together." Eph. iv. 3–6, "Endeavoring to keep the unity of the Spirit in the bond of peace. There is one body, and one Spirit; even as ye are called in one hope of your calling; one Lord, one faith, one baptism, one God and Father of all, who is above all, and through all, and in you all." Ver. 16, "The whole body fitly framed together and compacted, by that which every joint supplieth, according to the effectual working in the measure of every part, maketh increase of the body, unto the edifying itself in love."

As it is the glory of the church of Christ, that she in all her members, however dispersed, is thus one holy society, one city, one family, one body; so it is very desirable, that this union should be manifested, and become visible; and so, that her distant members should act as one, in those things that concern the common interest of the whole body, and in those duties and exercises wherein they have to do with their common Lord and head, as seeking of him the common prosperity. It becomes all the members of a particular family, who are so strictly united, and have in so many respects one common interest, to unite in prayer to God for the things they need: it becomes a nation, in days of prayer, appointed by national authority, at certain seasons, visibly to unite in prayer for those public mercies that concern the interest of the whole nation: so it becomes the church of Christ, which is one holy nation, a peculiar people, one heavenly family, more strictly united, in many respects, and having infinitely greater interests that are common to the whole, than any other society; I say, it especially becomes this society, visibly to unite, and expressly to agree together in prayer to God for the common prosperity; and above all, that common prosperity and advancement that is so unspeakably great and glorious, which God hath so abundantly promised to fulfil in the latter days.

It is becoming of Christians, with whose character a narrow

selfish spirit, above all others, disagrees, to be much in prayer for that public mercy, wherein consists the welfare and happiness of the whole body of Christ, of which they are members, and the greatest good of mankind. And union or agreement in prayer is especially becoming, when Christians pray for that mercy, which above all other things concerns them unitedly, and tends to the relief, prosperity and glory of the whole body, as well as of each individual member.

Such a union in prayer for the general outpouring of the Spirit of God, would not only be beautiful, but profitable too. It would tend very much to promote union and charity between distant members of the church of Christ, and a public spirit, and love to the church of God, and concern for the interest of Zion; as well as be an amiable exercise and manifestation of such a spirit. Union in religious duties, especially in the duty of prayer, in praying one with and for another, and jointly for their common welfare, above almost all other things, tends to promote mutual affection and endearment. And if ministers and people should by particular agreement and joint resolution, set themselves, in a solemn and extraordinary manner, from time to time, to pray for the revival of religion in the world, it would naturally tend more to awaken in them a concern about things of this nature, and more of a desire after such a mercy; it would engage them to more attention to such an affair, make them more inquisitive about it, more ready to use endeavors to promote that which they, with so many others, spend so much time in praying for. . . .

. . . If it would be a lovely sight in the eyes of the church of Christ, and much to their comfort, to behold various and different parts of the church united in extraordinary prayer for the general outpouring of the Spirit, then it must be desirable to them that such a union should be visible, that they may behold it; for if it be not visible, it cannot be beheld. But agreement and union in a multitude in their worship becomes visible, by an agreement in some external visible circumstances. Worship itself becomes visible worship, by something external and visible belonging to the worship, and no other way: therefore union and agreement of many in worship becomes visible no other way, but by union and agreement in the external and visible acts and circumstances of the worship. Such union and agreement becomes visible, particularly by an agreement in those two visible circumstances, *time* and *place*.

. . . Though it would not be reasonable to suppose, that merely such a circumstance of prayer, as many people's praying at the same time, will directly have any influence or prevalence with *God*, to cause him to be the more ready to hear prayer; yet such a circumstance may reasonably be supposed to have influence on the minds of *men;* as the consideration of it may tend to encourage and assist those in praying, that are united in prayer. Will any deny, that it has any reasonable tendency to encourage, animate, or in any respect to help the mind of a Christian in serving God in any duty of religion, to join with a Christian congregation, and to see an assembly of his dear brethren around him at the same time engaged with him in the same duty? And supposing one in this assembly of saints is blind, and sees no one there; but has by other means ground of satisfaction that there is present at that time a multitude of God's people, that are united with him in the same service; will any deny, that his supposing this and being satisfied of it, can have any reasonable influence upon his mind, to excite and encourage him or in any respect to assist him, in his worship? The encouragement or help that one that joins with an assembly in worshipping God, has in his worship, by others being united with him, is not merely by any thing that he immediately perceives by sight, or any other of the external senses (for union in worship is not a thing objected to the external senses), but by the notice or knowledge the mind has of that union, or the satisfaction the understanding has that others, at that time, have their minds engaged with him in the same service: which may be, when those unitedly engaged, are at a distance one from another, as well as when they are present. If one be present in a worshipping assembly, and is not blind, and sees others present, and sees their external behavior; their union and engagedness with him in worship, is what he does not see: and what he sees encourages and assists him in his worship, only as he takes it as an evidence of that union and concurrence in his worship, that is out of his sight. And persons may have evidence of this, concerning persons that are absent, that may give him as much satisfaction of their union with him, as if they were present. And therefore consideration of others being at the same time engaged with him in worship, that are absent, may as reasonably animate and encourage him in his worship, as if they were present.

There is no wisdom in finding fault with human nature, as God has made it. Things that exist now, at this present time, are in themselves no more weighty or important, than like things, and of equal reality, that existed in time past, or are to exist in time to come: yet it is evident that the consideration of things being present (at least in most cases) does especially affect human nature. . . .

Another objection, that is very likely to arise in the minds of many against such extraordinary prayer as is proposed for the speedy coming of Christ's kingdom, is that we have no reason to expect it, until there first come a time of most extreme calamity to the church of God, and prevalence of her Antichristian enemies against her; even that which is represented, Rev. xi., by the slaying of the witnesses. . . .

. . . This opinion, with such persons as retain it, must needs be a great restraint and hinderance, with regard to such an affair as is proposed to us in the memorial. If persons expect no other, than that the more the glorious times of Christ's kingdom are hastened, the sooner will come this dreadful time, wherein the generality of God's people must suffer so extremely, and the church of Christ be almost extinguished, and blotted out from under heaven; how can it be otherwise, than a great damp to their hope, courage and activity, in praying for, and reaching after the speedy introduction of those glorious promised times? As long as this opinion is retained, it will undoubtedly ever have this unhappy influence on the minds of those that wish well to Zion, and favor her stones and dust. It will tend to damp, deaden, and keep down, life, hope, and joyful expectation in prayer; and even in great measure, to prevent all earnest, animated and encouraged prayer, in God's people, for this mercy, at any time before it is actually fulfilled. For they that proceed on this hypothesis in their prayers, must, at the same time that they pray for this glorious day, naturally conclude within themselves, that they shall never live to see on the earth any dawning of it, but only to see the dismal time that shall precede it, in which the far greater part of God's people, that shall live until then, shall die under the extreme cruelties of their persecutors. And the more they expect that God will answer their prayers, by speedily bringing on the promised glorious day, the more must they withal expect themselves, to have a share in those dreadful things, that nature shrinks at the thoughts of, and also expect to see things that a renewed nature shrinks at and dreads; even the prevailing of God's enemies, and the almost total extinguishing the true religion in the world. And on this hypothesis, these discouragements are like to attend the prayers of God's people, until that dismal time be actually come: and when that is come, those that had been prophesying and praying in sackcloth, shall generally be slain: and after that time is over, then the glorious day shall immediately commence. So that this notion tends to discourage and hinder all earnest prayer in the church of God for that glorious coming of Christ's kingdom, until it be actually come; and that is to hinder its ever being at all.

It being so, this opinion being of such hurtful tendency, certainly it is a thousand pities it should prevail and be retained, if truly there be no good ground for it.

Therefore in answer to this objection, I would, with all humility and modesty, examine the foundation of that opinion, of such a dreadful time of victory of Antichrist over the church, yet to be expected: and particularly shall endeavor to show that the slaying of the witnesses, foretold Rev. xi. 7–10, is not an event that remains yet to be fulfilled. To this end, I would propose the following things to consideration.

1. The time wherein the *witnesses lie dead in the streets of the great city,* doubtless signifies the time wherein the true church of Christ is lowest of all, most of all prevailed against by Antichrist, and nearest to an utter extinction; the time wherein there is left the least visibility of the church of Christ yet subsisting in the world, least remains of any thing appertaining to true religion, whence a revival of it can be expected, and wherein all means of it are most abolished, and the state of the church is in all respects furthest from any thing whence any hopes of its ever flourishing again might arise. . . .

Now, if we consider the present state of mankind, is it credible, that a time will yet come in the world, that in these respects exceeds all times that were before the reformation? . . . If there should be another universal deluge, it might be sufficient to bring things in the world to such a pass; provided a few ignorant barbarous persons only were preserved in an ark: and it would require some catastrophe, not much short of this, to effect it.

2. In the reformation that was in the days of Luther, Calvin and others, their contemporaries, the threatened destruction

of Antichrist, that dreadful enemy, that had long oppressed and worn out the saints, was begun; nor was it a small beginning, but Antichrist had fallen, at least half way to the ground, from that height of power and grandeur, that he was in before. Then began the vials of God's wrath to be *poured out on the throne of the beast,* to the great shaking of its foundations, and diminution of its extent; so that the Pope lost near half of his former dominions: and as to degree of authority and influence over what is left, he is not now possessed of what he had before. God now at length, in answer to the long continued cries of his people, awaked as one out of sleep, and began to deliver his church from her exceeding low state, that she had continued in for many ages, under the great oppression of this grand enemy, and to restore her from her exile and bondage in the spiritual Babylon and Egypt. —And it is not agreeable to the analogy of God's dispensations, that after this, God should desert his people, and hide himself from them, even more than before, and leave them more than ever in the hands of their enemy, and all this advantage of the church against Antichrist should be entirely given up and lost, and the power and tyranny of Antichrist be more confirmed, and the church brought more under, and more entirely subdued than ever before, and further from all help and means to recover. This is not God's way of dealing with his people, or with their enemies: his work of salvation is perfect: when he has begun such a work he will carry it on: when he once causes the day of deliverance to dawn to his people, after such a long night of dismal darkness, he will not extinguish the light, and cause them to return again to midnight darkness; when he has begun to enkindle the blessed fire, he will not quench the smoking flax, until he hath brought forth judgment unto victory. . . .

49 · *Jonathan Mayhew*

(1 7 2 0 – 1 7 6 6)

"THE RIGHT AND DUTY OF

PRIVATE JUDGMENT"

In 1750, the year of Edwards' dismissal from Northampton, Jonathan Mayhew preached a sermon against unlimited submission that has been called "the morning gun of the Revolution." His sermon on the repeal of the Stamp Act is likewise celebrated as a ringing declaration of the self-evident truths of John Locke's *Second Treatise of Government*. To note that Mayhew, in his recorded thoughts on the domestic affairs of Massachusetts, was possibly even more conservative than Charles Chauncy, is not necessarily to challenge his credentials as an apostle of liberty and advocate of the "rights of man." But the fact is that this most outspoken of Liberals did defend the provincial Establishment—political as well as ecclesiastical—against all the popular radicalisms of his day. Mayhew's Liberalism emerged most clearly in his rejection

---

Jonathan Mayhew, *Seven Sermons . . . Preached at a Lecture in the West Meeting-House in Boston, . . . in August, 1748* (Boston, 1749; reprinted London, 1750), pp. 18–21, 29–33.

of the "repressive" dogmas of Calvinism. While a student at Harvard he had been personally touched by the Awakening, but he quickly and violently reacted against enthusiasm and all its corollary beliefs. Even before receiving his degree Mayhew enjoyed a considerable reputation as a brilliant, and unorthodox, thinker. None of the Boston ministers would participate in his ordination as pastor of Boston's West Church in 1747. He returned the compliment by refusing thereafter to join the local ministerial association. But Mayhew differed from most of his colleagues only in his greater willingness to entertain, and to discuss publicly, the full doctrinal implications of "rational religion." In the 1750's he openly attacked the orthodox doctrine of the Trinity and became the archenemy of American Calvinists. In reply to his critics, Mayhew made no effort to hide his utter contempt—his usual attitude toward all less gifted than himself—and he even questioned their right to espouse their enthusiastic notions. The "right of private judgment" that Mayhew invoked in his first publication is thus not to be confused with "religious liberty." The latter, in the context of eighteenth-century America, was the cause of the evangelical multitude. Mayhew spoke for each man's right to reason for himself—not the right of any number of men to hear the preachments of enthusiasts. For his own reasons, and from his own premises, Mayhew was the first American to challenge articulately what Alexis de Tocqueville was to call "the tyranny of the majority." He helped, in sum, to found a tradition just as American as the one which

Edwards fathered. Whether speaking of human salvation or of the social good, Mayhew focused, like all Liberals, on the capacities of the individual—or, at least, of the few as distinguished from the many.

. . . [Since] *truth* and *right* have a real existence in nature, independent on the *sentiments* and *practices* of men, they do not necessarily follow the multitude, or major part: nor ought we to make *number* the *criterion* of the true religion. Men are fickle and various and contradictory in their opinions and practices: but truth and moral rectitude are things fixed, stable and uniform, having their foundation in the nature of things. They will not change their nature out of complaisance to the most numerous and powerful body of men in the world. We may *conform* to them; but they will not *condescend* to us. Were number the mark of truth and right, religion itself would be a perfect *Proteus*, sometimes one thing, and sometimes another, according to the opinion that happens to prevail in the world. But if one man may err, why not two? and if two, why not two thousand? . . .

The *multitude* may *do evil,* and the *many, judge falsly. . . .*
. . . But nevertheless we daily see that the principal argument with which some endeavour to propagate their opinions, is, that they are generally received, *i. e.* in that particular place or country: and if they can but add, that they were the doctrines embraced by their pious fore-fathers, this they reckon such demonstration as no man in his senses can resist. Such idle, superficial cant may gull the thoughtless multitude; but will be despised by all others.

If we must needs be governed by number in the choice of our religion, it is certainly reasonable to be governed by the *greatest* number. And if so, we must be neither *Calvinists* nor

Arminians; Trinitarians nor *Unitarians; Quakers* nor *Anabaptists; Churchmen* nor *Presbyterians; Papists* nor *Protestants;* nor *Jews,* nor *Mahometants;* but we must even turn *Heathens* at once, *Paganism* being the most universal *Orthodoxy* in the world.

It will be observed, that I have said nothing for, or against, any of the different parties here enumerated: All I propose, is to shew the unreasonableness of chusing our religion by vote. This, considering the fickleness and capriciousness of mankind, amounts to much the same thing with chusing it by *lot*. For whether the major or minor part shall have truth and right of their side, is intirely precarious: To-day it may be so: To-morrow, otherwise.

Nor is it needless for us to be upon our guard in this matter, considering how natural it is to the generality of mankind, especially to such as are of an indolent, incurious make, to follow the most numerous and powerful party, both in principle and practice, without troubling themselves about the merits of the cause. Many would almost shudder at the thoughts of an unfashionable vice, or an unpopular doctrine, who would nevertheless readily embrace the same vice and the same doctrine, when unattended with the disadvantage of being contrary to the *mode*. What we abhor when out of date and fashion, we are apt to admire upon a change of times, when it comes to be reputable. It is most agreeable to us to herd with the multitude; to believe and act as they do, right or wrong. This gratifies our innate propensity towards *Society:* and many advantages naturally attend him that has the majority on his side. He procures the good-will of all about him, by falling in with their favourite opinions and practices, while the *dissenter* is either ridiculed or railed at, and labours under innumerable inconveniencies. Hence it often comes to pass, that we are insensibly attached to such corrupt opinions and practices as we should have abhorred, had they not been reputable and popular. For the sake of being with *the many*, we daily see some not only renounce their reason and understanding; but break through all the ties of honour, friendship, humanity, charity and piety, making intire shipwreck of a good conscience. Afterwards they imagine that number is the principal criterion of truth; and flatter themselves that they are always secure of being in the right, while they adhere to that side that can carry the vote. This *conforming* humour is too prevalent in the world at present; and always was. . . .

Nor is there more room for *scepticism* in relation to morals and religion, than in common life; nor indeed so much, with regard to the principal branches of our *duty*. . . . The being and perfections of God may be known without much difficulty; and these being known, it is as easy to know how we ought to conduct ourselves towards him in general, as it is for a servant to know how to please a master whose temper and character he is acquainted with. And it is at least as plain that the Sovereign of the world will make a distinction betwixt the righteous and the wicked, as that a wise and good prince will make a distinction between dutiful subjects and rebels.

Thus it appears, in general, that men are able to distinguish between truth and falshood, right and wrong. But I shall now make several observations upon this proposition, in order to farther explain the real intention of it, to obviate some objections against it, and to guard it against those abuses to which it may appear liable. And

1. It is not intended in this assertion, that all men have *equal abilities* for judging what is true and right. The whole creation is diversified, and men in particular. There is a great variety in their intellectual faculties. That which principally distinguishes some men from the beasts of the field, is the different formation of their bodies. Their bodies are *human,* but they are in a manner *brute* all beside. Whether the difference that there is in the natural powers of men, proceeds from the

original make of their minds, or from some difference in those bodily organs upon which the *exercise* of the rational faculties may be supposed to depend; it is apparent that there is, in fact, such a difference. And therefore when it is said that men are able to judge what is true and right, it must be understood in such a sense as is consistent with this fact. Those of the lower class can go but a little way with their inquiries into the natural and moral constitution of the world. But even these may have the power of judging in *some degree*. However, upon supposition that some were wholly ignorant of their own existence, it does not follow that all must be so, any more than that all bodies must be round, because some are of that particular figure. From the most dull and stupid of the human species, there is a continual rise or gradation, there being as great a variety in the intellectual powers of men, as in their bodily and active powers. And so it may be true of some in an higher and more proper sense than of others, that they may *even of themselves judge what is right*. Many things are obvious, and, in a manner, first principles to *them*, which to others are mysterious and incomprehensible.

2. As a farther limitation of this assertion, I would observe, that it does not imply, that the *same persons* are equally adequate judges of truth and right, in all conditions and circumstances. There is a great difference in the powers of different men: But no one differs more from another than he does from himself, considered in childhood and mature life, before and after his mind is cultivated by study and exercise. The *man* knows what the *child* was ignorant of. We come into the world ignorant of every thing. But he that, in his natural, rude and uncultivated state is unqualified to judge what is true and right, unless it be in a few obvious cases, is capable of considerable improvements by study and experience. Our intellectual faculties were given us to improve: they rust for want of use; but are brightened by exercise. Exercise strengthens

and invigorates our mental faculties as well as our bodily. And the more a man habituates himself to intellectual employments, the greater will be his aptness and facility in discovering truth, and detecting error. Without some previous study and application, it is as impossible that men should be accurate judges of truth and right, as it is that they should be compleat artificers in any mechanical business, without spending time to learn the trade. They may bungle and cobble; but can do nothing that will bear the inspection of a *master-workman*. It is the unhappiness of a great part of mankind that they do not sufficiently consider this natural weakness, ineptitude and awkwardness of human reason before cultivation; but sit down contented with their imaginary sagacity and promptness of understanding, without using the proper means to qualify them for judging of things that may come under their consideration. Hence it is that we have so many *quacks* and ignorant pretenders in all arts and sciences— What need of study to come at an acquaintance with those subjects which we may understand at any time only by opening our eyes? Who will descend into the bowels of the earth to dig for gold, while it lies in plenty within his reach upon the surface of the ground? Who will dive for pearls, while he imagines they float upon the waves? Or what need has that field of tillage, whose soil is so fertile, that, like that of *Eden*, it produces spontaneously the richest fruits? When men imagine that the depths of science may be fathomed by a single glance of thought, without any previous application to intellectual exercises, it cannot be expected that they should be able to determine justly upon any points but some of the most familiar and obvious. In this case, he that was *born like the wild asses-colt*, must needs continue to be so? or, at best, come to maturity, and grow up into an ass himself.

The alteration which time and study make in the abilities of men for judging concerning truth and right, is sufficient to account for the diversity of sentiments entertained by the *same persons* at different periods of their life, without having recourse to *scepticism*, or supposing all our notions, from first to last, to be mere fancy and illusion. A man may err once without erring always. Nor can we argue from the reveries of youth, and the absurd conceits of the illiterate, that all mankind are but a mighty nation of fools and lunaticks, pleasing themselves with idle dreams and delusive appearances, instead of realities.

3. That men are able *even of themselves to judge what is right*, does not imply, that they can receive no assistance from books, and the conversation of learned men; Or that they may judge as well without these helps, as with them. Although all men are capable of discerning truth and right in some degree, by the bare exercise of their own natural faculties, it does not follow that they can stand in no need of any foreign aid, in order to their judging in a more perfect manner. The more knowing may be helpful to others in their pursuit of knowledge. And the abilities of men for reasoning justly, and judging truly, may depend, in a great measure, upon the method of their education, the books they read, and the genius and abilities of the persons they converse with. Who will pretend that the natives of *Greenland*, or the *Cape of Good Hope*, enjoy the same, or equal, means of knowledge, with those that are born in the polite and learned nations of *Europe?* Who imagines that one brought up at the plough is as likely to form right notions of things, as if he had been educated at a university? Or that a man who has conversed only with ordinary Mechanics, has the same advantages with those who have enjoyed the familiarity of the greatest proficients in literature? To suppose these things, is to contradict daily experience. And, therefore, to decline all assistances from others in the search of knowledge, under a notion, that we are able to *judge even of ourselves what is right,* is pride

and vanity, and not the part of an ingenuous inquirer after truth. This may be allowed by the most strenuous asserter of mens natural abilities, and natural right, to judge for themselves, without any appearance of inconsistency or contradiction. For it amounts to no more than this, that some men are superior to others, and may help them to the knowledge of some things which they would not have known without their assistance.

50 · *Thomas Darling*

(1720–1789)

REMARKS ON THE DOCTRINES

OF NEW ENGLAND

As ways of thought evangelicalism and rationalism endured long after the Awakening was barely remembered.
George Bancroft saw the two philosophies at work in the
Democrat-Whig divisions of his day. The intellectual split
of the Awakening was directly translated into political
partisanship only in Connecticut, where politics was dominated by New Lights and Old Lights well into the
Revolutionary era. By the mid-1750's new issues, some of
them not directly related to the revival, had modified the
party structure, and the New Lights included not a few
who had never celebrated the glorious Awakening. One
such was Thomas Clap, who had joined in the Yale attack
on Whitefield and, as president of Yale, had expelled students for flirting with Separatism. Less than a decade later
Clap was more concerned with the degree to which his

Thomas Darling, *Some Remarks on Mr. President Clap's History and
Vindication of the Doctrines of the New-England Churches, &c* . . .
(New Haven, 1757), pp. 36–39, 48–53, 68–69.

students were being tempted by Anglicanism and with the rise, within Congregationalism itself, of a rationalist spirit. In 1755 Clap published what he conceived to be a complete exposé and refutation of this "new scheme" of religion. He urged the clergy of the colony to use the Saybrook Platform, as he was using the powers of the Yale Corporation, in defense of orthodoxy.

Clap's effort to unite the Calvinists of Connecticut against the threat of rational religion showed him to be no more the libertarian than he had been when confronted with revival enthusiasm. Other Connecticut ministers, especially those less recently converted to New Light-ism, saw the battle of the 1750's, and the value of ministerial associations, in terms of forcing crypto-Arminian ministers to show their true colors, thus permitting a presumably orthodox laity to stand in judgment on hateful doctrines. This was the situation as understood by Clap's most vigorous critic, Thomas Darling, a spokesman of those "respectable" citizens of Connecticut who both wanted Yale to be a more "cosmopolitan" institution and resented being made the objects of a Calvinist heresy-hunt. Darling had been a practicing lawyer at the age of seventeen, but after studying at Yale he was licensed to preach and from 1743 to 1745 was a tutor at the College. Shortly after joining in the faculty rebuke of Whitefield, Darling resigned his tutorship and entered on a mercantile career. He closed his prosperous life as a Tory opposed to the political enthusiasms of the Revolution. His social attitudes were likewise revealed in his 1757 attack (published anonymously) on Clap's effort to defend the old New England Way. Though Darling complained of Calvinist "priestcraft," his argument was in fact a defense of the prerogatives of intellectuals, the clergy among them, against the laity whose authority Calvinists proclaimed. What most disgusted Darling about Calvinism was its tendency to invoke, and bow to, the preferences of the multitude.

People understand from reading this Piece of Mr. *Clap*'s, and indeed 'tis the honest Understanding of it, that there are many Men in this Country who believe these Errors contained in his new Scheme; and that They are engaged with all their Power to promote and propagate them. I have heard People ask the Question (having read this Piece) is it possible that there should be any Men in the Country or in *New-Haven*, ('tis generally understood tha*t New-Haven* is especially aimed at) who believe such monstrous inconsistent Principles? Now I believe it may be said with Truth, that there is not one Man in *New-Haven* or in this Country, that believes these Errors; his Representation therefore, must be looked upon as injurious and un-Christian-*like*. This Representation that he has made, I take to be without any just Foundation; and that it was done with a studied fixed Design, to blacken a Number of Gentlemen in the Government, and particularly, in *New-Haven*. The President never could have thought it worth his Pains, to have made this Bustle about his *new Scheme*, had it not been his Design to persuade the People to believe, that there were Numbers who had imbibed these Errors, in the Country. I would therefore ask Mr. President some Questions, and desire that if he should ever write a Supplement to his new Religion, he would answer them. "Who are the Men that say, the only Design and End God had in the Creation, is the Happiness of the Creature? . . . Who are the Men, *in this Country* (for this is to be understood in every Question) that affirm GOD has no Right over his Creatures as Creator; but only as Benefactor? Who are *They* that affirm, that the only Criterion of Duty to God, is Self-Interest? Who are the Men who say, that the natural Tendency which Things have to promote our own Interest, is the sole Criterion of moral Good and Evil, Truth and Falsehood, Duty and Sin? Who are They that say we ought to have no Regard to GOD; but so far as he may be a Means or Instrument of promoting our own Happiness? Who says, that every Man is now born into the World in as perfect a State of Rectitude, as *Adam* was created, and has no more a Disposition to Sin than he had; and in all Respects stands as fair for the Favour of GOD as *Adam* did, not being obliged to be conformed to any Standard of moral Perfection; but only to pursue his own Interest and Happiness? Who are They that say, that GOD's Foreknowledge don't extend to the Actions of free Agents, because they are not Fore-knowable? Who are They that say, since Sin is nothing else but a Man's not pursuing his own Interest so well as he might, no Punishment is properly and justly due to him, but only that he should suffer the natural ill Consequences of his own Misconduct; consequently no Satisfaction is necessary in Order to the Forgiveness of Sin, and therefore CHRIST did not die to make Satisfaction for Sin? Finally, who are the Men in this Country that believe the Salvation of Devils?"

Now these Questions, containing the Bulk of the Errors in the Presidents new Scheme, I should be glad he would attempt to Answer them; but I never expect to see an Answer to these Questions particularly, for I believe there is no Answer to be given to them that will suit the President's Scheme, that will be satisfactory to any honest Man provided he is judi-

cious.—I would add, that after the President has said, that
there are Numbers of Men who believe the Errors contained
in his new Scheme, he proceeds to say, that these Men believe, "there are no fundamental Principles in Religion, or
any certain Set of Doctrines necessary to be believed in
Order to Salvation," that that is Truth to every Man, that
he believes to be Truth, &c. And represents them as making
little or no Difference between *Christianity*, and *Mahometism*,
and refined *Heathenism*, except in some external Rites and
Ceremonies; and that in their Belief, *Moses, Zoroaster, Jesus
Christ, Apollonius Tyaneus* a heathen Magician, and *Mahomet*
the grand Impostor, are about upon a Par. In a Word that
They had embraced a Scheme that is intirely subversive of
the Gospel of Christ.

Now this is the Character, the President would have his
Readers believe, some Men in the Country justly deserve.
How base the Representation! 'Tis or should be, beneath a
Gentleman to make such a One, and a Dishonour to the
President of a *Christian College*. 'Tis so contrary to the Spirit
and Temper of our Religion, that none but an ill-natured
Christian could be guilty of it. In fact this Piece of the President's, is nothing but a motly Mixture of Errors, thrown together with a View to render a Number of Men odious to
the rest of Mankind; and this done under a Cloak of Orthodoxy: For while he pretends to serve Religion, he does in
the most unchristian Manner, slur and defame his Neighbour.
Men's Characters, more than Life, are valuable; but as valuable as they are, and notwithstanding they are so well secured
by sacred Authority, and tho' our Attempts to deprive our
Neighbours of their good Name, generally meet with universal
Abhorrence; yet some Men to serve a Scheme, will run the
Venture of all these Things, to attack and destroy the Reputation of their Neighbour. And this Piece of the President's
is in my Opinion full Proof of this Fact: For 'tis the most

apparent Violation of all the Rules of christian Charity, that can well be imagined. . . .

I suppose it will be thought, that I am of too suspicious jealous a Temper: However 'tis my Opinion that the Government will soon be convinced, that my Suspicions are well founded. 'Tis well known that the President some Years passed, was violently set against, what has by Way of Contempt been called *New-light.* And that he shewed his abundant Zeal this Way, in expelling the two *Cleaveland's* from the *College* for attending upon a separate Worship at *Canterbury* on the *Sabbath-day.* And that he justified his Conduct by this *Argument,* that it was absurd to suppose the Government would support the *College,* while at the same Time its Members countenanced and upheld Meetings for publick Worship, set up in Opposition to the Constitution of the Government; which the Government as such, neither knew or owned; for this had a direct and natural Tendency, to introduce all the Confusion and Disorder into the BODY POLITICK, that could well be imagined. . . .

Those Gentlemen in the Country, who have known the President, in Years past, to have been a BARRIER against NEW-LIGHT and its Practices; will be surprised to hear, that Men of that Principle, are now the only Men proper to represent him at the *General Assembly,* and that he constantly votes for such. Han't the Government as much Regard for their Constitution as they used to have; or has the President less? What is the Reason of this? The President's uncertain fickle Conduct.— The President I suppose will say in Excuse for himself, that the Gentlemen he used to vote for, now appear to be *Hereticks.* They are no more *Hereticks,* than they were when he did vote for them. They are the same Men they used to be, Men of the same Good Sense, Honour and Integrity; and if there be any Change, 'tis in the President and not in them. When Men change their own Situation, with Regard to visible

Objects, they then view those Objects under different Angles; which Objects, for that Reason, cease to appear in every Particular just as they did before: These Men therefore are apt to imagine, for want of Consideration, that there has been some Change or Alteration, in those Objects; tho' the Change has been only with Regard to themselves.—

THE Truth I fear is, that all the Pranks that have been play'd in the Government, and through the Country, by the scheming and political *New-lights*[1]; are now a going to be acted over again (and possibly with this Difference only, that there are some new Actors) under this more sacred Name Orthodoxy, which probably will produce ten Times the Disorder, the Confusion, that the First has done. All Men therefore of Sense, Order and Religion, should double their Guard ten Times. . . .

I TAKE the Liberty to give a short Dissertation on Christian Charity, that we may see how well the President has comported himself with this important Precept.

CHARITY, is a kind benevolent Temper in the Soul, which persuades and urges Men to do Good, (as Opportunity presents) to All; but by a Christian Statute, it is to be extended, in a special Manner to Christians: By which we are enjoined *to do Good to All, as we have Opportunity, especially to the Household of Faith*: This Charity as a Principle, is the Support and Foundation of the Christian Religion: For as Unity is the Strength and Security of every Body of Men, so Charity is the best Foundation of this Unity: For which Reason CHRIST when he incorporated the Church into one Body with Himself, *he* being the Head, *they* the Members, made this Charity (which is truly so in the Nature of Things) a great and

---

[1] Those that espouse the separating Party, not from Principle and Conscience, but from political Views; who have been called political *New-lights,* and should be distinguished from those honest People who went off from our Communion from religious Principles only.

fundamental Principle; and by thus doing, founded his Church and Kingdom, upon a Basis worthy it's Author: Accordingly we see, he every where inculcates this Principle, *By Love* (says our LORD) *serve one another, for all the Law is fulfilled in one Word, even in this, thou shalt love thy Neighbour as thyself.* This Charity is essentially necessary; not only to the Being of a Christian, but to Christianity it self. It is the *Commune Vinculum,* the common Tie, the Christian Connection, it is that Principle, that good practical Rule of Action, which holds and binds Christians together; and in exact Proportion, as this Principle governs or not; so the Church of CHRIST increases or decreases in the World: This is the very Characteristick of a Christian; *By this* (says our LORD) *shall all Men know that ye are my Disciples, if ye love one another.* Charity is a great Christian Principle, and as 'tis the best Foundation of Unity, without which the Church could not stand; it may justly be esteemed a fundamental Principle. . . . How far now has the President made this Principle the Rule of his Conduct? *Charity* (says the Apostle) *thinketh no Evil;* but the President not only thinks, but says, his Neighbours have embraced a Scheme of Religion, unknown to the Gospel of CHRIST. *Charity believeth all Things, hopeth all Things,* says the Apostle, by which we are to understand, that a truly charitable Man, is really disposed to believe and hope the Best of his Neighbour: But the President, not only believes, but says, and writes the Worst of his Neighbours; by Representing of them as being no better than *Mahometans.* . . .

The President goes on to say, "when a Minister has a Call to a Church, it is upon this Supposition in the View of Those who call him; that he believes and will preach to Them and Their's, those Doctrines which *they* believe and declare to be the Truth, and if he does not, he is guilty of Delusion, Deception, and Breach of Covenant."

THIS is a fine Compliment paid to the *Laity:* And will

doubtless be pleasing to Those, *who* are afraid of being Priest-ridden. But if They survey the President's Scheme fully, they will not have so much Reason to be pleased, as they imagine. —This is the President's Scheme, that the Clergy should make Creeds and Confessions of Faith and impose them upon the People, and then that the Clergy should be obliged to preach the Principles that the People believe.

A MINISTER of the Christian Religion, is obliged to preach the Gospel of *Christ. Unto us, says the Apostle, are committed the Words of Reconciliation. Wo to me if I preach not the Gospel,* says St. Paul. As a Minister receives his *Commission* from *Christ,* he is obliged in Consequence of *that,* to receive *those Doctrines* that he is to preach, from *him* also. "And the *Ministry,* says the Apostle, *which I have received from the Lord Jesus, to testify the Gospel of the Grace of GOD."* And for this Reason, I believe it to be an Affront to the Author of our holy Religion, who *commissionates* Men to be Ministers in his Kingdom; for any such Minister upon his *Designation* to any particular Cure, meanly, and for want of true Christian Courage and Fortitude, to oblige himself to preach either the Principles of his People, or the Articles of the *Savoy* or *Westminster* Confession, or the Principles of any former Councils, or the Principles of any Body of Men whatsoever. For having received his Authority as a Minister from *Christ,* he is bound to preach the Gospel, and that alone: And has therefore no Right to oblige himself to preach the Principles of any Man or Body of Men, living or dead: Consequently if he does, he so far forth forfeits the *Character* of a *Minister* of *Christ:* For says the Apostle, *"which Things also we speak, not in the Words which Man's Wisdom teacheth; but which the Holy Ghost teacheth."* A Minister of the Gospel, is no more obliged to preach the Gospel in that *Sense* of it in which his People believe it; then a Justice of the Peace is obliged to execute the Laws of this *Colony,* in that *Sense* of them, in *which* those People understand them, over whom his Jurisdiction extends: But as in the one Case, the Justice is obliged to execute the Laws in *that Sense* of them, in *which* Those that made them, and put him in Power, understand them; so in the other Case a Minister is obliged to preach the Gospel in that *Sense* of it, in which *he* (meaning *Christ*) understood it, who made him a Minister.—So that a Minister is under Obligations to preach the Doctrines of the Gospel, whether his People believe them or not; whether they will hear or whether they will forbear.—

This Principle of the President's, is big with many Absurdities: For First it supposes that Those that are to be taught, are wiser and better Judges of the Doctrines of the Gospel, than their Teachers. . . .

51 · *Ezra Stiles*

(1727–1795)

A DISCOURSE ON THE

CHRISTIAN UNION

Not all who resisted the sway of orthodoxy became Tories. Indeed Thomas Darling's own student and friend, Ezra Stiles, was a steadfast Whig who contributed to the impulse toward American Independence. Stiles was one of the most learned of colonial Americans. He studied for the law and was for two years a practicing attorney, and he had a lifelong and, for his day, remarkable interest in science and literature. In 1755 Stiles entered the ministry and, though touched by skepticism, preserved an unquestionable religious faith. As a preacher and as Yale's post-Revolutionary president Stiles moderated an inherited Puritanism with many of the ideas and much of the vitality of the Enlightenment. Like his Old Light father, Isaac Stiles, he considered religious enthusiasm reprehensible;

Ezra Stiles, *A Discourse on the Christian Union: the substance of which was delivered before the Reverend Convention of the Congregational Clergy in the Colony of Rhode Island* . . . (Boston, 1761, pp. 50–55, 85–86, 89–93, 96–97, 102, 115–149.

but as a minister in Rhode Island, Ezra Stiles became an ardent and consistent advocate of religious liberty. Along with many of his Old Light friends, however, Stiles was persuaded that the Episcopal Church, which seemed intent on the creation of an American bishop, threatened the freedom of the colonies. In 1760, in an address to the clergy of Rhode Island, Stiles called for a defensive "confederacy" of American dissenters. Over the next decade he worked to implement his vision of an anti-Episcopal alliance of the churches of New England and the Middle Colonies and to perfect his notion of an "American Church." Stiles was a careful ecclesiastical historian, but he was also offended by the partisanship that blighted the church in his day. He defined the New England Way, and the faith that all Americans were to defend, as the purest of Congregationalisms. Yet his program appealed to many leaders of Old Side Presbyterianism, perhaps because he conceived his confederacy as united, not by vital piety, but in "mutual forebearance." His vision did not prove compelling to those Americans who saw in the communion of evangelical churches and saints a power capable of redeeming American society. But his latitudinarianism (as indeed the Revolution that he helped to foster) was a welcome relief to all who, perhaps tiring of the rigors of evangelical religion, were happy to obscure or forget the battle lines of the Awakening.

. . . [Our] churches . . . were willing and desirous to walk together as equal sister churches, not in subordination and subjection, but in universal protestant liberty and communion.

Having thus exhibited a summary view of the doctrine and policy on which our churches have a very general agreement, I procede

To mention some things on which there is among us some real or supposed difference of opinion, and to shew that these differences need not obstruct the general harmony recommended in the text: and that these real and suppostitious differences may be lessened by benevolent and honorable concessions.

1. One source of different sentiment, were the unhappy excesses into which our churches have been transported in the late enthusiasm that prevailed since the year 1740. In the public mistaken zeal, religion was made to consist in extravagancies and indecencies, which were not according to the faith once delivered. Multitudes were seriously, soberly and solemnly out of their wits. The scriptures were in danger of being neglected for the indistinguishable impulses of the Spirit of God; sober reason gave way to enthusiasm; the terrors of eternal damnation, instead of subserving rational and sober convictions, were improved to throw people into that confusion, frenzy and distraction, which unfitted them for the genial illuminations of the holy spirit. Besides this, the standing ministry were aspersed, and represented under abusive suspicions of being unconverted, legalists, arminians. And as they were thus publicly and indecently vilified, so it was taught as a duty to forsake their ministrations, and form into separate assemblies. And as was natural to expect, our churches were hereby rent and torn and thrown into convulsions and confusions, to the great dishonor of the general cause. Much of this indeed was piously meant, and honestly intended, and proceded from a zeal for the cause of God. Thus there was no doubt an intermixture of good, and it is

to be hoped many were savingly converted. Our churches have now in some measure cooled and recovered themselves, tho' the spirit of enthusiasm is not altogether extinguished as yet, but operates and influences under different pretexts, and in a different form. But it is to be remarked with gratitude to the over-ruling disposer of events, that amidst the religious convulsions which threatened the subversion of congregationalism, an augmentation of above 150 new churches has taken place in that period, founded not on the separations, but natural increase into new towns and parishes. These differences into which good and pious men were involved, have indeed made so deep an impression, as not to be easily effaced in the present generation, notwithstanding it is so much our interest to unite in love and harmony; nor can we so easily, heartily and sincerely unite as if nothing of this nature had happened to disturb the common benevolence. But it is to be hoped that the spirit of alienation will more and more subside, and not be transmitted to succeeding generations. On all sides there have doubtless been errors and indiscretions, let us put on condescention and charity; and nobly forgive one another.

2. Another source of differences is that of *calvinism* and *arminianism*. Many great and pious men are alarmed at a supposed prevalence of arminian principles through the churches of New-England: and other suppose calvinism greatly erroneous. Under these banners they respectively enlist, combat, conquer, and are conquered. The pretext of these names serves to legitimate mutual aspersions which neither party deserve. To me it appears that these jealousies are founded almost intirely on mistake: nor am I aware of any very essential or general alteration of the public sentiment on what we all agree to be the fundamental principles of revelation. From some considerable acquaintance with the ministers of New-England, I cannot perceive any very essential

real difference in their opinions respecting the fundamental principles of religion. I may be mistaken—but their different manner and phraseology in explaining the same principles appears to me to be their chief difference. We are apt indeed to attribute to one another consequences of our peculiar explanations which we by no means adopt. Thus those who are called arminians say of those called calvinists, that their doctrine of *original sin* makes God the author of moral evil—of *election* implies, that we are to sit still and do nothing towards our salvation—of *justification* by the imputation of Christ's righteousness, that it precludes the necessity of *faith, regeneration, inherent righteousness* and *good works,* and so far resolves this great affair into a matter of strict *justice,* as to preclude the rich free grace and sovereign mercy of the father—of *irresistible grace* as destructive of and inconsistent with the moral liberty and free agency of man.—And so on for the rest of the controverted points. And yet none that I ever conversed with who are called calvinists, by any means admit these consequences from their principles. Again, those reputed calvinists say of those reputed arminians, that their doctrine of *moral freedom* implies a natural power to become good and do all that heaven requires of man without the supernatural influence and power of the divine spirit imparted to the soul—that their interpretations of *original sin* implies a denial of the universal depravity of human nature, universal impotency and debilitation of the moral powers, and perversion of affection, with loss of the image and communion of God—that with them *election* is founded on foreseen *meritorious* conditions in man—that their idea of Christ's *atonement* is destructive of the true nature of satisfaction and atonement for sin in the propitiation of the obedience and death of Jesus—that they trust to the *works of the law for justification,*—that they substitute our obedience instead of the obedience of Christ, for the basis and meritorious foundation of justification—in a word, that their notions and sentiments imply that man is not totally depraved, and tho' fallen, yet by Christ recovered to even a better state at present than Adam in innocency was in; and that there is no need of atonement, renovation of nature, or of the spirit's operation. But all reputed arminians I have conversed with strenuously deny these consequences. And I find both reputed calvinists and arminians, especially of the clergy, agree in admitting the depravity of human nature in all its powers and affections—the absolute inability to faith and holiness, without the special influences, assistances and operations of the spirit on the human mind, over and above the elucidated and inspired discoveries of revelation, I do not mean to reveal new truths, but to enable us to an efficacious apprehension and discernment of those already revealed—that to his enlightning energies is to be attributed the principle of *regeneration*—that we are *justified* in the sight of God, not for good works, but alone for the sake of Christ and his atonement: tho' they may differ in defining the nature of atonement, yet all agree in making it the sole foundation of justification—that the benefits of Christ's righteousness are appropriated to believers by *faith*, as the condition of our receiving the atonement.

Some perhaps entertain sentiments *really* different on these important subjects. Their conviction however is not to be laboured by the coertion of civil or ecclesiastical punishment, but by the gentle force of persuasion and truth—not by appeals to the tenets of parties and great men; not by an appeal to the positions of Arminius or Calvin; but by an appeal to the inspired writings. And I am persuaded if all would freely and candidly compare their sentiments to this rule, they would be very soon found not very variant.

. . . The only way is to examine our sentiments by scripture; then candidly and benevolently inquire how far we are agreed in reality; to walk together by the same amiable rule so far

as we have attained to think alike; and to forbear real differences in love, where there appears a sincere love of truth,
candor and piety. Remembering we all have the unalienable
right of private judgment in religion; and that liberty of thinking and chusing our religion, *liberty of conscience* was the
great errand of our pious forefathers into America. And as to
real differences, I believe we might amicably adjust them by
honorable and benevolent concessions, by studying and comparing the written word which we all agree to be a sufficient
rule, instead of human systems on which we all justly differ.
In the search after truth it should be our perpetual motto,
"*nullius addictus jurare in verba magistri.*"[1] For after all, the
question ought not to be what is *calvinism*, or what *arminianism?*—what was the opinion of *calvin*, or what the opinion of
arminius? but what is real christianity? what is the truth as
Jesus and his inspired apostles delivered it?

3. There are some differences of opinion among us respecting the nature and authority of ecclesiastical councils, and
the powers of particular churches. . . .

[It] appears that all claims of councils or consociations, with
respect to jurisdictions and decisions in opposition to the
sense of particular churches and parochial congregations, may
be fruitless and to little purpose, besides a temporary em-
broiling of the churches. Besides, that through some unhappy
principles respecting the terms of communion and the qualification of communicants, by which multitudes of sober, pious
and virtuous christians are deterred from the ordinances, our
churches are often but a small part of the parochial congregations. And it is the congregation in its parochial congrega-

---

[1] "I am not bound to swear as any master dictates." The statement, a
quotation from Horace's Epistles (*l.* 1.14), suggests how a rationalist
minister, deriving his ideals as much from classic as from Christian
sources, could give rather fretful and negative connotations to the word
"liberty." [Ed.]

tional capacity that the law considers: And this as such does not enough partake of an ecclesiastical nature to be subject to ecclesiastical jurisdictions; or to have the validity of any of its acts dependent on the decisions of an ecclesiastical council. And even as to the influence of these decisions on the churches as such, they perhaps had better be left as those of the congregational councils *advisory* only, according to the sense in which it is probable that the Connecticut churches received their platform. All that is beyond this, till the public spirit be subdued, must endanger contests and oppositions, in which the public benevolence and liberty may suffer. And it is to be remarked, that even consociated churches have often called in congregational councils to advise on difficulties; which shews that they did not understand themselves restricted to the consociated councils. And it is further to be remarked, that the churches of the apostolic age knew nothing of consociated or congregational councils, nor their powers; but subsisted in the full enjoyment of unembarrassed liberty. No apostolic church had authority over another, either in an individual or aggregate capacity. The claims of authority in consociated councils over the churches, are not only contrary to the primitive pattern, but probably will not prevail in New-England, unless the legislatures enact that no congregational churches shall have benefit of the laws. It is said that there are several churches in Connecticut which have not acceded to the platform, most of which are congregational; and yet have the same immunities and privileges with the others. And any may renounce the platform when they please, as has been done in some instances, and yet are in full charity and communion with the consociated churches. It might be happy if they could all walk together on the consociated form, as they probably would do in time, if the consociation subsisted for fellowship only, and not for dominion, which essentially interferes with the stipulated equality of churches. . . .

The churches are at present above 500, and increasing amain. They might form 20 consociations besides those of Connecticut. And if formed without jurisdiction, they would nobly subserve the purpose of cementing us together into a respectable body. But the moment jurisdiction enters, like the creating *Cesar* perpetual DICTATOR, the beginning of the absolute loss of liberty commences. Let the consociations be *advisory* only to the churches, as the privy council to his majesty, the assembly of the states to the *united provinces;* even general provincial consociations of the same import *advisory only,* might have a friendly influence *salva Libertate & Jure Ecclesiarum universalium*[2]. . . . The exigencies of the christian church can never be such as to legitimate, much less render it wise, to erect any body of men into a standing judicatory over the churches. If on some extraordinary occasions it may be necessary to cede up the united power into an extraordinary commission; yet when the public work designed is accomplished, let the commission end, the power revert and rest in the bosom of the churches. Never suffer the united force and power of the churches to be at the call, especially at the command of a standing body of men, even if part subsist on constitutional delegates from the churches. The ends of civil and ecclesiastical polity are so widely different, that however this may be expedient in the one, it is by no means so in the other. If the united force of the churches can be constitutionally collected and directed to such objects and ends as a standing council (liable to corruption and undue influence) shall command, without and contrary to the consent of individual churches, whether the policy be a monarchy, or an oligarchy, it is indifferent—liberty is gone, tyranny and

---

[2] "in the sound [or saving] liberty and law of the universal churches." The use of the plural (*"Ecclesiarum"*), hardly an echo of any church father, testifies to the limited scope of Stiles' ecclesiastical vision. [Ed.]

intestine oppression may be the fate of succeeding generations. Our churches have not as yet given up their powers and liberty into foreign hands, at least the main body have not, and it is questionable whether any have designedly and bona fide done it. Let them be taught to stand fast in the liberty wherewith Christ has made them free. Heaven is giving us an opportunity to plant a noble body of free churches in America, and has charged us with a part to act for posterity. The *love of dominion* which reigns in every breast, and thus becomes a general principle, is almost too mighty for that other general principle the *love of liberty*, which it is designed to balance. Take either away out of human nature, and confusion arises. There is no need of cultivating the former, it is inextinguishable: but there is great need of cultivating the latter, especially in religion. Liberty and dominion are in opposite balances on the scale of human nature—both necessary: the latter is dangerous unless well guarded; the former generally safe excepting when collecting for one public burst on tyranny. They are designed by God to counterpoise and balance one another. There is no danger but the wanton licentiousness of the one will be corrected by the artifice and force of the other. Neither let liberty be extinguished nor dominion; both have their proper spheres; when the one degenerates into tyranny and unnecessary restraints, and when the other becomes anarchy, they are both equally pernicious to society. The principles of both and their balance ought to be well understood, settled and defined, and . . . their rationale publicly taught and explained thro' the community.

The body of the clergy in New-England might easily adopt a system of ecclesiastical management, which in a century or two, with moderation and attention to the public spirit, would gently gain the submission of the churches, and insensibly steal away their liberty. But I rejoice to believe they are not inclined to it. Yet let me say that measures may be honestly, and with pious intent, gone into, which effect this as surely as if with the design and foresight of a *Machiavel,* a *Richlieu,* or a *Mazarine.* The system adopted designedly or undesign-edly, however looks with undeviating operation to the same end. Any thing of this nature may be wisely opposed. Let us remain true and firm to our first principles, the unsurrendered power of the churches. And indeed there is need of the exer-cise of but little power here; for christianity is not a system of human power and dominion, but of liberty and benevolence.

. . . But in general our churches appear to me to be nearly on the same footing with the primitive churches, as left by the apostles, who doubtless left them completely instituted. Most other protestant churches are under embarrassments from which we are free. If there be more liberty for free in-quiry at present in some of them, it does not flow from the nature of their policy, but from the laudable moderation of their clergy, or other less honorable motives—and besides, the avenues to this liberty are embarrassed with dishonorable compliances and submissions. Any embarrassments in our churches procede not from the nature of their policy, but from the spirit of the times, which must and will alter. If there be any true way of worshipping the deity, the supreme Lord of nature, it may be in our manner: even deists must confess that our way is or may be natural and rational. And being possessed of the precious jewel of religious liberty, a jewel of inestimable worth, let us prize it highly, and esteem it too dear to be parted with on any terms; lest we be again en-tangled with that yoke of bondage[3] which our fathers could not, would not, and God grant we may never submit to bear. The lesser differences among ourselves, which will at times unavoidably spring up in this imperfect militant state, and afford a temporary disturbance to the best constituted

---

[3] STAR-CHAMBER and HIGH COMMISSION.

churches, will again subside, and finally terminate in defining the limits of power, and in more accurately ascertaining the terms of communion and universal benevolence. Providence has planted the british America with a variety of sects, which will unavoidably become a mutual balance upon one another. Their temporary collisions, like the action of acids and alcalies after a short ebullition, will subside in harmony and union, not by the destruction of either, but in the friendly cohabitation of all. An antecedent fermentation may take place, as it has done in the philosophic world, but generous inquiry and liberal disquisition will issue all in this. Resplendent and all-prevailing TRUTH will terminate the whole in universal harmony. All surreptitious efforts and attempts on the public liberty will unavoidably excite the public vigilance of the sects, till the terms of general communion be defined and honorably adjusted. The notion of erecting the polity of either sect into universal dominion to the destruction of the rest, is but an airy vision—may serve to inflame a tempory enthusiasm—but can never succede—all the present sects will subsist & increase into distinct respectable bodies, continuing their distinctions for a long time yet to come in full life and vigor. Indeed mutual oppression will more and more subside from their mutual balance of one another. Union may subsist on these distinctions, coalescence only on the sameness of public sentiment, which can again be effected in the christian world only by the gentle, but almighty power of truth. It has been effected in past ages, but can never be effected again on the former measures—so great an alteration is made among mankind by science and letters. The sects cannot destroy one another: all attempts this way will be fruitless— they may affect a tempory disturbance, but cannot produce a dissolution—each one subserves the mutual security of all. The advantages taken by any one sect over the security and indolence, or intestine broils of another, will soon eno' awaken its sensibility or moderation, and excite the spirit of self-defence—and so for the whole. Such is human nature, especially enlightened with the pure light of revelation and sciences. Nothing however will content us but actual experiment—this experiment will be made in one century, and then perhaps we shall be satisfied.

. . . It is truly important that this vine, which God hath planted with a mighty hand in this american wilderness, should be cultivated into confirmed maturity. You are very sensible, that there is a formal attempt on the chastity and order of our churches, which is vigilantly to be guarded against, at present, till our churches grow into one cemented, large, pure, defensible body. It is incumbent upon us to watch and guard their infancy with a paternal godlike fidelity. God has betrusted us with a part to act for posterity and the public; let us not supinely desert it, but act it well, consecrate and transmit the purity of religion to generations yet unborn. It is evident nothing tends more to enervate and moulder down our cause, than differences and animosities: nothing tends to strengthen and form it to defensible maturity like union and benevolence. If we have any public benevolence, any bowels of compassion, any tender affection for pure and undefiled religion—by the tender mercies of Jehovah! by the love of Jesus!—let us bury and lay aside our trifling differences, and harmoniously unite in carrying on and perfecting the one same great and noble work.

. . . In a century from this time we may have 5000 churches, even with allowances for emigrations to new provinces. But in order to this the love of liberty, and a zeal for pure and undefiled religion must be diffused and propagated with unremitted fidelity and vigilance. Should our intestine dissentions unhinge the minds of the rising generations, and disengage or render them indifferent to the cause, it might be attended with unhappy consequences. Union and diffusive harmony are truly important, during this infancy of the churches, and this period of rapid increase. The error of Balaam in the snare he laid for Israel, effectually wrought a confusion, from which omnipotence alone could recover them. Let us not be caught by any similar error. If we adhere to our principles, even the undefiled, the uncorrupted principles of revelation, with the utmost charity and benevolence to others, and without encroaching upon, or interfering with, the peculiarities of our protestant brethren of the other sects, if we are and continue united in faith and fellowship—providence is advancing us in a swift progress to figure and defensible maturity. The present increasing state of our churches, and the dependence of their future glory on harmonious union in their increasing infancy, appear to me a very powerful recommendation to walk together by the same rules, in love and harmony, so far as we have attained, and attentively to *mind the same thing;* that is, ourselves to respect, and to teach our children to mind the same great interest of the same common cause—never to desert it, but faithfully pursue it: that the public spirit be animated, guided and governed by the *same* public principles which are our common interest. It ought particularly to be inculcated upon our friends going from us to the settlement of new towns or provinces, to carry religion with them, to *settle early in church order, and furnish themselves with a ministry of the word and ordinances, for the benefit of themselves and their children.* Great encouragement should be given to our colleges and nurseries of literature, which grow more and more important every day. We should often relate to our posterity the history of the wonderful providences of God in the settlement of this country; and remark the growth of our churches, and engage them by all the honorable motives of christianity to steadfastness in the faith once delivered to the saints, and in the liberty wherewith the gospel has made us free. Let our children be often taught to read the sixth, seventh, eighth, and ninth verses of the twenty-sixth chapter of Deuteronomy with parallel application to the history of our ancestors. Let the great errand into America never be forgotten. Let them be well acquainted among other parts of sacred history, with the history of the Hebrew nation; in which they will see examples of public reward and public chastisement of providence in a very striking light. From the antient example let our churches be warned, very carefully to avoid the two capital errors which proved the ruin of the Hebrew republic, and which will never fail eventually to subvert the best constituted empire—I mean CORRUPTION in RELIGION and the public VIRTUE; & DISUNIONS. These two things operated with full strength among God's antient people, on the revolt of Jeroboam and introduction of idolatry, upon which in a very little time there were not found above 7 or 8000 men out of above a million who had *not bowed the knee to baal*. The pure religion becoming thus corrupted, Israel was ripe for that extirpation, which was effected upon their calling in the foreign aid of Damascus and Assyria. See this in 2 Kings 17. And before this the immediate effect of national dissention was the loss of half a million of men, being near half the kingdom of Israel which fell in one day, the greatest battle that history records. Even Judah forsook the *law of the Lord;* and within five years after the death of Solomon, the corruption he introduced in complaisance to foreign wives, had overspread the empire—so fatal is the ill example of princes. Judah also *"built them high places and images, and groves, on every high hill and under every green tree:"* on which Shishak, with the Egyptian and Ethiopian army, penetrated even to Jerusalem, and carried off the treasures of the temple and the king's house, the opulence amassed by Solomon. What prosperity attended God's people when they turned to the Lord and united in his ways? The whole treatment of divine providence towards that people from Moses to this day, has been exactly according to the 28th chapter of Deuteronomy. And excepting in one thing, there may be an analogy between the divine treatment of this and all other states, especially his conduct toward that kingdom wherein dwelleth righteousness. We may then reap great advantage in consulting and duly applying that history, which may be in some measure typical of our own. In a word, we have in the sacred and common histories of providence assistance to become assured in what point of view the PUBLICK VIRTUE and UNDEFILED RELIGION appear to the sovereign mind. If we conform ourselves to these notices and supernal assurances, we may depend with absolute certainty on the smiles and defence of Jesus our omnipotent patron.

52 · Joseph Bellamy

THE MILLENNIUM

Among evangelical Americans the bright promise of the Awakening was succeeded in the 1750's by the desperate sense that the tendency of history had suddenly moved downward. Arminianism and other rationalist "heresies" seemed to be growing increasingly fashionable, and, as both cause and consequence of this intellectual change, "vices of all sorts" abounded. In this time of "terrible darkness," made all the darker by the French and Indian War, pious Americans began to ask if the millennium promised by Edwards would ever arrive. According to Joseph Bellamy, they even asked whether, considering the obvious prospering of "sinners," Calvinism itself were not a fiction. In these circumstances in 1758 Bellamy published two treatises which he was certain would, when read together, make Christians "feel better and behave right." One was *The Wisdom of God in the Permission of Sin,* in which Bellamy argued that God allowed sin in order that the good would have a more dramatic and aesthetically appealing victory—much as the sun seems all the brighter, he explained, when it breaks through the darkest clouds.

Joseph Bellamy, *Works,* I, 495–516.

In the companion piece, a sermon on the millennium, Bellamy portrayed the same darkness as a time of testing, in which men could prove their claims to sainthood by not giving way to envy or to sloth. Only by right actions could men assure themselves of being among the elect when the Church Militant triumphed over the earthly powers of darkness, Bellamy argued, and he closed his sermon with an eloquent appeal for volunteers to encourage and hasten the victorious establishment of God's Kingdom on earth.

Bellamy's sermon, which represented the ultimate fusion of the doctrines of "experimental religion" with the Calvinist vision of the Work of Redemption, had, in the context of the 1760's remarkable effects. In 1762 the New Lights of Connecticut gained control of the lower house of the legislature, and Bellamy was asked to give the Election Sermon. In his discourse Bellamy placed the Calvinist ethic in judgment on all the affairs of the province. He called on all Christian citizens—populace as well as magistrates and ministers—to drive "sin" of every sort out of the colony, to "stone it until it is dead." Three years later, during the Stamp Act Crisis, pious mobs roamed the Connecticut countryside, despoiling Episcopal chapels, attacking Arminians, and declaring it more delightful to serve "in the Church Militant than in the Church Triumphant." This had been the intention neither of Bellamy's sermon nor of his doctrinal discourses. But considering the rhetoric of his immensely popular sermon, *The Millennium*, it is not difficult to imagine how evangelical doubts and anxieties, once offered a single opening, exploded into violence.

REVELATION xx. 1, 2, 3.

And I saw an angel come down from heaven, having the key of the bot-tomless pit, and a great chain in his hand. And he laid hold on the dragon, that old serpent, which is the devil and satan, and bound him a thousand years. And cast him into the bottomless pit, and shut him up, and set a seal upon him, that he should deceive the nations no more, till the thousand years should be fulfilled.

In a great variety of respects, the BIBLE is the most remarkable book in the world. In it we have God's moral character clearly exhibited to view, by a history of his conduct, as moral Governor of the world from the beginning: and the nature of fallen man painted to the life by a history of their behaviour for four thousand years. In it we have opened the glorious and astonishing method, that has been entered upon to disappoint all satan's designs, by the interposition of the Son of God; and are informed of his birth, life, death, resurrection, ascension, and exaltation, and of the glorious designs he has in view. And the whole is so contrived as to be admirably suited to all the circumstances and needs of a good man; that, as it were designed to be the good man's book, in a peculiar sense, so it is perfectly suited to his case. It is "profitable for doctrine, for reproof, for correction, for instruction in righteousness, that the man of God may be perfect, thoroughly furnished to all good works." (2 *Tim.* iii. 16, 17.)

That sincere concern for the cause of truth and virtue, for the honour of God and interest of true religion, which is peculiar to a good man, whose character it is to love Christ above father and mother, wife and children, houses and lands, yea, better than his own life, must naturally subject him to a peculiar kind of solicitude. Even as a child of a truly filial spirit, is pained when it goes ill with his father's family, to whose interest he is closely attached; and has a whole system of inward sensations, that a stranger intermeddles not with—the BIBLE, the good man's book, is therefore wisely adapted to ease the good man's pained heart, and afford consolation in this interesting and most important point; as it gives the strongest assurances that the cause of virtue shall finally prevail.

How insupportable must the grief of the pious Jews have been, sitting on the sides of the rivers of Babylon! "There we sat down," say they, "yea, we wept when we remembered Zion." And "on the willows they hung their harps," nor could any thing divert their minds. "If I forget thee, O Jerusalem, let my right hand forget her cunning. If I do not remember thee, let my tongue cleave to the roof of my mouth." (*Psal.* cxxxvii.) How insupportable, I say, must their grief have been, while their glorious holy temple, and their holy city, the place of all their sacred solemnities, were laying desolate, and God's people in captivity, had it not been for that promise, so often repeated, that after seventy years God would visit them, and cause them to return to their own land. God knew before-hand the anguish which would be apt to fill their hearts, the sinking discouragements, and all the train of dark and gloomy thoughts, they would be incident to; and before-hand provided a remedy. Yea, no sooner had he denounced their doom in the 39th chapter of *Isaiah*, but immediately in the next chapter, and for ten or twenty chapters together, does he provide for their support. "Comfort ye, comfort ye my people; speak comfortably to Jerusalem," &c.

So, how insupportable would have been the grief of the church of Christ, through the long, dark, cruel reign of mystical Babylon, while they beheld error and wickedness universally prevail, satan getting his will in almost every thing, and to appearance no signs of better times, but all things wearing a dreadful aspect before their eyes: how great their grief; how sinking their discouragements; how almost insuperable their temptations to apostatize, and forsake a cause that heaven seemed to forsake, had not the day of deliverance been expressly foretold, and the glory that should follow opened to view, by the spirit of prophecy! But in a firm belief that the cause they were engaged in, and for which they spilt their blood, would finally prevail, and prevail in this world, where they then beheld satan reigning and triumphing, I say, in a firm belief of this, the whole army of martyrs could march on to battle courageously, willing to sacrifice their lives in the cause, not doubting of final victory, although they themselves must fall in the field.

Indeed, were the salvation of his own soul the only thing the good man had in view, he would naturally be quite easy, upon a full assurance that this was secured. So, had Moses cared for nothing but the welfare of himself, and of his posterity, he might have been satisfied, while the whole congregation of Israel were destroyed, if he might become a great nation, and that without any solicitude for the honour of the GREAT NAME of the GOD of Israel. Yea, although the idolatrous nations round about were fully established in the belief of the divinity of their idols, and brought to look upon the GOD of the Hebrews with ever so great contempt by the means. But, attached as he was to the honour of the God of Israel, nothing could give him satisfaction, but a prospect that that would be secured. The welfare of himself and of his family was of no importance in his esteem, compared with this. (See *Exod.* xxxii.)

It must, therefore, be remembered, that, as the SON of God left his Father's bosom, and the realms of light and glory, and expired on the cross in the utmost visible contempt, that he might spoil principalities and powers, bruise the serpent's head, destroy the works of the devil; so his true disciples have imbibed a measure of the same spirit; and, as volunteers enlisted under his banner, have the same thing in view: they long for the destruction of satan's kingdom; and these petitions are the genuine language of their hearts, "Our father which art in heaven, hallowed be thy name, thy kingdom come, thy will be done on earth as it is in heaven." Nor can the salvation of their own souls, although ever so safely secured, satisfy their minds, without a clear view and fair prospect of Christ's final victory over all his enemies. "But if our great GENERAL, who has sacrificed his life in the cause, may but at last obtain a complete victory, notwithstanding all the present dark appearances; this is enough," says the Christian soldier: "I am willing to risk all in his service, and die in the battle too. But if satan were always to carry the day, Oh who could live under the thought!"

This having been the temper of good men, more or less, even from the early ages of the world, and through all successive generations to this day, they have evidently wanted a peculiar support, which the rest of mankind stood in no need of, to carry them comfortably through such a long scene of darkness; wickedness prevailing, God dishonoured, satan triumphing, the world perishing, the true church of God more generally in sackcloth. And accordingly, the final victory of the cause of truth and virtue was intimated in the very first promise made to fallen man. And from time to time God repeated this comfortable prediction to his church and people; and finally, made it the chief subject of the last book of holy scripture he ordered to be wrote for the use of his church.

Now let us take a brief view of the whole series of these divine predictions, from the beginning of the world, even down to this in our text, contained in one of the last chapters in the bible; that we may see what full evidence there is of this truth; and so what abundant cause for consolation to all the people of God.

I. Immediately after the fall, when the serpent, even that old serpent the devil, had just seduced mankind to revolt from God, and had, to all appearance, laid this whole world in perpetual ruin, even in the depths of this midnight-darkness, a ray of light shone down from heaven. *The seed of the woman shall bruise the serpent's head.* (*Gen.* iii. 15.) As if God had said, "I see the scheme that satan has laid to ruin the world, and establish his impious, malicious, cause: I see it, and I am determined to defeat it. The feebler woman he has over-matched, but her almighty seed shall conquer him, and as effectually subdue him, and prevent all future mischief by him, as a serpent is subdued and incapacitated for further mischief, when his head is crushed to pieces under the indignant heel of one determined on his death." This was a complete doom indeed denounced against satan, at the head of the kingdom of darkness. And it fully implied, that the cause of light, truth, and righteousness, should finally obtain a complete victory.

II. After this gracious and glorious promise had been the chief foundation of all the hopes of God's people for two thousand years, God was pleased to point out the particular family from whence this mighty deliverer should spring, and to intimate what a universal blessing he should be to all the nations of the earth. *And in thy* SEED *shall* ALL *the families of the earth be blessed,* said God to Abraham. (*Gen.* xii. 3.) Which again plainly supposed, that the cause of truth and righteousness, notwithstanding the dark state the world then was in, all sinking fast into idolatry, and would for many ages be in, buried in heathenish darkness, should yet in due time universally prevail over the whole earth. For *in thy seed shall* ALL *the families of the earth be blessed.* This same promise was repeated again and again to Abraham, and afterwards to Isaac and to Jacob.

III. Hitherto God had supported his people's hopes chiefly with promises, with verbal predictions; but from the days of

Moses to the days of Solomon, king of Israel, to assist his people's faith, God did, besides repeated promises of the same thing, by a great variety of wonderful works, shadow forth the glorious day: and at the same time show, that he had sufficient wisdom and power to accomplish the greatest designs. That his people might be convinced, that he could easily bring to pass, for the good of his church, whatsoever seemed good in his sight.

Israel, in the Egyptian bondage, were a designed type of a fallen world under the dominion and tyranny of satan. Nor was Pharaoh more loath to let Israel go, than satan is to have his subjects desert him, and his kingdom go to ruin. But notwithstanding all the seeming impossibilities in the way of Israel's deliverance, infinite wisdom knew how to accomplish the divine designs. God could even cause a member of Pharaoh's family to educate one to be an instrument of this designed deliverance. And in due time, behold, all the armies of Israel march forth from the land of Egypt, out of the house of bondage; and Pharaoh, and his chariots, and all his host, lie buried in the Red sea! So easily can God bring forth his people even out of the anti-christian kingdom, which is spiritually called Sodom and Egypt. And, if he pleases, raise up the instruments of this glorious work, even in the court of Rome.

And when the name of the true God was almost forgotten through all the earth, and the devil worshipped in his room, in idols of various names, through all the nations, God knew how to make his name known, and to cause his fame to spread abroad, and fill the whole earth with his glory, by wonders wrought in the land of Ham, by descending on Mount Sinai, by leading the armies of Israel forty years in the wilderness, in a pillar of cloud by day, and of fire my night, giving them bread from heaven and water out of the flinty rock, dividing Jordan, delivering up one and thirty idolatrous kings to the sword of Joshua, raising up judges one after another in a miraculous manner to deliver his people, until the days of David and Solomon, types of Christ. Of David, who, Messiah-like, subdued the enemies of Israel all around: of Solomon, who built the holy temple, and filled Jerusalem with riches and glory. He, who hath done all these things, can easily accomplish all the designs of his heart, preserve his church, raise up deliverance, break to pieces the kingdoms of the earth for her sake, make truth victorious, and set up the new Jerusalem in all her spiritual glory, build up his Church as a glorious holy temple, and set the son of David upon the throne; by whose hands, satan and all the powers of darkness shall be subdued, chained, sealed up in the bottomless pit, as much afraid, and as much unable to attempt any mischief, as the subdued nations around Israel were in the very height of David's power.

But when shall the son of David reign, and the church have rest? When shall the cause of truth and righteousness thus prevail? Perhaps the very time was designed to be shadowed forth in the law of Moses, in the institution of their holy days. The *seventh day*, said God, who always had this glorious season of rest in view, "the seventh day shall be a sabbath of rest, the seventh month shall be full of holy days, the seventh year shall be a year of rest:" so, perhaps, after *six thousand* years are spent in labour and sorrow by the church of God, the *seven thousandth* shall be a season of spiritual rest and joy, an holy sabbath to the Lord. And as God the Creator was *six days* in forming a confused chaos into a beautiful world, and rested the *seventh;* so God the Redeemer, after *six thousand* years labour in the work of the new creation, may rest on the *seventh*; and then proclaim a general liberty to an enslaved world, and grant a general pardon to a guilty race; as in the year of *Jubilee,* among the Jews, every enslaved Jew was set at liberty, and the debts of all the indebted were cancelled.

IV. These things, thus shadowed forth in types, were also expressly declared by the mouths of the ancient prophets, from the days of David, and forward to the end of that dispensation: and the same things are hinted here and there in the New Testament, and largely opened to view in the revelation of St. John. So that both the Old and New Testaments join to raise in us, who live in these ages, the highest assurance, that it is God's design to "give to his Son the heathen for his inheritance, and the uttermost parts of the earth for his possession. (*Psal.* ii. 8.) For all kings shall bow down before him, and all nations shall serve him. (*Psal.* lxxii. 11.) And the mountain of the Lord's house shall be established in the top of the mountains, and shall be exalted above the hills, and all nations shall flow unto it. (*Isai.* ii. 2.) They shall beat their swords into plow-shares, and their spears into pruning-hooks, and learn war no more. (*ver.* 4.) For the earth shall be full of the knowledge of the Lord, as the waters cover the sea. (*Isai.* xi. 9.) A nation shall be born in a day. (*Isai.* lxvi. 8.) All Thy people shall be righteous. (*Isai.* lx. 21.) They shall all know the Lord, from the least to the greatest. (*Jer.* xxxi. 24.) And holiness to the Lord shall be written on every thing. (*Zech.* xiv. 20, 21.) Kings shall become nursing fathers, and queens nursing mothers, (*Isai.* xlix. 23.) and there shall be nothing to hurt or offend. (*Isai.* xi. 9.) The inhabitants shall not (so much as) say, I am sick. (*Jer.* xxxiii. 24.) And this kingdom shall fill the whole earth. (*Dan.* ii. 35.) And all nations and languages shall serve him. (*Dan.* vii. 14.) And the kingdom and dominion, and the greatness of the kingdom under the whole heaven shall be given to the people of the saints of the most high God. (*Dan.* vii. 27.) And the Jews shall be called in, and the fulness of the Gentiles. (*Rom.* xi. 12–32.) For the gospel shall be preached to every nation, and kindred, and tongue, and people. (*Rev.* xiv. 6.) And satan shall be bound, and Christ shall reign on earth a thousand years." And as surely as the Jews were delivered out of the Babylonish captivity, and Babylon itself destroyed; even so surely shall all these things be accomplished in their time. And mystical Babylon shall "sink as a mill-stone into the sea, and shall be found no more at all." (*Rev.* xviii. 21.)

V. But when shall these things be? I answer, in the first place, it is plain, as yet they have not been, these great things have not been accomplished. They were not accomplished when the Jews were brought out of their Babylonish captivity; for, from thence to the coming of Christ, they never were in so flourishing a state as they had been before. They were not accomplished in the apostolic age: for St. John, when most, if not all, of the other Apostles were dead, spake of these things (in the *Revelation*) as yet to come to pass. They were not accomplished in the three first centuries; for, that was almost one continued scene of blood. They were not accomplished in the days of Constantine the great; for, it is since then that *the man of sin has been revealed.* Nor are they accomplished to this day: for satan is still walking to and fro through the earth, and going up and down therein; Babylon is not fallen; the Jews are not called; nor is the fulness of the Gentiles come in; but the greatest part of the earth to this day sit in heathenish darkness.

When then shall they be accomplished? Not till "the holy city has been trodden under foot forty-two months." Not till "the witnesses have prophesied a thousand, two hundred and threescore days, clothed in sackcloth." (*Rev.* xi. 2, 3.) And not till "the woman has been in the wilderness a time and times and half a time." (*Rev.* xii. 14.) Now a time and times and half a time, i. e. three years and a half, is equal to forty-two months; which is equal to one thousand two hundred and sixty days; which doubtless means 1260 years, a day for a year. As the event has proved was the case in the prophecy of Daniel, who declared it to be 70 weeks, from the going forth of the commandment to build Jerusalem, to the death of Christ. For it proved to be 490 years, which is 7 times 70, a day for a year. (*Dan.* ix. 24.)

So that there is no difficulty in determining the downfall of Antichrist, but what arises from the uncertainty we are at when to date the beginning of his rise and reign. The bishops of Rome were some hundred years rising gradually from the honest character of a scripture-bishop to the grand title of *universal Pope*, which was obtained, *A. D.* 606. And it was a long time from this, before they got to the height of their grandeur, and the Pope was constituted a *temporal Prince*, which was not till *A. D.* 756. And perhaps he may fall as gradually as he rose. And as now he has been falling 240 years, even ever since the beginning of the *reformation;* so we may rationally expect he will continue to fall, till *Babylon* sinks *as a mill-stone into the sea.* And then "the mountains and the hills shall break forth into singing, and all the trees of the field shall clap their hands." (*Isai.* lv. 12.) And all the hosts of heaven as loud as thunder, shall say, "Hallelujah! For the Lord God omnipotent reigneth. Let us be glad and rejoice, and give honour to him; for the marriage of the Lamb is come, and his wife hath made herself ready." (*Rev.* xix. 6, 7.)

And thus we have taken a brief view of the scripture-evidence, that the cause of truth and righteousness will finally become gloriously victorious.

VI. Nor is there the least reason to doubt the accomplishment of these things. For God in all times past has been faithful to his word, and is evidently sufficiently engaged in this affair; knows how, and can easily accomplish it; and it will be much to the honour of his great name to do it.

God has been faithful to his promises to his church from the beginning of the world. To all human appearance, it was a very unlikely thing, that the Hebrews, enslaved in Egypt, under Pharaoh, a very powerful monarch, and sunk down into idolatry, and very low-spirited, should arise, and go forth with all their flocks and herds, and march through the wilderness, and conquer the seven nations of Canaan, and possess their land. And so it was to all human appearance equally unlikely, that the Jews in Babylon should ever return to their own land. But God had promised in both cases, and God performed. And an event more surprising than either of these, yea, the most astonishing that could have happened, has also come to pass, just as God had said. The promised SEED has been born, and the serpent has *bruised his heel;* and methinks now not only God's faithfulness, but even the nature of the case itself, should lead us to believe, that *the* SEED *shall bruise his head.*

For, after God has appeared to be so *infinitely engaged* to destroy the works of the devil, as to give his only begotten Son, it can surely never once be imagined, that he wants sufficient resolution to carry him through what yet remains to be done.

And he, who could send Pharaoh's daughter to take up Moses, when an infant, out of his basket of bulrushes, and educate him in Pharaoh's court, that he might be skilled in all the arts of government; and when he had spent forty years in this situation, banish him into the land of Midian, that in the solitary life of a shepherd for another forty years, he might attain to be the meekest man on earth; that he might, by both, be thoroughly qualified for the work designed him. And he, who could take David from feeding his father's sheep, and, after a course of trials, so exceeding necessary to prepare frail man for high honours and great usefulness, exalt him to the throne of Israel, so thoroughly furnished to head their armies and subdue their foes, advance their external grandeur, and put great honour upon their religion. And he, who could take Daniel, one of the Jewish captives in Babylon, and raise him to such high honour and great authority, to be a father to his people through their seventy years' captivity, and by his means (perhaps) influence Cyrus so generously to release them, and assist them in their return.[1] And finally, he who could take a number of poor illiterate fishermen, and the persecuting Saul, and by them lay the foundation of the Christian Church, in spite of the united opposition of earth and hell; and after their death cause the Christian Church to live through, yea, at last to triumph over, the ten bloody persecutions, and even conquer the Roman Empire; and that which is still more wonderful, to subsist to this day, notwithstanding all the subtle and cruel methods, which have for so many hundred years been taken by antichrist to extirpate Christianity out of the world. I say, he who could do these things, cannot be at a loss for means, or want power, to effect the glorious things foretold, which yet remain to be accomplished.

And what if mankind are ever so estranged from God? And what if they are ever so averse to a reconciliation? And what if satan reigns in the courts of princes, in the councils of the clergy, as well as in the cottages of the poor? And what if even the whole world in a manner lies in wickedness? So that a general conflagration might rather be expected, as it is so eminently deserved; are these things any bar in the way?

What if mankind have abused divine grace from the beginning of the world? What if they have murdered his prophets,

---

[1] As Daniel understood the prophecies of Jeremiah, which had determined the time of the captivity to be seventy years, (*Dan.* ix. 2.) and had his heart so much in the affair of their return, as to *set his face to seek the Lord by fasting and prayer;* (*ver.* 3.) and being the chief man in the kingdom, must have free access to Cyrus; (*Dan.* vi.) so nothing could be more natural than to show him an ancient Jewish prophecy, wherein he was mentioned by name, near two hundred years ago, and pointed out as the person who was to let go the Jewish captives, build Jerusalem, and lay the foundation of the temple. *Isai.* xliv. 28. xlv. 1–3. To which Cyrus no doubt refers in his proclamation. *Ezra* i. 2, 3, 4. "Thus saith Cyrus, king of Persia, The Lord God of heaven hath given me all the kingdoms of the earth, and he hath CHARGED me to build him an house at Jerusalem, which is in Judah. Who is there among you," &c.

his Son, and his apostles? What if they have resisted and grieved the Holy Spirit, and perverted the doctrines, and gone counter to the precepts of his holy word? Yea, what if it appears that mankind are really on satan's side? And this after all the kind methods God has taken to reclaim a guilty world? so that even the best man on earth, or the kindest angel in heaven, might be discouraged, totally and finally discouraged, and think it never worth while to take any more pains with such a perverse race, but that it were more suitable to the rules of good government to resign them to destruction? Are any, or all these things together, a sufficient bar to the accomplishment of God's designs, whose goodness is absolutely infinite?

What! After the Son of God has been offered as a sacrifice of atonement, to secure the honour of the divine government, and open a way for the honourable exercise of his grace! What, after the Messiah has been exalted to be a Prince and a Saviour, to give repentance and remission of sins! And after all power and authority in heaven and earth is given into his hands, on purpose to destroy the kingdom of satan, and bring every nation, kindred, and tongue, to bow the knee to God? yea, when the infinitely wise Governor of the world has before determined to permit the wickedness of mankind to come out and stand in so glaring a light, and to suffer satan so long to practise and prosper; to this very purpose, that his power, wisdom, and grace might be the more effectually and the more gloriously displayed, in the accomplishment of all his glorious designs!

Instead of being discouraged, from a view of the past or the present state of the world, as without the light of divine revelation we should naturally have been; methinks now, viewing all things in the light of holy scripture, it must be perfectly rational to conclude, that all these things are only preparatory, as an introduction to the glorious day; even as all the cruel bondage of Israel in Egypt, and all the haughty conduct of

Pharaoh, were but preparatory, as an introduction to the glorious event that God had then in his eye. And what unspeakable honour will redound to God most high, if after all the vile conduct of this apostate world, and notwithstanding all their ill-desert, and after all the subtle methods satan has taken to make his kingdom strong; I say, what unspeakable honour will redound to God most high, if after all this he should accomplish his glorious designs? And when things have been ripening these five or six thousand years, and are now so nearly every way prepared for God to get himself a great name in the total destruction of satan's kingdom, can we once imagine that God will let the opportunity slip? Or rather, ought we not firmly to believe, that when every thing is quite ripe, then God will arise, make bare his arm, and fill the whole world with his glory?

Especially, considering, that as things stand, the honour of all his glorious perfections lies at stake. For ever since the ALMIGHTY gave out the word, that *the seed of the woman should bruise the serpent's head,* even from that very day, that old serpent, with all his subtilty, has employed his whole power to defeat the divine designs, maintain his kingdom in the world, and escape the dreadful blow. He stirred up Cain to kill his brother, and never left till the whole earth was filled with violence, which brought on the general deluge. And after the flood he was industrious to divert mankind from the knowledge and worship of the true God, and to establish idolatry and the worship of devils in all the kingdoms of the earth. And since christianity appeared, he has turned himself into every shape to defeat the gracious designs of the gospel, and has prevailed and reigned above a thousand years, at the head of the grand antichristian apostacy. And should the Almighty suffer him to go on and prosper, and finally prevail, what would become of his own great name? And how great would be their triumph in the infernal regions, to think, that in spite of God and of his Son, from the beginning to the end of the world, they have held out in a constant war, kept the field, and at last come off victorious? Wherefore, as when God repeats the wonderful works, which he had done for Israel in the days of old, in the 20th chapter of *Ezekiel,* he constantly says, *I wrought for mine own great name,* so here, in this case, will he do it again, and that in the most eminent manner. As it is written, the ZEAL *of the Lord of Hosts will perform this. Isai.* ix. 7.

So that, in a word, if almighty power and infinite wisdom, at the head of the universe, infinitely engaged, are a sufficient match for the guilty, impotent powers of darkness, then we may depend upon it, satan will meet with an overthrow, as notable as did Pharaoh and his host in the Red sea. And as proud Babylon, once the mistress of kingdoms, is now no more; so mystical Babylon shall sink as a millstone in the sea, and rise no more for ever. And,

VII. Whatever mistakes the Jewish rabbies might fall into, in their interpretation of Daniel's 70 weeks, and in their attempts to fix the precise time of the Messiah's coming; and whatever mistaken notions any of them had about the nature of his kingdom, as though it was to be of this world, and he to appear in all earthly grandeur; and although his coming, to some, might seem to be so long delayed that they began to give up all hopes of it, and to contrive some other meaning to all the ancient prophecies, or even to call in question the inspiration of the prophets; yet neither the mistakes of some, nor the infidelity of others, at all altered the case. Days, and months, and years, hastened along, and one revolution among the kingdoms of the earth followed upon another, till *the fullness of time* was come, till all things were ripe; and then, behold the MESSIAH was born. Even so it shall be now.

Whatever mistakes christian divines may fall into, in their interpretation of 666, the number of the beast, or in their endeavours to fix the precise time when the 1260 years of Antichrist's reign shall begin and end; or whatever wrong notions some have had, or may have about the nature of the Millennium, as though Christ was to reign personally on earth; and if some, meanwhile, begin to think, that all things will go on as they have done, and to conclude, that the expectation of these glorious days, which has prevailed in the christian church from the beginning, is merely a groundless fancy; yet none of these things will at all alter the case. Days, and months, and years, will hasten along, and one revolution among the kingdoms of the earth follow upon another, until the fullness of time is come, till all things are ripe for the event; and then the ministers of Christ will accomplish, in reality, what St. John saw in his vision. *I saw an angel fly in the midst of heaven, having the everlasting gospel to preach unto them that dwell on the earth, and to every nation and kindred, and tongue, and people.* (*Rev.* xiv. 6.) And then shall it come to pass, that *the vail* of ignorance, which hath so long spread over all nations, *shall be destroyed,* (*Isai.* xxv. 7.) and knowledge shall so greatly increase, that it shall be as though the *light of the moon* were *as the light of the sun, and the light of the sun seven fold,* (*Isai.* xxx. 26.) until *the knowledge of the Lord cover the earth, as the waters do the sea.* (*Isai.* xi. 9.) And then there *shall be nothing to hurt or offend in all God's holy mountain.* For Babylon shall fall, satan be bound, and Christ will reign, and truth and righteousness universally prevail, a thousand years.

REMARKS and INFERENCES.

1. When therefore, our Saviour, in the days of his flesh, denominated his followers *a little flock,* from the smallness of

their number, he had no design to teach us, that this would always be the case, for although it was very true, that his flock was at that time *a little flock;* yet the day was coming, when that *little leaven* should *leaven the whole lump,* (*Mat.* xiii. 33.) and *the stone cut out without hands* should become *a great mountain, and fill the whole earth;* (*Dan.* ii. 25.) so although it was a saying very applicable, not only to our Saviour's day, but to most other periods of the Church, that *many are called and few are chosen;* yet it does not hence follow, that this will be the case when *a nation shall be born in a day,* and *all the people shall be righteous.* And although it has commonly been so, that of the *many* who have sought *to enter in at the strait gate,* but *few have been able,* and the *generality* have from age to age gone *in the broad way, which leads down to destruction:* yet it shall be quite otherwise, when *satan is bound, that he may deceive the nations no more;* and when *all shall know the Lord from the least to the greatest,* when *the kingdom and the greatness of the kingdom under the whole heavens shall be given to the people of the saints of the Most High.* For it is very plain, that these and such like expressions used by our Saviour, which were applicable to the then times, and to most other periods, when the number of true converts hath been comparatively very small, were never designed to be applicable to that glorious period yet to come, which is to be the grand harvest-time, when *the Jews,* (who are to this day for that very purpose, no doubt, by divine Providence preserved a distinct people,) and *the fulness of the Gentiles shall come in.* Nor can it be right to interpret such expressions in such a sense, as to render them inconsistent with what the scriptures so plainly teach shall be the case in the latter days. Therefore,

2. Notwithstanding hitherto but few have been saved, there is no evidence but that yet the greater part of mankind may

be saved. Nothing can be argued against this from such expressions as have been just mentioned, for the reason already suggested. Nor can any thing be argued from any other passages of Scripture; for the Scripture no where teaches, that the greatest part of the whole human race will finally perish. I am sensible, many seem to take this for granted, and they are greatly strengthened in this belief, from a view of the awful state mankind have been in from the beginning of the world to this day. But if we should even grant, that hitherto not one in ten thousand have been saved, yet it may come to pass, (there may be time enough for it, and men enough yet born,) I say, it may yet come to pass, that by far the greatest part of mankind may be saved.

For, as the Scriptures constantly teach, that in these glorious days universal peace shall prevail; and instead of war, the nations shall employ their time in useful labour, *shall beat their swords into plow-shares, and their spears into pruning-hooks;* so it will naturally come to pass, that mankind, who are now in vast multitudes destroyed in the wars from one generation to another, will be greatly increased in numbers, and plentifully provided for. Only remove wars, famines, and all those desolating judgments, which the sins of mankind have from age to age brought down on a guilty world, and let that universal peace and prosperity take place, which indeed will naturally result from the sincere practice of pure christianity, and mankind will naturally increase, and spread, and fill all the earth. And while every one improves his time well, and is diligent in his calling, according to the rules of our holy religion, and all luxury, intemperance, and extravagance are banished from the nations of the earth, it is certain that this globe will be able to sustain with food and raiment, a number of inhabitants immensely greater than ever yet dwelt on it at a time. And now if *all* these shall *know the Lord from the least to the greatest,* as the scripture asserts, so that *the knowledge of the Lord shall fill the earth as the waters cover the sea,* for a thousand years together, it may easily, yea, it will naturally come to pass, that there will be more saved in these thousand years, than ever before dwelt upon the face of the earth from the foundation of the world.

Some indeed understand the thousand years in the *revelation* agreeable to other prophetical numbers in that book, a day for a year. So *the time, and times, and half a time,* i. e. three years and an half, and the *forty two months,* and the 1260 *days,* are no doubt to be reckoned. And if the dark period is to be reckoned by this rule, it should seem that the light period should likewise. For otherwise the dark period which in that book is represented to be the shortest, will indeed be the longest; the 1260 days longer than the 1000 years; and if the 1000 years is reckoned a day for a year, as the scripture-year contains 360 days, so the 1000 years will amount to 360,000 years. In which, there might be millions saved, to one that has been lost. But not to insist upon this, if this glorious period is to last only a thousand years literally, there may be many more saved than lost.

If it be granted that it is difficult to compute with any exactness in such a case as this, yet it is easy to make such a computation as may satisfy us in the point before us. For in Egypt the Hebrews doubled at the rate of about once in 14 years; in *New-England* the inhabitants double in less than 25 years; it will be moderate, therefore, to suppose mankind, in the Millennium, when all the earth is full of peace and prosperity, will double every 50 years. But at this rate, there will be time enough in a thousand years to double twenty times; which would produce such a multitude of people, as that although we should suppose all who live before the Millennium begins, to be lost; yet if all these should be saved, there would be above seventeen thousand saved, to one that would be lost. As may appear from the table below.

1	2
2	4
3	8
4	16
5	32
6	64
7	128
8	256
9	512
10	1024
11	2048
12	4096
13	8192
14	16384
15	32768
16	65536
17	131072
18	262144
19	524288
20	1048576

In the first column we have the 20 periods, which 1000 years will make, at 50 years to a period. In the second column, we see in what proportion mankind will increase, if they are supposed to double in every 50 years. At the end of the first 50 years, there will two for one. And so on: At the end of the twentieth period, there will be above a million for one. Now suppose the world to stand 6000 years before the Millennium; and suppose it in every age to be as full as inhabitants as it will be when the Millennium begins; and suppose, through all the 6000 years, all the inhabitants of the earth to have died off, and new ones come in their room, at the rate of once in 50 years; 6000 years, at 50 years to a period, will be 120 periods: 120 worlds full; all lost, suppose; yet by the table we see, that the seventh period alone, (which is 128), would more than counterbalance the whole.

Suppose all before the Millennium lost, $=$ 120

Sum total, 2,097,150

Suppose all in the Millennium saved, $=$ 2097150

Then, 120 : 2097150 : : 1 : $17476\frac{30}{120}$

Q. E. D.

That is, above 17000 would be saved, to no one lost; which was the point to be proved. Therefore nothing hinders, but that the greatest part of mankind may yet be saved, if God so pleases. There is time enough for it, and may be men enough yet born. And if these calculations may serve to clear up this, they answer the end proposed. What proportion of mankind will finally be saved, and what lost, none can tell. It is no where revealed. God was not obliged to save one out of all this guilty, lost world. Hitherto the generality may have perished: and the Lord is righteous. But who can tell to what a degree God may yet glorify his grace? The holy scriptures encourage us to look for things exceeding great and glorious; even for such events as may put a new face on all God's past dispensations. (See the Sermons on *the Wisdom of God in the Permission of Sin.*)

3. The periods past, that have been so dark, ought to be considered as introductory to this bright and glorious scene, and in various respects as preparatory thereto.

An apostate race, who had joined with the fallen angels in a course of rebellion against the Governor of the universe, might justly have been forsaken of God, and given up to a state of perfect darkness and wo, from generation to generation, entirely under the power of the prince of darkness. What has happened, in dark ages past, may help us a little to realize what might justly always have been the woful state of a fallen world. We have had a specimen of the dreadful nature and tendency of satan's government, in all the idolatry, wickedness, and wo, which have filled the world. And we have seen a little what is in the heart of fallen man, who have slain the Lord's prophets, crucified his Son, and shed the blood of thousands, yea, of millions of his servants. And what has happened may help us to realize a little what must have been the state of a fallen world, if grace had never interposed. At the same time it hath appeared, after the best contrived experiments have been sufficiently tried, that it is not in the heart of fallen man to repent, nor can he be brought to it by any external means whatsoever; whereby the absolute necessity of the interposition of supernatural grace hath been set in the most glaring light. And now, if after all God should effectually interpose, destroy the influence of satan, scatter the darkness which fills the world, recover mankind to God, and cause truth and righteousness at last to prevail; it would appear to be altogether of God, of his own mere self-moving goodness and sovereign grace. And after so long and sore a bondage, mankind will be the more sensible of the greatness of the deliverance. Nor can it ever be said by a proud and haughty world, "we did not need the influences of divine grace to bring us right;" when all other methods had been sufficiently tried, and tried in vain. But God may justly say, "what could have been done more to reclaim mankind, that I have not done? And to what purpose would it have been, to have taken one step further? I tried them enough. There was no hope. Their heart was a heart of stone. Therefore, behold, I, even I, will take away the heart of stone, and give an heart of flesh; and an apostate world shall be ashamed and confounded, and shall never open their mouth, when I shall do all these things for them."

We are apt to wonder why these glorious days should be so long delayed, if God indeed intends such mercy to men. But God, infinitely wise, knows what is best; knows how to conduct the affairs of the universe; knows when is the fittest time to introduce this glorious state of things; knows when matters will be all ripened, and every thing in the moral world prepared; so that this glorious day may be ushered in to the best advantage, in a manner most suited to honour God and his Son, to humble a haughty world, and to disappoint satan most grievously, after all his wily schemes, great success, and high expectations: I say, God knows when this will be. And this is the very time he has fixed upon for this glorious work.

4. It therefore becomes all the followers of Christ, in their several spheres, under a firm belief of these things, to be of good courage, and exert themselves to the utmost, in the use of all proper means, to suppress error and vice of every kind, and promote the cause of truth and righteousness in the world; and so be workers together with God.

If one stood at the head of this glorious army, which has

been in the wars above these five thousand years, and has lived through many a dreadful campaign, and were allowed to make a speech to these veteran troops upon this glorious theme, he might lift up his voice, and say, "Hail, noble heroes! brave followers of the Lamb! Your general has sacrificed his life in this glorious cause, and spoiled principalities and powers on the cross! and now he lives and reigns. He reigns on high, with all power in heaven and earth in his hands. Your predecessors, the Prophets, Apostles, and Martyrs, with undaunted courage, have marched into the field of battle, and conquered dying! and now reign in heaven! behold, ye are risen up in their room, are engaged in the same cause, and the time of the last general battle draws on, when a glorious victory is to be won. And, although many a valiant soldier may be slain in the field; yet the army shall drive all before them at last. And satan being conquered, and all the powers of darkness driven out of the field, and confined to the bottomless pit, ye shall reign with Christ a thousand years; reign in love and peace, while truth and righteousness ride triumphant through the earth. Wherefore lay aside every weight, and, with your hearts wholly intent on this grand affair, gird up your loins, and with all the spiritual weapons of faith, prayer, meditation, watchfulness, &c. with redoubled zeal and courage, fall on your spiritual enemies. Slay every lust that yet lurks within, as knowing your domestic foes are the most dangerous: and with gentleness, meekness, and wisdom, by your holy conduct, your pious examples, your kind instructions, your friendly admonitions, spread the savour of divine knowledge all around you, as ye are scattered here and there through a benighted world; labouring to win souls to Christ, to induce the deluded followers of satan to desert his camp, and enlist as volunteers under your prince, MESSIAH. And if the powers of darkness should rally all their forces, and a general battle through all the Christian world come on; O, love not your lives to the death! Sacrifice every earthly comfort in the glorious cause! Sing the triumphs of your victorious general in prisons and at the stake! And die courageously, firmly believing the cause of truth and righteousness will finally prevail."

Surely it is infinitely unbecoming the followers of Him who is *King of kings and Lord of lords,* to turn aside to earthly pursuits, or to sink down in unmanly discouragements, or to give way to sloth and effeminacy, when there is so much to be done, and the glorious day is coming on. How should those who handle the pen of the writer, exert themselves to explain and vindicate divine truths, and paint the Christian religion in all its native glories! How should the pulpit be animated, from sabbath to sabbath, with sermons full of knowledge and light, full of spirit and life, full of zeal for God, and love to men, and tender pity to infatuated sinners! Christ loves to have his ministers faithful, whether the wicked will hear or not. And let pious parents be unwearied in their prayers for, and instructions of their children, and never faint under any discouragements; as knowing, that Christ is exalted to give repentance and remission of sins, and can do it for whom he will. Bring your children and friends, with all their spiritual diseases, and lay them at his feet; as once they did their sick, when this kind Saviour dwelt on earth. Let pious persons of every age, and in every capacity, awake from sleep, and arise from the dead, and live and act worthy their glorious character and high expectations; and in their several stations exert themselves to the utmost to promote the Redeemer's glorious cause. Let this age do their share, as David, although the temple was not to be built in his day, yet exerted himself to lay up materials for that magnificent edifice, on which his heart was intently set; as knowing, that in his son's day it would be set up in all its glory. So let us rise up, and with the greatest alacrity contribute our utmost towards this building, this living temple, this temple all made of lively stones, of stones alive, in which God is to dwell, and which will infinitely exceed in glory the temple of Solomon, that was built of dead timber and lifeless stones. And let this be our daily prayer, an answer to which we may be assured of, whatever other requests are denied us, *our Father which art in heaven,* &c. *for thine is the kingdom, the power, and the glory, for ever.* Amen.

53 · *Hermon Husband*

(1 7 2 4 – 1 7 9 5)

SOME REMARKS ON RELIGION

A relationship between the Great Awakening and the
Revolution is discernible no matter what approach is
taken to eighteenth-century American life and thought.
What must always be kept in mind, however, is that in the
realm of politics as in all others the most enduring of the
Awakening's legacies was the change it wrought in the
quality of American life. A central fact of the time was
that many men pursued a happiness that could not be
measured by wealth, nor wholly realized in political privileges and rights, but was ultimately internal. An illuminating instance of the Awakening's effect on American
aspirations is observed in the career of Hermon Husband.
He "was undoubtedly the most prominent agitator in the
Regulator movement" which in the 1760's protested
against the government of North Carolina, and later took
up arms to seek redress of their grievances. After the de-

Hermon Husband, *Some Remarks on Religion, with the Author's Experience in Pursuit thereof. For the Consideration of all People, Being
the real Truth of what happened. Simply delivered, without the Help
of School-Words, or Dress of Learning* (Philadelphia, 1761), pp. 11–19,
22–26, 37–38.

feat of the Regulators at the Battle of Alamance, Husband fled to Pennsylvania, where he subsequently agitated against British imperial policy and, in his last years, was involved in the Whiskey Rebellion, the backcountry uprising against Alexander Hamilton's system of taxation. None of Husband's activities can be fully appreciated unless viewed against the background of his *Remarks on Religion,* which Husband published just as he was about to begin his battles against what he considered social, political, and economic injustice. Written about 1750, Husband's unpolished tract recalls the spiritual joys of the Awakening, and it traces his torments as the illumination of the revival dimmed, and his pilgrimage in quest of further light. Husband eventually joined the Quakers, but his own words attest his inability to be fully or permanently satisfied with the quiet and gradual enlightenment of the Friends. His longing for a more abrupt and soul-ravishing experience hints at why he, along with other Americans for whom the Great Awakening was still a vivid recollection, responded as they did to the next great "crisis" in the life of their society.

. . . Being now turned of fifteen Years of Age; . . . there came News of a Man, a Preacher, newly come from *England,* that both Men and Women were ready to leave all their Livings to follow him. At first I wondered does he want them to follow him, and what could it be he said or preach'd. I had not long to think on it, for in two or three Days after the first Report there came Tidings, he was to preach within fifteen Miles To-morrow, and his Fame coming, confirm'd also with the

Tidings I could not conceive what he said; for I little thought he spake of a sanctifying Work of God's Spirit on the Soul; having yet no Notion of the Pronunciation of the Work, or by what Name outwardly to call it. I imagined he spake as a Prophet of some strange Time at hand; may be he tells us when the Day of Judgment is to be.

My Father and Mother went however to hear him, and took me along, we went early, and got to the Place before he came; and I heard One ask another, what does this Man preach? any Thing that is News? who answered No; nothing but what you may read every Day in your Bible: For what is this great Cry then? who was unanswered after this Manner, stay, you will hear him by and by, you never heard the likes before. Here I was puzzled, what sure, what can this be he says? when in the Instant comes the Man, George Whitefield by Name, and he took a Text about the wise and foolish Virgins.

I presently understood him, for the Spirit of God witnessed to me, and speaking in me says, thy Argument against me is now come to Nought; thou thoughtest, there were none who kept their Lamps lighted as I wanted thee, yet, now here is One who bears a Testimony to the Truth, and methought I could feel and believe there were Numbers besides him; I also observed some of the People called *Quakers* present, and still having that gross Opinion of them beforementioned, thinks I, now you have heard something of the Movings or Inspirations of the Spirit indeed.

Being now fully convinced that this was the Way to Happiness to yield Obedience to Christ in me. I became now willing to take up the Cross; but a Fear was in me that I had rejected him so long, yea, I was now ashamed to think how I would not believe in him for all his Strivings with me, and thus I returned willing, I had hearkened to his Reproofs in Day of my Visitation, lest I were now too late.

I longed to see some of Whitfield's Writings, that I might more certainly know his Opinion in this Matter; for, in his Discourse he had not explain'd this otherwise than "That we must come to Christ, if ever we attain'd Happiness: That we must be born again of the Spirit, having Oil in our Lamps, or Grace in our Hearts, witnessing the Old Man crucified, and a putting on of the New: With some Threats to Sinners, and of the fearful Day of Judgment";—as well as I remember.

However, my Exercise after this became, how I might come to Christ, and if the Day of my Visitation was not past. And in a little Time we had News of a Presbyterian Minister, who was said to be of the same Doctrine as W————d: I went to hear him preach, not out of Curiosity, but to learn how to come to Christ. He thundered out against Sin, and pronounc'd Death, Damnation, &c. to Sinners, and that there was no Salvation but by Christ. I lik'd him much for thundering out against Sin and Sinners, for I now looked on myself as a very wicked Sinner withal, I patiently waited to know if I was likely ever to become a new Man, or how I might obtain to that State.

Thus for some Time hearing him and others of the same Society, and searching the Scriptures after these Things, and disputing with such as opposed the Workings of the Spirit of God, and continually praying that I might be one of the Elect; for, by this Time I had heard them preach, that none but the Elect could be converted, and endeavoured to give the Marks of the Converted from the Unconverted and if one Mark given of the Converted did not answer my Condition, I would conclude I was still unrenew'd; and on the other Hand, when the Marks of a Sinner were given I would take that to myself if possible; and when they threatened the Unconverted and cry to them, to fly to, and accept of Christ, I would count myself One, and earnestly wait to hear what I should do.

The Custom of those Ministers was generally, to divide their Discourses into Heads of particular Branches, telling us beforehand the Substance of Doctrine each Branch was to contain, and many Times one would be to tell us the Way of Christ. This would rejoice me, and I waited to hear.

Yet it proved to no Satisfaction; they told us to fly to Christ, to accept of him on his own Terms: All this I was willing to do, if I knew how, or where to find him; and that we must throw away our own Righteousness and accept of his. This would concern me how this was to be done, or whether or no I had, I was willing to do any Thing I thought: Yet could do nothing, nor yet from all the Discourses learn what to do.

This led me again to pray to God the Father of Mercies, to pardon my Sins, and lead and direct me again by his good Spirit how to do; thus I soon began to desire his Presence, and to be taught by him alone, and I notwithstanding, firmly believed he was the Teacher of those Ministers, and at Times (when as I now believe Truth prevailed in an eminent Manner) they would speak to this Effect: "To look to God alone, and observe the Motions and Leadings of his Spirit, and not to quench the least Sparks thereof, but cherish, improve, and kindle into Flame by Obedience those inward and heavenly Calls." These like Discourses were generally in what they call'd an Application, seldom in what they call'd the Doctrinal Part.

Our Minister, or the Church Minister (so called) would now and then preach in our Neighbourhood, who I went also to hear, from whom I could learn little or nothing at all, for the *New-Lights,* (as they began to be called) would tell us the Marks, at least some Marks of a Christian, and that we must be born again of the Spirit, and proving it from Scripture, and explain the Works of Conversion, describe the State of the new Man by Similitudes and Parables, thunder against sin with some Life and Power; But this Church Minister seemed to know nothing at all about the Matter, nay he would speak against it, and signify as much as that Water Baptism was the

New Birth, and that a Life of Morality was a Christian Life, without any sensible Workings of God's Spirit on the Soul; so that I got quite sick of him, yet when he came my Father would have us all go to Church.

One Day when he was to preach, there was also a Meeting that Day at the *New Presbyterian* Meeting-House, to which was my Desire to go; but whether I should displease my Father in refusing to go with him I could not resolve; after some Reasoning in myself, I concluded to leave it entirely to God, would he vouchsafe to enlighten me. Here I mounted on Horse-back, not yet knowing which Way I should go, the Ways kept together through a Gate, when they immediately parted, and as I opened the Gate I yet knew not if I should then turn to the Right or Left; but was no sooner through, when I had a perfect Freedom to go and hear the Church-man, and I think this was also contrary to my Expectation, and as I had no Dependence on him, it became wholly on God who had given me such Freedom of Mind to go, and when I got to the Chapel House, among the People, they kept such ado to answer the Priest, and to find the Place of the Book he was in, being up and then down, the Minister speaking alone, then all suddenly speaking aloud; this did not suit my solid Condition, it seem'd to me there was no true Worship in Spirit among them, he seemed the best Fellow who first found the Place of the Book the Minister was in, and to answer him, and to know when to rise up and sit down, (for the Minister had come so seldom, the People were not well practised in the Business.) But let not the Reader think I was a Stranger to them; for I had been One of the foremost in this Exercise in this same Place and among the same People, and once it had so happened that all had miss'd the Place of the Book, or forgot their Books at Home, except me: And I had to, and did answer the Priest alone (but as I had come for another Employment this Day I had brought no Book,) I sought how I might worship

God in Spirit, in Heart, and in Truth. As I said being uneasy at all this Noise, with so little Appearance of Solidness and true Sincerity I walked out a little Way into the Woods where I kneeled down, my Desires being to God for myself, not in the least despairing or even pitying them, for I knew not which Way to go myself; my Desires were to draw nigh to God, to know and worship him in Reality, which I longed for, and as much desired as a thirsty Creature does for Water. Here I was enabled to supplicate the Throne of Grace, and then came in again, and stayed till they were done. After returning, and Dinner being over, I retired into a Field of Rye, and was filled with Thanksgivings, with Praises, with joy unspeakable, and full of Glory, with Peace and Joy in the Holy Ghost, nor did this arise from any Thing that I had done, or Righteousness that I had acted, so far it was from that, for I was much cast down, and looked on myself as a disobedient sinful Wretch.

Yea it was so far from proceeding from any Thing I attributed to my own Actions, that I could hardly accept the blessed Favour, and went away praising and adoring that God, who had taken Notice of so unworthy a Creature.

And now the same Power and Light of Christ, which I witnessed in the Beginning, began to operate again in the same Manner, and I was now reproved for wicked Thoughts as well as Actions, and notwithstanding I had thought I was so willing to do any Thing if I knew what, I still found a Backwardness in taking up the Cross, which again brought Self Condemnings over me; and I have to repent such Backwardness to this Day. . . .

Yet at other Times I have felt the Spirit of God work so irresistably, that I have wondered all the World was not converted; as to that Difference of Opinion among Men, whether God forces the Will I shall not dispute. I will give here two instances of my own Experience, by which the Reader may judge my Sentiments.

One was, as I remember in this Manner: Coming one Evening to the House where I lodg'd and it had become dark, I was called of God to turn aside and pray; but a great unwillingness arose in me, and I must needs come nearer the House first, and as it press'd clearer and clearer I grew of a great Hurry and could not stay, as it was growing late and getting darker, and I could as well pray by the Bed-Side or in a more convenient Place than this; in this Interim, a certain Woman was meeting me, and it was not so dark but I saw her some Distance, and Satan suggested instantly in my Mind, assisted by the Lust of the Flesh also, as ready to take Hold of the Woman as she pass'd me, but yet nothing immodest: The Light and Power of God withdrew immediately, as soon as I gave the Temptation a Hearing, when nothing but Bashfulness was left to oppose, which made but a small Resistance. This Conflict all pass'd in about one minute's Time, when the Woman was nigh meeting me, and seem'd not to give the Way, which help'd to furnish me with an Excuse: Bashfulness being thus overpowered by the Flesh and the Devil, and observe, my great Hurry was now all over, and nothing was left to oppose. Yet this Light returned again so quick, and with severe Power like unto Lightning, so as to drive Lust and the Devil out of Hearing, in the twinkling of an Eye.

And I thought they never more would venture to return, at which Instant I pass'd the Woman by, and neither touch'd nor spoke to her, and presently ashamed, especially when I remembered how great a Hurry I had been in, but how I had slack'd my Pace to consult with the Flesh and the Devil, nor could I now pray for Shame and Confusion of Face: I fell to the Earth where I lay some Time, while the Spirit made Intercession for me, with Groanings, which I could not utter into Words. And I felt Peace afterwards, but not so full and satisfactory as if I had yielded to a true Obedience.

And now some may perhaps be ready to say, these Trials

are for our Experience. If I were to advise, it would be for every One to give up to God with full Obedience at first in all his Calls and Leadings, which they never will repent of. I have found none, nor read of any who have ventured to say, they had to repent following its Motions, while thousand repent they did not. And though God's Mercies may be extended to some, and we may arrive to the Land of Promise at last, for which I hope, yet many fall short and die in the Wilderness, besides, how happy is the Man who goes this Journey in forty Days! which the rebellious House of *Israal* was forty Years a going and then not peaceable Possession, and that because they did not wholly follow God's Command to utterly drive out the Inhabitants. Though I would warn any from taking Pattern by this, yet it is to be feared that there are too few now a-Days who come up with *Israel* of old, yea, methinks happy would it be for this Generation if the spiritual Enemies of spiritual *Israel* were as far subdued as they were of old, and yet the Gospel Dispensation is certainly more glorious. Be encouraged O Ye! who is entered on this spiritual Journey, to out-do the Jews in that less glorious Day, remember it was God's Command, to utterly drive out the Inhabitants. We are prone to think we can't be so good now as in former Times, especially in the Apostles Days; but I have to observe this to have been the Case in their Time, or the Apostle would not had Occasion to tell the People of his Day, that in former Times they were Men of like Passions as we are. It is quite safe to strive to excel our Predecessors in Virtue, much more to come even. I am in down-right Earnest, and would encourage any One into whose Hand this may happen to fall, in the Beginning of the Work of Christ in them to encounter the Devil, the World and the Flesh, at once, and wholly submit in Obedience to the Cross, and daily bear it after Christ. I am ready sometimes to wish, I had my Time to go over again, yet am afraid if I should, I might not come so well on as I have; but I am firmly of the Belief, that if I had wholly followed him at least in some of his clearest Discoveries, I should, at this Day, have been more nearly acquainted with him, and not a whit behind the Primitive Believer. So would I encourage others, being willing they should be before me, yet, if I know my Heart at all, I am desirous if it would be the Will of God, not to be behind One.

I would to God I were attain'd to that State of Perfection, which I believe is attainable in this Life, and that sometimes I have had a Taste and Sight of. For I remember, before I had any knowledge of the great Opposition this Spirit meets with in the World, among those who call themselves its Friends, I had walked some time wholly by its Directions in all Things, and likely might have stood in that State, had I been amongst its true Friends. However, I have to believe I ought to have stood there, in which State was no Occasion *to take Thought for To-morrow,* I mean even temporal Affairs, and wordly Employments: It would even put me forward in my Business, reprove my Slothfulness, excite Activity, bring to my Mind Things necessary to be done in the Things of outward Employment, as well as inward Exercises of Religion. And as I have witnessed a Time of this State, as also a falling therefrom again. I have plainly to observe, that our temporal Affairs are carried on much more to Advantage; it even enlivens the Body to Exercise, cause our Business to be delightsome and pleasant withal, every Thing under this Direction will be attended with Success. When I would be sent of Errands before Strangers and Great Men, (so called) as I was little and young, it would look difficult how to express myself, deliver my Message, and to behave myself; then I would look to my Leader, and wholly depend on him; to direct my Way, and order my Business, which I can give this Testimony of, and well remember, was always attended with Success and Peace to myself, and in my Return, I would have to praise his Holy Name.

This, I doubt not, but will look childish and silly to some of our old and wise Men, but mark by the Way, that in old Time old Men had their Eyes to God, to direct them and guide them in their Undertakings, both in their own, as also when they were sent by either Father or Master, witness *Abraham's* Servant, when he went for *Rebeccah*. I gained the Affections of all Company while under the Guidance of this Power.

But I observe, our Wise Men of this Age can tell us from whence all this ariseth, and write whole Volumes about the natural Causes thereof, but notwithstanding them, I know what I say to be true.

And also can see, yea, and comprehend them all, even the learnedest Writings extant, both Divinity, Mathematics, Astronomy, and the highest Philosophy of the Day, so far as I give myself the Time to study them, that I have good Reason to believe, my Capacity is not below them of the first or greatest Magnitude, nor have I been less curious than most to examine the Truth of our holy Religion, without Prejudice or Partiality; but find this little Stone the touch Stone of all Truth, and the other Nought in Comparison of this Wisdom of God; and 'tis not without some View of convincing some of the greatest Deists of this Day, that I throw this simple little Piece into the World, especially if I am, or shall be able to produce the second Part.

But to return in this State, which resembled the Sabath of Rest, or Sight of the Promiss'd Land, I had some Ups and Downs, occasioned in Part from my Unwillingness to bear the Cross, though it was become both pleasant and easy. But those who should have been my Helpers in this Travel rather helped to pull me down, yet under those Disadvantages I kept pretty steady some Time in the narrow Way, daily arguing against those that oppos'd the Workings of the Spirit, and exhorting Sinners, both by speaking some myself, and reading to them Portions of Scripture and Books of Divinity, mostly those of Whitfield's Writings and the *New-Presbyterians*, (so called) there being a Constraint laid on me so to do. And now having thus briefly gone over some Part of my Time, I come again to Particulars, which occasioned a new Conflict and Soul Exercise. . . .

Sometimes I sat down by the Fire, sometimes I stood up, being so uneasy and restless, I knew not what to do; it looked so deplorable a Case, it seemed unrecoverable: Which forced me to attempt to rest satisfied, with the Loss of GOD. But, O the Flames of Hell! represented with Flames of Sulphur and Brimstone, seemed Nothing in Comparison of the Wrath of God, of an angry God! I thought, I could endure the Thoughts of everlasting Fire, could I be hid from the Presence of an angry God: And I am sure, they, who have tasted of the Wrath of God, have no Need for Hell to be represented with burning Flames. . . .

I have also known at Times when my sinful Inclinations as Lying, Pride, Anger, Passion and the like would get the better of me, so as to cause Fear and Self-condemnings and afraid to bring my Deeds to the Light; thus sometimes they would gether on me on all Sides, and I had to behold my Sins as Mountains. I have yet escaped the condemning Power and had to behold those Mountains consumed, as by the very Breath of his coming, and in a Moment has laid them even with the Valley and embraced me in the Arms of divine Love, without the Sentence of Condemnation as at some other Times.

I was now a constant Adherent to the new Presbyterians or *Whitefieldians* so called, who became now greatly opposed by the World and Pharise Doctors of Divinity. I was according to my Age zealous against them, in contending for the Authority and Necessity of the inward and sensible Inspirations of the Holy Spirit, which was the grand Quarrel between us. The Scriptures proved this in the Apostles Days, but it was objected we was not to look for such in this Age.

The chief Objection of Weight with me was, if this be true: How comes we never heard of it before, and what has become of all our Forefathers? There was no such Doctrine preached in their Days, and I had seen no Book as yet except the Bible which held forth the same, though I had searched all I could come at; this would put me pretty much at a stand, how any in former Ages could have witnessed this Work and not declared it to others. I had conceived thereof if I could prove it not now, I thereby would prove it true. And as I was once in a Dispute with one who I had heard had a Book of *Martin Luther's* Works, after a pretty long Dispute, I asked him what *Luther* said of the Workings of the Spirit for I understood *Luther* had been one of the first Reformers from Popery; the Man said he, holds much the same in that as you do; I thought very strange at that that he would not believe for all that. I had a Desire and intended to get *Luther's* Works; but before I did, I met with *Sewell's* History,[1] a Book giving an Account of the Rise and Progress of a People called in Scorn *Quakers*, which was like the Sun breaking out of Darkness into Noonday. Me thought I found Truth in plain Characters, and though it might not convince the Wicked, whom one from the Dead would not; yet I was rejoiced beyond Measure and confirmed in the Truth of all I had been taught before of God, and was pleased to think how my Companions the *Whitefield-ians* would rejoyce with me also. Now, as I have already observed, my Notions of the *Quakers* were, that they knew nothing of the inward Inspirations of the Spirit. I had read also in *Whitefield's* Journal, where he says, "Their Notion about the Spirit, was right." But he calling them Notions, I thought they were only so without the experimental Knowledge thereof. And now on reading this History of *Sewell's*,

---

[1] William Sewel, *History of the Rise, Increase, and Progress of the Quakers* (London, 1725), several times reprinted in the colonies. [Ed.]

I was persuaded the *Quakers* of this Day were degenerate and fallen from the real Life, only retaining a Notion thereof in words. But I thought had *Whitefield* come across this Book, how much he would said in its Praise, as he had some I had not seen.

I was very impatient however to see some of my Friends, to shew them the Prize; and on Sunday as we called it, one of my Friends came, or one of the new Sort (as they began to be called), I soon began to read to him some of the Book, and he presently opened on me Lion like saying, it was the Works of the Devil, Delusions, and Witchcraft, and I wot no more than I now remember, adding as a great Crime, that the *Quakers* would read that Book on the Sabbath Day as soon as the Bible. Which I took to myself, and laid by the Book, thinking I would search it more narrowly, before I ventured to show it to any of them again. The Man charged me to read no more in it, whatever I did, for it was exceedingly bewitching; nevertheless I read a great deal therein. And as *Whitefield* had observed, I thought their Belief concerning the Spirit, was wholly agreeable to our *New Presbyterians*. Now I had no familiar Acquaintance with any of the Ministers, there being no settled One of that Sort in our Parts, but chief of some of the Elders and others, I began to dispute with concerning the *Quakers*, in order that they might rightly understand the *Quakers* Belief, concerning the grand Article of our Salvation, *to wit,* the New Birth, not doubting but then they would think more charitable of them; for I was sure it was the Spirit of Christ that brought us from Darkness to Light, by an inward Work, that was sensible to him in whom it was wrought, and not because of our own Works, or outward Performance, or Ceremonies. . . .

. . . I likewise told my Friends plainly, I had more Charity for the *Quakers* a great deal, then I had for the *Old Presbyterians;* for this Reason: As we hold, and truly believe it, to be by converting and sanctifying Grace, that we are made fit for the Kingdom, and not by the Performance of this or the other Ceremony, and seeing the *Quakers* owned and believed in the powerful Work of God, it might be the Ceremonies only, they differed with us about. But the *Old Presbyterians,* if once they come to own and experience this Work of God, this Power, which teaches, redeems, and sanctifies the Soul, then there is nothing more between us, seeing as to Outwards, we are all the same. If so they could not oppose the very Ground and Pillar of Truth, on which the Church of God is built, *to wit,* the Revelation of the Spirit, and call the Workings thereof, diabolical, enthusiastical, and spiritual Phrensy's. Imbibed Notions of spiritual Calls to the Ministry, and much more with writing malignant Satyrs against the very Power of God, such as the Description of the wandering Spirit: All which shews their Enmity to the Gospel of Christ. As there is no outward ceremonial Difference between us, some would own the Substance of all this to be true: but still deny the *Quakers* Salvation, and would have it, they knew nothing of the Work of God, but only some deluding Notions of the Devil, and wanted to prove it, by saying, they denied the Scriptures, and deny'd Christ's Coming in the Flesh; and would go start Naked about the Streets, both Men and Women, daubing themselves with Filth, and going into our meetings: And that they wholly depended on their own Works, and said, they were Holy and Perfect, and needed not the Blood of Christ: That they seldom prayed, and never for a Forgiveness of their Sins. Thus are these People represented to any One, who seems to have a Liking to their Ways, in order to frighten him from any further Search; for I am of Opinion, that there are few who are truly seeking the Kingdom of Heaven, who impartially look into, and examine the Principles of the *Quakers,* but ten to one he is convinced of the Truth of them; though many may fall back again, because by and by, for the Word's sake, they are offended, because their Doctrines testify to the Truth of that Word in their Conscience, which is deviding between a Man and his Lovers, and the Way becoming too narrow.

I also found there was a little or nothing in the above Slanders; this caused my Love for them the more, seeing there was all Manner of Evil spoke of them falsely for his Name sake. The Reader may have an Idea of a true *Quaker* by the foregoing Discourse, at least of that Power which makes a true *Quaker*. For now I saw plainly there was a certain Power, and that of some Spirit (chuse from whom), that whomsoever suffered himself to led thereby, became sober, honest, just, faithful, merciful, humble, low, meek, temperate, abundantly given to Prayer and Meditations, hating Sin, and delighting and desiring Holiness. And what is very remarkable, what it taught of old it taught now, what it taught one the same another being the same, Yesterday, to Day and forever. Speaking the same in *China as America*, being in Substance this, "Love the Lord thy God with all thy Heart, with all thy Soul, and with all the Strength, and thy Neighbour as thyself." Besides this saying none other; he that understands may read the whole in this small Lesson, but he who understands not, may imagine this is an old Lesson, and that many other Nicities and Ceremonies are since added. But I can tell thee O man! and that by Experience, thou canst not learn this one short Lesson from the Letter; but by the Spirit thou art first convinced, that thou lovest not God, or thou wouldest forsake thy Sin at his Reproof, and when thou forsakest by Degrees, he will also shew thee that it must be with all thy Heart, and with all thy Soul, and will be thy Helper as well as thy Teacher, to put out all thy Strength. And if thou plottest out against thy Neighbour, saying to thyself, he may do the same to me, and it is nothing but just, and that the Law will justify the same. Here thou mayest darken the Letter, but the Spirit will testify it to thy own Face; thou oughtest not to do so, but love thy Neighbour as thyself. Thus it brings all thousands and ten thousands to be of one Heart and one Soul, be their Profession as to Ceremonies or Forms what it may. I can safely say I never knew it take Part in one disputed Form or other, though to some others it may, but more likely. I believe we are apt to strive to shelter ourselves under ceremonious Forms when the Way becomes too narrow.

And I believe thousands of those who bear the Name of *Quakers,* know nothing of this saving Power of God. They having as well as others trampled it under Foot, setting up Forms to shelter under, and loving the Pleasures of Life under the Form of Holiness, whose God is their Bellies, their Sweet Hearts, their costly and grave Apparel, the Esteem of Man, and their fellow Mortals, besides others having no other concern but to maintain their Right to Society. . . .

Yet I believe many of all Denominations do own and believe in Christ within: As to their Particulars, even while small in Appearance, and like into a Mustard-Seed, though despised by their wise Rabbies, who will have great and splendid Notions of him outward, and above the Clouds, where their Belief of him without them will profit them nothing except they become Children and Fools, and believe in this Light, take up the Cross. However little and silly it may seem to be, and as they may think fit only for Children, yet if they, while really Fools and Children, (in whom I always believe it strives) did not believe in most (when Men, and grown Wise) again became Children and Fools; and indeed the only Time is when we are Children, to *remember our Creator in the Days of our Youth,* before our wise Notions are grown so high. Yet is this Power able to subdue the stoutest Soul, and wisest, or Self-righteous *Paul* in being.

Now though I thus argued, I had no Thought of leaving the *Presbyterians,* I rather expected from what I could learn from their Preaching, for I had the Opportunity of hearing many; for there was no settled One in those Parts, but Plenty of Travellers and Supplies from other Parts. . . .

I went now by Turns to both Meetings; the *Presbyterians* gave out from the Pulpit, "That the Power of God had left them, and said, it was from the great Opposition it met with by the World," meaning those that oppos'd the *New-Lights.* I thought for my own Part, the Opposition in myself was the most material. But I remember the Minister took much Pains from the Pulpit, to encourage his Hearers to depend on their former Experiences, and not throw away their Confidence, assuring them there was no Possibility of falling from Grace, and he preached much from a Text, where it says: *If thy Heart condemns thee, God is greater; but if thy Heart condemns thee not, then hast thou Confidence in God.* After much Stuff, the Whole he made of it was, "That God was greater, and would justify; but if our Hearts condemn'd us not, it was as well, and then we had Confidence, &c." All this Shuffling would not do with me, if my Heart condemns me, God is greater, and so much more and greater, the Condemnation would be, Conscience is here meant no Doubt; and the Answer of a good Conscience was, the saving Baptism, a pure Conscience and undefiled, is what we are to press to. They owned God's Power was gone, save at certain Times, and I saw they could preach without it; they were turning back to *Old Presbyterianism,* and a State of dead Forms. Thus I left them, and was the more confirm'd in the Truth of the Christian Religion, as I have all along plead for, nor was my Faith on Man, it matter'd nothing to me, that this did so, and the other so, for if it was Evil, I knew it was done in Opposition to that Power. When I had to remember how the Lord watch'd over me from one Year's End to another, Night and Day, exceeding the Care of a Mother over her sucking Child. I speak the Truth Friends, I lie not, I am not able to set in forth to the Full, it was not possible I could believe this Spirit was to blame for the Sins of the Disobedient, I mean that Spirit testified of by the ancient *Quakers,* for I am as sure the Spirit they witness'd of was the same, as I am of my Hand being Part of my Body, and I have known it strive so much against my yielding to Sin, that the Thoughts of bringing Dishonour to his Name has been a greater Motive to restrain me therefrom; than all the Terrors of Hell and Damnation.

So my Faith being not built on Man, the Fall of Man did not stumble me, for that will be Truth, tho' all Men deny it. I went now altogether to the *Quakers* Meeting, and been much ever since a quiet Spectator; and have seen my Beloved at Times, who would touch the Handles of the Lock and withdraw, and peep as it were through the Lettice of the Window, or through the Roof of the House; sometimes appear on the Way, but withdraw as soon as I came in Sight of the City, or Assembly of the People: Like a Mother who weaneth her Child from the Breast, so is my Beloved; nor may he *be stirr'd up till he please.* Satan now plan'd his Designs against me, and was more than seven Years advancing by such slow Degrees, as scarcely discernably his nearer approach. At length he *stirred up my Beloved: O ye Daughters of* Jerusalem! *stir the affectionate Son of my Bosom,* and has promised, *that then my Soul shall live!* stir him not up, he will come in the Time when it shall please him, and be *as a Wind in the Forrest among the Trees.*

INDEX